International Series in Operations Research & Management Science

Volume 181

For further volumes:
http://www.springer.com/series/6161

James H. Bookbinder
Editor

Handbook of Global Logistics

Transportation in International Supply Chains

Springer

Editor
James H. Bookbinder
Department of Management Sciences
University of Waterloo
Waterloo, ON
Canada

ISSN 0884-8289
ISBN 978-1-4419-6131-0 ISBN 978-1-4419-6132-7 (eBook)
DOI 10.1007/978-1-4419-6132-7
Springer New York Heidelberg Dordrecht London

Library of Congress Control Number: 2012943370

Printed on acid-free paper

Springer is part of Springer Science+Business Media (www.springer.com)

Preface

History

About 10 years ago, I began work on a special issue of *Transportation Research E*. The topic was "Global Logistics." There were to be papers on Logistics in all sectors of the world, and on flows between those regions. That topic did come to pass; the special issue (Vol. 41, No. 6) was published in 2005. (See http://authors.elsevier.com/sd/article/S1366554505000529)

I noted (Bookbinder 2005), in my editorial at that time, that we published the best of the manuscripts submitted, after helping those authors to revise. But it was pretty naïve to expect the international balance I had sought, without soliciting articles from researchers in specific geographic areas.

Thus, the idea of the present edited volume was born. Rather than issue a "Call for papers" and hoping for the best, the book would consist strictly of chapters that had been *commissioned*. I designed a rough list of chapters that would include applications from every continent, plus attention to all the modes of transport pertinent to international shipments.

It was my good fortune that so many of the authors I contacted were interested in preparing a chapter. As he or she saw fit, each principal contributor chose one or more co-authors with whom to collaborate. Together we worked on refining the content of the respective chapters, often with the aid of the referees named below.

Subject Matter

Consider the title of this edited volume, *Global Logistics*, and its subtitle, *Transportation in International Supply Chains*. No difficulties arise, until one tries to define the key terms and their relationships!

More seriously, let us now discuss the sections of this book. The geographic divisions are self-explanatory.

Part I Logistics and Supply Chains in Asia

The first four chapters involve Asia, reflecting that continent's importance today and tomorrow. We begin with "Logistics in China." Professors Feng Chen and Chung-Yee Lee are there, on the ground. They summarize the current situation and present two case studies. The near-term prospects are highlighted. These include improved Chinese logistics infrastructure to support the shift of industrial activities from eastern to middle or western areas.

Chapters 2 and 3 concern, respectively, India and the Asia Pacific region. Compared to Chap. 1, the emphasis here is a little more specific. R.P. Sundarraj and Komal Kumari deal with Electronic Procurement Systems in India, and their influence on supply chain operations in that country. The authors report on several case studies of firms in which innovative Logistics enables a unique blend of Indian customs with modern business practices. In Chap. 3, Amrik Sohal and Shams Rahmen focus on the uses of 3PL services in the Asia Pacific. Through surveys and published results, the enhanced use of outsourcing in that sector of the world is related to the growth of Manufacturing and Logistics there.

Ruth Banomyong, in Chap. 4, considers the progress in economic integration of the Greater Mekong Sub-region (GMS). All or portions of the six countries have significant commercial interactions, whose growth will depend on enhanced Logistics within and between those nations. Detailed comparisons across the GMS are made for each transportation mode, and for the various economic corridors in the region.

Part II Logistics and Supply Chains in Latin America

Chapters 5 and 6 present important Operations Research applications, respectively in Argentina and Brazil. Gustavo Braier and Javier Marenco describe an optimization model for the Argentine sugar industry. They provide details on a software tool to manage the data and analyze multiple scenarios for sugar production and distribution by a major Argentinean firm. A brief summary is also given of Logistics in that country.

Hugo Yoshizaki et al. formulate and solve a model that combines water-based domestic container shipments in Brazil with international movements of containers destined to that country. Their results show increases in vessel capacity utilization and in the gross margin of the particular liner company. The latter benefit could be obtained despite volatile currencies. (Domestic services are quoted in Brazilian *Real*; long-distance freight rates are in US Dollars.)

Chapters 5 and 6 are thus examples of the good Operations Research applications that abound in Latin American Logistics. Paul Mant and I take this a step further in Chap. 7. We give a detailed survey of various analyses of Latin American supply chains. The point-of-view is that of articles published in the *research literature*, whether involving OR models or empirical research. The papers are categorized by the country of application, the managerial issues, and the analytical approaches employed.

Part III Logistics and Supply Chains in Europe

The European Union, currently with 27 members, is not at all homogeneous. Indeed, only Chap. 11 concerns an application in just a single country. Chapters 8–10 deal with regional issues or comparisons further afield.

Britta Gammelgaard and Aseem Kinra discuss Logistics in the Oresund Region (Chap. 8). In that portion of Scandinavia, the national boundaries between Denmark and Sweden are blurred. Synergies that go beyond an individual country or government are created because the region targets emerging consumer needs around sustainability and macroeconomic competence. Harilaos Psaraftis et al., in Chap. 9, present the importance and significance of "Green Corridors." Such a corridor is characterized by a concentration of freight traffic between major hubs, and by relatively long distances of transport. They summarize an ongoing venture, entitled "Project SuperGreen," involving 22 partners from 13 European countries that seeks to identify and promote such corridors for the surface transportation of goods throughout Europe.

Jean-Paul Rodrigue and Theo Notteboom (Chap. 10) compare Europe to North America along several dimensions. Containerized freight is important in "intermediacy," i.e., in the linking of country pairs that would not be directly connected by water transportation service. Coastal and inland waterways, for example, exemplify differences in freight regionalism between North America and Europe.

Chapter 11 concerns an eye-catching topic, the production of beer. Haldun Süral and co-authors model the redesign of that supply and distribution network for a particular brewery. They also give an overview of Turkish Logistics in general.

Part IV Logistics and Supply Chains in the Developing World

Arnold Maltz et al., in Chap. 12, discuss the issues in the purchase of goods from Developing Countries. Those authors also present a case study that spans the US/Mexico border. The chapter's theme is the interdependence between global sourcing and global logistics. Emerging markets perhaps lack infrastructure and capable logistics service providers. But key opportunities for growth are in those nations: ones that may look difficult now, but will likely bloom later.

Chapter 13 pertains to the "last mile," not for the delivery of products but for the delivery of Healthcare. The difficult conditions in Gambia required an innovative approach to transportation. Hau Lee et al. recount in an enthusiastic way the use of *motorcycles* by health care workers. Careful practices in vehicle acquisition and maintenance, spare parts inventory management, and in scheduling the visits of these workers are described. Those practices, plus motorcycle-related training for the healthcare workers, resulted in striking productivity improvements (e.g. number of health-visits made to remote areas).

Part V Transportation Modes and their (Land) Interfaces

International shipments often involve transport by air. In Chap. 14, Aisling Reynolds-Feighan carefully compares the air freight networks through which those goods move. She identified the top five "freight-airports" in each of Asia, Europe, and North America, and the top ten freight carriers in each region. The networks of those main carriers are contrasted through intriguing visual displays. Important conclusions concern the future directions of the air freight industry and the role of integrated carriers.

Shipments that arrive at the main airport or seaport must still get to the "hinterlands." Peter de Langen and Jan Fransoo (Chap. 15) describe the network and business models for such an application in the Netherlands. They present a nine-level framework for the activities in international transport and logistics, in which Barge Operators and Terminal Operating Companies are among the key players. The authors emphasize the concept of an *extended gate*, whereby an inland hub becomes the "virtual gate" of a deep sea terminal.

James Higginson studies in detail the various challenges that a (global) shipment must overcome in crossing a border. He concentrates in Chap. 16 on the most important spots where (people or) freight can traverse between the United States and Canada, summarizing the statistical results published for specific crossings. James also reviews the academic literature on border crossings in general, and provides guidance on the OR modeling of border-related events and processes.

Chapter 17 concerns those countries plus Mexico: Wilbert Wilhelm and collaborators analyze tradeoffs in an international supply chain linking the nations of the North American Free Trade Agreement (NAFTA). They study the connections between the choice of transportation mode, the siting of facilities in the network, and the costs to enable the flow of product.

Part VI Innovative Features and Recent Global Developments

The final four chapters of this volume describe novel approaches or newer application areas that are becoming prominent. I am certainly proud of the innovations represented by Parts I through V. But the material in Part VI is neither particular to one area of the world, nor are these chapters specialized to a single mode of transportation.

Serhan Duran and co-authors (all formerly or presently at Georgia Tech) deal with Humanitarian Logistics in Chap. 18. A disaster can strike anywhere on the globe. The benefits of purchasing the required relief items ahead of time, and storing them in strategic locations, are analyzed.

Yossi Sheffi (Chap. 19) presents the case for Logistics-Intensive "Clusters." A logistics park, or extensions thereof, enable firms that are customers or suppliers of services to one another, to locate nearby. This co-location facilitates regional growth, and enables those firms collectively to be more competitive in an international sense.

In Chap. 20, Teodor Crainic and collaborators formulate and solve an optimization model for the grouping of orders in the context of global procurement. (This is in contrast to the typical shipment consolidation models, which are based on the grouping of "loads.") The authors make the case for their approach, and estimate the benefits in an application for a client in the grocery-products industry.

Most references that an author would cite describe what "is," or show how to improve a current system. Fewer publications deal with what could be or should be. But Chap. 21 ("The Future") attempts to do just that. Barry Prentice and I speculate on what the Logistics and Supply Chain universe may look like in 2025. Arguments are offered in support of various points-of-view, sometimes controversial ones. The book thus concludes with some food for thought.

Uses of the Book

Here are some remarks on how the present volume might be of benefit, and to whom. The geographical parts or sections of the book consist of chapters that are self-contained, yet can be the basis on which to begin a comparison of Logistics/SCM between countries in that region. That will occasionally take some *work* on behalf of the student or reader: Successive chapters, even in the given section, are not following a template! But those differences indicate the work required (by oneself or a professor) to perform a meaningful comparison.

As another example, particular issues or concepts recur throughout the volume. "Borders" is the clear focus of Chap. 16. But Border issues are also important in Chap. 4, for the various nations in the Greater Mekong Sub-region of Southeast Asia. And again in Chaps. 17 and 8. Borders are prevalent in the former chapter because the model was applied in the context of a NAFTA supply chain. The latter is because of the obvious influence of the two countries, Denmark and Sweden, in the Oresund Region.

Chapter 8 deals with the Oresund region of Scandinavia, in which a "Cluster" (treated in detail in Chap. 19) is formed by entities in the two distinct but adjacent nations. Chapter 7 notes the advantages that clusters have brought to certain supply chains in Latin America.

Now consider the functions of transportation carriers, and the shippers and 3PLs with whom they work. The influence and decisions of shippers are present in every chapter: A supply chain exists to move the goods dispatched by shippers to be received by consignees (buyers). Similarly, the third party logistics providers and carriers recur in most chapters. But 3PLs are the obvious focus of Chap. 3; carrier issues are prevalent in Chaps. 6, 14 and 15.

Chapters 10 and 15 (respectively on "intermediacy" and "hinterland transport") contain multiple layers of relationships. I, for one, intend to try and flesh those out in the future!

Acknowledgments and Appreciation

Elsewhere in the front matter, we thank a number of the referees whose work improved the quality of the various chapters. Here, I wish to thank others who helped me overcome particular challenges.

Fred Hillier, the acquiring editor of the series of books that includes the present volume, persisted in encouraging me to undertake this project. I'm glad that he did.

Neil Levine of Springer offered valuable advice at several meetings along the way. Matthew Amboy of Springer has provided aid in some of the final details, furnishing assistance in a number of aspects of the publication process.

I have worked with Bev Rodgers at the University of Waterloo since 2003. (She probably feels that was the year we began work on this book!) Bev did the major word-processing tasks on the chapters I co-wrote. She was especially active in the initial reports to the nineteen corresponding authors; other communications with them and the publisher; and in preparing the edited versions of the chapters that we submitted to Springer. Without Bev Rodgers, I could not have completed this project.

Finally, let me thank my wife Susan and our daughters, Amy and Lisa, for their love and support.

Waterloo, ON, Canada, February 2012 Jim Bookbinder

Contents

Referees

Every chapter in this volume was commissioned in advance. The review process thus differed from the "adversarial" one used by most journals. Some topics I felt comfortable to critique on my own, with the occasional consultation of an anonymous colleague.

Other chapters involved subject matter for which the following researchers provided detailed comments and suggestions. I am grateful for their help.

Aruna Apte, Naval Postgraduate School
André Bergsten Mendes, University of Sáo Paolo
Marc Goetschalckx, Georgia Tech
Anne V. Goodchild, University of Washington
Peter de Langen, Eindhoven University of Technology
Alain Martel, Université Laval
Charles McMillan, York University
David Pyke, University of San Diego
Jean-Paul Rodrigue, Hofstra University
Brian Slack, Concordia University

Part I
Logistics and Supply Chains in Asia

Chapter 1
Logistics in China

Feng Chen and Chung-Yee Lee

Abstract China is undergoing exciting economic changes. Many of these will impact, or are impacted by, Logistics. In this paper, we summarize the current status of Chinese Logistics. We discuss issues related to the various transport modes: water, rail, road, air and intermodal, and their use by firms and by 3PLs (third party logistics providers). Two case studies are presented. Possible paths are formulated for the future development of Logistics in China.

1.1 Introduction

With GDP increasing at an average rate of 10.8 % per year from 2001 to 2010, China became the second largest economy after the second quarter of 2010, and now has a GDP of USD 6,123 billion (Statistical Communiqué of the People's Republic of China 2010). Even under the economic recession in 2008, the gross volume of exports and imports of China were still USD 1,201 billion and USD 1,005 billion, respectively (Wang 2007a). This large GDP naturally needs considerable support from Logistics. It is reported that logistics cost takes around 18 % of GDP in China; that seems too high because the rate is only about 10 % for developed countries (Xu 2009). High logistics cost may thus have become an obstacle for economic development in China. The Chinese government has seen

F. Chen
Department of Industrial Engineering and Logistics Management,
Shanghai Jiao Tong University, Shanghai, China

C.-Y. Lee (✉)
Department of Industrial Engineering and Logistics Management, Hong Kong
University of Science and Technology, Kowloon, Hong Kong
e-mail: cylee@ust.hk

J. H. Bookbinder (ed.), *Handbook of Global Logistics*, International Series
in Operations Research & Management Science 181, DOI: 10.1007/978-1-4419-6132-7_1,

Table 1.1 Percentage for different transportation modes (%)

Years	Rail	Road	Water	Air
2000	13.14	76.46	9.01	0.01
2001	13.78	75.35	9.46	0.01
2002	13.82	75.25	9.56	0.01
2003	14.33	74.14	10.10	0.01
2004	14.59	72.96	10.98	0.02
2005	14.46	72.06	11.80	0.02
2006	14.15	71.98	12.21	0.02
2007	13.81	72.04	12.36	0.02
2008	12.77	74.08	11.38	0.02
2009	11.80	75.32	11.29	0.02
2010	11.38	75.78	11.38	0.02

Source http://www.stats.gov.cn

such a gap, and hopes to improve by developing the logistics infrastructure of railways, ports, airports, and roads. Indeed, logistics service capacities in China are believed to have been improved dramatically during the past ten years. However, while on the one side logistics facilities and technologies have been improved, on the other side the logistics cost still lingers around 18 % of GDP.

Table 1.1 shows that road takes the biggest ratio, about 3/4 of total logistics volume, and air takes the smallest ratio. In comparison, air logistics could be neglected. Rail takes a little more than water. Moreover, it is seen that the ratios for rail and road logistics have annually decreased, while the ratios for water and air have mostly increased. This indicates that water logistics plays a more and more important role in China.

This chapter mainly discusses rail, road and water logistics. It is organized as follows. Section 1.2 reviews literature. In Sect. 1.3, we separately discuss the status of China logistics by water, land, rail, air, multimodal, third party logistics and others. Two case studies are given in Sect. 1.4. Section 1.5 provides the current trend of logistics shifting in China.

1.2 Literature Review

Various publications have addressed different aspects of Chinese logistical issues. Paleari et al. (2010) analyze the most beneficial *network* for final passengers in terms of travel time. A time-dependent minimum path approach is employed to calculate the minimum travel time between each pair of airports in the three networks, inclusive of flight times and waiting times in intermediate airports. They evaluate each fastest indirect connection in terms of waiting times and routing factors to consider the effect of the hubs' coordination and locations. Particularly they point out that the Chinese network provides the quickest travel for passengers, but this performance is explained by a small number of airports per inhabitant. They also compare the logistics network in China with those in US and EU.

Zhang and Figliozzi (2010) discuss the performance of international and domestic transport and logistics systems as perceived by Chinese importers and exporters. Results and analysis of in-depth interviews with those importers and exporters are presented. Li et al. (2009) did a survey to study the current status of the logistics systems of Japanese companies in China; results show the characteristics and trends of these systems. Moreover, the survey also shows the current Chinese logistics service situation. Tongzon and Nguyen (2009) use a computable general equilibrium (CGE) model to examine the effects of China's continued economic rise on the Australian logistics sector. Dalya and Cui (2003) conduct interviews to examine the reality of issues surrounding *e-commerce and logistics* in China today. Some challenges are identified both for today and in the future.

Bai and Qian (2010) consider the development of the electricity, highway, and railway sectors in China, with special emphasis on *investment incentives*. Statistical summary of the development of these sectors is offered, followed by a detailed description of the institutional background, including investment and pricing mechanisms. They further analyze investment incentives based on the institutional background, and present estimates of the rates of return to investment in these sectors. It is observed that some of the current practices may serve as useful transitional arrangements, even though they are not desirable in the long run.

Cheng and Masser (2003) present a spatial data-analysis method to seek and model major determinants of urban growth in the period 1993–2000 through a case study of Wuhan City in China. The method comprises exploratory data analysis and a spatial logistic regression technique. Their study shows that the major determinants are urban road infrastructure and developed area, while master planning was losing some of its role during that period. Wang (2007a) provides his view from four aspects on challenges in developing modern logistics in China: (1) Huge geographical variations. (2) Absence of a fully integrated national transport network. (3) Multiple jurisdictions and local protectionism and (4) Old-fashioned wholesale market places remaining competitive.

Wu (2009b) discusses logistics services provided to domestic and foreign customers by manufacturing suppliers in China, and how the need to serve different customers affects their organization. This study is from the viewpoint of those Chinese suppliers, by attempting to understand customer logistics service criteria, IT services, customer selection criteria, and the difficulties and future challenges facing Chinese enterprises.

There is also literature concerning the logistics of sea ports in China. Cullinane and Wang (2007) study the historical context for the country's concurrent reform of its port industry, and discuss three distinct phases of development. They also point out that it is still too early to tell whether the latest phase of reforms will prove to be successful in solving China's port problems– particularly the capacity issue—and suggest possible implications of the reforms for overseas investment and future levels of concentration within the market.

Railway logistics has played an important role in Chinese logistics development in the past. Li and Cai (2007) give an empirical analysis of the statistical properties of the China Railway Network (CRN) consisting of 3,915 nodes (train stations) and 22,259 edges (direct track connections between stations). Wang et al. (2008) perform a similar detailed analysis, investigating the path length that every train runs, the distribution of the railroad path lengths and the optimal distribution of stations.

Li and Cai (2007) display two explicit features already observed in numerous real-world and artificial networks. Logistic curves and Gaussian curves are used to predict China's coal peak; results show that this peak demand will be between the late 2020s and the early 2030s. A regional survey of shipping companies and owners employed factor analysis to reveal that port service, hinterland condition, availability, convenience, logistics cost, regional center and connectivity are the determining factors in these regions.

Zhu et al. (2010) study residual deformation laws and a model of the permafrost subgrade under train traffic, based on dynamic triaxial tests at low temperature of the frozen clay from the Beiluhe permafrost subgrade along the Qinghai–Tibet Railway (QTR). Wang et al. (2009) analyze the expansion of China's railway network, the evolution of its spatial accessibility, and the impacts on economic growth and urban systems over a time span of about one century (1906–2000). Their study indicates that railway network expansion has significantly improved economic development and heavily influenced the formation of Chinese urban systems.

Rong and Bouf (2005) address the issue of railway reform in China with a description of the strengths and the weaknesses of Chinese railways. There follows a review of the different ways of putting competitive pressure on railways and an analysis of their application to railways in China. Intermodal competition, parallel competition, and competition for and in the market are analyzed from this perspective.

Publications have also studied air logistics in China. Wang (2007b) uses quality function deployment to integrate quality technology and the voice of outside consumers. He illustrates the service performance of Chinese air-cargo sector and offers suggestions for improvement. Yang et al. (2008) review the privatization and commercialization of China's airports. They look at the ways in which change has been brought about. There remain a number of challenges that constrain further development of the airports. In the long run, greater diversification and commercialization of airport ownership structures may be necessary. Lack of transparent performance indicators to gauge policy successes or failures is hampering the reform process of China's Aviation Industry.

Goh and Ling (2003) discussed the status, developments and challenges related to the transportation modes of highway, rail, water and air, and to telecommunications, warehousing and customs administration. They pointed out that the lack of physical high-tech warehouse structures and a computerized customs system were indeed logistics impediments, and that greater challenges lay in cultivating a skilled and knowledgeable labor force.

Fig. 1.1 Map of China

For road-related logistics in China, Fan and Kang (2008) estimate the impact of road investments on overall economic growth, rural and urban growth, and rural and urban poverty reduction. An econometric model that captures the different channels through which road investment impacts growth and poverty is developed and estimated using Chinese provincial-level data. Low-grade (mostly rural) roads have benefit/cost ratios for national GDP that are about four times larger than the benefit/cost ratios of high-grade roads. Low-grade roads raise far more rural and urban poor above the poverty line per RMB invested than do high-grade roads. Road investments yield their highest economic returns in the eastern and central regions of China, while their contributions to poverty reduction are greatest in western China (especially the southwest region).

When we mention the eastern, middle or western regions of China, the corresponding provinces or cities are as follows (Fig. 1.1). **Eastern region**: Liaoning, Hebei, Beijing, Tianjin, Shandong, Jiangsu, Shanghai, Zhejiang, Fujian, Guangxi.
Middle region: Helongjiang, Jilin, Shanxi, Henan, Hubei, Hunan, Anhui.
Western region: Inner Mongolia, Guangxi, Sichuan, Chongqing, Guizhou, Yunnan, Tibet, Shannxi, Gansu, Ningxia, Qinghai, Xinjiang.

Generally, both the economy as well as logistics are more developed in the east, followed by the middle region, and least developed in the west.

1.3 Logistics Status in China

In this section, we briefly review the current status of Logistics in China (See also Wang 2007a).

Table 1.2 Waterway logistics facilities

Years	Inland navigation length (thousands of kilometers)	Number of ports	
		Production quay and berth	Above 10 K tons
2001	122	33441	810
2002	122.6	33600	835
2003	124	34289	899
2004	123.3	35108	944
2005	123.3	35242	1034
2006	123.4	35453	1203
2007	123.5	35947	1337
2008	122.8	31050	1416
2009	123.7	31429	1554
2010	124.2	31634	1661

Source http://www.stats.gov.cn

1.3.1 Waterway Logistics

China has two major navigable rivers, the Yangtze River and the Yellow River. The Yangtze River Valley has a population of 440 million (Basics of Yangtze River Valley and its position in China economic developments. 2004) and GDP of RMB 6987 billion (Yangtze River Valley's economy took an upstanding start and grew stably in 2010). (The approximate conversion rate between Chinese RMB and US dollar since March 2011 is 6.5635.) Population is about 107 million in the Yellow River Valley, where the GDP is around RMB 484 billion. Most regions in these two valleys are undeveloped. If China wants to develop the economies there, the importance of the inland waterway navigation system must be recognized. That is because the status of railway and truck transportation is still primitive, and cannot be improved in a relatively short time.

From Table 1.2, we can see that at the end of 2010, China had approximately 124,200 km of navigable inland waterways, to rank first in the world. About 50 % are standard waterways (An update on the transport infrastructure in China 2010). On the other hand, Table 1.2 shows that the total lengths of inland navigation have not increased. In fact, the number of berths or quays is even in a decreasing trend, although the number of large ports has grown. The latter is due to enhanced demands for large vessels for their greater efficiency. At the same time, customers pursue cost reductions by increasing the transportation batch size, and prefer to select waterway logistics if large-berth capacities are available.

Table 1.3 shows that the number of vessels is decreasing and net weight is increasing. Improvements in the efficiency of water logistics are thus based on economies of scale in transportation batch size.

Inland waterways are still in a less-developed state. Only 12.3 % of them permit ships with loads of more than 300 tons. Some inland navigation berths have lagged behind in equipment and have poor loading efficiencies, and are not even deep enough to match the requirements of large vessels.

Table 1.3 Water logistics vessels

Years	Number (thousands)	Net weight (thousands of tons)	Average weight (thousands of tons)
2001	211	54495	2583
2002	203	57056	2811
2003	204	70616	3457
2004	211	86173	4090
2005	207	101786	4910
2006	194	110257	5673
2007	192	118815	6196
2008	184	124169	6741
2009	177	146088	8260
2010	178	180409	1011

Source http://www.moc.gov.cn

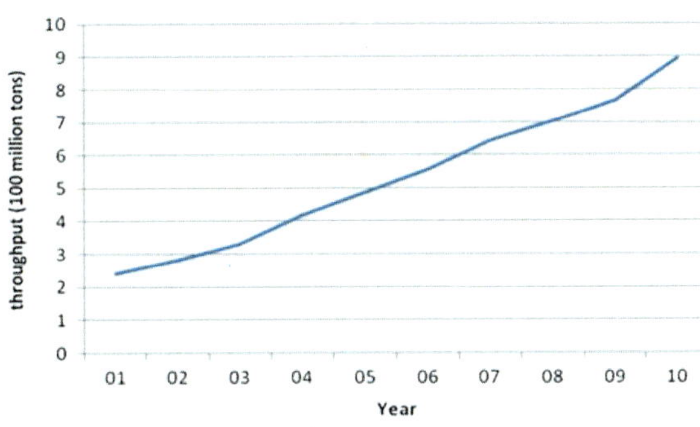

Fig. 1.2 Port throughput from 2001 to 2010. *Source* http://www.moc.gov.cn/

Port throughput can be recognized as following a trend of economic development. By Fig. 1.2, it is seen that port throughput is increasing continuously at almost a linear rate. China's demand from global contract manufacturing may slow down, which will affect the sea cargo logistics. However, if domestic logistics does grow, waterway logistics is also expected to do so during the period of the 12th five year plan. Actually, China has six of the ten largest (in terms of cargo-container throughput) ports in the world; in 2010, Shanghai, Shenzhen and Hong Kong were ranked numbers 1, 3 and 4 respectively.

1.3.2 Land Logistics

The efficiency of transport by land depends mainly on the overall road length, total number of trucks and the road density. Table 1.4 shows that the total road length has continuously increased during the first decade of this century, and the increases

Table 1.4 Road length and density

Years	Total road length (thousands of kilometers)	Length of grade highway (thousands of kilometers)	Road density (kilometers/ hundred square kilometers)
2001	1698	1336	17.7
2002	1765	1383	18.4
2003	1810	1439	18.9
2004	1871	1516	19.5
2005	1931	1592	20.1
2006	3457	2283	36.0
2007	3584	2535	37.3
2008	3730	2779	38.9
2009	3861	3056	40.2
2010	4008	3305	41.8

Source http://www.moc.gov.cn/

are mainly from grade highways. (Here, "grade highway" means a road or highway of better quality.) Road density also increased accordingly.

The highest rate of increase occurred at the turnover year of 2006, from the 10th to the 11th five-year planning period. This correctly indicates the importance of policy in China, because unfinished but scheduled activities are expected to be implemented at the end of each five-year interval under the centralized control of the Chinese government. Hence, we expect that the land conditions will have also been improved in the years 2010 and 2011.

Figure 1.3 shows that both the number of cargo vehicles (trucks) and the number of passenger vehicles generally increased during the past ten years. The exception, in 2005, is due to the adoption of a different statistical method that year. For example, different from the method from 2005 to 2009, the statistical number of passenger vehicles for 2010 excludes buses and taxis within city. Actually, the quantity of passenger vehicles has been increased by 5.9 % from 2009 to 2010. One can find details in the statistical communiqué of China transportation developments on road and waterway in 2010 (http://www.moc.gov.cn).

Table 1.5 summarizes the rapid growth in road freight traffic. Transportation accounts for the largest component of total logistics costs, at around 55 percent (RMB 2.1 trillion),followed by inventory storage costs (RMB 1.2 trillion) and management costs(RMB 500 billion) (Logistics in China. 2008). Gasoline and toll payments are the two main fees in transportation cost. The proportion of gasoline in the total transportation cost was 25 % in 2004, increasing to 40 % in 2008 with the rise in oil price (Xu 2009). However, the greatest cost is not from gas or oil but rather in paying tolls.

Requiring the payment of tolls can control and guarantee the quality of traffic flow, helping the highway system play its important role in developing the national economy. But when toll payments comprise 30–50 % of transport cost, the overall logistics expense may negatively impact road utilization and transportation efficiency. It is thus reasonable to seek feasible ways of reducing toll and gasoline expenses.

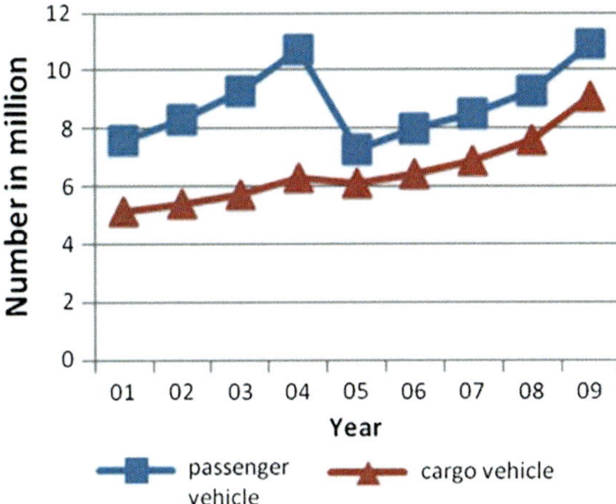

Fig. 1.3 Number of passenger and freight vehicles from 2001 to 2009

Table 1.5 Road freight traffic

Years	Freight traffic (billions of tons)
2001	9.4
2002	9.8
2003	9.8
2004	10.9
2005	11.9
2006	14.7
2007	16.4
2008	19.2
2009	21.3
2010	24.5

Source http://www.stats.gov.cn

With the loans for many highways having been paid off, toll charges are expected to be canceled or reduced. For example, in the year 2005, the Jing-shi highway connecting Beijing and Shijiazhuang accumulated RMB 1.7 billion in toll fees. After paying off the highway's loan principal and interest, almost RMB 600 million were left. The government could thus lengthen the payment period or construct a new system of tolls with different prices for various spaces, seasons and times (Cai 2008).

It should be noted that since highways always charge a significant toll, truck drivers prefer to choose roads with no charge rather than highways. However, the current road capacity is quite limited. For example (Shanxi Coal Shipping 2010), during the busy summer season for coal shipping, traffic is extremely heavy at the border of Shanxi province on Qing-yin road. The daily traffic in coal trucks could easily be in the thousands; the resulting traffic jam can reach 50 km. Blocking of the road for more than four days is very normal (see Fig. 1.4).

Fig. 1.4 Heavy traffic for coal transport in China

In 2004, China State Council approved a 7918 Network plan, in which 7 radial (from Beijing), 9 vertical (north–south) and 18 horizontal (east–west) roads will be constructed. The plan will extend the road network from 1.9 to 3 million kilometers and the expressways from 34 K to 85 K kilometers by 2020. It will cover most areas of China, whose population is one billion. The plan will connect all the provincial capitals, large cities with a population over 500,000 and medium-sized cities over 200,000. We expect that this plan will have a great impact on China's logistics, as well as on business, defense and security.

1.3.3 Railway Logistics

After three decades of rapid economic growth, both freight and passenger traffic volumes increased significantly, and reached or exceeded the designed capacity of the railway network. The relative importance of rail travel has declined over time. Specifically, the percentage of passenger trips by railway in China declined from 77 % in 1950 to 6.1 % of all passenger trips in 2007. By contrast, the respective percentage of trips by road and air passengers increased from 11.3 to 92.1 %, and from 0.005 to 0.83 %, of all passenger trips. The railway administration is more centralized and strictly controlled by the state than are other transportation modes. Railroads have faced increasing pressure from market-oriented reforms and decentralization. High-speed railway development and railway deregulation have been proposed as possible remedies to improve its competitiveness. Given the advantages in energy efficiency and environmental impact, railways should receive favorable governmental attention over air and highway transportation (Wang et al. 2008).

Railway logistics is suitable to transport low-value and large-batch goods such as coal and food. For the western regions to develop and compete with other developed regions, the most feasible way is to enhance the railway facilities in the west.

Table 1.6 Railway Freight Traffic

Years	Volume (millions of tons)
2001	1926
2002	2044
2003	2235
2004	2481
2005	2684
2006	2871
2007	3145
2008	3259
2009	3320
2010	3640

Source http://www.stats.gov.cn

From Table 1.6, we can see that Chinese railway freight traffic has continuously increased from 2001 to 2009. By the end of 2010, the total length of track was 91,000 km, placing China second in the world, just behind the US (An update on the transport infrastructure development in China 2010). (By comparison, China had just 22,000 km of track in 1949). Moreover, the total track length of high-speed (above 200 km/h) railways reached 8358 km; that was ranked *first* in the world. By 2012, China will have constructed eight high-speed railway routes, with four running between east and west and the other four connecting north and south. The total track length of high-speed railways will be 13,000 km; this includes 5000 km with speeds of 250 km/h and 8000 km with a speed of 350 km/h (Micro investigation of Chinese high-speed railway 2010). By 2020, the total passenger railway system will comprise 18,000 km (An update on the transport infrastructure development in China: railway transportation 2010).

With the high-speed rail system, geographic distance will no longer be an obstacle for economic development. By 2012,the high-speed railway will closely connect the Yangtze River Delta, Pearl River Delta, Bohai Bay and other cities. It will take only four hours from Beijing to Shanghai, seven hours from Beijing to Guangzhou, five hours from Hangzhou to Shenzhen, and six hours from Nanjing to Chengdu. Three urban circles, Jing-Jin, Hu-Ning-Hang, and Guang-Shen respectively will be finally formed. There are also three relatively small economic circles: The middle-south urban circle of Zhengzhou, Wuhan and Changsha; The west-north urban circle of Xi'an and Baoji, and the west-south urban circle of Chengdu and Chongqing.

High-speed railway development will make it easy for passengers to reach a large hub airport. Hence, via advanced systems of communication, the airlines and high-speed railways can use their advantages together. In fact, there are many airports in the world where such air-railway models are adopted, with even a special railway waiting room set up for passengers in the airport. But in China, the biggest obstacle for air-railway allied transportation comes from "non-smooth" communication channels between the different administrative departments to which they belong. Recently, China has opened a communication hub center in Shanghai. That furnishes not just an air-rail connection, but also connects the subway and highway systems of Shanghai.

The Wuguang high-speed railway, linking Wuhan and Guangzhou, was set up in 2009. It increases not only the passenger capacity but also the freight capacity. During the spring festival of 2010, the frequency of trains between Wuhan and Guangzhou was decreased by 9.4 % compared to the same period of 2009, but the passenger train traffic *increased* by 17.5 %, reaching 2.133 million people. Total freight traffic belonging to the Wuhan railway bureau increased by 22.8 % in 2010, or by 10.63 million tons compared to 2009.

Moreover, high-speed rail service will greatly affect the airline business (High-speed vs airline, changes of a time on transportation 2009). Because most high-speed railways are located in the eastern regions and most airlines and air traffic also operate there, there exists much airline-railroad competition in these regions. For middle or short-distance trips (200 to 1000 km), high-speed rail is competitive to air. Indeed, over such distances, rail's total travel time is even shorter than that by air, and transportation capacity with high-speed is far greater. Moreover, high-speed rail is not sensitive to climate and has excellent on-time rate and safety. Although this may threaten the business of airlines, it will also provide much room for airline development. In China, as elsewhere, a given railway may have many stations, and most are in those cities with airports. So it is easy to construct a hub-spoke transportation structure in which goods are collected by railroads to airport hubs, and the long distance transport carried out by airlines. We also believe that such a hub-spoke structure is helpful for China to implement an economic transfer from the eastern to western regions. Short-distance transportation can be done by railway in the inner eastern region or the western region, while airlines would address the long-distance transportation between the eastern region and the west (Chen et al. 2010).

We remark that a high-speed railway has no explicit impact on water transportation. While the development of railways and roads around rivers may reduce initial demand for river transportation, the progressing of railways and improved roads will greatly enhance the demands for water logistics (Qi et al. 2006).

Although no specific high-speed *freight* railway has been constructed, the high-speed rail passenger service releases much capacity for freight traffic (High-speed vs airline, changes of a time on transportation 2009). Apart from the Shen-Qin special passenger railway, almost all other railways in China serve both passengers and freight. However, from the experiences of US, Japanese or European countries, it is better to separate the freight and passenger traffic (Rong and Bouf 2005). High-speed railways will increase the current capacity for passengers. This may help to release some rail service to be used only for freight. As a result, the capacity, speed, and safety of cargo transportation will be improved (Li and Qi 2007).

Although Chinese high-speed rail has bright prospects, there are still several challenges, all related to pricing. Expensive ticket prices may exclude many

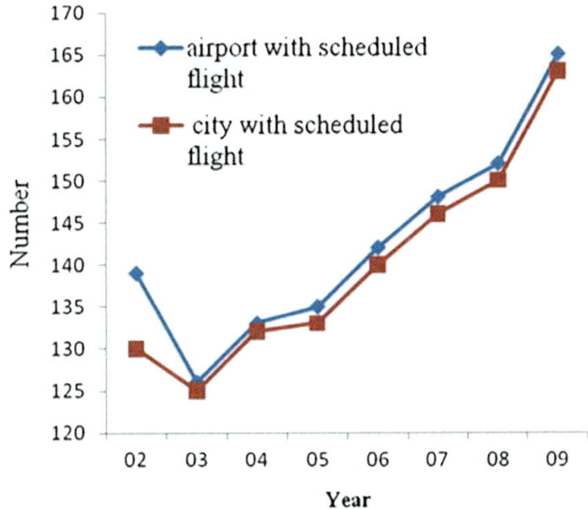

Fig. 1.5 Number of airports and cities with scheduled flights. *Source* http://www.moc.gov.cn/

Source: http://www.stats.gov.cn

customers. China has not found a reasonable pricing mechanism, whether in the peak periods or in the off-peak hours, to ensure profit for high-speed railways.

China's rail density at the end of 2010 was 0.95 km of track per 100 km^2; by contrast, the 2009 figure was 6.14 km for Japan and 2.26 km for the United States. The other measure is *traffic density*, which is calculated by the number of traffic units (i.e., the sum of ton-kilometers and passenger-kilometers) per kilometer of railroad. China's traffic density is three times that of American railroads and seven times that of European Union railways. High traffic density shows the relative scarcity of railway infrastructure in China (Rong and Bouf 2005).

There is little double-tracking and average train speed is still low. The heavy haul railway, high-speed railway, and the operations management systems are at an initial stage, to be improved. It is known that six hundred container freight stations exist (Zhu et al. 2010). However, many are reconstructed from ordinary cargo stations, and therefore equipment or facilities are not very appropriate for containerized freight. Moreover, these container stations may not be located at the best sites.

1.3.4 Air Logistics

Reynolds-Feighan (2013), in the present volume, presents a comprehensive review of air freight networks around the world. In China, the number of airports and cities with scheduled flights has been increasing significantly since 2003 (see Fig. 1.5). Airline industrial infrastructure is also sharply improving. There are many connections among cities (Table 1.7). A growing number of airports now handle more than 10,000 tons of cargo annually (Table 1.8).

Table 1.7 Annual throughput and number of flights

Years	Goods throughput (millions of tons)	No. flights (millions)
2001	3.4	1.7
2002	4.0	1.9
2003	4.5	1.9
2004	5.5	2.5
2005	6.3	2.8
2006	7.5	3.1
2007	8.6	3.5
2008	8.8	3.8
2009	9.5	4.4
2010	11.3	5.5

Source http://www.caac.gov.cn

Table 1.8 Number of airports with more than 10,000 ton annual throughput

Years	Number	Percentage of total number of airports
2002	35	97.2
2003	38	98.3
2004	39	98.4
2005	39	98.5
2006	39	98.4
2007	43	98.7
2008	44	98.8
2009	45	98.8
2010	47	98.8

Source http://www.caac.gov.cn

Compared to the EU and US, China's network has fewer airports per capita and per unit area, and offers a lower level of service to passengers to get access to the network (Paleari et al. 2010). The geographical density of airports in China has an uneven distribution. There are only 1.5 airports per 100,000 km^2 in China compared with 6.4 airports per 100,000 km^2 in US. Airports are mainly located in eastern regions, particularly the Yangtze River Valley, Pearl River Valley and Bohai Bay, while the western regions have only about 1.0 airport per 100,000 km^2. The lowest density is in the Xinjiang region, where that ratio is only 0.6 (Yang et al. 2008).

1.3.5 Multimodal Transportation

As far back as 1962, the Chinese government strongly encouraged alliances between road and waterway transportation (Current status of multimodal transport in China 2010). In 1989, the government further funded a "973" project concerning the multi-modal international container transportation system. This work was sponsored by the ministry of transport of the People's Republic of China, the water transportation institute and the Shanghai municipal government. The project in fact played an important role in developing container regularization and its modernization, as well as multimodal transportation in China. In addition, since 2000, China has pursued collaboration with developed countries such as Canada and the United States on multimodal transportation.

Recently, in order to meet demands for international trade, China has encouraged several modes to open transportation links with some countries or regions including Japan, United States, Africa, Western Europe, Australia, and Russia. The routes include those from Mongolia or Russia to Iran, and the Siberian Land Bridge between western and northern Europe. For example, China has adopted three transportation types: rail–rail, rail-sea and rail-road for Siberian Land Bridge businesses, for which container transportation has been developed quickly with 10,000 TEU per year (Current status of multimodal transport in China 2010).

However, the distribution of different transportation types is not reasonable to support multimodal transportation. Road transportation takes more than 74 % of total logistics traffic. The other shares are 13 % for rail, from 10 to 12 % for water, and less than 1 % for air. Table 1.1 shows that such a division is relatively stable.

Multimodal transportation of international containers started in the 1970s. To this point, there are three organizational types: sectional transportation, international allied transportation and multimodal transportation. The sectional type accounts for more than 90 % of international container transportation (Guo 2010). This also means that the multimodal transport of international containers is still in the initial stages for China.

Sea-rail is a main type of intermodal transportation for most of the world. The rapid development of China's economic and international trade has enhanced the demands for container transportation. In China, however, the percentage of sea-rail transportation is low compared to water-and-road transportation. This limits the opportunities for multimodal development there. In fact, for much of the globe, containerized rail shipments constitute a large percentage of rail logistics, e.g., about 49 % in the United States, 40 % in France, 30 % in England, 35 % in India. However, that figure is only 2.2 % for China. In developed countries, the sea-rail percentage can reach from 20 to 40 %, while it is only 1.5 % in China (Sea-rail logistics 2008).

The pioneering Shanghai Hongqiao communication center has realized an almost-zero transfer-time between railway (high-speed) and airline. Such a new model will bring airline and high-speed rail together and provide air-rail service. We admit that in China, airlines and railroads are separately managed by different governmental departments. Hence, some obstacles still exist for such an alliance. However, the successful model in Shanghai will shed light on a bright perspective for other cities, such as Tianjin and Shenzhen, to develop their multimodal transportation, particularly rail-sea.

The other modes (waterway and road) are also managed by different Chinese divisions. It is thus hard to bring all departments together when making a decision on infrastructure construction. Consequently, the capacities of each type are not synchronized, which limits the development of multimodal transportation. Moreover, managerial efficiency is lower in China than elsewhere, and market barriers persist. The famous example is that many sizes of container are in use. China currently has 1-, 5- and 10-ton, and 20- and 40-foot rail containers. Only the 20- and 40-foot sizes can be employed for rail-sea multimodal transportation (Zhou 2007). But other container types are not easy to eliminate. There are still many small vehicles, but few large or special vehicles, such as frozen trucks, van trucks and flat-bed trucks. The number of special cars or unit trains is limited for rail transportation.

China's multimodal transport shows a lack of connection between different partners compared to western developed countries. There is no "multimodal transportation operator" to manage the transport when two or more modes are involved. Only in the regions of Shanghai, Zhejiang, Jiangsu and Jing-jin-tang, are the bills and documents signed by carriers or agents. Rail container transportation cannot connect with port and other foreign departments in a smooth way, thus causing multimodal problems that cannot be solved in the near future.

The system of freight collection, distribution and transportation is not well organized. Freight equipment is insufficient; bill of lading cannot be shared with others. Empty containers cannot even be returned from inland locations, thus affecting loading efficiency. The main reason is lagging information technologies. For example, electronic data interchange (EDI) is still in the process of development for many logistics partners. There is no unified system in China to connect customs and the department of inspection and quarantine. Multiple transportation styles are not easily integrated in a business-like manner. The Chinese government, realizing these deficiencies, is trying to reform its policies. It is investing in process improvements to reduce the gap with developed countries.

1.3.6 Third Party Logistics

The annual rate of capital turnover is between 10 and 20 in developed countries (Hu 2009). That figure in China is 2.1 overall and 2.8 for manufacturing and key materials-trading companies. This leads to increased holding costs, reduction in revenue, and decreasing competition. As a result of the economic recession, 2009 was the toughest year for Chinese logistics over the past thirty years. The logistics profit rate is currently less than 10 %, down from 30 % in 2000. Profit rates for inventory and transportation are respectively about 4 and 3 %. Logistics volume in international trade has indeed decreased about 20 %, but *domestic* logistics has increased by over 20 % (Blue print: profit rate of logistics 2010). Third party logistics in China accounts only for 2 % of the total logistics market, compared to

30 % in developed countries (Demand analysis and development strategy of third party logistics in China 2009).

Based on an investigation conducted by the Chinese Logistics and Purchasing Association, 76 % of companies employ an integrated logistics model. 20 % of enterprises use "90 % self-operation and little outsourcing," while 11 % utilize "from 70 to 90 % self-operation and outsourcing". Another 20 % of firms use "40 to 70 % self-operation and outsourcing", and 25 % practice "10 to 40 % self-operation and outsourcing". Various enterprises invest differently in 3PL and focus on distinct issues. Automotive companies, including Changan and Ford, care more about inventory-level reduction by 3PL. Garment and textile enterprises, including Jeanswest, Nike, and Younger, focus more on how to reduce production cycle time.

Electrolux, Haier, Hessense, Konka, Meiling, Philips and Sharp are consumer electronics firms. Their goal is reduction in logistics cost. Food enterprises (e.g., Kraft; Shanghai Bright Dairy and Food; Qingdao Beer) worry more about green logistics and cold-chain logistics. Service enterprises, among them Siemens, BenQ, Acer, HP, Huawei, Lenovo, Lucent, Motorola and ZTE require IT and communication aid from their 3PL providers.

Once China joined the WTO in 2001, global logistics service providers such as DHL, UPS, TNT, and APL Logistics have established their businesses in China through joint ventures. We believe that the trend of outsourcing logistics operations to a 3PL will continue.

1.3.7 Other Issues

1. **Free Trade Zones**

In a free trade zone (FTZ), an enterprise can make its supply chain simple and efficient, as well as have access to a low cost and high quality logistics infrastructure (Zhang and Figliozzi 2010). Doing so can avoid a complex supply chain with undeveloped logistics facilities and local policy restrictions. In 2006, the gross freight volume passing through free trade zones accounted for 6.2 % of total volume in China (Economics development analysis for free trade zone 2010).

There are fifteen free trade zones whose performance has been uneven. Shanghai, Shenzhen, Tianjin, Zhangjiagang, Ningbo and Dalian have developed better than others. Some FTZs have been impacted by the high price of materials, thereby experiencing slow growth. Meanwhile, trading companies are heavily affected by national policies, which cause free trade zones some challenges in absorbing customers. Furthermore, export processing zones, free trade port zones and special customs supervision zones also have some functions as a free trade zone. This further increases the pressure on those FTZs in China.

2. **Logistics Parks**

Logistics-intensive clusters, and logistics parks in particular, are discussed in the present volume by Sheffi (2013). A logistics park can provide a synergistic location for 3PLs, transportation carriers or DCs that all service distribution-oriented industrial firms. Such a location could also be synergistic for particular companies that perform most or some of their own distribution activities themselves. Sheffi lists a number of significant logistics parks in various countries, including China.

Here we limit ourselves to pointing out that China has about 475 logistics parks. Among them, 122 are running, 219 are in the process of construction and 134 parks are in the planning stage. Integrated service parks represent the highest percentage with 75 %, while cargo service takes 18 % and manufacturing service has 3 %. Trade parks comprise 2 %, and others 2 %. Among them, 84 % have some sort of management information system (Tongzon and Nguyen 2009).

Many Chinese logistics parks were built in a rush, without sufficient justification and with no definite objectives. The value of current logistics parks in China needs to be reevaluated. Since many are in the process of construction or planning, they are still far from full implementation of all functions. But Sheffi (2013) makes a case for the value of such parks when there is a mature logistics infrastructure.

3. **Education and Training**

In 2008, Logistics was designated as one of the ten industries for development in China, and where related education will be provided. There is a lack of *six million* people specifically trained in logistics (China Logistics and Purchasing Association 2009). Among them, the shortage of advanced managers is about 30 to 50 thousand, and more than 100 thousand others in operations or sales could benefit from logistics training.

In order to regularize the human resources market in Logistics, the Chinese Logistics and Purchasing Association began in 2003 to assist the Ministry of Labor and Social Security. National standards were established for training and or degree requirements in certificate Logistics. In 2004, training and examination locations were set up in over 25 provinces or regions. Since then, more than 5,000 people have obtained Bachelors or Masters degrees (Wu 2009a). About 340 universities and 730 advanced polytechnic schools have now set up a logistics major. In the polytechnic case, approximately 35,000 students have graduated or are presently enrolled in that major. Today, other organizations in 37 cities offer training in logistics (China Logistics and Purchasing Association 2009). Those organizations include training companies, logistics research institutes and universities, and consulting firms that will invite academic or industrial experts to provide help in training.

1.4 Case Studies

Case 1. OEM Company

Company A is an original equipment manufacturer (OEM). It provides multinational design, manufacturing and logistics services for the computer, communications and consumer electronics (3C) industries. Its gross revenue exceeds RMB 400 billion per year. Inbound and outbound logistics are very important for Company A to serve its customers. The firm outsources a portion of its inbound logistics to a 3PL provider who uses VMI (vendor managed inventory) to control stocks. However, Company A itself owns a logistics firm (we denote it by DL). 90 % of the inbound logistics of Company A is operated by DL. And DL is in turn managed by an internal logistics department of Company A.

Its outbound logistics is also operated by the same logistics firm, DL. Company A has even set up a distribution center for DL in a logistics park, where DL turns LTL loads into FTL loads by consolidation. Nevertheless, this does not mean that Company A can control all its inbound or outbound operations. Because Company A is an OEM company, it will respect the customers' choices. For instance, some large international companies may appoint their own logistics provider. In such cases, the inbound or outbound logistics are performed by the appointed 3PL. Recently, due to lower-cost labor, Company A set up a new factory at an inland city in the middle of China. This change greatly increased the internal logistics flow among factories. Now, to ship their products overseas, Company A prefers a good sea-rail intermodal logistics system. Logistics cost has risen to between 13 and 18 % of the total cost for Company A to provide its products to customers. They do hope that this percentage can approach the 9–10 % seen in US.

Company A views the main reasons for high transportation costs to be too many toll stations, each requiring large payments. Company A has even suggested that the Chinese government privatize some nation-owned logistics companies, such as the China Railway Container Co. Moreover, it is said that modern information technologies would help improve logistics efficiency in China. For instance, use of such technology by toll stations would surely speed up each station's operation. Company A is very concerned about training its staff, and so has set up its own internal training school. As for logistics staff, language ability is the most important skill, and Company A has called for a deep coordination between universities and industrial firms to provide the best logistics education.

Case 2. 3PL Company

Company B is one of the largest 3PLs that provide automotive logistics service. It offers customers the inbound and outbound logistics for parts receiving and the shipment of finished cars respectively. Inbound, Company B collects parts every day from suppliers located less than 300 km from the car manufacturers. After those receiving processes, a line-feeding operation is performed to provide parts into buffers near the production lines. Company B also ships over 2,000 cars to more than 100 cities in the largest regions of China per day. The firm was surprised to see that their outbound logistics had negative profits, and only a 3–4 % profit margin for their inbound logistics and line-feeding operations.

High toll payments contributed most to their negative profit in outbound logistics. Actually, company B has a decision support system to schedule outbound logistics resulting in almost no waste in truck capacity. This fact reveals just how greatly the high toll payments have affected the survival of 3PLs. Another point we have learned from Company B is that Chinese firms are not so willing to outsource their logistics. Company B's main customers (i.e., car manufacturers) actually own a significant share of this 3PL. We found out that Company B did try, unsuccessfully, to extend its business to other customers during the past 10 years. Moreover, Company B owns a berth for exporting cars overseas. They have a good land-sea arrangement for multimodal transportation, with a warehouse in a free trade zone near that berth.

1.5 Future Trends of Logistics in China

The position of China as the world's factory is being threatened by countries such as Vietnam and India. Nevertheless, the following three "from-to" changes for the Chinese economy are observed, and will lead the logistics futures there.

1. **From eastern to middle or western**

With China's government focusing on balanced development over all the country, and under the pressure of high labor cost in developed regions, industries have begun to transfer from eastern to middle or western regions (Promoting industrial transfer from eastern to western region in China 2009). Although the infrastructural facilities in the latter regions have been improved in recent years, they are still far behind those in the developed east. For example, the railway density in the middle and western regions is 47 % below the average level in China. Only some major cities in the west have highway connections; transportation there depends mainly on lower-class roads. This leads to higher transportation costs in western regions than in the east (Yao and Ren 2009). Therefore, if China wants to grow the economies of its western regions, logistics within those regions, and logistics between there and the developed east, must be improved in advance. This poses a challenge, but also an opportunity, for the Chinese logistics industry.

2. **From global to domestic**

The financial recession of 2008 severely affected China's logistics industry through the impact of contract manufacturing. The Chinese government realizes that global economic recovery cannot happen within a short period. Actually, its domestic market has always been more substantial than the global market. Hence, China's "Twelfth Five-Year Plan" has clearly indicated that China will turn its economic development attention from the international market to the domestic one. However, infrastructure for domestic logistics is deficient compared to that for the global arena. China must therefore invest in its own logistics market to ensure the success of domestic developments. Taking into account these requirements, in 2009 China's government approved the construction of *seventeen* free trade logistics centers in the northwest region (Seventeen bonded logistics centers are approved 2009). Xi'an set up a state-level bonded logistics center in 2010; Xi'an can now extend its logistics service with a port function, via an intermodal connection to eastern sea ports (e.g., Tianjin).

International logistics companies also see such potential developments (Xi'an bonded logistics center 2010). For example, UPS has submitted an application to the State Post Bureau of China for a domestic license. Once approved by China's government, UPS will roll out a next-day delivery service and second- and third-day delivery products. UPS believes the Chinese domestic market could be as large as 5 million packages per day. (By comparison, in countries other than China and the US, UPS delivered a total of only 1.2 million packages daily in 2009.) (UPS eyeing China domestic parcel service market 2010).

3. **From urban to rural**

Urbanization has become the most important engine for China to stimulate its domestic economy (Hu 2003). It is easier to provide efficient logistics service for an urban population than for rural people who live far away geographically. There were 607 million urban residents, i.e., 45.7 % of the whole Chinese population, at the end of 2008 (China's urban population 2009). There are 655 cities in China. Among these, 118 cities have more than one million people; 39 are "super-big" cities with more than four million residents. China's urban population will rise to over 700 million people by 2015, when city dwellers will outstrip the rural population for the first time (Some 1.4b Chinese 2010).

Urbanization has changed people's shopping style and created huge opportunity for retail chain stores and for the logistics industry. Modern living definitely needs an efficient logistics system. But China's citizens still live mainly in undeveloped regions except for the east and southeast. However, as pointed out in the previous paragraph, the logistics infrastructure there is insufficient, nor is it efficient. Furthermore, with local municipal governments' protectionism and potentially different jurisdiction systems, the implementation of integrated logistics in rural areas remains challenging and difficult. So, we believe that is where there exists huge opportunities for China's logistics industry.

Acknowledgments We would like to thank Editor James Bookbinder for his extensive comments and suggestions which helped to improve significantly the presentation of this chapter.

References

An update on the transport infrastructure development in China: railway transportation. China distribution and trading, 2010, 68. LI&FUNG research centre

An update on the transport infrastructure in China: water transportation. China distribution and trading, 2010, 69. LI&FUNG research centre

Bai C, Qian Y (2010) Infrastructure development in China: the cases of electricity, highways, and railways. J Comp Econ 38:34–51

Basics of Yangtze River Valley and its position in China economic developments. http://www.cjw.com.cn/news/detail/20070413/85427.asp. 2004

Blue print: profit rate of logistics >20 %, survive after price war. http://info.02156.cn. 2010

Cai X (2008) Analysis on derating highway charge to lower logistic expense and restrain inflation (in Chinese). China Market 45:139–140

Chen W, Kuang X, Yang Y, Li H (2010) Analysis of the development of high-speed railway and the effects upon aviation logistics. Logistics Technol 4:8–10

Cheng J, Masser I (2003) Urban growth pattern modeling: a case study of Wuhan city, PR China. Landscape Urban Plann 62:199–217

China logistics and purchasing association. Annual report for China logistics annals. 2009, 399–410

China's urban population exceeds 600 million. http://www.chinadaily.com.cn/china/2009-06/16/content_8288412.htm. 2009

Cullinane K, Wang T (2007) Port governance in China. Devolution, port governance and port performance. Research in Transportation Economics 17:331–356

Current status of multimodal transport in China. http://www.examda.com/hydl/fudao/wuliu/20100107/103520546.html. 2010

Dalya SP, Cui L (2003) E-logistics in China: basic problems, manageable concerns and intractable solutions. Ind Mark Manage 32:235–242

Demand analysis and development strategy of third party logistics in China. http://www.chinawuliu.com.cn. 2009

Economics development analysis for free trade zone of the first half of 2010. http://www.cfea.org.cn/show_news.asp?id=8523. 2010

Fan S, Kang C (2008) Regional road development, rural and urban poverty: evidence from China. Transp Policy 15:305–314

Goh M, Ling C (2003) Logistics development in China. Int J Phys Distrib Logistics Manage 33:886–917

Guo Q (2010) Some thoughts on multimodal transport development in China. Logistics Eng Manage 4:3–4

High-speed vs airline, changes of a time on transportation. http://money.163.com/special/00253TN5/gaotie.html. 2009

Hu A (2003) Civilization is the main factor in promoting economic development of China. Population Sci China 6:1–8

Hu J (2009) Study on development status and strategies of third party logistics. Mod Bus Trade Ind 24:12–14

Li W, Cai X (2007) Empirical analysis of a scale-free railway network in China. Phys A 382: 693–703

Li Z, Qi R (2007) Influences of high-speed railway on logistics development of Hebei province. Hebei Enterp 4:23

Li R, Mao M, Zhang J (2009) An insight about logistics strategies and logistics systems of Japanese companies in China based on results of a questionnaire survey. Working Paper. Faculty of economics, University of Toyama, Japan

Logistics in China. http://www.kpmg.com/CN/en/IssuesAndInsights/ArticlesPublicationsPages/logistics-china-200804.aspx. 2008

Micro investigation of Chinese high-speed railway. http://www.peoplerail.com/gaotie/gtgk/201048/n06127451.html. 2010
Paleari S, Redondi R, Malighetti P (2010) A comparative study of airport connectivity in China, Europe and US: Which network provides the best service to passengers? Transp Res Part E 46:198–210
Promoting industrial transfer from eastern to western region in China (2009). J China Natl Sch Adm (in Chinese) 100–104
Qi Y, Qiao L, Hu G (2006) On the rapid railway and freeway network along the Yangtze River that influence the water transportation of the Yangtze River. Journal Chongqing Jiaotong University (Soc Sci Ed) 6:38–41
Reynolds-Feighan A (2013) Comparative analysis of air freight networks in regional markets around the globe. In: Bookbinder JH (ed) Global logistics. Springer, New York
Rong Z, Bouf D (2005) How can competition be introduced into Chinese railways? Transp Policy 12:345–352
Sea-rail logistics, key for reducing consolidation cost. http://www.chinaports.org/info/200807/110242.htm. 2008
Seventeen bonded logistics centers are approved. http://www.moc.gov.cn/zhuzhan/jiaotongxinwen/xinwenredian/200901xinwen/20090/t20090105_549425.html. 2009
Shanxi Coal Shipping: more than thousand of trucks are blocked. http://www.chinadaily.com.cn/dfpd/shanxi/2010-06-04/content_414769.html. 2010
Sheffi Y (2013) Logistics-intensive clusters: global competitiveness and regional growth. In: Bookbinder JH (ed) Global logistics. Springer, New York
Some 1.4b Chinese by 2015 http://www.straitstimes.com/BreakingNews/Asia/Story/STIStory_549540.html. 2010
Statistical Communiqué of the People's Republic of China on the 2010 National Economic and Social Development.http://www.stats.gov.cn/tjgb/ndtjgb/qgndtjgb/t20110228_402705692.htm
Tongzon J, Nguyen H-O (2009) China's economic rise and its implications for logistics: the Australian case. Transp Policy 16:224–231
UPS eyeing China domestic parcel service market: report. http://news.yahoo.com/s/nm/20100928/bs_nm/us_ups_china. 2010
US-China business council. US-China trade statistics and China's world trade statistics. http://www.uschina.org/statistics/tradetable.html. 2009
Wang J (2007a) Logistics in China. Chapter 24 in Waters D (ed): Global logistics—new directions in supply chain management, 5th edn. Kogan Page Publishers, London
Wang R (2007b) Improving service quality using quality function deployment: the air cargo sector of China airlines. J Air Transp Manag 13:221–228
Wang R, Tan J, Wang X, Wang D, Cai X (2008) Geographic coarse graining analysis of the railway network of China. Phys A 387:5639–5646
Wang J, Jin F, Mo H, Wang F (2009) Spatiotemporal evolution of China's railway network in the 20th century: an accessibility approach. Transp Res Part A 43:765–778
Wu F (2009a) Educational comparison between domestic and international logistics. J Jiangxi Inst Educ (Soc Sci) 30:30–33
Wu J (2009b) Logistics and IT services in China outsourcing in the manufacturing industries. In: de Pablos PO, Lytras MD (eds) The China information technology handbook, Springer Science, Berlin pp 311–333
Xi'an bonded logistics center has passed the acceptance. http://news.cnwest.com/content/2010-04/21/content_2962969.htm. 2010
Xiong M (2010) Lessons for China from a comparison of logistics in the U.S. and China. Master's Thesis, Sloan School of Management, MIT
Xu Y (2009) Affect and influence of fuel tax innovation on transportation. Transp Enterp Manage 6:7–9
Yang X, Tok S, Su F (2008) The privatization and commercialization of China's airports. J Air Transport Manage 14:243–251

Yangtze River Valley's economy took an upstanding start and grew stably in 2010. http://www.stats.gov.cn/was40/gjtjj_detail.jsp?searchword=GDP&channelid=6697&record=26. 2010

Yao H, Ren Z (2009) China western economic development report (2009). Social Science Academic Press (China), Beijing

Zhang Z, Figliozzi MA (2010) A survey of Chinese importers and exporters: China's logistics industry developments and the impacts of transportation system performance on supply chain costs and operations. Transport Rev 30:179–194

Zhou G (2007) Analysis of development of the multi-modal transport. Logistics Sci-Tech 30: 99–100

Zhu Z, Ling X, Chen S, Zhang F, Wang L, Wang Z, Zou Z (2010) Experimental investigation on the train-induced subsidence prediction model of Beiluhe permafrost subgrade along the Qinghai-Tibet railway in China. Cold Reg Sci Technol 62:67–75

Chapter 2
Electronic Procurement Systems in India: Importance and Impact on Supply Chain Operations

R. P. Sundarraj and Komal Kumari

Abstract Electronic Procurement Systems (EPS) are being acknowledged by researchers as promising technological enablers for achieving a responsive supply chain, and thereby, for gaining a competitive advantage in today's global marketplace. A number of empirical studies have focused on the adoption of EPS in different countries. There is, however, a scarcity of work related to EPS adoption in India, even though information technology and the Internet play a significant role in that country. To fill this gap, we first discuss the potential supply chain benefits of EPS, especially as they relate to large multinational companies. Then, we specifically consider the Indian context. We highlight several firms whose innovative logistics operations permit the respective supply chains to function, uniquely blending Indian customs with modern business practices. We report on an empirical survey, as well as three case-studies relating to the importance and impact of EPS adoption in India.

Part of this work was done while the authors were at: Great Lakes Institute of Management, East Coast Road, Manamai, 603102; India.

R. P. Sundarraj (✉) · K. Kumari
Department of Management Studies, Indian Institute of Technology Madras,
Chennai 600036, India
e-mail: rpsundarraj@iitm.ac.in

J. H. Bookbinder (ed.), *Handbook of Global Logistics*, International Series in Operations Research & Management Science 181, DOI: 10.1007/978-1-4419-6132-7_2,

2.1 Introduction

Effective supply chains are crucial for a firm to remain competitive in today's market. This effectiveness is driven by striving for proper synchronization and coordination of all activities across the entire supply-chain network, ranging from end-customers to suppliers. As a result, once-relegated functions such as procurement, a primary determinant for the organization's relationship with suppliers, become important.

With the growth of electronic commerce (Carter et al. 2000), procurement processes have also evolved by being enabled electronically. Perhaps, the first step toward that evolution has come in the form of enterprise resource planning (ERP) systems, aimed primarily at integrating the internal value chain of an organization. With its roots in traditional manufacturing systems such as MRP II, ERP systems have now metamorphosed into information technologies that seek to manage the extended enterprise as well (i.e., the entire supply chain). Thus, conceptually, these new-generation ERP systems (also sometimes known as ERP II) encompass not only the core intra-organizational features but have expanded into a number of domains such as supplier-management, customer management etc. Today, owing to advances in software technology, the implementation of ERP II has often involved a core ERP system such as SAP together with a number of specialized "best-of-breed" systems (Soh et al. 2000; Poba-Nzaou et al. 2008) that seamlessly integrate with one another using open-systems architecture. This chapter pertains to one such genre of systems, known as electronic procurement systems (EPS). Perceptions of managers in India are brought out regarding the importance and impact of EPS on the supply-chain.

Research looking into EPS adoption has been conducted across various geographies and industries/sectors, such as construction, manufacturing, healthcare and government. For example, Hawking et al. (2004) consider the barriers against the adoption of EPS in Australia. Gunasekaran and Ngai (2008) study the EPS adoption in Hong Kong, as applicable to medium-size enterprises, while the research of Gunasekaran et al. (2009) is based on small industries in the southern coast of United States (US). Reddick (2004) discusses how US state governments are utilizing EPS. Results based in Singapore are given by Kheng and Al-Hawamdeh (2002), while Tatsis et al. (2006) describe the benefits of EPS for the Greek food-chain industry.

In the Indian situation, however, awareness and adoption of EPS, and studies on its adoption are scarce, although information technology and the Internet play a significant role in the Indian economy. Aiming to fill this gap, we define an EPS and provide a framework of how such systems work in an organization. §§2 and 3 provide the background materials pertaining to supply chains and EPS, respectively. In §4, the supply chain benefits of an EPS are described and illustrated by cases of well-known successful EPS implementations in the US. This sets the stage for us to survey the perceptions of Indian managers about EPS, based on past studies (Lee et al. 2001; Pearcy and Giunipero 2008; Soares-Aguiar and Palma dos-Rois 2008). The results of this survey are then followed by three case-studies (§5). Implications for Indian supply chains are contained in §6.

2.2 Supply Chains in India

To provide the context for EPS in India, we briefly compare supply chains in that country with those in North America.

As compared to North American countries, India is a complex diverse country. Even though India is the fifth largest country in terms of gross national product, the 2010 report from the World Economic Forum places India at the 51st position (WEF 2010). This ranking is in part due to the infrastructure deficiencies, in terms of roads, ports and electricity. For example, even though India has one of the world's largest road networks, only 47 % is paved and only 20 % of the paved roads are in good usable condition (Sundar et al. 2009). A sizeable proportion (as much as 95 %) of India's labor force belongs to the unorganized sector (Chopra et al. 2010). The Indian middle class is 350 million strong, but is not a homogeneous lot either.

This diversity poses peculiar challenges for supply chain design. Thus, transplantation of pure North American models of retailing and supply chain management can result in failure. One well-known example is that of Subiksha, a chain of supermarkets that was supposed to be set up in every nook and corner of metropolitan cities. After expanding to set up over 1600 stores in two years, the chain faced a cash-crunch and eventually closed down. Other examples of companies that pulled out or re-oriented their operations include UK companies Argos, and Marks and Spencer (Chopra et al. 2010).

The following cases illustrate how some companies have dealt with the challenges pertaining to Indian supply chains.

Example 1 *(Jaipur Rugs, Jaipur, India).* Jaipur Rugs (JR) is a company that sells exclusive rugs to customers in over twenty countries. JR focuses on connoisseurs of ancient classical hand-woven rugs. A key challenge facing the company is to bridge the unorganized weaver community with customers primarily from developed nations such as US, Australia and Canada.

JR employs a two-pronged supply chain design (Chopra et al. 2010; Jaipur 2011). To maintain its exclusivity, JR uses CAD software to develop innovative carpet designs, which are then communicated to its sourcing, production and distribution operations through an Enterprise Resource Planning (ERP) software. Quality is maintained by adhering to ISO 9001 standards throughout its operations.

While such technologies and processes are important to the success of JR, what is different herein is the behavioral element of the supply chain. Realizing that its success hinges on its artisans, JR assumed responsibility for the social and economic development of its 35,000 weaver community, by improving their standard of living, by reducing social injustices and wage-inequities, and providing skills-training. This cultivated an "extended familial relationship", thereby winning the confidence of the weavers and eliminating middlemen. JR is now able to deal directly with the weavers who work on 7,000 looms spread across remote Indian villages, yet are connected with one another through ERP software.

Example 2 (Gopaljee Milks, Noida, India). Gopaljee, a 20 year-old company that initially started with products like biscuits, is now a household name for dairy products in the northern part of India. The company's vision is to use clean milk sourced from villages, and produce safe and pure dairy products such as ghee (clarified butter), milk powder and long-life milk. Gopaljee's strategy to support this vision lies in its interaction with its suppliers.

With the cooperation from the government, Gopaljee set up 4,000 village societies to collect milk from 125,000 farmers (Gopaljee 2011). The company further helped the farmers with subsidized veterinary medicines and vaccines, materials for testing milk quality, high-quality seeds and cattle feed. It also provided training on farming methods. Finally, farmers were given prompt payment. These measures facilitated Gopaljee to have a symbiotic relationship with its suppliers.

The company's supply chain begins with milk collected directly from farmers. Within three hours of milking, the milk is chilled and transported to a milk-plant, wherein it is processed and sent by refrigerated truck to sale depot and stores. Clearly, all these require advanced technologies and processes, in order to work successfully.

To summarize, at this juncture, Indian organizations must contend with a fragmented supply chain, as opposed to that in North America wherein both suppliers and customers are well-connected. Both JR and Gopaljee given above (as well as other successful companies), seem to have realized this issue, and thus, have merged modern supply chain concepts with traditional ways of people-engagement that are rooted in Indian ethos and socioeconomic realities.

2.3 E-Procurement Systems

The supply chains outlined above can be made more efficient by implementing technologies such as EPS. The purpose of this section is to briefly define an EPS and describe its features.

Definition

The literature has seen varied definitions of what constitutes an EPS. For example, Davila et al. (2003) define EPS "as any technology designed to facilitate the acquisition of goods by a commercial or a government organization over the Internet. E-procurement technologies [...] are focused on automating workflows, consolidating and leveraging organizational spending power, and identifying new sourcing opportunities through the Internet". Raghavan and Prabhu (2004) expand this definition somewhat: EPS is "the electronic acquisition of goods and services including all processes from the identification of a need to purchase of products, to the payment for these purchases, including post-contract/payment activities such as contract management, supplier management and development".

Examples of EPS include Ariba, as well as IBM's and SAP's E-procurement system. These packages provide an environment for buyers and supplier to collaborate with each other. SAP's system is integrated with the company's ERP system, while other packages can be stand-alone systems. EPS facilitates supplier discovery, sourcing, supplier management, requisitioning, procurement, order receiving, and contract management. A comparison of the focus of each package is in Rodovilsky (2010).

Framework and Features

Perhaps the varied definitions given above stem from distinct conceptualizations of an EPS. First, since the procurement process inherently involves multiple organizations, Johnston and Vitale (1988) have provided a framework that classifies an EPS on a *continuum* involving the extent to which it can link organizations together. This classification also mirrors the classification of organizational relationships between buyers and suppliers. On the one hand, there are EPSs providing support for transactional activities such as online searches and order entry. Once an order is placed, it is processed by the systems that are exclusively operable only by the supplier. In the other end of the continuum, not only can the EPS perform order-entry activities, but it is also linked to the supplier's database, and can therefore transmit the order directly into the manufacturing/operations processes of that supplier.

While the preceding classification is used in the literature (see, for example, Wu et al. 2007), it does not include details that relate to the functionality of an EPS. In this functional view (Subramaniam 2004; Soares-Aguira and Palma-dos-Reis 2008), buyers/suppliers use an electronic gateway to interact with the system's processes consisting of: (1) procurement management entailing web-support for user interaction, product cataloging etc. (2) transactional support in the form of searches and other order-management activities; and (3) features such as auctions/negotiation. Of these three levels, levels (1) and (2) are the most visible and prevalent parts of EPS technologies, while level (3) relates to advanced functionality (see shaded parts of Fig. 2.1) for which models are beginning to be proposed (e.g., Talluri et al. 2007; Sundarraj and Mok 2010).

Based on this functional view, a detailed range of EPS features can be shown, as in Table 2.1.

2.4 EPS Impact on Supply Chain and Logistics

Irani and Love (2002) discuss general issues in evaluating investments in Information Technology. However, Section 2.3 brings out the fact that an EPS is more complex than classical information systems. Hence, its benefits have been classified in a variety of ways, including organizational, IS and financial perspectives (see, for example, Piotrowicz and Irani 2010).

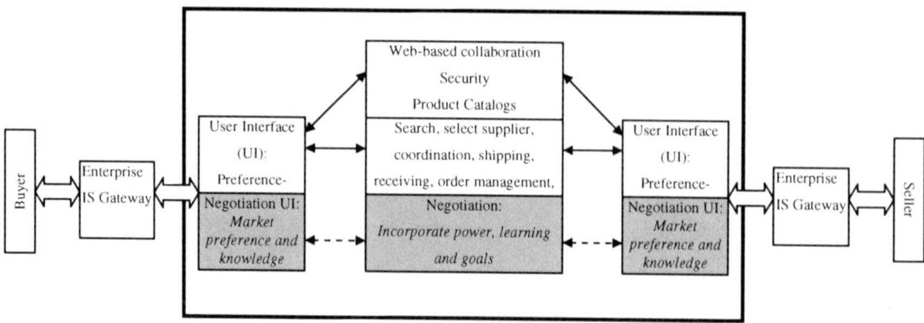

Fig. 2.1 Framework of an electronic procurement system. *Source* adapted from Soares-Aguiar and Palma-dos-Reis (2008)

Table 2.1 Collection of features of an electronic procurement system

Feature	Explanation
eCatalog	Database of supplier's products/services
Punch-out	Access to supplier's website directly from buyer's system
E-request for quotes	Buyer's invitation to suppliers for quotes
Approval workflow	Automatic routing of orders to financial/business authorizers
Order dispatch	Creating purchase order automatically and sending to suppliers
E-goods receipt	Record product/service deliveries in the system
E-invoice matching	Store invoices electronically/Generate payments automatically
E-marketplace	Third party marketplace where buyers and suppliers transact and/or exchange information
E-tendering	Manage tendering process online
E-auction/ negotiation	Suppliers posting competitive bids; buyers/suppliers negotiating online
E-evaluation	Tender evaluation against pre-agreed criteria
E-collaboration	Establish, manage, monitor, renew contracts and collate histories of suppliers

Also serves as the basis for the questions on perceived importance of EPS feature

An EPS is important from the viewpoint of commercial transactions, but more so in the transformation of internal systems, leading to subsequent influences in terms of cost, productivity and supply chain performance (Chopra et al. 2010). At the strategic level, the benefits of EPS are in the realm of the subjective and intangible, while at the operational level, benefits tend to be tangible. The following is a short list of the benefits that EPS provides, according to the literature (e.g., Bakos 1997; Croom 2000; Barua et al. 2001; Boer et al. 2001; Subramaniam 2004; Puschmann and Alt 2005; Gunasekaran and Ngai 2008; Soares-Aguiar and Palma-dos-Rois 2008; Gunasekaran et al. 2009; Chopra et al. 2010; Pietrowicz and Irani 2010).

Operational SCM Benefits

- Acquisition-cost reduction. Research reveals that the use of EPS significantly reduces the cost to acquire goods and services (Croom 2000; Boer et al. 2001). These reductions can be to the tune of 50–80 % (Puschmann and Alt 2005).
- Shorter purchasing cycle time. The Internet reduces the time to search for a proper supplier (Bakos 1997). As well, orders placed are instantly received at the supplier, thus lowering purchase time.
- Order-cost reduction. It is acknowledged by a number of authors that the Internet provides access to large volumes of information at lower costs. Thus, the use of EPS can help with the lowering of order cost.
- Reduced inventory costs. Since EPS reduces the fixed ordering cost, and since lot size is often proportional to the square root of the order cost, the optimal order size will be lower. This and other features given below lower the cycle inventory costs.

Strategic SCM Benefits

- Design Collaboration with suppliers. With an EPS, organizations can synchronize their design efforts with those of their suppliers. This can be an advantage, since about 80 % of the part's cost is fixed during the design stage (Chopra et al. 2010). Thus, collaboration with one's supplier in finding existing parts/designs can help with integrating the supply chain and in keeping costs low.
- Faster response to changes. Organizations can use an EPS to share their production plans with their suppliers. Thus, collaborative planning forecasting and replenishment can be easily done, and in turn, this can reduce information uncertainty and the amount of inventory.
- Consolidation of purchasing activities. In many organizations, especially large ones, a certain product is likely to be ordered by multiple departments. An EPS could consolidate such purchases, and avoid duplication of efforts. In addition, pricing discounts can be availed.
- Elimination of unnecessary activities. EPS implementation is sometimes seen as an enabler for making process changes. Organizations could, for example, simplify the authorization of orders, and the returning of parts (Pierson 2002).
- Use of marketplaces. By using the catalog management of EPS, companies can drive their procurement strategy by taking advantage of external multivendor catalogs. This strategy has been pursued by Bayer and SAP (Raisch 2001).
- Other intangible benefits. EPSs also offer other intangible benefits such as process decentralization, improved transparency of process, and improved relationships with suppliers.

One example of successful EPS implementation is the oft-cited integration of Daimler Chrysler with Johnson Controls, and extending in turn to Johnson's suppliers themselves. Several hundred times each day, Johnson received its orders from Chrysler in regards to various combinations of colors and other attributes. These orders were then passed on to the 35 suppliers of Johnson for assembly and delivery of the finished module to Chrysler (Peirson 2002). Johnson used

Commerce One (Commerce One 2011) as its EPS and integrated it with their existing Oracle ERP system, resulting in a listing of more than one million catalog items, 10,000 purchase orders and $25 million in annual purchases.

Cisco uses a combination of Ariba, and Oracle (Cisco 2010). The company provides a punchout solution to its customers, whereby complex orders are configured, integrated, and automated through the use of reusable configurations and order templates. At the other end of the supply chain, Cisco also integrates almost 2,000 of its suppliers, distributors and contract manufacturers through its trading network (see also Grosvenor and Austin 2001).

Such success stories have prompted other companies, such as Rockwell International and Walt Disney, to follow suit and benchmark their procurement performance as well (Piotrowicz and Irani 2010).

2.5 Survey and Case-Study in India

One question stemming from the above discussion is the extent to which the lessons from Cisco and Johnson apply to India, given its supply chain realities. We use an empirical survey and three case-studies to answer this question. Implications of the results are brought out in §6.

2.5.1 Empirical Survey

This section summarizes the results of a survey of Indian managers, as pertinent to the goals of this chapter. Details concerning survey administration and analysis will be forthcoming in a fuller report.

Our survey consists of: (1) basic queries about the respondent; (2) perception questions about the importance of EPS features (listed in Table 2.1); and (3) items on firm-specific characteristics such as size, financial position, top-management support and customer-orientation (for more details on these terms, as well as the questionnaire for measuring them, see, for example, Lee et al. 2001; Pearcy and Giunipero 2008; Soares-Aguiar and Palma dos-Rois 2008). The survey was administrated to managers working in different sectors of Indian industry. Overall, 101 responses were received. Some of them had nonsensical values, while with a number of other responses, the participants were from the same organization. Hence, the data from all such participants did not essentially differ on variables such as firm size. To handle this difficulty, response data coming from the same company were averaged out. This gave us a total of 66 responses for further analysis. The major findings are as follows.

- Most respondents accord a high level of importance to EPS features. For example, 48 % of respondents view an e-catalog to be *very important*, and 38 %

consider this feature to be *important*. Likewise, 88 % of people view *Request for quotes* to be very important or important. Despite this, only about 10 % of the companies have adopted an EPS system.

- Participants view the EPS features to consist of four categories: e-catalog and electronic request for quotes (Stage 1); workflow approval, order dispatch, electronic good receipt and invoicing (Stage 2); items such as auctions and market places (Stage 3); and e-collaboration and e-contracts (Stage 4). Roughly speaking, this categorization appears to be according to the degree of sophistication of the application; for example, auctions and contracts are more sophisticated uses of an EPS than catalog searches.
- Perception of the importance of Stage 2 features differs based on firm-size and the level of top-management support available at the firm; importance of Stage 3 features differs based on top-management support and customer orientation of the company.

2.5.2 Case Studies in India

The survey results summarized above reveal that even though participants saw different stages of EPS functions and felt that those features are important for organizations in general, actual adoption of a system is still low; the importance of EPS features is not explicable by the various organizational characteristics. To understand this result, we study three Indian companies, by using a structured interview process for one and secondary sources for the other two.

Medium Company

The first case is based on XYZ Group.[1] Having a combined turnover of US$ 4 billion, XYZ group comprises over 25 companies and has a total of 25,000 employees on its payroll. Since its founding in early the 1900s, XYZ has followed a steady path of expansion and diversification. It now operates in such areas as automotive, finance, and electronics. A common thread with the entire group is the importance given to quality and customer service. As such, several companies of this group have won the coveted Deming award.

The particular firm chosen for our study is the electronics business. Considered medium-sized in the Indian context, this business was founded about 25 years ago and faces companies such as Epson India as its competitors. XYZ electronics focuses on various types of input–output computer peripherals such as keyboards, POS terminals and printers, as well as consumable parts needed for such devices. Put together, these products have a demand of tens of thousand per month.

[1] XYZ is a pseudo-name.

Table 2.2 Structure of interview questions

Questions related to context:
1. What is your company structure?
2. What products are marketed by your company?
3. What is your position within the structure and hierarchy?
4. Has your company adopted an e-procurement system? Why or why not?
Importance of features:
5. What are the different features of EPS?
6. What is the importance of each of these features?
Supply chain benefits:
7. What are the strategic benefits of EPS to SCM?
8. What are the tactical benefits?
9. What are the operational benefits?

The person we talked to is a senior manager, with about 2 years of experience in the company and over a decade in the industry. He is familiar with EPS and its features. Table 2.2 lists the set of questions asked by the interviewer.

In terms of IS implementations, XYZ has the SAP system that links orders from customers with the manufacturing activities of the plants. However, XYZ does not have an EPS, nor does it have any plans for such an implementation, as indicated by the respondent's comments below:

> Activity through web-based [ordering] will not be helpful
> At this point of time, we do not need such a system

When asked about the reason for the above statement, the respondent analyzed it from multiple perspectives. First, in terms of demand, product variety at XYZ is small. Also, components are designed to be modular and can therefore be used in multiple product-lines with only minor modifications. Moreover, variations within a product-line involve only a small number of parts. Therefore, the respondent felt that product demands can be forecast with a fair degree of accuracy, especially because large orders get sufficient lead time. Second, from the supply perspective, most of the sub-assemblies are ordered through tier-1 suppliers, who in turn order components from tier-2 vendors that are pre-qualified by XYZ, thus reducing the need for an EPS. Thirdly, at this point in time, suppliers are not familiar with an EPS and may not be ready in terms of the infrastructure needed to implement such a system. Thus, for these reasons, the utility of EPS is somewhat low.

The procurement process followed by XYZ is to periodically collect customer-orders from SAP, and then batch its purchases by email to one among the few pre-qualified suppliers. Finished goods are then delivered by using milk-runs from the factory to the various customers.

Following these questions about his own company, the respondent was asked to extrapolate his experiences for the industry. His comments indicate that notwithstanding India's growing economy, the volumes at which Indian organizations operate are still low by global standards; therefore, EPS functionalities such as auctions/negotiations do not have as much utility as one might expect for a large multinational company.

This raised the natural question as to how XYZ and other such companies could gain internal acceptance for a significantly more expensive ERP system without the added functionality of an EPS. The following interview-transcript aptly contextualizes the problem of EPS with respect to the justification that XYZ might have undertaken for an ERP system.

Interviewer:
How long have you had SAP?
Respondent:
Maybe about two years now.
Interviewer:
Were there some arguments posed against the implementation of SAP, at some point in time?
Respondent:
No ..., and yes, maybe it was there when Baan was introduced—we had Baan before [SAP].
Over a period of time, every industry is looking at the other industry and see the benefits they get ... whereas the e-procurement is still at a very raw stage now.
Very large-scale industry may have implemented, *but all others are in a wait-and-watch mode right now*.

Large Indian Organization

This opinion of our interviewee—about the utility of EPS for large organizations–is supported by our follow-up research on Indian Railways[2] (IR). IR, a state-owned organization with a 150 year history, is one of the world's largest organizations with a network of about 64,000 km. As the national carrier, it plays a key role in India's social and economic development, by providing affordable transportation to about 19 million passengers and 2.3 million tonnes of bulk freight every day (see, for example, IRYB 2010; www.ireps.gov.in for more information).

IR provides a key link to other modes of transportation. Owing to its access to remote areas of the country, IR can extend the reach of the fast growing airline industry. IR is also linked to India's extensive road network. For example, Konkan Railway, one of the zonal branches of IR, introduced an intermodal system whereby trucks are transported on flatbed IR trailers (Konkan 2011). Finally, in addition to the above, the IR-port interface provides great economic benefits to a globalizing India. About 95 % of the country's international trading is through the thirteen major ports of India (Sundar et al. 2009), and goods from/to ports are transported by IR. Figure 2.2 conceptually gives these connections.

IR and ports also interact for carrying intra-country freight, with the coal industry as one of the major beneficiaries. Coal is the second largest commodity handled at ports. Coal accounts for US$ 1.2 billion of ports' import-revenue, and constitutes over 45 % of the goods transported by IR, in terms of both tonnage and revenue (Raghuram et al. 2004). Moreover, coal is a key raw material for steel,

[2] Another such example is Coal India, a Government of India undertaking.

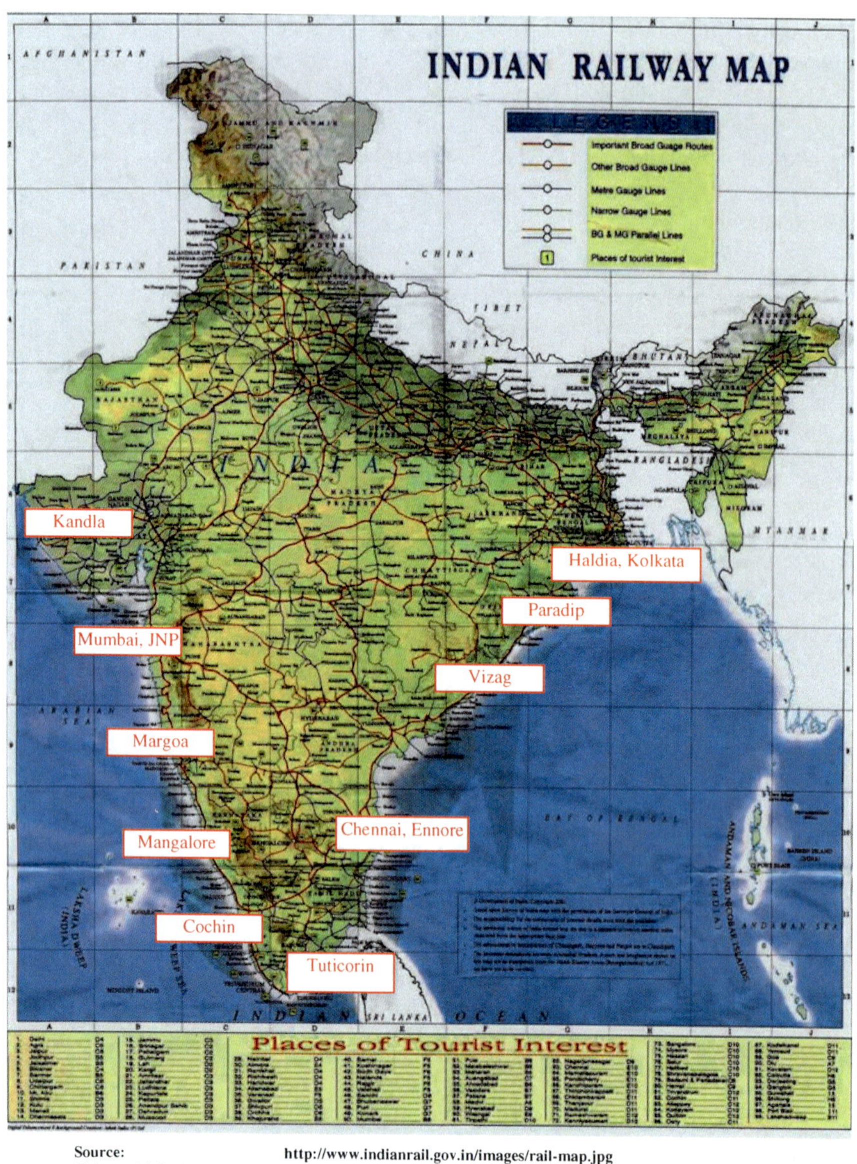

Source: http://www.indianrail.gov.in/images/rail-map.jpg
Thirteen Major Ports: Kandla, Mumbai, JNP, Margoa, Mangalore, Cochin, Tuticorin, Chennai, Ennore, Vizag, Paradip, Haldia, Kolkota

Fig. 2.2 Railway routes overlaid with major ports

cement and power industries. To give an example, coal from Talcher mines (in Orissa) is a raw material for the power plant at Ennore. One option is to send the coal through IR's network, which will take 1350 km. The other option is to send the coal to Paradip by rail (200 Kms) and then use waterways for 1025 Kms between the Paradip and Ennore ports (see Fig. 2.2) Raghuram et al. (2004) found that the latter intermodal option provides over 40 % savings.

While the aforementioned discussion establishes the importance of IR to India's transportation sector, it is the case that the organization's market-share predominance has steadily eroded from over 80 % in the 1950s to less than 40 % in 2005 (Sundar et al. 2009). Hence, to improve, IR has been reengineering itself, including its logistics and materials management operations that play a crucial role.

IR has 220 stocking-depots that contain about 300,000 components. Expenditure on purchases is over US$ 500 million. Recognizing the importance of procurement to IR's logistics and in turn to India's social and commercial interests, IR has developed and implemented a secure EPS for procuring and managing its materials effectively. This system permits vendors to search and download tender-information, and submit online offers into the system (www.ireps.gov.in) in a fair, secure, confidential and transparent manner (See also Lin and Hsieh 2000).

Every online bid is submitted with a valid digital signature certificate, and is acknowledged by the system, by including the date and time of the bid-receipt. Vendors cannot access submitted bids, but they can add a revised bid superseding their original bid. While cost-effectiveness is the role of procurement in the private sector, for public organization such as IR, the larger "public good" is an important goal of implementing an EPS. Thus, all vendors who have submitted e-bids can view every offer made by each vendor, along with the respective timestamp. Another feature provided for the sake of transparency is to ensure a proper payment procedure (i.e., electronic funds transfer), so that the lag between good-receipt and payment is uniform for all vendors.

Incidentally, the IR case brings out the importance of intangible benefits as well (e.g., transparency and process decentralization), as given in §4, in order to justify and implement an EPS system.

Public–Private Partnership of ITC's e-choupal. ITC is a hundred-year-old company that was established under the name of Imperial Tobacco Company, and that later re-named itself to ITC Limited (for more details on the information given below, see Upton and Fuller 2004).

In 1999, to grow its agricultural part, ITC's chairman, Y. C. Deveshwar, commissioned a plan to use technology for improving the competitiveness of the value chain. At that point in time, after the harvest, farmers brought their produce to a local shop (called *mandi*) where agents bought the goods and then sold them to ITC (generally at a much higher price). ITC processed these goods and delivered them to stores. Farmers had little connection amongst one another, and therefore lacked the knowledge of their harvest's market price. Thus, with this process, middlemen (i.e., agents) ended up getting a substantial part of the proceeds.

As a way to break this inefficiency, ITC established a total of 1,695 kiosks or e-choupals (*choupal* means meeting place in the Indian language, Hindi). The choupals were setup in the villages of one Indian state, namely Madhya Pradesh. Each kiosk contained a printer, as well as a microcomputer that was connected to the ITC's website through dial-up or VSAT terminals. The website provided information on such matters as the weather, crop-cultivation practices, and more importantly, on market prices. A lead farmer was picked, and was provided training to operate the website and then post a printout of the above information on a notice board.

Farmers benefited from that information, because it provided them a very easy way to know the prices at remote locations of the country. Previously, this knowledge required time-consuming travel, which was seldom undertaken. Further, this price-discovery allowed them to make informed decisions about where to sell their produce—they could sell to the agents as before (at *mandis*) or directly to ITC hubs, which were located to be within convenient distance of every farmer. Third, unlike agents, the hubs provided prompt payment to farmers. Finally, the hubs also featured facilities such as soil-testing that was previously available only at a remote government lab.

For its part, ITC's direct contact with farmers entailed several benefits. First, it provided ITC with a reliable supply-source. Second, ITC was able to understand the current farming technique employed and thus gauge the quality of its purchase. Third, it was able to influence the farmer to practice improved techniques. Finally, direct contact reduced the chances of adulteration by middlemen. In turn, the improved quality fetched a higher price for ITC at international markets.

To grow this successful concept further, ITC then expanded to other states as well (ITC 2011). Partners from the village communities, non-governmental organizations, and the government itself were involved in this effort. For example, in the states of Andhra Pradesh and Rajasthan, ITC collaborated with the state government to develop over 8,000 hectares of previously unused land. Overall, this gave ITC enormous coverage–ten states, 4 million farmers, six different crops, 40,000 villages and 6,500 e-choupals. Thus, in 2006–07, the company was cited by the Government of India's Economic Survey for its transformational impact on rural lives.

To summarize, the implementations at both IR and ITC were somewhat home-grown, and do not fit the high-end commercial systems that were put in place at companies such as Cisco. In terms of the EPS framework given in Fig. 2.1, the ITC system helps with searches and information provision, while the IR system entails specific applications such as auctions. In both cases, volume appears to be an important commonalty for adoption.

2.6 Supply-chain Implications

Our first finding is that EPS adoption can be imagined to consist of different stages, with each higher level being more complex in function and use than the lower one. The stages are: (1) eCatalogue and Electronic Request For Quotes; (2) Approval Workflow, Order Dispatch, Electronic Goods Receipt and Electronic Invoice Matching; (3) Electronic Marketplace, eTendering, eAuction & Negotiation and eEvaluation; and (4) eContract Management and eCollaboration. Firms with more management support are more likely to adopt the features of Stage 2, while those having Customer Orientation and Top Management Support adopting the Stage 3 features. These results indicate that the Indian view of EPS features matches that in the literature.

Our interview and survey results provide several lessons about the adoption of EPS in India. First, most benefits listed in §4 are aimed at reducing the complexity of operating the supply chain, which in turn is related to uncertainties existing in the chain. However, it appears that medium-size Indian companies are not yet focused on the delivery of highly customized products to customers. There is thus less need to reduce uncertainties, nor a need for complex procurement systems. Alternatively, the volume of transactions in an organization can provide the required economy of scale, so that overall savings in transaction costs (e.g., inventory, order, acquisition costs etc.) can justify the use of an EPS system.

As of this writing, select Indian organizations meet the latter criterion. In IR's case, it is clear that large bulk is involved, whereas with ITC's e-choupal, the volume lies in the sheer number of farmers and villages covered by the system. Thus, lessons from IR are potentially applicable to organizations such as Coal India, while the ITC case has implications for JR and Gopaljee, owing to the suppliers being spread out. It should be remarked, however, that both systems offer only a subset of the EPS features discussed in §3.

To facilitate the adoption of EPS, suppliers must be engaged and be made aware of the benefits of using EPS, along with the infrastructure needed to operate such systems. This is a crucial point for the Indian context, since the supply chain is fragmented and the workforce is unorganized. Thus, simple systems with possible facilitated use (as was the case with ITC) are likely to gain user-acceptance and thereby provide the anticipated supply chain benefits.

2.7 Summary

Supply chains can be globally competitive only if all of its links work together in an efficient coordinated fashion. This coordination can be facilitated by the use of electronic procurement technologies, which offer a number of strategic benefits (e.g., design collaboration) and operational ones (e.g., order cost reduction). Thus, multinational firms, which tend to be part of a well-connected supply chain, have incorporated EPS into their processes and have reported enormous savings as a result. In India, our study shows that such systems are known to a wide section of managers, and are beneficial to organizations that deal with large volume. Given the attributes of Indian supply chains, relationship-cultivation with various stakeholders can serve as an important precursor to generating the required volume, and in turn, to actual implementation. The EPS set-up itself must be focused on practical targeted use, rather than on a full set of sophisticated functionalities. Finally, medium and small companies appear to be observing industrial trends and are likely to adopt such packages, as the Indian economy grows and gets more globally oriented.

References

Bakos J (1997) Reducing buyer search costs: Implications for electronic marketplaces. Manage Sci 43(12):1676–1692

Barua A, Prabhudev K, Andrew W, Fang Y (2001) Driving e-business excellence. MIT Sloan Manage Rev 43(1):36–44

Boer L, Harink J, Heijboer G (2001) A model for assessing the impact of electronic procurement forms. In 10th International Annual IPSERA Conference, pp 119–130

Carter P, Carter J, Monczka R, Slaight T, Swan A (2000) The future of purchasing and supply: a ten year forecast. J Supply Chain Manage 36(1):14–26

Chopra S, Meindl P, Kalra D (2010) Supply chain management. Pearson Education, Noida

Cisco (2010) www.cisco.com. Accessed Oct 2010

Commerce One (2011) www.commerceone.com. Accessed 2011

Croom S (2000) The impact of web-based procurement on the management of operating resources supply. J Supply Chain Manage 36(1):4–13

Davila A, Gupta M, Palmer R (2003). Moving procurement systems to the internet: the adoption and use of E-procurement technology models. Eur Manage J 21(1):11–23

Gopaljee (2011) www.gopaljee.com. Accessed Feb 2011

Grosvenor F, Austin T (2001) Cisco's eHub Initiative. Supply Chain Manage Rev pp 18–26

Gunasekaran A, Ngai EWT (2008) Adoption of E-procurement in Hong Kong:an empirical research, Int J Prod Econ 113(1):159–175

Gunasekaran A, McGaughey R, Ngai E, Rai B (2009) E-procurement adoption in Southcoast SMEs. Int J Prod Econ 122:161–175

Hawking P, Stein A, Wyld CD, Foster S (2004) E-procurement: is the ugly duckling actually a swan down under? Asia Pac J Mark Logistics 16(1):3–26

Irani Z, Love PED (2002) Developing a frame of reference for ex-ante IT/IS investment evaluation. Eur J Inf Syst 11(1):74–82

IRYB (2010) Indian Railway Year Book 2008–09 at http://www.indianrailways.gov.in/indianrailways/directorate/stat_econ/pdf/Year_Book_English2008-09.pdf. Accessed 2 Nov 2010

ITC (2011) http://www.itcportal.com/sustainability/lets-put-india-first/echoupal.aspx. Accessed Feb 2011

Jaipur (2011) www.jaipurrugs.com. Accessed Feb 2011

Johnston H, Vitale M (1988) Creating competitive advantage with interorganizational information systems. MIS Quarterly 12:153–165

Kheng CB, Al-Hawamdeh S (2002) The adoption of electronic procurement in Singapore. Electron Commer Res 2:61–73

Konkan (2011) http://pib.nic.in/newsite/erelease.aspx?relid=68761. Accessed Feb 2011

Lee E-K, Ha S, Kim S (2001) Supplier selection and management system considering relationships in supply chain management. IEEE Trans Eng Manage 48(3):307–318

Lin B Hsieh C-T (2000) Online procurement: implementation and managerial implications. Hum Syst Manage 19(2):105–110

Pearcy DH, Giunipero L (2008) Using E-procurement applications to achieve integration: what role does firm size play? Supply Chain Manage: Int J 13(1):26–34

Pierson J (2002) Johnson Controls Journal to E-procurement. Supply Chain Manage Rev, January–February pp 56–62

Piotrowicz W, Irani Z (2010) Analysing B2B electronic procurement benefits: information systems perspective. J Enterp Inf Manage 23(4):559–579

Poba-Nzaou P, Raymond L, Fabu B (2008) Adoption and risk of ERP systems in manufacturing SMEs: a positivist case study. Bus Process Manage J 14(4):530–550

Puschmann T, Alt R (2005) Successful use of E-procurement in supply-chains. Supply Chain Manage: Int J 10(2):122–133

Raghavan SNR, Prabhu M (2004) Object-oriented design of a distributed agent-based framework for E-procurement. Prod Plann Control 15(7):731–741

Raghuram G, Verma S, Dixit K, Kapshe S (2004) Strategies for improving indian railways' market share of port based coal traffic: a diagnostic study, Indian Institute of Management Ahmedabad Report, Vastrapur, Gujarat, India

Raisch WD (2001) The E-marketplace: strategies for success in B2B E-commerce. McGraw-Hill, New York

Reddick CG (2004) The growth of E-procurement in American state governments: a model and empirical evidence. J Public Procurement 4(2):151–176

Rodovilsky Z (2010) Electronic procurement. In: Bidgoli H (ed) The handbook of technology management: supply chain management, marketing and advertising, and global management, vol 2. Wiley, Hoboken, New Jersey pp 53–67, 07030

Sundar S, Agarwal V, Chawla R, Diljun G, Garg A, Ghate A, Krithika P (2009) Competitive issues in regulated industries: the case of indian transport sector. The energy and resource institute, Project Report No 2007CP21, Darbaro Seth Block, Lodhi Road, New Delhi 110003

Soares-Aguiar A, Palma-dos-Reis A (2008) Why do firms adopt E-procurement Systems? Using logistic regression to empirically test a conceptual model. IEEE Trans Eng Manage 55: 120–133

Soh C, Kien S, Tay-Yap J (2000) Cultural fits and misfits: Is ERP a Universal solution? Commun ACM 43(4):47–53

Subramaniam C (2004) The effects of process characteristics on the value of B2B E-procurement. Inf Technol Manage 5:161–180

Sundarraj R, Mok W (2010) Models for human negotiation elements: validation, and implications for electronic procurement. To appear in IEEE Transactions of Engineering Management

Talluri S, Narasimhan R, Viswanathan S (2007) Information technologies for procurement decisions: a decision support systems for multi-attribute e-reverse auctions. Int J Prod Res 45:2615–2628

Tatsis V, Mena C, Van Wassenhove LN, Whicker L (2006). E-procurement in the Greek food and drink industry. J Purchasing Supply Manage 12:63–74

Upton D, Fuller V (2004) The ITC eChoupal initiative. Harvard Business School Case 9-604-016. Boston, MA, 02163

WEF (2010) http://gcr.weforum.org/gcr2010/. Accessed Feb 2011

Wu F, Zsidisin G, Ross A (2007) Antecedents and outcomes and e-procurement adoption: an integrative model. IEEE Trans Eng Manage 54:576–587

Chapter 3
Use of Third Party Logistics Services: An Asia-Pacific Perspective

Amrik S. Sohal and Shams Rahman

Abstract We compare trends in the use of 3PLs (Third Party Logistics Providers) in the Asia-Pacific region, mostly among four countries: Australia, India, Malaysia, Singapore. These comparisons are based upon published results and surveys by us and by other researchers. The enhanced use of outsourcing is related to the growth of Manufacturing and Logistics in the Asia-Pacific. Another important factor is the skills required of Logistics managers. Those necessary competencies are detailed, with particular emphasis on China and Australia.

3.1 Introduction

Over the past 2 decades, we have witnessed a massive growth in the Asia-Pacific region in terms of manufacturing and the related logistics and supply chain activities. Following the rapid growth and success of manufacturing industries in Japan and South Korea during the last quarter of the 20th century, China and other nations in South East Asia have now emerged as the new power-houses of manufacturing. In the 21st century, manufacturing activity is becoming a very different game, not only because of the availability of new and advanced manufacturing technologies and practices, but also because of location and resource (human and materials) differences.

A. S. Sohal (✉)
Department of Management, Monash University, Melbourne, Australia
e-mail: Amrik.Sohal@buseco.monash.edu.au

S. Rahman
School of Business IT and Logistics, RMIT University, Melbourne, Australia
e-mail: Shams.Rahman@rmit.edu.au

J. H. Bookbinder (ed.), *Handbook of Global Logistics*, International Series in Operations Research & Management Science 181, DOI: 10.1007/978-1-4419-6132-7_3,

Table 3.1 US imports (billions of dollars) from selected countries between 2000 and 2005 (adapted from Carter et al. 2008)

US imported from	2000	2005	Percentage increase
China	100.0	244.0	144
Mexico	135.0	170.0	25.9
Brazil	14.0	24.4	74.3
India	10.7	18.8	75.7
South Africa	4.2	5.9	40.5
Czech Republic	1.1	2.2	100
Romania	0.5	1.2	140

A growing number of multinationals have established manufacturing and logistics operations in the Asia Pacific region—here we are including China, India and several emerging South East Asian countries, specifically Malaysia and Singapore. Also included is Australia, which now sees itself as part of Asia. Another major shift that has occurred over the past 2 decades is the outsourcing of logistics functions to primarily third-party logistics (3PL) providers. Many 3PLs can now offer services that span the entire logistics process.

In this chapter, we discuss a number of issues relating to the following:

- The growth of manufacturing and logistics in the Asia-Pacific region
- Increase in outsourcing and Third Party Logistics
- Trends in the Asia-Pacific region
- Skill requirements for logistics managers (in particular, those in Australia and China)

3.2 Growth of Manufacturing and Logistics in the Asia-Pacific Region

As a result of globalization and the developing economies in the Asia-Pacific, trade in terms of exports and imports grew rapidly during the last 3 decades. Manufacturing firms in the region became capable of designing and producing products for the global market. Many of these companies thus export manufactured products and components to *developed* economies. Table 3.1 shows US imports from selected countries for 2000 and 2005, including China and India. Imports from those two nations increased by 144 and 76 %, respectively, over the 5 year period and continue to increase. Other countries in the Asia-Pacific, for example Malaysia and Thailand, have also made significant improvement in their manufacturing and hence export activity. [Maltz et al. (2011), in the present volume, take the perspective of the *purchaser* of those goods from developing nations.]

Firms source globally for a variety of reasons. Carter (2005) found five principal motives for which a firm would establish, plan and execute global procurement. These are to:

- achieve cost-effective growth in the supply base for goods, services and technologies in their value chains;
- focus on core competencies and reduce capital investment;
- match the outsourcing activities of competitors;
- improve non-competitive cost structures; and
- establish a future sales footprint in a low-cost country.

With a substantial increase in external trade, demand for logistics services also grew rapidly. Singapore took the lead in investing heavily in logistics infrastructure, developing its port and transportation. In 1996, it was estimated by Singapore's Economic Development Board that the logistics sector in Singapore had committed a record S$1.1 billion in fixed assets, a hefty 70 % increase over 1995. Total business spending of the logistics sector in Singapore rose 40 % in 1996 to more than S$280 million.

Turning now to China, the authorities there also realized that an efficient logistics system is of paramount importance for the further economic growth and modernization of the country. The Chinese Government has designated Logistics as a strategic industry. China invested heavily in the development and improvement of logistics infrastructure such as multi-modal transportation networks and distribution centers (Trunick 2003). The average annual growth rate of the logistics industry in China between 1994 and 2004 was 22.2 % (China's Logistics Report 2005). In spite of such impressive growth, the logistics market remains highly fragmented, and the largest providers have less than 2 % market share. Logistics costs account for around 20 % of GDP, compared to 9 % in Australia and the USA, and 11 % in Japan (Jones Lang LaSalle 2007).

The logistics industry was also impacted during the 1980s by the increased emphasis on time-based competition. This refers to the speed with which products are manufactured, delivered to the market, and serviced. The ability to compete on the basis of time has become an important source of competitive advantage for many corporations. This is especially the case in markets where organizations can achieve technological parity on the various aspects of product processing.

During the 1980s and 1990s, in their quest for time-based competence, many firms adopted a variety of new manufacturing methods and technologies such as just-in-time production, flexible manufacturing systems, and computer-aided manufacturing. These delivered significant improvements in manufacturing performance through their focus on lead-time reduction and improved quality. However, it was realized that further enhancements in time-based competitiveness required a focus on the logistics function and the entire supply chain. Improving the flow of information amongst both upstream and downstream was recognized as a key activity; supply chains could then become more responsive to changes in demand and supply. Expediting logistics activities, such as storage and delivery of materials/products through the entire supply chain, received extra attention in satisfying customers.

Developing a highly efficient logistics system requires managers to consider a number of issues. Often a tradeoff is necessary between the need to reduce overall supply chain inventory and lead times, and the opportunity to capture economies of scale in logistics functions such as warehousing and transportation. Such a tradeoff becomes considerably complicated due to the increasing uncertainty that plagues global supply chains. This randomness typically arises due to variability in supplier, manufacturing and demand processes. However, other stochastic effects relating to climate change, conflicts in particular countries/regions of the world and global health issues can greatly impact supply chains, resulting in serious disruptions.

The typical response by many companies to cope with uncertainty has been to carry inventory. However, the costs of holding inventory, in increased obsolescence and of investing in warehouse operations, have become unsustainable. The use of appropriate logistics practices has become imperative for all types of organizations. Firms are therefore challenged to improve their performance on inventory and lead-time-related characteristics, while simultaneously capturing economies of scale and enhancing customer service (Bhatnagar et al. 1999).

3.3 Growth of Outsourcing and Third Party Logistics

3.3.1 *Growth of Outsourcing*

Evidence from the studies on outsourcing conducted in the late 1980s and early 1990s indicates that organizations turned to outsourcing in an effort to capture cost savings and gain competitive advantage. Results of later research imply that organizations are focusing to a greater extent on developing capabilities through outsourcing to spur value creation and to gain competitive advantage. Hence, the earlier publications suggest that outsourcing decisions tended to rely on economic factors, and therefore, the transaction cost view (TCV) had been the dominant theory to explain outsourcing decisions (Williamson 1979).

On the other hand, some recent studies infer that an organization's motivation for outsourcing can be more appropriately explained using the resource-based view (RBV) rather than TCV. The RBV emphasizes value creation and competitive advantage for the firm. According to Walker and Poppo (1991), however, a suitable approach would be a hybrid relationship which combines the economic aspects of TCV and the relational view of RBV. This hybrid view has been supported by current research, suggesting that TCV and RBV are complementary to one another (Hoetker 2005; Jacobides and Winter 2005). Therefore, it is becoming apparent that an effective understanding of what motivates outsourcing decisions requires investigation from both the transaction-cost-based and resource-based perspectives.

3.3.2 Growth of Outsourcing Logistics

Third party logistics first became popular amongst European and North American organizations. The use of external providers to perform some or all of a firm's logistics functions had a key rationale: with intensified global competition, that firm could concentrate its energies on core activities that are critical to survival, and leave the rest to specialists. Fuller et al. (1993) suggest that one important reason for the growth of 3PL services is that companies compete in a number of businesses that are logistically distinct, due to varied customer needs. Such distinct services can be offered more efficiently by the integrated providers that grew rapidly during the 1990s. These 3PLs offer differentiated service through their investments in dedicated assets and technologies, and their structured methods. The nature of such relationships between the manufacturing firms and logistics service providers encompasses a variety of options, ranging from narrow (limited to specific activities like transportation) to broad (covering substantive activities in the entire supply chain).

Terms such as "contract logistics", 3PL and "logistics alliances" have been used to describe contracting out of logistics activities that were previously performed in-house (Lieb 1992; Lieb et al. 1993; Sink et al. 1996). As a result, several definitions and interpretations of 3PL have evolved (Holldorsson and Skjott-Larsen 2004). They can be studied from different angles such as the scope of service, its time frame and the nature of the relationship (Knemeyer and Murphy 2005). From the point of view of scope, a few definitions have a wide focus. Bagchi and Virum (1996) take a narrower view but suggest that, in an outsourcing context, "the shipper and the logistics provider see themselves as long term partners" (p. 193), thus adopting a long-term perspective. Bagchi and Virum (1996), and others that consider a long-term view in the definition of 3PL, tend to be more strategic than tactical (Skjott-Larsen 2000). In this chapter, we have adopted the Lieb (1992) definition of outsourced logistics services, which is as follows:

> Third-party logistics involves the use of external companies to perform logistics functions that have traditionally been performed within an organization. The functions performed by the [3PL provider] can encompass the entire logistics process or selected activities within that process.

This definition expresses the meaning of 3PL services in a manner which is easy to understand, while taking a broader view of 3PL.

There have been three waves of entrants into the 3PL market. The first dates back to the 1980s or even earlier with the appearance of 'traditional' logistics providers, whose activities usually emerged from a fundamentally strong position in either transportation or warehousing. The second wave began in the early 1990s, when companies operating significant networks, for example DHL, TNT and FedEx started to offer logistics services. The third wave dates from the late 1990s, where a number of players from the areas of information technology, management consultancy and even financial services worked together with providers from the first and second waves (Sohail and Sohal 2003).

3.4 Third-Party Trends in the Asia Pacific Region

In discussing the Asia-Pacific growth in outsourcing logistics, we draw on several studies conducted in that region over the past 10–15 years. Information presented in this section focuses on Singapore (Bhatnagar et al. 1999), Malaysia (Sohail and Sohal 2003), India (Sahay and Mohan 2006), and Australia (Sohal et al. 2002; Rahman 2009). Elsewhere in this book, the chapter by Sundarraj and Kumari (2013) gives an overall discussion of Logistics in India, especially electronic procurement systems. Our remarks of course emphasize outsourcing.

In Australia and Singapore, the services provided by 3PLs are comparable to those offered by their counterparts in the USA and Europe. A number of Australian logistics service providers now operate in Asia and are achieving considerable success. Examples are Linfox and Toll Logistics, who are also setting standards for the rest of the Logistics industry in Australia and other Asian countries.

We will now analyze the 3PL trends based on:

- Motivations for outsourcing;
- Type of logistics functions being outsourced;
- Expenditure on logistics outsourcing;
- Average length of 3PL contracts;
- Organizational impact of 3PL;
- Percentage of full-time Logistics positions eliminated as a result of using 3PL, and
- Level of satisfaction with 3PL providers' services.

3.4.1 Motivations for Logistics Outsourcing

The motivation to outsource logistics services comes from several factors. Studying the US companies, Sheffi (1990) suggested that cost savings, the need to concentrate on core business, and improved services are the main reasons. Similar justifications were reported by Richardson (1990), Bardi and Tracey (1991), Sink et al. (1996) and Rabinovich et al. (1999). Richardson (1992) and Fantasia (1993) found that reduction in capital investment in equipment, facilities and human resources, and on-time delivery improvement are among the important motives for outsourcing. Factors such as gaining access to sophisticated technology, flexibility of operations, and risk reduction have also been proposed. For instance, Gooley (1997), van Laarhoven et al. (2000) and Larson and Gammelgaard (2001) found that a principal factor for outsourcing the logistics functions in Europe is to retain flexibility in logistics operations. Bhatnagar et al. (1999) mentioned that, along with cost savings and customer satisfaction, flexibility of operations is the main reason for outsourcing in the context of Singaporean manufacturing firms. Recently, Arroyo et al. (2006) reported similar findings on outsourcing in Mexico.

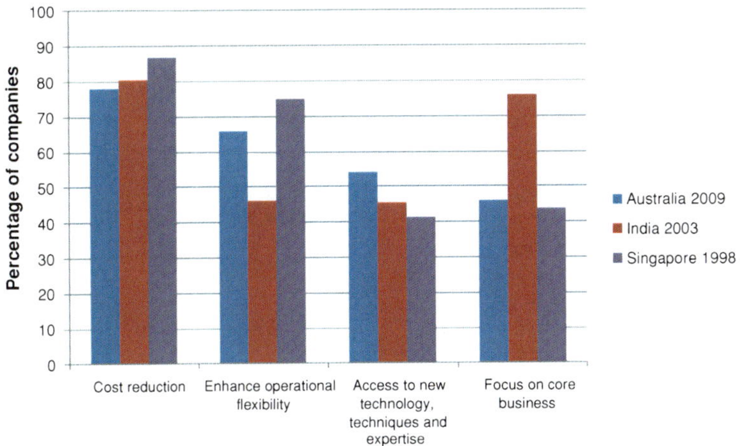

Fig. 3.1 Motivations for outsourcing/3PL (*Sources* Rahman 2009, Sahay and Mohan 2006 and Bhatnagar et al. 1999, respectively in Australia, India and Singapore.)

Lynch (2004) and Arroyo et al. (2006) noted that along with flexibility of operations, the opportunity to reduce uncertainty is also a major determinant in the outsourcing of logistics services.

Results relating to motivation for logistics outsourcing are compared in Fig. 3.1 for three countries, namely Australia, India and Singapore. Cost reduction was reported as the main reason to outsource logistics services across the three nations—identified by around 80 % of the responding firms. Enhancing operational flexibility was reported to be the second most important factor in Australia and Singapore, but not in India, where focusing on core business was identified as second most important. The need to focus on their core business was reported by around 75 % of the Indian respondents, compared with around 45 % of the Australian and Singaporean organizations. In all three countries, access to new technologies, techniques and expertise was ranked fourth amongst the four reasons for logistics outsourcing.

3.4.2 Types of Services Outsourced

Based on four different studies, Table 3.2 shows the types of logistics services being outsourced by companies in Australia, India and Malaysia—categorized under transportation and distribution; warehousing and inventory; and information systems/technology. A wide range of logistics services is outsourced in these countries, with fleet management, shipment consolidation, warehouse management and order fulfilment being the most popular services outsourced across the three nations.

3.4.3 Expenditure on Logistics Outsourcing

Figure 3.2 shows the percentage of total corporate logistics expenditure by organizations in Australia, India, Malaysia and Singapore. Just over 60 % of the Indian firms allocate up to 20 % of their logistics budget to third-party logistics providers, compared to between 25 and 42 % for the other three countries. Except for India, around 30 % of the firms from Australia, Malaysia and Singapore allocate over 60 % of their logistics budget to third-party logistics companies. Although these four studies were conducted in different time periods, the results presented do illustrate the size of the 3PL industry that has continued to grow over the past decade.

3.4.4 Average Length of 3PL Contracts

Figure 3.3 shows the average length of 3PL contracts used by clients in Australia, India, Malaysia and Singapore. Contracts of three plus years are the most common, particularly in Australia, Malaysia and Singapore, with 61, 63 and 84 % of the companies using them respectively in these three countries. In India, just over half the firms reported using contracts of 1 year or less.

3.4.5 Organizational Impact of Third Party Logistics

Figure 3.4 shows the effects of the use of 3PL services in Australia, India, Malaysia and Singapore. Between 70 and 90 % of the firms reported impacts on logistics cost (this item was not included in the Indian study), customer satisfaction and on internal logistics. A higher proportion of companies in Malaysia (95 % of the respondents) and Singapore (81 % of those responding) reported effects on employee morale, compared to firms in Australia and India (around 50 % of firms in each country). These results indicate that logistics outsourcing may influence organizations in a number of different ways, and hence can deliver positive results.

3.4.6 Percentage of Full Time Logistics Positions Eliminated by Using 3PL

Figure 3.5 shows the percentage of full-time logistics positions eliminated due to the use of 3PL in Australia, Malaysia and Singapore. Over three-quarters of the Australian and 70 % of the Malaysian respondents reported eliminating up to 20 % of the positions. In Singapore, 25 % of the firms reported that between 21

Table 3.2 Outsourced logistics functions in Australia, India and Malaysia—summary of recent academic works (numbers in parentheses refer to percentages in use of services)

Type of outsourced logistics service	Australia (Sohal et al. 2002)	Malaysia (Sohail and Sohal 2003)	India (Sahay and Mohan 2006)	Australia (Rahman 2009)
Transport and distribution related	• Fleet management (52) • Shipment consolidation (40) • Carrier selection (38) • Freight payment (14)	• Shipment consolidation (58) • Fleet management (49) •Freight payment (42) • Carrier selection (39) • Rate negotiation (37)	• Outbound transportation (56) • Inbound transportation (52) • Fleet management and consolidation (29) • Distribution (23)	•Fleet management (41) • Shipment consolidation (27) • Carrier selection (23)
Warehousing and inventory related	• Warehouse management (43) • Order fulfilment (34) • Product returns (28) • Order processing (18) • Inventory replenishment (11)	•Warehouse management (33) • Order fulfilment (30) • Inventory replenishment (24) • Product return (20)	• Customs clearance and forwarding (52) •Outbound warehousing (34) • Inbound warehousing (30) • Labelling and packaging (29) •Order picking (27) • Inventory management (24) • Reverse logistics (22) • Order fulfilment (20) • Order processing (19)	•Warehousing management (64) • Order fulfilment (59) •Order processing (27) • Product returns (27) • Product assembly/ installation (9)
Information systems/ technology	• Logistics information systems (17)	• Logistics information systems (21)	–	–

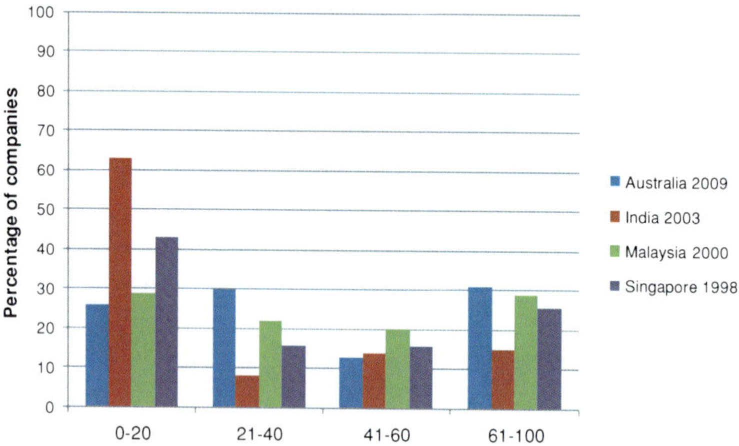

Fig. 3.2 Percentage of total corporate logistics expenditures paid to third party logistics providers. *Sources* Rahman (2009), Sahay and Mohan (2006), Sohail and Sohal (2003), and Bhatnagar et al. (1999), respectively for Australia, India, Malaysia and Singapore

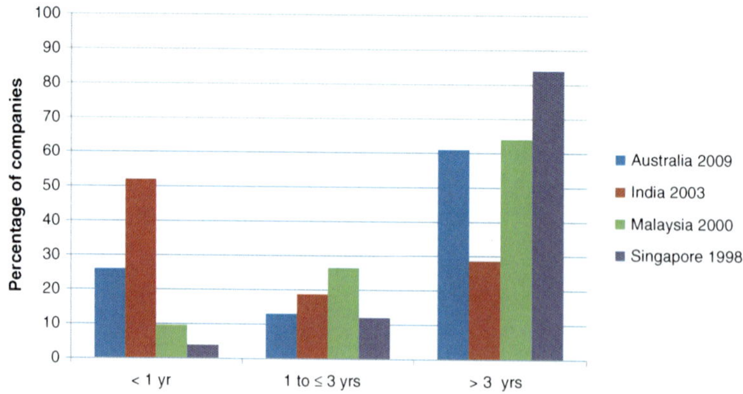

Fig. 3.3 Average length of 3PL contracts. *Sources* Rahman (2009), Sahay and Mohan (2006), Sohail and Sohal (2003), and Bhatnagar et al. (1999), respectively for Australia, India, Malaysia, and Singapore

and 40 % of full-time positions had been eliminated. There is no doubt that using 3PL will impact jobs, and this is an area where must pay particular attention.

3.4.7 Level of Satisfaction with Services of 3PL Providers

As indicated in Fig. 3.6, clients generally are 'satisfied' with the services of 3PL providers. In Malaysia and Singapore, around 85 % indicated that they were

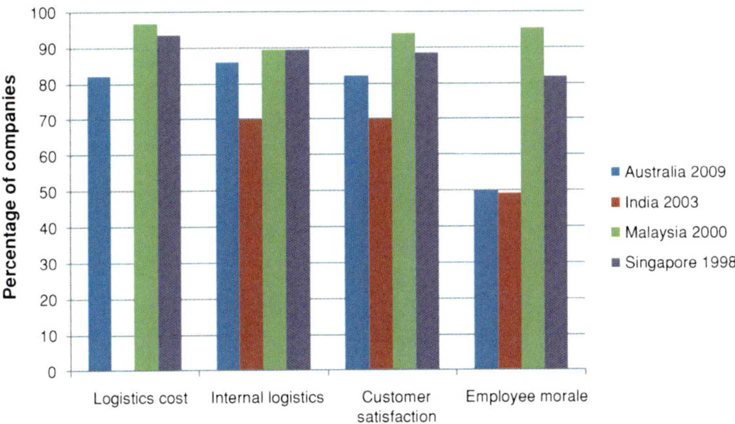

Fig. 3.4 Impact of the use of 3PL services. *Sources* Rahman (2009), Sahay and Mohan (2006), Sohail and Sohal (2003), and Bhatnagar et al. (1999), respectively for Australia, India, Malaysia, and Singapore

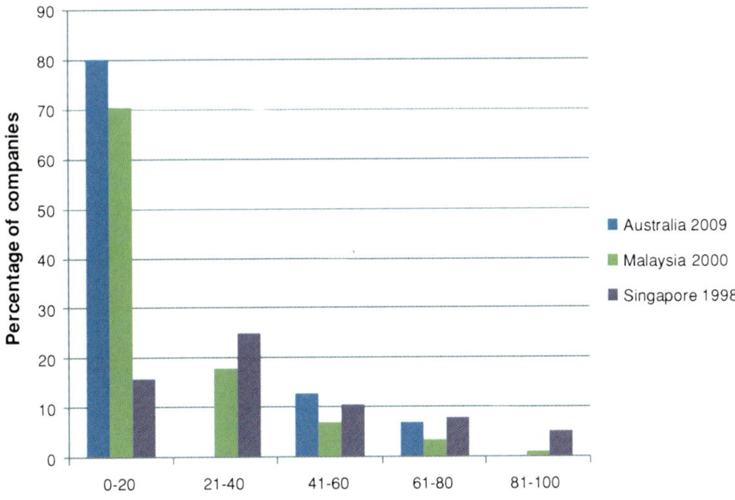

Fig. 3.5 Percentage of full-time positions eliminated due to use of 3PL. *Sources* Rahman (2009), Sohail and Sohal (2003), and Bhatnagar et al. (1999), respectively in Australia, Malaysia, and Singapore

satisfied, whilst the figure was somewhat lower for Australia (64 %) and India (72 %). Compared to in India, Malaysia and Singapore, nearly twice as many Australian firms (18 %) were 'very satisfied'. Similarly, twice as many Australian firms (14 %) were 'dissatisfied' with the providers' services, relative to their counterparts in India, Malaysia and Singapore.

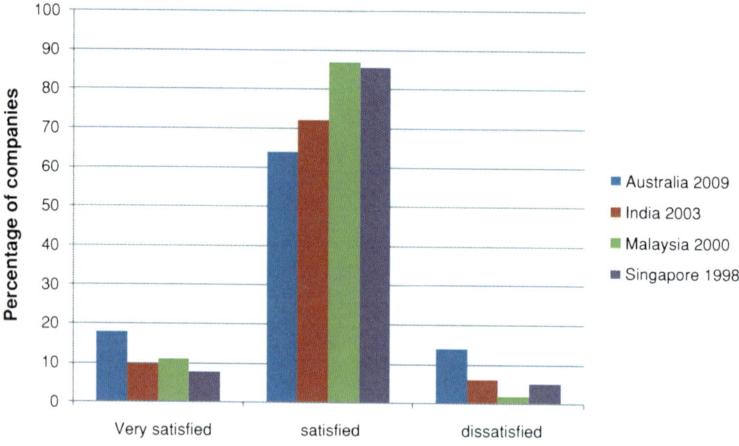

Fig. 3.6 Level of satisfaction with services of 3PL providers. *Sources* Rahman (2009), Sahay and Mohan (2006), Sohail and Sohal (2003), and Bhatnagar et al. (1999), respectively for Australia, India, Malaysia, and Singapore

3.5 Competencies of Logistics Managers

3.5.1 New Logistics Skills Required

Given the challenges and difficulties faced by modern logistics managers, both practitioners and academics have recognized the need for them to acquire new skills. Murphy and Poist (1994, 1998) proposed that senior-level logisticians required three kinds of skills, namely those pertaining to business, logistics and management. The findings of their survey of executive search firms, logistics practitioners and logistics educators indicated that management skills were the most important, followed by skills in logistics and business.

Research by Gammelgaard and Larson (2001) added another layer to the skill requirements of logistics professionals. Those authors put forward a three-factor model of skill areas for SCM practitioners, viz basic interpersonal/managerial skills, those of a quantitative/technological nature, and SCM core skills. In addition, they emphasized that logisticians also need to be good at communication, to be able to coordinate across functions and organizations in order to promote SCM, as well as to manage the upward and downward flows of information within the firm. It is noteworthy that good management skills appear to be of critical importance for supply chain professionals.

Another contribution in this area was by Mangan and Christopher (2005). They adopted a triangular research approach to obtain the views of three different stakeholders, i.e. providers of education and training, students/participants in programmes, and corporations that purchase these programmes. Mangan and Christopher thus determined the skills and key knowledge areas required by logistics and supply chain managers. The major competencies that emerged from the research were analytical, interpersonal, leadership, change management, and project management.

Giunipero and Pearcy's (2000) study, conducted in the US, also illustrated the critical skills required of supply chain professionals. The five most important ones identified concerned interpersonal communication, decision making, ability to work in teams, negotiation skills, and customer focus. Subsequent research on large US-based businesses, conducted by Giunipero et al. (2006), demonstrated the progression towards a strategic set of competencies in supply chain management. Those authors recognized five areas, namely skills in team building, strategic planning, communication, technical abilities, and broader financial skills.

3.5.2 Results from an Australian Study

A recent study of logistics and supply chain managers, conducted by Monash University (Australian Supply Chain Management Research Unit) and GS1 Australia, covered a number of issues. Those included area of responsibility, skills and competencies, use of technologies, and future challenges. The present section presents the main findings of that study.

3.5.2.1 Areas of Responsibility

The top four areas of responsibility relate to what are typically regarded as logistics/distribution activities: warehousing, inventory control, distribution, and transportation. Supply chain/business analysis and planning activities such as quality management (including control and improvement) and production planning and scheduling are important areas of responsibility from an organizational, tactical perspective. Inventory control and warehousing each continue to be a key focus, as they are critical to the success or failure of many supply chains.

3.5.2.2 Skills and Competencies

Communication and Team Work Skills—The ability to work effectively with individuals and groups was considered the most important competence in communication and team work. This was followed by the ability to manage relationships in diverse contexts: cross-culturally, intra- and inter-organizationally. Those skills were identified as the most significant. That demonstrates the perceived requirements for successful integration of different businesses along the supply chain, both domestically and globally.

Technology Skills—Ability to employ quantitative techniques for decision making (e.g. forecasting and scheduling), and the competence to lead major projects, are very important for logistics managers. In addition, the skills to solve complex and novel SCM problems (such as issues of tracking and tracing, product authentication), and to understand the interconnection of SCM with other disciplines (e.g. information systems, industrial engineering, human resources) are also of significance. SCM professionals require knowledge of a broad range of technologies to achieve a high level of integration along the supply chain.

Initiative and Enterprise Skills—The ability to manage risk in the supply chain is the most important skill in this category. The management of change within the local context, and the ability to develop and implement long term business strategies, are also of significance. Advancing SCM knowledge through professional engagement has a medium level of importance.

Compliance and Legal Knowledge—The understanding of contractual and legal or regulatory aspects of business; an awareness of ethical issues at the national and international levels; and a respect for diversity, social justice principles, the environment, and corporate governance have medium levels of importance for Australian supply chain managers. In many organizations, such activities are the responsibility of specialists with a legal background. However, we believe that the SCM professional of the future should be reasonably conversant in this area.

Supply Chain Competencies in Small/Medium/Large Enterprises—A comparative analysis, across small, medium and large enterprises, of the abilities and skills for supply chain professionals, indicates significant differences between small and large enterprises with regard to the importance of a few competencies. The following are some examples of those differences:

- SCM has stronger interconnection with other disciplines (e.g. information systems, industrial engineering and human resources) in large organizations than in small ones.
- Larger firms have greater ability to manage change within the local context.
- The competence to develop and implement long-term business strategies is stronger in large companies than in small ones.
- Larger organizations have more ability to apply continuous improvement and customer-focused concepts.

3.5.2.3 Use of Logistics/Supply Chain Technologies

Information and communication technology (ICT) has increasingly impacted on SCM, particularly in the process of collaboration between supply chain partners. ICT has made possible the sharing of large amounts of information along the supply chain. This has enabled real-time collaboration and integration between partners, thus providing organizations with forward visibility and improvements in production planning, inventory management and distribution.

A noticeable shift can be observed in supply chains, as the "build-to-order" model replaces the "build-to-forecast" method. Supply Chain Management is more critical in the former case, as it involves close communication between various agencies in the chain and the ability to respond accordingly. Adoption of supply chain technologies, e.g. enterprise resource planning (ERP), extranets, and B2B markets, to name a few, enables companies to improve their operations and effectively integrate the various links in the chain (Dawson 2002; Jacobs et al. 2011). Recent years have witnessed a tremendous growth in supply chain management software, such as systems for transportation management, supply chain planning and execution, and warehouse management (e.g. Higginson and Bookbinder 2008). The use of third-party software systems, collaborative technology, and use of expert systems are also important (Green 2001).

Technologies such as electronic data interchange (EDI) have been used by businesses as a tool for efficient replenishment and improved coordination with suppliers, rather than for integrating supply chains (Hill and Scudder 2002). However, EDI is expensive and can restrict the exchanged information. The retail sector, for example, has moved towards new ways of information exchange such as electronic marketplaces (Sparks and Wagner 2003).

A study of suppliers-retailers in Taiwan suggested that existing relationships between partners can either enable or constrain the positive effect of IT on interorganizational collaborations. It is essential for managers to understand that a socio-technical approach is required for successful supply chain collaborations (Chae et al. 2005).

Internally/Externally Focused Supply Chain Technologies—The major technologies that were used in supply chains in Australia are primarily internally-focussed technologies, and include warehouse management systems, data-capture systems (e.g. bar-code scanning), and enterprise resource planning. These results are quite surprising, given the fact that data capture is at the heart of any technologically-based initiative in supply chain integration.

In the externally-focused category, EDI and e-messaging are common. By contrast, other technologies like global positioning systems, radio frequency identification (RFID), online auctions or reverse auctions, online bidding/tendering, and public e-marketplaces are not yet very popular. That of course indicates low adoption of these technologies.

Supply Chain Technologies Used by Small/Medium/Large Enterprise—There are significant differences across small, medium and large enterprises in their adoption of supply chain technologies. Examples such as ERP, advanced planning and optimization (APO), data-capture systems, and warehouse management systems are employed to a greater extent in large organizations than in small ones. Similarly there are significant differences between medium and large Australian organizations in their use of those technologies. Also, there is a significant difference in the usage of scan packing applications between end-product manufacturers and downstream entities.

3.5.2.4 Logistics/Supply Chain Performance Measurement

The key performance indicators are more operational than strategic in nature. According to Lambert and Pohlen (2001), this is largely due to a disconnect between the strategies of an organization and its supply chain, as a result of which managers are driven by operational measures. Performance indicators that are very important, and which are customer focused, include service level, percentage delivered in full on time (DIFOT) in specification, and the costs of transportation and distribution. Likewise, measures such as delivery speed, inventory turnover, and procurement lead time are considered important. In contrast, indicators such as cash-to-cash cycle and procurement costs are of lesser importance.

Due to supply chain complexity, it can be difficult to categorize metrics for evaluating SC performance (Shepherd and Gunter 2006). Earlier research has grouped supply chain measures based on different criteria such as (a) Quantitative and qualitative indicators, e.g. resources, output, and flexibility, as identified by Beamon (1999); (b) Cost vs non-cost measures; and (c) Strategic, tactical, or operational focus (Gunasekaran et al. 2001). Stephens (2001) suggested that supply chain performance be measured by five dimensions: reliability, responsiveness, flexibility, cost, and efficiency.

At the other end of the spectrum lie criticisms against the performance measurement systems in supply chain management, for reasons such as their weak connection with the strategic goals of the organization, the focus on cost as a primary criterion (Beamon 1999), an un-balanced approach between financial and non-financial indicators, a lack of system thinking, and loss of supply chain context (Chan 2003). It is essential for both managers and employees to take custody of, and be actively involved in, the design of a simpler and more effective performance measurement system.

It is also important to realize that not every criterion can be a Key Performance Measure. A combination of strategic performance metrics, managerial performance outputs, and operational performance statistics is required, and should be linked to the expectations of shareholders and customers. The future of performance measurement in the supply chain needs to emphasize certain areas of change. These include the shift of economic hubs for world manufacturing and trade to non-western parts of the globe. This in turn will require accounting for the cultural interactions in supply networks.

Moreover, the ability to monitor and predict changes in the world's climate and its impact on both local and international trade will necessitate different types of performance indicators in the future. Lastly, rising price levels due to declining reserves of fossil fuels will force companies to address aggregate supply network costs. That will be done via comparison of financial performance measurements and agreement on criteria and standards across organizations (Morgan 2007).

3.5.2.5 Future Challenges

A number of future challenges to Logistics in Australia were identified. They have been categorized under the following headings: environment, globalization, supply chain integration, supply chain training and development, and supply chain responsiveness/agility. These are briefly discussed below.

Impact of Environment—Transportation costs (due to geographical distance and petrol supply/price) are identified as having a large effect on supply chains in the future. Other environmental issues relating to the management of scarce resources, such as lean concepts in the supply chain, environmental (green) impact of products and processes, and limited natural resources will have a medium degree of influence.

Impact of Globalization—Effects of globalization, such as international supply and distribution channels and complexity of the structure of logistics networks, will greatly influence supply chains in the future. In contrast, factors such as a shift of centre of gravity of supply chain activities to China and India, and obstacles to world trade, including legislation and tariffs, will have a medium level of impact on supply chains.

Supply Chain Integration—Challenges relating to greater visibility requirements of the supply chain, and integrating processes with SC partners, will have a medium to high influence on the future of supply chains. The low usage of various SC technologies indicates that supply chain professionals may not yet have fully recognized the major impediments to integration.

Supply Chain Training and Development—SCM has become very complex due to a number of issues that affect business in general. Supply chain education, training and career development, and the shortage of skills in an aging population, are two areas that will have a medium degree of impact on supply chains in the future.

Supply Chain Responsiveness/Agility—An agile supply chain is required for companies to stand above their competitors. Top areas of concern, which will have a medium influence on future supply chains, relate to measuring SC performance (qualitative and quantitative metrics), responsiveness and agility, as well as fragmentation and the variety of each customer's needs, and the end-to-end lead-time compression of the supply chain pipeline.

Future Challenges for Supply Chains in Small/Medium/Large Enterprises—There are significant differences between small and large Australian organizations in their perception of challenges for SCs in the future. Concerns related to closed loop supply chains, integrating organizational functions through supply chain processes, and greater visibility requirements of the SC were identified by large organizations to have a significantly higher impact on their future supply chains as compared to small organizations. Similarly, there were noticeable differences between wholly domestically-owned and wholly foreign-owned companies in their perceived challenges for tomorrow's supply chains. The latter differences especially concerned global supply and distribution channels, and volatile demands and markets.

3.6 Skill Requirements of Chinese Logistics Managers

The chapter by Chen and Lee (2013), earlier in this volume, concentrates on "Logistics in China." We thus limit ourselves here to some general remarks on 3PL and the training of Logistics managers in China, viewed from its perspective as an Asia-Pacific nation, as supported by the recent survey co-authored by one of us (Rahman and Yang 2009).

Substantial efficiency improvements could be achieved if China's logistics industry were to consolidate. The sector has considerable inefficiencies, with poor inventory management, low on-time delivery, high damage rates and sub-standard tracking. Most warehousing is, in general, ill equipped, and characterized by little or outdated technology. These issues are compounded by a shortage of staff that have the required logistics skills (both professional and manual). Training is weak on both a practical and strategic level. Whilst shipment of goods out of the country is relatively easy and straightforward, moving goods within the country is fraught with difficulties. Inadequate infrastructure outside the main coastal cities is only the beginning.

China has one of the most highly regulated logistics markets in the world—at a number of different tiers (national, regional and city). This hinders the creation of an integrated national network. Due to the division of China into provinces, with significant local powers, provincial governments protect their interests by setting up complicated regulatory requirements, and stringent border controls. As goods cross provincial borders, there are often high road tolls (both legal and illegal), and complex customs processes. It is often necessary to use more than one haulage company to move goods across multiple regions. Many cities restrict the access of trucks from other provinces.

Fortunately, recent developments are starting to improve matters, on the domestic front as well as for export-based logistics. The sector is expected to grow by about 30 % per year. Experts predict that there will be substantial increase in 3PL activities, with more international operators getting involved in moving goods inside China. It is also felt that China's liberalization measures are likely to be sustained and extended. As large 3PLs develop their Chinese networks, they will create growing pressure for change. Recent studies point to a shift away from warehousing for storage purposes towards other uses, notably higher-value services, transhipment and consolidation. Enhanced importance of specialist warehousing and greater use of information technology are also anticipated (Jones Lang Lasalle 2007).

One of the main implications of the preceding trends is that the Chinese Logistics industry will require more skilled managers to run those activities. Unfortunately, the inefficiency of the 3PL sector in China is also compounded by a shortage of managers with relevant logistics skills, and poor training on both the practical and strategic levels. To identify the skills required by logistics and supply chain managers in China, a survey was conducted in 2008 in the Shanghai Region

Table 3.3 Ten most important skills (based upon Rahman and Yang 2009)

Skill item	Average perception	Standard deviation
Inventory Management	7.58	1.35
Supply chain awareness	7.57	1.10
Cross-functional awareness	7.57	1.08
Customer service	7.57	1.25
Supply chain cost minimization	7.56	1.38
Ability to see "Big Picture"	7.51	1.22
Transport management	7.48	1.48
Cross-functional coordination	7.38	1.13
Team work	7.34	1.22
Integration of information flow	7.30	1.01

(Rahman and Yang 2009). Another purpose of that study was to suggest the key knowledge areas that require improvement.

From the 200 firms selected, a total of 54 managers responded to the survey. Among the respondents, 17.7 % were line mangers, 70.6 % were middle managers and 11.7 % were senior managers. Of the 54 managers who participated, 62.7 % were male and 37.3 % were female. The average age of the respondents was 32.54 years. Their average work experience was over 10 years; their average work experience in the area of logistics exceeded 7 years. A large proportion of the firms (84.9 %) had more than 1,000 employees, while 4.3 % had fewer than 100. About 6.5 % of the companies had between 501 and 1,000 employees.

The respondents were asked to rate the importance of 45 specific skill items on a scale from 0 (none) to 9 (very high). In this study, the word 'importance' refers to the degree that those skills were needed to perform logistics functions efficiently, as perceived by the managers. We identified 10 most important and 5 least important skills, in the opinions of those Chinese logistics managers.

Ten Most Important Skills—Table 3.3 shows the top ten skills in terms of mean importance ratings. These concern the management of inventory, supply chain awareness, cross-functional awareness, customer service, supply chain cost minimization, ability to see the 'big picture', transport management, cross-functional coordination, team work, and integration of information flow. It is important to note that the respondents appreciated the soft skills such as cross-functional coordination, team orientation, supply chain concept, and ability to see the big picture as some of the critical skills required by logistics managers.

Five Least Important Skills—Table 3.4 shows the five least important skills as perceived by the respondents. A vast majority of them (about 71 %) were middle level managers, and therefore it is not surprising that they gave low priority to computer programming. Other less important skills are salvage and scrap disposal and ISO 14,000 standards.

That study provided an assessment of the skills required by supply chain managers in China. The results indicated that generally all "individual skills" are highly rated with regard to their importance in performing logistics functions.

Table 3.4 Five least important skills (adapted from Rahman and Yang 2009)

Skill item	Average perception	Standard deviation
Computer programming	4.81	2.59
Salvage/scrap disposal	5.15	1.86
ISO 14,000 standards	5.23	1.80
Parts support	5.62	1.91
Material handling	5.62	1.84

However, some of the skill items belonging to the "environment awareness" skill-category, such as ISO 14,000, salvage and scrap disposal, were not assessed highly. Environmental issues in logistics in general, and reverse logistics in particular, are becoming challenging areas for the corporate world. It is important that Chinese supply chain managers be trained in the areas of reverse logistics, and in environmental issues such as closed-loop remanufacturing, life cycle analysis, and product take-back policies.

3.7 Conclusions

This chapter has focussed on a number of key points concerning the use of Third Party Logistics (3PL) in the Asia-Pacific region. Resulting from the shift of manufacturing from North America and Europe to Asia, the demand for Logistics services has grown substantially over the past two decades in various countries in this region. Trends in 3PL were compared amongst four countries, namely Australia, India, Malaysia and Singapore.

Cost reduction and enhancement of operational flexibility are the two main reasons why firms outsource logistics—with fleet management, shipment consolidation, warehouse management and order fulfillment being the most popular services outsourced. The positive impact of the use of 3PL reported by firms has been substantial in terms of logistics costs, customer satisfaction, internal logistics and employee morale. However, there is also a negative impact in terms of full-time logistics positions eliminated as a result of using 3PL. Generally, companies have been 'satisfied' with 3PL service providers.

China is experiencing rapid growth overall, and in particular, in the demand for Logistics services. However, the country's logistics providers face a number of challenges that need to be addressed. These include relationships with highly-demanding customers, dealing with government and legal restrictions, and coping with the rapidly changing external environment.

A somewhat similar picture emerges for India. This nation is also experiencing rapid growth. Inadequate road infrastructure, state government regulations, and highly-demanding customers are factors that 3PLs must face in India too.

Within the Asia-Pacific region, Australia and Singapore are well developed in terms of the availability of 3PLs. Clients of these firms are generally satisfied with the services provided.

This chapter also reported on the results of recent studies focusing on the skills of logistics/supply chain managers in China and Australia. Communication and teamwork, as well as knowledge of a broad range of technologies, both intra-company and inter-company technologies, were identified as the key competencies required.

Environmental issues relating to the management of scarce resources will have a significant impact on supply chains in the future. Logistics managers will thus need to possess a diverse set of skills to tackle the varied perceived challenges expected in years to come.

An important topic for further research concerns the potential disruptions to local and global supply chains. 3PLs will need to better understand how these effects can be mitigated. We also feel that the impact of climate change will remain a significant area, for 3PLs and the supply chains they serve.

References

Arroyo P, Gaytan J, de Boer L (2006) A survey of third party logistics in Mexico and a comparison with reports on Europe and USA. Int J Oper Prod Manage 26(6):639–667

Bagchi PK, Virum H (1996) European logistics alliances: a management model. Int J Logistics Manage 7(1):93–108

Bardi EJ, Tracey M (1991) Transportation outsourcing: a survey of US practices. Int J Phys Distrib Logistics Manage 21(3):15–21

Beamon BM (1999) Measuring supply chain performance. Int J Oper Prod Manage 19(3):275–292

Bhatnagar R, Sohal AS, Millen R (1999) Third party logistics services: a Singapore perspective. Int J Phys Distrib Logistics Manage 29(9):569–587

Carter JR (2005) Outsourcing strategically for sustainable competitive advantage. Research monograph, Centre for Advanced Purchasing Studies, Tempe, AZ.

Carter JR, Maltz A, Yan T (2008) How procurement mangers view low cost countries and geographies—a perceptual mapping approach. Int J Phys Distrib Logistics Manage 38(3):224–243

Chae B, Yen HR, Sheu C (2005) Information technology and supply chain collaboration: moderating effects of existing relationships between partners. IEEE Trans Eng Manage 52(4):440–448

Chan FTS (2003) Performance measurement in a supply chain. Int J Adv Manuf Technol 21:534–548

Chen F, Lee C-Y (2013) Logistics in China. In: Bookbinder JH (ed) Global logistics: transportation in international supply chains. Springer, New York

China's Logistics Report (2005) Logistics Information Centre of China and China Federation of Logistics and Purchasing, vol Jan–June

Dawson A (2002) Supply chain technology. Work Study 51(4):191–196

Fantasia JJ (1993) Are you a candidate for third party logistics? Transp Distrib 34:30 (Jan)

Fuller JB, O'Connor J, Rawlinson R (1993) Tailored logistics: the next advantage. Harvard Bus Rev 71(3):87–98

Gammelgaard B, Larson P (2001) Logistics skills and competencies for supply chain management. J Bus Logistics 22(2):27–50
Giunipero LC, Pearcy DH (2000) World-class purchasing skills: an empirical investigation. J Supply Chain Manage 36(4):4–15
Giunipero LC, Handfield RB, Eltantawy R (2006) Supply management's evolution: key skill sets for the supply manager of the future. Int J Oper Prod Manage 26(7):822–844
Gooley TB (1997) The state of third party logistics in Europe. Logistics Manage 36(1):80A–81A
Green FB (2001) Managing the unmanageable: integrating the supply chain with new developments in software. Supply Chain Manage Int J 6(5):202–211
Gunasekaran A, Patel C, Tirtiroglu E (2001) Performance measures and metrics in a supply chain environment. Int J Oper Prod Manage 21(1/2):71–87
Higginson JK, Bookbinder JH (2008) Chapter 2: Warehouse management systems and product flow: reconciling the two. In: Lahmar M (ed) Facility logistics: approaches and solutions to next generation challenges. Auerbach Publications, New York, pp 17–38
Hill CA, Scudder GD (2002) The use of electronic data interchange for supply chain coordination in the food industry. J Oper Manage 20:375–387
Hoetker G (2005) How much you know versus how well I know you: selecting a supplier for a technically innovative component. Strateg Manag J 26(1):75–96
Holldorsson A, Skjott-Larsen T (2004) Developing logistics competencies through third party logistics relationships. Int J Oper Prod Manage 24(2):192–206
Jacobides MG, Winter SG (2005) The co-evolution of capabilities and transaction costs: explaining the institutional structure of production. Strateg Manag J 26(5):395–413
Jacobs FR, Berry WL, Whybark DC, Vollmann TE (2011) Chapter 1A: Enterprise resource planning (ERP). In: Manufacturing planning & control for supply chain management, 6th edn. McGraw-Hill Irwin, New York
Jones Lang Lasalle, Ltd (2007) China logistics: the geography of opportunity. World winning cities series: emerging city winners. China Supply Chain Council, Shanghai
Knemeyer AM, Murphy PR (2005) Is the glass half full or half empty? An examination of user and provider perspectives towards third-party logistics relationships. Int J Phys Distrib Logistics Manage 35(10):708–727
Lambert DM, Pohlen TL (2001) Supply chain metrics. Int J Logistics Manage 12(1):1–19
Larson PD, Gammelgaard B (2001) Logistics in Denmark: a survey of the industry. Int J Logistics: Res Appl 4(2):191–206
Lieb RC (1992) The use of third party logistics services by large American manufacturers. J Bus Logistics 13(2):29–42
Lieb R, Millen R, van Wassenhove L (1993) Third-party logistics services: a comparison of experienced American and European manufacturers. Int J Phys Distrib Logistics Manage 23(6):35–44
Lynch CF (2004) Why outsource? Supply Chain Manage Rev 8(7):44–49
Maltz AB, Carter JR, Villalobos JR (2011) Procurement from developing countries. In: Bookbinder JH (ed) Global logistics: transportation in international supply chains. Springer, New York
Mangan J, Christopher M (2005) Management development and the supply chain manager of the future. Int J Logistics Manage 16(2):178–191
Morgan C (2007) Supply network performance measurement: future challenges? Int J Logistics Manage 18(2):255–273
Murphy P, Poist R (1994) Educational strategies for succeeding in logistics: a comparative analysis. Transp J 33(3):36–48
Murphy P, Poist R (1998) Skill requirements of senior-level logisticians: practitioner perspectives. Int J Phys Distrib Logistics Manage 28(4):284–301
Rabinovich E, Windle R, Dresner ME, Corsi T (1999) Outsourcing of integrated logistics functions: an examination of industry practices. Int J Phys Distrib Logistics Manage 29(6):353–373

Rahman S (2009) Outsourcing third-party logistics services by Australian firms. Int J Logistics Supply Chain Manage 1(1):41–49
Rahman S, Yang L (2009) Skills requirements for logistics managers in China. IIBM Manage Rev 21(2):140–148
Richardson HL (1990) Explore outsourcing. Transp Distrib 31:17–21 (July)
Richardson HL (1992) Outsourcing: the power worksource. Transp Distrib 33:22–24 (July)
Sahay BS, Mohan R (2006) 3PL practices: an Indian perspective. Int J Phys Distrib Logistics Manage 36(9):666–689
Sheffi Y (1990) Third party logistics: present and future prospects. J Bus Logistics 11(2):27–39
Shepherd C, Gunter H (2006) Measuring supply chain performance: current research and future directions. Int J Prod Perform Manage 55(3/4):242–258
Sink HL, Langley CJJ, Gibson BJ (1996) Buyer observations of the US third party logistics market. Int J Phys Distrib Logistics Manage 26(3):38–46
Skjott-Larsen T (2000) Third-party logistics—from an interorganisational point of view. Int J Phys Distrib Logistics Manage 30(2):112–127
Sohail MS, Sohal AS (2003) The use of third party logistics services: a Malaysian perspective. Technovation 23:401–408
Sohal AS, Millen R, Moss S (2002) A comparison of the use of third-party logistics services by Australian firms between 1995 and 1999. Int J Phys Distrib Logistics Manage 32(1):59–68
Sparks L, Wagner BA (2003) Retail exchanges: a research agenda. Supply Chain Manage Int J 8(3):201–208
Stephens S (2001) Supply chain operations reference model version 5.0: a new tool to improve supply chain efficiency and achieve best practice. Inf Syst Frontiers 3(4):471–476
Sundarraj RP, Kumari K (2013) Electronic procurement systems in India: importance and impact on supply chain operations. In: Bookbinder JH (ed) Global logistics: transportation in international supply chains. Springer, New York
Trunick PA (2003) Logistics links are critical in China. Transp Distrib 44(8):50–53
van Laarhoven P, Berglund M, Peters M (2000) Third party logistics in Europe—five years later. Int J Phys Distrib Logistics Manage 30(5):425–442
Walker G, Poppo L (1991) Profit centres, single source suppliers and transaction costs. Adm Sci Q 36:66–87
Williamson OE (1979) Transaction cost economics: the governance of contractual relations. J Law Econ 22:233–261

Chapter 4
The Greater Mekong Sub-region of Southeast Asia: Improving Logistics Connectivity

Ruth Banomyong

Abstract Traders in the Greater Mekong Sub-region (GMS) require efficient logistics services that can move their goods to the proper place, at the promised time, in the right condition, and at a suitable price. The GMS in Southeast Asia is composed of Cambodia, Lao People's Democratic Republic, Myanmar, Thailand, Vietnam, as well as Yunnan Province and the Guangxi Zhuang Autonomous Region of the People's Republic of China. It is, therefore, of great importance that regional linkages among neighbouring countries be enhanced, in order to facilitate trade and develop logistics for better access to the "global" market. The purpose of this chapter is to provide a description and rating of the GMS logistics system. The Greater Mekong Sub-region has focused on an "economic corridor" approach to economic integration; assessment of the logistics performance of these corridors is thus needed. Even though there is a GMS agreement that was ratified to facilitate the crossing of borders, it was still observed during our study that the weakest links in the various economic corridors remain the border crossings.

4.1 Introduction

Manufacturers and traders in the Greater Mekong Sub-region (GMS) require efficient and effective logistics services that can move their products to the appropriate place, at the desired time, in good condition, and at the price offered. To establish production and economic networks and develop logistics for better

R. Banomyong (✉)
Thammasat Business School, Bangkok, Thailand
e-mail: ruth@banomyong.com

J. H. Bookbinder (ed.), *Handbook of Global Logistics*, International Series in Operations Research & Management Science 181, DOI: 10.1007/978-1-4419-6132-7_4,

access to international markets, it is therefore of great importance that regional linkages within and between GMS nations be strengthened.

The GMS comprises Cambodia, Lao People's Democratic Republic (Lao PDR), Myanmar, Thailand, and Vietnam, as well as Yunnan Province and Guangxi Zhuang Autonomous Region of the People's Republic of China (PRC). In 1992, with assistance from the Asian Development Bank (ADB), the six countries entered into a program of sub-regional economic cooperation, designed to enhance economic relations among themselves.[1] The GMS countries are illustrated in Fig. 4.1.

In the GMS, inadequate transport infrastructure and high logistics connectivity costs have constrained economic integration (Fujimura 2008). As a remedy, major infrastructure investments are already being undertaken by these nations, and more are planned. Physical connectivity in the GMS will be significantly improved upon completion of those investments. Enhanced quality of infrastructure, coupled with expanded cross-border cooperation among these countries, will help accelerate the process of regional integration, as well as give better access to global markets.

With physical connectivity along the GMS economic corridors significantly progressing, greater emphasis is being placed on addressing many of the "soft" areas of cooperation to increase speed and smoothness. There is particular focus on tackling behind-border obstacles, such as regulatory practices, licensing, standards or other types of restrictive policies and methods that add cost, impede business processes, or create barriers to entry (Banomyong 2008).

This chapter aims to describe and rate the GMS logistics system. The sub-region has emphasized economic corridors[2] as a means to economic integration. It is now necessary to rank the logistics performance of these corridors (Banomyong 2010). Although a GMS accord, entitled the GMS Cross Border Transport Agreement[3] (CBTA), was passed to improve the crossing of borders, we nevertheless found in our research that those border crossings were the least impressive elements in most economic corridors (Banomyong et al. 2010).

4.2 Logistics Conceptual Framework

It is important to understand that "logistics," as a business concept, has traditionally been implemented and managed at the *firm* level. Governments in the GMS have now started to recognize the general importance of logistics in supporting and sustaining competitive advantage. However, the majority of those Governments are still struggling with the idea of logistics, and how it can be improved in a holistic manner (Banomyong et al. 2008).

---

[1] www.adb.org/GMS accessed on January 15, 2011.

[2] http://www.adb.org/GMS/Economic-Corridors/default.asp accessed on January 15, 2011.

[3] www.adb.org/GMS/Cross-Border/about.asp accessed on January 15, 2011.

Fig. 4.1 The Greater Mekong Sub-region. *Source* Asian development bank

In this chapter, the scope of logistics relates to the interaction between four key logistics dimensions as described in the conceptual model of Fig. 4.2 (Banomyong 2008; Banomyong et al. 2008). That interaction between those four facets provides a preliminary understanding of the current logistics capability of a country or a region.

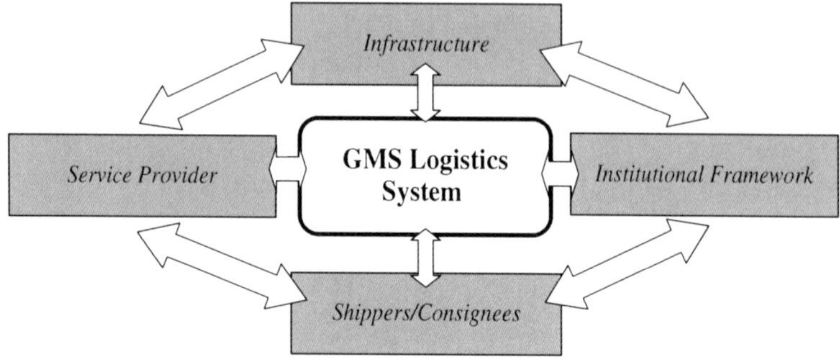

Fig. 4.2 Model of the scope of logistics

Logistics is not just confined within national borders or markets because within each country or region, there are export and import firms that face logistics requirements that may differ from those experienced domestically (Grant et al. 2006). In an international logistics system, a multitude of state agencies and, in particular, customs and other departments entrusted with border-control functions play a very important role in shaping the logistics system and determining its level of efficiency (Kieck 2010). There is also a heavy reliance on specialized service providers, such as freight forwarders or customs brokers, that can facilitate the flow of goods across frontiers.

The four logistics dimensions need to be interlinked, to improve the effectiveness and efficiency of the GMS logistics system as a whole. It is only through integration of those aspects that the Greater Mekong Sub-region can strengthen its logistics capability and performance. The four dimensions of logistics are thus:

- Quality and capacity of the GMS infrastructure
- An enabling GMS institutional environment
- The capability of GMS logistics service providers
- Access of GMS traders and manufacturers to competitive logistics services.

4.3 Status of GMS Logistics Development

Logistics systems and services vary significantly from country to country in the GMS. In general, logistics in the Greater Mekong Sub-region is still in its early development. Quality of services and availability of infrastructure often lag behind best practices observed in more advanced trading nations, both outside and within Southeast Asia. This section describes the rank or standing of key logistics infrastructure in the GMS.

4.3.1 GMS Ports and Maritime Issues

Access to a functioning, well-developed maritime transport network determines the degree of participation of countries in the global trading system. Additionally, that access provides an increasingly important element in the implementation of working agreements on regional trade and integration. The influence of regional sea transport for the promotion and attainment of GMS integration objectives is gradually being realized, notwithstanding the fact that GMS transport activities are still very much centered on improvements in land transportation.

According to ESCAP (2005), modern and efficient ports are necessary and powerful tools for facilitating and fostering trade and development. Ports must offer ships and cargo effective and reliable services, including communication systems, documentation, and customs procedures to allow the timely flow of goods through the transport supply chain. Therefore, ports are no longer simply a place for cargo handling, but are major functional elements in dynamic logistics chains. Ports are also nodal points where national and international transportation systems meet, hence are increasingly called upon to ensure system compatibility and avoid undue rupture of the total supply chain.

The small number of direct services in Cambodia and Myanmar, or the lack of them, reflects the relatively low container volumes compared to those in more developed GMS countries such as China and Thailand. Cambodia, Myanmar, and to some extent Vietnam are mostly served by feeder services to main regional hubs such as Singapore or Hong Kong. The growth of Guangxi's port system in China will increase the shipping capability of the GMS. Development of ports in Vietnam, especially in the South of the country, has provided enhanced connectivity with the main markets through newly designed end-to-end shipping linkages.

Port systems in the GMS can be categorized as either operating or "landlord" ports. Under the operating port system, the port is managed and operated by a state or public port authority, whereas under the landlord port system, the port authority provides the land, but operations are administered by the private sector. In Thailand, the port of Bangkok is managed and operated by the Port Authority of Thailand, while the operations at its deep sea port of Laem Chabang are supervised by private operators under a concession system. Similarly, the Myanmar International Terminals Thilawa (MITT) of Yangon port is operated by Hutchinson Port Holding from Hong Kong, as is Saigon International Terminals Vietnam (SITV). The Port of Singapore Authority International operates SP-PSA International Port Vung Tau container terminal, while Dubai Port World manages Saigon Premier Container Terminal and APM Cai Mep International Terminal (CMIT), all in the South of Vietnam.

Port information and communication technology (ICT) play an important role in the integration of the port and its stakeholders, including the shipping lines, exporters, importers, and customs. However, Cambodian, Myanmar and Vietnamese ports are still at an early stage of ICT development, with Guangxi and Thailand being the most advanced among the GMS. Certain ports in Vietnam,

Table 4.1 GMS port and maritime matrix

	Cambodia	Myanmar	Thailand	Vietnam	Guangxi (PRC)
Direct mainline services	No	No	Yes	Limited	Yes
Feeder services	Yes	Yes	Yes	Yes	Yes
Regional services (>1,500 TEU)	No	No	Yes	Yes	Yes
Landlord port	No	No	Yes	Planned	No
Container terminal concessions	No	Yes	Yes	Yes	No
Fixed day of the week shipping services	Yes	Limited	Yes	Yes	Yes
Port Community systems–Portnet or others	Planned	Planned	Partial	Limited	Yes
Post-Panamax gantry cranes	No	No	Yes	Planned	Yes
Computerized terminal control system	Yes	Planned	Yes	Yes	Yes
Automated gate entry	Partial	No	Partial	Planned	No
Off dock container yard	No	No	Yes	Yes	Yes
Bonded distribution facilities	Planned	No	Yes	Yes	Yes
Full truck scanners	Yes	Yes	Yes	Planned	Yes
Rail links to port	No	No	Yes	No	Yes

mostly private ones, do have computerized information systems that enable ports and port users to exchange information on regulatory procedures or on the status of cargo in transit. Here again, Myanmar lags behind in terms of port and maritime development, with Thailand and Guangxi seemingly the most advanced. There is also an observed lack of rail links with the main ports in Cambodia, Myanmar and Vietnam. Modal integration is generally limited to providing the road and sea interfaces in the GMS. Table 4.1 summarizes port issues in the Greater Mekong Sub-region.

4.3.2 GMS Rail Transport

The railway system in the GMS is not connected, even though there are concrete plans to develop the Singapore to Kunming rail link (ADB 2010). Table 4.2 provides a description of existing and new requirements for railway construction in the missing sector/routes and spur lines along the Singapore-Kunming Rail Link (SKRL) network (see Fig. 4.3). To complete the SKRL network, new railway construction will be required in Cambodia, Lao PDR, Myanmar and Vietnam, with further rehabilitation in Thailand and China. It is to be noted that the maximum length of new construction is required in the least developed nation, Lao PDR, to achieve the spur line.

Table 4.2 New construction required for missing routes and spur line

Country	Missing sector/Route and spur line	Existing (km)	New construction (km)
Cambodia	Poipet (Thailand border) -Sisophon	–	48
Cambodia	Phnom Penh -Loc Ninh (Vietnam border)	32	254
Vietnam	Loc Ninh (border)–Ho Chi Minh City	20	129
Myanmar	Thanbyuzayat–Three Pagoda Pass	–	110
Thailand	Three Pagoda Pass–Nam Tok	–	153
Lao PDR	Vientiane-Thakhek-Mu Dia	–	466
Vietnam	Mu Dia–Tan Ap- Vung Anh	6	119

Source Adapted from the feasibility study for the Singapore-Kunming rail link

Fig. 4.3 Singapore-Kunming rail link (SKRL) route network. *Source* Secretariat of the association of South-East Asian nations (SKRL fact sheet)

Table 4.3 GMS rail matrix

	Cambodia	Lao PDR	Myanmar	Thailand	Vietnam	Yunnan	Guangxi
Standard gauge	No	No	No	No	Planned	Yes	Yes
Double track	No	No	Yes	Limited	No	No	No
Dedicated track for freight services	No	No	No	No	Planned	Planned	Planned
Centralized train control	No	No	Planned	Limited	Limited	Yes	Planned
Electrified lines	No	No	No	Planned	Planned	Yes	Yes
Heavy Load Wagons	No	No	No	No	No	Yes	Yes
Long trains (over 60 TEUs)	No	No	No	No	No	No	Yes
Modern locomotives	No	Limited	Yes	Planned	Limited	Yes	Planned
Unit container train operations	No	Planned	No	Yes	Yes	Yes	No
24 h freight terminal operations	No	Planned	Yes	Yes	Limited	Yes	Yes
Privately owned rail wagons	Planned	Planned	Limited	Planned	No	No	No
Private freight train operations	Planned	Planned	No	Planned	Limited	No	No

Rail logistics is complex, as it requires the management of capacity, schedules, shipment characteristics, origins, and destinations. Table 4.3 outlines the rail situation in the Greater Mekong Sub-region.

The GMS railway system is based mostly on the meter-gauge system, except in Yunnan and in Guangxi province of China. There exists rail connectivity with freight traffic moving between Guangxi and Northern Vietnam. The link between Yunnan province and Vietnam is under restoration. The GMS rail freight system is characterized by:

- Access charges that are high compared to direct road transportation. This means that to use rail transport, goods usually must first move by road to rail terminals for intermodal transfers, thus increasing the charges to access rail transport;
- Almost no international routes, leading to excessive transit time and inferior service quality; and
- Lack of priority given to timetables, resulting in poor reliability except in China.

Apart from physical constraints, there is a general requirement for GMS railways to be more customer-oriented, particularly in terms of pricing flexibility and contract arrangements. Efforts to improve and integrate the GMS rail network will need to be based on long-term support, as the network capability is currently constrained by limited infrastructure and lack of management skill. Completion of the missing portions in the Singapore-to-Kunming rail link is still very much behind schedule, as illustrated in Fig. 4.3.

Table 4.4 GMS road transport matrix

	Cambodia	Lao PDR	Myanmar	Thailand	Vietnam	Yunnan (PRC)	Guangxi (PRC)
Multilane dual carriageway	No	Planned	No	Yes	Yes	Planned	No
Limited access highway	No	Planned	No	Partial	No	No	No
Toll roads	Limited	Planned	Yes	Yes	Yes	Yes	No
Ring road capital	Limited	Planned	Yes	Yes	Limited	Limited	Yes
Ring road major cities	Limited	Planned	Yes	Yes	Limited	Limited	Yes
Partial truck ban	Limited	Planned	Yes	Yes	Yes	Yes	No
Control axle load limit	Partial	Yes	Yes	Partial	Planned	Yes	Yes
Limit enforced by police	Partial	Planned	No	Partial	No	Yes	Yes
Articulated trucks	Yes	Limited	Yes	Yes	Yes	No	Limited
Modern commercial trucks	Limited	Planned	Yes	Yes	Yes	Yes	Yes
Road worthiness certificate	Partial	Limited	Yes	Yes	Planned	Yes	Yes
Pollution control	No	Planned	Yes	Yes	Yes	Yes	Yes
Test failed but still on road	Partial	Yes	Yes	Yes	Yes	No	No

4.3.3 Road Transport in the GMS

Road transportation is the principal mode in the Greater Mekong Sub-region. However, its management and operations still need to be harmonized and standardized. The challenge is that road infrastructure in Cambodia, Lao PDR, Myanmar and Vietnam continues to lag behind that of Thailand and China. Multilane dual carriageways (divided highways) exist only in Vietnam; limited access highways are *non-existent* in Cambodia, Lao PDR, and Myanmar. Toll roads and ring roads around major cities do exist in Myanmar and Vietnam, where urban congestion has hindered the efficient flow of goods carried by trucks, especially during peak hours. This is also among the reasons behind implementation of total or partial truck bans in the GMS, with the only exception being Guangxi province. Table 4.4 describes road transport considerations in the Greater Mekong Sub-region.

Overloading of cargo is a major issue faced by many nations of the GMS. Axle load limits do exist, but enforcement is frequently lacking. In terms of compliance, roadworthiness certificates are theoretically required in most GMS nations, but again observance is often absent. There is the same difficulty with pollution control. Substandard trucking is as much a general problem as insufficient equipment for container transport in the GMS, and constitutes a formidable barrier

Table 4.5 GMS IWT matrix

	Cambodia	Lao PDR	Myanmar	Thailand	Vietnam	Yunnan (PRC)	Guangxi (PRC)
Scheduled service	Yes	No	Yes	Limited	Yes	Yes	Planned
Links to main seaport	No	No	No	Limited	No	No	Planned
Container vessel for IWT	Limited	No	No	Planned	Yes	No	Yes
Container terminal	Yes	No	No	Planned	Limited	No	Yes
Computerized terminal control system	Yes	No	No	No	No	No	Yes
Automated gate entry	Limited	No	No	No	Yes	No	No
Off-dock yard	Limited	No	Limited	Planned	Yes	Yes	No
Bonded distribution facility	No	Limited	No	Planned	Planned	No	No
Rail lines to IWT terminal	No	No	No	No	Yes	Yes	Yes

to the widespread introduction of door-to-door multimodal movement of containers.

Countries in the Greater Mekong Sub-region are thus characterized by inadequate capability to enforce road regulations. The exception is China, where rules are strictly monitored. (However, that observation needs to be interpreted with great care, as usually these instances occur on a case-by-case basis). Nevertheless, the inability to enforce regulations appears to have important consequences for sector competitiveness and sustainable development.

4.3.4 GMS Inland Waterway Transport

The Mekong River links Jinghong (in Yunnan, China) with Ho Chi Minh City, Vietnam. Apart from the Mekong, however, inland waterways in the GMS serve mostly domestic traffic. Table 4.5 compares inland water transportation (IWT) systems among countries in the Greater Mekong Sub-region.

Some scheduled *international* inland waterway services do exist in the Northern Mekong area between Yunnan, Lao PDR, Myanmar and Thailand, as well as between Cambodia and Vietnam. Connections to the main seaports are not readily available except in the case of Phnom Penh to Ho Chi Minh. Deficiency of key inland waterway transport has hindered growth of the GMS logistics system. Linkages to principal seaports are currently being developed, e.g. between Phnom Penh Port in Cambodia and the new port network in Southern Vietnam, but these IWT connections will face strong modal competition from road transport.

When compared to maritime ports, inland waterway port facilities, equipment, and ICT systems are sorely missing, with most cargo transported in bulk. There is a general lack of container vessels and container-handling capability, although some river ports do handle containers on an *ad-hoc* basis.

4.3.5 Air Cargo in the GMS

The ASEAN[4]-China air transport agreement is currently being finalized. Its objective is to remove restrictions on air services, based on the perspective of achieving full liberalization between ASEAN and China. The author has conducted a survey of Government officials. According to that survey, only Myanmar has not liberalized air freight services, even though it has a commitment based on the ASEAN Multilateral Agreement on the Full Liberalization of Air Freight Services (MAAFS). Myanmar ratified that Agreement in August of 2009.

Pure freighter services are not common in the GMS, but Lao PDR is keen to operate them. Myanmar and Vietnam also would hope to be considered as major air freight hubs for the region, as gleaned from their national air development policies. However, pre-requisites of an airfreight hub are the improved on-site operations at airports and cargo villages. These facilities do not exist or are limited in Myanmar and Vietnam. As well, capabilities to handle cold storage and dangerous-goods storage, and competitive ground handling services, are important factors in the development of an airfreight hub.

It is interesting to note that Yunnan province does not position itself as such a hub. However, that province wishes to become the "flower capital of Asia" and compete with the Netherlands on the global market. There will thus be a need for Yunnan to have at least one airfreight hub facility to support this objective. (A statement or intention of the desire to become a hub is in itself not sufficient.) Table 4.6 describes the air cargo transport capability between GMS nations.

4.3.6 Infrastructure Summary

The growth of logistics in the Greater Mekong Sub-region has been very uneven. Countries such as Thailand and China are more developed than other GMS members in terms of logistics. However, the case of China is interesting, as an in-depth exploration of logistics characteristics in Yunnan and Guangxi provinces shows that local providers still have to improve their capability. Vietnam is emerging as a country where logistics is rapidly maturing, while in Cambodia,

[4] ASEAN (Association of South-East Asian Nations) is a regional economic grouping that is composed of Brunei, Cambodia, Indonesia, Lao PDR, Malaysia, Myanmar, Philippines, Singapore, Thailand and Vietnam.

Table 4.6 GMS air cargo transport matrix

	Cambodia	Lao PDR	Myanmar	Thailand	Vietnam	Yunnan (PRC)	Guangxi (PRC)
Liberalized air freight services	Yes	Yes	No	Partial	Yes	No	No
Pure freighter services	No	Planned	No	Yes	Limited	Yes	No
Hub for air freight	No	Planned	Yes	Yes	Yes	No	Planned
Cargo village	No	Planned	Planned	Yes	Limited	Yes	Yes
On-airport cold storage	Limited	Planned	Limited	Yes	Yes	No	Planned
Competitive ground handling services	No	Limited	Limited	Limited	No	Yes	No
Large pallet scanners	No	Planned	No	Yes	Yes	Yes	No
Quick clearance	Yes	No	Yes	Yes	Yes	Yes	Limited
EDI for cargo manifest	No	No	No	Yes	Planned	Yes	Limited

Lao PDR and Myanmar, the logistics sector mostly continues to offer conventional services focused on transport and warehousing.

The challenge for the GMS remains the *integration* of logistics in the region. Based on questionnaire data obtained by the author, it was easy to see the wide discrepancies between GMS countries. An integrated logistics system can only be as strong as its weakest link. This is why special attention is required in less developed countries, to enable them to achieve the minimum standard necessary for GMS logistics integration.

That minimum standard concerns not only the infrastructure for logistics, but also *implementation* on the institutional side. The capabilities of local logistics providers need to be upgraded. These firms must better utilize the existing infrastructure within the current GMS institutional environment, so as to meet and exceed the demands of their customers.

4.4 GMS Economic Corridor Development

The Asian Development Bank (ADB) offers technical assistance to countries of the Greater Mekong Sub-region on issues related to logistics improvement. The Bank concluded that logistics policy, infrastructure enhancements and the capacity of logistics service providers are very uneven among those countries (Banomyong and Faust 2010). Additionally, the capabilities of "indigenous" 3PLs in the GMS are generally limited to traditional logistics activities such as warehousing and transportation, with relatively few value-added services. The current offerings of

Table 4.7 Corridor development framework

Stage	Corridor	Definition
Level 1	Transport corridor	Corridor that physically links an area or region
Level 2	Logistics corridor	Corridor that not only physically links an area or a region, but also harmonizes the corridor institutional framework to facilitate the efficient movement and storage of freight, people, and related information
Level 3	Economic corridor	Corridor that is able to attract investment and generate economic activities along the less developed area or region. Physical linkages and logistics facilitation must first be in place

local 3PLs are therefore unable to meet the increasing need for integration of global/regional supply chains.

This holistic assessment of GMS logistics system capability may not sufficiently reflect logistics realities on the ground. The ADB therefore adopted an economic-corridor approach to developments.[5] Such an approach recognizes that development entails infrastructure integrated with other economic activities such as logistics. It is therefore important to understand the types of existing corridors in the GMS; Table 4.7 proposes a corridor development framework.

The purpose of a transport corridor is to physically link areas within a country or region that were not previously connected. A logistics corridor focuses not only on that physical connection, but also on how the flow and storage of freight, people and vehicles is *optimized* in the corridor, with the support of capable service providers and a facilitating institutional environment furnished by relevant agencies. It is impossible to establish economic corridors at the outset. There is a gradual evolutionary phase that must be followed if establishment of those corridors is to be sustainable.

The main stakeholders in a logistics corridor are shippers and consignees using the various routes along the corridors. 3PL providers of diverse types of logistics services are also significant. Governmental agencies have important involvement in the infrastructure, as well as in setting the rules and regulations on movement and storage of freight along the logistics corridor.

The potential strength of logistics corridors lies primarily in the possibilities they offer in confronting the concerns and interests of all relevant stakeholders, public and private. The parties can focus on policies and initiatives to cater to specific routes and border crossings. These corridors thus make it feasible to tackle logistics issues in a holistic manner (institutional, administrative, and infrastructural), initiating and accomplishing changes that otherwise may be difficult to achieve at a wider national and/or regional level.

Investment will not be concentrated solely in the large cities along an economic corridor. Investment and economic development will need to reach smaller towns and rural areas located on the route. Incentives to attract private sector investments

[5] 8th GMS Ministerial Meeting, Manila, 1998.

must be reviewed and harmonized between the different countries of the corridor, to facilitate economic activities in less-developed areas. Success of an economic corridor will therefore depend on attraction of investment. That attraction will in turn rely on appropriate infrastructure and facilitation policies.

Figure 4.4 provides a graphical illustration of the key economic corridors under development in the Greater Mekong Sub-region. There are currently three main corridors:

1. The Southern Economic Corridor (SEC), from Thailand to Southern Vietnam via Cambodia.
2. The East West Economic Corridor (EWEC) that connects Myanmar to Vietnam via central Thailand and Lao PDR
3. The North South Economic Corridor (NSEC). It links Yunnan province in China with Bangkok, the capital of Thailand, via Lao PDR and Myanmar.

Currently the SEC is the most under-developed corridor and no logistics assessment has been made, while the NSEC and the EWEC have been subject to a number of studies related to their logistics performance over the past few years (Banomyong 2008; Banomyong et al. 2010). Our discussion will thus focus solely on NSEC and EWEC; the following sub-sections provide further details related to the logistics assessment of each corridor.

4.4.1 Corridor Logistics Assessment Methodology

The corridor logistics assessment model presented here includes both transport (road, rail, inland waterway) and intermodal transfer (ports, rail-freight terminals, inland clearance depots, border crossings) as cost and/or time components (Fig. 4.5). This model has been adapted by the present author from one that was originally formulated by Beresford and Dubey (1990) and later improved by Beresford (1999). Cost and time data collected for a particular product along a given corridor can be graphically exhibited through the model in Fig. 4.5. That model helps to describe the cost and time components of movement from origin to destination by each available route and mode, as well as to illustrate the delays at borders or other inspection points up to the destination within the corridor.

The model assumes that unit costs of transportation vary between modes. The steepness of the cost curves reflects the fact that, for volume movements, sea transport should be the cheapest per ton-kilometer, road transport should normally be the most expensive (at least beyond a certain distance), and waterway and rail costs should be intermediate. At ports, inland terminals and border crossings, a freight handling charge is levied without any substantial progress being made along the supply chain; a vertical "step" in the cost curve thus represents the costs incurred there.

Similarly, by plotting time against distance, the relative speed of transit for each leg (or mode) can be compared, and the bottlenecks at transshipment points can be

Fig. 4.4 GMS economic corridors. *Source* Asian development bank

identified. As a rule of thumb: the higher the vertical step, the more likely that the border crossing or the nodal link is a bottleneck in the logistics corridor.

The corridor cost model that we are presenting in this chapter is subject to limitations with regard to the reliability dimension. The significance of deviations

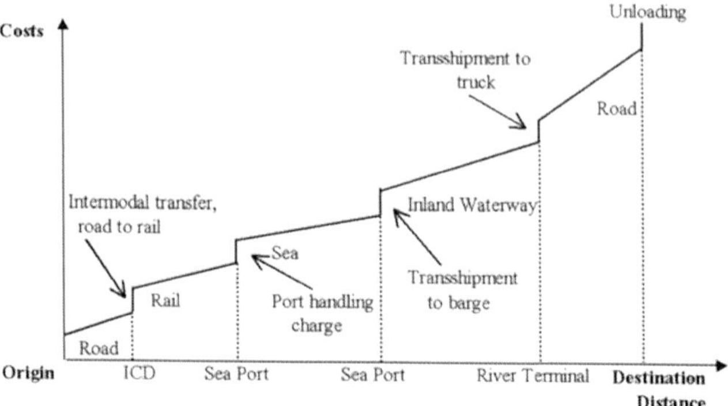

Fig. 4.5 Corridor Logistics Assessment Model (*ICD* Inland Clearance Depot). *Source* Adapted from Beresford (1999)

or randomness for a decision situation depends on the cost of reversing a commitment, once made. It is when great uncertainty is coupled with high cost that this uncertainty needs to be acknowledged and allowed for in the analysis.

4.4.2 Logistics Assessment of the NSEC

The NSEC or the Bangkok (Thailand) to Kunming (Yunnan, China) corridor is expected to become important for the infrastructure in the sub-region. It will function as a land bridge between Yunnan province in China and other GMS countries, particularly Thailand. Once the corridor is fully operational, significant impact such as shifts in transportation mode, with short and long-term economic and sociological changes, can be anticipated.

Along the Bangkok-Kunming corridor, three routes currently provide the connection between both cities:

- Route No.3 West, via Myanmar (R3 W): Bangkok (Thailand)–Chiang Rai–Mae Sai (Thailand)–Tachilek (Myanmar)–Mengla (Myanmar)–Daluo (China)–Jinghong–Kunming (China).
- Route No. 3 East, via Lao PDR (R3E): Bangkok (Thailand)–Chiang Rai–Chiang Khong (Thailand)–Houay Xay (Lao PDR)–Luang Namtha–Boten (Lao PDR)–Mohan (China)–Kunming (China).
- Route via the Mekong River: Bangkok (Thailand)–Chiang Rai–Chiang Saen (Thailand)–Mekong River–Jinghong (China)–Kunming (China).

Assessment of the NSEC (Table 4.8) showed that no Level-3 or established economic corridors are yet in place on this path. For the various sub-routes in the Bangkok-to-Kunming corridor, our overall assessment was that of Level 1, the weakest links. This means that, currently, there are only transport corridors in the NSEC.

Table 4.8 Assessment of levels of NSEC

From	To	Level
Bangkok (Thailand)	Chiangrai (Thailand)	2
Chiangrai (Thailand)	Mae Sai (Thailand)	2
Chiangrai (Thailand)	Chiangsaen (Thailand)	2
Chiangrai (Thailand)	Chiangkhong (Thailand)	2
Mae Sai/Tachilek (Thailand/Myanmar)	Mongla/Da Luo (Myanmar/Yunnan, China)	1
Daluo (Yunnan, China)	Kunming (Yunnan, China)	2
Chiangsaen (Thailand)	Jinghong (Yunnan, China)	1
Jinghong (Yunnan, China)	Kunming (Yunnan, China)	2
Chiangkhong/Houay Xay (Thailand/Lao PDR)	Boten/Mohan (Lao PDR/Yunnan, China)	1
Mohan (Yunnan, China)	Kunming (Yunnan, China)	2
Overall level		1

Source Compiled from industry data

Characteristics of the Bangkok-Kunming corridor are summarized in Table 4.9. The lengths of the three routes are not significantly different. At present, the route via the Mekong River is the most popular; the R3W route is never used for "official" transit purpose, due to the political situation and the transit fee in Myanmar.

Figures 4.6 and 4.7 describe graphically how cost and time increase along the three routes of the Bangkok-Kunming corridor.[6] The route via the Mekong River has the lowest total cost but takes the longest time. The route via Myanmar (R3W) has the greatest uncertainty from a user's perspective. Border crossings seem to be where there is the largest increase in cost and time, without any movement of goods. This clearly shows that actual transport in itself is not a major impediment. However, effectiveness and efficiency very much depend on the cost at which, and how quickly, borders can be traversed. Full implementation of the GMS Cross Border Transport Agreement (CBTA)[7] will play a crucial role in the reduction of border-crossing cost and time.

Tables 4.10 and 4.11 provide more details on border-crossing charges as a proportion of total transit and border-crossing costs. The pure transport cost on all three routes is less than the charges for border crossing and transit. This again shows that transportation, even though a critical component of the corridor cost, is not the biggest factor.

---

[6] The individual cost- and time-elements, upon which Figs. 4.6 and 4.7 are based, are contained in Tables 4.15, 4.16 and 4.17 of the Appendix.

[7] The Cross Border Transport Agreement (CBTA) is a regional transport and transit agreement that is supposed to facilitate the movement of people, freight and vehicles within the GMS area. One of the main contributions of the CBTA is the requirement for single-stop inspection at border crossings. This single-stop restriction will reduce cost and time at those crossings.

Table 4.9 Characteristics of Bangkok-Kunming routes

Segment	Logistics infrastructure	Route choice (distance in km)		
		via Myanmar (R3W)	via Lao PDR (R3E)	via Mekong River
Bangkok–Chiang Rai	4-lane highway	830	830	830
Chiang Rai–Mae Sai	4-lane highway	60		
Chiang Rai–Chiang Saen	2-lane highway			60
Chiang Rai–Chiang Khong	2-lane highway		110	
R3W	2-lane highway	253		
Mekong River	Mekong River Ports			360
R3E	2-lane highway		228	
R3W/R3: Daluo to Kunming	6-, 4-, and 2-lane highway	674		
R3: Jinghong to Kunming	6- and 2-lane highway			534
R3E/R3: Boten/Mohan to Kunming	6-, 4-, and 2-lane highway		688	
Total length		1,817	1,856	1,784

Notes Approximate distances after all projects are *completed*
Bullets near the start of Sect. 4.4.2 show the three routes in detail

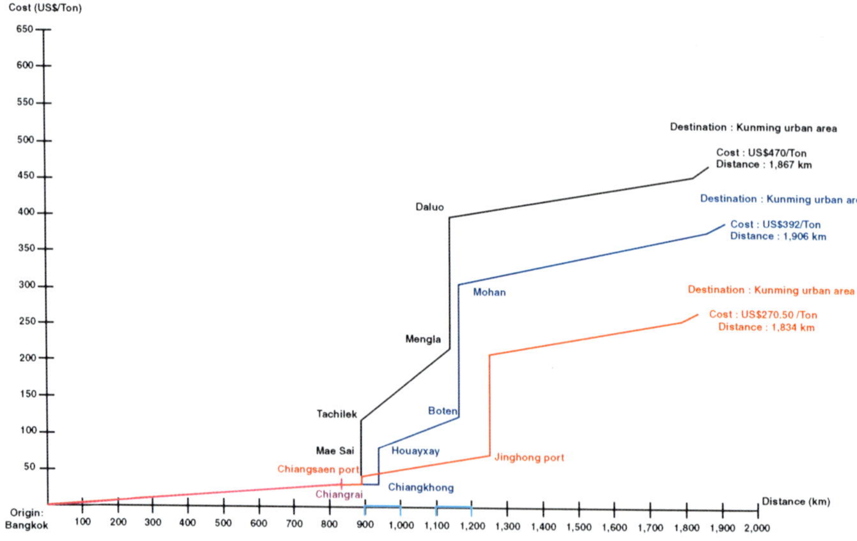

Fig. 4.6 Cost Model of Route No. 3 from Bangkok to Kunming. *Source* Compiled from Jinxin (2007) and industry data

Tables 4.12 and 4.13 give the proportion of total route time represented by transport and border crossing. Transport takes more than 80 % of total corridor time, but when the infrastructure is completed, this will probably be reduced.

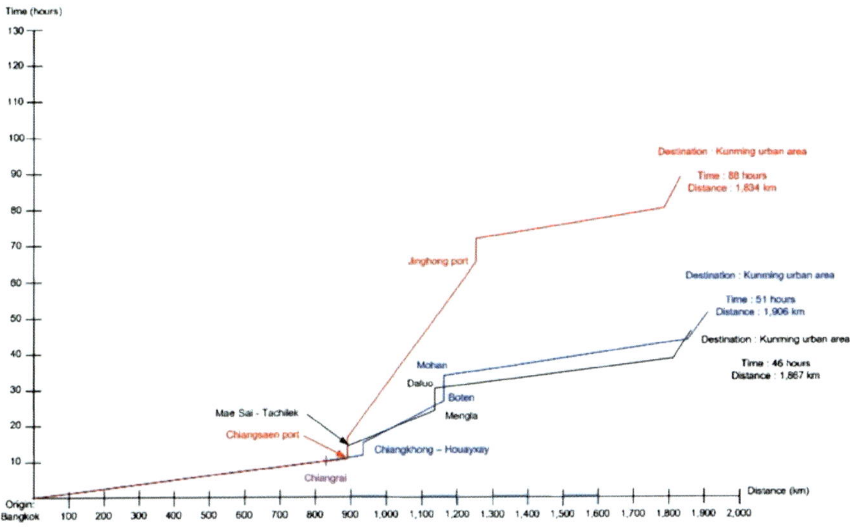

Fig. 4.7 Time Model of Route No. 3 from Bangkok to Kunming. *Source* Compiled from Jinxin (2007) and industry data

Table 4.10 Bangkok-Kunming cost summary

Route	Transport and distribution (%)	Border crossing and transit fees (%)
R3W	42	58
R3E	40	60
Via Mekong river	Road 32 River 15	53

Table 4.11 R3 border cost summary

Route	Border 1 Thailand (%)	Border 2 Myanmar Lao PDR (%)	Border 3 Myanmar Lao PDR (%)	Border 4 PRC (%)	Total border cost (%)
R3W	Mai Sai 1	Tachilek 33	Mongla 15	Daluo 51	100
R3E	Chiangkhong 2	Houay Xay 20	Boten 18	Boharn 60	100
Via Mekong river	Chiangsaen 3	N/A	N/A	Jinghong 97	100

N/A not applicable

4.4.3 Logistics Assessment of the EWEC

The East–West Economic Corridor (EWEC) is another key GMS initiative, aimed at enhancement of infrastructure to enable development and sharing of resources, promoting the flow of goods and people within the sub-region. The East–West Economic corridor is named after the physical linkage connecting four GMS

Table 4.12 Bangkok–Kunming time tummary

Route	Transport and distribution time (%)	Border crossing time (%)
R3W	80	20
R3E	85	15
Via Mekong river	Road 32 River 54	14

Table 4.13 Bangkok–Kunming: summary of border times

Route	Border 1 Thailand (%)	Border 2 Myanmar Lao PDR (%)	Border 3 Myanmar Lao PDR (%)	Border 4 PRC (%)	Total time spent at borders (%)
R3W	Mae Sai 12	Tachilek 22	Monglar 22	Daluo 44	100
R3E	Chiangkhong 12.5	Houay Xay 12.5	Boten 25	Mohan 50	100
Via Mekong river	Chiangsaen 46	N/A	N/A	Jinghong 54	100

nations. The corridor stretches from Mawlamyine in Myanmar to Danang in Vietnam, through several cities in Myanmar, Thailand, Lao PDR and Vietnam (See Figs. 4.1, 4.4 and 4.8). This 1,110 km route is currently utilized, albeit missing some links. Infrastructure was built within the EWEC to support physical linkages such as the 2nd Lao-Thai friendship bridge between Mukdahan (Thailand)-Savannakhet (Lao PDR), and the Hai Van tunnel[8] in Danang. Today, physical connections within the EWEC are almost complete, with some links in Myanmar needing rehabilitation. In the following, we discuss key characteristics of the EWEC sections in each country.

Roads still constitute the dominant infrastructure for transport in all EWEC nations. Thailand presently possesses the most developed road network and facilities. A relatively new international airport, Suvarnabhumi, and modern seaports, such as Laem Chabang, encourage the movement of international freight. Myanmar and Lao PDR, on the other hand, are comparatively less developed. Even though the EWEC road in Lao PDR is physically complete, supporting logistics facilities remain limited. Vietnam's infrastructure has been improved to cope with the new trade flows, but maintenance issues will become critical in the near future.

In the EWEC, the basic approaches to expedite trade and transport are in place, but their implementation is still lacking. There is also a myriad of understandings that have coverage over different geographical areas. The four EWEC nations are parties to both the Cross Border Transport Agreement and the ASEAN Framework Agreement for the facilitation of goods in transit (signed in 1998 in Hanoi). There are also bilateral accords to smooth the flow of goods in transit between Thailand and Lao PDR, as well as between Vietnam and Lao PDR.

[8] The longest tunnel in Southeast Asia.

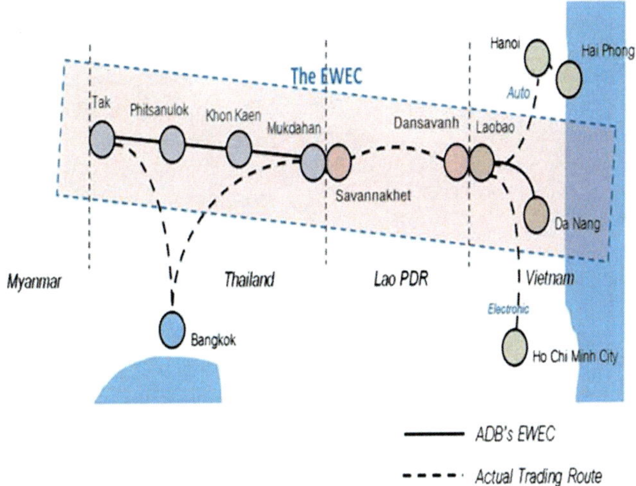

Fig. 4.8 Policy EWEC vs. Actual EWEC. *Source* Based upon Banomyong et al. (2010)

The roles of 3PL service providers, and the uses of outsourcing and information technology in managing logistics, are relatively well developed in Thailand. These practices are insufficient in Lao PDR, Myanmar and Vietnam, where modern logistics ideas have not yet been fully carried out. Thai, Lao, and Vietnamese logistics service providers have grown rapidly and have played a strong supporting role in the manufacturing sectors. However, those 3PL companies are often small and cannot compete directly with multinational firms (e.g., UPS, TNT, FedEx, and DHL).

Logistics service providers in the EWEC countries have a variety of strengths and weaknesses, although a common strength is their in-depth knowledge of the local market. Vietnam is currently facing an acute shortage of qualified human resources; the market in Lao PDR is still based on traditional logistics services such as customs brokerage and physical transportation. 3PL providers in Thailand may seem to be more competitive, but this is true only with respect to third party firms from elsewhere in the EWEC. The case of Myanmar is more difficult to assess, due to limited data and an ongoing US-led embargo.[9]

It can be said that Lao PDR and Myanmar are lagging behind Thailand and Vietnam in terms of logistics. Vietnam and Thailand should not be considered as "world-class," but their national logistics systems can be rated as "fair" (i.e. more or less adequate). Nevertheless, both countries still require massive infrastructure and institutional improvements, to meet the ever-increasing international standard and sustain their competitiveness in the global market.

---

[9] The visit to Burma (i.e. Myanmar) in November 2011 by US Secretary of State Hillary Clinton was the first in more than 50 years by such a high-ranking American official. The embargo now seems on its way out.

Table 4.14 EWEC corridor assessment levels

Section	Corridor type	Level
Mawlamyine–Myawady (Myanmar)	Transport Corridor	1
Myawady (Myanmar)–Tak (Thailand)	Transport Corridor	1
Tak–Mukdahan (Thailand)	Logistics Corridor	2
Mukdahan (Thailand)–Savannakhet (Lao PDR)	Transport Corridor	1
Savannakhet–Dansavanh (Lao PDR)	Logistics corridor	2
Dansavanh (Lao PDR)–Lao Bao (Vietnam)	Transport corridor	1
Lao Bao-Danang (Vietnam)	Logistics corridor	2
Overall assessment	Transport corridor	1

This framework is used to evaluate the existing development level of the EWEC corridor. The approach yields a segmented perspective of the EWEC, where every individual leg/section in each EWEC country is identified and graded. A rating of the EWEC is presented in Table 4.14.

Overall assessment of the EWEC is determined by the weakest link of the corridor. It must be noted that logistics corridors do exist, but only within the boundary of a nation, not at the EWEC or cross-border scale. The current status of EWEC border crossings is still based solely on existing physical links, as the institutional framework facilitating border crossing has not been totally implemented. There are two main veins that exist within the EWEC:

1. The route from Tak (Thailand) to Danang (Vietnam), part of the originally agreed-upon EWEC route that was designated for support from ADB. Linkages with Myanmar cannot be considered, due to international sanctions and embargo. The logistics assessment can therefore only be made between Thailand and Vietnam.
2. The EWEC route developed by the private sector. This links Bangkok and its surrounding industrial estates in Thailand with Hanoi and Ho Chi Minh City in Vietnam, as the respective origin and destination points.

Until recently, commodity flows on ADB's EWEC have been almost nonexistent (Than 2005). Presently the main flows of goods within EWEC consist mostly of automotive products, from/to Bangkok/Laem Chabang port of Thailand and from/to Hanoi/Hai Phong port, and electronics items (between Bangkok and Ho Chi Minh City in Vietnam). Currently-existing flows are illustrated by the dotted lines in Fig. 4.8. However, when appraising freight flows on ADB's version of the EWEC, note that in reality there is no movement of goods between Danang and Tak province at the border with Myanmar.

A "snapshot" of the EWEC route, based on information collected, will now be presented. As will be seen from the model, transportation in itself is quite dependable; there is not much difference in terms of service time. From the graphical model, the less predictable areas are the border crossings and the entry into Vietnam. This wide variation stems from a number of factors. The element that most often decreases reliability within the EWEC is a lack of appropriate import or transit documentation.

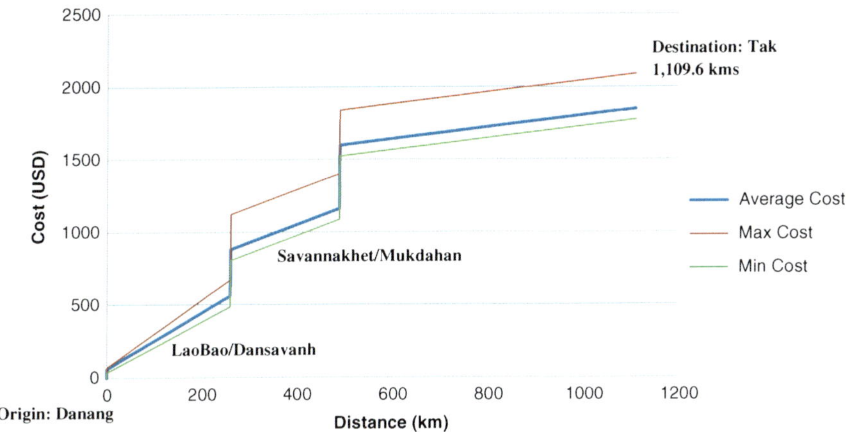

Fig. 4.9 Cost model: Danang to Tak

From empirical evidence collected on the route between Danang and Tak, it is observed that nearly half (18 h) of the 41.3 h total transit time is in fact taken at customs or border crossings, based on each country's administrative formality. The non-synchronization and complicated institutional framework are clearly bothering the smooth flow of goods across frontiers. From a cost perspective, 43 % of the door-to-door transport costs are collected at customs and border crossings. That amount is almost equivalent to the cost of physical transportation. This result is frightening and must be solved.[10] The international, institutional frameworks must be better arranged or implemented, if they have already been agreed upon.

Figures 4.9 and 4.10 illustrate logistics comparisons for the EWEC. The origin in this example is Danang (Vietnam), with destination at Tak (Thailand). The graphical output also presents the minimum, maximum and average cost (to transport one TEU), and the corresponding times taken on this particular corridor. Details are in Table 4.18.

It is noticed that Thailand and Vietnam are slightly more dependable than Lao PDR in terms of infrastructure and administrative and business activities. However, as a corridor, the lack of trust in administrative processes is still evident in a majority of the EWEC area. There is not much confidence in those practices. Reliability of local business operators is also considered to be limited, compared to the multinational firms that are now entering the EWEC logistics market.

[10] Earlier in this book, Chen and Lee (2013) note a similarly dis-proportionate amount of tolls and fees, when freight is shipped between different provinces in China.

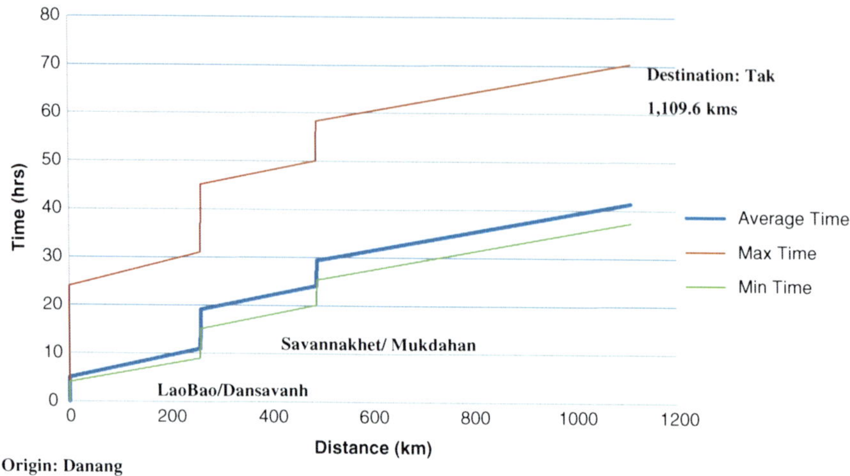

Fig. 4.10 Model of the time between Danang and Tak

4.5 Summary

It is expected that by 2015, the physical and institutional foundations will be in place within the Greater Mekong Sub-region. Freight charges may increase or decrease. Either way, the key logistics bottlenecks, the border crossings, still need to be sorted out. Time is of the essence because infrastructure improvement is moving much more quickly than the institutional arrangements between GMS nations.

The lack of standardized and harmonized border and transit trade procedures is the Achilles' heel of the GMS corridors; special attention must be paid to those border issues.[11] This shortcoming, together with poor infrastructure connections, is currently hindering progress toward an integrated regional logistics system that can satisfy customers while controlling or even lowering total costs. The backbone of logistics development in the GMS is the infrastructure linkages. Upgrading that framework must be done in conjunction with the facilitation of trade, transit, and transport services to create an effective and efficient GMS logistics system. Incidentally, although transit trade is currently minimal compared to border trade, transit can become an important component of trade along the NSEC (Than 2005).

An integrated attack is necessary to answer the questions posed in this chapter. Such an approach should combine explanations of the physical or "hardware" infrastructure phase with solutions to "software" rules and the regulatory aspects. Most difficulties in enhancing the logistics system for cross-border and transit trade are related to import/export and transit processes of the GMS countries. Infrastructure is still considered a constraint, but its impact may seem insignificant.

---

[11] Later in the present volume, Higginson (2013) discusses the corresponding difficulties at a number of crossings of the frontier between Canada and the United States.

Table 4.15 Route R3 via Myanmar (R3W)

Route via Myanmar	Activity	Cost (USD/Ton)	Distance (km)	Time (h)
Bangkok–Chiangrai	Transport	28	830	10
Chiangrai–Mae Sai	Transport	28	60	1
Mae Sai	Inspection	1.5	N/A	1
	Clearance	1.5		
Tachilek	Transload	5	N/A	2
	Clearance transit fee	13		
		70		
Tachilek–Mengla	Transport	100	253	10
Monglar	Clearance transit fee	40	N/A	2
Daluo	Inspection	75	N/A	4
	Import VAT	60		
	Transload	5		
Daluo–Kunming	Transport	57	674	8
Kunming urban area	Warehouse	7	50	8
	Distribution	7		
Total	N/A	470	1,867	46

Source Compiled from Jinxin (2007) and field data

That is due to the relatively low volumes involved, as well as to a commitment by member nations to link the corridors physically and institutionally by 2015.

It is very important to continually assess and monitor the situation along corridors in the Greater Mekong Sub-region. Turmoil in a country, revisions in national or regional policies, or infrastructure upgrading can have a noteworthy impact on the selection of a particular logistics corridor. If changes do occur, there will be a need to re-evaluate which logistics corridor is the most effective and efficient under the new circumstances.

The challenge remains on how to transform these GMS corridors into full-fledged *economic* corridors through the development of logistics. The goal is to attract investment and generate economic activities in remote areas of the corridors.

Appendix

Here we offer further details to support numerical results presented earlier in the chapter. Tables 4.15, 4.16 and 4.17 disclose the individual components of cost and time, summarized respectively in Figs. 4.6 and 4.7. Those give the three routes of the Bangkok-Kunming corridor, the North–South economic corridor between Thailand and Yunnan Province, China.

Table 4.18 shows the elements of cost and time for the corridor between Danang, Vietnam and Tak, Thailand. Figures 4.9 and 4.10 are the respective graphical displays.

Table 4.16 Route via Lao PDR (R3E)

Route via Lao PDR	Activity	Cost (USD/Ton)	Distance (km)	Time (h)
Bangkok–Chiangrai	Transport	28	830	10
Chiangrai–Chiangkhong	Transport	28	110	2
Chiangkhong	Inspection	1.5	N/A	1
	Clearance	1.5		
Chiangkhong–Houay Xay	River crossing	5	1 km	1
Houay Xay	Clearance	2	N/A	1
	Transload	5		
	Transit fee	40		
Houay Xay–Boten	Transport	40	226	12
Boten	Clearance	2	N/A	2
	Transit fee	40		
Mohan	Inspection	75	N/A	4
	VAT	60		
	Transload	5		
Mohan–Kunming	Transport	71	688	10
Kunming urban area	Warehouse	7	50	8
	Distribution	7		
Total	N/A	392	1,906	51

Source Compiled from Jinxin (2007) and field data

Table 4.17 Route via the Mekong river

Route via Mekong River	Activity	Cost (USD/Ton)	Distance (km)	Time (h)
Bangkok–Chiangrai	Transport	28	830	10
Chiangrai–Chiangsaen port	Transport	28	60	1
Chiangsaen port	Loading/ Unloading	3	N/A	6
	Inspection fees	1.5		
Chiangsaen port–Jinghong port	Transport	42	360	48
Jinghong port	Loading/ Unloading	2	N/A	7
	Inspection	75		
	VAT	60		
Jinghong port–Kunming	Transport	45	534	8
Kunming urban area	Warehouse	7	50	8
	Distribution	7		
Total	N/A	270.5	1,834	88

Source Compiled from Jinxin (2007) and field data

Table 4.18 Data for Danang (Vietnam) to Tak (Thailand)

Activity	Avg.Time	Range of Time	Avg. Cost ($/TEU)	Range of Cost ($/TEU)	Actors	Documents/Operations	Distance (km)	Notes (from/to)
1	5 h	4 h–1 day	60	35–70	Port operator/Freight forwarder	Unloading, customs clearance	N/A	Danang port
2	6 h	5–7 h	500	450–600	Freight forwarder	Goods in transit	260	Danang–Laobao
3	2 h	2–6 h	70	60–100	Exporter/Freight forwarder	Export customs procedure	N/A	Vietnam customs (Lao Bao)
4	5 min	–	–	–	Freight forwarder	Goods in transit	0.6	Laobao–Dansavanh
5	6 h	4–8 h	250	200–350	Importer/Freight forwarder	Import customs procedure	N/A	Lao customs (Dansavanh)
6	5 h	N/A	280	N/A	N/A	Road transport	229	Dansavanh-Savannakhet
7	1 h	1–4 h	200	200	Freight forwarder	Transloading from Vietnamese to Thai truck	N/A	Savannakhet (Friendship Bridge)
8	2 h	N/A	150	N/A	N/A	Transit clearance	N/A	Lao customs (Savannakhet)
10	15 min		30	N/A	N/A	Bridge Fee	1	Friendship bridge
11	2 h	N/A	57	N/A	N/A	Customs clearance	N/A	Thai customs at Mukdahan
12	12 h	N/A	250	N/A	N/A	Road transport	619	Mukdahan-Tak

Source Compiled from industry sources

References

ADB (2010) Connecting Greater Mekong Sub-region railways: a strategic framework. Asian Development Bank, Manila

Banomyong R (2008) Logistics development in the Greater Mekong Sub-region: a study of the north-south economic corridor. J Greater Mekong Sub-region Dev Studies 4:43–58

Banomyong R (2010) Benchmarking economic corridors logistics performance: a GMS border crossing observation. World Customs J 4(1):37–46

Banomyong R, Cook P, Kent P (2008) Formulating regional logistics development policy: the case of ASEAN. Int J Logistics Res and Appl 11(5):359–379

Banomyong R, Faust P (2010) GMS logistics development strategy. Asian development bank, RETA 6450 Enhancing transport and trade facilitation. Unpublished report, Manila

Banomyong R, Sopadang A, Ramingwong S (2010) Logistics benchmark study of the East West economic corridor. Bus Manage Q Rev 1(2):1–12

Beresford, AKC (1999), Modelling freight transport costs: a case study of the UK-Greece corridors. Int J Logistics Res Appl 2(3):229–246

Beresford AKC, Dubey RC (1990) Handbook on the management and operations of dry ports. RDP/LDC/7, United Nations Conference on Trade and Development, Geneva

Chen F, Lee C-Y (2013) Logistics in China. In: Bookbinder JH (ed) Global logistics. Springer, New York

ESCAP (2005), Free trade zone and port hinterland development. Economic and social commission for Asia and the Pacific, United Nations, New York, ST/ESCAP/2377

Fujimura M (2008) Economic integration in the Greater Mekong Sub-region and cross border transport infrastructure. J Greater Mekong Sub-region Dev Studies 4:21–42

Grant DB, Lambert DM, Stock JR, Ellram LM (2006) Fundamentals of logistics management. McGraw Hill, European Edition

Higginson JK (2013) Border issues and research. In: Bookbinder JH (ed) Global logistics. Springer, New York

Jinxin L (2007) Handbook of the logistics study tour of China-Myanmar-Thailand-Laos highway, Mar 5–11, 2007. Foreign affairs office of the people's government of Yunnan Province, China

Kieck E (2010) Coordinated border management: unlocking trade opportunities through one stop border post. World Customs J 4(1):3–14

Than M (2005) Myanmar's cross-border economic relation with the People's Republic of China and Thailand in the Greater Mekong Sub-region. J GMS Dev Studies 2(1):37–54

Part II
Logistics and Supply Chains in Latin America

Chapter 5
Strategic and Tactical Modeling in the Argentine Sugar Industry

Gustavo Braier and Javier Marenco

Abstract This chapter describes the application of linear programming techniques to the automatic planning of manufacturing and distribution decisions at the main sugar producer in Argentina. We summarize the production and logistics chain for the sugar business of this company, and present a linear programming model representing the key planning decisions within these processes. We provide details on the implementation of a software tool for managing the data, solving the model, and analyzing the results. That software tool and embedded model allowed the sugar planning team to improve the planning decisions by having a global comprehension of a very complex decision structure and analyzing multiple scenarios. At the same time, the team obtained a better understanding of the limits and potential of the available industrial and logistical facilities.

5.1 Introduction

5.1.1 The Company

Ledesma SAAI is an Argentine company that is a leader in the sugar, paper, citrus fruits, and citric juice markets of Argentina. Since starting its operations in 1908, Ledesma transformed its original sugar mill and refinery into an agricultural/industrial complex, involving different activities in eight provinces. The firm is the

G. Braier (✉) · J. Marenco
Braier & Asociados Consultores, Caseros 2040, 1636 Olivos, Buenos Aires, Argentina
e-mail: braier@papyro.com

J. Marenco
e-mail: jmarenco@papyro.com

J. H. Bookbinder (ed.), *Handbook of Global Logistics*, International Series in Operations Research & Management Science 181, DOI: 10.1007/978-1-4419-6132-7_5,

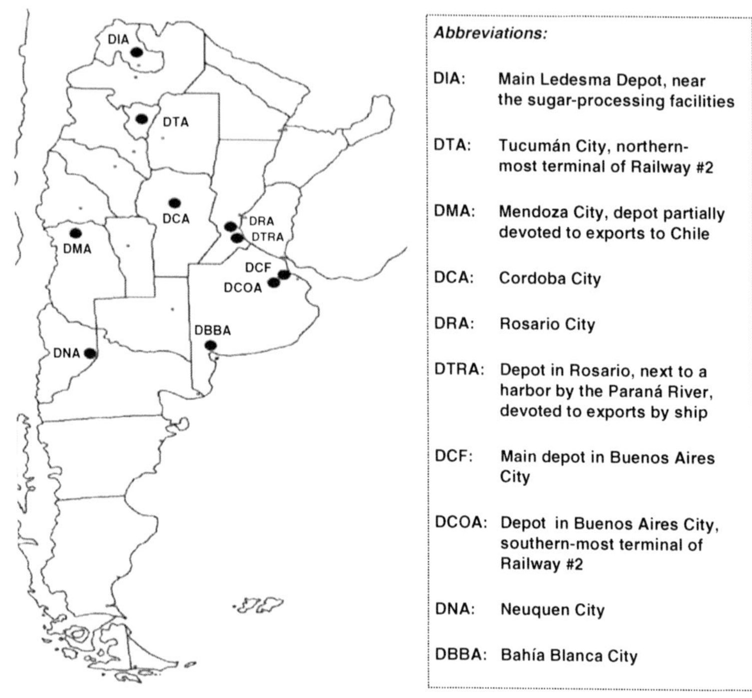

Fig. 5.1 Ledesma's sugar depots in Argentina. DIA is the main Ledesma depot, next to the unique location of the industrial complex in Jujuy province. DCF and DCOA are two separate depots in Buenos Aires City, the only ones there. DTRA is a depot beside a harbor in the Paraná River, devoted to exports by ship

main Argentine producer of raw and refined sugar, covering 20 % of the Argentine sugar market and being actively involved in sugar exports. Ledesma manufactures packaged products ranging from 1 kg home bags to 1,250 kg *big bags* for industrial purposes.

Ledesma currently has more than 6,000 employees, with its main sugar-processing facilities located in the Jujuy Province in the northwest of Argentina (depicted as DIA in Fig. 5.1). This agricultural and industrial complex includes over 37,000 hectares planted with sugar cane, and with sugar, alcohol, and pulp and paper plants. The sugar crops involve at least 600 km of internal roads built and maintained by the company, and about 1,400 km of irrigation channels.

The harvest period runs from May to November; the sugar refinery is active from May to February/March, stopping for maintenance in March and April. The refinery produces and packs over 50,000 tons (tn) of refined sugar during each of the harvest months, and around 46,000 tn in each of the non-harvest months, the difference being due to the availability of energy generated by steam sources during the harvest. The packing plant is located in the industrial complex in Jujuy Province.

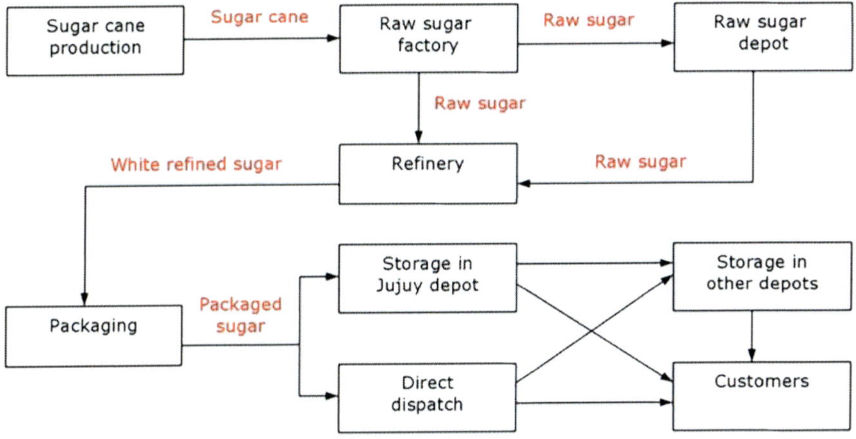

Fig. 5.2 The production and logistics process

Ledesma has 10 depots throughout the country (see Fig. 5.1), four of them devoted to exports besides the local market. Two companies provide railroad transportation, and transportation by truck is also allowed among the depots. Transshipment procedures between railroad and truck transportation are routinely performed.

5.1.2 The Production Process

Manufacturing begins with the harvest of sugar cane, which is transferred by trucks to the *raw sugar factory*. This factory performs a first processing of the sugar cane, by separating the molasses from the cellulose components of sugar cane (bagaze). The molasses goes through a processing stage which outputs *raw sugar*, whereas the bagaze is stored for paper manufacture and energy production (see Fig. 5.2). Raw sugar can either go directly to the *refinery* or be stocked in the *raw sugar depot*, a specially-adapted facility which can hold up to 164,000 tn of non-packaged raw sugar. During the harvesting period, the output of the raw sugar factory exceeds the production capacity of the refinery; hence a fraction of the raw sugar produced goes to the refinery, while the remainder is stored at the raw sugar depot. Input for the refinery is extracted from that depot during the non-harvest period, when the raw sugar factory does not operate.

The refinery produces two kinds of *white refined sugar*. Approximately 37 % of production represents standard-quality refined sugar, with around 63 % corresponding to premium-quality refined product. These percentages are determined by the installed machinery, and cannot be changed without seriously affecting the sugar quality. Refined sugar goes directly to the *packing plant*, which includes separate facilities for *small bags* (6.25 g small sachets, and 0.5 and 1 kg home bags), *bags* (25 and 50 kg), and *big bags* (1,000, 1,100, and 1,250 kg). The refinery and the packing plant work as a single production line, meaning that an unexpected shut-down at the packing plant implies that the refinery must stop, involving major quality issues and an important setup time to resume production.

The *packaged sugar* can either be stored at the main depot in Jujuy, or be directly dispatched to customers (we also refer to the export requirements as originating from "customers") or to other depots. There is a daily limit to the number of direct dispatches. But these are preferred over storage in the Jujuy depot as they avoid holding costs.

Data on customer demands and export requirements are known in advance. Demand from the internal market is quite stable and can be predicted with a reasonable degree of certainty. On the other hand, as the Argentine sugar market includes export quotas for the main sugar producers, the export possibilities can also be anticipated. Nevertheless, cancellations of export operations, late arrivals of ships, and other unexpected events are quite frequent.

5.1.3 The Planning Team

The planning process is under the direction of the so-called *planning team*. This was established in 2001, and is composed of the manager of the packing plant (who also speaks on behalf of the refinery manager), the manager of the Jujuy main depot, and representatives from each of the logistics division and the sales division. The planning team holds monthly meetings whose main inputs are the demand forecast and planned export operations (which are prepared by the sales manager), and whose main objective is to design a production and logistics plan for the following months. Usual constraints to this process include availability of raw sugar, production capacities, and the stock levels in the depots.

An important intangible benefit derived from the creation and monthly meetings of the planning team is the interaction among usually-separated divisions in the company, and the understanding by the team's members of each division's problems and constraints. Since those members represent areas with clashing objectives, conflict among these areas was not uncommon prior to the introduction of this team.

For example, a typical conflict arises when there is plenty of raw sugar and not enough immediate demand. The depots then have high inventories (and, therefore, greater technical management problems), but the refinery cannot slow down the manufacturing process too much, as that would involve quality costs and a shortened recess time for maintenance. Another important source of disagreement comes from requests of the sales division, which in many cases involve immediate manufacturing and logistic decisions so as to meet an urgent delivery. Those requirements cannot always be covered by the latter divisions without compromising their own objectives. These "natural" clashes did not disappear with the introduction of the planning team, but have clearly decreased.

Moreover, creation of that team was a key point on the way towards introducing operations research techniques to aid the planning decisions. Introduction of a linear-programming-based computational tool to assist the manufacturing and logistics decisions of Ledesma would have been impossible without the previous experience gathered by the planning team, both in technical issues and in understanding the sugar business of the company as a whole.

5.1.4 Logistics in Argentina

Argentina is located in the so-called "Southern Cone," between the Andes mountain range to the west and the Atlantic Ocean to the east. It is the second largest country in South America and the eighth-largest in the world by land area, comprising over 2,700,000 km^2 with its greatest straight distance of about 3,900 km along the north–south axis. Argentina has slightly more than 40 million inhabitants, 31 % of which are located in Buenos Aires City and its surroundings. In contrast, the second-largest urban area is Cordoba City, whose population is nearly 10 times as small as that of Buenos Aires City. The southern region of Patagonia is scarcely populated, with large areas hosting less than one inhabitant per square kilometer.

Transport in Argentina is based on a network of roads across the country, together with a few railways and two main fluvial courses. Most cargo transportation in Argentina is performed by truck, involving in some cases up to three-day trips. There are highways connecting the main cities and the remaining roads are two-lane paved routes, although not all of them are in perfect condition. Truck robberies are not uncommon, and roadblocks are frequent, especially in the surroundings of Ledesma's industrial complex in Jujuy Province. There is a well-coordinated mechanism with local police stations in Jujuy to monitor roadblocks, so the trucks going to and from the industrial complex can avoid these situations. Nevertheless, these facts introduce a high level of uncertainty in the logistic operations.

The Argentine railway network was the longest and most prosperous in South America up to the first half of the 20th century. Unfortunately, due to critical declines in railway profitability and the lack of support, the rail network has progressively diminished to the current state, with just a few railways providing cargo services. The current railroads span to the north and center of the country from Buenos Aires City and Rosario City. With some minor exceptions, there are no active railways in Patagonia.

Water transportation is mainly performed through the Paraná River, which is navigable by up to Panamax-sized ships. The Uruguay River, bordering with Uruguay and Brazil, also hosts some transportation. Fluvial transport, consisting mostly of cargo, is relatively inexpensive, but not heavily used. The Paraná River is mainly devoted to agricultural exports.

Finally, there is a number of local and international airports operating throughout the country, although air transportation is mostly used for passengers and postal services. Buenos Aires city is the principal flight hub, Cordoba City being a minor hub for connections.

5.1.5 Brief Description of Argentine Facilities in the Company's Region

Ledesma faces very particular conditions concerning its logistics operations. There are two railways providing transportation services from the north-western part of Argentina. One of them has a rail siding ending right at the finishing line of the packing plant. Thus, there can be direct dispatches of sugar, without going to and from the main depot in Jujuy. Due to a lack of locomotives and to contract specifications, the other railroad usually has long delays.

Although transportation by train is much cheaper than movement by truck, the contracts of both railways devote only limited capacity to Ledesma's transport requirements. Therefore, the company usually resorts to the two railroads, each at their upper bound. The remaining goods movements are dispatched by truck. Trips with long travel times are usually devoted to non-critical products, thus introducing an additional consideration into logistics operations. However, it is interesting to note that a long trip can be regarded as a "virtual depot", which may even be beneficial if inventories at the actual depots are high. Indeed, if those depots are full, then loading stock onto a railway with a huge travel time can ease the logistics operations at the depots for some days.

Sugar exports to Chile, Paraguay, and Uruguay are made by truck through Mendoza City (1,350 km south–west of Jujuy; designated as DMA in Fig. 5.1), directly from Jujuy, and from Buenos Aires City, respectively. Exports to other countries are performed by ships, which are loaded in Nuevo Alberdi harbor in the Parana River (depicted as DTRA in Fig. 5.1). This harbor is located 1,200 km south–east of Jujuy, and can also be directly reached from Tucuman by train.

5.1.6 Review of Previous Works

Many research efforts have been conducted in the past for the planning of operations within the sugar industry. The harvesting process has received much attention in the literature, in particular with the objective of maximizing sugar cane production. A number of simulation-based approaches have been reported; see, for example, the works by Díaz and Pérez (2000), Lejars et al. (2008) and Le Gal et al. (2009). A sophisticated model to optimize the harvest-date and crop-cycle decisions is given by Higgins (1999), who implemented a tabu search heuristic for solving a large model. Further approaches based on optimization techniques have been pursued by Higgins (2002), who presents a mixed integer programming formulation for harvesting decisions, and by Taechasook et al. (2008), who propose a genetic algorithm for harvesting decisions.

Concerning the manufacturing process, Higgins et al. (2006) propose a mixed integer programming model for optimizing the production and shipping of sugar exports by several mills in Australia. Chiadamrong and Kawtummachai (2008) consider production, transportation, and storage issues for the export channel of the Thailand sugar industry, and implement a genetic algorithm for the associated problem. Finally, Kostina et al. (2010) present a mixed integer programming model for optimizing capacity expansions of manufacturing and storage facilities over time, along with the associated sales decisions. By contrast, in the present work, we employ linear programming techniques.

5.2 The Linear Programming Model

In 2004, Ledesma deployed an initiative to incorporate operations research into the planning process, with the objective of aiding the monthly operations of the planning team. To this end, we developed a linear programming model for representing the production, packing, and logistic decisions for the sugar business, by modeling the decisions regularly made by the planning team.

The linear programming model features monthly decisions with a 13 month planning horizon. The model is essentially a multi-commodity multi-period network flow model, which takes as its inputs the production of the raw sugar factory and the purchases of raw sugar. The model's outputs correspond to deliveries of sugar to customers and exports. The decisions within the raw sugar factory are beyond the scope of the planning team, hence the operation of this factory is excluded from the model.

The demand forecast for the 30 products manufactured by Ledesma is updated every month, and has a monthly level of detail for each product. Demands of the national market are aggregated over all depots, although each customer is delivered from a prespecified depot (usually the one closest to that customer's reception point). For planning purposes, the national demand is therefore de-aggregated by suitable coefficients for each product and depot. Exports involve some of the standard products packed by the packing plant; each export operation includes (indicates) the month, product, quantity, and depot for the delivery.

The linear programming model has quite an involved set of variables and constraints. However, a good idea of that model can be obtained by inspecting the underlying network structure. To this end, in the following subsections we describe this network and the relevant details concerning the flow.

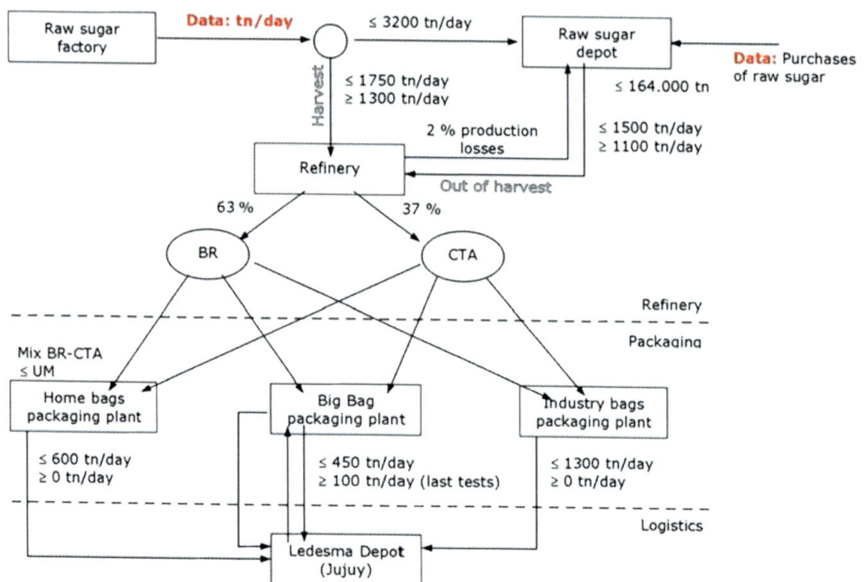

Fig. 5.3 Modeling of production and packing decisions

5.2.1 Production and Packaging Decisions

Figure 5.3 shows the multi-commodity network structure for the modeling and packing decisions. For each monthly planning period, the inputs are given by the production of raw sugar (which is zero in the non-harvest months) and the purchases of raw sugar, which go directly to the raw sugar depot. There are lower and upper bounds on the amounts of raw sugar that can be moved among the raw sugar factory, the raw sugar depot, and the refinery, as depicted in the figure. Stock at the raw sugar depot cannot exceed 164,000 tn in any month, and cannot exceed 10,000 tn at the end of April. The latter corresponds to sugar left over from the previous year's harvest.

The refinery takes raw sugar and manufactures white refined sugar, divided into 63 % of premium-quality sugar (shown as BR in Fig. 5.3) and 37 % of standard-quality sugar (indicated there by CTA). Moreover, 2 % of the raw sugar goes back to the raw sugar depot; that sugar was lost during production and has to be refined again. (This is considered as raw sugar for planning purposes.) The white refined sugar goes to the three packing facilities, each of which has a maximum packing capacity and also a lower bound on the daily packed amounts. In addition, there are individual minimum and maximum production levels for each stock keeping unit (SKU). Furthermore, some of those involve a mixture between standard- and premium-quality refined sugar. For such products, an upper bound UM on the percentage of each kind of sugar is also specified.

"Big bags" involve a special re-packing procedure, in order to keep sugar hardening under control. In production tests, it was found that sugar stored in big bags developed unacceptable hardening properties, making the final product very difficult to extract from the bag. To solve this problem, big bags are initially kept for ten days at the Jujuy depot, then taken to a special re-packing facility. The sugar is removed from each of the big bags, and re-packed in new ones. This procedure ensures that the final big bag does not suffer from hardening effects. Since the model treats the months as atomic periods, we simulate this procedure by adding a special category of *intermediate big bags*, which return to the repacking facility to be converted into regular big bags. We also add a constraint asking for a stock level of intermediate big bags of exactly one third the production of the corresponding big-bag product at the end of each month. Assuming that production of big bags is evenly distributed among all days in the month, such a stock level represents the number of intermediate big bags produced in the last ten days of the month (which will be re-packed in the following month).

Several conditions stated by the planning team would give rise to binary variables, hence they cannot be included in an LP model in a straightforward way. To illustrate, there are some low-demand products (e.g., items with special quality standards for pharmaceutical purposes) for which it is desirable to manufacture at least a minimum amount or to manufacture nothing at all. Moreover, some pairs of SKUs should not be manufactured together in the same month, due to technical restrictions. These additional constraints would have given rise to binary variables, and perhaps compromised the possibility of solving the resulting model in practice. Fortunately, we could avoid introduction of those binary variables by allowing the user to forbid production of a specific product in certain periods. This way, the user chooses in which months each of these special low-demand items will be manufactured (avoiding product clashes), and the model solution will determine the particular amount to produce in those months. This solution is heuristic and represents a compromise, but it turned out to be very effective. That allowed us to remain within a linear programming environment.

5.2.2 The Manufacturing/Distribution Interface

Figure 5.4 shows the connections between production and logistics. These take place in Jujuy at the output of the packing plant and the input to the main Jujuy depot. The manufactured items can be directly dispatched, either on one of the railways or by truck. These *direct dispatches* are routed through the transportation network (to be described in Sect. 5.2.3) to other depots or to the final customers, that being the exit point for flow in the network. As the demands are given, the output of each product at a given depot in any period must not exceed the corresponding demand. A penalty is added to the objective function whenever some portion of demand cannot be met. This demand depends on the item (mass-

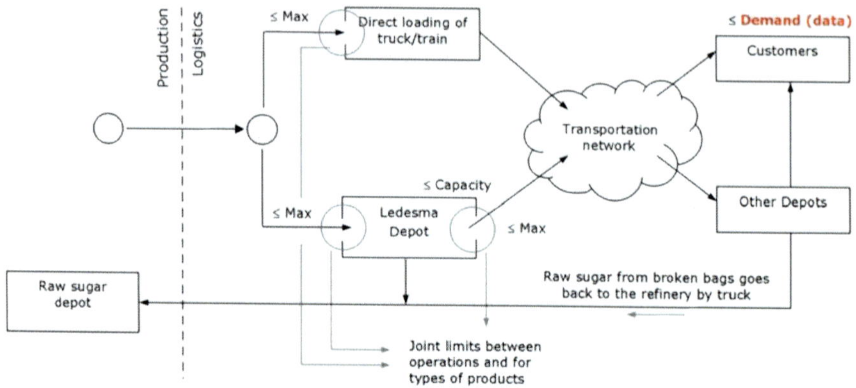

Fig. 5.4 The production/logistics interface

consumption 1 kg bags are critical) and on the customer (exports are more important than deliveries to national customers).

If a manufactured product is not directly dispatched, then it is stored in the main Ledesma depot in Jujuy. With the exception of SKUs with special quality requirements, most items are stacked directly on the depot floor. Direct dispatch, stacking, and de-stacking operations involve a specified amount of human resources, which are measured in labor-hours. There are constraints imposing an upper bound on the number of labor-hours devoted to each of these operations for every type of package (small bags, bags, and big bags), and a joint upper bound for the total labor-hours for each operation. Furthermore, for the operations on small bags and big bags, the depot manager has a certain number of available labor-hours (since they correspond to monthly-salaried employees), and any additional labor-hours are charged on a proportional basis (those involve paid-per-hour employees). Those labor-hour constraints apply only to the main depot in Jujuy, as the stacking and de-stacking operations at the remaining depots are not extremely critical and involve smaller quantities of products.

Finally, it must be mentioned that the direct dispatch, stacking, and de-stacking operations usually generate some broken bags. This sugar is not disposed, but instead is collected, stored, and sent back to the industrial complex in Jujuy as raw sugar. Each time a logistic operation is performed in some depot, the model generates a small user-defined percentage (of about 0.5 %) of the involved sugar as broken bags. Sugar coming from broken bags is kept at each depot. We explicitly model transportation by truck of this sugar back to the raw sugar depot, where it is added to the existing raw sugar and is eventually re-refined. It is interesting to note that these movements correspond to 1.5 days of additional refinery during the year, so inclusion of this feature in the model was indeed necessary.

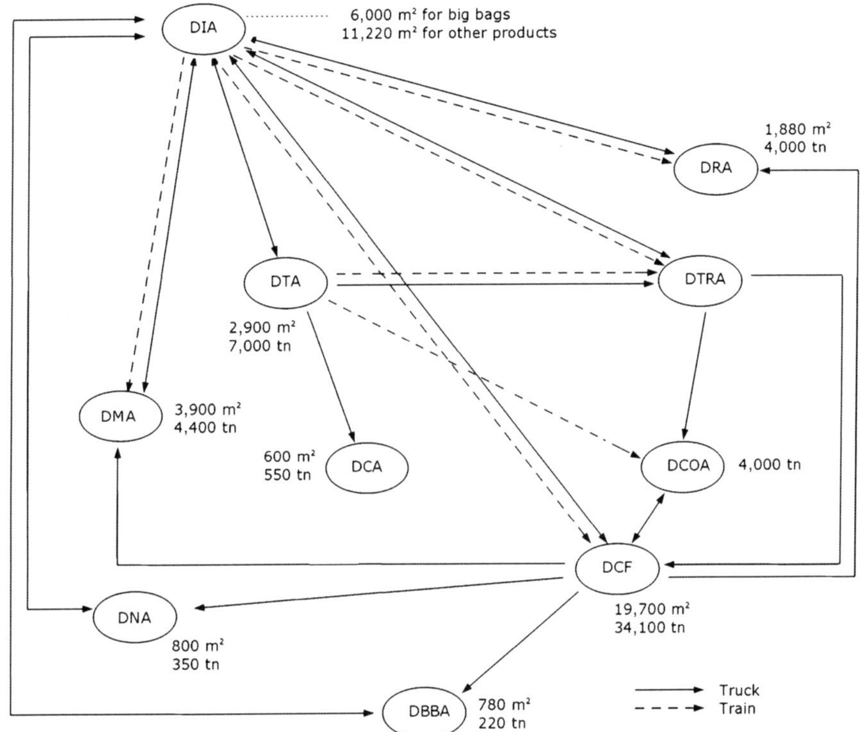

Fig. 5.5 The transportation network

5.2.3 The Transportation Network

Figure 5.5 depicts the current transportation network, which can be represented by a directed graph. The nodes correspond to depots, solid arrows to the admissible transportation routes by truck, and dashed arrows indicate rail lines. Arcs going in both directions correspond to transport by truck from/to the DIA depot, next to the industrial complex in Jujuy. Transportation back to DIA carries sugar coming from broken bags into the raw sugar depot.

Each depot has a maximum storage capacity (expressed in square meters for the main Jujuy depot, and in tons for the remaining depots). Each railroad route has an upper bound on capacity per month, due to existing contracts. There is also a maximum monthly joint capacity for each railway company. Each route has a price per ton; the routes by truck have a different price scheme for the high season (approximately from May to September), which corresponds to the fruit-harvesting months in the north of Argentina. Within the model, we allow the user to define two prices for each kind of transportation, and to define in which months the higher price applies (i.e., which months correspond to the high season).

We explicitly keep track of the inventory of each product at every depot at the end of any period. Respective products have minimum and maximum global stock levels (i.e., sum of the existing stock over all depots), and minimum and maximum stock levels for each depot. These stock levels are expressed in terms of *demand periods*. For example, a minimum stock level of 2 demand periods means that at the end of each month, the stock must be greater than or equal to the demand of that item in the next two months. Such demand periods need not be integers, and the associated constraints are elastic (i.e., can be violated, but in that case a penalty is added to the objective function). This way, we can adapt the inventory requirements to the seasonal demands of each product. Finally, special coefficients associated with particular periods are added. These enable us to relax the preceding requirements during the harvest months (when the stock is easily replaced), and in the two months where the refinery is stopped (when stock levels are allowed to be lower).

Transshipment costs are incurred for the dispatches by the railroad operating the routes DTA-DTRA and DTA-DCOA. The sugar going through these routes must first travel by truck from the industrial complex to DTA, then be transshipped onto the train at DTA, hence we add those charges to the costs of the associated rail routes.

5.2.4 Objective Function

The objective function is composed of a *cost term* and a *penalty term*. The former includes the refinery costs, labor costs for logistic operations in the Jujuy main depot, and transportation costs. Refinery costs are proportional to the refinery speed, which can vary between some limits. No costs are added for the packing activities, dispatches to customers, and the stacking and de-stacking at the remaining depots, as these activities must always be performed and thus they would only add a constant term to the objective function.

The penalty term includes a penalty for not meeting the demand (note that demand should always be met within the production and logistics plan, since satisfying the demand or not is not a decision taken by the planning team), and penalties for not respecting the minimum and maximum stock levels for each product. If demand for an SKU cannot be fully satisfied in a certain period, unsatisfied demand carries over to the next period. Tuning the penalty coefficients turned out to be a critical task as, e.g., too small a penalty for not meeting demand may make production and transportation "uneconomical", but too high a penalty may force inconvenient logistic movements to meet the demand at any cost.

The linear programming model from the May, 2010 scenario has about 75,000 variables, around 72,000 constraints, and 318,000 non-zero elements. It is interesting to note that the density of the associated matrix is quite low, being 0.0058 % in this particular scenario. The model was coded in a GAMS-like proprietary modeling language, and involves 53 groups of variables and 134 blocks of

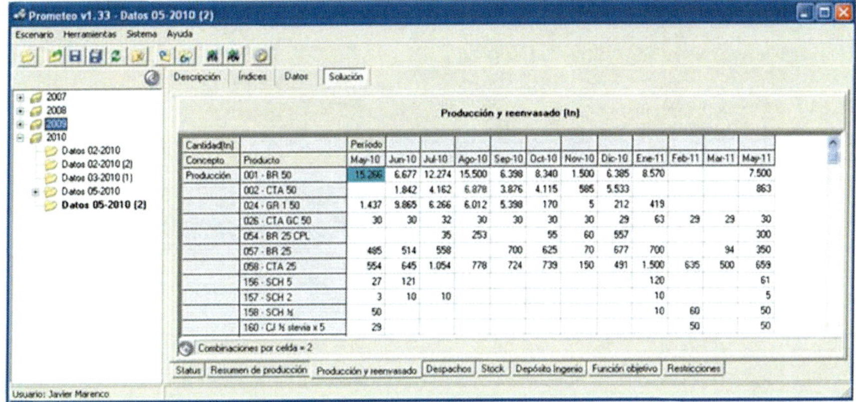

Fig. 5.6 The scenario-based computational tool

constraints. We routinely generate the model with a proprietary software tool within 4 min on a regular desktop PC. We employ Mosek 3 to solve the model, a task that is performed in less than 30 s. For more details about this LP solver, please see Mosek (2010).

5.3 The Software Tool

We implemented a scenario-based software tool to manage the data, solve the model, and analyze results (see Fig. 5.6). Each scenario consists of the whole set of data needed to run the model and, if available, the solution obtained by the last execution of the algorithmic procedures. This way, the users can generate many scenarios at each meeting of the planning team, in order to perform "what-if" analyses and explore the effect of different constraints on the final solution.

The Microsoft Windows application was coded in the C++ Builder 5 environment—see e.g., Hollingworth et al. (2000)—and employs an SQL-Server 2005 database to centrally store the scenarios. Each user can access those scenarios in the database and, additionally, can save or recover scenarios to/from files in his or her local workstation. This way, a user can "play around" with a scenario or variations of a scenario without affecting the "official" scenarios recorded in the database. This last feature turned out to be useful for helping users when they found an unexpected behavior in some scenario: In such a situation, he/she would save the scenario to a file, e-mail that scenario to us, and we could analyze it and eventually e-mail the corrected scenario back.

Data management is performed through Microsoft Excel-like pivot tables. This is a natural tool for users to manage the information: All members of the planning team are highly skilled in Microsoft Excel. The ability to copy and paste data from or to Excel was also very welcome, as it is common that users perform small data

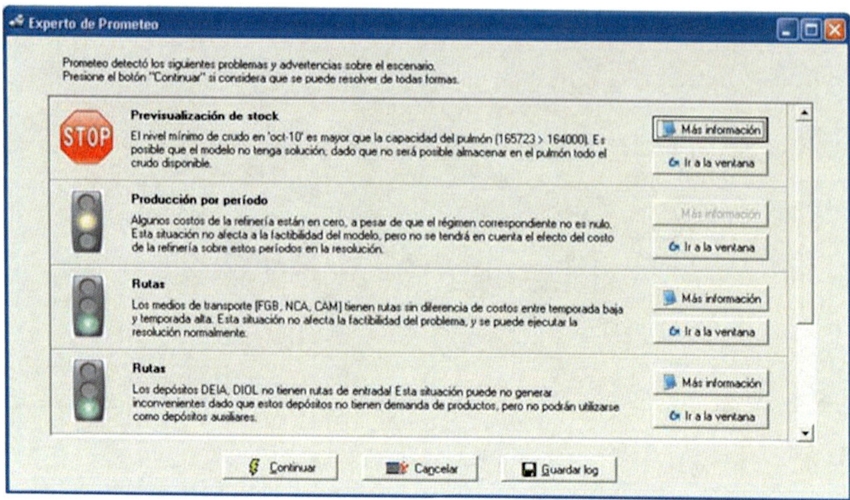

Fig. 5.7 Alerts given by the pre-solving "expert system"

analyses in temporary Excel tables. The software includes interfaces to import stock levels from the existing computational systems at Ledesma, and to import demand forecasts from a standard Excel table which is updated every month by the sales manager.

We have implemented a pre-solving "expert system" which helps to detect data that may generate an infeasible model (see Fig. 5.7). During our experience installing and helping the users to get started with the software, we identified many data combinations which can make the model infeasible. This expert system checks for all those situations, and provides a warning when it finds some possible infeasibility (also giving a user the possibility of going directly to the data table containing the problematic data). Identifying potential infeasibilities in the model before attempting solution turned out to be a crucial feature: The presence of so many constraints can make the model infeasible, and users frequently run into trouble when that happens. This way, the user can instead correct potential data errors, thus ensuring a feasible result from the solution process.

A primary source of infeasibilities is the balancing of the available sugar and the implied use of the raw sugar depot (e.g., if the amounts to be refined are too small, the storage capacity of the raw sugar depot may then be exceeded in the months following the harvest). To properly uncover this situation, the application includes an interface to project the stock levels of raw sugar and packed sugar, highlighting the periods where raw-sugar inventory capacity is violated. This way, a user can easily detect that the model will be infeasible, and correct the data and parameters prior to solving.

We have also implemented a tool to analyze the results after solving the model, in such a way that potential difficulties are identified and presented. The user gets a list of the shortcomings that the solution may have, so he/she does not have to go through many tables packed with numbers to assess whether the production and logistics plan provided by the model is acceptable or not. Typical examples of cases tested and found by this "post-solving" analyzer include:

- an important fraction of the demand is not satisfied,
- the minimum or maximum stock levels are violated for too many products,
- the manufactured amounts of a particular SKU vary by too much during a certain number of consecutive periods (suggesting that narrowing the production limits for that item may be a good idea),
- a product is at its maximum possible production level for many periods (suggesting that enabling a greater production rate of this SKU may be a good idea).

Finally, the application includes an interface to investigate shadow prices and reduced costs. The goal is to enhance the capability of a user, who may not have specific knowledge of linear programming, to perform economic analyses over the whole problem. Figure 5.8 depicts this interface. It includes suitable filters to query the constraints by their respective indices (periods, products, depots, and transportation providers), and provides information about the activity level and shadow price of each active constraint. This interface allows the analysis of unexpected behaviors in the solution. For example, if demand for a product is not fully satisfied during the first periods, then we can query the constraints associated with this SKU to determine which active constraints are limiting the production of this specific item (e.g., an upper bound on its allowable monthly production, a limit on the amount that can be directly dispatched, etc.).

5.4 Implementation and Benefits

5.4.1 The Implementation Process

It can be difficult to implement an operations-research-based tool for aiding the regular decisions of a planning team. A key point during the development work was to make the users a part of that model development. In particular, we implemented a preliminary Excel-based prototype to rapidly develop an initial model and to grow this model into a mature model of the planning decisions. This way, after the initial interviews and requirement-eliciting activities, we were able to quickly come up with a fully-functional first version of the model, which moreover allowed us to perform changes and add parameters quite efficiently.

With the help of this prototype (and with our assistance, as the interface in this prototype was not fault-tolerant), users could introduce the model data, solve the model, analyze the solution, propose changes, and see the results of those changes. This way, the model adjustments were performed effectively, and users could watch the model grow according to their observations and comments. Once the prototype evolved to a mature model that provided acceptable solutions to the

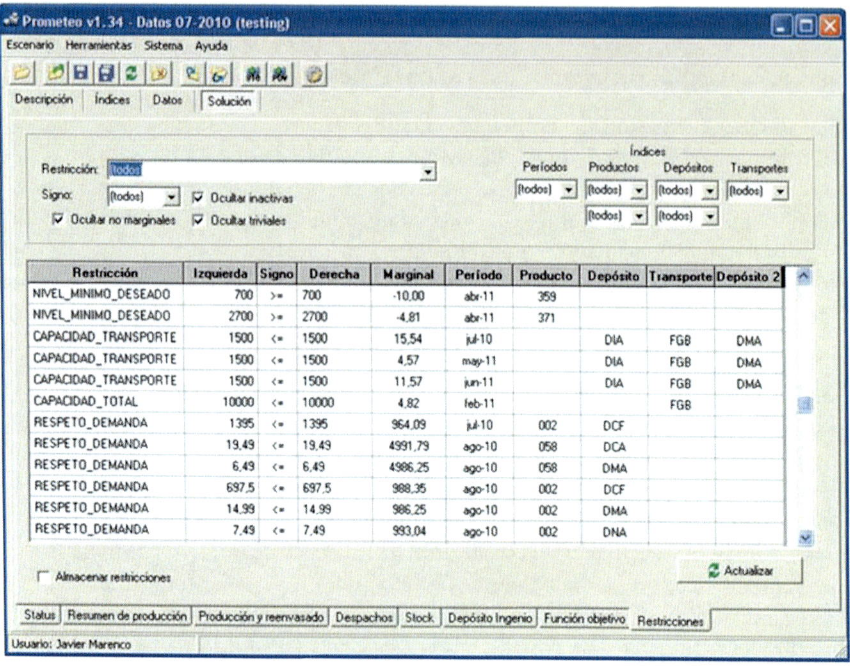

Fig. 5.8 Interface for querying shadow prices

users, we developed the Windows application with greater certainty that requirements were quite stabilized.

The users did not immediately express confidence in the results provided by the model. In the first experiments, solutions contained many unacceptable characteristics, as some features were missing in the model or the parameters were not properly tuned. However, by performing the tuning process and enabling the users to be part of the development activities, we could see a growing confidence in the model results. This general feeling was enhanced by the replacement of some team members (due to internal employee movements at Ledesma), at which point existing members of the planning team introduced the benefits of model-based decision-making to the incoming members. The latter received those techniques not as a novelty, but as a standardized planning practice.

A key point within the computational tool is the possibility of fixing some decisions prior to solving the model. If the planning team decides to produce a certain amount of a particular product in some period (usually the first or second months in the planning interval), then the users can plug these values into the scenario, the corresponding variables are fixed, and the model will solve for the remaining decisions. This way, a user can incorporate into the solution specific decisions arising from technical or commercial considerations not contemplated in the model.

5.4.2 Tactical Benefits and Strategic Impact

A main benefit of the introduction of the linear programming model embedded within a computational software system has been the possibility of generating production and logistics plans which take into account many constraints simultaneously. Such a task could not be performed previously. The detailed consideration of many months in advance is a feature which has now been incorporated into the decision-making process. Prior to introduction of this model, just the first two months were planned in a detailed way, and the following months were loosely considered.

The linear programming model is a medium-term tactical tool. It is interesting to note, however, that the model has been used several times to aid in long-term strategic decisions, e.g. to analyze the impact of depot upgrades, depot rentals, and the acceptance/rejection of exports. For example, near the end of the harvesting months in 2009, several proposals were under consideration for changing the traditional March–April refinery-stopping period. The planning team generated four different scenarios for each such proposal, and prepared graphical visualizations of the evolution of stock levels under each proposal. That information was available at the management meeting where this issue was to be decided. The added value was that the predicted inventory levels were not rough estimates, but rather had instead been generated with the same model which assisted the monthly planning decisions.

An intangible benefit is the creation of a unified framework for modeling all the areas involved in the planning process. This is a step forward in the overall vision of Ledesma, as obtained by each member of the planning team. Since the creation of that team, the entire production and logistic process is not only understood by each of the participants, but also modeled in a detailed way. Additionally, the application becomes an arena where some values are shared, enabling a better understanding of interrelationships between the costs of different areas.

On the down side, the model requires a huge amount of data, and parameters which must be properly tuned so as to provide acceptable solutions. Users are expected to "experiment" with those parameters in order to do "what-if" analyses, but there is room for spoiling a good scenario by mistakenly setting a wrong value for a key parameter. Introduction of the pre-solving "expert system" helped to avoid many of these situations, but the potential danger remains.

Finally, in the last months we have gone through joint analytical activities with the planning team, in order to study the introduction of further operations research-based tools within the decision-making process. Due to the inherent uncertainties in logistics operations of this company in Argentina, we do not believe that an automated decision support system is possible for the daily operations. However, we think that a planning tool that considers *weekly* periods instead of monthly periods is indeed possible. The production and logistic constraints involved in the weekly decisions seem to be amenable to suitable modeling by linear programming (or even reasonably-sized integer programs, if period- or product-aggregation techniques are employed), hence this approach may be viable.

Acknowledgements The authors would like to thank Fabio Bardín, Miguel Casares, Hugo Díaz, Miguel Kremer, Alejandro Peuchot, Rodolfo Roballos, Alberto Salvado, and Alejandro Serrano from Ledesma SAAI. The authors are indebted to Prof. James Bookbinder for his valuable comments and remarks, which greatly improved this chapter.

References

Chiadamrong N, Kawtummachai R (2008) A methodology to support decision-making on sugar distribution for export channel: a case study of Thai sugar industry. Comput Electron Agric 64(2):248–261

Díaz J, Pérez I (2000) Simulation and optimization of sugar cane transportation in harvest season. In: Proceedings of the 32nd winter simulation conference, pp 1114–1117

Higgins A (1999) Optimizing cane supply decisions within a sugar mill region. J Sched 2(5): 229–244

Higgins A (2002) Australian sugar mills optimize harvester rosters to improve production. Interfaces 32(3):15–25

Higgins A, Beashel G, Harrison A (2006) Scheduling of brand production and shipping within a sugar supply chain. J Oper Res Soc 57:490–498

Hollingworth J, Allsop J, Butterfield D, Swart R, Smith M, Woodbury W, Turnbull K, Bonavita J, Chandler D, Banks D, Almannai K, Cashman M, Blanton II P, Wu S, Winters C (2000) C++ builder 5 developer's guide. Sams Professional, New York

Kostina A, Guillén-Gosálbeza G, Meleb F, Bagajewiczc M, Jiméneza L (2010) Integrating pricing policies in the strategic planning of supply chains: a case study of the sugar cane industry in Argentina. Comput Aided Chem Eng 28:103–108

Lejars C, Le Gal P, Auzoux S (2008) A decision support approach for cane supply management within a sugar mill area. Comput Electron Agric 60:239–249

Le Gal P, Le Masson J, Bezuidenhout C, Lagrange L (2009) Coupled modelling of sugarcane supply planning and logistics as a management tool. Comput Electron Agric 68(2):168–177

Mosek ApS (2010) The MOSEK optimization tools manual. Mosek ApS, Copenhagen

Taechasook P, Sethanan K, Bureerat S (2008) Application of genetic algorithms for sugar cane harvesting decision. Proceedings of the technology and innovation for sustainable development conference, pp 172–177

Chapter 6
Integration of International and Cabotage Container Shipping in Brazil

Hugo Tsugunobu Yoshida Yoshizaki, Celso Mitsuo Hino and Daniel Chebat

Abstract This chapter concerns the integration of liner container shipping and short sea service (cabotage) in Brazil. The methodology is based on a linear programming model, which maximizes the gross contribution margin and evaluates the consequences of mixing international and domestic loads. Firstly, the text presents an overview of Brazilian cabotage. Then the problem and the model are presented. The method is applied to a real case, where through sensitivity analysis, impacts on the performance of a liner company are measured. Thus, different scenarios are compared using a set of key performance indicators. The results show that this integration is quite attractive, and they also provide the shipping company with a solid background to support strategic and operational decisions.

6.1 Introduction

Due to a strong bias toward trucking in Brazil's transportation matrix, that country has seen a renewed interest in short sea shipping. The Brazilian government intends to increase the current share of water transportation (inland and short sea)

H. T. Y. Yoshizaki (✉)
Department of Production Engineering, EPUSP, University of São Paulo, Av. Professor Almeida Prado 128, Cidade Universitária, 05508-900 São Paulo, SP, Brazil
e-mail: hugo@usp.br

C. M. Hino
Department of Naval and Oceanic Engineering, EPUSP, University of São Paulo, Av. Professor Mello Moraes, 2231, Cidade Universitária, 05508-030 São Paulo, SP, Brazil
e-mail: cmhino@usp.br

D. Chebat
Department of Production Engineering, EPUSP, University of São Paulo, São Paulo, Brazil

J. H. Bookbinder (ed.), *Handbook of Global Logistics*, International Series in Operations Research & Management Science 181, DOI: 10.1007/978-1-4419-6132-7_6,

from 13 to 29 % in ton-miles by 2025, while decreasing the share of truck transportation from 58 to 30 % (Ministry of Transportation 2009). However, figures from the Syndicate of Brazilian Maritime Shipping Companies (SYNDARMA) show that container short sea trade has experienced a significant expansion, from 90,000 twenty-feet equivalent units (TEU's) in 2000 to 630,000 TEU's in 2008 (SYNDARMA 2009). Because Brazilian laws allow foreign ships to operate on short sea routes under some specific conditions, the integration of international and domestic container trade could be an attractive alternative for ocean liner carriers.

This work analyzes the feasibility, from the perspective of an ocean container carrier, of transporting cabotage cargoes in Brazil. That would utilize a portion of the transportation capacity of long distance service vessels that currently carry only international freight (Costa et al. 2009). Thus, our objectives are the following:

- To evaluate potential synergies of integrating national and international shipping; in other words, vessels that operate on international routes would use part of their capacity to haul domestic loads;
- To evaluate the competitiveness of hauling containers along the Brazilian coast by ship, compared to road transportation.

6.2 Short Sea Shipping (Cabotage) in Brazil

Brazil's coast is 8,000 km long, and most people live within two hundred miles of the Atlantic coast. These two simple figures exemplify the potential advantages of short sea transportation for this large nation. However, historical problems have conspired against that mode of transport, including the ineffectiveness of state-owned Brazilian ports, a former de facto state monopoly of coastal shipping, and, most damaging of all, the priority given to road transportation as the impetus of Brazilian industrialization in the 1960s. With the demise of the Brazilian state shipping company, Lloyd Brasileiro, in the 1980s, general cargo cabotage virtually came to a standstill.

General cargo short sea operations gradually bounced back with the large-scale introduction of container shipping on international routes, which led to a revival of Brazilian ports in the 1990s. Figure 6.1 shows the current Brazilian ports.

Ono (2001) claims that approval in 1993 of Federal Law 8630, known as the Bill of Port Modernization, marked a new beginning for Brazilian ports because it allowed the establishment of private terminals and therefore, allowed for private investments. Container operations benefited greatly from these new private players. Ono (2001) also mentions Law 9611 from 1998, which deals with Multimodal Transportation, enabling shippers to profit from more efficient logistics. That law regulates the offering of door-to-door services in the country. However, cabotage suffered from a lack of regular container service, as well as low port

Fig. 6.1 Major Brazilian ports. *Source* Ministry of Transportation

frequency; at that time, there were just a few vessels in operation and only two shipping companies. In addition, the work force has been on ongoing issue because many of the major ports are under the control of unionized labor, which imposes constraints on shifts, minimum group composition, and working hours. In practice, Brazilian ports face problems in dismissing workers because of union pressures.

The growth of container cabotage service from the beginning of the twenty-first century is a salient fact. According to SYNDARMA (2009), the demand has increased from 20,000 TEU's in 1999 to 630,000 TEU's in 2008 (Fig. 6.2).

A 2006 survey by the Brazilian Confederacy of Transportation Syndicates (CNT 2006) states that the main advantages of short sea shipping are (Fig. 6.3) the following: reduced freight cost; increased security; lower lead-time variation; less damage; freight storage; and ancillary services. Freight cost is the dominant issue.

A previous survey by CNT (2002) focused on the main problems facing maritime carriers. The number one difficulty is the high cost of warehousing, cited by 62.6 % by those interviewed as a critical or very critical problem. The second most important problem, by a very small margin, is excessive bureaucracy (61.8 % considered it as critical or very critical), followed by lack of financing for the

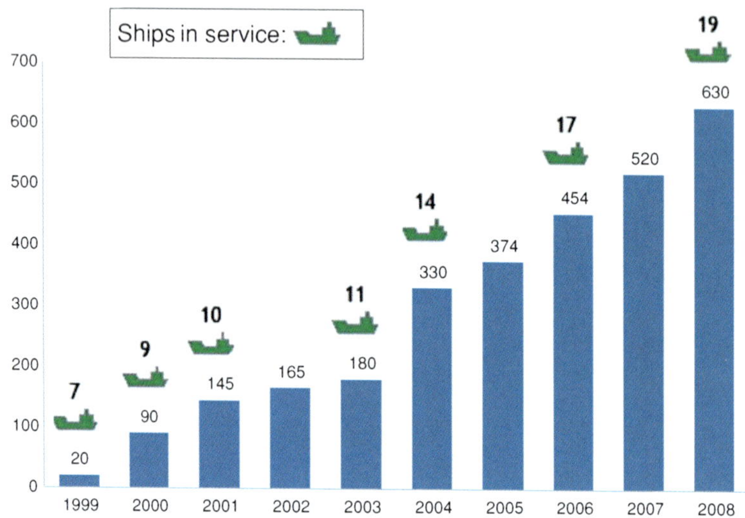

Fig. 6.2 Total freight moved by cabotage (thousand TEU's)

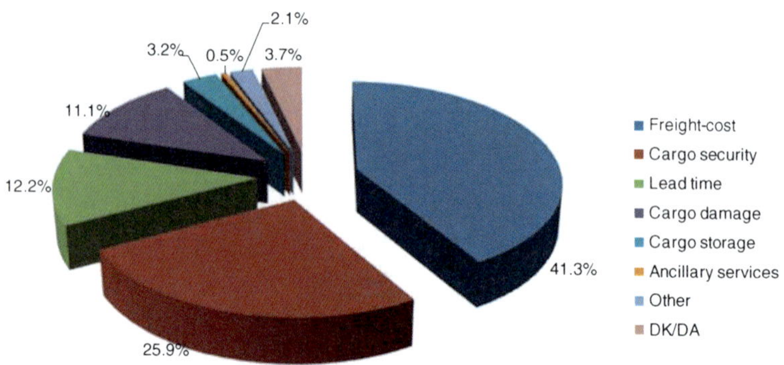

Fig. 6.3 Competitive advantages from short sea shipping. *Source* Water transportation survey CNT 2006: Maritime ports: long haul and cabotage. Brasília: Confederacy of Transportation Syndicates 2006

industry and inefficiency of ports, with 39.7 and 35.9 %, respectively, of evaluations being critical or very critical. The lack of regular lines is also cited, although it is considered not as crucial as the others. This is evaluated by 3.1 % of interviewed carriers as a very critical problem, and by 17.6 % as critical (CNT 2002).

Article 178 of the Brazilian Constitution states that specific legislation should regulate the use of foreign vessels in short sea and interior water navigation. Federal Law 9432 allows the use of foreign vessels for cabotage if these ships are owned or leased by a Brazilian carrier, and when Brazilian-flag ships are not available for service. That law does not allow foreign carriers, with foreign or open flags and with a foreign crew, to operate in cabotage trade.

Another survey, by the Maritime Administration (MARAD) of the US Department of Transportation, established in 1987, then updated in 2004, and cited in the US Evaluation of Maritime Policy in 2009, showed that, in a sample of 56 countries, it is commonplace for a nation to protect cabotage shipping. Some examples are listed:

- **United States**: Short sea shipping must be performed by vessels made and registered in the US, the vessels must be owned by US citizens, and their crews must have at least 75 % US citizens (the Jones Act).
- **European Economic Community (EEC)**: Ship owners are allowed to operate in short sea shipping of any Member State, as long as their vessels are registered and navigate under the flag of one of the Member States (Resolution n. 3577/92 of the EEC Council).
- **China**: The Maritime Code of the People's Republic of China states that cabotage must be performed by ships under the Chinese flag. Foreign investments, as well international partnerships that involve short sea or interior navigation, need specific authorization.
- **Canada**: Short sea navigation is protected using two sets of laws: the Coastal Trade Act and the Customs Tariff. The main purpose of these laws is to develop Canadian domestic navigation without exposing it directly to international competition.
- **Japan**: The country's maritime laws state that transportation of cargo and passengers between national ports is reserved to vessels under the Japanese flag. Limited access to Japanese cabotage is possible for ships from countries that have trade, friendship, or navigation relations with Japan, under the principle of reciprocity.
- **Mexico**: Cabotage and maritime support services are reserved for Mexican-flag vessels. The federal government states that the transportation of cargoes is also the prerogative of Mexican-flag ships. In the case of lack of capacity through national means, service may be performed by foreign ships, under specific authorization by Mexican authorities.
- **Argentina**: Only vessels owned by Argentinean maritime carriers are allowed.
- **Chile**: The Bill for Development of the Merchant Marine of Chile establishes that cabotage is a prerogative of Chilean vessels, but foreign ships may carry cargo lighter than 900 tons, if bid at public auction.

The main reasons for the preceding market protection are thus "to develop a merchant marine," "to give preference to labor and national industry," "to generate employment for nationals," "to support national security," and "to protect the domestic economy."

In Brazil, after implementation of the Law for Modernization of Ports, there has been a sharp increase since 2000 in the number of Brazilian short sea containers moved since 2000 (see Fig. 6.2). The cabotage freight rates became relatively cheaper than trucking for long distances on coastal routes (i.e., those along a sea shore) (ANTAQ 2005, 2009).

In 2005, a report by the Brazilian Federal Research Institute of Applied Economics (IPEA) estimated the potential for cabotage in that country. This study had three objectives. The first was to determine, from the total cargo moved by all transportation modes, which portions can be moved by cabotage. Then it identified, by product category, the potential loads of transshipment freight (feeder service) that could be transported by cabotage. Transshipment freight originates from international trade. Lastly, it identified key aspects that influence the expansion of goods transportation along the Brazilian coast, taking into consideration both macroeconomic matters and specific conditions of the cabotage sector.

To determine the possible quantity that could be transported by cabotage, the IPEA (2005) considered three major conditions, beginning with geography. It eliminated freight flows connecting states located in the interior of the country (and distant from the coast) from its estimate of potential cabotage cargo. The other two conditions concerned the following two questions. First, are the overall characteristics of the goods suitable for the maritime mode? Second, is the distance involved greater than one thousand kilometers (the minimum distance beyond which cabotage transport is competitive with road transport)? After applying all these conditions, the IPEA (2005) roughly calculates that R$ 311 billion of goods (about US$ 182 billion) could have been transported by cabotage in 2004. This amount represents 17 % of the 2004 Brazilian GDP, as estimated by the Brazilian Federal Institute of Geography and Statistics (IBGE).

In addition, the study states that approximately another R$ 50 billion of freight (about US$ 29 billion) that originated from international trade (transshipment) could have been transported by cabotage in 2004. These are goods that could be profitably integrated with international trade.

The IPEA (2005) also observed that, to transport new cargo, carriers should focus on the following economic activities: wholesale trade; chemical products; beverage and food production; vehicle production and assembly; and electronic equipment manufacturing. According to this study, those are the largest economic activities in terms of inter-state financial flows, in the order presented.

That study states that the growth potential of the short sea market is huge, approximately ten times that of the present market, but there are important barriers that would render this accomplishment difficult. Obstacles do not stem from macroeconomic issues, which today favor growth of the cabotage market. Rather, severe restrictions are caused by specific problems in the short sea trade.

Based on information from interviews conducted with the three major companies that operate in the Brazilian cabotage market, the IPEA (2005) states that the current limitation on cabotage transportation capacity is due to lack of vessels. The study highlights the fact that *all three firms* interviewed declared that a shortage of cabotage ships is the bottleneck in this sector. Still, according to the study, the vessel deficit in Brazilian cabotage has two causes that have been identified. Firstly, national shipyards must present guarantees of federal financing

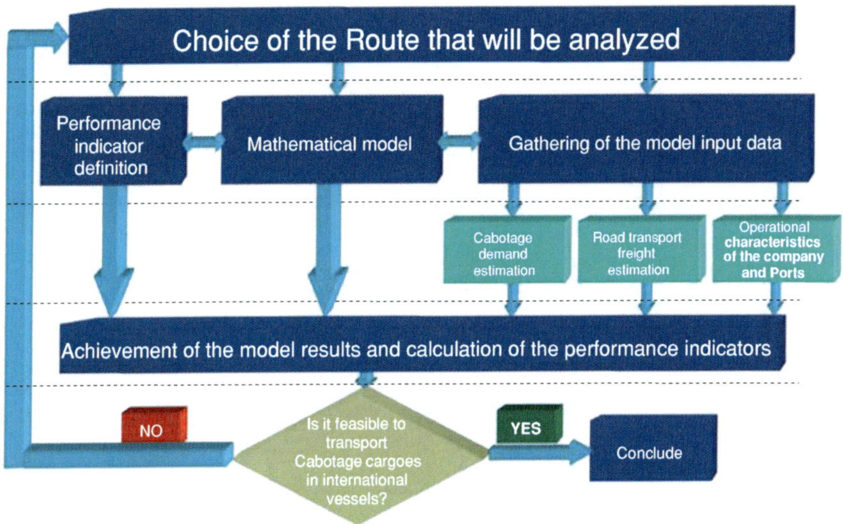

Fig. 6.4 Study methodology

to order new vessels. Secondly, the growth of international trade, led by China, has provoked a scarcity in the supply of ships and has raised time-charter rates. Thus, integration of international and short sea container trade could help alleviate this capacity deficiency.

In addition, the IPEA (2005) states two other difficulties faced by the short sea service: high port costs and a port infrastructure that is unsatisfactory to handle general cargo (container) cabotage.

Therefore, the study concludes that conditions are very favorable to increase Brazilian cabotage services. Additionally, the IPEA (2005) mentions that the growth of international trade represents an opportunity to implement a hub port that would enhance transshipment operations by short sea feeder services. This is robustly contradicted by Aversa et al. (2005), who showed that hub ports and feeder services are not attractive to shipping companies operating on the East coast of South America (Brazil, Uruguay, and Argentina). Thus, a different strategy, focused on the integration of international and domestic trade, must be considered.

6.3 Methodology

The methodology, shown in Fig. 6.4, employs the following three steps: route and potential cargo-type choices; model development; and evaluation of integrating international and domestic cargoes on a given route.

The first step analyzes road freight transportation in Brazil, focusing mainly on legs that are direct competitors of short sea routes. To do this, a freight survey was conducted with companies considered to be possible clients of Brazilian cabotage. This enabled the formulation of a method to justify potential cabotage demand to be used in the last step of our methodology.

In the second part, a mathematical programming model was developed and tested. This model maximizes the company's contribution margin through selection of the best cargoes. The model permits an evaluation of cabotage alternatives from the point of view of a carrier (shipping company) that operates in international and short sea transportation routes. In others words, given the company's current service structure over long-distance routes, the model is able to identify if and which cabotage cargoes contribute positively when integrated into the firm's freight portfolio, and the impacts of this change.

In the third and last step, the data gathered in the initial survey was applied using the mathematical model to determine the influence generated by the integration of transportation of international and Brazilian cargoes. The objective was to evaluate the changes that take place when a portion of the capacity of vessels that operate on long-distance routes is used to transport cabotage cargo.

6.3.1 Mathematical Model

The problem can be defined as the following: given a route, a homogeneous fleet of vessels, the demand, the revenues and costs related to full container operations, and the costs associated with empty container logistics, determine which cargoes should be selected and loaded in each port to maximize the contribution margin of all freight over the planning horizon of the given carrier.

Indices and sets:

$p \in P$ Set of all ports;
$i \in I$ Set of all loading ports;
$j \in J$ Set of all discharging ports;
$k \in K$ Set of all container types;
K^R Subset of K ($K^R \subset K$) with all reefer-type containers;
K^F Subset of K ($K^F \subset K$) with all 40′ -size containers;
$c \in C$ Set of all cargo types;
$t \in T$ Set of all periods

Parameters

$D^F_{i,j,k,c,t}$ The demand for type k containers, with type c cargo, from the loading port i to the discharging port j, in period t;
$R^F_{i,j,k,c,t}$ The revenue (freight and taxes), for one type k container, with type c cargo, from the loading port i to the discharging port j, in period t;
$C^F_{i,j,k}$ The loading and discharging cost of one type k container, from the loading port i to the discharging port j;

$C^{E}_{i,j,k}$ The loading and discharging cost of one empty type k container, from the loading port i to the discharging port j;
C^{M}_{c} The attendance cost for type c cargo;
C^{S}_{k} The storage cost for one type k container, for one period;
$W^{F}_{k,c}$ The average weight of a type k container with type c cargo;
W^{E}_{k} The average weight of an empty type k container;
H_{p} The maximum cargo deadweight in the port of index p;
$M_{p,i,j}$ The predecessor matrix, with binary values. $M_{p,i,j} = 1$, if a container loaded in port i with destination port j is on board when the vessel arrives at port p, and zero otherwise;
$S^{F}_{j,i,k,\delta}$ Represents the fraction of type k containers that, loaded full in port i and discharged at port j, returns empty to the empty-container terminal of port j after δ periods of time, counted from the time of loading at port i. (It is assumed that the Liner Carrier has an empty-container terminal close to each port j of the route.)

To maintain the general balance of the model, we assume that relations (6.1)–(6.4) are all satisfied.

$$\sum_{\delta \in \Delta} S^{F}_{j,i,k,\delta} = 1 \; \forall j \in J, \forall i \in I, \forall k \in K \tag{6.1}$$

$S^{E}_{j,i,k,\delta}$ Represents the fraction of type k containers that, loaded empty at port i and discharged at port j, becomes available for utilization after δ periods of time, counted from the loading time at port i.

$$\sum_{\delta \in \Delta} S^{E}_{j,i,k,\delta} = 1 \; \forall j \in J, \forall i \in I, \forall k \in K \tag{6.2}$$

$L^{F}_{j,k,\delta}$ Represents the fraction of type k containers that, released for export at the empty-container terminal in port i, returns full to this port after δ periods, counted from the release time.

$$\sum_{\delta \in \Delta} L^{F}_{j,k,\delta} = 1 \; \forall j \in J, \forall k \in K \tag{6.3}$$

$L^{E}_{j,k,\delta}$ Represents the fraction of type k containers that, released for empty positioning at the empty container terminal of port i, returns empty to this port after δ periods, counted from the release time.

$$\sum_{\delta \in \Delta} L^{E}_{j,k,\delta} = 1 \text{ para } \forall j \in J, \forall k \in K \tag{6.4}$$

$P^X_{c,t}$ The maximum fraction of the Liner Carrier share of type c cargo in period t;

$P^I_{c,t}$ The minimum fraction of the Liner Carrier share of type c cargo in period t;

N^V The number of vessels allocated by the Liner Carrier to the route considered;

T^C The round trip time for the route, measured in periods of the set T; ($T^C = 1, 2, \ldots$)

N^T The vessel capacity in TEU;

N^D The vessel capacity in cargo deadweight;

N The maximum flow in TEU between consecutive ports. It is a function of the number of vessels and the round trip time for the route. The calculation of N is determined using the following formula:

$$N = \left(\frac{N^V \times N^T}{T^C}\right) \tag{6.5}$$

N^P The number of plugs for reefer containers in the vessel;

N^F The vessel capacity for 40′ container stowage;

N^E_i The storage capacity of empty containers, in TEU, in the port i;

N^C_k The fleet of type k containers;

Q_k The quantity of TEU occupied by one type k container;

$T^R_{t,\delta,t'}$ Represents those periods of index t' that are predecessors to the periods of index t. The parameter assumes the value one if the period of index t' possesses a relation of antecedence (represented by the index δ) to the index t, and assumes the value zero otherwise.

Decision Variables

The following are decision variables in the mathematical model proposed:

C^T Total contribution margin of freight for the evaluated system;

$F^F_{i,j,k,c,t}$ Quantity of full type k containers, with type c cargo, loaded at port i and discharged at port j, in period t;

$F^E_{i,j,k,t}$ Quantity of empty type k containers, loaded at port i and discharged at port j, in period t;

$E_{j,k,t}$ Quantity of empty type k containers, stored at port j, at the end of period t;

$R_{p,t}$ Quantity of TEU on board the vessel, at the entrance to the port of index p, in period t. It represents the sum of the full and empty containers on board;

$R^{SF}_{j,k,t}$ Quantity of empty type k containers, returned in period t to the empty-container terminal of port j, previously loaded at all ports of index i (this is a function of the parameter $S^F_{j,i,k,\delta}$). They are returned by the import clients;

$R^{SE}{}_{j,\,k,\,t}$ Quantity of empty type k containers, received in period t after an empty repositioning at the empty-container terminal at port j, previously having been loaded at any port i (it is a function of the parameter $S^{E}{}_{j,\,i,\,k,\,\delta}$);

$R^{LF}{}_{j,\,k,\,t}$ Quantity of empty type k containers released, for export clients, in period t at the empty-container terminal of port j;

$R^{LE}{}_{j,\,k,\,t}$ Quantity of empty type k containers released in period t at the empty-container terminal for repositioning at port j

Objective Function

$$C^T = \begin{bmatrix} \sum_{i\in I}\sum_{j\in J}\sum_{k\in K}\sum_{c\in C}\sum_{t\in T}\left(R^F_{i,j,k,c,t} \times F^F_{i,j,k,c,t}\right) - \\ \sum_{i\in I}\sum_{j\in J}\sum_{k\in K}\sum_{c\in C}\sum_{t\in T}\left(C^F_{i,j,k} \times F^F_{i,j,k,c,t}\right) - \\ \sum_{i\in I}\sum_{j\in J}\sum_{k\in K}\sum_{c\in C}\sum_{t\in T}\left(C^M_c \times F^F_{i,j,k,c,t}\right) - \\ \sum_{i\in I}\sum_{j\in J}\sum_{k\in K}\sum_{t\in T}\left(C^E_{i,j,k} \times F^E_{i,j,k,t}\right) - \\ \sum_{j\in J}\sum_{k\in K}\sum_{t\in T}\left(C^S_k \times E_{j,k,t}\right) \end{bmatrix} \tag{6.6}$$

The terms on the right side of Eq. (6.6) represent, from top to bottom, respectively, the revenue, the costs of loading and discharging full containers, costs to service the cargo types, the costs of loading and discharging empty containers, and costs to store empty containers.

Constraints

The decision variables are subject to the following constraints:

Maximum Share of the Liner Carrier in the cargo type, Constraint (6.7), sets an upper bound on the share that the carrier has of any cargo type.

$$F^F_{i,j,k,c,t} \leq \left\lfloor P^X_{c,t} \times D^F_{i,j,k,c,t} \right\rfloor \quad \text{for } \forall i \in I, \forall j \in J, \forall k \in K, \forall c \in C, \forall t \in T \tag{6.7}$$

The function $f(x) = \lfloor x \rfloor$ was used in Eq. (6.7), returning the greatest integer less than or equal to x. Minimum Share of the Liner Carrier in the cargo type, Constraint (6.8), imposes a lower bound on the share of cargo of type c.

$$F^{F}_{i,j,k,c,t} \geq \left\lfloor P^{I}_{c,t} \times D^{F}_{i,j,k,c,t} \right\rfloor$$
$$\text{for } \forall i \in I, \forall j \in J, \forall k \in K, \forall c \in C, \forall t \in T \tag{6.8}$$

Balance of empty containers at all ports of the route:

$$E_{j,k,t} = E_{j,k,t'} + R^{SF}_{j,k,t} + R^{SE}_{j,k,t} - R^{LF}_{j,k,t} - R^{LE}_{j,k,t}$$
$$\text{for } \forall j \in J, \forall k \in K, \forall t \in T, t' \middle| T^{R}_{t,\delta=1,t'} = 1 \tag{6.9}$$

The initial storage of empty containers is set free, to be chosen by the model.

Calculation of the number of empty containers returned from import status, Constraint (6.10), calculates how many empty containers were returned in period t by import clients, at each port j, for each container type k.

$$R^{SF}_{j,k,t} = \sum_{i \in I} \sum_{c \in C} \sum_{\delta \in \Delta} \sum_{t' \in T} \left(T^{R}_{t,\delta,t'} \times S^{F}_{j,i,k,\delta} \times F^{F}_{i,j,k,c,t'} \right)$$
$$\text{for } \forall j \in J, \forall k \in K, \forall t \in T \tag{6.10}$$

Determination of the number of empty containers received from empty container repositioning, Constraint (6.11), finds how many empty containers are available in period t after repositioning, at each port, for each container type.

$$R^{SE}_{j,k,t} = \sum_{i \in I} \sum_{\delta \in \Delta} \sum_{t' \in T} \left(T^{R}_{t,\delta,t'} \times S^{E}_{j,i,k,\delta} \times F^{E}_{i,j,k,t'} \right)$$
$$\text{for } \forall j \in J, \forall k \in K, \forall t \in T \tag{6.11}$$

Calculation of the number of empty containers released for export, Constraint (6.12), holds in any period t, at each port, for every container type.

$$R^{LF}_{j,k,t} = \sum_{i' \in I | i'=j} \sum_{j' \in J} \sum_{c \in C} \sum_{\delta \in \Delta} \sum_{t' \in T} \left(T^{R}_{t,\delta,t'} \times L^{F}_{j,k,\delta} \times F^{F}_{i',j',k,c,t'} \right)$$
$$\text{for } \forall j \in J, \forall k \in K, \forall t \in T \tag{6.12}$$

Calculation of the number of empty containers released for repositioning, Constraint (6.13), applies in period t, to each port i and container type k.

$$R^{LE}_{i,k,t} = \sum_{i' \in I} \sum_{j \in J | j'=i} \sum_{\delta \in \Delta} \sum_{t' \in T} \left(T^{R}_{t,\delta,t'} \times L^{E}_{i,k,\delta} \times F^{E}_{i',j,k,t'} \right)$$
$$\text{for } \forall i \in I, \forall k \in K, \forall t \in T \tag{6.13}$$

Maximum Storage, Constraint (6.14), limits the quantity of containers, in TEU, that can be stored at each port in any period.

$$\sum_{k\in K}\left(E_{j,k,t}\times Q_k\right)\leq N_j^E \quad \text{for } \forall j\in J, \forall t\in T \tag{6.14}$$

Flow Capacity, Constraint (6.15), enforces the maximum flow, in TEU, that the Liner Carrier is able to generate in the planning horizon. This maximum flow (N) in (6.16) is a function of the number of vessels and the round trip transit time of the route [see Eq. (6.5)].

$$R_{p,t}=\left[\begin{array}{l}\sum_{i\in I}\sum_{j\in J}\sum_{k\in K}\sum_{c\in C}\left(M_{p,i,j}\times Q_k\times F^F_{i,j,k,c,t}\right)+\\ \sum_{i\in I}\sum_{j\in J}\sum_{k\in K}\left(M_{p,i,j}\times Q_k\times F^E_{i,j,k,t}\right)\end{array}\right] \quad \text{for } \forall p\in P, \forall t\in T \tag{6.15}$$

$$R_{p,t}\leq N \quad \text{for } \forall p\in P, \forall t\in T \tag{6.16}$$

The maximum draft in the ports on each leg of the route is set by Constraint (6.17).

$$\left[\begin{array}{l}\sum_{i\in I}\sum_{j\in J}\sum_{k\in K}\sum_{c\in C}\left(M_{p,i,j}\times W^F_{k,c}\times F^F_{i,j,k,c,t}\right)\\ +\sum_{i\in I}\sum_{j\in J}\sum_{k\in K}\left(M_{p,i,j}\times W^E_k\times F^E_{i,j,k,t}\right)\end{array}\right]\leq \min\left\{\frac{N^V\times H_p}{T^C},\frac{N^V\times H_{p'}}{T^C}\right\} \quad \text{for } \forall p\in P, p'|\text{ predecessor of } p, \forall t\in T \tag{6.17}$$

The number of full reefer containers on board any vessel is limited, due to the quantity of electrical plugs for those containers on the vessel, by Constraint (6.18).

$$\sum_{i\in I}\sum_{j\in J}\sum_{k\in K^R}\sum_{c\in C}\left(M_{p,i,j}\times F^F_{i,j,k,c,t}\right)\leq\left(\frac{N^V\times N^P}{T^C}\right) \quad \text{for } \forall p\in P, \forall t\in T \tag{6.18}$$

The quantity of 40′ containers on board a vessel must obey the restriction (6.19), due to the stowage plan for this type of container.

$$\left[\begin{array}{l}\sum_{i\in I}\sum_{j\in J}\sum_{k\in K^F}\sum_{c\in C}\left(M_{p,i,j}\times F^F_{i,j,k,c,t}\right)+\\ \sum_{i\in I}\sum_{j\in J}\sum_{k\in K^F}\left(M_{p,i,j}\times F^E_{i,j,k,t}\right)\end{array}\right]\le\left(\frac{N^V\times N^F}{T^C}\right) \quad (6.19)$$

for $\forall p\in P,\forall t\in T$

Finally, the complicated constraint (6.20) limits the size of the container fleet, for each type of container.

$$\begin{aligned}&\sum_{i\in I}\sum_{j\in J}\sum_{c\in C}F^F_{i,j,k,c,t}+\sum_{i\in I}\sum_{j\in J}F^E_{i,j,k,t}+\sum_{i\in I}E_{i,k,t}+\\&\sum_{i\in I}\sum_{j\in J}\sum_{c\in C}\sum_{t'\in T|T^R_{t,\delta,t'}=1}\sum_{t''\in T|T^R_{t',\delta',t''}=1}\sum_{\delta\in\Delta|\delta>1,\ \delta<\Delta}\sum_{\delta'\in\Delta|\delta'>\delta}\begin{pmatrix}T^R_{t',\delta',t''}*\\S^F_{j,i,k,\delta'}*\\F^F_{i,j,k,c,t'}\end{pmatrix}+\\&\sum_{i\in I}\sum_{j\in J}\sum_{t'\in T|T^R_{t,\delta,t'}=1}\sum_{t''\in T|T^R_{t',\delta',t''}=1}\sum_{\delta\in\Delta|\delta>1,\ \delta<\Delta}\sum_{\delta'\in\Delta|\delta'>\delta}\begin{pmatrix}T^R_{t',\delta',t''}*\\S^E_{j,i,k,\delta'}*\\F^E_{i,j,k,t'}\end{pmatrix}+\\&\sum_{i\in I}\sum_{j\in J}\sum_{c\in C}\sum_{t'\in T|T^R_{t,\delta,t'}=1}\sum_{t''\in T|T^R_{t',\delta',t''}=1}\sum_{j'\in J|j'=i}\sum_{\delta\in\Delta|\delta>1,\ \delta<\Delta}\sum_{\delta'\in\Delta|\delta'>\delta}\begin{pmatrix}T^R_{t',\delta',t''}*\\L^F_{j',k,\delta'}*\\F^F_{i,j,k,c,t'}\end{pmatrix}+\\&\sum_{i\in I}\sum_{j\in J}\sum_{t'\in T|T^R_{t,\delta,t'}=1}\sum_{t''\in T|T^R_{t',\delta',t''}=1}\sum_{j'\in J|j'=i}\sum_{\delta\in\Delta|\delta>1,\ \delta<\Delta}\sum_{\delta'\in\Delta|\delta'>\delta}\begin{pmatrix}T^R_{t',\delta',t''}*\\L^E_{j',k,\delta'}*\\F^E_{i,j,k,t'}\end{pmatrix}\\&\le N^C_k,\ \text{ for } \forall k\in K,\forall t\in T\end{aligned} \quad (6.20)$$

The summation groups on the left of Eq. (6.20) represent, respectively, the number of full containers on board; the quantity of empty containers on board; the number of empty containers stored at the ports; the quantity of full import containers in the ports and not yet returned empty; the amount of empty containers discharged from repositioning and not yet available; the number of empty containers released for export and not yet loaded full; and the quantity of empty containers released for repositioning, but not yet loaded.

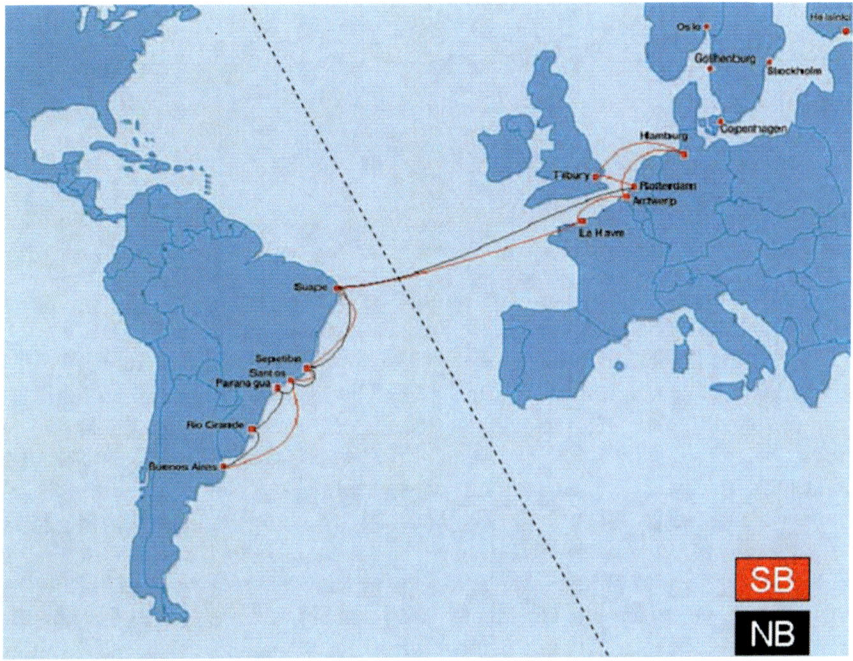

Fig. 6.5 Illustration of the route analyzed

6.4 Results

The evaluation was performed by comparing two alternatives: the current scenario, where the international route is operated the traditional way, with loading/unloading of only international cargo (base scenario—CB); and the integration of international and domestic freight (FF set of scenarios). Because the one degree of freedom for the Liner Carrier Company is the price for short sea transportation, nine different levels of the cabotage freight price (one for each FF scenario) were determined and compared to the base scenario.

6.4.1 Base Scenario

The base scenario represents an actual route that the company operates today, and it is thus used as a point of comparison. Figure 6.5 illustrates the route analyzed in that scenario.

This route has two bearings and eleven ports of call. Five ports are located in Europe and six in Latin America. The direction defined as Southbound (SB)

Table 6.1 Characteristics of the vessel fleet considered by the model

Type	Value	Unit
Quantity	6	Vessel
Entire voyage duration	42	Days
Capacity in TEU	1,850	TEU
Capacity (deadweight)	27,000	Tons
Capacity of plugs	264	Plugs
Capacity of 40 feet	550	Containers

represents voyages from Northern Europe to the east coast of Latin America. Northbound (NB) naturally indicates voyages in the opposite direction.

Four container types are considered. The type is classified according to two criteria: container size (20 or 40 feet) and cargo type (dry or reefer). To fulfill the route demand, the company employs a six-vessel fleet, which has weekly calls at every port. The detailed characteristics of the vessels are presented in Table 6.1.

"Entire Voyage" denotes the time necessary for the vessel to cover (call at) all the ports involved. The vessel fleet considered in the mathematical model is homogeneous. Each vessel has the same characteristics, which can be described in a general way by four different capacities: maximum number of containers that can be transported (Capacity in TEU), maximum number of reefer containers possible (Capacity of plugs), maximum number of 40 foot containers that can be transported (Capacity of 40 feet) and, finally, maximum weight that can be accommodated by the vessel (Capacity deadweight).

The cargo types considered in this study involve the two-digit code of the "Codigo Harmonizado de Mercadorias" (Merchandise Harmonization Codes), present in the DATALINER (2006) database. The transport demand for international cargoes, over the planning horizon, was gathered from this database. The mathematical model works with 12 time periods in months of 30 days (T_01 to T_12), which characterizes the planning horizon.

6.4.2 *Series FF*

A number of scenarios here analyze how a gradual decrease in cabotage freight rates influences the attractiveness of shipborne cargo. In other words, this series aims to determine the lowest cabotage freight rates that could be offered, yet still contribute positively to the overall margin of the company.

Nine scenarios were determined and studied. In each, the cabotage freight rates are gradually reduced, from current long distance (truck) prices (zero reduction) to an 80 % reduction, in steps of 10 %. The initial scenario of this series, scenario FF-00, considers cabotage freight rates equal to the road transport freight rates estimated in the first step of the methodology. Further scenarios therefore consider a gradual decrease in those cabotage rates, which means that eventually cabotage freight costs 20 % of truck freight for the same origin–destination.

Table 6.2 Indicators: Comparison between CB and FF-00 (Financial figures in thousands of US Dollars)

Financial indicators	CB	FF-00	Variation (FF-CB) %
Contribution margin	221,297	252,164	14.0
Total revenue	283,154	358,809	26.7
Total variable cost	61,858	106,545	72.2
Description of the variable costs	**CB**	**FF-00**	**Variation**
Cost of loading and discharging full containers	52,205	93,003	78.1
Cost of cargo service	1,622	1,578	−2.7
Cost of loading and discharging empty containers	7,862	11,874	51.2
Cost of container storage	179	90	−49.6
Share of each cost in total variable cost	**CB (%)**	**FF-00 (%)**	**Variation (%)**
Cost of loading and discharging full containers	84.8	87.3	3.4
Cost of cargo holding	2.6	1.5	−43.5
Cost of loading and discharging empty containers	12.7	11.1	−12.2
Cost of container storage	0.3	0.1	−70.7

The introduction of cabotage demand directly implies an increase in container fleet size, generating an increase in costs as well. These costs are therefore considered in calculating each financial indicator for this series of scenarios.

Comparison of financial indicators

Table 6.2 compares those indicators obtained from the base-scenario, CB, with those of FF-00. Note that this first scenario considers cabotage freight rates to be equal to the average road freight rates that are currently available in the Brazilian transportation market.

It is important to emphasize the difficulties that cabotage transport companies would face in offering freight rates equal to those for road transport: Cabotage clients would also have to pay for inland transportation. Clients who want to transport a certain cargo by sea have to consider the freight rates for inland transport between the cargo's origin and its port of departure, as well as between its port of arrival and final destination. Thus, the FF-00 scenario defines an upper bound for potential profits of the Liner Shipping carrier.

The FF series turns out to be somewhat interesting. It is necessary for the carrier to determine a lower bound on the quantity of cabotage freight that can be transported, so that this freight can continue to be attractive for the company. By determining the attractiveness of cabotage cargo, the carrier is able to verify the freight rate that should be offered to clients. It is then possible to analyze the prices and service levels, to verify the company's competitiveness in the transport market.

Table 6.2 shows that the transport of cabotage cargo in long-distance vessels improves the logistics of transporting containers, reducing the variable costs of repositioning and stocking empty containers (by 12.2 and 70.7 %, respectively). Moreover, cabotage transport reveals itself to be a great revenue generator (potential increase of 26.7 %). Figure 6.6 demonstrates that even a sharp reduction

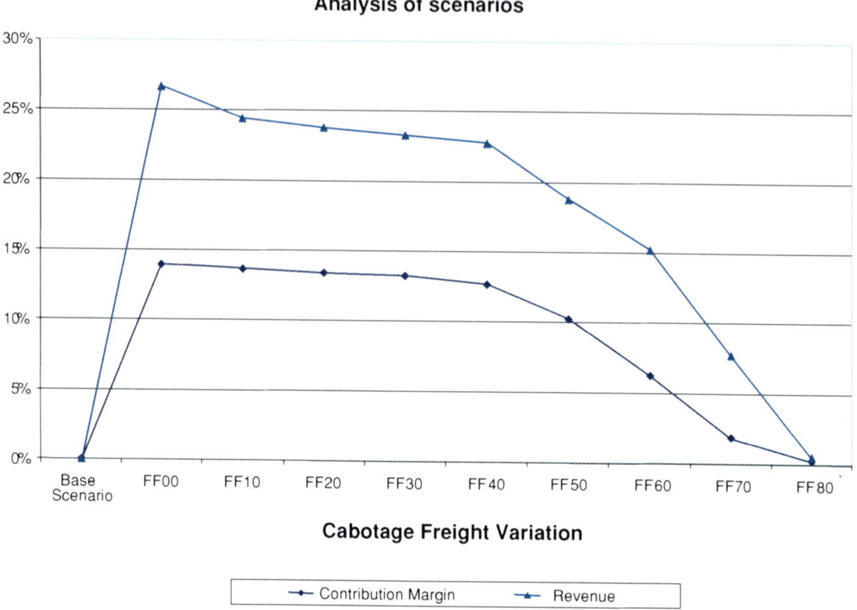

Fig. 6.6 Variation in contribution margin and revenue due to reduction of cabotage freight rates

in cabotage freight rates diminishes the attractiveness of only a portion of cabotage cargoes for the company. Some cabotage cargo continues to contribute positively to the contribution margin of that firm.

Utilization indicators

These indicators enable analysis of the vessel's degrees of idleness. Indicators related to participation of the cabotage cargoes are not considered for the base-case scenario (CB) because, naturally, there is no cabotage demand in it. The base scenario is run to reproduce the company's current operations.

These indicators are shown in a table whose rows represent the port of entrance of the vessel, and where the columns denote the time period considered. The sequence of rows, from top to bottom, indicates the vessel route.

Table 6.3 demonstrates the vessel performance in its Latin America-Europe trajectory, proceeding from the port of Suape (NB_SUA) to the port of Rotterdam (SB_RTM), utilizing its full capacity, in deadweight, for all time periods considered (row SB_RTM of Table 6.3). However, in the opposite direction of voyage, Europe—Latin America, the vessel does not use its full transport capacity, in deadweight, as presented in row SB_SUA of that table.

Another important characteristic is shown in rows NB_SSZ and NB_SPV. It is demonstrated that the port of Santos has a huge share of the export of cargo, unbalancing the transport flows, and causing idleness of vessels on particular legs, represented mainly by the shaded cells of Table 6.3.

Table 6.3 Utilization of vessel capacity, regarding the weight transported, for the base-case scenario (all entries in %)

Port of entry	T_01	T_02	T_03	T_04	T_05	T_06	T_07	T_08	T_09	T_10	T_11	T_12
SB_RTM	100	100	100	100	100	100	100	100	100	100	100	100
SB_TIL	76	76	75	75	76	75	81	77	77	77	78	77
SB_HAM	74	75	73	73	73	72	78	76	75	75	75	74
SB_ANR	67	70	58	69	68	67	73	71	69	69	70	69
SB_LEH	79	81	78	78	81	77	82	81	77	77	77	78
SB_SUA	78	81	76	77	80	76	81	80	76	76	76	75
SB_SPB	76	79	74	76	78	74	78	79	74	74	74	75
SB_SSZ	74	76	72	73	75	72	74	75	71	71	71	72
NB_BUF	58	57	58	61	57	64	61	55	55	55	58	58
NB_RIG	36	37	34	41	39	37	41	37	33	33	38	39
NB_PNG	38	40	36	42	41	39	43	41	33	33	44	40
NB_SSZ	39	42	38	45	43	41	45	44	36	36	45	42
NB_SPV	92	94	94	92	91	92	92	91	91	88	90	90
NB_SUA	98	99	99	97	98	98	98	98	97	97	98	98

lower than 50% | between 50% to 90% | Higher than 90%

Table 6.4 Utilization of vessel capacity, regarding the weight transported, for the scenario FF-00 (all entries in %)

Port of entry	T_01	T_02	T_03	T_04	T_05	T_06	T_07	T_08	T_09	T_10	T_11	T_12
SB_RTM	100	100	100	100	100	100	100	100	100	100	100	100
SB_TIL	75	74	72	73	74	73	77	75	77	76	76	75
SB_HAM	73	74	71	71	73	70	75	74	75	75	75	73
SB_ANR	64	69	66	66	67	65	68	68	69	69	69	66
SB_LEH	75	81	79	76	82	75	79	79	80	77	77	78
SB_SUA	73	80	76	75	79	74	78	78	79	75	75	77
SB_SPB	73	79	77	74	78	72	78	77	78	74	74	76
SB_SSZ	71	75	73	68	75	69	72	73	72	71	71	71
NB_BUF	100	100	100	100	100	100	100	100	100	100	100	100
NB_RIG	71	69	70	72	72	73	68	70	69	66	68	70
NB_PNG	94	94	94	93	93	97	93	94	96	87	94	95
NB_SSZ	96	98	96	95	95	99	98	98	97	92	96	97
NB_SPV	96	99	99	95	95	98	95	93	99	95	96	97
NB_SUA	99	99	100	97	97	99	98	97	100	99	98	99

lower than 50% | between 50% to 90% | Higher than 90%

The fact that European legs lower vessel utilization (Table 6.4) can be explained by the types of freight exported from Europe. Usually, these goods are lighter than those exported by Latin America countries, and moreover, there is a need to reposition empty containers in Latin America because of imbalance.

Comparison of logistic indicators

All logistic indicators were calculated for each scenario in series FF. Table 6.5 compares those indicators from the base-scenario with those obtained in series FF-00.

It is important to remark that the previous analysis, concerning the variation of contribution margin and total revenue, considered growth in the container fleet; related costs were calculated for each type of container.

Table 6.5 Logistic indicators: comparison between CB and FF-00

	Container type	CB	FF-00	Variation (%)
Fleet size	K20_D	7,127	10,616	49.0
	K20_R	1,735	2,676	54.2
	K40_D	6,580	7,293	10.8
	K40_R	932	1,355	45.4
Percentages	K20_D	45.5	48.4	11.2
	K20_R	10.6	12.2	15.1
	K40_D	40.2	33.2	−17.3
	K40_R	5.7	6.2	8.5
Productivity index	K20_D	8.93	10.64	19.1
	K20_R	5.63	9.34	65.8
	K40_D	9.29	10.51	13.2
	K40_R	6.52	8.38	28.6
Stock indices (%)	K20_D	17.6	3.3	−81.2
	K20_R	15.9	3.0	−80.9
	K40_D	21.3	12.5	41.6
	K40_R	70.7	34.5	51.1
Repositioning index	K20_D	1.42	1.89	32.8
	K20_R	4.59	3.00	−34.6
	K40_D	1.89	1.53	−19.1
	K40_R	3.28	3.00	−8.5

Table 6.5 shows that the container productivity indices for the FF-00 scenario increase for all types of containers, while the container stock and repositioning indices decrease for each type.

Considerations about the FF series

It is important to emphasize that the carrier's strategy is to fulfill cabotage demand by making use of idle or marginal capacity of long-distance vessels. Even if cabotage freight rates were 70 % cheaper than road transport rates, cabotage freight would have contributed positively to the company's contribution margin. By transporting cabotage cargo in long-distance vessels, the company is able to improve vessel utilization, both in volume and in weight, mainly due to a better balancing of cargo transport flows.

Cabotage freight rates are stated in Brazilian currency (Real), while long-distance transport services have their freight rates indicated in USD (dollars). In the case of a variation in exchange rates and depreciation of the Brazilian currency, cabotage cargo becomes less attractive. However, with an appreciation of the national currency, cabotage demand becomes even more attractive. In addition, foreign exchange variations greatly impact the flows of international shipment because they directly affect the imports and exports of a country.

6.5 Conclusions

The transport of cabotage cargo by vessels that operate on long-distance routes was shown to be feasible and also capable of providing financial, productive and logistical improvements to a carrier. Our analysis demonstrates that an increase in combinations of cargo flows, due to cabotage transport demand, generates important synergies for the company's business. The utilizations of vessel capacity and container productivity are both increased, resulting in improvements to cost structure, and especially enhancing revenues generated from cabotage. The firm is thus able to offer cabotage at very competitive freight rates.

Recall the difference in currencies, in which the freight rates of long-distance services are given in USD, while cabotage services are in Real. The carrier should thus pay attention to exchange volatility. It is necessary to adopt a "protectionist" strategy aimed at reducing losses caused by this variation.

Admittedly, the analyses presented here do not consider other characteristics of each mode of transport, such as safety, transit time, and costs of inland transport before and after sea transport. Nevertheless, the significant difference in freight rates between the two modes indicates the importance of this study.

With the integration of cabotage cargo on long-distance routes, the comparative importance of the costs for moving empty containers decreases. Some flows of empty-container repositioning are substitutes for cabotage cargo, generating revenue for the company.

References

ANTAQ—Agência Nacional de Transportes Aquaviários (National Agency of Water Transportation) (2005) Anuário Estatístico da Navegação Marítima—2005 (Annual Maritime Navigation Statistical Report). Brasília, ANTAQ. Available at: www.antaq.gov.br accessed on 10 Jun 2010

ANTAQ—Agência Nacional de Transportes Aquaviários (National Agency of Water Transportation) (2009). Anuário Estatístico da Navegação Marítima—2009 (Annual Maritime Navigation Statistical Report). Brasília, ANTAQ. Available at: www.antaq.gov.br accessed on 10 Jun 2010

Aversa R, Botter RC, Haralambides HE, Yoshizaki HTY (2005) A mixed integer programming model on the location of a hub port in the East Coast of South America. Marit Economics Logistics 7(1):1–18. doi: 10.1057/palgrave.mel.9100121

CNT—Confederação Nacional do Transporte (Brazilian Confederacy of Transportation Syndicates) (2002). Pesquisa Aquaviários CNT 2002—Relatório Analítico (Water transportation Survey CNT 2002—Analytical Report). Brasília, CNT. Available at: www.cnt.org.br accessed on 10 Jun 2010

CNT—Confederação Nacional do Transporte (Brazilian Confederacy of Transportation Syndicates) (2006). Pesquisa Aquaviários CNT 2006—Portos Marítimo: Longo Curso e Cabotagem (Water transportation survey CNT 2006—Maritime ports: long haul and cabotage). Brasília, CNT. Available at: www.cnt.org.br accessed on 10 Jun 2010

Costa GAA,Brinati MA, Hino CM (2009) Contribution margin model applied to the marketing planning of a container liner carrier. Proc Inst Mech Eng Part M J Eng Marit Environ 223(1):63–90. doi: 10.1243/14750902JEME109

DATALINER (2006) Plate area foreign trade statistics system 2006 and Brazil foreign trade statistics system 2006

IPEA—Instituto de Pesquisa Econômica Aplicada (Institute of Applied Economics) (2005) Perspectiva do crescimento do transporte por cabotagem no Brasil (Perspectives for the growth of short sea shipping in Brazil). Brasília, IPEA, p 37

Ministry of Transportation, Brazil (2009). Plano Nacional de Logística e Transportes—PNLT (National Plan for Logistics and Transportation). http://www.transportes.gov.br/PNLT/CD_RE/Index.htm accessed 30 July 2010

Ono RT (2001) Estudo de viabilidade do transporte marítimo de contêineres por cabotagem na costa brasileira (Economic feasibility analysis of container short sea shipping in the Brazilian coast), p 132. M.Sc. Thesis. Department of Naval Engineering, University of São Paulo

SYNDARMA—Sindicato Nacional das Empresas de Navegação Marítima (Syndicate of Brazilian Maritime Shipping Companies) (2009) http://www.syndarma.org.br/index.php accessed 30 July 2010

Chapter 7
Latin American Logistics and Supply Chain Management: Perspective from the Research Literature

James H. Bookbinder and Paul Mant

Abstract This article aims to classify and critique the research and applications that have been conducted concerning supply chain management and logistics in Latin America. We assess the countries in Central and South America according to their capabilities in transportation infrastructure and various demographic and economic characteristics. A third objective is to identify additional research opportunities. Use of a variety of scientific databases covering major journals in logistics, supply chain management, transportation, and the management sciences led to an original list of 250 references. That was reduced to about 90, the great majority from 1997 onward. These were appraised and categorized along multiple dimensions. While the countries in Latin America are quite diverse, and a number of impediments to logistics exist, various regional trading blocs are facilitating progress in supply chains there. Five "lessons for business decisions" are emphasized which will aid companies that operate within, or may become part of, a Latin American supply chain. Moreover, summaries of the pertinent facts and country characteristics on infrastructure, trade, etc. enable us to identify top-performing nations as possible points of strategic entry, for a global firm wishing to conduct operations in Central America or in South America. Finally, several Propositions on Latin American logistics are formulated and proposed for future empirical testing.

Research supported by the Natural Sciences and Engineering Research Council of Canada. It is a pleasure to thank Tiffany Matuk and Tracy Kong for their assistance in updating the references and data.

J. H. Bookbinder (✉)
Department of Management Sciences, University of Waterloo, Waterloo, ON N2L 3G1, Canada
e-mail: jbookbin@uwaterloo.ca

P. Mant
Canadian Pacific Railway (Domestic Intermodal), Mississauga, ON L5C 4R3, Canada

J. H. Bookbinder (ed.), *Handbook of Global Logistics*, International Series in Operations Research & Management Science 181, DOI: 10.1007/978-1-4419-6132-7_7,

7.1 Introduction

Latin America is fascinating in so many ways. Large territories are often rich in resources. Striking contrasts exist between big cities and rural lands, and between wealthy and poor. (See, e.g. Encyclopedia Britannica Inc 2010)

A glance at a map suggests that Central America and South America are obvious extensions of the NAFTA domain. Implementation of the North American Free Trade Agreement has led to enhanced trade between the countries involved, i.e. Canada, the United States and Mexico. Interest in Latin America certainly preceded NAFTA. However, that agreement has motivated increased enthusiasm about the remainder of the Americas. Indeed, there has even been some talk about a possible FTAA (Free Trade Area of the Americas).

The present chapter adopts the perspective of academic literature, and has three goals or objectives. First, we summarize important background material on Latin America and the state of research in Logistics. This would lay the groundwork for a more fundamental study of issues pertinent to FTAA, by improving researchers' knowledge of logistics applications there.

The extremes in Latin America are far greater than within the NAFTA region. A second goal here is thus to discuss the countries in Latin America according to their transportation infrastructure and various demographic and economic characteristics (Tables 7.1 and 7.2), and to understand the extent of the published literature on Central and South American supply chains and logistics. In doing so, we must recognize that many other issues constrain logistics activities, or modify the form that those functions can take.

Our third objective in this work is to propose additional research. Based upon the literature review, we identify missing themes and raise new research questions. Particular application areas, where normative modeling could be done to support the empirical research already carried out, are indicated. We also formulate several propositions on Latin American Logistics that should be tested empirically.

Zinn (1996) notes that "Latin America" traditionally means the Spanish- or Portuguese-speaking countries in the American continent, hence excludes e.g. Belize, Guyana, Suriname and Haiti. We have thus omitted these nations from Tables 7.1 and 7.2, and have carefully listed in the captions to the maps (Figs. 7.1 and 7.2) only those countries to which our review pertains. With the preceding clarifications, however, no confusion should result when for variety we refer to (South America + Central America) as Latin America.

Table 7.1 presents some pertinent facts or data on South American Countries; Table 7.2 does the same for Central America and the Caribbean. Tables 7.1 and 7.2, although fairly detailed, are introduced this early in our chapter for several reasons. Consider the discussion of an article whose application takes place in Argentina, say. While reading those paragraphs, the reader may wish to consult Table 7.1 on the significance of the particular industry in that country. Are the products involved the major ones for import or export? Are the countries in the given supply chain the prominent trading partners of Argentina?

Table 7.1 South America

Country	Area (000 km^2)	Population (Millions)	Population below the poverty line (%)	GDP (Billions of US$)[a]	GDP (Thousands US$) per Capita[a]	Inflation rate (% Increase in CPI)[a]	GDP % composition by sector[a]	Major industries
Argentina	2,780	41.8	30 (2010)	596	14.7	22 % 16 % (2009)	Agriculture: 8.5 Industry: 31.6 Services: 59.8	Food processing, motor vehicles, consumer durables, textiles, chemicals and petrochemicals, printing, metallurgy, steel
Bolivia	1,098	10.1	30.3 (2009)	47.88	4.8	2.5 % 3.3 % (2009)	Agriculture: 12.0 Industry: 38.0 Services: 50.0	Mining, smelting, petroleum, food and beverages, tobacco, handicrafts, clothing
Brazil	8,515	203.4	26 (2008)	2,172	10.8	5.0 % 4.9 % (2009)	Agriculture: 5.8 Industry: 26.8 Services: 67.4	Textiles, shoes, chemicals, cement, lumber, iron ore, tin, steel, aircraft, motor vehicles and parts, other machinery and equipment
Chile	757	16.9	11.5 (2009)	257.9	15.4	1.4 % 1.5 % (2009)	Agriculture: 5.1 Industry: 41.8 Services: 53.1	Copper, lithium, other minerals, foodstuffs, fish processing, iron and steel, wood and wood products, transport equipment, cement, textiles
Colombia	1,139	44.7	45.5 (2009)	435.4	9.8	2.3 % 4.2 % (2009)	Agriculture: 9.2 Industry: 37.6 Services: 53.1	Textiles, food processing, oil, clothing and footwear, beverages, chemicals, cement, gold, coal, emeralds

(continued)

Table 7.1 (continued)

Country	Major exporting partners (%)[a]	Export commodities	Major importing partners (%)[a]	Import commodities	Railways (1,000 km)[a]	Highways (1,000 km)[a]	Waterways (km)[a]	Airports[a]
Argentina	Brazil 21.2 China 9.1 Chile 7.0 US 5.4	Soybean and derivatives, petroleum and gas, vehicles, corn, wheat	Brazil 34.5 US 13.8 China 11.4 Germany 5.0	Machinery, motor vehicles, petroleum and natural gas, organic chemicals, plastics	Total: 37.0 Broad gauge: 26.5 Standard gauge: 2.8 Narrow gauge: 7.7	Total: 231.4 Paved: 69.4 Unpaved: 162.0 (2004)	11,000	Total: 1,141 Paved: 156 Unpaved: 985
Bolivia	Brazil 43.5 US 12.3 Peru 6.8 Columbia 5.5 Japan 5.1 Argentina 4.8	Natural gas, soybeans and soy products, crude petroleum, zinc ore, tin	Brazil 27.4 Argentina 17.3 US 11.9 Peru 9.6 Chile 7.8 China 4.1	Petroleum products, plastics, paper, aircraft and aircraft parts, prepared foods, automobiles, insecticide, soybeans	Total: 3.7 Narrow gauge: 3.7	Total: 13.6 Paved: 5.0 Unpaved: 8.6 (2004)	10,000	Total: 881 Paved: 16 Unpaved: 865
Brazil	China 15.2 US 9.6 Argentina 9.2 Netherlands 5.1 Germany 4.0	Transport equipment, iron ore, soybeans, footwear, coffee, autos	US 15.0 China 14.1 Argentina 7.9 Germany 6.9 South Korea 4.6	Machinery, electrical and transport equipment, chemical products, oil, automobile parts, electronics	Total: 28.5 Broad gauge: 5.6 Standard gauge: 0.2 Narrow gauge: 22.7	Total: 1,752 Paved: 96 Unpaved: 1,655 (2004)	50,000	Total: 4,072 Paved: 726 Unpaved: 3,346

(continued)

Table 7.1 (continued)

Country	Major exporting partners (%)[a]	Export commodities	Major importing partners (%)[a]	Import commodities	Railways (1,000 km)[a]	Highways (1,000 km)[a]	Waterways (km)[a]	Airports[a]
Chile	China 23.8 Japan 10.2 US 10.0 Brazil 6.0 South Korea 5.9	Copper, fruit, fish products, paper and pulp, chemicals, wine	US 17.0 China 13.6 Argentina 8.5 Brazil 7.9 South Korea 5.8 Japan 5.0 Germany 4.0	Petroleum and petroleum products, chemicals, electrical and telecommunications equipment, industrial machinery, vehicles, natural gas	Total: 7.1 Broad gauge: 3.4 Narrow gauge: 3.6	Total: 80.5 Paved: 16.7 Unpaved: 63.8 (2004)	N/A	Total: 366 Paved: 84 Unpaved: 282
Colombia	US 42 EU 12.6 China 5.2 Ecuador 4.5	Petroleum, coffee, coal, nickel, emeralds, apparel, bananas, cut flowers	US 25.5 China 13.4 Mexico 9.4 Brazil 5.9 Germany 4.1	Industrial equipment, transportation equipment, consumer goods, chemicals, paper products, fuels, electricity	Total: 0.874 Standard gauge: 0.15 Narrow gauge: 0.724	Total: 141.4 Paved: N/A Unpaved: N/A	18,000	Total: 990 Paved: 116 Unpaved: 874

(continued)

Table 7.1 (continued)

Country	Area (000 km^2)	Population (Millions)	Population below the poverty line (%)	GDP (Billions of US$)[a]	GDP (Thousands US$) per Capita[a]	Inflation rate (% Increase in CPI)[a]	GDP % composition by sector[a]	Major industries
Ecuador	283	15.0	33.1 (2010)	115	7.8	3.6 % 5.2 % (2009)	Agriculture: 6.4 Industry: 35.9 Services: 57.7	Petroleum, food processing, textiles, wood products, chemicals
Paraguay	407	6.5	18.1 (2009)	33.31	5.2	4.7 % 2.6 % (2009)	Agriculture: 21.8 Industry: 18.2 Services: 60.1	Sugar, cement, textiles, beverages, wood products, steel, metallurgic, electric power
Peru	1,285	29.2	34.8 (2009)	275.7	9.2	1.5 % 2.0 % (2009)	Agriculture: 10.0 Industry: 25.0 Services: 55.0	Mining and refining of minerals and metals, steel, metal fabrication, petroleum extraction and refining, natural gas, natural gas liquefaction, fishing and fish processing, cement, textiles, clothing, food processing

(continued)

Table 7.1 (continued)

Country	Area (000 km^2)	Population (Millions)	Population below the poverty line (%)	GDP (Billions of US$)[a]	GDP (Thousands US$) per Capita[a]	Inflation rate (% Increase in CPI)[a]	GDP % composition by sector[a]	Major industries
Uruguay	176	3.3	20.9 (2009)	47.99	13.7	6.7 % 7.1 % (2009)	Agriculture: 9.2 Industry: 22.3 Services: 68.5	Food processing, electrical machinery, transportation equipment, petroleum products, textiles, chemicals, beverages
Venezuela	912	27.6	37.9 (2005)	345.2	12.7	28.2 % 27.1 % (2009)	Agriculture: 4.0 Industry: 36.0 Services: 60.0	Petroleum, construction materials, food processing, textiles, iron ore mining, steel, aluminum, motor vehicle assembly

(continued)

Table 7.1 (continued)

Country	Major exporting partners (%)[a]	Export commodities	Major importing partners (%)[a]	Import commodities	Railways (1,000 km)[a]	Highways (1,000 km)[a]	Waterways (km)[a]	Airports[a]
Ecuador	US 37.3 Panama 13.0 Peru 6.2 Columbia 4.5 Chile 4.2 Russia 4.2	Petroleum, bananas, cut flowers, shrimp, cacao, coffee, wood, fish	US 29.6 Columbia 9.3 China 8.1 Venezuela 5.9 Brazil 5.3 Venezuela 5.3	Industrial materials, fuels and lubricants, nondurable consumer goods	Total: 0.965 Narrow gauge: 0.965	Total: 43.7 Paved: 6.5 Unpaved: 37.2 (2007)	1,500	Total: 428 Paved: 105 Unpaved: 323
Paraguay	Uruguay 16.2 Brazil 12.8 Chile 10.0 Argentina 8.1 Italy 5.0 Netherlands 4.4 Spain 4.3 Turkey 4.2 Germany 4.2	Soybeans, feed, cotton, meat, edible oils, electricity, wood, leather	Brazil 27.7 China 17.6 US 16.6 Argentina 15.2	Road vehicles, consumer goods, tobacco, petroleum products, electrical machinery, tractors, chemicals, vehicle parts	Total: 0.036 Narrow gauge: 0.036	Total: 29.5 Paved: 15.0 Unpaved: 14.5 (2001)	3,100	Total: 800 Paved: 15 Unpaved: 785
Peru	China 18.4 US 16.1 Canada 11.7 Japan 6.6 Germany 4.5 Spain 4.0	Copper, gold, zinc, tin, iron ore, molybdenum; crude petroleum and petroleum products, natural gas; coffee, potatoes, asparagus and other vegetables, fruit, apparel and textiles, fishmeal	US 24.7 China 13.0 Brazil 7.4 Ecuador 4.7 Chile 4.3 Colombia 4.2	Petroleum and petroleum products, chemicals, plastics, machinery, vehicles, color TV sets, power shovels, front-end loaders, telephones and telecommunication equipment, iron and steel, wheat, corn, soybean products, paper, cotton, vaccines and medicines	Total: 2.02 Standard gauge: 1.89 Narrow gauge: 0.13	Total: 102.89 Paved: N/A Unpaved: N/A (2007)	8,808	Total: 211 Paved: 58 Unpaved: 153

(continued)

Table 7.1 (continued)

Country	Major exporting partners (%)[a]	Export commodities	Major importing partners (%)[a]	Import commodities	Railways (1,000 km)[a]	Highways (1,000 km)[a]	Waterways (km)[a]	Airports[a]
Uruguay	Brazil 21.0 Nueva Palmira Free Zone 10.2 Argentina 7.5 Chile 5.5 Russia 5.3	Beef, soybeans, cellulose, rice, wheat, wood, dairy products, wool	Argentina 18.6 Brazil 16.7 China 13.5 Venezuela 9.1 US 8.3 Russia 4.2	Crude oil, refined oil, passenger vehicles, transportation vehicles, vehicles parts, cellular phones, insecticides	Total: 1.6 Standard gauge: 1.6	Total: 77.7 Paved: 7.7 Unpaved: 69.9	1,600	Total: 58 Paved: 9 Unpaved: 49
Venezuela	US 38.7 China 7.7 India 4.8 Cuba 4.1	Petroleum, bauxite and aluminum, minerals, chemicals, agricultural products, basic manufactures	US 26.6 Colombia 11.4 Brazil 9.6 China 9.1	Agricultural products, raw materials, machinery and equipment, transport equipment, construction materials	Total: 0.806 Standard gauge: 0.806	Total: 96.2 Paved: 32.3 Unpaved: 63.9 (2002)	7,100	Total: 409 Paved: 129 Unpaved: 280

Data for this table based on US Central Intelligence Agency, The World Factbook, as of October 13, 2011
(That source for Tables 7.1 and 7.2 also contains many other facts not relevant to the present paper.)
[a] 2010, unless specified otherwise

Table 7.2 Central America and the Caribbean

Country	Area (000 km^2)	Population (Millions)	Population below the poverty line (%)	GDP (Billions of US$)[a]	GDP (Thousands US$) per Capita[a]	Inflation rate (% Increase in CPI)[a]	GDP % composition by sector[a]	Major industries
Costa Rica	51.1	4.6	16 (2006)	51.17	11.3	5.7 % 7.8 % (2009)	Agriculture: 6.5 Industry: 22.5 Services: 71.0	Microprocessors, food processing, medical equipment, textiles and clothing, construction materials, fertilizer, plastic products
Cuba	111	11.0	N/A	114.1	9.9	2.9 % 1.4 % (2009)	Agriculture: 4.0 Industry: 21.8 Services: 74.2	Sugar, petroleum, tobacco, construction, nickel, steel, cement, agricultural machinery, pharmaceuticals
Dominican Republic	48.7	9.9	42.2 (2004)	87.25	8.9	6.3 % 1.4 % (2009)	Agriculture: 7.1 Industry: 28.3 Services: 64.6	Tourism, sugar processing, ferronickel and gold mining, textiles, cement, tobacco
Guatemala	109	13.8	56.2 (2004)	70.15	5.2	3.9 % 1.9 % (2009)	Agriculture: 13.2 Industry: 23.8 Services: 63.0	Sugar, textiles and clothing, furniture, chemicals, petroleum, metals, rubber, tourism

(continued)

Table 7.2 (continued)

Country	Area (000 km^2)	Population (Millions)	Population below the poverty line (%)	GDP (Billions of US$)[a]	GDP (Thousands US$) per Capita[a]	Inflation rate (% Increase in CPI)[a]	GDP % composition by sector[a]	Major industries
Mexico	1,973	113.7	18.2 (2008)[a]	1,567	13.9	4.2 % 5.3 % (2009	Agriculture: 3.9 Industry: 32.6 Services: 63.5	Food and beverages, tobacco, chemicals, iron and steel, petroleum, mining, textiles, clothing, motor vehicles, consumer durables, tourism
Nicaragua	103.3	5.7	48 (2005)	17.71	3.0	5.5 % 3.7 % (2009)	Agriculture: 18.5 Industry: 25.9 Services: 55.6	Food processing, chemicals, machinery and metal products, knit and woven apparel, petroleum, refining and distribution, beverages, footwear, wood
Panama	75.4	3.5	25.6 (2010)	44.36	13.0	3.5 % 2.5 % (2009)	Agriculture: 4.6 Industry: 16.7 Services: 78.7	Construction, brewing, cement and other construction materials, sugar milling
Puerto Rico	13.8	4.0	N/A	64.84	16.3	2.5 %	Agriculture: 1.0 Industry: 45.0 Services: 54.0 (2005)	Pharmaceuticals, electronics, apparel, food products, tourism

(continued)

Table 7.2 (continued)

Country	Major exporting partners (%)[a]	Export commodities	Major importing partners (%)[a]	Import commodities	Railways (1,000 km)[a]	Highways (1,000 km)[a]	Waterways (km)[a]	Airports[a]
Costa Rica	US 33.6 Netherlands 11.7 China 11.7 UK 11.5	Bananas, pineapples, coffee, melons, ornamental plants, sugar, beef, seafood, electronic components, medical equipment	US 40.1 Mexico 6.6 Japan 5.6 China 5.3	Raw materials, consumer goods, capital equipment, petroleum, construction material	Total: 0.278 Narrow gauge: 0.278 (none of network in use)	Total: 38.0 Paved: 9.6 Unpaved: 28.4 (2008)	730	Total: 151 Paved: 39 Unpaved: 112
Cuba	China 25.5 Canada 23.3 Venezuela 10.0 Spain 5.6	Sugar, nickel, tobacco, fish, medical products, citrus, coffee	Venezuela 35.2 China 11.7 Spain 8.5 Brazil 4.6 Canada 4.2 US 4.1	Petroleum, food, machinery and equipment, chemicals	Total: 8.6 Standard gauge: 8.3 Narrow gauge: 0.3 (2008)	Total: 60.8 Paved: 29.8 Unpaved: 31.0 (2001)	240	Total: 136 Paved: 65 Unpaved: 71
Dominican Republic	US 52.0 Haiti 13.6	Ferronickel, sugar, gold, silver, coffee, cocoa, tobacco, meats, consumer goods	US 44.0 Venezuela 7.0 China 6.1 Mexico 4.9 Colombia 4.8	Foodstuffs, petroleum, cotton and fabrics, chemicals and pharmaceuticals	Total: 0.142 Standard gauge: 0.142	Total: 19.7 Paved: 9.8 Unpaved: 9.9 (2002)	N/A	Total: 35 Paved: 16 Unpaved: 19
Guatemala	US 36.8 El Salvador 10.3 Honduras 8.8 Mexico 7.5	Coffee, sugar, petroleum, apparel, bananas, fruits and vegetables, cardamom	US 34.6 Mexico 11.8 China 7.9 El Salvador 5.3	Fuels, machinery and transport equipment, construction materials, grain, fertilizers, electricity	Total: 0.332 Narrow gauge: 0.332 (2009)	Total: 14.1 Paved: 4.9 Unpaved: 9.2 (2001)	990	Total: 372 Paved: 13 Unpaved: 359

(continued)

Table 7.2 (continued)

Country	Major exporting partners (%)[a]	Export commodities	Major importing partners (%)[a]	Import commodities	Railways (1,000 km)[a]	Highways (1,000 km)[a]	Waterways (km)[a]	Airports[a]
Mexico	US 73.5 Canada 7.5	Manufactured goods, oil and oil products, silver, fruits, vegetables, coffee, cotton	US 60.6 China 6.6 South Korea 5.2	Metalworking machines, steel mill products, agricultural machinery, electrical equipment, car parts for assembly, repair parts for motor vehicles, aircraft and aircraft parts	Total: 17.2 Standard gauge: 17.2	Total: 366.1 Paved: 132.3 Unpaved: 233.8 (2008)	2,900	Total: 1,819 Paved: 250 Unpaved: 1,569
Nicaragua	US 58.2 El Salvador 7.7 Canada 6.4 Venezuela 4.2	Coffee, beef, shrimp and lobster, tobacco, sugar, gold, peanuts, textiles and apparel	US 23.4 Venezuela 16.7 Costa Rica 8.8 China 7.2 Mexico 6.7 Guatemala 6.9 El Salvador 4.6	Consumer goods, machinery and equipment, raw materials, petroleum products	N/A	Total: 19.1 Paved: 2.0 Unpaved: 17.1 (2009)	2,200	Total: 143 Paved: 11 Unpaved: 132

(continued)

Table 7.2 (continued)

Country	Major exporting partners (%)[a]	Export commodities	Major importing partners (%)[a]	Import commodities	Railways (1,000 km)[a]	Highways (1,000 km)[a]	Waterways (km)[a]	Airports[a]
Panama	Venezuela 20.6	Bananas, shrimp, sugar, coffee, clothing	Japan 25.3	Capital goods, foodstuffs, consumer goods, chemicals	Total: 0.76	Total: 11.9	800	Total: 118
	South Korea 18.2		China 19.6		Standard gauge: 0.76	Paved: 4.3		Paved: 54
			Singapore 12.3					
	Ecuador 6.3					Unpaved: 7.6 (2002)		Unpaved: 64
	India 6.2		US 10.0					
	Japan 5.6		South Korea 9.3					
	Greece 5.3							
	US 5.3		Ecuador 4.1					
Puerto Rico	N/A	Chemicals, electronics, apparel, canned tuna, rum, beverage concentrates, medical equipment	N/A	Chemicals, machinery and equipment, clothing, food, fish, petroleum products	N/A	Total: 26.6	N/A	Total: 29
						Paved: 25.3		Paved: 17
						Unpaved: 1.3 (2008)		Unpaved: 12

Data for this table based on US Central Intelligence Agency, The World Factbook, as of October 13, 2011

[a] By the definition of food-based poverty; asset-based poverty was more than 47 %

Fig. 7.1 South America: Argentina, Bolivia, Brazil, Chile, Colombia, Ecuador, Paraguay, Peru, Uruguay, Venezuela. *Source* WorldAtlas.com http://worldatlas.com/webimage/countrys/sa.html

Each country in Tables 7.1 and 7.2 was therefore classified and analyzed on almost 50 pieces of information, such as the level of transportation infrastructure and current demographic and financial data. Later, following the literature reviews, our discussion contains inferences from these tables to permit selection of "top-performing nations," important to a global firm wishing to expand to Latin America.

We take this opportunity to summarize certain comparative information, gleaned from the same source as Tables 7.1 and 7.2, but not included there. In 2010, most countries in South America experienced annual growth rates averaging 3–7 % in GDP. (Corresponding figures were 1–6 % in most Central American nations.) Some exceptions were Peru and Uruguay (each about 9 %); Panama and the Dominican Republic (both around 8 %.); and Venezuela (−2 %). Even more extreme were Paraguay (+15 %) and Puerto Rico (−6 %). Contrast those numbers to the more-similar rates of GDP growth at that time in the NAFTA countries: USA and Canada (∼3 %), and Mexico (5 %).

Unemployment rates in South America during 2010 were typically below 10 %. Colombia and Venezuela, at 12 %, had the highest figures, while Equador (5 %) and Paraguay (∼6 %) were lowest. In Central America, the ranges in rates were generally comparable that year, between the Dominican Republic (13 %) and Cuba at 2 % unemployment.

Fig. 7.2 Central America and the Caribbean: Costa Rica, Cuba, Dominican Republic, Guatemala, Mexico, Nicaragua, Panama, Puerto Rico. *Source* WorldAtlas.com http://worldatlas.com/webimage/countrys/carib.htm

It is interesting that, within all of South and Central America, only Bolivia and Paraguay are landlocked. This is seen in Figs. 7.1 and 7.2. We remark that most of our material will pertain to South American countries; they are the subject of a greater number of logistics publications.

This chapter is structured as follows. After a brief discussion of the methodology, successive sections present our review and summarize the findings; offer a few lessons for business decisions; and discuss tentative conclusions. We note the various regional trading groups (ones that do not extend *throughout* Central or South America), and their influence and that of particular strong countries. Suggestions are made for future research; these include several testable propositions and some opportunities for normative modeling.

7.2 Study Design and Organization

In this review, we focus on publications which address specific issues in Central and South America concerning supply chain management or logistics. Some articles deal solely with Latin American countries. Other papers, such as Diener (1997), discuss the Central or South American operations of a multi-national supply chain. Different articles pertain to international logistics, applying a general principle to Latin American industry (e.g. Merchant 2004).

Table 7.3 Relating particular publications to Latin American nations

Country	Corresponding references
Argentina	Alexander et al. (2000), Braier and Morenco (2013), Carranza et al. (2002), D'Andrea et al. (2000), Fuller et al. (2003), Garcia Martinez et al. (1998), Ó hUallacháin and Wasserman (1999), Scenna and Santa Cruz (2005)
Brazil	Alexander et al. (2000), Campos (2001), Cunha and Silva (2007), Dagnino (1995), Fleury (2007), Fukasawa et al. (2002), Fuller et al. (2003), Georgiou and Vargus (2009), Ivarsson and Göran Alvstam (2005), Kawamura et al. (2006), Li et al. (2008), Ó hUallacháin and Wasserman (1999), Ojima and Yamakami (2006), Petersen and Taylor (2001), Rigatto et al. (2005), Wanke and Hijjar (2009), Yoshizaki et al. (2013)
Chile	Agosin and Bravo-Ortega (2007), Bianchi and Ostale (2005), Contesse et al. (2005), D'Andrea et al. (2000), Donoso and Singer (2007), Garrido and Leva (2003), Giuliani and Bell (2004), Martínez et al. (2000), Maturana and Contesse (1998), Weintraub et al. (1999)
Costa Rica	Altenburg and Meyer-Stamer (1999), Brenes et al. (1997), Diener (1997) Ickis et al. (2000), Saiz (2006)
Cuba	Alligood (1995), Enoch et al. (2004), Milan et al. (2006), United Nations: Human Development Report (2009), United States Central Intelligence Agency (2010), Van Bodegraven (2001)
Guatemala	Brenes et al. (1997), Ickis et al. (2000), United Nations: Human Development Report (2009), United States Central Intelligence Agency (2010)
Mexico	Alexander et al. (2000), Altenburg and Meyer-Stamer (1999), Biles et al. (2007), Bookbinder and Fox (1998), Campos (2001), Carranza Torres (2007), Drake and Diaz Rojo (2008), Francis et al. (2009), Giuliani et al. (2005), Ivarsson and Göran Alvstam (2005), Rajagopal (2009), Robinson and Bookbinder (2007), Sargent and Matthews (2001), Trostel and Light (2000)
Panama	Montero Llácer (2004), Montero Llácer (2006), United Nations: Human Development Report (2009), United States Central Intelligence Agency (2010)
Puerto Rico	United Nations: Human Development Report (2009), United States Central Intelligence Agency (2010), Van Bodegraven (2001)
Dominican Republic	United Nations: Human Development Report (2009), United States Central Intelligence Agency (2010), Van Bodegraven (2001)
Venezuela	Grunow et al. (2007), Nicholson et al. (1994), United Nations: Human Development Report (2009), United States Central Intelligence Agency (2010), Veenstra et al. (2005)
Multiple/other regions of South America	Harper et al. (2006), Jones et al. (2003), Martínez et al. (2000), Román and Martín (2004), Terg and Jamarillo (2006), Vantine and Marra (1997), Vexler et al. (2004)
Multiple/other regions of the Caribbean and Central America	Hans et al. (2007), McCalla (2008), Veenstra et al. (2005), Vexler et al. (2004), Walecki (2007)
Multiple/other regions of Latin America in general	Altenburg and Meyer-Stamer (1999), Baer et al. (2002), Barbier (2004), Bontekoning et al. (2004), Brown et al. (2005), Clark et al. (2004), Frankel (1995), Giuliani et al. (2005), Henson and Loader (2001), Kimura and Ando (2003), Kotabe et al. (2000), Madani (1999), Mellor and Hyland (2004), Merchant (2004), Prasad et al. (2005), Sim and Ali (1998), Trostel and Light (2000), Vonortas (2002), Zinn (1996)

With this scope in mind, we looked for major journals in logistics and supply chain management, transportation, and management science and operations research. Details of the search procedure are in the Appendix. There we give the full set of databases consulted (Table 7.5) and the keywords used (Table 7.6). For now, let us summarize our thought process on how an article was chosen to be included or omitted.

Electronic searching yielded a preliminary set of references. Recent publications which cited the latter could then be obtained. Having found a more current paper, the previous one was kept if both were interesting and there was little overlap between them. When a newly-located article employed an alternative keyword, a further search was initiated.

From the variety of sources, the result was a list of 250 references. That was reduced, through the winnowing process in the Appendix, to about 90; all but a few are from 1997 and later. Table 7.3 relates that literature to the particular countries involved. One half of those articles will be summarized in detail here.

The most common decisions to which the studies relate or the models are applied include site selection; determination of partners or supply chain collaborators; analysis of production, transportation or distribution; and choice of supplier. Table 7.4 notes the correspondence between those functions and the references that we cite. Tables 7.3 and 7.4 together permit the reader an overall perspective on the literature: To which countries do the applications pertain, and what decisions have been analyzed?

Aspects of international logistics or supply chain management have of course been covered in a number of earlier review papers. Our objective differs as we seek to study specifically the research on supply chains and logistics in Latin American countries. Previous authors, such as Meixell and Gargeya (2005), analyze the design of "global" supply chains, in whatever section of the world may be pertinent; Bookbinder and Matuk (2009) emphasize logistics and transportation in global supply chains.

Our focus is also quite different from that of Zinn (1996). Building upon detailed knowledge of logistics practices by local firms in each Latin American country, Zinn establishes a series of rules for logistics decision making and strategies that may offer opportunities for growth in Latin American logistics. These principles and policies are indeed insightful, leading for example to the importance to a given company of improvements in information technology. The emphasis of our chapter is communicated by its sub-title. The *research literature* of the past 15 years contributes a perspective which complements that of Zinn (1996).

We stress that papers in the research literature do permit inferences about Latin American countries, their infrastructure, and the status of Logistics in the region. Here are two examples. Suppose a paper concerns shortest path calculations (Maturana and Contesse 1998; Cunha and Silva 2007). Are the transportation times between origin and destination small or large? Are they roughly constant or more variable? This has some relationship to those data that could actually be obtained, but has more to do with the speed and reliability of transport over a given distance in that region.

As a second illustration, consider an optimization model for the choice of suppliers (e.g. Prasad et al. 2005). Such a manuscript shows the size of the model

Table 7.4 Correspondence Between Logistics Applications and Literature Cited

Applications	References	
	Normative modeling	Empirical or case-study research
Site selection	Robinson and Bookbinder (2007), Román and Martín (2004)	Clark et al. (2004), D'Andrea et al. (2000), Fleury (2007), Ickis et al. (2000), Mellor and Hyland (2004)
Determination of partners or supply chain collaborators	(Garrido and Leva (2003), Giuliani and Bell (2004)	Altenburg and Meyer-Stamer (1999), Bontekoning et al. (2004), Fleury (2007), Giuliani et al. (2005), Hans et al. (2007), Ivarsson and Göran Alvstam (2005), Kotabe et al. (2000), Merchant (2004), Rigatto et al. (2005), Sim and Ali (1998), Terg and Jamarillo (2006)
Production, transportation, Distribution	Bookbinder and Fox (1998), Braier and Morenco (2013), Contesse et al. (2005), Cunha and Silva (2007), Fukasawa et al. (2002), Garcia Martinez et al. (1998), Garrido and Leva (2003), Grunow et al. (2007), Jones et al. (2003), Kawamura et al. (2006)	Alligood (1995), Barbier (2004), Bontekoning et al. (2004), Brenes et al. (1997), Carranza et al. (2002), Clark et al. (2004), Diener (1997), Drake and Diaz Rojo (2008), Estache et al. (2002), Fleury (2007), Francis et al. (2009), Frankel (1995), Georgiou and Vargus (2009), Harper et al. (2006), Kawamura et al. (2006), Madani (1999)
	Li et al. (2008), Maturana and Contesse (1998), Meixell and Gargeya (2005), Nicholson et al. (1994), Ojima and Yamakami (2006), Robinson and Bookbinder (2007), Scenna and Santa Cruz (2005), Weintraub et al. (1999), Yoshizaki et al. (2013)	Martínez et al. (2000), McCalla (2008), Milan et al. (2006), Ó hUallacháin and Wasserman (1999), Prasad et al. (2005), Saiz (2006), Sim and Ali (1998), Terg and Jamarillo (2006), Veenstra et al. (2005), Vexler et al. (2004), Wanke and Hijjar (2009)
Choice of supplier		Bontekoning et al. (2004), Carranza et al. (2002), Diener (1997), Fleury (2007), Frankel (1995), Harper et al. (2006), Prasad et al. (2005), Rajagopal (2009), Sim and Ali (1998), Terg and Jamarillo (2006)

utilized, implying that the state of the industry has attained at least that capability level in the particular country.

Our review of the literature could have been organized through the application areas of Table 7.4, but several references concern more than one type of application. Perhaps more importantly, the rows of Table 7.4 could describe subjects or studies conducted elsewhere. The fact that a case study takes place in Central or South America is more fundamental to some articles in the literature than to others. This is why we have chosen the following categories instead.

The references we cite can be viewed on a scale of four possibilities: The application occurs in a single nation in Latin America; several countries there are compared on a logistics function or practice, or multiple logistics functions are contrasted in a given nation; the article involves activities of specific firms doing business in the region; or the paper discusses general issues in transportation and international trade concerning Latin American supply chains. Those headings describe the four subsections in our review which follows.

7.3 Survey and Discussion

7.3.1 Supply Chain/Logistics Applications in a Single Country

Every case study or problem example has an associated geographic location. This may be a company head office, the site of potential distribution centers, or nodes in a supply chain. Articles in this section describe analyses and case studies that are set in Latin America.

One sees in Tables 7.1 and 7.2 that Agriculture is often a prominent sector. Nicholson et al. (1994) and Garcia Martinez et al. (1998) present applications of optimization to cattle production in Venezuela and Argentina, respectively. Barbier (2004) discusses general issues in agriculture and their relationship to economic expansion in Latin America.

Fukasawa et al. (2002) examine the flow of (Brazilian) rail freight cars within specified time parameters. Once feasible routes are identified, the authors present a methodology to obtain optimal (profit-maximizing) routes for those cars, with computational results on real instances reported for large freight railroads. This research paper resulted in an actual software product, 'OptVag', currently in use within a major Brazilian railway.

The preceding operations research study could have occurred in Europe or the United States; the setting of the network model was in fact Brazil. Similarly, Cunha and Silva (2007) design a less-than-truckload network for a Brazilian company, while Li et al. (2008) discuss truck scheduling for solid waste collection in Brazil. Other applications in that country include Kawamura et al. (2006) concerning the distribution of ethanol, Ojima and Yamakami (2006) for a quadratic programming approach to the marketing of Brazilian soybean, and Yoshizaki et al. (2013) on the integration there of domestic and international container shipping. Rigatto et al. (2005) discuss alternative supply chain designs in the case of peach canning in Brazil.

Garrido and Leva (2003) consider the selection of carriers and port destinations in the United States for exporters of (Chilean) fruit. Analysis is based on a stochastic choice process with time and space interactions, via a probit model. The authors found that temporal effects played a large role. The end result is a modeling approach successfully applied by exporters of Chilean grapes. Additional Chilean case studies are those of Maturana and Contesse (1998) regarding optimal logistics for sulphuric acid, of Weintraub et al. (1999) concerning emergency-vehicle dispatch, of Contesse et al. (2005) on the supply chain for natural gas, and of Agosin and Bravo-Ortega (2007) on export growth in the food and forestry sectors.

Merchant (2004) builds on Sim and Ali (1998), which compared characteristics and performances of joint-ventures between American firms and firms operating in developing countries (Argentina, Brazil, Chile, Colombia, Mexico and Venezuela). Merchant classifies two-party equity joint-venture partnerships into three distinct categories: the partners are from developed countries, from newly industrialized countries, or from developing countries. The structure of joint-venture performance varied significantly across each partnership category.

Prasad et al. (2005) differentiate between the traditional Make-to-Stock and the emerging Build-to-Order environments, comparing operations of the latter type in developed and developing countries. Although 57 % of the firms and plants selected were located in the US, Latin America (30 %) had the next largest sample. Results of this study may provide managers with specific direction for aligning supply chains in a Build-to-Order environment across the globe. Those results can also be applied to the formation of clusters, discussed below.

Clark et al. (2004) found, for Latin American countries wishing to trade with the United States, transport costs can be a greater barrier to market access than import tariffs. The paper noted that an overall empirical improvement in port efficiency, from the 25th to the 75th percentile, reduces shipping costs by 12 %; and for the average country, 'bad' ports are equivalent to being 60 % farther from markets. Excellent ports could thus be critical in enabling Latin America to enhance its efficiency overall. A similar significance of port operations was seen by Wanke and Hijjar (2009) in a survey of large exporters in Brazil.

Bontekoning et al. (2004) observed a steady increase in freight-transport research, contending that a new field is emerging in *Intermodal* applications. Those authors reviewed 92 publications, four specifically from Latin America, to classify the characteristics of this knowledge base. A few aspects of their approach were incorporated in our work.

7.3.2 Comparative Studies Concerning Latin America

Some articles will identify various regions in illustrating a general theory or practice. The publications we now summarize mention one or more countries in Latin America in this way.

Alexander et al. (2000) apply previous research, on market risk and pricing strategies, to operations in Latin America of American railroads: Burlington Northern (now Burlington Northern Santa Fe) in Argentina, and Kansas City Southern/Illinois Central (now Kansas City Southern Lines) operating throughout Mexico. Fuller et al. (2003) classify the infrastructure for export-grain corridors within Argentina and Brazil, identifying possible impacts of enhanced transportation-system efficiency on each nation's global competitiveness and incorporating spatial models from the corn and soybean economies. With the preceding transport improvements, producer revenues increased by a reported \$1 billion per year.

Extension of the Andean Trade Preference Act (ATPA) will allow many consumer products, including apparel, to be exported to the US duty free. Terg and Jamarillo (2006) believe that small and medium sized firms from the South American textile industry could thus become major collaborators in the US apparel supply chain, by acting as manufacturing sub-contractors. From a survey carried out in six countries, Terg and Jamarillo found however that quality demands by US firms were typically higher than standards in South America, but that the textile industry there would benefit from expanding its customer base to include US partners.

Henson and Loader (2001) study the impact of sanitary and phytosanitary (SPS) requirements imposed by developed countries, when they import agricultural and food products from developing countries including several South American nations. "Phytosanitary" pertains to a certificate issued by the export country's government, indicating that the shipment has been inspected and is free of harmful pests and plant diseases. The authors find that requirements such as the WTO's SPS Agreement can act as non-tariff trade barriers for developing nations.

Kotabe et al. (2000) identify Brazil, Chile and Mexico as "newly industrialized countries," for which (as a group) significant economic gains are expected. To enhance competitively, local companies from NICs may form alliances with foreign firms. Kotabe et al. differ from previous authors by exploring productivity solely from the viewpoint of NICs, rather than all developing countries. As one example, a North American organization may pass along second-generation technology in exchange for exclusive access to the NIC's home market. Technology transfer in Brazil and Mexico is also discussed by Ivarsson and Göran Alvstam (2005).

The latter reference concerns a Swedish firm. As another illustration that more than North-American companies are involved, Kimura and Ando (2003) present the case of Japanese multinationals in Latin America.

Mellor and Hyland (2004) compare the application of technologies and improvement programs in countries in the OECD (Organization for Economic Co-operation and Development) to the practice in developing, non-OECD nations. Do businesses in the latter countries use management programs such as TQM? Data from 700 companies in 23 nations, e.g. Argentina, Brazil, Chile, Mexico and Peru, demonstrate that larger businesses in non-OECD countries do utilize those technologies, closing the profitability gap relative to OECD companies. But smaller firms in the same non-OECD countries remain far behind. (We note that Vonortaz 2002 treats competitiveness and new technology specifically in Latin America.)

Caribbean trade in the metal, copper, is discussed by Vexler et al. (2004). Veenstra et al. (2005) consider the Caribbean as a cross-road for international and regional transshipments. A detailed matrix on container and port flows is analyzed for Costa Rica, Cuba, the Dominican Republic, Guatemala and Puerto Rico. To those, McCalla (2008) adds Jamaica and Trinidad, where ports compete for the six million TEUs transshipped annually in the Caribbean basin.

7.3.3 Companies Operating in Latin America

The previous section comprised pertinent studies in various countries. We now turn to logistics activities of specific *firms*. Indeed, the titles of some of the next papers simply contain a company name. These deal with a particular application, either empirical or analytical, to a firm operating in Latin America. Case studies of greatest relevance include the following.

J. M. Textiles is a trans-national subsidiary of a British corporation. Brenes et al. (1997) investigate Guatemala and Costa Rica as possible sites for a new plant, and comprehensively compare the two nations in terms of infrastructure, political, economic and demographic characteristics. D'Andrea et al. (2000) prepare a case study for Rheem-Saiar, a manufacturer of water heaters and the dominant firm in Argentina; Rheem-Saiar wished to determine appropriate distribution channels for newly-identified global markets. The benchmarking of Argentinean companies by Carranza et al. (2002) also concerns transportation operations. Scenna and Santa Cruz (2005) present another transportation application in Argentina.

Portico S.A. (Diener 1997) of Heredia, Costa Rica, manufactures high-end residential exterior-use doors, made mostly of mahogany. In 1994, the firm considered enlarging the product line to include an additional premium wood, American Red Oak, in its new line of doors. Portico would purchase oak from the United States, ship it to Costa Rica where the doors would be produced, then re-export finished doors to the US and global markets.

Ickis et al. (2000) conduct a case study of Tabacalera Nicaraguense (Tanic), a subsidiary of British American Tobacco. Sales were exclusively within Nicaragua until 1995, when Tanic looked outside the country for new distribution channels, and possible sources of raw materials in Guatemala and Honduras. The firm also opened a regional office in Costa Rica. The result was development of "mini-factories," a scheme based on self-motivated work teams operating their own businesses, obtaining inputs from other mini-factories and selling to external clients.

Martínez et al. (2000) discuss Virutex-Ilko, a Chilean company with a dominant share in the domestic market for household cleaning products and kitchen bakeware. Should Virutex-Ilko seek new markets in Argentina, Bolivia, Mexico, Paraguay, Peru and Uruguay? Differences in the transport system of each market necessitated a separate importer for every country chosen.

Jones et al. (2003) analyze the European company, Syngenta Seeds Inc, which produces over 50 seed-corn hybrids. Proper geographical conditions, e.g. the right climate and temperature and the absence of insects, are required to promote seed growth. The authors developed a "second-chance production-planning model," allowing Syngenta to control for uncertainties in geographical conditions and consumer demands before major commitments are undertaken. The firm currently uses this model to plan the production corresponding to 80 % of its total sales.

Milan et al. (2006) study the supply chain for Cuban sugar. A mixed-integer linear programming model identifies a cost-minimizing method of sugar cane removal, the optimal route and transport capacities required, by road or rail, to ensure the supply of cane to the mill. Grunow et al. (2007) analyze issues for Venezuelan sugar concerning the cultivation, optimization of sugar-cane supply and harvesting. Braier and Morenco (2013), in the present volume, propose and implement an optimization model for sugar production in Argentina.

Trostel and Light (2000) prepare a case study of Carrier Mexico, a producer of air conditioners for Latin American sales. The firm had been operating under a philosophy of Kaizen or continuous improvement. Several changes to the market forced Carrier to adopt a "product delivery system," whereby all models of air conditioner would be produced in one plant. Manufacturing space was reduced by 32 %; production increased 38 %.

Francis et al. (2009) study the financial and organizational variables that impact profitability for a sample of smaller firms, each operating on both sides of the US-Mexican border. Robinson and Bookbinder (2007) optimize the location decisions and modal choices for a client company of this type. That work, in the context of NAFTA logistics, also includes Canada.

7.3.4 Trade, Transportation and Latin American Supply Chains

The preceding discussion emphasized company-specific examples. Let us now concentrate on articles dealing with a particular supply chain in Central or South America, or ones that discuss *general* issues in Latin American transportation.

Bianchi and Ostale (2005) observe that while many retailers from developed nations wish to expand into foreign markets, a number of major firms had attempted unsuccessfully to penetrate the Chilean market. These include Home Depot, Royal Ahold, Carrefour and J.C. Penny. Biles et al. (2007) consider international supermarket chains that expanded to Mexico, where results were not as uniformly negative.

Peterson and Taylor (2001) determine optimal timing and cost-minimizing routes for a new railroad connecting Northern and Southern Brazil. Existing rail and water transport systems, plus possible new railway links, are modeled together as a network. Campos (2001) describes the railway restructuring processes in Brazil and Mexico. Following a detailed background on the privatization during the 1990s of the rail systems for both nations, the authors identify obstacles to rail reform, such as regulatory problems, the management of interline traffic and ensuring access. For the cases of railroads in Brazil and Argentina, Estache et al. (2002) study the impact of privatization on efficiency. More recently, Georgiou and Vargus (2009) classify other factors in Brazilian railway development, including railway decision-making.

Some references (e.g. Carranza Torres 2007; Fleury 2007) have titles (*Global Perspectives—Mexico*; *Global Perspectives—Brazil*) leaving no doubt on the subject areas: Those works are from an ongoing CSCMP series on Logistics/SCM in selected countries.

Enoch et al. (2004) analyze the Latin American nation of Cuba, and how physical, economic and social factors influence development of its transportation system. Implications are drawn for other developing nations. A detailed categorization is given of Cuban roads, railways and forms of public transit. Alligood (1995) discusses the degree to which Cuba's airports and seaports could meet the challenge if the US trade embargo, imposed since the 1960s, were lifted. Van Bodegraven (2001) offers interesting observations on Cuban Logistics in general.

Saiz (2006) notes the puzzling fact that, in countries which are more democratic, highways and roads tend to be inferior to those in less democratic countries. It is believed that changes toward democratic government are associated with slower growth of road infrastructure. In the specific case of highways and roads in Costa Rica, the author suggests that dictatorships find paved roads and highways to be more useful for military and repressive purposes.

Harper et al. (2006) study zinc extraction and production cycles in several Latin American countries. A material-flow analysis identifies trade associated with production of zinc. Brazil and especially Peru are the primary exporters of zinc in the channel, while Argentina, Chile, Colombia and Venezuela produce the material for domestic consumption only.

Montero Llácer (2004) considers the strategic position of the Panama Canal and elaborates on the nation's inter-oceanic waterway. The paper indicates changes, successfully implemented, aimed at unifying Panama's maritime policies. In Montero Llácer (2006), a detailed view is given of the Panama Canal's growth since privatization of terminal ports in 1995. Positive results of reform include gains in terminal efficiency.

Altenburg and Meyer-Stamer (1999) distinguish the types of clusters possible in Latin America. By *cluster* is meant a group of companies generally within a similar industry or the same supply chain, positioned fairly close geographically to save on shipping time and expenses. The authors describe examples of best-practice clusters including the auto industry around Puebla, Mexico, and the electronics industry in Guadalajara and in Costa Rica.[1]

Giuliani et al. (2005) analyze the degree to which clusters benefit the participating firms. Positive impacts include ability to overcome growth constraints and to compete in distant markets. Results show that more effort is needed to link local clusters to external global partners, and that sectoral details are the main influence in the cluster's modal choice. Other Latin American supply chain clusters include

---

[1] Later in this book, the chapter by Sheffi (2013) gives a wide-ranging discussion of clusters. Naturally, his examples cover a greater diversity of geography and industries.

the textile industries of Coahuila, Mexico and Medellin, Colombia, as well as the furniture industry in Serra Gaucha and Espirito Santo, Brazil.

Giuliani and Bell (2004) study the supply chain cluster for the Chilean wine market. Results of a social-network analysis demonstrate that knowledge and technology are not evenly diffused, but rather are evident mainly within a core group of participants in the chain. Policy implications, such as how to change a firm's role within its supply cluster, are noted.

7.4 Lessons for Business Decisions

Several papers have thus shown the importance of clusters. That is one of our overall "lessons learned," five influential factors analogous to the "decision making rules" of Zinn (1996). Next, the size and unpredictability of inflation rates affect the entire region. Then, besides clusters, there are three positive lessons for Business to learn: How quality and trust can influence supply chain partners; the significance of Export Processing Zones, especially in combination with a trade agreement; and the impacts of various trade agreements themselves.

We emphasize the regional trade agreements because Latin American Logistics and SCM are *facilitators* of trade. Trade in turn enhances them. Similarly, Supply Chain activities, and the Logistics industry, can make major progress in Latin America if the questions we pose about quality, below, can be resolved.

7.4.1 Instability of Inflation Rates

Almost every Latin American nation has experienced periods of extraordinary inflation over the last few decades. Specifically in the period 1997–2010, we observed instability in inflation rates in many countries, e.g. the larger economies of Brazil, Argentina and Chile. As an adjunct to the data in Table 7.1, Brazil's annual rate of inflation in late 2008 was 5.7 %, having reached a decade-high 14.8 % in 2003. Corresponding figures in Argentina are 8.6 and 25.9 % (in 2002). Chile has done well relative to the rest of Latin America: At the end of 2005, it had an inflation rate of a mere 2.4 %, but reached a decade-high figure of 8.7 % in 2008. (Each of the percentages in this paragraph is from US Central Intelligence Agency 2010).

Comparison to North America reveals that Latin American countries still have a way to go in attaining stability in inflation. Rates for Canada and the US in late 2008 were 1.3 and 2.7 %, respectively, and for the decade prior, neither country averaged an inflation rate over 3.1 % (IMF 2009). This is roughly two-thirds the rate of inflation even in Brazil's best year. Instability in inflation rates is a major problem in supply chain management. When prices of inputs are not only increasing, but by *random amounts*, it is difficult to plan for the costs of production.

7.4.2 *Quality and Trust*

Rajagopal (2009) conducted an empirical study of buyer–supplier relationships in the Mexican office-equipment industry. "Trust" was found to be an important dimension in its impact on the quality of service and supplier performance.

In the gap analysis prepared by Terg and Jamarillo (2006) for the US-South American textile/apparel industry, two major problems were uncovered: Quality demands by US firms, and American companies' desire to trust their South American partners. The latter authors believed that both concerns could easily be addressed if South American companies registered with a quality board, such as ISO 9000, the way organizations often do in Europe and North America.

Terg and Jamarillo (2006) noted that many South American firms did not wish to register, even though their product quality may have made them eligible. (See Dagnino 1995 for a description of criteria underlying a Brazilian award similar to the Baldridge award for quality.) Numerous South American firms failed to recognize the benefits, and instead focused solely on the costs of registration, i.e. monetary expenses and lost time.

We suggest that, even on a temporary basis, a "South American/Latin American ISO registration board" should be developed. Its primary purpose would be to demonstrate to Latin American industry the advantages, ensuring as simple a process as possible. This type of registration system would enable American companies, wishing to expand their business, to easily identify Latin American firms producing the desired quality of output.

7.4.3 *Clusters*

Altenburg and Meyer-Stamer (1999) and Giuliani and Bell (2004) have studied clusters in detail; Giuliani et al. (2005) mention several benefits associated with cluster formations. Cost and time savings from shortened travel distances permit the cluster companies to grow and thus compete internationally. We agree with these three papers that inclusion of cluster relationships in a supply chain can be a comparative advantage for firms embracing them, and that once organized, those clusters should be linked to global partners to foster upgrading at the local level. Kotabe et al. (2000) note the merits associated with external linkages. Linkages can be established through a variety of avenues, many of which are outlined in Merchant (2004).

7.4.4 *Export Processing Zones*

An Export Processing Zone (EPZ) may be defined as "a region within a country, designed to encourage development of labour-intensive exports that use a high proportion of imported inputs. "[Most] activity in EPZs [thus involves] the use of labour which 'processes' imported inputs to then be exported" (Terg and Jamarillo 2006). Firms that end up locating in EPZs are often multinational corporations, or have some affiliation with one.

EPZs furnish numerous rewards to the countries employing them, the primary ones being, "to provide foreign exchange earnings by promoting non-traditional exports, to provide jobs to alleviate unemployment ... and assist in income creation, to attract foreign direct investment ... and ... act as catalysts for domestic entrepreneurs to engage in production of non-traditional products" (Madani 1999). In fact, Sargent and Matthews (2001) study the possible combination of EPZs with another common initiative, that of the regional trade agreement. Both are utilized by governments of developing nations to increase the wealth benefits received from international trade and investment.

Mexico has successfully integrated its EPZs (Maquiladora regions) within the terms of the NAFTA free trade agreement. Sargent and Matthews (2001) find, however, that NAFTA has not significantly altered the competitive dynamics of Mexico's EPZs. To ensure that developing countries can hold politically powerful multi-national corporations to the EPZs' rules and regulations, those authors recommend tax incentives, minimum-wage standards or the altering of domestic tariffs. By such means, Latin American nations may be able to combine the two initiatives and successfully increase their trade capabilities.

7.4.5 Trade Agreements

Trading blocs in the Americas have been discussed by Frankel et al. (1995), and by Salazar-Xirinachs (2002) concerning sub-regional agreements leading to those blocs. In particular, *CAFTA* is the 2003 Central American Free Trade Agreement. Hans et al. (2007) discuss the impact of that agreement on the apparel supply chain in the region. Walecki (2007) places CAFTA in the general context of controversy on free trade.

Mercosur is a 1991 trading agreement between Brazil, Argentina, Uruguay, Paraguay and Venezuela. Its purpose is to promote free trade and the fluid movement of goods, labour and currency throughout South America. Vantine and Marra (1997) identify 45 impediments to the transportation and logistics integration that would be required by Mercosur. Some of these include operations and information technology, but are often at the more fundamental level of a lack of customs services and poor transportation infrastructure.

Ó hUallacháin and Wasserman (1999) investigate the effects of trade policies, mainly those of Mercosur, on Brazil's automobile-component parts industry and its locations chosen for manufacturing. Large tier-one suppliers within Brazil and Argentina assemble chassis, engines and body subsystems. Those firms are directly affected by development of new trade policies. The authors conclude that Mercosur led to decreased tariffs levied on the South American automobile sector, which in turn increased the demand for automobiles. Vehicle assemblers thus restructured existing facilities in Sao Paulo, Brazil to make operations more flexible, and built new plants in southern Brazil and northern Argentina.

The regions covered under Mercosur are significant economies, with more than 220 million consumers and combined Gross Domestic Product above one trillion dollars per year (Center for Popular Economics 2010). Baer et al. (2002) questioned, however, why such a trade agreement has not lived up to expectations for individual member countries. Although there had been some effort by the NAFTA countries to coordinate their macroeconomic policies, no such attempts were made in South America, to the detriment of those nations. This gap is particularly obvious between the major participants, Argentina and Brazil, where lack of coordination has strained the trade agreement. Key problems found by Baer et al. (2002) include unpredictable inflation rates, erratic behavior of exchange rates, as well as instability of many political regimes.

Mercosur announced in late 2005 that Bolivia would progress from an associate to a full member. (Other associate members of Mercosur include Chile, Colombia, Ecuador and Peru.) It is worth observing the overlap between this group and another bloc called the "Andean Community of Nations," comprising Bolivia, Colombia, Ecuador and Peru. Associate members of that trading bloc include Chile plus all of Mercosur's full members except Venezuela.

The Andean Community and Mercosur began negotiating a merger in 1999. They signed an agreement of cooperation in 2004, with a view to create a South American Free Trade Area (SAFTA). It is important to note that such an expanded organization could well pre-empt the Free Trade Area of the Americas: A majority of current Mercosur member countries rejected the FTAA proposal at the IV Summit of the Americas in Argentina in 2005. (See Brown et al. 2005 for a numerical study of economic issues concerning the FTAA.)

7.5 Conclusions

In this chapter, we have discussed the research and applications concerning Latin American supply chain management and logistics, as reflected in the academic literature. Upon perusal, that literature divided naturally into several themes: Models and analyses in a single country; comparisons in Latin America to illustrate a broad theory; case studies of specific firms in the region; and general issues (transportation and trade) for Latin American supply chains.

Following that review, we discussed lessons for business decisions overall. Those pertained to effects of inflation, the roles of quality and trust among supply chain partners, the influence of clusters, and combined significance of export processing zones and trade agreements.

In the present section we now mention important issues not specifically dealt with in the publications reviewed, but ones inferred from our detailed study of the literature. These final points involve the "top-performing nations" in Latin America; propositions that we suggest be tested empirically; and additional modeling opportunities. We end with general remarks on the state of Latin American Logistics.

7.5.1 Top-Performing Nations

To aid in our literature review, we had conducted a synopsis for countries within South and Central America (Tables 7.1 and 7.2). Those tables were developed to help a reader understand a logistics application in its wider context, e.g. the significance of the products moved or the supply chains involved. Nevertheless, the summaries for each country in Tables 7.1 and 7.2 enable selection of "top-performing nations" as possible points of strategic entry, for a global firm desiring to conduct operations in Latin America. The following nations consistently ranked in the best five on each criterion within South America: Argentina, Brazil, Chile and Venezuela. They are perhaps no surprise. Less obvious are the corresponding top countries in Central America and the Caribbean: Costa Rica, Cuba, the Dominican Republic, Guatemala, Panama and Puerto Rico.

7.5.2 Testable Propositions

Possibilities for future research include the empirical testing of the following Propositions:

- North American companies that wish to expand their operations to Latin America are more likely to offer profitable business to Latin American firms that qualify for ISO 9000 registration, than to firms that do not.
- Consider a group of Latin American firms that has formed a cluster. There is an increased likelihood of cluster profitability:
  - the stronger their tie to a well-known international partner
  - the more mature their industry.
- A Latin American nation that belongs to a regional trade agreement can utilize its Export Processing Zone to greater advantage, than can a nation in Latin America that is not part of such an agreement.

With respect to the latter, we can think of several ways to operationalize "greater advantage." These include an enhanced Gross Domestic Product within the EPZ; or a larger number of new firms might be established there; or that the increases in employment may be superior within that Export Processing Zone.

7.5.3 Opportunities for Normative Modeling

The four categories of functional applications in Table 7.4 have been divided into those that emphasize normative modeling, and others whose focus is empirical or case-study research. It is clear that a good deal of normative modeling has concentrated on Production, Transportation and Distribution. In this way, Latin America is similar to other areas of the world.

Considerable empirical or case-study research has been done in the three other functional categories, but that has been accompanied by little or no normative modeling. Some published models do exist which are applicable to the sparsely-populated cells of Table 7.4. The challenge to researchers in Central or South America is to apply these tools there, in a precise setting.

7.5.4 State of Logistics

"Logistics" is of course a set of functional processes (inventory, transportation, ...). Those activities can be performed by a shipper, carrier or consignee; our list of references contains a number of examples for each. In those instances, the functions of transportation or inventory management, etc. are conducted within a distinct supply chain.

Our discussion did not often differentiate between logistics papers and those on supply chain management. Naturally, Logistics and SCM are not synonymous, but the *context* aids a reader to distinguish between them. To us, the most important aspects of a published article are the particular application and those countries to which it pertains. Indeed, our review includes papers whose geographic settings (Table 7.3) involve all major Latin American nations.

We remark that the term "Logistics" can also apply to the capabilities of a given nation, or of a region (e.g. Bookbinder and Tan 2003). The United States envisions a Free Trade Area of the Americas. If a supply chain for this hemisphere is to be viable, the calibre of Logistics that is possible must be satisfactory.

In the major Latin American countries, it seems to be. That is demonstrated by the entries in Table 7.4. There we note European- or North-American-scale applications in site selection (Clark et al. 2004); choosing supply chain collaborators (e.g. Merchant 2004; Giuliani et al. 2005); appointment of transportation carriers (Garrido and Leva 2003) and network design (Cunha and Silva 2007); and the determination of suppliers (Prasad et al. 2005).

What appears absent to a degree, however, is the *public logistics infrastructure*. The three NAFTA countries were "ready" for a possible free-trade arrangement. Many of the intermodal routes for containerized shipments between Canada and Mexico via the US have non-dominated time–cost tradeoffs (Bookbinder and Fox 1998). There were potential doubts about some highways in Mexico in the early days of NAFTA, and issues today about security at border crossings. But a company would not wonder whether its supply chain can be supported by the NAFTA region. Incorporation of those countries into a supply chain is strictly a *business decision* for the firm to make.

Now consider South America, where most applications we discussed are within a single nation. A trade bloc clearly involves two or more countries, and Latin America does have a number of *bilateral* Free Trade Agreements. We also stressed Mercosur and the Andean Community. While their potential combination as SAFTA still encompasses less than all of South America, those are the trade agreements for which the countries seem ready.

Table 7.5 Electronic sources and databases consulted

ABI/Inform	ISI Web of knowledge
Business week online	Lexis Nexis
Canada Institute for Scientific and Technical Information (CISTI Source)	ProQuest
CSA Illumina	Scholarly journal archive (JSTOR)
Google Scholar	Science direct
International abstracts in operations research	Scopus

Table 7.6 Selected keywords[a] for electronic searches[b]

Distribution	Central America
Facilities	Latin America
Free Trade	South America
Location	Individual Country[c]
Logistics	
Production	
Purchasing	
Routes	
Supplier	
Transportation	
Warehousing	

[a] Other specialized keywords were occasionally utilized when an article that used them was found

[b] A search typically employed one keyword from the left (functional) group **AND** one keyword from the right (geographical) group

[c] Example: Argentina, Bolivia, Brazil, … (one country at a time)

Even if Latin America as a whole favored an FTAA, more is required than desire for trade. An infrastructure enabling Logistics processes between countries is necessary. Yet rail lines may use different gauges in one nation and the next; there is considerable variation in the available highways (Tables 7.1 and 7.2). Drake and Diaz Rojo (2008) cite statistics which point out that, although Logistics in Mexico is generally not up to the standard in the US or Canada, Mexico's import and export operations are still fastest among Latin American countries. The interaction of Logistics with all the factors in Tables 7.1 and 7.2 seems to cause Logistics in Latin America to be far more diverse than, say, in Europe. And that is why Latin America continues to be fascinating.

Appendix: Details of the Search Methodology

We began by consulting a number of databases (Table 7.5). It is easy to do a computer-based literature search. Too easy; one quickly can be swamped with the references found. After browsing, however, it was straightforward to eliminate some articles: An author's interpretation of one or more keywords (see Table 7.6) could have differed from our own. The paper may have lacked sufficient focus on Logistics/SCM. A research orientation might have been missing, or perhaps the topic was not so stimulating.

It may also be worthwhile to summarize the complementary criteria by which we decided to include a given paper. The work needed to involve Central or South America in one of a few major ways (noted in our main text). It should have been published within the past 15 or 20 years in a "research" (i.e. refereed) journal. We sought articles that employed an up-to-date methodology with some analytical content, and where portions of that methodology and content were discussed in a technical or academic way. Of course applications related only to SCM or Logistics were considered; each paper had to be judged as "interesting."

Articles in Trade Magazines, often quite topical, can have a "half-life" shorter than the lead time to publication of a paper accepted by a typical academic journal. It was thus decided to omit discussion of the thought-provoking trade articles we found. Indeed, the sub-title of the present chapter reinforces an intended focus on the research literature.

For our subject area, a reader may wonder about the necessity of *translation*. Some trade articles on Latin American Logistics are of course in Spanish or Portuguese. However, very few *research* papers are. Academic authors, from Central and South America or elsewhere, do tend to publish in English.

Thus, while our search procedures and databases at first may seem skewed toward English papers, in fact hardly any academic articles on Latin American Logistics are written in Portuguese or Spanish. Moreover, the references Dagnino (1995), Ojima and Yamakami (2006), and Wanke and Hijjar (2009), each in Portuguese, came up during searches in English. Several other papers located were deemed less pertinent to our topic.

Another writer may not agree fully on our choice of publications. But the articles we have selected are analytical, and are diverse in their geographic settings and the types of application (Tables 7.3 and 7.4).

References

Agosin MR, Bravo-Ortega C (2007) The emergence of new successful export activities in Latin America: The case of Chile. Working Paper No 236, Department of Economics, Universidad de Chile. http://econ.uchile.cl/public/Archivos/pub/f5ba4950-b592-4285-8c58-decd6ea07234.pdf

Alexander I, Estache A, Oliveri A (2000) A few things transport regulators should know about risk and the cost of capital. Util Policy 9:1–13

Alligood A (1995) Cuba's seaports and airports: Can they handle a post-embargo cargo boom? Colombia J World Bus 30(1):66–73

Altenburg T, Meyer-Stamer J (1999) How to promote clusters: policy experiences from Latin America. World Dev 27(9):1693–1713

Baer W, Cavalcanti T, Silva P (2002) Economic integration without policy coordination: the case of Mercosur. Emerg Markets Rev 3:269–291

Barbier EB (2004) Agricultural expansion, resource booms, growth in Latin America: implications for long-run economic development. World Dev 32(1):137–157

Bianchi C, Ostale E (2005) Lessons learned from unsuccessful internationalization attempts: examples of multinational retailers in Chile. J Bus Res 59(1):140–147

Biles JJ, Brehm K, Enrico A (2007) Globalization of food retailing and transformation of supply networks: consequences for small-scale agricultural producers in South-eastern Mexico. J Latin Am Geogr 6(2):55–75

Bontekoning YM, Macharis C, Trip JJ (2004) Is a new applied transportation research field emerging?—A review of intermodal rail-truck freight transport literature. Transp Res A 38:1–34

Bookbinder JH, Fox NS (1998) Intermodal routing of Canada–Mexico shipments under NAFTA. Transp Res E 34(4):289–303

Bookbinder JH, Matuk TA (2009) Logistics and transportation in global supply chains: review, critique and prospects. In: Oskoorouchi MR (ed) Tutorials in operations research. Hanover, MD: Institute for Operations Research and the Management Sciences Chapter 9 (pp 182–211). doi:10.1287/educ. 1090.0059

Bookbinder JH, Tan CS (2003) A comparison of Asian and European logistics systems. Int J Phys Distrib Logistics Manage 33(1):36–58

Braier G, Morenco J (2013) Strategic and tactical modeling in the Argentine sugar industry. In: Bookbinder JH (ed) Global Logistics. Springer, New York 2011

Brenes ER, Bryant K, Castro R, Ruddy V (1997) J.M. Textiles. J Bus Res 38(1):67–75

Brown DK, Kiyota K, Stern RM (2005) Computational analysis of the Free Trade Area of the Americas (FTAA). North Am J Econ Financ 16(2):153–185

Campos J (2001) Lessons from railway reforms in Brazil and Mexico. Transp Policy 8(2):85–95

Carranza O, Maltz A, Antún JP (2002) Linking logistics to strategy in Argentina. Int J Phys Distrib Logistics Manage 32 (6):480–496

Carranza Torres OA (2007) Global perspectives—Mexico, Council of Supply Chain Management Professionals, Lombard

Center for Popular Economics (2010) CPE Globalization Briefs on-line. Available at: http://www.populareconomics.org/globalization/briefs.html

Clark X, Dollar D, Micco M (2004) Port efficiency, maritime transport costs, and bilateral trade. J Dev Econ 75(2):417–450

Contesse L, Ferrer JC, Maturana S (2005) A mixed-integer programming model for gas purchase and transportation. Ann Oper Res 139(1):39–63

Cunha CB, Silva MR (2007) A genetic algorithm for the problem of configuring a hub-and-spoke network for a LTL trucking company in Brazil. Eur J Oper Res 179(3):747–758

Dagnino BV (1995) O uso dos Critérios do Premio Nacional da Qualidade para auto-avaliação no Brasil (The use of National Quality Award Criteria for self-assessment in Brazil). Gestão Produção 2(1):87–96

D'Andrea G, Postigo S, Florin J (2000) Rheem-Saiar. J Bus Res 50(1):47–55

Diener BJ (1997) Portico, S.A. J Bus Res 38(1):89–96

Donoso P, Singer M (2007) Internal supply chain management in the Chilean sawmill industry. Int J Oper Prod Manage 27(5):524–541

Drake MJ, Diaz Rojo N (2008) The current state of Mexican logistics operations. J Int Manage Stud 3(2):92–97

Encyclopedia Britannica Inc (2010) Encyclopedia Britannica on-line. Available at: www.britannica.com

Enoch M, Warren JP, Valdés Ríos H, Henríquez Menoyo E (2004) The effect of economic restrictions on transport practices in Cuba. Trans Policy 11(1):67–76

Estache A, González M, Trujillo L (2002) What does "privatization" do for efficiency? Evidence from Argentina's and Brazil's Railways. World Dev 30(11):1885–1897

Fleury P (2007) Global perspectives—Brazil. Council of Supply Chain Management Professionals, Lombard

Francis J, Mukherji A, Mukherji J (2009) Examining relational and resource influences on the performance of border region SMEs. Int Bus Rev 18(4):331–343

Frankel J, Stein E, and Wei S (1995) Trading blocs and the Americas: The natural, the unnatural, and the super-natural. J Dev Econ 47(1):61–95

Fukasawa R, Poggi de Aragão MV, Porto O, Uchoa E (2002) Solving the Freight car flow problem to optimality. Theor Comput Sci 66(6):1–11

Fuller S, Yu TH, Fellin L, Lalor A, Krajewski R (2003) Transportation developments in South America and their effect on international agriculture competitiveness. Transp Res Rec 1820:62–68

Garcia Martinez A, Rodriquez Alcaide JJ, Ruiz DEM (1998) Optimization of the bovine fattening in grazing in the Pampas region (Argentina) using linear programming. Investigacion Agraria Produccion y Sanidad Animales 13(1/3):99–117

Garrido RA, Leva M (2003) Port of destination and carrier selection for fruit exports: a multi-dimensional space-time multi-nomial probit model. Transp Res *B* 38(7):657–667
Georgiou I, Vargus G (2009) Mapping railway development prospects in Brazil. Transp Rev 29(6):685–714
Giuliani E, Bell M (2004) Paper No. 115–when micro shapes the meso: learning networks in a Chilean wine cluster. *SPRU Working Paper Series* The Freeman Centre, University of Sussex, pp 1–36
Giuliani E, Pietrobelli C, Rabellotti R (2005) Upgrading in global value chains: lessons from Latin American clusters. World Dev 33(4):549–573
Grunow M, Günther H-O, Westinner R (2007) Supply optimization for the production of raw sugar. Int J Prod Econ 110(1–2):224–239
Hans J, Morley GP, Kessler S, Piñeiro V, Sánchez A, Torero M (2007) The Impact of the Central America free trade agreement on the Central American textile maquila industry. International Food Policy Research Institute (IFPRI) 720
Harper EM, Bertram M, Graedel TE (2006) The contemporary Latin America and the Caribbean zinc cycle: one year stocks and flows. Resour Conserv Recycl 47(1):82–100
Henson S, Loader R (2001) Barriers to agriculture exports from developing countries: the role of sanitary and phytosanitary requirements. World Dev 9(1):85–102
Ickis JC, Edelberg G, Morales M (2000) Tanic. J Bus Res 50(1):123–137
International Monetary Fund (2009): World Economic Outlook October 2009, as of February 9, 2010 on-line. http://www.imf.org/external/pubs/ft/weo/2009/02/pdf/text.pdf
Ivarsson I, Göran Alvstam C (2005) Technology transfer from TNCs to local suppliers in developing countries: a study of AB Volvo's truck and bus plants in Brazil, China, India, and Mexico. World Dev 33(8):1325–1344
Jones PC, Kegler G, Lowe TJ, Traub RD (2003) Managing the seed-corn supply chain at syngenta. Interfaces 33(1):80–90
Kawamura MS, Ronconi DP, Yoshizaki H (2006) Optimizing transportation and storage of final products in the sugar and ethanol industry: a case study. Int Trans Oper Res 13:425–439
Kimura F, Ando M (2003) Fragmentation and agglomeration matter: Japanese multinationals in Latin America and East Asia. North Am J Econ Finan 14(3):287–317
Kotabe M, Teegen H, Aulakh PS, Countinho de Arruda MC, Santillán-Salgado RJ, Greene W (2000) Strategic alliances in emerging Latin America: a view from Brazilian, Chilean, and Mexican companies. J World Bus 35(2):114–132
Li J-Q, Borenstein D, Mirchandani PB (2008) Truck scheduling for solid waste collection in the City of Porto Alegre, Brazil. Omega 36(6):1133–1149
Madani D (1999) A review of the role and impact of export processing zones. World Bank: Policy Research Working Paper Series # 2238, pp 1–108
Martínez JE, Báez RK, Salinas FP (2000) Virutex-Ilko S.A. J Bus Res 50(1):83–95
Maturana S, Contesse L (1998) A mixed integer programming model of the logistics of sulphuric acid in Chile. Int Trans Oper Res 5(5):405–412
McCalla RJ (2008) Site and situation factors in transshipment ports: the case of the Caribbean basin. Tijdschrift voor Economische en Sociale Geografie 99(4):440–453
Meixell MJ, Gargeya VB (2005) Global supply chain design: a literature review and critique. Transp Res E 41(6):531–550
Mellor R, Hyland PW (2004) Manufacturing management programs: are developing economies bridging the strategic gap? Technovation 25(8):857–863
Merchant H (2004) The structure-performance relationship in international joint ventures: a comparative analysis. J World Bus 40(1):41–56
Milan EL, Fernandez SM, Pla Aragones LM (2006) Sugar cane transportation in Cuba, a case study. Eur J Oper Res 174(1):374–386
Montero Llácer FJM (2004) Panamanian maritime sector management. Marine Policy 28(4):283–295
Montero Llácer FJM (2006) Port privatization in Panama. Marine Policy 30(5):483–495
Nicholson CF, Lee DR, Boisvert RN, Blake RW, Urbina CI (1994) An optimization model of the dual-purpose cattle production system in the humid lowlands of Venezuela. Agric Syst 46(3):311–334
Ó hUallacháin B, Wasserman D (1999) Vertical integration in a lean supply chain: Brazilian automobile component parts. Econ Geogr 75(1):21–42
Ojima ALRO, Yamakami A (2006) Quadratic programming model in the analysis of the logistical movement and marketing of Brazilian soybean [Modelo de programação quadrática para análise

da movimentação logística e comercialização da soja Brasileira] *Engenharia Agricola* 26(2):552–560

Petersen ER, Taylor AJ (2001) An investment planning model for a new North-Central railway in Brazil. Transp Res *A* 35(9):847–862

Prasad S, TataJ, Madan M (2005) Build to order supply chains in developing countries. J Oper Manage 23(5):551–568

Rajagopal A (2009) Buyer-supplier relationship and operational dynamic. J Oper Res Soc 60(3):313–320

Rigatto P, Padula AD, Larson DW (2005) Differences between supply-chain structures within a given industry: insights from the Brazilian peach canning industry. Int J Logistics Syst Manage 1(4):311–330

Robinson AG, Bookbinder JH (2007) NAFTA supply chains: facilities location and logistics. Int Trans Oper Res 14(2):179–199

Román C, Martín JC (2004) Analyzing competition for hub location in intercontinental aviation markets. Transp Res 40(2):135–150

Saiz A (2006) Dictatorships and highways. Reg Sci Urban Econ 36(2):187–206

Salazar-Xirinachs JM (2002) Proliferation of sub-regional trade agreements in the Americas: an assessment of key analytical and policy issues. J Asian Econ 13(2):181–212

Sargent J, Matthews L (2001) Combining export processing zones and regional trade agreements: lessons from the mexican experience. World Dev 9(10):1739–1752

Scenna NJ, Santa Cruz ASM (2005) Road risk analysis due to the transportation of chlorine in Rosario City. Reliab Eng Saf Syst 90(1):83–90

Sheffi Y (2013) Logistics-intensive clusters: global competitiveness and regional growth. In: Bookbinder JH (ed) Global Logistics. Springer, New York

Sim A, Ali Y (1998) Performance of international joint ventures from developing and developed countries: an empirical study in a developing country context. J World Bus 3(4):357–376

Terg SG, Jamarillo H (2006) Integrating the US textile and apparel supply chain with small companies in South America. Supply Chain Manage Int J 11(1):44–55

Trostel A, Light A (2000) Carrier Mexico S.A. de C.V. J Bus Res 50(1):97–110

United Nations: Human Development Report (2009) on-line. Available at: http://hdr.undp.org/en/reports/global/hdr2009/. 9 Feb 2010

United States Central Intelligence Agency (2010) The world Factbook. Available at: https://www.cia.gov/library/publications/the-world-factbook/. 9 Feb 2010; and again, 13 Oct 201

Van Bodegraven A (2001) The state of logistics in Cuba—Not just sugar cane anymore. J Bus Logistics 22(2):209–218

Vantine JG, Marra C (1997) Logistics challenges and opportunities within MERCOSUR. Int J Logistics Manage 8(1):55–66

Veenstra A, Mulder HM, Sels RA (2005) Analysing container flows in the Caribbean. J Transp Geogr 3(4):295–305

Vexler D, Bertram M, Kapur A, Spatari S, Graedel TE (2004) The contemporary Latin American and Caribbean copper cycle: 1 year stocks and flows. Res Conserv Recycl 41(1):23–46

Vonortas NS (2002) Building competitive firms: technology initiatives in Latin America. Technol Soc 24(4):433–459

Walecki JM (2007) Changing business environments, international trade and regional integration: who needs CAFTA? Econ Aff 7(2):73–77

Wanke PF, Hijjar MF (2009) Brazilian exporters: exploratory study on perceptions about logistics infrastructure quality [Exportadores brasileiros: Estudo exploratório das percepções sobre a qualidade da infraestrutura logística] Producao 19(1):143–162

Weintraub A, Aboud J, Fernandez C, Laporte G, Ramirez E (1999) An emergency vehicle dispatching system for an electric utility in Chile. J Oper Res Soc 50(7):690–696

Yoshizaki HTY, Hino C, Chebat D (2013) Integration of international and cabotage container shipping in Brazil. In: Bookbinder JH (ed) Global Logistics. Springer, New York

Zinn W (1996) The new logistics in Latin America: an overview of current status and opportunities. Int J Logistics Manage 7(1):61–71

Part III
Logistics and Supply Chains in Europe

Chapter 8
Logistics in the Oresund Region of Scandinavia

Britta Gammelgaard and Aseem Kinra

Abstract Much has been documented about the logistical efficiencies created in the traditional European trade corridors. Those corridors, spanning countries like the UK, the Netherlands, Germany, France, Italy and Spain, thereby create an important economic region of its own. This is, however, to the detriment of the informational content of decision making on site selection. It is also to the disadvantage of other important regions that offer unique competitive advantages to foreign firms trying to base their value proposition on location in the sub-continent, especially those regions that have not yet matured in their place-branding initiative. The Oresund region is one such logistics hotspot in Scandinavia, where "Oresund" is the name of the narrow strait between the eastern part of Denmark and Southern Sweden. The two countries have been connected via ferries for centuries, but economic integration activities really took off when the fixed link (bridge and tunnel) was established in 2000. The Oresund region not only performs the important logistical function of connection and coordination between mainland Europe, the Baltic states and some important parts of Central Europe—it also makes a good logistical location for firms that target emerging consumer needs around sustainability, green supply chain management, and macroeconomic competence and stability. This chapter describes the potential offered by the Oresund region by charting its development, documenting those of its main features related to logistics infrastructure and practices, and tracking its performance on all major levels of logistics decision categories.

B. Gammelgaard (✉) · A. Kinra
Department of Operations Management, Copenhagen Business School,
2000 Frederiksberg, Copenhagen, Denmark
e-mail: bg.om@cbs.dk

A. Kinra
e-mail: aki.om@cbs.dk

J. H. Bookbinder (ed.), *Handbook of Global Logistics*, International Series in Operations Research & Management Science 181, DOI: 10.1007/978-1-4419-6132-7_8,

8.1 Introduction

As individual countries, Denmark, Sweden, Norway and Finland consistently rank very highly on aggregate performance criteria in all well-known competitiveness indices. At the same time, when it comes to setting up shop in Europe, it is no secret that Germany, the UK and the Netherlands have traditionally occupied the top awareness of most professionals. These countries have been viewed as engines of economic growth, and because of their high population density, they have offered logistical efficiencies in the movement and distribution of goods. Notwithstanding economic arguments related to size, Bergqvist (2007) equally attributes the choice and performance of specific countries and regions to marketing and place-branding initiatives. It seems, however, that the traditional argument of logistics and transportation as being a "derived demand" holds well in this instance: Logistical requirements are largely expected to follow trade patterns and corridors. For example, the trade corridor created through the above countries is referred to as the *European Banana* (RECLUS-Datar (1989) in Matthiessen (2000)).

However, and especially since the major enlargement of the EU in 2004, when a high proportion of the Eastern European countries—formerly under Soviet rule – were incorporated into the EU, the character of Europe has seen a fundamental change, and trade corridors have expanded as a result. This means, for example, that with the exception of Russia, the countries around the Baltic Sea are now part of the European economy. There seems to be emerging a new corridor of buying power, connectedness and logistical expertise, which includes new locations in northern, central and Eastern Europe. Figure 8.1 seeks to illustrate these changes. They imply that European growth is based on many more economies than just those included in the traditional trade corridors. That growth should therefore be visualized in a perspective of these newer corridors, such as the *European Snail* (Boevé 2010).

Furthermore, each (global) supply chain has its own peculiarities in terms of market demands and supply conditions. Decision makers should thus in any event consider a range of factors and sites, in addition to the all-important ones, when locating their supply chains in specialized economies, be they countries or regions. In this instance, individual economies and economic regions, small or large, play an important role in the site-selection considerations of multinational corporations on the basis of specific benefits furnished by their global value chains. From this viewpoint, the European Banana represents only a few spatial areas that offer specialized advantages that have been fairly well-documented in the logistics discipline. Other geographical areas could be of particular interest to decision makers in international SCM. For example, the decision and information needs of those managers of global value chains who seek to locate in Europe will remain incomplete, to the point that not all such specialized location alternatives are described (e.g. Min 1994; Kinra and Kotzab 2008). That approach is further clarified later in this chapter.

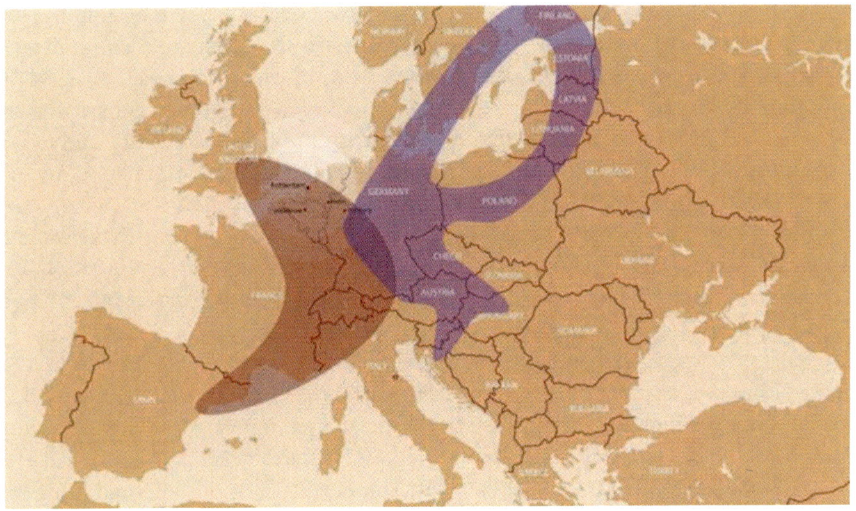

Fig. 8.1 "Disclosing economic hotspots". *Source* Boevé 2010

In other words, it is justifiable to raise an argument for logistics and transportation possessing *integrated* demand (Hesse and Rodrigue 2004) for creating interest, and describing European locations other than the traditional ones. Oresund is one such new/specialized economic region in Europe that can provide specific advantages to firms that target emerging consumer needs around sustainability, green supply chain management, and macroeconomic competence and stability. The aim of this chapter is thus to create an awareness of the Oresund region, "the largest hub in Scandinavia for transportation of goods and persons within sea, road, air and railway".[1]

8.1.1 Existing Knowledge and the Emergent Nature of the Oresund Region

There are other good reasons to enhance the recognition of Scandinavia, and more specifically the Oresund region's logistics-related expertise, at this juncture. First, given that previous (academic) literature on this topic is scanty from the point of view of business logistics and supply chain management and provides limited information to managers of global value chains, this chapter furnishes a timely description of the region. For example, while one of the first and most important contributors to knowledge of the region, Skjött-Larsen et al. (2003), adopt multiple

[1] http://www.oresund.org/logistics/projects/ecomobility accessed at 10:32 on 23/08/10.

perspectives in the understanding of logistics in a regional context, their findings are (perhaps therefore) more significant for overall socioeconomic and cultural integration of the region. Similarly, although the work of Matthiessen (2000, 2004) is important in this direction, it tends to address issues of transportation geography and the broader questions of transportation, rather than of business logistics and SCM.

Similarly, some good knowledge is to be found in academic publications targeted towards professionals and policy makers. For example, *Global Perspectives*, a trade periodical by the Council of Supply Chain Management Professionals (CSCMP), takes "an in-depth look at a particular country or region".[2] *Global Perspectives Scandinavia* (Gammelgaard et al. 2009) may be used as a source of knowledge to examine complexities facing global supply chain management in this context. However, the limited description of the Oresund region in that publication and its practitioner orientation warrant a more detailed account here.

The final justification, and probably the most important one, involves consideration of the developing nature of the region. It must be remembered that this region practically came into existence with the inception of the Oresund bridge in 2000. Given the factors noted here, and now on the tenth anniversary of the much celebrated bridge, and in light of the renewed importance of southern Scandinavia in connecting a much wider Europe, it therefore becomes interesting to describe the region once again from the perspective of global logistics and supply chain management. This point therefore relates to the fact that the existing information on the region is currently in need of an update.

Many suitable perspectives could be used to document a specific economic territory. As noted, immediately above, the main one chosen here is region's the attractiveness from the point of view of *business logistics and supply chain management*. Location in this regard is important, and may be understood from a number of angles. For example, and as also implied in the previous paragraph, the design of extended supply chains is highly dependent on market-specific demands (e.g. Fisher 1997) and uncertainties (e.g. Lee 2002), where geographies are chosen based on cost and responsiveness in planning operations. Similarly, location is important from the perspective of *geographical proximity* to specialized suppliers, customers and other significant industry players (e.g. Porter 1990), where geographical *clusters* are chosen for the competitive advantages they provide. (See also the chapter by Sheffi (2013) in the present volume.) For a more comprehensive overview of research approaches that may be adopted for the study of location at the regional level, we refer to Bergqvist (2007).

Location may, however, also be viewed from a perspective in which countries and regions are chosen on the basis of their individual distances (e.g. Ghemawat 2007) in relation to the company's host location. Since global supply chains span multiple countries and regions, a major question is how the environment at each of these macroeconomic levels impedes or expedites the flow of goods. In other

[2] http://cscmp.org/MemberOnly/Perspectives.asp accessed at 17:48 on 14/09/10.

words, it becomes important to capture the distance and differences between various countries and regions in terms of logistical environment and practices.

Regardless of whether the latter distinctions between supply chains are the result of conscious design considerations by key decision makers, as is implied by Fisher (1997) and Lee (2002), or they prove to be emergent, the interesting issue is that these differences exist and make every global supply chain peculiar. Those distinctions tend not only to provide competitive advantages, but also challenges for each organization in adopting the value-creation logic (Porter 1985; Stabell and Fjeldstad 1998) embedded in long-linked (Thompson 1967) or extended supply chains, as they are known in the domain of logistics and SCM (Mentzer et al. 2001). Because of these differences between particular countries, conditions of environmental uncertainty can then appear when locating internationally or expanding globally, regardless of individual companies' original intentions with respect to expansion. To counter or exploit conditions of environmental uncertainty, managers of global value chains need more information on specialized locations (Kinra 2009). That is therefore one of the main reasons for documenting specific regions in the world. This is also the chief perspective adopted in the present chapter.

8.1.2 Structure and Approach of the Chapter

The description of a particular location can be structured in alternative ways, and can focus on various information components that are useful for decision makers. Since the main theme of the book is *global logistics*, we find it useful to structure this description according to the main roles of logistics in global supply chain management, namely the *connecting and coordinating role* and the *strategic role* of improving performance (Wood et al. 2002). Furthermore, when describing and analysing spatially dispersed logistics systems, it is not enough to simply document performance related to individual nations (e.g. infrastructural and macro-economic criteria). These systems are, in fact, embedded in larger logistics networks and partnerships spanning multiple countries and regions (Kinra 2009).

When discussing the Oresund Region of Scandinavia in a decision-making perspective, there are thus several aspects to consider. We take the point of departure in the model of Skjött-Larsen et al. (2003.) that depicts several layers in the transport system. This model sees material flows as connected to transport infrastructure through what they call "transport operation". Between these layers of the transport system, markets with demand and supply are created. The model also includes markets for information, which are closely linked to the transport system, but that is not considered further in this chapter. Figure 8.2 thus graphically illustrates a global supply chain that traverses multiple geographies. The figure is based on the value proposition embedded in the Oresund region of

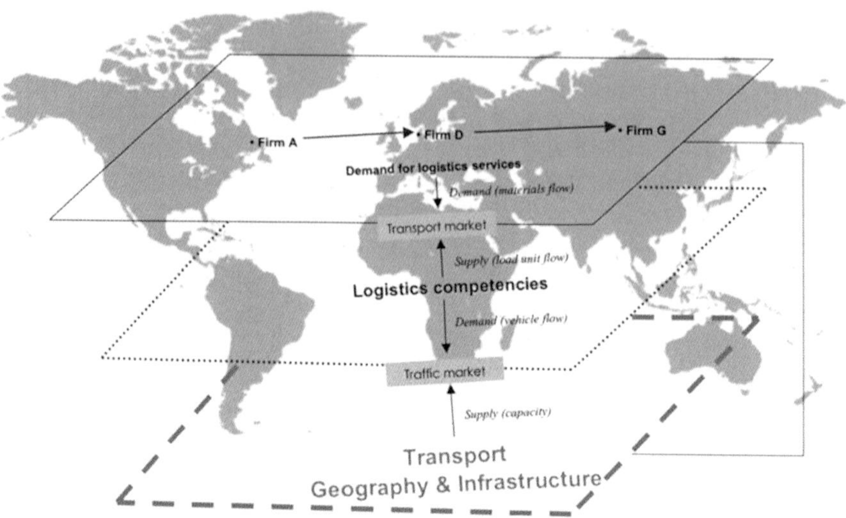

Fig. 8.2 Logistics-oriented decision categories impacting global supply chains. *Source* adapted from Skjött-Larsen et al. (2003) and Kinra (2009)

Scandinavia. It is therefore important that decision makers understand its specificities in terms of the layers in Skjött-Larsen et al. (2003).

The preceding model was developed for analyzing transport systems. Figure 8.2 converts to a terminology for decision making in logistics operations. We see the upper layer of the model, the material flow, as drawing on demand for logistics services, among them of course transportation. These material flows are inbound flows—materials and components—for further production and assembly, and also outbound flows of finished goods for consumers and end users. In the specific model underlying our chapter, we call this layer, "Demand for logistics services". The middle layer—transport operations—is translated into competencies in providing those services. We use the specific term "Logistics competencies" for that layer. And finally, the basis for having both material flows and logistics competencies is the transport infrastructure of the region, which can be seen as the bottom layer of the freight transport model. For this layer, we prefer the specific term "Transport geography and infrastructure".

Seen from a decision maker's perspective—a decision maker who might have to design and organize a global value chain—it is important to know whether there are economic activities in a region, whether there are logistics competencies, and finally whether there is a sufficient infrastructure to support the operations. This model will now be used to describe logistics operations in the Oresund region.

Fig. 8.3 The Oresund region. *Source* The Oresund bridge and its region, p. 5, Øresundsbrokonsortiet (2009)

8.2 Demand for Logistics Services

The demand for logistics services depends firstly on a certain population in need of supplies. The total population of the Oresund region is about 3.7 million,[3] 2.5 million of whom live on the Danish side with 1.2 million on the Swedish side of the strait. The population of Denmark is 5.5 million and that of Sweden 9.1 million.[4]

As both Denmark and Sweden are among the wealthiest countries in the world, the region represents considerable purchasing power. The 2009 per capita GDP averages were US$ 34,664 in Sweden and US$ 34,952 in Denmark. On economic

[3] (Tendens Øresund 2010; Population) http://www.tendensoresund.org/en accessed 15/09/2010 12:21 h.

[4] CIA, The World Factbook.

performance, the two countries rank 15 and 30 in the world in 2010 respectively. In terms of overall competitiveness, Sweden ranks 6 and Denmark ranks 30.[5]

Geographically, the Oresund Region includes Scania on the Swedish side of the strait. Malmo is the largest city with 280,000 inhabitants. On the Danish side is Copenhagen, the capital of Denmark; the population is 1.2 million in the greater Copenhagen area. Zealand plus Lolland, Falster and Bornholm are included in the region, as indicated in Fig. 8.3.

Secondly, industry creates the demand for logistics services. Industrial structure varies somewhat throughout the region because of the presence of the Danish capital. Manufacturing industries are limited in the Greater Copenhagen area, whereas manufacturing is still significant in the rest of the Danish section despite considerable outsourcing and offshoring of manufacturing activities in Denmark[6] (IBU Øresund 2010, based on Eurostat). Manufacturing in Scania is on the same level as in Zealand, but generally more than 20 % of the region's value added is created in R&D and business services.[7] The wholesale and retail industries account for about 13 % of value added in the region, with health care and the medical sector contributing around 8 %.

It is not surprising that Copenhagen, the capital of Denmark accounts for a disproportionately high share of the value added in financial and telecommunication services compared to the other parts of Oresund. These statistics are mirrored in how the region seeks to develop and market itself at the Oresund Science Region platform (www.oresund.org), where knowledge platforms covering the industrial strengths of the region are set up and developed. These platforms include, for example, ICT, food science, clean technology and material sciences, medical industries and logistics. The main purpose of the organization is to coordinate interests, work and projects among approximately 12,000 researchers and 160,000 students in the region. The Oresund Science Region seeks to coordinate knowledge among the nine universities, municipalities and private and public companies in the region. Oresund has also been chosen by the EU to build the world's largest neutron microscope, the ESS—European Spallation Source. The facility will be located at Lund University. It will be completed in 2020, and is expected to attract a large number of international researchers to the region.

In summary, demand for logistics services *into* Oresund is generally characterized by the distribution of high value products to a population with superior education and spending power. The demand for logistics services *out of* the region is similarly characterized by high value items such as pharmaceuticals, and in general products containing advanced knowledge and information. It is therefore reasonable to expect that the logistics skills in demand will most likely be related to strong levels of consciousness and transparency concerning the global supply chains supplying Oresund with food and consumer goods. This transparency will

[5] IMD World Competiveness Online, accessed 13/09/2010.

[6] IBU Øresund 2010 based on Eurostat.

[7] (Tendens Øresund 2010; Industry).

concern ethical and environmental issues potentially surpassing governmental and EU regulation. Furthermore, it is also reasonable to expect that the population will demand logistical efficiency where products should be available 24/7 with no delays. But at the same time, the vagaries of practical logistics—traffic, noise and pollution—will be tolerated less and less. The other side of this picture is the fact that the region also serves as a transit corridor for Swedish and Norwegian industrial goods southwards, and supplies to these industries northwards. That is the inherent dilemma in connecting Oresund to the rest of Scandinavia, and in the future also to continental Europe.

8.3 Logistics Competencies

Several aspects of the regions logistical competence will now be analyzed. This will be done in terms of a fit between the economic performances of individual *supply chain players*, such as specialized logistics service providers (LSPs); at the level of *industries*, e.g. the logistics industry as a whole and economic competitiveness of individual *countries* and of entire regions such as Oresund. The performance of the region at each level is now discussed separately, while at the same time linking it to performance at other tiers.

In 2008, the size of the national market for logistics services, measured by revenues of the ten largest service providers in each country, was approximately 6.2 billion euros in Sweden and 3.9 billion euros in Denmark (Klaus et al. 2009). Swedish logistics services in particular have been subject to the wave of consolidation in that sector that has resulted from intensification of EU integration and the subsequent liberalization of transport markets. On the top ten lists of largest LSPs in Sweden, four are of Swedish origin. In Denmark, the top two of the top ten are Danish, and of these top ten, six are of Danish origin (Klaus et al. 2009). The Danish logistics service industry is also strong at European level, where two of the top ten logistics service providers are Danish (Klaus et al. 2009).

The shipping industry includes such players as A. P. Møller-Maersk, number three in the top 100 logistics companies in 2008 according to Klaus et al. (2009). That industry is especially strong in a Danish national setting (Berlingske Nyhedsmagasin 2009). So too is freight forwarding, which has considerable international scope via such players as DSV (number nine on the same list). In Sweden, the Green Cargo railway has a fairly high international ranking in terms of size. Volvo Logistics (contract services), a spin-off from the Swedish car industry located principally in the Gothenburg area, is also worth mentioning.

It is, then, no surprise that both countries comprising the Oresund region, namely Denmark and Sweden, consistently perform well on industry-related and other micro-logistical indicators. For example, the Logistics Performance Index (LPI 2010) ranks the two countries highly on factors specific to the industry such as international shipments, logistics quality and competence, tracking and tracing, and timeliness (Sweden is ranked number three and Denmark number 16 in the overall rankings). Nor is it a surprise that both countries consistently perform well on most macro-logistical indicators. For example, the World Economic Forum's Global Competitiveness Index (2010) ranks Sweden and Denmark as two and nine respectively and categorizes both as innovation-driven economies, while the IMD's World Competitiveness Index (2010) ranks these countries at six and 13 respectively. Similarly, a study comparing Asian and European logistics performed by Bookbinder and Tan (2003) ranks Denmark and other Scandinavian/Nordic countries as Tier 1 countries in terms of their logistical systems.

All these advantages make Oresund an attractive transit point for international shipments and global value chains. However, there are also constraints that prevent the region from performing at its capacity. Factors such as access to financing, inefficient government bureaucracy, and restrictive labor regulations can still be accommodated by locating on either side of the Oresund, depending on individual preferences. Professionals in these countries, however, generally perceive factors such as tax rates and tax regulations as the most problematic in doing business in the entire region (Global Competitiveness Report 2010–11, pp. 142 and 310). For a decision-maker, those constraints must be put in the context of the range of benefits mentioned here, including the demand for specialized, innovative, high-value services that were noted in the previous section.

8.4 Transport Geography and Infrastructure

The Danish straits have been of major strategic and military importance for centuries. They were and still are the gate to the Baltic Sea, and thus to the seaway to the eastern part of northern Germany, Poland, Lithuania, Latvia, Estonia, Russia and Finland. Today the straits are open waters. Historically, the Oresund strait between Denmark and Sweden was especially important because the Danish capital is on the Oresund coast, and because the strait meant easy access by sea to international trade and warfare from the Swedish capital, Stockholm. Whoever controlled the Oresund was able to collect tolls from vessels passing through the strait. Denmark and Sweden have not, however, been at war with each other for more than 350 years. Today, the discussion is about integration of the two countries, physically and economically, through new and improved infrastructure.

Sweden and Denmark have traditionally been connected via ferries at several places in the Oresund; there is still a ferry connection at the narrowest point in the strait, i.e. at Elsinore in northern Zealand and Helsingborg in Sweden. This crossing takes 20 min, and more than two million vehicles annually are carried across the strait here (Øresundsbron 2010). The big breakthrough in regional thinking, however, came with the opening of the 16 km Oresund bridge and tunnel in 2000. This fixed link is jointly owned and operated by the Danish and Swedish states through the Øresundsbro Konsortiet. The connection takes both vehicles and trains: An estimated 2.7 million individuals cross the Oresund annually via the bridge. Figure 8.4 illustrates the growth in crossings over the Oresund since 1990.

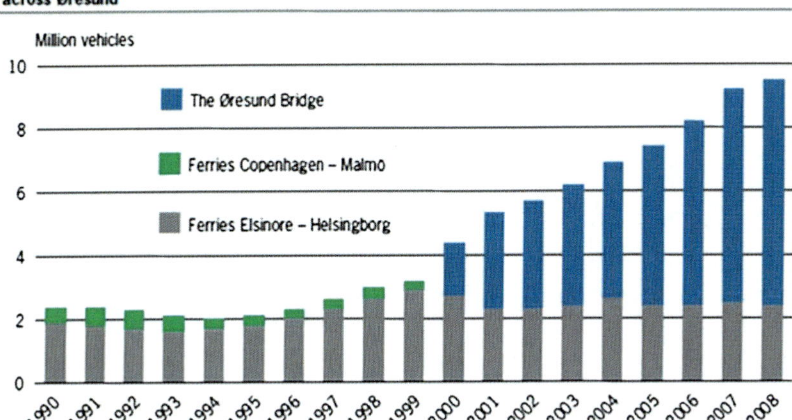

Fig. 8.4 Traffic across the Oresund. *Source* The Oresund bridge and its region, p. 4, Øresundsbrokonsortiet (2009)

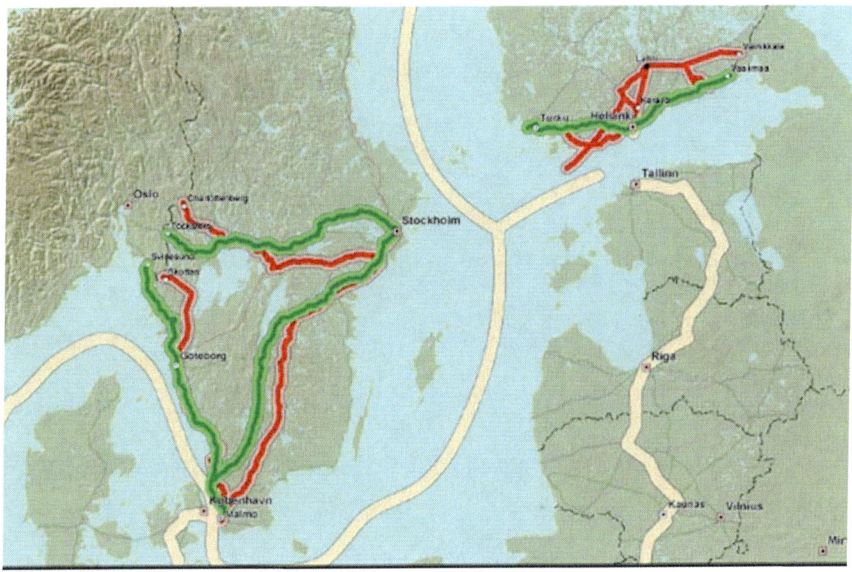

Fig. 8.5 The Nordic triangle. *Source* TEN-T PP progress report of the EC, DG-MOVE, TENtec Information System

An estimated 16 % of the trucks out of Sweden move via the Oresund bridge; ferries from the South of Sweden (Trelleborg) to Germany are the leaders with a 48 % market share (Oresundsbron op. cit.).

Fig. 8.6 The Oresund fixed link. *Source* TEN-T PP progress report of the EC, DG-MOVE, TENtec Information System, p. 46

The Oresund Bridge is well connected to waterway, railway and motorway systems, among them the so-called "Nordic Triangle". This is an EU-prioritized transport axis, connecting the Oresund Region to Norway via Gothenburg, which houses the largest port and the only deep-sea port in Scandinavia (Global Perspectives Scandinavia), and eastwards to Stockholm and via ferries to Finland, Russia (St. Petersburg) and the Baltic states. Figure 8.5 shows these connections within EU member states. The motorway and ferry connections from Denmark to Germany are illustrated in the map of Fig. 8.6.

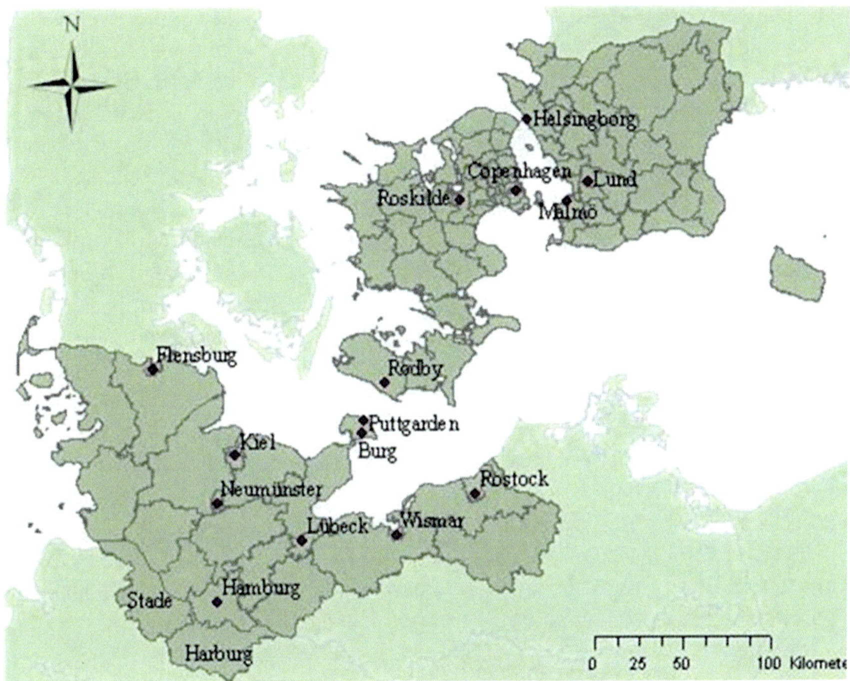

Fig. 8.7 A new region with a Fehmarn Belt fixed link. *Source* Matthiessen (2010), front page

The region is also well connected to the world via airports, where Copenhagen Airport is by far the largest, followed by Roskilde Airport in Zealand and Malmo-Sturup Airport in Scania. Copenhagen Airport has a cargo division and is in the process of building a so-called cargo city adjacent to its facilities, located next to the Oresund Bridge and motorway. The railway is integrated into the airport buildings.

The seaway to and from the region goes through the Copenhagen-Malmo Port (CMP) and the Port of Trelleborg on the south coast of Scania. The CMP is a port jointly owned by Swedish and Danish interests. The port is operated on both sides of the Oresund, but as development opportunities in the Copenhagen section are limited and relatively expensive, the CMP is expanding its cargo activities primarily on the Swedish side in the Norra Hamnen. This will be completely connected to the motorway system in the region and will have a container and combi-terminal, a distribution center and a ferry terminal. The Copenhagen section of the CMP is dedicated largely to cruise ships that can dock alongside quays very close to the inner city of Copenhagen because of its historic location.

Today the Oresund region is connected to Puttgarten, Germany via a ferry link across the Fehmarn Belt from Rødby, Denmark. However, in 2009 the Danish government voted, after a mutual agreement with the German government, for a *fixed link* between those two locations. This will be 18 km long, with rail and motorway, projected to open in 2018. The map of Fig. 8.7 illustrates the Swedish, Danish and German regions that will then be connected by the two fixed links.

The new fixed link will connect the Oresund region to the north German states Schleswig–Holstein and Mecklenburg-Vorpommern. The long term vision of regional politicians is that Oresund will be extended by about six million people. It should also be noted that Fig. 8.7 omits the fixed links between Zealand, Funen and Jutland in Denmark. The fact is, however, that because of those links, the infrastructural integration of Scandinavia and northern Germany will be even more extensive. Of further importance is the fact that ferry lines between the northern part of Jutland and Norway and Sweden also connect Scandinavia physically.

In summary, the fixed links between Denmark and Sweden, and between the Oresund Region and Germany, lay a foundation for the further economic development of Scandinavia. To some extent, that will compensate for the lower population density and longer distances compared to Central Europe. This means that global supply chains will have easier and cheaper access to a population that was previously considered to be on the periphery of Europe. That market may be reached within a day or two from a centralized distribution centre in the middle of Europe. However, another choice may be to set up local DCs to avoid congestion in Central and Western Europe (e.g. out of Rotterdam), and at the same time, for efficiency and environmental reasons, avoid partly-empty trucks on the motorways.

8.5 Conclusions

8.5.1 Summary and Discussion

Continued enlargement of the EU has created new trade patterns in Europe. Huge infrastructure projects are now emerging to connect countries which were previously either geographically remote from continental Europe or outside the EU's borders. In this part of Europe, trade has become and is still becoming easier.

The Oresund fixed link (bridge and tunnel) is one such infrastructure project that was created to facilitate trade in Scandinavia, giving birth to what is now termed the Oresund region. That connects the eastern part of Denmark, including the capital, to Scania, the southern part of Sweden. This fixed link is integrated into motorways, ports and airports so that access to and from Oresund is easy and efficient.

The region has a population of 3.7 million well-educated people, with considerable purchasing power, and international ranking on lists of economies and competitiveness. From a decision-making perspective in global supply chains, this means a potential advantage in the selling and distribution of high value goods. And it is also possible to buy knowledge-intensive goods developed and manufactured in the region. Logistics competence and connectedness are high and convenient for businesses, despite differences in legislation (on taxes in particular) and labor regulations across the Oresund.

8.5.2 *Future Prospects*

It is critically important to continuously develop connections to and from the Oresund region, in order to promote mobility of a population that most likely will develop more and more industries and institutions that are based on knowledge and science. This has been facilitated by investing heavily in infrastructure projects during the last couple of decades, now including a fixed link (to open in 2018) between the region and northern Germany (the Fehmarn Belt). It is of vital significance for Oresund that Germany be ready to invest in sufficient infrastructure on the German side, thereby enabling faster connections e.g. to Hamburg and the capital Berlin (Lohse and Jespersen 2010). At this point in time, those decisions have not yet been made.

The region's solutions to the dilemma of being a place that should attract highly educated people that need logistics, but who do not want the disadvantages of transport and the prospects of intensifying the transit character of Zealand, are also important for the future. The Fehmarn Belt fixed link will facilitate the connectedness of Swedish and Norwegian industry with Continental Europe through Zealand. The extension of the CMP port on the Swedish side of the Oresund will, however, expand the possibilities of sea transport to and from the region.

Apart from relative buying power, it is important for Oresund to bring together a considerable volume of people with a high degree of mobility, so that companies can attract the necessary labor with the desired educational profiles. On this point, the region is still somewhat constrained because of its location in two countries, and possibly three in the future. Tax and labor regulations are different. Each country has to take its *whole* country into consideration when deciding e.g. on taxes in the region, despite the fact that all countries are EU members. This is yet another dilemma. Its solution will impact the future prospects of the Oresund region.

References

Bergqvist R (2007) Studies in regional logistics: the context of public-private collaboration and road-rail intermodality. Phd Dissertation, Göteborg University

Berlingske Nyhedsmagasin, Guldnummer no. 33, 30 Oct 2009

Boevé W (2010) European gateway services; the sustainable network presented at CSCMP Europe 2010. Rotterdam, The Netherlands

Bookbinder JH, Tan CS (2003) Comparison of Asian and European logistics systems. Int J Phys Distrib Logistics Manage 33(1):36–58

CIA The World Factbook www.cia.gov/library/publications/the-world -factbook, Accessed Sept 2010

Fisher M (1997) What is the right supply chain for your product? Harvard Bus Rev 75(2):105–116

Ghemawat P (2007) Redefining global strategy. Harvard Business School Press, Boston

Gammelgaard B, Landborn J, Vestergaard M (2009) Scandinavia, CSCMP Global Perspectives, Council of Supply Chain Management Professionals. Oak Brook, IL

Hesse M, Rodrigue J-P (2004) The transport geography of logistics and freight distribution. J Transport Geogr 12(3):171–184

IBU-Øresund, Intereg IVA (2010) Megatrends: drivkræfer bag udviklingen af transport og mobilitet i Øresundsregionen
IMD World Competiveness Yearbook 2010 www.worldcompetetiveness.com
Kinra A (2009) Supply chain (logistics) environmental complexity. Phd Dissertation, Copenhagen Business School
Kinra A, Kotzab H (2008) Understanding and measuring macro-institutional complexity of logistics systems environment. J Bus Logistics 29(1):327–346
Klaus P, Hartmann E, Kille C (2009) Top 100 in European transport and logistics services—2009/2010, Deutscher Verkehrsverlag
Lee H (2002) Aligning supply chain strategies with product uncertainties. California Manage Rev 44(3):105–119
Lohse S, Jespersen PH (2010) The perception of the Fehmarn Belt connection among German stakeholders. Summary (draft), Roskilde University
Mentzer JT, De Witt W, Keebler JS, Min S, Nix NW, Smith CD et al. (2001) Defining supply chain management. J Bus Logistics 22(2):1–26
Min H (1994) Location analysis of international consolidation terminals using the analytic hierarchy process. J Bus Logistics 15(2):25–44
Matthiessen CW (2000) Bridging the Øresund: potential regional dynamics. J Transport Geogr 8(3):171–180
Matthiessen CW (2004) The Øresund area: Pre- and post-bridge cross-border functional integration: the bi-national regional question. GeoJournal 61(1):31–39
Matthiessen CW (2010) Fast Femern Bælt-forbindelse. En ny dynamisk regional udvikling i Nordeuropa. Femern Sund and Bælt, juni
Øresundskonsortiet (2009) The Oresund bridge and its region
Øresund Bridge (2010) www.oresundsbron.com
Porter ME (1985) Competitive advantage. The Free Press, New York
Porter ME (1990) The competitive advantage of nations. Harvard Bus Rev 68(2):73–91
Schwab K (ed) (2010) The Global Competitiveness Report 2010–2011. World Economic Forum, Geneva
Sheffi Y (2013) Logistics-intensive clusters: global competitiveness and regional growth. In: Bookbinder JH (ed) Global Logistics. Springer, New York
Skjött-Larsen T, Paulsson U, Wandel S (2003) Logistics in the Øresund region after the bridge. Eur J Operational Res 144(2):247–256
Stabell CB, Fjeldstad ØD (1998) Configuring value for competitive advantage: on chains, shops and networks. Strategic Manage J 19(5):413–437
Thompson JD (1967) Organizations in action. Mc Graw-Hill, New York
The Logistics performance index (LPI) 2010
Ten-T PP Progress report of the EC, DG-MOVE, TENtec Informaiton System, June 2010
Wood DF, Barone AP, Murphy PR, Wardlow DL (2002) International logistics. AMACOM, New York
World Economic Forum's Global Competitiveness Index 2010

Chapter 9
Green Corridors in European Surface Freight Logistics

Harilaos N. Psaraftis, Atle Minsaas, George Panagakos, Christopher Pålsson and Ilkka Salanne

Abstract In the European Commission's Freight Transport Logistics Action Plan of 2007, a number of short- to medium-term actions are presented that will help Europe address its current and future challenges, and ensure a competitive and sustainable freight transport system there. One action is the "Green transport corridors for freight". A *Green Corridor* is characterized by a concentration of freight traffic between major hubs and by relatively long distances of transport. Green Corridors should in all ways be environmentally friendly, safe and efficient. Green technologies and smart utilization of Information and Communication Technologies (ICT), where available, may even improve those corridors. Where not available, new R&D may be required to further develop what is needed. Given the above policy goals, project "SuperGreen" has been launched. This is Coordination and Support Action co-funded by the European Commission in the context of the 7th Framework Programme for Research and Technological Development, and coordinated by the National Technical University of Athens. The project involves 22 partners from 13 European countries. The purpose of this chapter is to address the key issues involved in the development of Green Corridors for European Freight Logistics, describe the SuperGreen project, and give an overview of main results to date.

H. N. Psaraftis (✉) · G. Panagakos
National Technical University of Athens, Athens, Greece
e-mail: hnpsar@mail.ntua.gr

A. Minsaas
Marintek, Norway

C. Pålsson
IHS Fairlpay, Sweden

I. Salanne
Sito Ltd, Espoo, Finland

J. H. Bookbinder (ed.), *Handbook of Global Logistics*, International Series in Operations Research & Management Science 181, DOI: 10.1007/978-1-4419-6132-7_9,

9.1 Introduction

The European Commission has stated in its Freight Transport Logistics Action Plan, launched in October 2007, that "Logistics policy needs to be pursued at all levels of governance" (EU 2007a). This plan is one in a series of policy initiatives to improve the efficiency and sustainability of freight transport in Europe. In the Freight Transport Logistics Action Plan, a number of short–to medium-term actions are offered to aid Europe meets its challenges. The goal is a competitive, sustainable system of European freight transport. Among those actions is the "Green transport corridors for freight". In such a corridor, freight traffic between major hubs is concentrated and transport distances are relatively long.

Green Corridors should be environmentally friendly, safe and efficient. But what really is a Green Corridor? A precise definition of the term is still elusive; one of the most important contributions of ongoing research would be to develop an explicit and workable definition. Still, one can mention a couple of high-level definitions:

According to the European Commission, "Green Corridors are a European concept denoting long-distance freight transport corridors where advanced technology and co-modality are used to achieve energy efficiency and reduce environmental impact." [By *co-modality*, one usually means the use of different modes on their own and in combination, with the aim of obtaining an optimal and sustainable utilization of resources in the supply chain (Guthed and Jobenius 2009)].

The Swedish Ministry of Transport characterizes a Green Corridor by:

- Sustainable logistic solutions.
- Integrated logistic concepts with utilization of co-modality.
- A harmonized system of rules.
- National/international goods traffic on long transport stretches.
- Effective and strategically placed transhipment points and infrastructure.
- A platform for development and demonstration of innovative logistic solutions.

These definitions are not very precise, perhaps deliberately. However, in the quest for sustainable transport solutions, there is a clear need to move to a definition level that can ultimately help both policy-makers and the industry achieve verifiable progress towards a more environmentally friendly supply chain.

The environmental performance of the various modes of transport, in terms of energy use and emissions, is quite diverse (Table 9.1).

Figure 9.1 shows the contribution of each transport mode, and of other energy-consuming industries, to the overall level of Greenhouse Gas (GHG) emissions worldwide. It is seen that among transport modes, road is by far the main contributor of GHGs (21.3 %), with international shipping second but far behind (2.7 %), and rail the least contributor (0.5 %). On a per ton-km basis, maritime transport fares the best among modes while air transport fares the worst.

Table 9.1 Energy efficiency and emissions to the atmosphere (by mode)

Energy use	11,000 TEU container vessel	6,600 TEU container vessel	Rail-electric	Rail-diesel	Heavy truck	Boeing 747–400
kWh/tkm[a]	0.014	0.018	0.043	0.067	0.18	2.00
Emissions (g/tkm)	11,000 TEU container vessel	6,600 TEU container vessel	Rail-electric	Rail-diesel	Heavy truck	Boeing 747–400
Carbon dioxide (CO_2)	7.48	8.36	18	17	50	552
Sulphur oxides (SO_X)	0.19	0.21	0.44	0.35	0.31	5.69
Nitrogen oxides (NO_x)	0.12	0.162	0.10	0.00005	0.00006	0.17
Particulate matters (PM)	0.008	0.009	n/a	0.008	0.005	n/a

[a] Kilowatt hours per tonne-km. The complete value chain for electrical production is considered in emissions for rail. *Source* Network for Transport and the Environment, Sweden

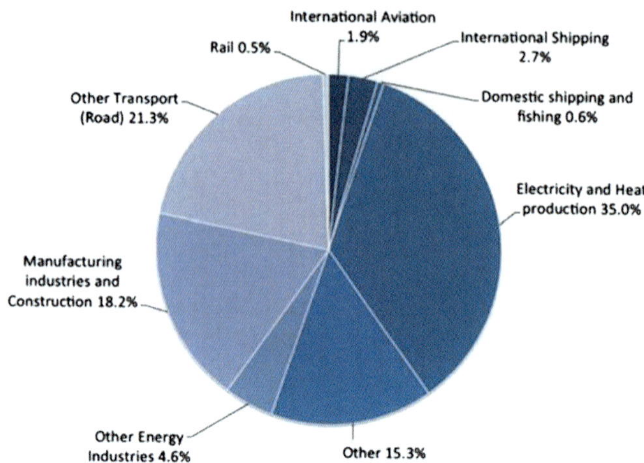

Fig. 9.1 Distribution of world GHG emissions for 2007 *Source* IMO 2009 GHG study (Buhaug et al. 2009)

Table 9.1 may be slightly misleading: container vessels are by far the most energy-consuming ship type due to their speed. That is for kilowatt hours per ton-km. But consider CO_2 emissions. A Very Large Crude Carrier (VLCC) emits 3.6 and a Capesize bulk carrier as few_2 as 2.7 g of CO_2 per ton-km. This means that if one were to move 120 tonnes of freight over a distance of 9,000 km, a typical payload/range combination for a B 747—400 freighter, that freighter would generate some 596 tonnes of CO_2. The equivalent figure for a Capesize bulk carrier, pro-rated for the same cargo volume, would be only 2.9 tonnes of CO_2.

When transport modes are combined, i.e. in an *intermodal* logistical chain, the result depends on the particular scenario and the chosen criteria. There is thus a clear need to develop a method to assess the environmental performance of the combined product. Such an evaluation needs to be coupled with traditional criteria of logistical performance, with a view to improve both, if possible.

To attain verifiable progress towards a more environmentally friendly supply chain, EU project "SuperGreen" has been launched (See Sjogren and Pedersen 2010). This is a so-called "Coordination and Support Action" co-funded by the European Commission in the context of the 7th Framework Programme for Research and Technological Development (FP 7). The project involves 22 partners from 13 European countries These include transport, logistics and infrastructure operators, shippers, environmental organizations and authorities responsible for social and spatial planning, consultants, academia and R&D.[1] Altogether, they committed to mobilize resources of more than 3 million Euros, with the European Commission contributing on the order of 2.6 million Euros. The timetable of the project is January 2010-January 2013. The project's web site, www.supergreen project.eu, includes all deliverables released to the public. That site is also on green surface logistics in general.

This chapter aims to address the key issues involved in development of Green Corridors for European Freight Logistics, and give an overview of the project's main results during its first year. Because the end of the SuperGreen project was some 2 years away (at the time of writing), the results described will be only partial. But these should give a good idea of the problems and challenges involved.

We remark that air transport is outside the scope of SuperGreen, and therefore also outside the scope of this chapter, which is organized as follows. Section 9.2 is a state-of-the-art section. A broad overview of the SuperGreen project is provided in Sect. 9.3. Section 9. 4 discusses the benchmarking of Green Corridors by describing the corridor selection process and defining Key Performance Indicators (KPIs). Sections 9.5 and 9.6 respectively present other relevant factors and the chapter's conclusions. In Appendix A, we summarize an additional dozen European Projects, each with some relationship to SuperGreen.

9.2 State-of-the-Art

9.2.1 Policy Framework

The issue of "Green Corridors" is still pretty much at an early maturity stage, but several distinct facets of transport policy formulation already touch upon green corridors, either directly or indirectly. The mid-term review of the 2001 "White paper—European transport policy for 2010: time to decide" (EU 2001) stressed the key role of logistics in ensuring sustainability and competitiveness in mobility in Europe, and how logistics contributes to other objectives (cleaner environment, security of energy supply, transport safety). Freight Transport Logistics, seen as a prime contributor to meeting the visions in the Lisbon agenda on growth and jobs, is about planning, organization, management, and control. Execution of transport

[1] SuperGreen partners: National Technical University of Athens (Greece, project Coordinator), Marintek (Norway), Sito Ltd (Finland), D' Appolonia Spa (Italy), Port Authority of Gijon (Spain), Det Norske Veritas (Norway), Via Donau (Austria), Newcastle University (UK), Consultrans (Spain), PSA Sines (Portugal), Straightway Finland, SNCF Italia, Procter and Gamble Europe (Belgium), VR Group (Finland), IHS Fairplay (Sweden), Hellenic Shortsea Shipowners Association (Greece), Dortmund University of Technology (Germany), TES Consult (Ukraine), Turkish State Railways, DB Schenker (Germany), and the Norwegian Public Road Administration.

operations in a supply chain comprises numerous actors and disciplines throughout the chain.

In December of 2009, a widely-attended Green Corridor conference was hosted by the European Commission in Brussels (See Huber 2009).[2] However, perhaps the most important institutional development was the 'new White Paper' on transport policy, announced in late March of 2011. A central pillar of this policy is the so-called 'decarbonisation of transport'. In fact, the ambitious goal of reducing GHG emissions from transport by at least 60 % by 2050 has been set.

To reach that goal, the 2011 White Paper stipulates, among other things, that *"30 % of road freight over 300 km should shift to other modes such as rail or waterborne transport by 2030, and more than 50 % by 2050, facilitated by efficient and green freight corridors. To meet this goal will also require appropriate infrastructure to be developed."*

In parallel, a so-called "Core network of strategic European infrastructure—A European Mobility Network" has been proposed. To arrive at the core network, one would have to:

- Define in the new guidelines of the Trans-European Transport Network (TEN-T) a core network of strategic European infrastructure, integrating the eastern and western part of the European Union and shaping the Single European Transport Area. Foresee appropriate connections with neighbouring countries.
- Concentrate EU action on components of the TEN-T network with highest European added value (cross-border missing links, intermodal connecting points, key bottlenecks).
- Deploy large scale intelligent and interoperable technologies to optimize capacity and the use of infrastructure.
- Ensure that EU-funded transport infrastructure takes into account energy-efficiency needs and climate-change challenges (climate resilience of the overall infrastructure, refuelling/recharging stations for clean vehicles, and choice of construction materials).

Green Corridors thus depend heavily on the characteristics of surface transportation modes. Section 9.2.2 summarizes the overall picture of those modes.

9.2.2 *Surface Modes of Transport*

European road transport has been the subject of successive EU legislation and fees. These include the introduction of Euro classes and highway tolls based on the internalization of external costs caused by traffic congestion, noise, accidents and pollution, according to SEC (2008) 2206/3, Commission Staff Working Document

[2] All 18 presentations from that conference can be found by visiting this link:http://ec.europa.eu/transport/sustainablesustainable/events/2009_12_09_green_corridors_conference_en.htm.

Table 9.2 Ten-T priority projects

Nro description	TEN-T priority projects
1.	Railway axis Berlin-Verona/Milano-Bologna-Napoli-Messina-Palermo
2.	High-speed railway axis Paris-Brussels-Köln-Amsterdam-London: PBKAL
3.	High-speed railway axis of South-West Europe
4.	High-speed railway axis East
5.	Betuwe line, railway Rotterdam-Dutch/German border
6.	Railway axis Lyon-Trieste-Divaca / Koper-Divaca-Ljubljana-Budapest-Ukrainian border
7.	Motorway axis Igoumenitsa /Patra-Athens-Sofia-Budapest
8.	Multimodal axis Portugal/Spain-rest of Europe
9.	Railway axis Cork-Dublin-Belfast-Stranraer: COMPLETED 2001
10.	Malpensa Airport: COMPLETED 2001
11.	The Oresund bridge: COMPLETED 2000
12.	Nordic triangle railway/road axis
13.	Road axis United Kingdom/Ireland/Benelux
14.	West coast main line, railway route in the UK, London-the West Midlands-the North West-North Wales
15.	Galileo
16.	Freight railway axis Sines/Algeciras-Madrid-Paris
17.	Railway axis Paris-Strasbourg-Stuttgart-Wien-Bratislava
18.	Waterway axis Rhine/Meuse-Main-Danube
19.	High-speed rail interoperability in the Iberian Peninsula
20.	Railway axis Fehmarn belt
21.	Motorways of the sea
22.	Railway axis Athens-Sofia-Budapest-Wien-Prague-Nurnberg /Dresden
23.	Railway axis Gdansk-Warszawa-Brno/Bratislava-Wien
24.	Railway axis Lyon /Geneva-Basel-Duisburg-Rotterdam /Antwerp
25.	Motorway axis Gdansk-Brno/Bratislava-Vienna
26.	Railway/road axis Ireland/United Kingdom/continental Europe
27.	Rail Baltica axis: Warsaw-Kaunas-Riga-Tallinn-Helsinki
28.	Eurocaprail on the Brussels-Luxembourg-Strasbourg railway axis
29.	Railway axis of the Ionian/Adriatic intermodal corridor
30.	Inland waterway Seine-Scheldt

Source European commission

on "Greening Transport" (EU 2008). Road transport must therefore increase energy efficiency, not only because of oil price volatility, but also due to continuous regulations (Euro class 6 expected to be in force starting 2014). Key measures thereto are improved engines and fuels, and fuel-efficient driving. Further, the optimal consolidation of road transport shall enable a reduction in the number of operating vehicles, as well as an increased load factor per vehicle. This is a special challenge for logistics companies with a dense transport network.

Regarding railways, the general EU policy has been to favor development of rail transport by increasing reliability, competition and capacity, and hence its attractiveness relative to other modes. The 2006 Mid-Term Review of the

Transport White Paper underlined the need to tackle low levels of interoperability, the lack of mutual recognition of rolling stock and products, and the weak coordination of infrastructure and interconnection of IT systems. Exploiting the potential of rail, therefore, has been a key focus of recent Commission initiatives, including development of a rail network, giving priority to freight. In the Communication, "Towards a rail network giving priority to freight" (EU 2007b), the Commission emphasized measures which contribute to creating that strong European rail network. This is part of the TEN-T. (Priority projects are summarized later, in Table 9.2.) The goal is that rail has a greater share of freight transport in Europe.

On maritime transport, the Commission is promoting the creation of a new "European maritime transport space without barriers" (EU 2007c), and a new strategy for maritime transport policy to 2018 (EU 2009). The challenge is to proceed in a way compatible to environmental goals. Recent developments at the IMO (International Maritime Organization) may have important ramifications. The IMO unanimously adopted amendments to the MARPOL Annex VI regulations, stipulating serious reductions in SO_x emissions. But on the negative side, progress regarding greenhouse gases has been slow. In the summer of 2011, the IMO adopted mandatory rules on the so-called Energy Efficiency Index (EEDI). This applies to new ships, and aims to assess their energy efficiency. However, effective application of this index will not be felt until several years later. Discussion has only started on the introduction of Market Based Measures (MBMs) (See Psaraftis and Kontovas 2010 concerning the balance between environmental and economic aspects of maritime transport).

The European Commission is following IMO developments very closely, and has stated quite clearly its intention to act alone if IMO's procedures take longer than previously anticipated. The end of 2011 is critical: any delay beyond that date will certainly trigger the EC's action. Indeed, the EC will almost certainly proceed with measures of its own, even though the IMD has adopted EEDI. It is not yet clears what these measures could be.

Significant as the IMO developments might be, these may have important impact on other, seemingly unrelated, policy subjects regarding alternative modes of transport, especially road. Already ECSA (European Community Shipowners' Association) has voiced concern that the use of fuel with lower sulphur within designated sulphur emissions control areas (SECAs) may have a reverse impact on the policy goal to shift cargo from land to sea. Short-sea shipping would become less favourable than road transport, ultimately leading to *more* CO_2 pollution overall (Lloyds List 2008). Measures to reduce emissions in ports (such as cold ironing[3]) may, if not implemented properly, increase the cost of moving freight through ports and again discourage co-modality from land to sea. Given the Commission's new port policy (EU 2007d), the question is, How can the

[3] "Cold ironing" is the use of shoreside electricity by a ship while in port, so as to avoid emissions from the ship's auxiliary engines.

environmental issue be handled so that all these policies converge in a 'win–win' fashion?

Inland navigation is considered to be a sustainable, safe and environmentally friendly mode of transport; however, its capacity is far from utilized. In the "Communication on the promotion of Inland Waterway Transport (NAIADES)" (EU 2006), the Commission sets out an integrated action programme to fully exploit the attraction and market potential of inland navigation.

9.3 The SuperGreen Project

9.3.1 Objectives: Overview

We now give a brief outline of the SuperGreen project. Its objectives concern supporting the development of sustainable transport networks by fulfilling requirements covering environmental, technical, economical, social and spatial planning aspects. These will be achieved by:

- Giving overall support, and recommendations on Green Corridors to EU's Freight Transport Logistics Action Plan.
- Conducting a programme of networking activities between stakeholders (public and private) and ongoing EU and other R&D projects. Networking would facilitate information exchange, dissemination of research results and communication of best practices and technologies at a European, national, and regional scale, thus *Adding value to ongoing programmes.*
- Providing a schematic for overall benchmarking of Green Corridors based on selected KPIs.
- Delivering a series of short- and medium-term studies addressing topics of importance to the further development of Green Corridors.
- Offering policy recommendations at a European level for the further development of those Corridors.
- Providing recommendations to the Commission concerning new calls for R&D proposals to support enhancement of Green Corridors.

9.3.2 Work Plan

Work packages WP 2 to WP 7 will next be described (WP 1 refers to the overall Project Management).

9.3.2.1 Benchmarking Green Corridors (WP 2)

This work package aims to determine the major development needs and possibilities for the greening of transport chains in selected transport corridors. It also provides information on Key Performance Indicators suitable to assess the economic efficiency, social acceptance and environmental sustainability of green corridors. The work is based on indicators developed for monitoring the sustainable development goals of the EU. WP 2 will utilize the studies done in member states on supply chain accounting and reporting, as well as test the sustainable development indicators for spatial and social planning. The current situation, the sustainability, plus the future development of transport corridors will be described.

Much of this chapter concerns results of WP 2. Specifically, Sects. 9.4.1 and 9.4.2 discuss the selection of corridors and the KPIs.

9.3.2.2 Sustainable Green Technologies and Innovations (WP 3)

The objectives of this work package are the identification, selection and benchmarking of Green Technologies, to be applied to solution of bottlenecks in operating specific Green Corridors. Investigations will be made of novel propulsion systems and engines, alternative fuels, cargo handling and transfer technologies, or any new concepts relevant to multimodal corridors. This work package will offer a sound coverage of the most promising technologies, techniques and procedures to be employed in Green Corridors, both over the different transport legs and at transshipment points. WP 3 will assess which techniques would help reduce the sustainability footprint of the overall logistics chain. Analysis will compare the different technologies on a set of applications, in terms of *what-where-how* use-case scenarios. Results will be stored in a web-based knowledge repository, and made accessible to stakeholders by means of a user-friendly wizard. WP 3 will continuously run throughout the project lifetime to include new technology developments.

9.3.2.3 Smart Exploitation of ICT-flows (WP 4)

WP4 seeks to define and exploit the role of Information and Communications Technology towards the goal of greener transport. As a complement to WP 3, WP 4 will identify 'win–win' solutions and best practices. That will be based on implementation of methodologies that achieve a cost-effective utilization of transport resources on the one hand, and a green supply chain management on the other. This goal seems simple to state; it will not be trivial to attain. Realistic and efficient solutions that reduce supply chain emissions and also enhance international trade, but will not unduly burden the intermodal transport industry, may not exist. WP 4 will furnish taxonomy of these problems. Together, a map of relevant alternatives and measures will be developed, in an attempt to facilitate policy recommendations (WP 6).

9.3.2.4 Recommendation for R&D Calls (WP 5)

The main objective is to identify and define calls for R&D proposals to the European Commission; such recommendations are among the main outputs from SuperGreen. The EC seeks support on Green Corridor issues in their work on implementation of the 2009 Freight Transport Logistics Action Plan, and, most recently, the 2011 White Paper. What makes a corridor green, in terms of benchmarks and key performance indicators? That is the subject of WP 2. Another question is, How can *available* green technologies (WP 3) and e-freight solutions contribute to make existing corridors green or even greener? If there are no such existing green technologies or e-freight solutions, there is a technology gap between what is available and what is needed to make the corridors green. This gap could be a basis for future R&D recommendations to be implemented in later calls of the Seventh Framework Programs. The main output of WP 5 is those R&D recommendations, which again give important input to WP 6 (Policy Implications) and WP 7, Dissemination and Awareness Raising.

9.3.2.5 Policy Implications (WP 6)

The transport of freight, ranging from raw materials to finished goods, is essential to economic activity and to the quality of life in the EU. The overall objective of the SuperGreen project is to give support on Green-Corridor issues to EU's Freight Transport Logistics Action Plan, and, ultimately, to the 2011 White Paper. The main goal of WP 6 is thus to enhance the interaction between the regulatory policy framework and the findings produced within the project.

9.3.2.6 Dissemination and Awareness Raising (WP 7)

Dissemination activities will spread the SuperGreen project results to a wider audience outside the consortium. Those activities will create the right awareness of SuperGreen achievements and highlight the possible benefits, challenges and issues that the project will bring to the logistics sector and to society. To fulfill the above-mentioned objectives, dissemination will include specific events, press releases and newsletters, published both on paper and on the project's dedicated website. There is also a SuperGreen friends email (supergreen@martrans.org), and even a Green Corridors group at LinkedIn. Particular importance will be given to recommendations for R&D calls developed in WP 5.

Table 9.3 Criteria and scales used in corridor pre-selection

Scale				
1	2	3	4	5
Low		Transport volume (million tons)		High (>100)
Under 1,000		Length of corridor (kms)		10,000 or more
No bottlenecks		Transport infrastructure bottlenecks: Number and seriousness		Serious bottlenecks
Bad potential		Types of goods, multimodality		Good potential
No preconditions		Geographical preconditions		Many preconditions
Much		Used transport and information technology		Little
Good		Supply chains managements, transport clients		Poor
Under 3		Human habitat (million people)		20 or more

9.4 Benchmarking Green Corridors

Let us now summarize progress within WP 2, the most critical work package of SuperGreen thus far. More details on Sects. 9.4.1 and 9.4.2 can be found in Salanne et al. (2010) and Pålsson et al. (2010), respectively.

9.4.1 Methodology: Selection of Corridors

A critical task within WP 2 was to determine 10–15 corridors from which some (6–8 according to the description of work) would be selected for further benchmarking. Given the multitude of corridors in Europe, that process consisted of two steps: (a) pre-selection and (b) selection. Pre-selection is first described.

An initial database of corridors was obtained from the current TEN-T network. That programme consists of hundreds of projects—defined as studies or works—whose ultimate purpose is to ensure the cohesion, interconnection and interoperability of the trans-European transport network, as well as access to it. The TEN-T projects, located in every EU Member State, involve all modes (road, rail, maritime, inland waterways, and air) plus horizontal priorities such as logistics, co-modality[4] and innovation. Thirty *Priority* Projects (either transport axes or other horizontal priorities) were established to focus on European integration and development. Those 30 projects identified by EU Member States and included in the Community guidelines for development of the TEN-T as projects of European interest, are listed in Table 9.2.

[4] The term *co-modality* was introduced by the European Commission in 2006. It means the "use of different modes on their own and in combination," with the aim "of obtaining an optimal and sustainable utilisation of resources".

Table 9.4 Final selection of nine SuperGreen corridors

Acronym	Brief description- branches	Nickname	Explanation
BerPal	Malmo-Trelleborg-Rostock/Sassnitz- Berlin-Munich-Salzburg-Verona-Bologna-Naples-Messina-Palermo	Brenner	The Alpine pass that is the key of this corridor
	Branch A: Salzburg-Villach-Trieste (Tauern axis)		
	Branch B: Bologna-Ancona/Bari/Brindisi-Igoumenitsa/Patras-Athens		
MadPar	Madrid-Gijon-Saint Nazaire-Paris	Finis Terrae	point of Europe
	Branch A: Madrid-Lisboa		(in Galicia)
CorMun	Cork-Dublin-Belfast-Stranraer	Cloverleaf	Green grass that is a symbol of Ireland
	Branch A: Munich-Friedewald-Nuneaton Branch B: West Coast Main line		
HelGen	Helsinki-Turku-Stockholm-Oslo-Goteborg-Malmo-Copenhagen	Edelweiss	(also the shape of this Corridor)
	(Nordic triangle including the Oresund fixed link)- Fehmarnbelt-Milan-Genoa		
RotMos	Motorway of Baltic sea	Nureyeev	The top Russian ballet dancer of the
	Branch: St. Petersburg-Moscow-Minsk-Klapeida		
RhiDan	Rhine/Meuse-Main-Danube inland waterway axis	Strauss	Music composer of the famous blue Danube
	Branch A: Betuwe line		
	Branch B: Frankfurt-Paris		
AthDre	Igoumenitsa/Patras-Athens-Sofia-Budapest-Vienna-	Two seas	The Mediterranean seas
	Prague-Nurnberg/Dresden-Hamburg		
SinOde	Odessa-Constanta-Bourgas-Istanbul-Piraeus-Gioia Tauro-Cagliari-La Spezia-Marseille-Barcelona-Valencia-Sines	Mare Nostrum	Latin for Mediterranean sea
	Branch A: Algeciras-Valencia-Barcelona-Marseille-Lyon		
	Branch B: Piraeus-Trieste		
CNHam	Shanghai-Le Havre/Rotterdam-Hamburg/Goteborg-Gdansk-Baltic ports-Russia	Silk way	The classical name for the road to China
	Branch: Xiangtang-Beijing-Mongolia-Russia-Belarus-Poland-Hamburg		

Fig. 9.2 The nine selected corridors in 'metro' format

Besides the TEN-T network, the set of so-called Pan-European transport corridors was considered. Those ten corridors were defined at the second Pan-European Transport Conference, in Crete in March 1994, as routes in Central and Eastern Europe that required major investment over the next ten to 15 years. Additions were made at the third conference in Helsinki in 1997. (These corridors are thus sometimes referred to as either the "Crete corridors" or "Helsinki corridors", regardless of their geographical locations.) A tenth corridor was proposed after the end of hostilities between the states of former Yugoslavia. These development corridors are distinct from the Trans-European transport networks that include all major established routes in the European Union. This is despite the fact that there are proposals to combine the two systems; most of the countries involved are now members of the EU.

The corridor list was supplemented with the Pan-European corridors mentioned above (not listed here due to space limitations). Where applicable, a combination of TEN-T and Pan European corridors was made. A new list of 45 corridors was formed as a result of this consolidation.

An internal pre-selection workshop was then arranged. The aim was to pre-select 10–15 corridors for further work. Criteria for pre-selection are shown in Table 9.3. Assessment of the corridors according to these criteria was carried out using the Delphi method. Table 9.4 shows the final corridors selected.

It should be made clear that the above corridors were chosen only for purposes of the SuperGreen project. Selection by no means implies any endorsement, either by the SuperGreen consortium or by the EC, of these corridors vis-à-vis any other corridor, with respect to any criteria. Resources available were the main determinant of the number of corridors (9). Also, it must be stated that one criterion for choosing those corridors was their "greening potential", i.e. the chance for improvement in at least some of their segments according to environmental criteria. Balance in geographical coverage and in modal mix was also important Fig. 9.2.

9.4.2 *Key Performance Indicators*

Criteria for selection of the KPIs are dependent upon the latter's uses. The impact-assessment document of the Freight Transport Logistics Action Plan from the European Commission states that: "*Both trends, the economic and the environmental, call for the mobilisation of untapped efficiencies in logistics in order to make more judicious and more effective use of freight transport operations.*"

After discussion, it was decided that the KPI major groups should be: (a) Efficiency, (b) Service quality, (c) Environmental sustainability, (d) Infrastructural sufficiency, and (d) Social issues.

Details, including methodology, can be found in Pålsson et al. (2010). Below we give an overview of the main elements of each KPI group.

9.4.2.1 Efficiency

"Efficiency" deals with traditional economic costs, as these are reflected in the logistics operation. Both absolute unit costs and relative unit costs are envisaged. *Absolute* unit costs are used for comparisons of transport solutions on the same route. *Relative* unit costs enable comparisons of transport solutions, either on different routes within the same corridor or on different corridors.

Absolute unit costs

Absolute unit costs are often expressed in € per ton for the entire stretch from the origin (loading node) to the destination (discharging node). Solid arguments, however, can be made that for some types of goods, the unit should be € per m^3. But for the purposes of transparency and benchmarking, € per ton will be the preferred unit.

The total direct transport costs are needed for the entire stretch. These are then to be divided by the quantity of goods, to arrive at the absolute unit cost per ton. Actual costs are always preferred as input data, provided they are collected in a coherent and transparent way. This information is quite often difficult to obtain. We are then forced to rely on one or more cost-calculation models using representative values.

Cost-calculator tools, as described in Appendix A, provide both data and the instrument to facilitate the calculation. A formal assessment of the available tools is necessary prior to selecting those that will be used in corridor benchmarking.

Relative unit costs

Relative unit costs are expressed in € per ton-kilometre for the entire stretch from the loading node to discharging node. Relative unit costs are obtained by dividing the Absolute unit costs by that Distance of the entire stretch.

Stakeholders who are concerned about these KPIs obviously include carriers, shippers, logistics operators, terminal operators, producers and consumers at large. That set of KPIs is important to virtually *all* stakeholders. Perhaps environmental stakeholders would consider the KPIs here to be of lesser significance (vis-à-vis environmental criteria), but this does not mean that they are irrelevant.

9.4.2.2 Service Quality

The "Service Quality" group deals with attributes and perceptions that define the logistics service level. KPIs envisaged include transport time, reliability, frequency of service, and the safety and security of the cargo. ICT applications would also play a role in service quality.

Transport time

"Transport time" refers to the total time in hours or days, from loading at the origin to discharging at the destination. An alternative way to measure transport time is via the average speed for the same route. The Be- Logic project (see Appendix A) defined "Time" along the supply chain as the sum of loading time, driving/sailing time, waiting time at borders and terminals, and unloading time. Units can be in days, hours or minutes.

Reliability (time precision)

Reliability is a KPI often brought forward as important. The reliability indicator in the Be- Logic benchmarking tool is defined as the mean of: punctuality, transit time variation, reputation and complaints. For each of these, depending on data availability, a qualitative scale (1–5) or a quantitative representation can be used (for instance, percent of arrivals that are punctual).

The related quality objectives of the Brenner corridor, as defined in the BRAVO project, concern punctuality (maximum delay of 15 min for 90 % of the trains) and transit time variation (maximum train delay of 180 min for the 10 % non-punctual trains).

ICT applications

The presence and degree of sophistication of applications of information and communication technology is important from several aspects. From an operational point of view, it is about planning. From the perspective of shifting transports towards more sustainable alternatives, it is about facilitating change and improvements in efficiency.

Since ICT applications cover a wide range, this KPI is the assessed result of four performance indicators. Those broadly reflect the availability and degree of sophistication of goods-tracking services, as well as of other relevant ICT services. To summarize, the four indicators are: Availability of tracking services on nodes/links; Integration & functionality of tracking services; availability of other ICT services on nodes/links; and integration & functionality of other ICT services.

The assessment is the average according to numbered, graded scales, describing first the presence in terms of "non-existent" to "full coverage of transport stretch", then the degree of integration and functionality in similar terms.

Frequency of service

"Frequency of service" describes the number of shipments available per week for each individual transport solution. As frequency is closely related to the *flexibility* of transport, the Be- Logic KPI definition shall be equally considered. This is a composite indicator involving the following: (a) Ability to adapt to changes in demand/volume (scale 1–5) (b) ability to adapt to changes in size/special cargo (scale 1–5) (c) Ability to adapt to changes in time table (time needed to return to normal conditions/response time) (d) Robustness: ability to cope with serious disruptions such as cancellations or strikes (scale 1–5) (e) Availability: possibility of custom-made departure times (yes/no), and (f) Availability of fixed time tables (number of departures per week).

Cargo security

Cargo that is "secure" will experience minimal loss due to unlawful acts such as thefts or roadside robbery. The various transport modes have different security levels, measured qualitatively in terms of degree of security. The usual way to evaluate performance involves measuring the security incidents and comparing them to the total number of shipments.

A different approach is followed by Marintek in the Shipping KPI project (see Appendix A). A prevention-oriented approach has been selected for this project. The cargo security performance of a ship is described by an index that considers crew- and port state control-related aspects, in addition to security deficiencies recorded during external inspections of the vessel.

Cargo safety

Cargo "safety" refers to incidents that result in damage to the goods transported. As in the ease of cargo security, the cargo safety performance of a ship is expressed through an index combining the results of safety incidents with relevant preventive measures. The crew- and port state control-related aspects of the index are identical to those of the cargo security index discussed above. Furthermore, the safety index depends on fire and explosion, navigational, equipment failure, and cargo incidents, in addition to fatalities, injuries, lost workdays and safety deficiencies recorded during external inspections of the ship.

9.4.2.3 Environmental Sustainability

The "Environmental Sustainability" KPI group deals with climatic or atmospheric attributes defined in the logistics operation. Performance indicators are thus envisaged for the carbon footprint and for other pollutants.

Greenhouse Gases (Carbon Footprint)

The KPI specified for greenhouse gases is the emissions of CO_2-*equivalent*, as it takes into consideration emissions of other-than-CO_2 greenhouse gases. The unit is grams of CO_2 per tonne-km. Because the "price" of a tonne of CO_2 may fluctuate in time, emissions themselves are preferred to estimates of the relevant external costs for corridor assessment. Following the NTM tool logic on system boundaries (Appendix A), the system boundary B (well-to-wheel) is selected for this application, provided of course that the necessary data is readily available.

The chosen indicator is in reality a composite, its value being produced from those of three PIs according to the formula:

Specific emissions of GHG = (Fuel Emission Factor)(Specific energy consumption)/(load factor)*

The **Fuel Emission Factor** expresses emissions of GHG per energy unit of fuel and is measured in grams CO_2-eq/kWh. It depends on the type of fuel being used. The **Specific Energy Consumption**, the energy input to the vehicle (or vessel) per unit distance travelled, is measured in kWh/km. It is influenced by engine and vehicle technology, driving conditions (speed, congestion, topography, weather, driving pattern) and by load factors. Finally, the **Load factor** (capacity utilization factor) describes the cargo load in tons relative to the capacity of the vehicle/vessel, in ton-km/vehicle-km.

Pollutants

The assessment of indicators for pollutants with local and regional effects is done in the same way as for greenhouse gases. The KPI denotes specific emissions of the pollutants NO_X (nitrogen oxide) SO_X (sulphur oxide) and $PM_{2.5.}$ (particulate matter- PM) expressed in grams of pollutant per tonne-km. ($PM_{2,5}$ is the fraction of PM with a size below 2.5 micrometers).

For heavy vehicles, ships and trains, specific emissions (NOx and PM) are usually given in grams per kWh of engine power. That must be transformed to emissions per tonne-km through energy efficiency data and load factors similar to those employed for GHG above. Note that the gram per kWh in this case usually refers to the energy *output* of the engine, not the energy input as for GHG. Sulphur emissions are most commonly communicated through data on sulphur content in fuels and can be transformed to grams/tonne-km. Specific Emissions of NOx depend mainly on engine technology, although some differences can be attributed to fuels (relevant mainly for ships). Specific Emissions of SOx vary with the sulphur content in fuels. For road diesel, there is a common standard (10 ppm) within the EU; for ships the sulphur content may vary from below 1,000 ppm (0.1 %) (ships at berth in community ports and inland waterway vessels) to over

20,000 ppm (ships using heavy fuel oil outside SECAs). Specific Emissions of PM depend both on engine technology and on the fuel used, and increase with sulphur content.

Obviously, environmental groups and society at large are those with the highest stake in these KPIs. Individual carriers, shippers, logistics operators, and terminal managers would a priori appear to have a lower stake, particularly if the external costs of emissions are not reflected in the price these stakeholders pay to operate. In that sense, if these external costs are not internalized, some operators may not behave in a way consistent with optimal environmental performance.

9.4.2.4 Infrastructural Sufficiency

The "Infrastructural Sufficiency" KPI group concerns such measures as (a) Congestion, and (b) Bottlenecks. An indicator pertaining to energy balance of the infrastructure could also be considered. This would compare the energy produced (mainly through renewable sources) against the energy consumed during operation on an annual basis. It is more relevant to ports and inland terminals, but could also be applied to new road and rail projects.

Congestion

Congestion, an important component of transport-related external costs, is even more significant than emissions when it comes to road transport. Approaches in the literature to measure congestion include indicators based on (a) travel time (or speed), (b) traffic volume, and (c) area.

Examples of KPIs are the following:

- 'Total delay' to 'volume of traffic' ratio: Gives the "average amount of delay" for a vehicle travelling 1 km.
- Speed-based KPIs, especially relevant for motorways (e.g., a congested state exists when traffic speed is below 70 kph).
- The 'congestion reference flow', an index determined by capacity of the road, number of lanes, and other traffic-related variables.
- The 'level of service' indicator, a basic congestion scale running from A to F (with A being best) that describes conditions using variables such as speed, travel time, disruption to flows, and safety. It is widely employed in the United States.

Bottlenecks

The KPI for bottlenecks is the assessed result of an inventory of different types of bottlenecks per transport solution, which are further divided into a few categories reflecting the seriousness of each type of bottleneck. The objective of this KPI is to find the biggest bottlenecks per transport mode within corridors and estimate the seriousness of these bottlenecks. The target is to survey the development of the bottlenecks in time in different transport corridors.

Bottlenecks can be divided into three categories: Infrastructure, Capacity, and Geography. Those related to the first describe how many sections of transport infrastructure along the corridor are in bad condition. Capacity bottlenecks concern traffic jams, customs, and insufficient port or rail capacity. The final bottlenecks, those that pertain to geography, involve barriers along the corridor (ice conditions, mountains etc.).

Obviously most stakeholders would consider this set of KPIs important, but more so infrastructure operators and users, and most notably those who are asked to *pay* for infrastructure construction and maintenance.

9.4.2.5 Social Issues

Lastly, the "Social issues" KPI group deals with factors likely to impact society in a broader sense. Indicators envisaged include Corridor land use, Safety, and Noise.

Corridor land use

The literature contains a plethora of land use indicators, the most prominent being (a) size, density and proportion of population living along the corridor; (b) percent of built-up land by distance from the median line of the corridor; and (c) percent of new development on "brown field" (previously developed) land.

For the purpose of corridor benchmarking, it was decided to focus our analysis on urban areas (with their significant transport-related external costs) and environmentally-sensitive areas (due to potential effects on nature and endangered species). We believe that these two aspects combine to provide a sufficiently good picture of the external costs related to land use that transport activities impose on the general public.

The first step in forming the urban land KPI is to define different land use categories along the corridor. To get homogeneous data related to that land use, calculations can be made using the CORINE Land Cover spatial dataset. Within a buffer radius of 20 km from the median line of each corridor, the total area of urban land cover can be calculated; this will be put in relation to the total area of corridor occupied land. The radius of 20 km allows inclusion of the major parts of even the largest cities along the corridors, takes into account that transports are, in part, distributed to areas around the defined corridors.

Traffic safety

Safety here refers to the incident rate of accidents and/or fatalities. The approach is similar to the KPI for cargo safety. The unit is percent of the total number of shipments. (Alternatively, relative values could be expressed as percentages of the transport ton-km, as suggested by the NTM model.) For each transport solution within a corridor, the number of shipments that have been subject to an accident will be presented in relation to the total number of shipments.

One difficulty with this indicator might be that distinct definitions of what constitutes an "accident" apply on the different transport modes. An alternative indicator that bypasses this potential problem is to focus on *results* of the accidents, namely fatalities and serious injuries. Should this approach be followed, the indicator could be the sum of deaths and serious injuries over either total number of shipments or the total transport work (ton-km).

Noise

Noise pollution is commonly defined as the excessive or annoying degree of unwanted sound in a particular area. The "Environmental Noise Directive" (END), relating to the assessment and management of environmental noise, was adopted by the European Parliament and Council in 2002. This Directive guides and steers activities on noise in Member States. The acceptable noise level is set to 50 dB, except for trains (55 dB). The unit for this KPI on noise is percentage of the total distance that is exposed to noise levels above the 50/55 dB limit. There are available figures in existing databases.

9.4.3 Which KPIs are the Most Important?

In late 2010 and early 2011, the SuperGreen project had a series of consultations with industrial stakeholders and the project's Advisory Committee with a view to narrowing down the list of KPIs to a manageable set. A workshop session held in Malmoe, Sweden in March, 2011,[5] took place jointly with a panel discussion. That panel consisted of project managers of various Swedish initiatives on Green Corridors, representatives of the industry and was led by the SuperGreen project coordinator. Another objective was to finalize the methodology for benchmarking. Validation of the final filtering of KPIs with stakeholders was considered a very important outcome of this workshop. The change of methodology (to focus on individual transport chains and to analyze operations in corridors) was accepted (with minor changes) by the audience and members of the panel. Those KPIs that received the highest endorsement as the most relevant and important for corridor benchmarking were the following:

Indicator	Unit
CO_2 emissions	g/ton-km
SO_x emissions	g/1,000 ton-km
Relative transport cost	€/ton-km
Transport time	Hours[a]
Frequency, services per year	Number
Reliability, on time deliveries	%

[a] Alternatively, an average speed in km/h can be considered.

[5] This was one among a series of four regional workshops.

These KPIs are to be used for benchmarking of the selected corridors, a process that was ongoing as these lines were being written.

9.5 Concluding Remarks

This chapter has explored the concept of Green Corridors in European Surface Freight logistics by highlighting the main issues and by describing the means by which these issues can be tackled. The objectives, approach and some partial results of the EU project SuperGreen have been outlined. It is clear that more results will be available after this book has been published. Those results will be available on the project's web site.

Effort on this project is ongoing and is scheduled to continue in the foreseeable future. (What is not included here will be reported in subsequent publications.) In view of important policy implications and of the need of policy makers to be able to evaluate alternatives in an effective way, methods and tools specifically designed to tackle such problems seem more required than ever. It is hoped that studies such as the one described herein will help toward that goal.

Acknowledgments Work reported in this chapter was supported in part by EU project SuperGreen (grant agreement TREN/FP7TR/233573/"SUPERGREEN"). The assistance of Rein Jüriado and Fleur Breuillin, Project Officers at the European Commission (DG-MOVE), for technical and administrative support and for their advice in general, is gratefully acknowledged. Indrek Ilves should be credited with rendering the corridor maps in metro- format (Fig. 9.2). We are also thankful to (alphabetically) Sergio Barbarino, Niklas Bengtsson, Bianca Byring, Chara Georgopoulou, Even Ambros Holte, Konrad Pütz, Sanni Rönkkö, Anders Sjöbris, Andrea Schön, Panos Tsilingiris, Aud Marit Wahl, the members of the project's Advisory Committee and numerous other individuals, perhaps too many to mention by name, for their help.

Appendix A: Related Projects

The state of knowledge on emissions is immense, and so is the one on logistics. But not as much has been written on the interface between the two. The following (mostly European) logistics research projects are connected, directly or indirectly, to the objectives of SuperGreen. Pålsson et al. (2010) present further details.

"BE Logic" (www.be-logic.info) is the acronym of the "Benchmark Logistics for Co-modality" collaborative project funded by the European Commission under the 7th Framework Programme. It began on 1 September 2008 and was to last for 2.5 years. The nine partners are led by ECORYS Company. The project aims to improve efficiency of the different modes of transport, supporting the development of a quality logistics system. This is done through the benchmarking of: (a) transport policy, (b) transport chains and (c) inland and sea terminals.

"InteGRail" (Intelligent Integration of Railway Systems, www.integrail.info) was established in 2005 to address the growing demand for an efficient and integrated railway system in Europe. The project developed a method to assess performance of railways and to study the influence of changes in lower level performance indicators on the overall transport volume. The 40 project participants included railway and infrastructure companies, academic institutions, consultancies and technology providers. 11 million Euro out of a total project budget of 20 million was contributed by the European Union under FP6.

The **Shipping KPI** project (www.sintef.com/Projectweb/Shipping-KPI/) is based on a group of 18 leading ship-management and ship-owning companies that agreed to cooperate in establishing an international standard for Key Performance Indicators in shipping. A pilot project was initiated in January 2005 to test methodologies to measure the value of different KPIs. The pilot project was followed the "Shipping KPI Phase 1" sponsored by the research Council of Norway. The project was launched in January 2006 and ended in 2008.

The **Network for Transport and Environment** (NTM) is a non-profit organization that specializes in environmental performance assessment, establishing methods and data that enable credible calculations of transports' environmental, climate and energy performance. NTM was initiated in 1993 by a variety of transport providers and buyers of transport services. NTM has developed and offers web-based calculation tools for goods and passenger transportation.

"EcoTransIT World" (www.ecotransit.org), is an upgrade development of "EcotransIT", a project initiated in 2000 by five European railways: Railion AG (Germany), SBB (Switzerland), Green Cargo AB (Sweden), Trenitalia (Italy) and SNCF (France). New partners from Spain, Belgium and Germany have subsequently joined. EcoTransIT identifies the environmental impacts of freight transportation in terms of direct energy consumption and emissions during the operation of vehicles involved in freight transport (tank-to-wheel).

The **"Calculation of external costs for goods transport"** project was carried out at IVL with financial support by Vinnova, the Centre for Environmental Assessment of Products and Material (CPM) at Chalmers University and the Foundation for the Swedish Environmental Research Institute (SIVL). The member companies of CPM which co-financed the project were Schenker, Akzo Nobel, ABB and AB Volvo.

IHS Fairplay has developed **"COMPASS",** an acronym for comparison tool for co-modal transport assessments. COMPASS enables the entire transport chain to be modelled in steps and activities, with each chain including as many nodes and links as required.

The **NP Should** cost calculator was developed internally at Procter and Gamble 2009. The tool estimates transport costs, lead times and external costs. Calculations are based on collected data, which are linked to a user-specified intermodal transport chain. The model was improved in 2010 to include other modes of transport (e.g. inland waterways).

The German company Contargo has, since 1996, developed an **"Intermodal Tariff Information System"** (IMTIS), which helps evaluate the best transport mode and route. The system is permanently being updated and now possesses knowledge of more than 115,000 destinations in Europe. In 2007, the calculator was extended by a new factor: the CO_2 emissions of each mode of transport.

A similar tool is **GIFT**, Geospatial Intermodal Freight Transportation. It enables trade-offs between economic, environmental and energy impacts of freight transportation. GIFT, developed as a joint project between the University of Delaware and Rochester Institute of Technology, has been applied e.g. on East Coast freight studies and for the Great Lakes region. In the latter, implications of policies such as a carbon tax introduction were analyzed.

PROMIT is the acronym of the "Promoting Innovative Intermodal Freight Transport" Coordination Action, funded by the EC under the 6th Framework Programme. It promotes successful logistics approaches to intermodal transport. From the SuperGreen perspective, the following four cases are the most interesting.

BRAVO: The Brenner corridor, one of the busiest European freight corridors both by road and rail, transits the sensitive Alpine region (Austria, Germany, Italy). The objective is to raise the volume of environment-friendly combined rail-road transport and increase rail's market share along Brenner. "Action Plan Brenner 2005" contains a list of measures required to organize and ensure the short- to medium-term upgrading of the level of service provided in combined (rail-road intermodal) transport on this corridor.

RODER and AlpFRail: This supply chain case exhibits synergies between two separate developments in PROMIT. It concerns freight traffic between Turkey and Western Europe, where the previously-existing land-based routes were unattractive in respect to road distance, time, transport costs and environmental impact.

VOLVO: Recognising that Volvo's factories are "peripheral" in relation to customers, the company perceived a distance handicap compared to other vehicle manufacturers. In practice, these factories had to pay transport costs twice, both for sourcing of materials and for the distribution of finished products. To serve the Volvo factories and DCs in Umeå, Gothenburg and elsewhere, Volvo Logistics selected a train/short sea shipping (SSS) solution. That covered Volvo's transport needs with minimum environmental impact, by combining products (cabs) with production material.

The Viking Train: This offers a 1,735 km long link from the Baltic Sea region in Eastern Europe to the Black Sea Region (Caucasus and Turkey) in South-eastern Europe, and beyond to Central Asia. The Viking train makes use of the Pan-European corridor IX and circumvents the heavily congested western European north–south corridors, running through the countries of Lithuania, Belarus and Ukraine. The Viking train, as a road-SSS-rail intermodal connection improves security for long-distance trucks; reduces the disadvantage of a lack of through motorways; and enables the rebalancing of empty containers between northern and southern Europe.

PLATINA (www.naiades.info/platina/downloads) is the acronym of the "Platform for the implementation of NAIADES" project, financed by the European Commission under the 7th Framework Programme. The NAIADES action plan is an EC initiative to enhance the use of inland navigation as part of intermodal freight solutions, to create a sustainable European-wide transport network.

The **BestLog project** aimed to disseminate and promote logistics best-practice cases. Nine research institutes from as many European countries participated, establishing a basis for transport logistics decision making and reviewing trends such as the relation between growth in freight traffic and economic growth in the EU.

The **Swedish "Green Corridors"** initiative focuses on transport routes and collaboration among shippers, forwarders, industry and haulers to optimize the use of transport capacity. Better utilization of the transport resources will reduce the impact on the environment. The approach concerns all transport modes, and may lead to shifts from one mode to another. The project, managed by the Swedish Logistics Forum, began in 2008 and today features collaboration with the governments of Denmark, Finland and Norway. In addition, there are three international transport projects in the Baltic region, exhibiting important "greening" characteristics:

The **"East–West Transport Corridor" (EWTC)** project (www.eastwesttc.org/about-ewtc.aspx) was a cooperative venture between 42 different partners—local, regional and national authorities, universities, harbours and private stakeholders—in Denmark, Lithuania, Russia and Sweden. The project, begun in 2006, was co-financed by the project partners and the Interreg IIIB Baltic Sea 2000–2006 programme. EWTC aimed to strengthen the transport development through infrastructure improvements and cooperation between researchers.

The **SCANDRIA** project (www.scandriaproject.eu) is a cooperation of 19 partners from Germany, Denmark, Sweden, Finland and Norway, to develop a green and innovative transport corridor that connects capitals and metropolitan regions along the shortest path from Scandinavia to the Adriatic Sea. It is partly financed by the Baltic Sea Region Programme of the EU. Scandria fosters co-modality, rail transport and environmentally friendly solutions in road transport.

The **TransBaltic** project (http://transbaltic.eu/about/) is co-financed by the EU Baltic Sea Programme 2007–2013. Its overall objective is to provide regional-level incentives for creation of a comprehensive multimodal transport system in the Baltic Sea Region. This is to be achieved by means of joint transport development measures and jointly implemented business concepts.

References

Buhaug O, Corbett JJ, Endresen O, Eyring V, Faber J, Hanayama S, Lee DS, Lee D, Lindstad H, Mjelde A, Palsson C, Wanquing W, Winebrake JJ, Yoshida K (2009) Second IMO Greenhouse Gas Study. International Maritime Organization, London

EU (2001) European transport policy for 2010—time to decide, mid-term review COM (2006) 314 final—keep Europe moving -sustainable mobility for our Continent

EU (2006) Communication from the commission: COM (2006) 6 final—communication on the promotion of Inland Waterway Transport—an integrated European action programme for inland waterway transport (NAIADES)

EU (2007a) Communication from the commission: COM (2007) 607 final—freight transport logistics action plan
EU (2007b) Communication from the commission: COM (2007) 608 final—Towards a rail network giving priority to freight
EU (2007c) Communication from the commission: COM (2007) 575 final—an integrated maritime policy for the European union
EU (2007d) Communication from the commission: COM (2007) 616 final—communication on a European ports policy
EU (2008) SEC (2008) 2206/3, Commission staff working document on greening transport
EU (2009) COM (2009) 8 final- strategic goals and recommendations for the EU's maritime transport policy until 2018
Guthed A, Jobenius M (2009) Swedish corridor initiatives, presentation at the EU green corridor conference, Brussels, Dec 9
Huber W (2009) Green corridor brenner, presentation at the EU green corridor conference, Brussels, Dec 9
Lloyds List (2008) IMO sulphur limits deal could see more freight hit the road, Lloyds List, 10 April 2008
Pålsson C, Bengtsson N, Salanne I, Pütz K, Tsilingiris P, Georgopoulou C, Schön A, Minsaas A, Wahl A-M, Panagakos G (2010) Deliverable D2.2: definition of benchmarking indicators and methodology. Available at http://www.supergreenproject.eu/docs/public/SuperGreen%20 D2.2%20PUBLIC%20FINAL.pdf
Psaraftis HN, Kontovas CA (2010) Balancing the economic and environmental performance of maritime transportation. Transportation Research, Part D, 15(8):458–462
Salanne I, Rönkkö S, Byring B (2010) Deliverable D2.1: selection of Corridors. Available at http://www.supergreenproject.eu/docs/public/ FINAL%20PUBLIC%20Deliverable%20D2%201_WP%202_Super%20Green.pdf
Sjögren J, Pedersen J-T (2010) eFreight: one of the key facilitators for green corridors, presentation at the Super Green Helsinki workshop, June. Available at http://www.supergreenproject.eu/ docs/public/helsinki2010/eFreight-%20one%20of%20the%20key%20facilitators%20for%20 green%20corridors.pdf

Chapter 10
Containerized Freight Distribution in North America and Europe

Jean-Paul Rodrigue and Theo Notteboom

Abstract It is uncommon that country pairs would be directly connected by shipping services. The concept of "intermediacy" is thus important in regional or global freight distribution, as it addresses a whole range of network structures and nodes using to connect different market scales. In this chapter, the comparative intermediacy of transport nodes in Europe and North America is assessed over intermodal rail transport, and especially in container shipping. The respective cases of gateways, gateway port systems, and coastal and inland waterways are discussed. Each exemplifies a particular dimension of the intermediacy and freight regionalism that distinguishes North America and Europe.

10.1 Global Logistics and Regional Distribution

On par with globalization, logistics has evolved, both in terms of the range of activities it includes, as well as over its geography. What used to be labeled "global logistics" was mainly a collection of separate national strategies, since it was cumbersome to manage production and distribution over different

J.-P. Rodrigue (✉)
Department of Global Studies and Geography, Hofstra University,
Hempstead, New York 11549, USA
e-mail: Jean-paul.Rodrigue@Hofstra.edu

T. Notteboom
Institute of Transport and Maritime Management Antwerp (ITMMA),
University of Antwerp, Kipdorp 59, 2000 Antwerp, Belgium
e-mail: theo.notteboom@ua.ac.be

T. Notteboom
Antwerp Maritime Academy, Noordkasteel Oost 6, 2030 Antwerp, Belgium

J. H. Bookbinder (ed.), *Handbook of Global Logistics*, International Series in Operations Research & Management Science 181, DOI: 10.1007/978-1-4419-6132-7_10,

jurisdictions. Global logistics was mainly the organization of flows of raw materials and finished goods for markets where such goods were not readily available. This environment has irremediably changed from the 1980s: corporations were able to seek various input-cost reductions through global sourcing practices as well as expanded market opportunities. Multinational enterprises (MNE) have adopted flexible organizational structures on a global scale with an extensive network of globally dispersed inputs. The functional relations resulting in such a process are well beyond any nations with multilateral agreements in which jurisdictional and regulatory issues are harmonized. The base at which production and distribution processes took place has consequently moved away from a national and artificial construct based on regulatory constraints, to something that is much more regional and based on accessibility.

Leading-edge companies are taking a broader view of the parts of their business they seek to control and manage. The re-engineering of supply chain processes (including customer order management, procurement, production planning, distribution, etc.) to enhance performance typically resulted in collaborative networks with logistics partners. Modern global logistics thus thrive on complex international supply chains managed by third and fourth party logistics service providers (3PL and 4PL; Lieb et al. 1993). By the mid-1990s, third-party logistics became a separate industry characterized by several new entrants and various ways of value creation by logistics providers (see e.g. Berglund et al. 1999).

"Globalization" has gone hand in hand with the emergence of a global logistics market and global supply chain management practices, trying to reconcile a variety of price, capacity, efficiency and operational constraints, but with the benefits of standardization along transport chains. Thus, various factors and conditions of convergence have been the object of much interest. Modern supply chain management has favored investigations that seek to identify and understand how standardization and harmonization were diffusing along supply chains, helping to improve efficiency and productivity.

Against the backdrop of an evolving global logistics market, the global freight distribution system has been impacted by a *convergence* in terms of technology, infrastructure, modes and terminals. Containerization can be seen as the most salient example of convergence, with far reaching consequences over supply chains. With the standardization of load units, standardized modes (e.g. containerships) and terminals were massively developed (Levinson 2006; Rodrigue and Notteboom 2009). Intermodalism is associated with a higher level of integration between different systems of circulation. This integration leads to new functional structures, namely global production networks, each tending to have its own organizational and spatial behavior, depending on the supply chains (Coe et al. 2004; Rodrigue 2006).

It might be expected that the globalization of logistics has led to a convergence in terms of how regional freight distribution of container traffic takes place in North America and Europe. Both continents are treated as a whole, although large differences among sub-regions might exist. Still, global logistics enhances *regionalism* in freight distribution practices. It implies that geographical and market forces are inciting an organization of freight distribution over functional entities, such as port hinterlands, that are shaped by commercial flows and less so by jurisdictional oversight.

In spite of strong converging forces, logistical and freight distribution practices of containerized cargo flows are far from being uniform. When they take place over an extended area, they result in regional logistical strategies that have to take account of a large array of specific attributes linked with locations such as modal preferences, infrastructure ownership, policy and regulation. Historical path dependency in policy-making and firms' operational strategies heavily influence regional differences; regional distribution practices tend to endure in spite of technological and regulatory changes (Rodrigue and Notteboom 2010). The "regional effect" is thus significant, underlining the continuing relevance of the comparative analysis of freight transport systems, so that global logistics goes on par with regional distribution.

This chapter focuses on containerized freight distribution in North America and Europe. These two major markets share many commonalities, notably in terms of a strong import function (inbound logistics) and advanced freight distribution systems linking them to global trade flows. Yet, they also differ significantly in terms of how logistical strategies are taking place over their respective territories. Earlier comparative studies (e.g. Leinbach and Capinari 2007) have revealed Europe and North America are not walking the same paths when it comes to the configuration of transport and logistics networks, via operational decisions (see e.g. Slack 1996 on intermodal rail terminals in North America and Europe) and the setting of a regulatory framework (see e.g. Button 1997). The attributes of intermediary hubs, gateways, corridors, hinterlands, regulation, governance, and value chains help understand the regionalism of containerized freight distribution in the North American and European contexts, as well as anywhere else. More in particular, this chapter elaborates on the following characteristics of containerized freight distribution systems in Europe and North America. To:

- Understand how intermediary functions contribute to the regionalism of containerized freight distribution.
- See how North American and European gateways are embedded within their regional containerized freight transport systems.
- Look at the differences in inland freight distribution systems, namely corridors, inland logistics, and specific value-added functions that reflect North American and European logistics.

10.2 Intermediacy in Global Freight Distribution

Global and regional trade flows require appropriate transport networks to allow efficient freight movement by sea, in the air and over land. Transport operators such as shipping lines, rail operators, barge operators, trucking companies, and cargo handling companies aim at providing transport and handling services that meet the requirements of their customers. At the same time, those operators must take into account the possibilities and limitations linked to the infrastructural capacities at nodes (seaports, airports, intermodal terminals) and links (rail corridors, waterways) in the transport networks. The networks are shaped by a complex interaction between trade flows, the geography of consumption and production centers, government policy and the regulatory framework. Characteristics and capacity of nodes and links, the freight distribution strategies of global logistics service providers and transport operators, and competition between them, also have great impact on those networks.

One of the most interesting attributes of freight distribution networks is the inclusion of nodes that take up an "intermediacy" function. These nodes rely on traffic flows that are distantly generated by the interaction of widely separated places, and are dependent on the node's en-route location or intermediacy (Fleming and Hayuth 1994). An intermediate location can imply a location near the main maritime and land routes and/or near production and consumption centers. A good location is a necessary condition for attaining a high intrinsic accessibility. It becomes a sufficient condition when the favorable geographical location is valorized by means of the provision of efficient infrastructures and transport services (Notteboom and Rodrigue 2007). In this chapter, the intermediacy of transport nodes in North America and Europe is compared over two areas: container shipping and intermodal rail transport.

10.2.1 Intermediacy in Container Shipping

The role of intermediacy is very apparent in container shipping. The global maritime transport system operates mostly under the principle of intermediacy. Only 17 % of all country pairs are directly connected by container shipping services (UNCTAD 2009). This reflects a significant transshipment and interlining/relay function in global freight distribution, as 62 % of all country pairs require at least one transshipment. This intermediacy is not random. Rather, it takes place along transshipment markets that are essentially freight regions where ports compete for discretionary traffic.

Geography plays an important role in the setting of a transshipment market, which is often at the crossroads of north/south shipping routes and where there is a bottleneck such as a strait or a canal (Notteboom and Rodrigue 2010). Singapore is such a case, where the major Asia—Europe shipping lanes are constrained to pass through the Strait of Malacca. The Mediterranean has only two points of entry (Suez Canal and Straits of Gibraltar), both of which have significant transshipment and interlining activity (i.e. Tanger Med and Algeciras at the Straits of Gibraltar and Port Said, Damietta and Alessandria at the entrance of the Suez Canal). Ports that are the center of the basin show significant sea–sea transshipment flows

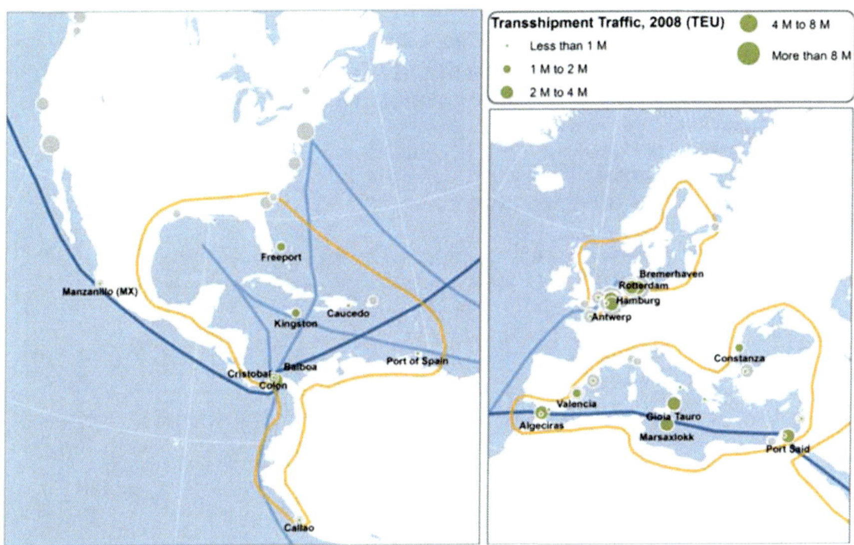

Fig. 10.1 North American and European transshipment markets

(e.g. Gioia Tauro and Taranto in the south of Italy, Marsaxlokk in Malta and Cagliari in Sardinia).

Although the Caribbean has a large exposure on the Atlantic side, it has one outlet for the Pacific, the Panama Canal, which has significant transshipment activities both on the Atlantic and Pacific sides. The North Sea and the Baltic are another transshipment market, but of lower incidence. That is because transshipment activities in ports like Rotterdam, Antwerp and Hamburg are combined with large gateway flows to the core regions in the European hinterland (Fig. 10.1).

Figure 10.2 reveals that the overall transshipment incidence in South Europe/Med reached a fairly high 44.6 % in 2008, but transshipment volumes remain small compared to Asia. In the Mediterranean, extensive hub-feeder container systems and short sea shipping networks emerged since the mid-1990s to cope with the increasing volumes and to connect to other European port regions. Quite a number of shipping lines rely on a hub-and-spoke configuration in the Med, with hub terminals located close to the main navigation route linking the Suez Canal with the Straits of Gibraltar. Major "pure" transshipment ports in the region are Algeciras, Taranto, Cagliari, Marsaxlokk and Gioia Tauro. Such hubs, with a transshipment incidence of 85–95 %, can only be found in the Mediterranean.

Northern Europe does not count any pure transshipment hub; overall transshipment incidence amounts to a moderate 24.2 %. Hamburg, the North-European leader in terms of sea–sea flows (mainly in relation to the Baltic), has a transshipment incidence of about 45 %, far below the elevated transshipment shares of the main south-European transshipment hubs (Notteboom 2010). A third transshipment market has emerged on the link between the UK and the mainland. Many

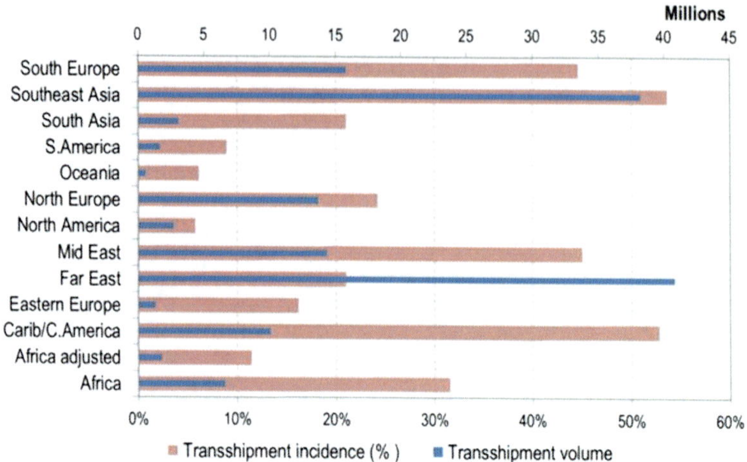

Fig. 10.2 Transshipment incidence (the share of the total traffic handled by a port which is moved from one ship to another) in port regions around the world. *Note* Africa adjusted = total for African ports excluding North African transshipment hubs Damietta, Alexandria, Port Said and Tanger Med. *Source* own compilation, based on data in Drewry (2009)

of the load centers along the southeast coast of the United Kingdom faced capacity shortages in recent years. Quite a number of shipping lines, therefore, opted for the transshipment of UK flows in mainland European ports (mainly Rotterdam, Zeebrugge, Antwerp and Le Havre), instead of calling at UK ports directly.

North America has no transshipment hubs (transshipment incidence of only 5.8 %), in spite of expectations from some ports (e.g. Halifax, Nova Scotia) to capture this role. The transshipment function takes place in a few offshore hub terminals along the Caribbean (Freeport, Bahamas or Kingston, Jamaica for instance). Well positioned to act as intermediary locations between major shipping routes (Asia-Europe, Europe-Latin America) and offering lower costs, this traffic is relatively small in comparison to total containerized traffic. In the US, many impediments in American shipping regulations gravitating around the US Merchant Marine Act of 1920 (also known as the Jones Act) have favored a process of limited (feeder) services between American ports. The Jones Act, which basically states that cargo may not be transported between two US ports unless it is transported by vessels owned by citizens of the US, built and registered in the US, and manned by a crew of US nationals, implies that the potential of domestic shipping in North America remains underutilized (Brooks 2009). The expansion of the Panama Canal by 2014 may trigger more transshipment activities in the Caribbean, which in 2008 handled about 10 million TEU of transshipment cargo representing a transshipment incidence of 52.8 % (Rodrigue 2011).

North America and Europe have thus followed different paths, both in their role as transshipment regions and in terms of the inclusion of intermediary port terminals in maritime networks.

Table 10.1 Modal split in land-based container flows of some major European container ports

Seaport	Total container throughput (including sea–sea transshipment)	Road	Rail	Inland barge
	Million TEU	%	%	%
Antwerp (Belgium)	8.66	56.6	11.0	32.4
Bremerhaven (Germany)[a]	5.50	34.0	62.9	3.1
Constanza (Romania)	1.38	69.6	27.8	2.6
Hamburg (Germany)	9.70	63.1	34.7	2.2
Le Havre (France)	2.45	86.2	6.6	7.2
Marseille (France)	0.85	81.0	13.0	6.0
Rotterdam (the Netherlands)	10.83	57.0	13.0	30.0
Zeebrugge (Belgium)	2.21	62.0	36.6	1.4

Source own compilation, based on data from respective port authorities and Schiffahrt Hafen Bahn und Technik, No. 1 (2010), p 68

[a] Figures for terminal operator Eurogate only

10.2.2 Intermediacy in Intermodal Rail Networks

European rail logistics are highly complex. A geographically, politically and economically fragmented Europe prevented the realization of a greater European-wide integrated intermodal rail network (Charler and Ridolfi 1994). Since the mid-1990s, the European intermodal sector has undergone major changes as a result of European rail liberalization and with it the entry of new market players (see e.g. Gouvernal and Daydou 2005; Debrie and Gouvernal 2006). The emergence of a new generation of rail operators not only made incumbent firms act more commercially, but also led to improvement in the endogenous capabilities of the railway sector. This in time could make rail a more widespread alternative in serving the European hinterlands, at least if some outstanding technical and operational issues (e.g. standardization of rail traffic management systems under the ERTMS scheme—European Rail Traffic Management System) facing cross-border services can be solved.

At present, a wide array of rail operators make up the supply of rail products out of European container ports. Hamburg's rail connections outperform all other ports in numbers (more than 160 international and national shuttle and block train services per week) and in traffic volumes by rail (1.89 million TEU in 2008). Rotterdam (rail volume of 1 million TEU in 2008) and Antwerp (8,37,000 TEU) each have between 150 and 200 intermodal rail departures per week. Other European seaports with substantial rail volumes include Bremerhaven (8,67,000 TEU), Zeebrugge (6,75,000 TEU), Gothenburg (3,42,000 TEU) and La Spezia (3,00,000 TEU). Still, rail transport typically represents a small share in the land-based container flows of many European containers ports, with German seaports and Zeebrugge as the notable exceptions (Table 10.1). Smaller container ports tend to seek connection to the extensive hinterland networks of the large-load seaports by installing shuttle services, either to rail platforms in the big container ports or to master rail hubs in the hinterland.

From a network perspective, intermodal rail transport in Europe has undergone an initial transition from a meshed network to a star or hub-and-spoke network based on intermediate rail hubs. Now the network is transformed to a system of direct lines. For example, the backbone of rail services out of the main European container ports is formed by direct point-to-point shuttle trains, with a unit capacity ranging from 45 to 95 TEU per shuttle (Notteboom 2008). However, the profitability of most individual direct shuttle trains, even to the immediate hinterland of European load-centre ports, remains uncertain. In the past, some carriers and rail operators resolved the problems related to the fluctuating volumes and the numerous final destinations by bundling container flows at rail hubs in the immediate hinterland. Numerous hub-and-spoke railway networks thus emerged in the 1990s. An example was the Qualitynet of Intercontainer-Interfrigo (ICF) with Metz-Sablon in north-eastern France as intermediate rail hub linking the Rhine-Scheldt Delta ports with the remainder of western Europe.

Such hub-and-spoke networks were revealed to be vulnerable, as the volumes on the spokes could be affected by (1) newcomers entering the market in the aftermath of European rail liberalization and (2) increasing intermodal volumes in seaports (Kreuzberger 2005; Notteboom 2009a). New railway operators often "cherry-pick" by introducing competing direct shuttle trains on a spoke of a competitor's established hub-and-spoke network. This has a negative effect on cargo volumes on the spoke, and can lead to a collapse of the whole hub-and-spoke system. That is what happened to ICF's Qualitynet in 2004; ICF launched its new strategy late that year. The intermodal traffic of the former Qualitynet hub in Metz is now handled by a set of direct shuttle trains going to fewer destinations. For eastern and south-eastern Europe, services are centered around the hub in Sopron (Hungary).

Rail hubs are progressively being abandoned. Nevertheless, some of the new systems being set up by operators still include massification centres. For instance, German intermodal operator BoxXpress uses Gmunden in Germany to connect trains leaving from Bremerhaven and Hamburg. However, these types of terminals are only "massifying gateways" on direct routes, and do not act as intermediate hubs for a large number of spokes.

The North American rail transport system shows a high level of geographical specialization: seven large rail carriers[1] service vast regional markets (Fig. 10.3). Each carrier has its own facilities, and thus its own markets along the segments it controls. The rail system is the outcome of substantial capital investments occurring over several decades with the accumulation of impressive infrastructure and equipment assets. The system was developed to support flows of commodities, particularly coal and grain. Competition has a strong regional connotation; over vast territories of track, only two rail operators have intermodal terminals.

[1] Often labeled Class I rail carriers.

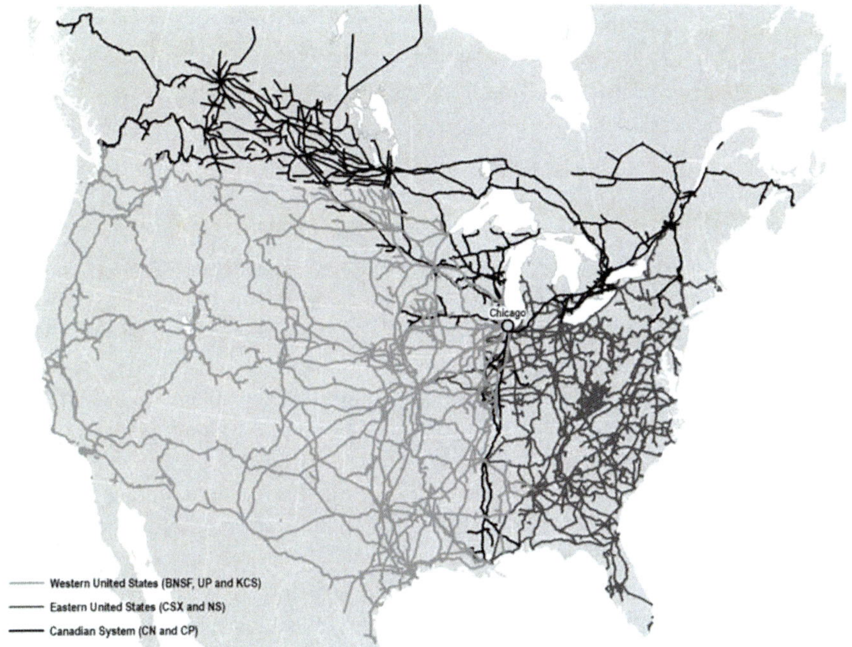

Fig. 10.3 The North American rail transport system. *Source* Oak Ridge National Laboratory

However, the growth of intermodalism created issues about *continuity* within the North American rail network, particularly in the United States.

Mergers have improved this continuity. But a limit has been reached in the network size of most rail operators. Attempts have been made to synchronize the interactions between those operators, with the setting of intermodal unit trains for long distance trade. Often bilateral, trilateral or even quadrilateral arrangements are made between rail carriers and shipping companies to improve the intermodal interface at major gateways, or at points of interlining between significant networks. Chicago is the largest interlining center in North America, handling around 10 million TEU per year. Chicago is located at the junction of the Eastern (NS and CSX), Western (UP, BNSF and KCS) and Canadian rail systems (CN and CP). Other leading interlining locations include Kansas City, St. Louis and Memphis.

10.3 Using Coastal and Inland Waters in Freight Distribution: Short Sea Shipping and Barge Transport

It is complicated to define "short sea shipping." That can involve diverse vessels (container feeder vessels, ferries, fast ships, etc.), tramp or liner operations, a variety of cargo handling techniques (horizontal, vertical or a mixture of both) and different types of ports of loading or discharge (Paixao and Marlow 2002). In an intermodal freight context, two main categories of short sea shipping can be distinguished:

- Feeder services from transshipment hubs to feeder ports, and vice versa. These services can be arranged on the basis of a direct hub port to feeder port, or can follow a line bundling set-up, with several feeder ports of call per vessel rotation;
- Cabotage services between ports of the same economic region.

About 6 % of the American freight tonnage is carried by short sea shipping services; the European figure is in the range of 41 %. In Europe, short sea shipping (SSS) is defined by the statistical office Eurostat as the transport of goods between ports in the EU-27, Croatia and Norway on one hand, and ports situated in geographical Europe, on the Mediterranean and Black Sea on the other. In North America, SSS is defined as domestic shipping taking place along the coasts, rivers and lakes. SSS also includes cross-border traffic between the United States, Canada and Mexico; it excludes any shipping which is transoceanic.

In 2007 total freight transport by short sea shipping in the EU-27 amounted to 1.86 billion tons or 61 % of total EU-27 maritime goods transport. The most important short sea countries are the United Kingdom (366 million tons), Italy (325 million tons) and the Netherlands (259 million tons). The majority of short sea flows take place between partner ports situated in the Mediterranean (28 %) and the North Sea (27 %), see also Fig. 10.4.

Liquid bulk (including liquefied gas, crude oil and oil products) is the most important cargo type, with almost half the total tonnage or 896 million tons. Short sea traffic of dry bulk amounted to 364 million tons. Containers accounted for 210 million tons, roll-on/roll-off ("roro") for 250 million tons, and other cargo for 142 million tons.

Rotterdam was the largest European short sea port overall with 186 million tons of short sea traffic. Antwerp was the largest European short sea port for containers, with 30.5 million tons, closely followed by Rotterdam with 30.2 million tons. Dover in the UK and Calais in France remained the top two roro short sea ports, with 24.6 and 18.3 million tons of roro short sea traffic, respectively (Eurostat 2009).

Restrictions to maritime cabotage have been lifted in Europe. By the late 1990s, the liberalization of cabotage services was virtually complete (only the Greek market remained partially protected until 2002). At present, an EU-flag ship is eligible to participate in the cabotage trades of any other EU state. This liberalization makes it possible for short sea to compete effectively with land-based transport.

The European Commission is supporting the development of short sea shipping in view of a modal shift from road to other transport modes. That would make use of the latter's underused available capacity, and reduce the environmental footprint of EU transport activities. The EC's short sea policy is supported by the creation of "Motorways of the Sea" (MoS) and funding mechanisms like the Marco Polo Program. The EC has set a clear policy objective to remove any remaining administrative and customs obstacles towards the creation of an EU maritime space (European Commission 2009).

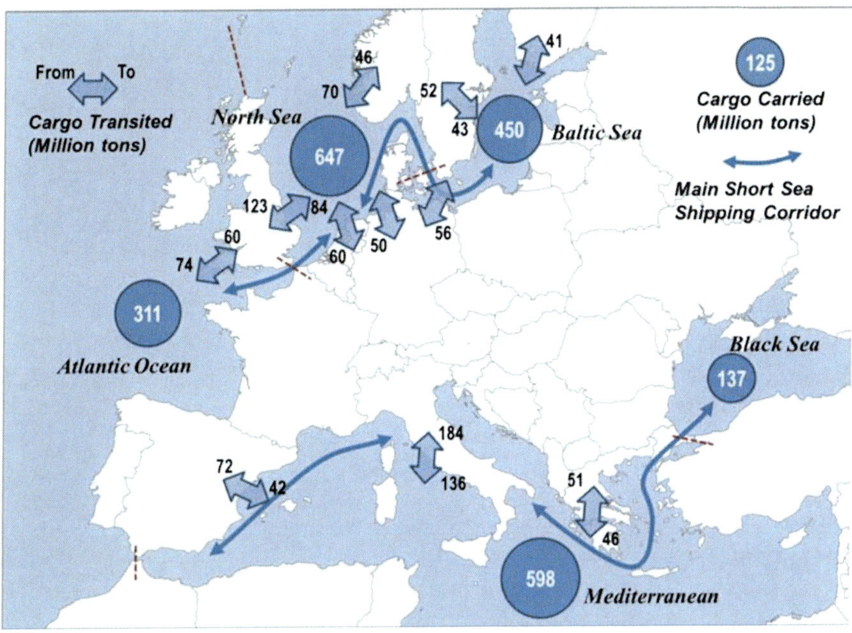

Fig. 10.4 Largest short sea flows (*top* 20) in Europe, figures for 2007. *Source* own compilation, based on Eurostat data

Basic requirements for improved services of short sea shipping relate to (see also OECD 2001; Paixao and Marlow 2002):

- Technical and infrastructural aspects, such as a shorter turnaround time in ports, more efficient customs operations and administrative procedures, more favorable port pricing;
- Commercial aspects: better integration of short sea shippingshort sea shipping in supply chain practices (data and information systems, frequency, reliability, etc.);
- Political aspects: e.g. policies to internalize the external costs of transport modes, ending of discriminative treatment by customs procedures of inner-EU shipping in favor of overland traffic, harmonization of rules for land and sea carriage of hazardous goods.

The transport of containers on European inland waterways is strongly concentrated on the respective main waterway axes. In 2008 these included 1,19,000 TEU on the Elbe in relation to Hamburg; 55,700 TEU on the Weser to/from Bremerhaven; 85,000 TEU on the Rhône to/from Marseille; 1,45,000 TEU on the Seine to/from Le Havre; and about 17,000 TEU on the Danube to/from Constanza. The main European barging ports, Rotterdam (2.34 million TEU in 2008) and Antwerp (2.64 million TEU) show a more diverse distribution of containerized flows: the axis Antwerp-Rotterdam, the Rhine Basin, Northern France and the Benelux. It is only in Rotterdam and Antwerp that barge transport

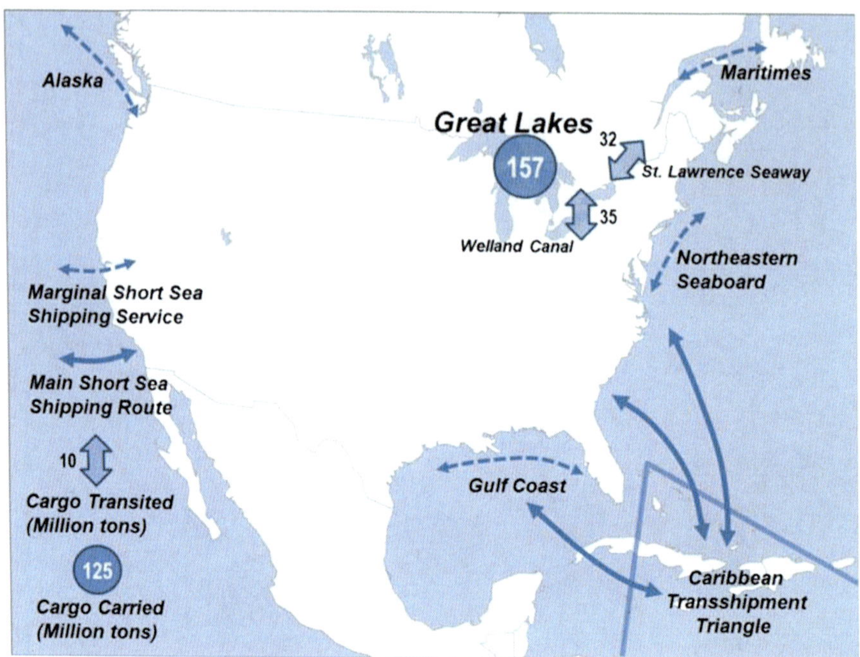

Fig. 10.5 The North American short sea shipping market—Figures for 2007. *Source* own compilation from the Lake Carriers' Association and the St. Lawrence Seaway Corporation

has succeeded in reaching a high market share in the modal split of inland container flows (see also Table 10.1). In other ports, policies have been developed to increase the barge share of inland freight distribution by coordination with relevant players such as barge operators, shipping lines and logistics service providers. For a more detailed discussion on the dynamics of container barge transport in Europe, we refer to Notteboom and Konings (2004) and Notteboom (2007) for river ports on the Rhine, and to Frémont et al. (2009) for river ports in France.

Unlike Europe, the potential of short sea shipping in North America is significantly curtailed by markets, policy and geography (Brooks and Trifts 2008). The prominence and efficiency of rail for long distances, and of trucking for short distances, mostly leaves to short sea the shipping to niche markets with limited growth potential (Fig. 10.5). Additionally, policy related to trade and custom regulations (advance manifest requirements, cabotage rules, tariffs and duties) undermine the operations of short sea shipping. For instance, the Jones Act prevents foreign carriers from carrying containers between American ports. Considering the configuration of pendulum routes along the coasts (a pendulum route typically calls at 2–4 ports), there is an untapped potential. If the cabotage rule were amended, it would replace some elements of North American freight distribution with a new form of regionalism.

The Eastern Seaboard, with the exception of the St. Lawrence/Great Lakes system, offers no significant navigable river system. The upper Great Lakes (Erie, Huron, Michigan and Superior) offer good navigation depths, but navigation is limited by the waterways between the lakes and by ice in winter. Still, they handled about 157 million tons of dry-bulk cargo in 2007. Further, access to the Atlantic is limited to the depth and lock size of the St. Lawrence Seaway (transiting 32 million tons of cargo), which is closed for a few months during the winter. The St. Lawrence enables a vessel to go deep inland, but maritime vessels can go up to Montreal, which is essentially at the same longitude as New York. The St. Lawrence/Great Lakes system, in spite of carrying substantial bulk volumes, remains a market that is not serviced by intermodal transportation. The Eastern Seaboard, however, has, in addition, a complex but underused coastal transport system. The setting of intermodal barge services is also an initiative not without challenges. For instance, the New York/Albany barge service, which started in April 2003, was suspended in February 2006 due to the lack of funding, which corresponded to the end of subsidies provided to help jump-start the service.

For the Gulf of Mexico, the Mississippi inland waterway system is extensive but generally limited to depths less than 15 feet. Under such circumstances, ports along the Mississippi are dominantly handling barges loaded with agricultural commodities, which implies a substantial but highly seasonal traffic. Moreover, the Mississippi system has a north–south orientation while most of the goods flows are east–west, implying a limited potential to service intermodal freight movements. Like the Eastern Seaboard, there is an Intracoastal Waterway ranging from Texas to Florida, served by limited short sea services.

The Western Seaboard has four major deep water gateways: Seattle, Portland, San Francisco and Los Angeles. However, there is poor waterway access to the interior because of the Sierra Nevada and Rocky Mountains. The only exception is the Columbia River basin, which is accessible to deep-sea ships up to Portland, about 160 km inland. The existing short sea services transport mostly containers and trailers between Tacoma and Anchorage. Except for a few very small instances, there are no inland maritime container services in North America.

10.4 Gateway Port Systems

10.4.1 Gateways: Agents of Freight Regionalism

Gateways represent the fundamental interface structure between regional and global transport systems (Van Klink and Van Den Berg 1998). Gateways are essential in connecting economic regions to overseas areas. This section aims at analyzing the influence that gateways have on freight regionalism, by focusing on gateway container ports and their relation to logistics zones and the development of intermodalism and corridors. The interface between regional and global container transport systems can be impacted by several factors, such as policies favoring specific ports of entry. If

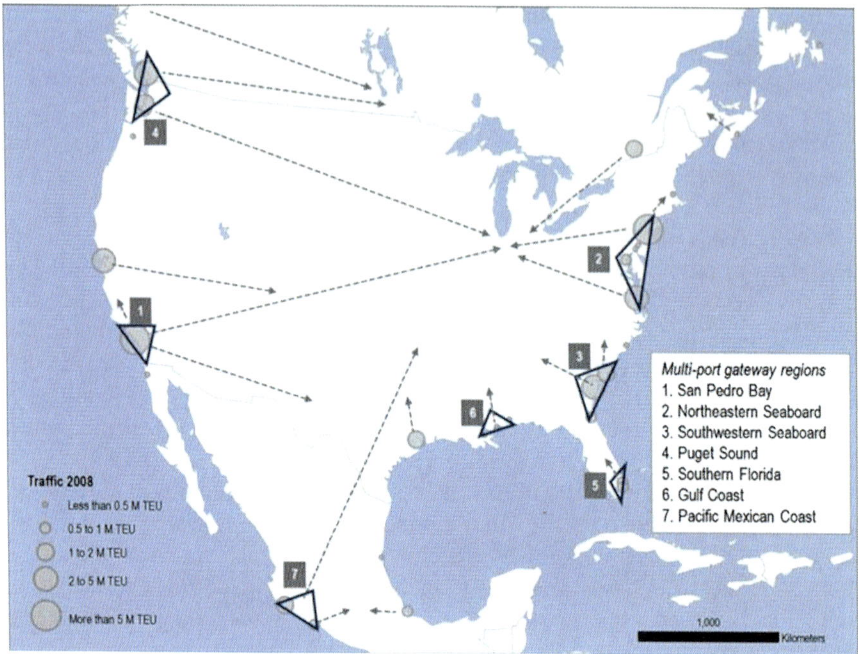

Fig. 10.6 Main gateway systems and corridors of North America

left relatively unimpeded, however, a natural gateway will be established based on the level of accessibility and economic activity of its hinterland.

As globalization increased in scale and scope, locations enabling an efficient articulation between different systems of circulation have become more relevant. Within global maritime shipping networks, hubs have emerged to connect regional and global systems, while creating functional regions on the maritime foreland (Rodrigue and Notteboom 2009). For the maritime/land interface, gateways have become significant logistical clusters. Gateways include terminal infrastructures such as ports, rail terminals and freight distribution centers, but supply chain management activities as well. That ensures continuity within global supply chains. Yet, the role and function of gateways and their corridors vary according to the geographical setting, which has an impact on modal and operational considerations.

Figures 10.6 and 10.7 provide a synthetic representation for North America and Europe and comparative functional maps of North American and European gateways and corridors, notably in terms of the major gateway systems.

10.4.2 Freight Regionalism at North American Gateways

In North America, there is a high level of concentration of economic activities along the East and West coasts, with significant resource and manufacturing hinterlands.

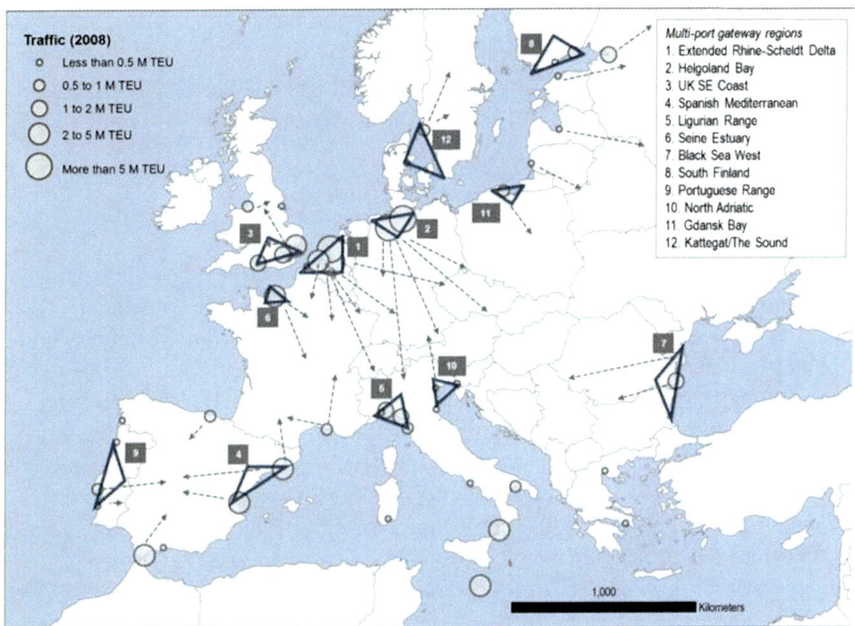

Fig. 10.7 Main gateway systems and corridors of Europe

Gateways tend to be the dominant markets, and this for all the two major maritime facades, with the Gulf Coast playing a more marginal role, particularly for containers. From the start, it was mainly commercial considerations that shaped the setting of North American gateways and corridors. These have remained quite stable in time, albeit with an ongoing trend of traffic concentration. North America relies on a relatively small number of gateways; less developed port ranges thus have few chances to fully take part in international shipping networks. Cargo concentrations in the North American container port system emanate from the increasing dominance of Long Beach/Los Angeles as the major gateways along the Pacific Coast, mainly catering to Asian import cargo. However, the extent to which this trend will endure is highly questionable, as evidenced by the economic slowdown that began in 2008.

Longitudinal long distance rail corridors from coastal gateways often take the form of a land bridge. Those corridors service a continental hinterland, articulated by major transportation and industrial hubs such as Chicago and Kansas City. The double stack trains have unit capacities of up to 400 TEU and a total length of well above 2 km. The large-scale inland rail freight transport system of North America is unique in the world, not only because of its sheer size, but also because of the direct link made between two different coastlines.

The major changes in North America's hinterlands, namely the decline of the industrial belt (which has been monitored for decades) and the industrialization of the "sun belt," are long-term shifts that are reflected in the gradual reorientation of the traffic. NAFTA also favors the setting of natural gateways and corridors, i.e.

through Canada (in particular Vancouver and Montreal) and Mexico (Lazero Cardenas) and a reorientation of traffic flows (Brooks 2008). This trend is, however, dwarfed by the restructuring taking place in Europe and its impacts on freight flows.

10.4.3 Freight Regionalism at European Gateways

In Western Europe, the hinterland is not only intense along the coastline but also in the interior. This is notable along the Rhine river system and its tributary rivers (Main and Neckar), Bavaria in the South of Germany, and the economic centers around Milan in Northern Italy and Madrid in central Spain. That trend is reflected from the major markets in Paris, the Liverpool-Manchester-Leeds belt in the UK and the belt reaching from Austria to the growing production clusters in Hungary, the Czech Republic and Southern Poland. Moreover, large parts of the European economic centers are somewhat remote from the main shipping lanes, as is the case for countries around the Baltic. European gateways are therefore relatively small markets and act as intermediary locations to reach inland markets, even if many gateways are important industrial centers (e.g. in the petrochemical industry).

The hinterland is accessed from coastal gateways such as Rotterdam, Antwerp, Hamburg, Bremerhaven, Le Havre, Barcelona, Marseille and Felixstowe by medium distance corridors involving various combinations of road, barge (where available) and rail services. Almost all the major European capitals are interior cities located along rivers. There is a particular disconnection between the nationality of the gateway and the nationality of the hinterland. This is an outcome of several decades of integration that have gradually let transport and supply chain considerations, as opposed to policies centered on national ports of entry, be the driving force for shaping hinterlands.

Thus, the role of gateways in developing functional freight regions within Europe is much more recent and profound than in North America. Cargo concentration levels in the European port system are slowly declining, whereby nearly all port ranges fully participate in international shipping networks. Each port range consists of a unique blend of load center ports and smaller facilities with a more local focus.

10.4.4 Gateway Specialization

Europe and North America also differ at the level of functional division of freight flows. The degree of specialization of European gateways in specific foreland regions is typically lower than in North America. Asian cargo is mainly being handled in the Mediterranean and the Le Havre-Hamburg range. Cargo flows on secondary routes such as Africa and South America also find their way throughout the vast European container port system. The geography of North America has led to route specialization among gateways. The bulk of Asian cargo flows is handled in the West Coast ports, in particular Long Beach and Los Angeles, but the use of the all-water route through the Panama Canal has accounted for a growing share in recent years.

Caribbean cargo finds its way to North America via the container ports in Florida and Georgia (Miami, Savannah). Liner shipping services between Europe and North America are primarily calling at ports north of Hampton Roads, VA. Construction of a new lock system in the Panama Canal would allow vessels of up to 12,500 TEU to offer "round-the-world" services. That is expected to increase this geographical specialization. However, the European port system is expected to remain more diffuse.

A last feature relates to the role of "path-dependency" in the development of respective port systems (Notteboom 2009b). In Europe, containerization started in the Le Havre-Hamburg range and its link with trans-Atlantic trade. In 2008, the ports in this range (mainly Rotterdam, Antwerp, Hamburg, Bremerhaven, Le Havre and Zeebrugge) handled more than 48 % of total European container throughput. In the new millennium, the position of the northern range has even gradually improved, while the Med ports and the UK port system lost market share (Notteboom 2010). The observed dominance of the Le Havre-Hamburg range is a combined result of first-mover advantages, scale economies, a high operational performance (terminals and onward inland transport) and the economic density of the immediate hinterland. First-mover advantages, together with the history of commercial relations (i.e. the impact of the colonial past) and the national strategic interest of individual EU Member States (i.e. the national borders) also contribute to the observed regional traffic dispersion among main European ports. These effects play a lesser role in cargo dynamics in the North American port system.

Although gateways are the fundamental structure of the maritime—land interface, terminals are the physical infrastructures through which functional regionalism is shaped. Port regionalization (Notteboom and Rodrigue 2005) underlines the emergence of new relationships between port terminals and their hinterland, with the setting of inland ports and distribution services. How port terminals establish their connections with the hinterland is influenced by regional characteristics. These include density and economic function, and also the physical performance of terminal facilities, the capacity and modes of inland connections as well as of inland ports. All of this is the realm of "inland logistics."

10.5 Inland Logistics

10.5.1 Logistical Structures

The logistical development in North America and Western Europe has been particularly driven by the growing needs at the level of inbound logistics, primarily from Asia. The differences between inbound and outbound logistics constitute a

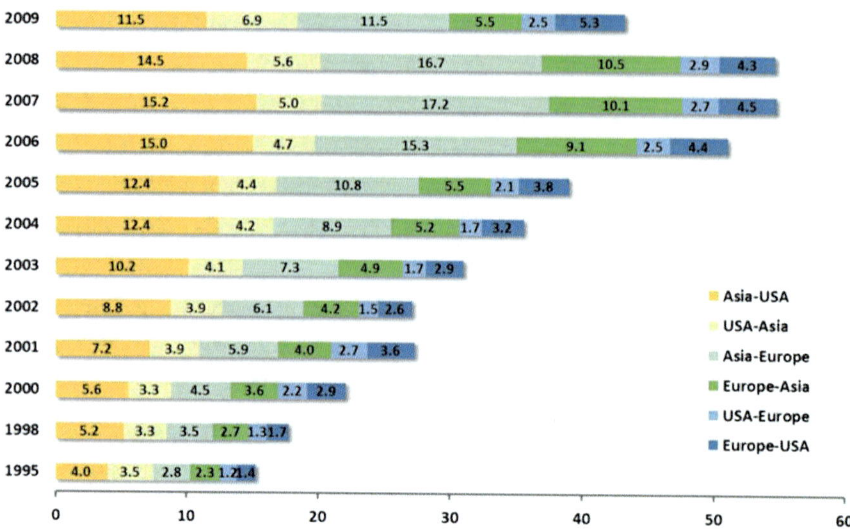

Fig. 10.8 Containerized cargo flows along major trade routes, 1995–2009 (in millions of TEUs). *Source* UNCTAD, Review of Maritime Transport, various years

very prevalent issue, particularly in North America where trade imbalances have traditionally been larger than in Europe (Fig. 10.8).

With global trade imbalances, the logistical hinterland has been facing acute pressures to cope with disequilibrium in transport flows. For instance, there are 2.5 times as many containers moving from Asia to the United States (14.5 million TEUs in 2008) than vice versa (5.6 million TEU). This implies a combined American imbalance of 12.3 million TEU with Asia and Europe, meaning that these containers have to be repositioned. By 2005, about 70 % of the slots of containerships leaving the United States were empty. Major container ports, such as Los Angeles handled large amounts of empty containers; 1.85 million TEU were exported in 2008 alone. The Asia-Europe trade route is facing a similar imbalance, but at a lesser level. The impacts on the regional geography of maritime transportation are major: the repositioning of empty containers is becoming a logistical challenge, particularly in North America, where imbalances have taken dramatic proportions in the mid-2000s. On the export side in Asia, this has resulted in frequent surges in the unavailability of boxes.

Supply chains are being redesigned to respond to varying customer and product service-level requirements. Value chains reflect the specific economic processes of the North American and European markets. The question is where value-added functions should be carried out and the form they should take. Again, distinct freight distribution strategies mark particular regionalism. When it comes to the inbound logistics of overseas goods, a general distribution structure does not exist. Differences in the economic geography of North America and Europe have led to specific characteristics in inland distribution networks, as depicted on Fig. 10.9.

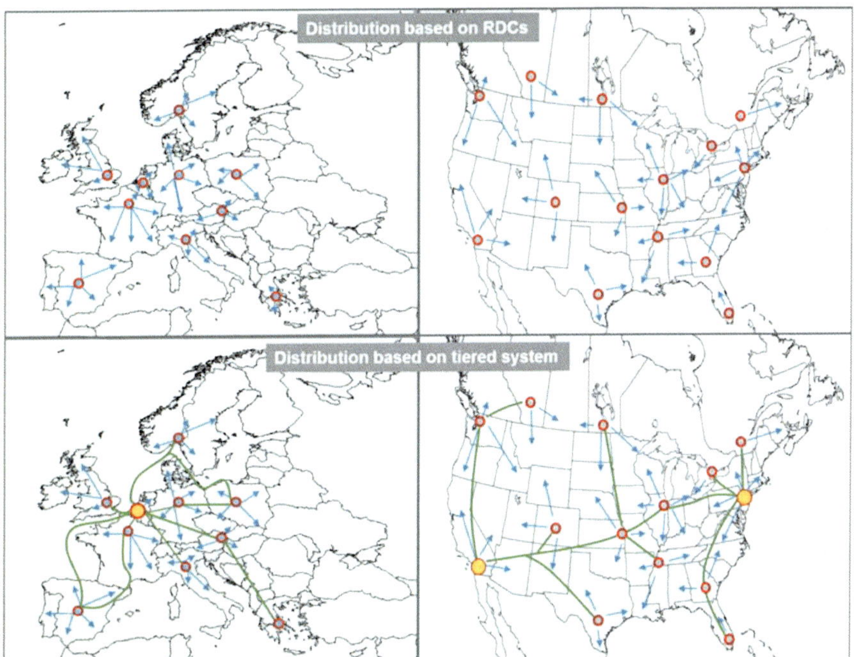

Fig. 10.9 Some distribution network configurations for containerized import cargo, Europe and North America. *Source* adapted from Rodrigue and Notteboom (2010)

The conventional distribution networks, both in Europe and North America, relied on a system of regional distribution centers. Over the last 15 years many barriers for cross-border transactions between countries within the EU and NAFTA have decreased. As a result, many companies consolidated their distribution operations into one central Gateway Distribution Center (GDC): in Europe, typically a European Distribution Center (EDC) covering all European Union countries and, in North America, a large distribution center servicing a part of the continent, often divided by coast. This meant longer distances to the final consumers and in some market segments, local market demand has led companies to opt for Regional Distribution Centers or RDCs.

More recently, a certain degree of decentralization of distribution structures has taken place. A tiered structure, consisting of one GDC in combination with some smaller local warehouses, 'merge in transit' concepts or 'cross docking' facilities, offers the best results in many cases in terms of high level of service, frequency of delivery and distribution cost control. Companies today often opt for a hybrid distribution structure of centralized and local distribution facilities. For instance, they use a GDC for medium- and slow-moving products and RDCs for fast-moving products. These RDCs typically function as rapid fulfillment centers, rather than holding inventories. The classical or multi-country distribution structures are being replaced by merge-in-transit, cross-docking or other fluid logistics structures, actively linked with inland ports.

The choice between the various distribution formulas depends on among other things the type of product, the variability in its demand, and the frequency of deliveries. In the fresh food industry for example, gateway or European distribution centers are unusual: The quickly-perishable product dictates a local distribution structure. In the pharmaceuticals industry, gateway or European distribution centers are common. Regional or local distribution centers are not present, because pharmaceuticals are often manufactured in one central plant and delivery times are less critical (hospitals often have their own inventories). However, in the high tech spare parts industry, all of the distribution center functions can be present. Spare parts need to be delivered within a few hours, and high-tech spare parts are usually very expensive (which would require centralized distribution structures).

At present, the majority of EDCs in Europe is still opting for a location in the Benelux region or northern France, but more and more regions are vying for a position as attractive location for RDCs and potentially EDCs. In Europe, inland distances are somewhat shorter, so maritime containers tend to move directly to their destined distribution centers through inland ports. In North America, gateway distribution centers are dominantly around the Los Angeles/Long Beach, New York/New Jersey and Savannah clusters. In spite of the similarities that Fig. 10.9 suggests, there are notable particularities in North American and European freight regionalism, beginning with customization.

Customization is an important aspect where different regionalisms impact freight distribution. Europe is a grouping of different cultures, implying a variety of tastes, preferences and languages. That leads to a higher need for customization for each specific market. Some added value customization functions (labeling, power supplies, manuals, etc.) must thus be performed in proximity of final markets (distribution centers), as market fragmentation renders particular source-based (factory) functions prohibitive for many ranges of goods (e.g. a change from ISO-pallet to a Europallet, or a change in packaging to meet local tastes and language). The North American market is much more homogeneous culturally (or at least linguistically). There is less culture-based customization, so the matter resides in distributional efficiencies. Customization can thus be performed at the source (e.g. Chinese free trade zone) or in the early stages of the supply chain. For a variety of consumer goods such as shoes, price ticketing is even done in China as the last step of the production process before shipping to North American distribution centers. For European markets, the customization at the source (China) is also a growing business, but it primarily involves more generic products.

10.5.2 North American Inland Freight Regionalism

In North America, longer distances, and the availability of a load unit greater than the standard forty foot maritime container, have favored an active transloading function at gateways. The equivalent of three forty-foot maritime containers can be transloaded into two domestic fifty-three footers. Maritime containers, after being transloaded, can be brought back to the port terminal and the maritime shipping network. The additional costs incurred by transloading are compensated by a consolidation of inland load units with the outcome of anchoring value-added function at gateways. The diffusion of slow steaming (ships reducing their average cruising speed from the 23–25 to 18–19 knots) as a prevalent practice for containerized maritime shipping will tie up a greater quantity of containers in transit and incite transloading at gateways. Containers (the majority owned by shipping companies) are thus kept within maritime circuits.

The North American freight distribution system conveys several opportunities to extract added value from distribution efficiencies. One notable form is *cross-docking*, in which a distribution center essentially acts as a high-throughput sorting facility where inbound shipments are reconciled with various outbound demands. Big-box stores are heavy users of this form of sorting of inbound freight flows to a multitude of large stores. For instance, the world's biggest retailer, Wal-Mart, delivers about 85 % of its merchandise using a cross-docking system. This structure takes advantage of the massification of shipment via long-distance rail corridors: a decomposition of shipments at a regional warehouse/cross-docking facility serves an array of stores with daily trucking services. This retailing structure is more dominant in North America. Europe has several large players (e.g. Carrefour), but tends to involve more locally-based companies (cultural market differentiation).

There are few new ports in North America. One exception is Prince Rupert, British Columbia, which exploits a niche market (shorter transpacific distances; or long-distance rail access to the Chicago hub, and then) to the Mexican Pacific coast, that has seen the setting of new terminal facilities such as in Lazero Cardenas (Randolph 2008). Several ports (e.g. Mobile, Jacksonville, Norfolk), have expansion projects that may capture a greater share of the traffic, but it remains to be seen to what extent these additional capacities will be used in freight distribution. There is also an entirely new terminal project at Melford, Nova Scotia, in collaboration with the same terminal operator as in Prince Rupert (Maher Terminals) but this project remains highly speculative.

Infrastructure investments tend to reinforce the existing efficiency of the inland transport system in which long distance is dominated by rail and where limited, if any, inland barge services are possible. The new heartland corridor linking the terminals of Norfolk to the Chicago hub is a salient example. The benefits of double-stacking were expanded with double (or triple) *tracking*, and the setting of inland load centers servicing their respective market areas. This also permitted the setting of large-scale intermodal rail terminals because such economies of scale were feasible. Thus, North American inland terminals tend to service large market areas.

10.5.3 European Inland Freight Regionalism

In Europe, there is a multiplication of terminals in new ports to cover the expansion of the EU as well as to take advantage of better hinterland accessibility. A prime example is the new eastern gateway of Constanza on the Black Sea. This implies the setting of entirely new distribution practices, such as inland barges and short sea shipping, to complement and substitute for trucking which has the dominant share. However, economies of scale are difficult to achieve for rail terminals because of the unavailability of double-stacking and of shorter unit trains (at most 95 TEU per shuttle train). Barge services are less impaired by such limitations with ongoing economies of scale where draft is permissible (Notteboom and Konings 2004). While the European hinterland for a long time was marked by a temporal stability, the impacts of European integration and changes in hinterland access are having significant consequences on the distribution of freight flows.

The enlargement of the European Union from 15 members in the 1990s to 27 members today reinforced trading links between countries in Eastern and Central Europe. It has, however, also led some manufacturing activities to move from Western Europe towards the low-cost eastern regions. The result is ever larger bi-directional East–West flows within the European Union of raw materials and consumer products. Those East–West flows are giving impetus to the creation of extensive infrastructures including corridors and terminals. Germany, the Czech Republic, Poland, Slovenia and Hungary have strong *rail* networks (road networks in the Eastern European countries are less well developed.) The Danube and the Elbe are emerging as new barge corridors, although total barge volumes remain small compared to the Rhine river and its tributaries and the North–South axis (the Netherlands, Belgium and Northern France). Northern ports, in particular Hamburg, up to now have benefited the most from EU enlargement, whereas new opportunities might arise for secondary port systems in the Adriatic and the Baltic Sea. The improvements in Eastern Europe are complemented by a strong enhancement of trade flows in the Baltic area and the Latin arc (stretching along the coastline from southern Spain to northern Italy).

At a policy level, the above developments have fuelled an intense discussion on distributional equity in the European port system. Market-related dynamics, such as maritime and intermodal connectivity and scale considerations, favor a concentration of European cargo flows on trunk lines between major (mostly north-European) container ports and the hinterland regions. Some political forces at the European-Union level, however, advocate more of an even balance, with a larger participation of Southern and Eastern European ports in freight distribution systems. This tension between centralization and a decentralized port system is a key input for future inland infrastructure development in Europe via the *TEN-T* program (Trans-European Network—Transport).

The possibility of economies of scale at terminals, linked with constraints on load availability and operational constraints (e.g. double stacking, unit train size, maximal truck load unit) is imposing a notable differentiation between North American and European inland terminals. While in both cases gateway systems tend to be similar, it is in their respective hinterlands that differentiation is taking shape. A larger number of inland terminals is required in Europe than in North America, to handle a similar volume.

Table 10.2 Gross revenue of the world's 25 leading 3PL companies (in million US$—figures for 2008)

3PL company	Country	Gross revenue (million US$)
Deutsche post world net (DPWN)	Germany	39,900
Kuehne & nagel	Switzerland	20,220
DB Schenker logistics	Germany	12,503
Geodis	France	9,700
CEVA logistics[a]	The Netherlands	9,523
Panalpina	Switzerland	8,394
Logista	UK	8,190
CH Robinson worldwide	USA	7,130
Agility logistics	Kuwait	6,316
UPS supply chain solutions	USA	6,293
Expeditors international of Washington	USA	5,650
Dascher and Co	Germany	5,377
DSV	Denmark	5,351
UTi worldwide	USA	4,996
Sinotrans	China	4,757
NYK logistics	Japan	4,723
Wincanton	UK	4,331
Bolloré	France	4,330
Hellmann worldwide logistics	Germany	4,209
Rhenus and co	Germany	3,940
Toll holding	Australia	3,125
JB Hunt transport services	USA	3,088
Logwin (formerly Thiel Logistik)	Luxemburg	3,081
Kitetsu world	Japan	2,991
Penske logistics	USA	2,910

Notes Gross Revenue for non-asset based logistics
Source SJ Consulting Group Estimates, www.jindel.com/aboutsjc.htm
[a] In 2006 TNT Logistics was sold and rebranded to CEVA Logistics. But TNT Express remains a big player in the global express and mail business

10.5.4 Third Party Logistics

The growing trend of outsourcing logistics activities in a wide variety of industrial sectors has led to a surge of academic interest and publications in the area of third party logistics (3PL). Selviaridis and Spring (2007) provide an extensive literature overview on the issue. Consolidation within the 3PL industry has resulted in the emergence of large companies that have the capabilities to offer logistics solutions on a regional or even global scale. North America and Europe are very active in this field.

Table 10.2 provides an overview of the world's top 3PL firms. Many of them are based in Europe or the USA. Deutsche Post World Net (DPWN), through its acquisitions, has become the leading 3PL in the European logistics market and the world. Its businesses include those formerly owned by such names as Danzas,

DHL, AEI, Airborne, ASG, Nedlloyd and Exel. Kuehne and Nagel is a global freight forwarder with an asset-light, high-financial-return business model. The other large European 3PL companies are mainly based in the core economic regions of Europe such as Germany, the UK, France and the Benelux countries. CH Robinson Worldwide is the largest North American 3PL, closely followed by UPS Supply Chain Solutions, Expeditors International of Washington and UTi Worldwide. At first look, it would appear that Western European firms are more committed than American organizations to outsourcing. This is evidenced by the substantially greater logistics budgets allocated to third-party firms in Table 10.2. However, giant American retailers (e.g. Wal-Mart, Home Depot, Target) tend to organize their supply chains "internally," with less reliance on 3/4PL, so the United States is under-represented. The issues faced by European and US firms are in fact very similar.

The position of Northwest European and North American 3PL companies in the worldwide global logistics service market is entwined with the strong growth of inbound logistics that took place in Europe and North America since the late 1980 s. Customers' service expectations are moving towards a push for higher flexibility, reliability and precision. 3PLs are challenged to deliver supply chain excellence, with superior customer service and lowest cost to serve.

10.6 Conclusion

Containerized freight distribution in Europe and North-America has largely been shaped by the effects of globalization, particularly at the level of inbound logistics. The logistics industry has to manage these freight flows via asset-based and non-asset based activities. The actual patterns of flows are determined by locational decisions made by a logistics industry which is guided by institutional, geographical and market factors. European and North-American 3PL companies are at the forefront of developing global logistics solutions. However, in terms of total freight volumes moved and related deployment of assets, Asia and in particular China has surpassed the two continents. Chinese container ports (including Hong Kong) handled a total of 150 million TEU, in 2008, more than Europe and North America combined: Total European container throughput reached 90 million TEU in the same year (Notteboom 2010), while North American container ports (USA and Canada) recorded a volume of 47.5 million TEU (figures from the Association of American Port Authorities).

In recent years, containerized freight distribution dynamics in North America and Europe has been characterized by a more modest development than their Asian counterparts, but also by a high level of regionalism, as shown in this chapter. Such regionalism underlines that, in spite of powerful forces towards standardization and the convergence of supply chain management practices, the region retains a significant affect on global logistics. In this chapter, we demonstrated that the main differences in freight distribution between North America and

Europe are found in the field of intermediacy (transshipment hubs, rail networks), the role of short sea shipping and inland waterway transport, the configuration of gateway port systems, and inland logistics structures.

Four factors, among others, are likely to influence the regionalism of North American and European containerized freight distribution:

- **A changing economic geography, and with it the emergence of new logistics hotspots.** Freight distribution in North America and Europe is impacted by the orientation of trade flows and the global distribution of value-added activities among logistics sites. Future regional freight distribution patterns in Europe are likely to see a growing importance of North Africa (Morocco in particular), Turkey and Russia, as well as the emergence of new logistics hotspots in East- and Central-European locations. The expanding logistics market is expected to result in renewed configurations of associated distribution networks, potentially implying a move away from the single EDC concept (see Sect. 5.1). These developments challenge the established large-gateway ports to enhance (rail) corridor connectivity to more-distant hinterlands, and provide opportunities to smaller and medium-sized gateway ports in the Med, the Black Sea and the Baltic to take a more prominent position in the European seaport system.
  However, despite the spread of large-scale logistics activities over an ever larger area, liner shipping economics and the benefits of cargo concentration are likely to consolidate the position of the North-West European ports (the so-called Hamburg-Le Havre range) as the main gateway system to Europe, and to provide chances to intermediate locations to capture some of the value creation in supply chains. For North America, the challenges of new gateways, such as Prince Rupert and Lazaro Cardenas, remain more marginal. Railways have invested massively in reinforcing the capacity of existing long-distance corridors. In cooperation with large logistics real estate firms, railways have co-located inland ports at strategic inland locations servicing large market areas so that economies of scale can be effectively achieved.
- **Rebalancing.** With the setting of export-oriented economies in the Asia–Pacific, global trade flows, notably with North America, have become significantly balanced (see Fig. 10.8). Since economic history underlines that imbalances are eventually rectified, the rebalancing (which could involve a drop in imports and a growth in exports) will have important consequences for global logistics. It has been shown in this chapter that complex regional freight distribution structures have been developed to accommodate this pattern. The recessionary period that began in 2008 may be the beginning of a phase of readjustment, with complex and unforeseen changes in logistics.
- **Slow steaming.** Initially adopted to accommodate the excess capacity in maritime shipping as a result of the financial crisis of 2008, the practice of lowering the operating speeds from about 22–24 knots to around 18–19 knots appears to have become an enduring trend. This may entail several changes in freight distribution; longer lead times for containerized supply chains and a greater quantity of containerized assets tied in transit are of concern. Both for Europe

and North America, that may incite a growth in transloading activities at gateways and greater difficulties to secure maritime containers inland. It remains to be seen how transshipment activities will be impacted. An observed trend is that shipping lines seem to shorten mainline European routes in with more transshipment activity in Benelux ports instead of North German ports, and an increase of interlining/relay operations near the Straits of Gibraltar (e.g. Tanger Med, Valencia and Algeciras). Surprisingly, slow steaming has not improved schedule reliability of liner services (Johnson 2010): on average about half of all vessels still arrive late, i.e. not on the scheduled arrival day. This challenges logistics planners and increases the costs of safety stock (see also Notteboom 2006; Vernimmen et al. 2007).

- **Panama Canal expansion.** Another relatively significant unknown remains the impact of the expansion of the Panama Canal, expected to be completed in 2014. For North America, it may favor an enhanced share of the all-water route from Asia, although this share has significantly grown in recent years. There may also be an increase in transshipment of the Caribbean. Freight, and regionalism along the American West Coast is expected to change. For Europe, the impacts of the Panama Canal are likely to be more marginal. However, it must be considered that with a parity in capacity between the Suez and the Panama canals, a greater reliance on circum-equatorial routes can be expected. Transshipment activities in the Mediterranean will thus be expanded.

References

Berglund M, van Laarhoven P, Sharman G, Wandel S (1999) Third-party logistics: is there a future? Int J Logistics Manag 10(1):59–70

Brooks M (2008) North American freight transportation: the road to security and prosperity, Edward Elgar, Cheltenham

Brooks M (2009) Liberalization in maritime transport, International Transport Forum, OECD, Paris, p 31

Brooks M, Trifts V (2008) Short sea shipping in North America: understanding the requirements of Atlantic Canadian shippers. Marit Policy Manag 35(2):145–158

Button K (1997) Lessons from European transport experience. Ann Am Acad Polit Soc Sci 55(31):157–167

Charler JJ, Ridolfi G (1994) Intermodal transportation in Europe: of modes, corridors and nodes. Marit Policy Manag 21(3):237–250

Coe NM, Hess M, Yeung HW-C, Dicken P, Henderson J (2004) 'Globalizing' regional development: a global production networks perspective. Trans Inst Br Geog 29(4):468–484

Debrie J,Gouvernal E (2006) Intermodal rail in Western Europe: actors and services in a new regulatory environment. Growth Change 37(3):444–459

Drewry (2009) Container market 2009/2010: annual review and forecast, Drewry Shipping Consultants, London

European Commission (2009) Communication and action plan with a view to establishing a European maritime transport space without barriers [COM (2009) 11 final]. <http://ec.europa.eu/maritimeaffairs/subpage_mpa_en.html#1>

Eurostat (2009) Statistics in focus, 58, Eurostat, Brussels

Fleming DK, Hayuth Y (1994) Spatial characteristics of transportation hubs: centrality and intermediacy. J Transp Geogr 2(1):3–18

Frémont A, Franc P, Slack B (2009) Inland barge services and container transport: the case of the ports of Le Havre and Marseille in the European context. Cybergeo, Espace, Société, Territoire, article 437, http://cybergeo.revues.org/index21743.html

Gouvernal E, Daydou J (2005) Container railfreight services in North-West Europe: diversity of organizational forms in a liberalizing environment. Transp Rev 25(5):557–571

Johnson E (2010) Time for a rethink. American Shipper, pp 32–37

Levinson M (2006) The box: How the shipping container made the world smaller and the world economy bigger, Princeton University Press, Princeton

Leinbach T, Capineri C (eds) (2007) Globalized freight transport: intermodality, E-commerce, logistics and sustainability, transport economic, management and policy series, Edward Elgar Publishing, Cheltenham

Lieb RC, Millen RA, Van Wassenhove LN (1993) Third party logistics services: a comparison of experienced American and European manufacturers. Int J Phys Distrib Logistics Manag 23(6):35–44

Kreuzberger E (2005) Hub and spoking in a process of changing bundling concepts of intermodal rail networks: current developments in the light of intermodal efficiency. In: Witlox F, Dullaert W, Vernimmen B (eds) Proceedings of the BIVEC-GIBET transport research day 2005, Nautilis, Ghent, pp 405–436

Notteboom T (2006) The time factor in liner shipping services. Marit Econ Logistics 8:19–39

Notteboom T (2007) Container river services and gateway ports: similarities between the Yangtze River and the Rhine River. Asia Pac Viewpoint 48:330–343

Notteboom T (2008) Bundling of freight flows and hinterland network development. In: Konings R, Priemus H, Nijkamp P (eds) The Future of intermodal freight transport, operations, technology, design and implementation, Edward Elgar, Cheltenham, pp 66–88

Notteboom T (2009a) The relationship between seaports and the intermodal hinterland in light of global supply chains: European challenges. Round Table no. 143, OECD—International Transport Forum (ITF): Paris, pp 25–75

Notteboom T (2009b) Path dependency and contingency in the development of multi-port gatewaygateway regions and multi-port hub regions. In: Notteboom T, Ducruet C, De Langen P (eds) Ports in proximity: competition and coordination among adjacent seaports, Ashgate, Alderschot, pp 55–74

Notteboom T (2010) Concentration and the formation of multi-port gateway regions in the European container port system: an update. J Trans Geogr 18(4):567–583

Notteboom T, Konings R (2004) Network dynamics in container transport by barge. Belgeo, 5:461–477

Notteboom T, Rodrigue J-P (2007) Re-assessing port-hinterland relationships in the context of global supply chains. In: Wang J, Notteboom T, Olivier D, Slack B (eds) Ports, cities, and global supply chains, Ashgate, Alderschot, pp 51–68

Notteboom T, Rodrigue J-P (2010) Foreland-based regionalization: integrating intermediate hubs with port hinterlands. Res Trans Econ 27:19–29

OECD (2001) Short sea shipping in Europe, OECD, Paris

Paixao AC, Marlow PB (2002) Strengths and weaknesses of short sea shipping short sea shipping. Mar Policy 26:167–178

Randolph D (2008) Preparing for the future Mexican land bridge to the United States. North American Transportation Competitiveness Research Council. Working Paper No. 6

Rodrigue J-P (2006) Transportation and the geographical and functional integration of global production networks. Growth Change 37(4):510–525

Rodrigue J-P (2011) Factors impacting North American freight distribution in view of the panama canal expansion. The Van Horne Institute, University of Calgary

Rodrigue J-P, Notteboom T (2009) The geography of containerization: half a century of revolution, adaptation and diffusion. Geo J 74:1–5

Rodrigue J-P, Notteboom T (2010) Comparative North American and European gateway logistics: the regionalism of freight distribution. J Trans Geogr 18(4):497–507

Selviaridis K, Spring M (2007) Third party logistics: a literature review and research agenda. Int J Logistics Manag 18(1):125–150

Slack B (1996) Along different paths: intermodal rail terminals in North America and Europe. In: Proceedings of the 7th WCTR conference. World Conference of Transport Research Society, pp 123–131

UNCTAD (2009) Transport Newsletter, No. 43, http://www.unctad.org/en/docs/webdtltlb20092_en.pdf

Van Klink HA, Van den Berg GC (1998) Gateways and intermodalism. J Trans Geogr 6(1):1–9

Vernimmen B, Dullaert W, Engelen S (2007) Schedule unreliability in liner shipping: origins and consequences for the hinterland supply chain. Marit Econ Logistics 9:193–213

Chapter 11
Network Redesign in Turkey: The Supply, Production, and Distribution of Malt and Beer

Murat Köksalan, Haldun Süral and Selin Özpeynirci

Abstract In this chapter, we consider a network redesign problem that contains decision problems of opening new malt plants and breweries in order to increase the malt and beer production capacities of a Turkish corporation, Efes Beverage Group. We briefly discuss several beer logistics applications in Turkey and other countries, and some location applications in Turkey. Some attention is also given to the overall status of logistics in Turkey. We construct a mixed integer programming model for the multi-period, multi-item, multi-level capacitated facility location/relocation problem of Efes. The model determines the locations of new malt plants and breweries as well as the distribution decisions for barley, malt, and different types of beer while minimizing fixed costs and annual transportation costs. We suggest a procedure to set effective capacities of breweries due to seasonality of demand. We solve the model under different parameter settings in order to obtain a variety of solutions that the decision makers may find useful. We discuss our results and experiences from this application process.

11.1 Introduction

Beer is one of the world's oldest alcoholic beverages. As early as 6000 BC, people were brewing beer in Mesopotamia, the land between the Tigris and Euphrates, rivers that originate in southeast Anatolia. Hittites, one of the most sophisticated

M. Köksalan · H. Süral (✉)
Department of Industrial Engineering, Middle East Technical University, Ankara, Turkey
e-mail: sural@ie.metu.edu.tr

S. Özpeynirci
Department of Industrial Systems Engineering, İzmir University of Economics, İzmir, Turkey

J. H. Bookbinder (ed.), *Handbook of Global Logistics*, International Series in Operations Research & Management Science 181, DOI: 10.1007/978-1-4419-6132-7_11,

civilizations 4000 years ago in Anatolia, were drinking beer. Today, the brewing industry is a huge business worldwide.

Beer is produced by the fermentation of carbohydrates in cereals, such as wheat, corn, rice, and most commonly barley. The main ingredients of Efes' beers, which are the most consumed beers in Turkey by far, are water, malted barley, hops and yeast. Malted barley is the processed grain that has begun germination by being soaked in water, and provides beer its body and color. Hops are used in small amounts as a preservative agent. It also gives beer a bitter flavor and a pleasant aroma. Yeast is composed of micro-organisms that convert sugar in malt juice to alcohol and carbon dioxide. From the start of the production process, it takes approximately 21 days until the beer is ready for consumption. Beer tastes best if consumed when fresh; soon after bottling.

11.1.1 Brewing Industries and Beer Logistics

The European brewing industry, covering 31 countries, includes 4,000 brewers and employs 2.5 million people, directly or indirectly. Its contribution to the European economy is about 0.43 % of total GDP (see The Brewers of Europe 2010). The U.S. brewing industry, the second largest producer of beer after China, includes more than 2,000 brewers, over 2,800 wholesalers, over 521,000 retailers, and roughly 1.9 million employees, including indirect employment (see Beer Serves America 2009). Its contribution to the economy is about 1.5 % of GDP (see The Beer Institute 2009). The Canadian brewing industry, including over 100 breweries and having one of the most highly taxed beer industries in the world, second only to Norway, contributes $4.3 billion annually (2.6 %) to tax revenue, employs 0.2 million people, amounting to 1.2 % of the workforce of Canada, and is among the top ten largest exporters by volume. Its contribution to the economy is about 1.1 % of GDP (see Brewers Association of Canada 2009).

An earlier overview of the European beer market can be found in Vrontis (1998). For an assessment of the role of branding in product management within the market, Vrontis uses three companies, the British Bass, the Danish Carlsberg, and the Dutch Heineken, in order to exemplify marketing issues. Houthoofd and Heene (1997) describe features of the Belgian brewing industry and present an analysis for strategic groups and firm performance relations in the industry. Beugelsdijk et al. (2002) discuss how Heineken has experienced different organizational changes due to different challenges such as a shift in origin of demand from pubs to supermarkets, which has radically altered distribution channels of beer. A comprehensive analysis of the German and the Croatian brewing industries with an emphasis on managerial implications is presented in Niederhut-Bollmann and Theuvsen (2008). A broad account of evolution of the U.S. brewing industry is provided in Warner (2010). Carroll and Swaminathan (2000) explain how microbrewery movement (i.e., a dramatic increase in the number of small brewers in the industry) emerged in the U.S. beer brewing industry in the late 1980s, following the domination of the industry by a few large brewing companies, and also show that these two opposite trends are essentially interrelated. Sass (2005) analyzes the effects of exclusive-dealing contracts between brewers and distributors in the U.S. beer industry, that prohibit distributors from selling the products of other brewers.

Kioulafas (1985) presents a multiple regression study to explain the relationship between the sales and advertisement of beer in Greece. Gelders et al. (1987) consider the beer distribution for a Belgian brewer and determine the number and locations of depots to be opened. Duran (1987) considers the integrated production and distribution problem of a Colombian brewer. These are examples of earlier studies using quantitative techniques to solve beer logistics problems. Ramirez-Beltran (1995) develops a production planning model to minimize the labor costs for a Puerto Rican beer producer. A time series study is presented by Lenten and Moosa (1999) to model trend and seasonality in the consumption of beer in the U.K. Bommer et al. (2001) propose a performance system for distributors in the U.S. beer and soft drink industry so that they develop a service strategy based on several service categories such as price, customer service, delivery, etc. for their retailers. In a reverse logistics study of U.K. industries including the beer industry, Breen (2006) finds that customer non-compliance, in returning distribution equipment back to their sources, damages the performance of the logistics system. Kant et al. (2008) report a Coca-Cola implementation to handle daily construction of routes for beverages and its extension to beer distributors like Carlsberg, Heineken, and Inbev. Implementation at Inbev in France and Belgium included finding optimal depot-retail outlet pairs and optimal frequency to deliver an outlet, and realized a 100 % return on investment within one year.

11.1.2 Brewing Industry and Beer Logistics in Turkey

Turkey, the 11th largest beer producer among 31 European countries, has more than ten breweries run by seven brewing companies. Turkey brews about 0.9 billion liters of beer annually, which is equivalent to 2.4 % of the total annual beer production in Europe (see The Brewers of Europe 2010). Having a domestic market share of about 78 %, Anadolu (Anatolian) Efes (or Efes in short) is the leader of the Turkish brewing industry. In the domestic beer market, Efes supplies a large number of popular flavors under license agreements. Efes, with a brewing capacity of 3.3 billion liters, and a malt production capacity of 0.2 million tons annually, also offers a wide variety of local brands with different tastes and appeals in the international markets, especially in the former Soviet Union, Southeast Europe, and the Middle East (see Efes Beverage Group, Anadolu Efes 2009).

There are several location and forecasting applications conducted for Efes that are reported in the literature. Köksalan et al. (1995) and Köksalan and Süral (1999) present their results on the locations of new breweries and malt plants, respectively. The former is one of the earliest studies in the literature that incorporate inventory issues into the location-distribution problem. Both studies aggregate beer types and costs, and consider liters of beer to study production and distribution decisions. Using their findings from an earlier application conducted for Efes, Köksalan et al. (2010) develop a case study that requires building a multiple linear regression model for explaining the monthly beer demand in Turkey to help Efes Group in its beer demand predictions.

Köksalan et al. (1999), in an earlier study on beer logistics in Turkey, present medium and short-term regression models to explain and forecast the beer demand in Turkey. Pamuk et al. (2004) develop a product delivery system of Efes in Ankara, and report a savings potential of up to 25 % in distribution costs.

11.1.3 Where does Turkey Stand in Worldwide Logistics?

The quality of logistics services differs from one country to another because of differences in customs regulations, infrastructure, policies, etc. We refer the reader to Schoenherr (2009) for an extensive review of logistics and its applications in the global context.

The logistics performance index (LPI), created by the World Bank, is a comprehensive index,[1] rated on a scale from one (worst) to five (best), that summarizes the performance of 155 countries in six areas.[2] This index captures the most important aspects of the current logistics environment (Arvis et al. 2010). Eight of the top 10 countries in this index are from Europe and the entire group of 31 European countries is within the top 50 percent of LPI performers. Croatia has the lowest rank of 74 among the European countries. The first-ranking country in this list is Germany. Turkey, ranked 39th in the list of 155 countries, with an index value equal to 71.4 % of that of Germany, has the 21st highest score within the European countries and is in the top 40 % of logistics performers worldwide. Furthermore, in an assessment that considers both country income and logistics performance, Turkey is the sixth logistics performer among upper middle-income countries (Arvis et al. 2010). Based on interviews with 428 logistics companies operating in Turkey, Agaran et al. (2010) find that increasing and improving information technology use, a worldwide current trend today, is seen as the most essential requirement to achieve strategic goals by all logistics parties in Turkey.

Of course, the above remarks do not directly indicate the performance of beer industry's logistics in Turkey because "an organization's- or industry's -logistics success is only partly due to the overall business environment," as explained in

---

[1] LPI is based on standard statistical techniques to aggregate the data into a single indicator (Arvis et al. 2010).

[2] These areas are 'efficiency of the customs clearance process', 'quality of trade and transport-related infrastructure', 'ease of arranging competitively priced shipments', 'competence and quality of logistics services', 'ability to track and trace consignments', and 'frequency with which shipments reach the consignee within the scheduled or expected time'(Arvis et al. 2010).

Bookbinder and Tan (2003). Perhaps its performance can be assessed by using findings of Ulengin and Nuray (1999) analyzing the status of logistics in Turkey. They argue that the beverage industry is one of the industries having a proactive logistics management compared to other industries in Turkey, which is consistent with Turkey's macro logistics indicators in the global context.

11.1.4 Supply, Production, and Distribution Network Redesign for Efes

In this study, we consider the (re)location decisions for malt plants and breweries of Efes, in addition to the decisions on transportation of barley, malt, and beer. We develop a multi-period, multi-item, multi-level capacitated location/relocation model. In addition to capacity restrictions on barley supply and malt production, we consider differences in transportation costs of, and capacity limits on, differently-packaged beer as distinct products. We develop a procedure to specify the effective yearly capacities of breweries in order to capture the seasonality in the monthly beer demand. Determining the effective capacities with this procedure prevents holding excessive inventories for long periods during the year.

Another aspect we consider is to maintain a homogeneous taste in the beer regardless of where it is brewed or where its barley is grown. This is achieved by either mixing different types of barleys, whose malt yields vary from 75 to 80 %, depending on the region, in the same proportions in each malt plant, or mixing various malts of different plants in the same proportions in each brewery. Considering the mixing of grains, however, causes nonlinearity in the mixed integer linear model. We formulate two types of linearization to solve the model.

Facility location problems have been mostly studied for single-level systems, as discussed by Şahin and Süral (2007) in the context of systems of different levels of interacting facilities. In a review of facility location and supply chain management, Melo et al. (2009) state that around two thirds of the surveyed papers model locations in a single level. The dynamic multi-item, multi-level location problem studied in Melo et al. (2006) is similar to our current work and involves several aspects that affect the network design. We refer the reader to Melo et al. (2006) for a list of studies in the literature on the dynamic location problems, and to Klose and Drexl (2005) for a review of the multi-item location problems.

11.1.5 Other Location Applications in Turkey

Şahin et al. (2007) develop a hierarchical design approach for the Turkish Red Crescent Society's blood service network, where regional facilities are located in the highest level and mobile units that are allocated to service regions are in the lowest level. Tan and Kara (2007) consider a hub location problem encountered by cargo delivery systems; they report that speed and reliability are more important than cost in cargo delivery. According to their interviews with different cargo delivery companies operating in Turkey, delivering the cargo in a timely manner is the key factor in the Turkish market. Alamur and Kara (2009) develop a mathematical model to design hub networks, focusing on needs of a cargo company operating in Turkey. Bozkaya et al. (2010) suggest a GIS-based optimization framework for a competitive multi-facility location-routing problem, and report their computational results for a supermarket store chain in Istanbul. Çetiner et al. (2010) consider the combined hubbing and routing problem in postal delivery systems and present the results of a case study for the Turkish postal services. Demirel et al. (2010) report an application of warehouse location selection for a Turkish logistic company, using an uncommon multi objective approach. Erden and Coskun (2010) study the selection of fire station locations in Istanbul. Their approach combines the analytic hierarchy process and geographic information systems to support the decision maker.

11.1.6 Outline

Let us now concentrate on the specifics of our problem. We define the problem in detail in Sect. 11.2, and discuss various problem parameters and assumptions in Sect. 11.3. Section 11.4 contains the development of our models. We discuss various solutions obtained with the model in Sect. 11.5, and present our concluding remarks in Sect. 11.6.

11.2 Problem Definition

Efes currently has two malt plants and five breweries in Turkey (as of December 2010). We consider seven and eight sites as the possible locations for the new breweries and malt plants, respectively. Locations of the existing sites, new potential sites, and the barley regions are shown in Fig. 11.1.

Due to confidentiality, we conceal the identity of the specific breweries, malt plants, and the barley regions in the rest of our discussions. Codes will refer to each facility and region. We assign a number to each city and add the letters, A for barley, ME for existing malt plants, MP for potential malt plants, BE for existing breweries, and BP for potential breweries before the numbers.

Efes' two malt plants are located close to main barley regions in central Anatolia at locations ME6 and ME7. The malt produced is either transported to Efes' beer breweries or exported. Existing breweries are located at BE1-BE5. The potential locations for the new malt plant are MP1, MP2, and MP7-MP12. Two

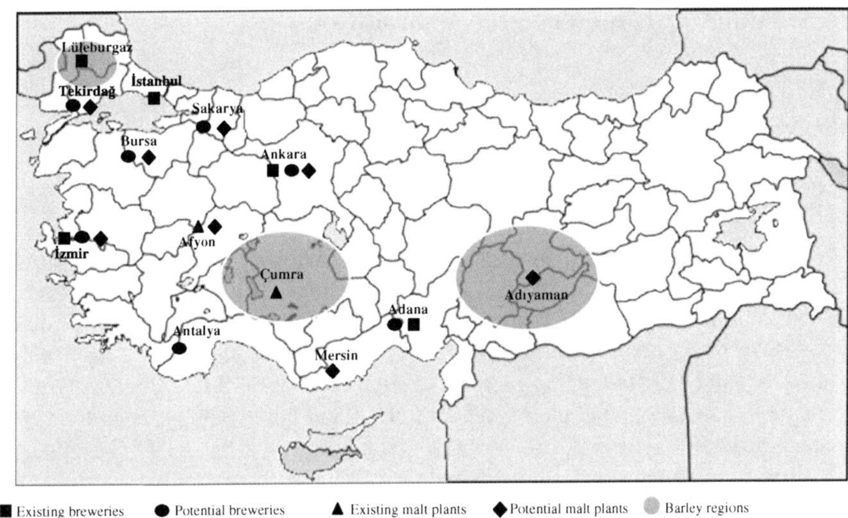

Fig. 11.1 The locations of existing and potential facilities

alternatives correspond to building next to the existing breweries and another alternative is to expand an existing plant. The potential locations for the new brewery are BP1-BP3, BP8-BP10, and BP13.

The problem is to determine where to locate the new brewery and malt plant as well as the amounts of barley, malt and beer to transport among different locations each year. In doing so, beer demands of all customers and malt demands of all breweries should be satisfied, necessary amounts of barley should be shipped to each malt plant, and the capacities of breweries and malt plants as well as barley availability in each region should be taken into account. The objective is to minimize the long term discounted total cost which includes the fixed cost of relocating a brewery and opening a new malt plant, and the transportation costs of barley, malt, and beer.

There are several complicating issues in this problem. The location of new breweries and malt plants is a strategic decision and has important long-term effects. Therefore, the decision should be made after a detailed analysis. In the analysis, the capacities of the new breweries are not fixed in advance and we want to choose the optimal capacity configuration by trying different scenarios. Another difficulty arises due to high seasonality of beer demand and necessity of producing the beer in a homogeneous taste in multiple locations. The former difficulty requires incorporation of inventory issues into decisions on capacity settings of the plants, whereas the latter requires considering balanced distributions of different barley types or various malts or both from their multiple origins to their multiple destinations. We further discuss and address these difficulties in the next section.

11.3 Model Parameters and Assumptions

There are about 40 barley supply regions and they are aggregated to four centers: A8, A6, and A12 represent north-west, central, and south-east Anatolia regions, respectively, and the imported barley is assumed to be transported from the closest harbor to each malt plant. Upper limits for barley supply amounts for each region are provided by Efes, and excess demand for barley is always satisfied by A12. Amounts of malt obtained from 100 kg of barley are approximately 78 kg for the barley of north-west and south-east Anatolia regions, 75 kg for the barley of the central Anatolia region, and 80 kg for the imported barley. Production of 1,000 liters of beer requires 0.136 tons of malt.

Efes has about 740 demand points and supplies beer in three different types of containers, namely, bottle, can, and barrel. Demand points are aggregated into 82 centers in addition to exports; demand is assumed to increase 4.5 % annually, based on other forecasting studies conducted by Efes. In order to determine the transportation costs for barley, malt, and beer types, the regression equation obtained in a previous study (Köksalan et al. 1995) is revised and used here. The production cost differs in the two malt plants due to using different technologies, but is approximately the same in all breweries.

We considered years 2008 and 2009 in detail, and used the transportation patterns of year 2009 to represent the long term after 2009. The plan of Efes was to open the new malt plant at the beginning of 2008 and the new brewery in June 2008. We used an annual opportunity cost of 10 % in calculating the discount factor.

11.3.1 Seasonality and Capacity

There is high seasonality in beer demand. Generally, consumption of beer increases during summer. The percentage of total beer demand that occurs each month in a typical year in Turkey is shown in Table 11.1. According to this table, operating a brewery at full capacity all year long would lead to stocking up in winter months to satisfy the peak demand of summer months. This is undesirable, not only because of the cost of carrying inventory, but also due to the fact that beer tastes best when consumed within several months after bottling. Efes tries to enforce this strategy. Since our model considers a medium term, its time periods are years. Due to seasonality effects and the Efes' strategy of selling fresh beer only, it is not straightforward to set the yearly capacity of a brewery. We need to determine an effective yearly capacity that leads to a desirable monthly brewing and stocking plan. The following applies to any brewery. We therefore omit the brewery subscripts to simplify the notation. Let

B: the effective yearly capacity (of a brewery).

p_t: the proportion of the effective yearly capacity (of the brewery) utilized in month t, where $0 \leq p_t$ and $\Sigma_t p_t = 1$.

Table 11.1 Percentage of yearly demand occurring in each month

Month	Jan.	Feb.	Mar.	Apr.	May	Jun.
% Demand	5.90	6.42	7.65	8.85	10.78	11.74
Month	Jul.	Aug.	Sep.	Oct.	Nov.	Dec.
% Demand	13.15	12.14	9.09	3.29	4.81	6.18

C the maximum amount that can be brewed (in the given brewery) in any month, where $p_t\, B \leq c$.

s_t the proportion of the yearly demand that occurs in month t.

Suppose that we decide to use full capacity several months before the summer, operate at that pace throughout the summer, and brew in proportion to the demand during the remaining months. More specifically, let us set the effective monthly capacity to c (i.e., $p_t\, B = c$) for months $M = \{m + 1,\ldots, m + k\}$ and set $p_t = s_t$ for the remaining months $\{1, \ldots, m, m + k + 1, \ldots\}$. Note that we would at least like to set the effective capacity for the month where the peak demand occurs (July) to full capacity.

Using the above, we can write $B = \sum_{t \notin M} s_t B + \sum_{t \in M} c = \sum_{t \notin M} s_t B + kc$ for $k \geq 1$. Simplifying, we obtain $B = kc/(1 - \sum_{t \notin M} s_t)$.

Using the s_t values given in Table 11.1 and setting $p_7\, B = c$ (i.e., using full capacity only in July) we obtain $B = c$ / (1-.0590-.0642-...-.1174-.1214-...-.0618) = 7.61c. In this case, even if the effective capacity is fully utilized, there will be no need to carry any inventory.

Alternatively, if we decide to use full capacity March thru August, the effective capacity will be $B = 6c$ / (1-.0590-.0642-.0909-.0329-.0481-.0618) = 9.33c. In this case, inventory will start to accumulate starting from March if the effective capacity is fully utilized. No inventory will be carried September thru February.

The above analysis can simply be generalized to represent different annual effective capacities by considering any demand seasonality throughout a year and willingness or policy of decision maker for how long to carry inventories in the planning year. In our experiments, we set the effective capacities to 9.33c, in accordance with the strategy of Efes, to avoid holding inventories for long periods.

11.4 The Mathematical Model

We formulated the problem as a mixed integer linear program. The model uses a year as the time period. We used an infinite planning horizon, but studied the first two years in more detail. The new brewery and malt plant are considered to start operating in 2008 and to reach full capacity in 2009. To represent the long-term transportation costs, we used the present worth of a representative year's cost as if it would repeat each year beyond 2009.

11.4.1 Indices and Parameters

L: Number of barley supply regions
K: Number of malt plants
J: Number of breweries
I: Number of demand points
P: Nature of beer container ($p = 1, 2, 3$ stand for bottle, can, barrel, respectively)
T: Length of planning horizon
d_{ipt}: Annual demand of point i for beer type p in year t (in kilo liters)
B_{jt}: Annual production capacity of brewery j in year t (in kilo liters)
D_{jpt}: Annual packing capacity of brewery j for type p in year t (in kilo liters)
M_{kt}: Annual production capacity of malt plant k in year t (in tons)
A_{lt}: Annual limit on barley supply at region l in year t (in tons)
α_l: Kg of malt produced from barley at region l
β: Kg of malt to produce one liter of beer
FM_k: Fixed cost of opening alternative malt plant k at the beginning of T
FB_j: Fixed cost of relocation and opening alternative brewery j at the beginning of T
ca_{lkt}: Present value of transportation cost of barley from barley region l to malt plant k in year t (in value of TL/ton)
cm_{kjt}: Present value of transportation cost of malt from malt plant k to brewery j in year t (in value of TL/ton)
cb_{jipt}: Present value of transportation cost of beer from malt plant k to demand point i in year t in terms of $t = 1$ prices (in value of TL/kilo liters)

11.4.2 Decision Variables

z_{lkt}: Tons of barley sent from barley region l to malt plant k in year t
y_{kjt}: Tons of malt sent from malt plant k to brewery j in year t
x_{jipt}: Kilo liters of beer type p sent from brewery j to demand point i in year t
u_k: 1 if malt plant k is built in the beginning of T; 0 otherwise
v_j: 1 if brewery j is built the beginning of T; 0 otherwise

11.4.3 The Model

The objective is to minimize the present value of the total transportation costs of barley, malt and beer, and the fixed costs of opening new malt plant and brewery, plus long term transportation costs:

$$\text{Minimize} \sum_{l=1}^{L}\sum_{k=1}^{K}\sum_{t=1}^{T} ca_{lkt}z_{lkt} + \sum_{k=1}^{K}\sum_{j=1}^{J}\sum_{t=1}^{T} cm_{kjt}z_{kjt} + \sum_{j=1}^{J}\sum_{i=1}^{I}\sum_{p=1}^{P}\sum_{t=1}^{T} cb_{jipt}x_{jipt}$$

$$+ \sum_{k=1}^{K} FM_k u_k + \sum_{j=1}^{J} FB_j v_j + [\text{long term transportation costs}] \quad (11.1)$$

The total amount of barley shipped from barley region l cannot exceed the capacity of that region each year.

$$\sum_{k=1}^{K} z_{lkt} \leq A_{lt} \quad \forall l, t \quad (11.2)$$

Each malt plant should obtain enough barley for its malt production.

$$\sum_{l=1}^{L} \alpha_l z_{lkt} = \sum_{j=1}^{J} y_{kjt} \quad \forall k, t \quad (11.3)$$

The total amount of malt produced at malt plant k cannot exceed its production capacity each year. Constraint 11.4 (11.5) below is for existing (candidate) malt plants.

$$\sum_{j=1}^{J} y_{kjt} \leq M_{kt} \quad \forall t, k \quad (11.4)$$

$$\sum_{j=1}^{J} y_{kjt} \leq M_{kt}u_k \quad \forall t, k \quad (11.5)$$

Each brewery should obtain enough malt for its beer production.

$$\beta \sum_{j=1}^{J} y_{kjt} = \sum_{i=1}^{I}\sum_{p=1}^{P} x_{jipt} \quad \forall j, t \quad (11.6)$$

The total amount of beer produced at brewery j cannot exceed its production capacity each year. Constraint 11.7 (11.8) is for existing (candidate) breweries.

$$\sum_{i=1}^{I}\sum_{p=1}^{P} x_{jipt} \leq B_{jt} \quad \forall t, j \quad (11.7)$$

$$\sum_{i=1}^{I}\sum_{p=1}^{P} x_{jipt} \leq B_{jt}v_j \quad \forall t, j \tag{11.8}$$

The total amount of beer type p packed at brewery j cannot exceed its packing capacity each year. As above, constraint 11.9 (11.10) is for existing (candidate) breweries.

$$\sum_{i=1}^{I} x_{jipt} \leq D_{jpt} \quad \forall p, t, j \tag{11.9}$$

$$\sum_{i=1}^{I} x_{jipt} \leq D_{jpt}v_j \quad \forall p, t, j \tag{11.10}$$

The total amount of beer type p shipped from all breweries to each demand point i must satisfy the demand at that point each year.

$$\sum_{j=1}^{j} x_{jipt} = d_{ipt} \quad \forall i, p, t \tag{11.11}$$

Only one malt plant and one brewery will be opened.

$$\sum_{j=1}^{j} v_j = 1 \tag{11.12}$$

$$\sum_{k=1}^{k} u_k = 1 \tag{11.13}$$

Constraints on variables

$$z_{lkt},\ y_{kjt},\ x_{jipt} \geq 0 \quad \text{and } u_k,\ v_j \in \{0, 1\} \tag{11.14}$$

11.5 Solutions

The above model was generated using Visual C++ and solved by CPLEX 8.1 on a Pentium 4, 2.80 GHz computer with 520 MB RAM. We solved the model under various scenarios. In this section, we discuss the results obtained and their comparisons.

Table 11.2 2009 malt capacity usage

Malt plant	ME7	ME6	MP9
% Usage	–	100	68

11.5.1 The Optimal Solution

The optimal solution of the scenario without mixing grains is to open both the new brewery and malt plant in city 9. According to the optimal solution, malt capacity usages in 2009 are given in Table 11.2. Malt plant ME6 works at full capacity and the remaining demand is satisfied by the new malt plant. It is not economical to satisfy the malt requirements of breweries from ME7. Production cost, included in the transportation costs of the model, in malt plant ME7 is higher than others.

The beer capacity usages for production and packaging in 2009 are given in Table 11.3. When BE4 is closed to relocate, opening the new brewery at the alternative city closest to city 4 gives the best solution. Also, the new brewery uses most of its production and packaging capacities. Can and barrel capacity usages are very low for almost all breweries. This is due to high packaging capacities of the two cases compared to demand.

Table 11.4 reports the distribution of transportation costs among different activities in 2009. Barley and malt transportation constitute around 19 % of total costs, while beer transportation constitutes approximately 81 %. Also a high portion of beer transportation cost belongs to bottled beer. As will be discussed later, the alternatives for the new malt plant result in slight differences in the total cost.

11.5.2 Comparison of Potential Breweries

The solutions obtained for alternative brewery locations are compared and are given in Table 11.5. We forced the model to open the new brewery in one of the alternative locations and solved for finding the best location of the new malt plant and the optimal distribution plan. In the last two rows of Table 11.5, even though city 4 is not a potential location for the new brewery, we searched for the answer to the question, "What happens if the new brewery could be opened at city 4?" In the first implementation we let the model select the new malt plant's location, and in the second implementation we force to open the new malt plant at city 4. In both implementations, the total costs are lower than the optimal total cost found in Sect. 11.5.1. Table 11.5 shows that the closer the new brewery is to city 4, the less the transportation costs will be.

Table 11.3 2009 beer capacity usage

Brewery	Production %	Bottle %	Can %	Barrel %
BE1	90	70	43	69
BE2	53	43	45	11
BE3	88	99	95	24
BE5	82	100	61	–
BP9	100	98	68	67

Table 11.4 2009 transportation cost proportions

	%	
Barley		13.5
Malt		5.8
Bottle	61.3	
Can	9.1	
Barrel	10.3	
Beer Total		80.7
Total		100.0

Table 11.5 Comparison of potential breweries (2009)

Beer	Malt	Percentage above the optimal
BP10	MP10	5
BP8	MP9	6
BP13	MP11	17
BP2	MP11	29
BP3	MP11	30
BP1	MP1	31
BP4	MP9	−6
BP4	MP4	−6

11.5.3 Comparison of Potential Malt Plants

We also compare the solutions obtained by opening the new malt plant in all potential locations. The results in Table 11.6 show that malt plant location has a small effect on the total cost, and the optimal brewery location BP9 is quite robust.

11.5.4 Capacity Alternatives for the New Brewery

As mentioned earlier, one of the decision problems that we dealt with in this study is the capacity of the new brewery. The previous models were solved assuming that the new brewery would be opened with a high capacity (and grains are not mixed). Another alternative is to open the new brewery with a small capacity

Table 11.6 Comparison of potential malt plants (2009)

Malt	Beer	Percentage above the optimal
MP2	BP9	1
MP11	BP9	1
MP6	BP9	2
MP12	BP9	3

Table 11.7 Results for opening the new brewery with small capacity

Malt	Beer	Percentage above the optimal
MP9	BP8	11
MP9	BP9	12

(almost half of the high capacity) and to expand when needed. Table 11.7 gives the comparison of these new results with the optimal solution, assuming high capacity. As seen in the first row of Table 11.7, the best locations are found to be BP8 for the brewery with small capacity, and MP9 for the new malt plant. The second row of Table 11.7 displays the optimal solution when a brewery with small capacity is opened at BP9. Note that these two solutions, with 11–12 % deviations from the optimal total cost found in Sect. 11.5.1, are very close to each other.

Building a brewery with a high capacity may not be advantageous due to making the high investment early. On the other hand, such a brewery may be advantageous due to savings in transportation costs and more production flexibility (having ability to adapt to unexpected situations). When these advantages are taken into account, we suggest opening the new brewery with high capacity.

11.5.5 Opening Second New Brewery

According to the long term demand forecasts, the brewery capacity of Efes will not be enough to meet demand in 2014. The model is solved to find the optimal location of the second new brewery, assuming that the first new brewery will be opened in BP9 and the second new brewery will start to work with full capacity in 2014. First, we let the model find the optimal malt plant location and MP11 turns out to be the best alternative. Then we consider opening the new malt plant in MP9. In both implementations, whose results are given in Table 11.8, BP13 is found as the (unique) optimal location for the new brewery.

Since the malt plant location does not significantly affect the total cost and city 9 is the optimal location of that plant before year 2014, opening the new malt plant in city 9 now seems more reasonable.

Table 11.8 Results for second new brewery

Malt	Beer	Percentage above the optimal
MP11	BP9 + BP13	0
MP9	BP9 + BP13	0.07

11.5.6 Barley or Malt Mix

It is important that Efes maintains the same quality and taste of products produced in different facilities. For this purpose, either the barley from different regions is mixed in malt plants in the same proportions (as given by constraint 11.15), or the malt supplied from different plants is mixed in breweries in the same proportions (as given by constraint 11.16).

$$z_{lkt} = \left(\sum_n z_{nkt}\right)\left(\frac{\sum\limits_p z_{lpt}}{\sum\limits_{n,p} z_{npt}}\right) \quad \forall l, k, t \tag{11.15}$$

$$y_{kjt} = \left(\sum_n y_{njt}\right)\left(\frac{\sum\limits_p y_{kpt}}{\sum\limits_{n,p} y_{npt}}\right) \quad \forall k, j, t \tag{11.16}$$

Both (11.15) and (11.16) are nonlinear. We can, however, linearize (11.15) as Efes works with barley producers on a contract basis. Considering the yearly agreements done in a given region, the amount of barley that would be supplied from that region is roughly estimated, and thus the total amount of barley supply from all regions is computed. For instance, the ratio of the annual total barley supply from region l to the total barley supply from all regions, $\left(\sum_p z_{lpt}\right)/\left(\sum_{n,p} z_{npt}\right)$ from Eq.(11.15), is computed. If we denote this ratio by rb_l for barley region l, that equation can be written as

$$z_{lkt} = \left(\sum\nolimits_n z_{nkt}\right) rb_l \quad \forall l, k, t \tag{11.17}$$

Alternatively, if we can assume that the amount of malt supplied from each plant is known, then we can find the ratio $rm_k = \left(\sum_p y_{kpt}\right)/\left(\sum_{n,p} y_{npt}\right)$ for every malt plant k. For instance, if we fix the supply amounts from malt plants at their supply amounts in the optimal solution of the case without mixing grains, we would have a linear approximation of (11.16), which can be written as

$$y_{kjt} = \left(\sum_n y_{njt}\right) rm_k \quad \forall k, j, t \tag{11.18}$$

Table 11.9 Effect of barley or malt mix on the transportation costs: Results when constraint (11.18) or (11.17), respectively, is appended to the model

	Malt plant	Percentage above the optimal
Malt mix	MP9	15
Barley mix	MP9	22

We add constraint (11.17) to solve the model enforcing the barley mix, and constraint (11.18) to solve the model enforcing the malt mix. As seen in Table 11.9, as expected, adding any of these constraints increases the transportation costs.

11.6 Conclusions

In their previous collaborations with Efes on the malt location problem, Köksalan and Süral (1999) conclude that "a more general approach to the problems of our client would be to consider the locations of the new malt plants together with the locations of the new beer breweries." We believe that the current work fulfills their desire of using a general combined approach.

The procedure developed in Sect. 11.3.1 gives an effective yearly production capacity setting that leads to desirable monthly production and inventory control plans for Efes. It may be applied to any similar problem with seasonal variations in demand over a year.

Searching for effective solution techniques for the dynamic combined location, distribution, and inventory management problem with nonlinear constraints may be an interesting future research area.

Acknowledgments We thank S. Bölükbaşı, L. Tomaç and A. Atılır from Efes for their excellent guidance and support throughout the current work. We are also grateful to James Bookbinder for his comments that substantially improved this manuscript.

References

Agaran B, Aktas E, Ulengin F, Onsel S, Kabak Ö (2010) A comprehensive analysis of the logistics sector in Turkey to identify the requirements for technological improvement", The 12th World Conference on Transport Research, Lisbon, Portugal

Alumur S, Kara BY (2009) A hub covering network design problem for cargo applications in Turkey. J Oper Res Soc 60:1349–1359

Arvis JF, Mustra AM, Ojala L, Shepherd B, Saslavsky D (2010) Connecting to compete 2010: trade logistics in the global economy, The World Bank, Washington

Beer Serves America (2009). http://www.beerservesamerica.org/.Accessed on Feb 28 2011

Beugelsdijk S, Slangen A, van Herpen M (2002) Shapes of organizational change: the case of Heineken Inc. J Organizational Change Manage 15(3):311–326

Bommer M, O'Neil B, Treat S (2001) Strategic assessment of the supply chain interface: a beverage industry case study. Int J Phys Distrib Logistics Manage 31(1):11–25
Bookbinder JH, Tan CS (2003) Comparison of Asian and European logistics systems. Int J Phys Distrib Logistics Manage 33(1):36–58
Bozkaya B, Yanik S, Balcisoy S (2010) A GIS-based optimization framework for competitive multi-facility location-routing problem. Netw Spat Econ 10(3):297–320
Breen L (2006) Give me back my empties or else! A preliminary analysis of customer compliance in reverse logistics practices (UK). Manage Res News 29(9):532–551
Brewers Association of Canada, 2009. http://www.brewers.ca/. Accessed on March 28 2011
Carroll GR, Swaminathan A (2000) Why the microbrewery movement? Organizational dynamics of resource partitioning in the U.S. brewing industry, Am J Sociol 106(3) 715–762
Çetiner S, Sepil C, Süral H (2010) Hubbing and routing in postal delivery systems. Ann Oper Res 181:109–124
Demirel T, Demirel NÇ, Kahraman C (2010) Multi-criteria warehouse location selection using Choquet integral. Expert Syst Appl 37:3943–3952
Duran F (1987) A large mixed integer production and distribution program. Eur J Oper Res 28(2):207–217
Efes Beverage Group, Anadolu Efes (2009). http://www.anadoluefes.com. Accessed on Jan 22 2010
Erden T, Coskun MZ (2010) Multi-criteria site selection for fire services: the interaction with analytic hierarchy process and geographic information systems. Nat Hazards Earth Syst Sci 10:2127–2134
Gelders LF, Pintelon LM, Van Wassenhove LN (1987) A location-allocation problem in a large Belgian brewery. Eur J Oper Res 28(2):196–206
Houthoofd N, Heene A (1997) Strategic groups as subsets of strategic scope groups in the Belgian brewing industry. Strateg Manage J 18(8):653–666
Kant G, Jacks M, Aantjes C (2008) Coca-Cola enterprises optimizes vehicle routes for efficient product delivery. Interfaces 38(1):40–50
Kioulafas KE (1985) An application of multiple regression analysis to the Greek beer market. J Oper Res Soc 36(8):689–696
Klose A, Drexl A (2005) Facility location models for distribution system design. Eur J Oper Res 162(1):4–29
Köksalan M, Erkip N, Moskowitz H (1999) Explaining beer demand: A residual modeling regression approach using statistical process control. Int J Prod Econ 58:265–276
Köksalan M, Özpeynirci BS, Süral H (2010) Forecasting beer demand at Anadolu Efes. INFORMS Trans Edu 10(3):140–145
Köksalan M, Süral H (1999) Location and distribution decisions: an application for malt plants. Interfaces 29:89–103
Köksalan M, Süral H, Kırca Ö (1995) A location-distribution application for a beer company. Eur J Oper Res 80(1):16–24
Lenten LJA, Moosa IA (1999) Modelling the trend and seasonality in the consumption of alcoholic beverages in the United Kingdom. Appl Econ 31:795–804
Melo MT, Nickel S, Saldanha-da-Gama F (2006) Dynamic multi-commodity capacitated facility location: a mathematical modeling framework for strategic supply chain planning. Comput Oper Res 33:181–208
Melo MT, Nickel S, Saldanha-da-Gama F (2009) Facility location and supply chain management—a review. Eur J Oper Res 196:401–412
Niederhut-Bollmann C, Theuvsen L (2008) Strategic management in turbulent markets: the case of the German and Croatian brewing industries. J East Eur Manage Stud 13(1):63–88
Pamuk S, Köksalan M, Güllü R (2004) Analysis of the product delivery system of a beer producer in Ankara. J Oper Res Soc 55:1137–1144
Ramirez-Beltran ND (1995) Integer programming to minimize labour costs. J Oper Res Soc 46(2):139–146

Sass TR (2005) The competitive effects of exclusive dealing: Evidence from the U.S. beer industry. Int J Ind Organization 23:203–225

Schoenherr T (2009) Logistics and supply chain management applications within a global context: an overview. J Bus Logistics 30(2):1–25

Şahin G, Süral H (2007) A review of hierarchical facility location models. Comput Oper Res 34:2310–2331

Şahin G, Süral H, Meral S (2007) Location analysis for regionalization of TRC blood services. Comput Oper Res 34:692–704

Tan PZ, Kara BY (2007) A hub covering model for cargo delivery systems. Networks 49:28–39

The Beer Institute (2009) Presentations 2008 Annual Industry Update—June. http://www.beerinstitute.org/. Accessed on Feb 28 2011

The Brewers of Europe (2010). http://www.brewersofeurope.org/. Accessed on Feb 28 2011

Ulengin F, Nuray N (1999) Current perspectives in logistics: Turkey as a case study. Int J Phys Distrib Logistics Manage 29(1):22–49

Vrontis D (1998) Strategic assessment: the importance of branding in the European beer market. Brit Food J 100(2):76–84

Warner AG (2010) The evolution of the American brewing Industry. J Bus Case Stud 6(6):31–46

Part IV
Logistics and Supply Chains in the Developing World

Chapter 12
Procurement from Developing Countries

Arnold B. Maltz, Joseph R. Carter and J. Rene Villalobos

Abstract In 2008, world trade amounted to over $15.8 trillion, and developing countries were the origin of 38 % of worldwide exports. In every case, a sourcing (buying) decision had to be made, and as we shall show, global logistics is both a logical and essential component in these decisions. This chapter first reviews the motivation for global sourcing/procurement and the role of logistics in executing this strategy. Then we indicate how procurement managers and their logistics service providers can obtain the necessary information to evaluate logistics capabilities throughout the world. Finally, we illustrate the importance of global logistics to sourcing/procurement through an Appendix, a case study that spans the U.S./Mexico border.

12.1 Global Sourcing: Motivation and Process

There are many reasons for the adoption of global sourcing as an integral part of an organization's operations. Almost all are directly related to gaining competitive advantage and market share by improving strategic positioning in response to a changing business environment. These reasons are shown in Table 12.1.

Given these compelling reasons to look for supplies and suppliers literally throughout the world, it is not surprising that, even 20 years ago, organizations

A. B. Maltz (✉) · J. R. Carter
Department of Supply Chain Management, W. P. Carey School of Business, Arizona State University, Tempe, AZ 85287-4706, USA
e-mail: arnie.maltz@asu.edu

J. Rene Villalobos
Fulton School of Engineering, Arizona State University, Tempe, AZ 85287, USA

J. H. Bookbinder (ed.), *Handbook of Global Logistics*, International Series in Operations Research & Management Science 181, DOI: 10.1007/978-1-4419-6132-7_12,

Table 12.1 Reasons to adopt global sourcing

Driver of global sourcing	Contribution of global sourcing to firm competitiveness
Intense global competition	Access to lower factors of production
Need for operational flexibility	Multiple suppliers with a variety of capabilities
Need for different service outcomes for different customers	Suppliers in multiple locations and at various levels of sophistication
Shorter product/service development cycles	24/7 operating capability and parallel processing
Stringent quality standards	Lower factor costs frees resources for increased quality
Ever-changing technology	Quicker access to new technology
Free organizational resources for other purposes	Multiple low cost suppliers allows concentration on core competencies (Prahalad and Hamel 1990)
Produce products for emerging markets	Use of emerging market suppliers allows production at local cost levels

interviewed for a study conducted by one of the authors all had established corporate supply management offices for global sourcing and procurement as a matter of corporate policy (Carter and Narasimhan 1990).

12.2 Global Sourcing Process

The supply management cycle for global sourcing has several distinct phases: (1) recognition of need; (2) source identification; (3) source evaluation; (4) evaluation of price quotations; (5) subjective analysis and negotiation; and (6) contract management. A supply management department may deal with hundreds of potential sources for thousands of items. Global sourcing involves a series of tasks similar to domestic sourcing, but these tasks are typically more complex and require more attention to detail. The principle differences are described below.

12.2.1 Source and Product Identification

There are several ways in which organizations interested in global sourcing can identify potential sources of supply. Information can be obtained from commercial attachés, large banks, government documents, global trading organizations and National State Departments, all of whom can be helpful in the evaluation process used by organizations engaged in global sourcing.

Global marketing of products and services is creating both opportunities and challenges for the overall organization and the supply management function. A number of considerations go into selecting products or services suitable for cross-border sourcing. One consideration is the length of supply lines (distance of suppliers); another is the need to clearly communicate specifications, terms and

Table 12.2 Considerations in deciding to source globally: factors related to the product to be purchased and the potential suppliers

(a) Product factors considered in evaluating global sourcing options
• Stability of design
• Whether or not the product requires continuous runs
• Completeness of engineering and other documentation
• Materials and tooling required
• Necessary visits
(b) Supplier factors considered in evaluating global sourcing options
• Duration of anticipated association with supplier
• Desired service levels
• Ability to provide technical/quality assistance
• Language proficiencies
• Physical distance to supplier
• Ability to provide assistance for various time zones

conditions of the purchase contract, and the extent of supplier development required (including site visits). Some of the criteria that may be used in selecting products or services for cross-border sourcing are shown in Table 12.2a and b.

Of course, internal company factors may also influence supplier and product selection. For example, buying from a subsidiary of one's organization may be mandatory. Similarly, the presence of a strategic partner in a key developing market may drive the supplier and supply product choice in that geographical region.

12.2.2 Example-Determining Supply Needs

At LG Electronics Corporation, supplier identification is preceded by an organizational needs analysis. This is done through a survey of organizational units by the office of the Director of Procurement. The survey identifies unmet needs pertaining to a product, technology, quality, and/or some service. Based on the needs assessment, a search is initiated to identify world class suppliers.

12.2.3 Qualifying Suppliers

Once the requirements/needs have been identified, as well as potential suppliers, further investigation is required. In the domestic market, an organization has legal recourse against a supplier who fails to honor contractual agreements. This same legal recourse either may not exist or be too burdensome when dealing with an international supplier. An organization's top management must establish the risk profile for the organization, and how this risk profile then gets translated down into real criteria that can be formulated by a supply management organization.

For example, what is the risk-cost tradeoff for adding a second (or nth) international supplier, and how does this match up with the organization's risk profile? A good rule of thumb is to reduce the risk of nonperformance by "qualifying" the international supplier, before allowing the supplier to bid on a contract. Any good risk analysis and management strategy allows for both contingency plans and exit strategies (Bhattacharyya et al. 2010).

Important considerations in international source qualification include experience of the supplier as an international source, financial strength of the supplier, the ease with which effective communication can be established, human resource policies of the country and supplier, and implications for inventories (e.g., size or location). These and related considerations are explained further below.

Experience. A majority of the respondents participating in a study of global sourcing principles and practices reported that a careful evaluation of the supplier's experience and management expertise was essential to selecting a reliable international supplier. The supply management professional should ask for and check references from organizations doing business with the international supplier (Carter et al. 1988). In particular, it may be appropriate to interview the logistics service providers to prospective suppliers, to verify that the latter have a history of meeting commitments.

Financial Strength. The financial strength of a supplier needs to be checked carefully. The potential supplier should be capable of meeting the increased expenditures necessary for equipment, marketing, and additional inventory. Two decades ago, a Director of Corporate Procurement for a multi-national organization suggested US $10 million in sales and 100 employees as the lower limit on the size of an international supplier to his/her operation (Carter et al. 1988). Absolute size limits no longer apply, but the care placed in ascertaining financial stability has definitely become more significant since the global recession of 2009.

Communication and Technology. It is essential that good communication lines exist. Multi-national organizations should require an international supplier to designate a global representative who can ensure that communication lines are kept open. As the involvement of an organization in global sourcing increases, the need for developing information systems and technology to support source identification, supplier development and qualifications, relocation of purchased materials, logistics, and inventory controls will also increase (Narasimhan and Carter 1990, Carter et al. 2007 and Ashenbaum et al. 2009).

Inventory. International sources must be willing and have the capability to maintain higher levels of inventory to compensate for longer supply lines, tight specifications, and stringent delivery requirements. Issues such as warehousing capabilities and locations, inventory containers to accommodate different modes of transportation (e.g. ship to rail), and inventory-tracking timeliness and accuracy must also be considered.

Longer-Term Orientation. Because of the length of time it takes to identify, develop, and qualify international sources, it is important for organizations to strive for a long-term association with an international supplier. The supplier should seek this as well.

Human Resource Management. Issues such as labor skills, labor practices, human rights considerations, and cultural differences need to be considered, addressed and continuously monitored.

Corporate Governance and Responsibility. Legal implications of international contracts, intellectual property protection and rights, and brand management, including the risk of product or service pirating, need to be addressed.

12.2.4 Analyzing Quotations from International Sources

Typically an international procurement office, a designated trading agent or broker, or a firm's local subsidiary will issue Requests for Quotation to potential international suppliers. Major manufacturing firms such as Honeywell International Inc. often staff field offices with engineers with considerable marketing experience. This joint engineering and marketing experience provides a necessary linkage between product/market (customer) needs and supplier requirements.

Proposals from suppliers in response to RFPs or RFQs[1] are routed through the issuer (often Procurement) and sent back to the operating division for evaluation. Some cost elements that should be considered in comparing proposals from international suppliers are shown in Table 12.3. Note that a number of these costs are related to logistics concerns and, as we shall show, even some of the non-logistics items can affect logistics costs.

In addition, information is requested on the business practices of the supplier. Among these are whether or not a letter of credit is required, the name of the bank handling the letter of credit, payment terms for open account transactions, principal customers of the international supplier, FOB point, and size and scope of a supplier's operation (number of employees, annual sales volume, market share, etc.). The responsibility of the operating supply management organization is to develop requirements specifications and statements of work, to elaborate supplier qualification criteria, perform analysis and provide negotiation assistance, place orders, and coordinate with the corporate global procurement supply management office. Logistics professionals and/or supply management personnel handle shipment details, global carrier control, and dealing with customs and customs brokers. Criteria for supplier qualification are often the same as for domestic suppliers. However, an understanding of the transportation, logistics and delivery schedules is more critical when international scope and coverage are part of the supplier offer.

---

[1] A Request for Proposal (referred to as RFP) is an invitation for suppliers, through a bidding process, to submit a proposal on a specific product or service. An RFP typically involves more than the price. The Request for Quotation (RFQ) is used where discussions aren't required with bidders (mainly when the specifications of a product or service are already known), and price is the main or only factor in selecting the successful bidder. RFQ may also be used as a step prior to going to a full-blown RFP to determine general price ranges.

Table 12.3 Cost elements for RFQ evaluation

- Unit price
- Supplier selection
- Supplier management
- Export taxes
- Global transportation costs
- Insurance
- Tariffs
- Brokerage costs
- Letter of credit
- Cost of money including currency conversion
- Inland (domestic and international) freight cost
- Risk of obsolescence
- Cost of rejects
- Damage in transit
- Inventory holding costs
- In-country transportation infrastructures
- Language skills
- Technical and communication support, and/or
- Employee travel costs
- Length of supply line
- Political climate
- Complexity of technology or other regional infrastructure considerations

12.2.5 Negotiating Prices and Terms

Negotiating prices and terms with an international supplier poses additional challenges. Cultural and language barriers exacerbate the task of negotiating with a supplier and might require the services of an interpreter. Preparation for the negotiation should include a study of costs, supplier management strengths, supplier growth potential, service provision history, currency exchange rates, and handling of rejected materials. It is common practice to turn to consulting companies for cost analysis and currency exchange rate projections. For example, one consulting firm uses a computer model that projects the cost of manufacturing a specific component by analyzing its material content, part characteristics, and manufacturing steps required to produce the component. The model utilizes data on labor, materials, energy, transportation, and factory overhead costs. This firm's database can project costs for products in several countries (see for example, http://www.mtisystems.com/cost_estimating_solutions.htm). Such a computer model equips a supply management organization with detailed knowledge of an international supplier's cost components, both present and future, for materials and services. It also sets the stage for determining whether the buyer should take responsibility for logistics costs, or whether these are best left with the supplier.

During the last 20 years, exchange rates for international currencies other than the Chinese Yuan have floated freely with respect to the dollar. Fluctuations have

Table 12.4 Non-cost considerations for RFQ evaluation

Non-cost consideration	Implications for logistics	Influence on decision
Mode and/or carrier selection	Critical factor in transport cost and service	Minimal to moderate, depending on item
Transportation insurance	Major factor in overall cost, and differs by mode	Significant for high value items
Provision for returns and/or replacements	Reverse logistics costs are sizable for consumer electronics, clothing, etc	Rarely considered, but can be affected by quality of supplier's goods and their return policies
Method of payment	Slow payment and/or complicated payment provisions can delay goods either at borders or at destination	Letters of credit, although still common, are now deemed somewhat expensive and less useful than before. Increasingly, open account arrangements are sought, even in developing markets
Intellectual property rights	Need to safeguard IP will complicate logistics procedures	Intellectual property issues are a major consideration for many advanced manufacturers
Corporate social responsibility, sustainability, etc	Logistics is a primary energy user and employer in many countries. Hence, these concerns could affect choice of logistics service provider	Increasingly important, especially when government regulations exist in these areas
National accounting and tax Policies	Taxes may be levied on inventory and specific countries are "tax advantaged"	Frequently, minimizing taxes requires extra steps in the logistics chain but the tradeoff is not always recognized

been, at times, precipitous. Before signing a contract, the supply management professional must work closely with finance to forecast scenarios on exchange-rate movements and methods likely to moderate the impact of such fluctuations. Arbitrarily contracting for payment in U.S. dollars makes little economic sense in most cases. Supply management professionals, in conjunction with finance, must also manage and monitor currency decisions for the European Community, as the EU continues to include additional member states.

Table 12.4 shows a further list of items that are often part of the RFQ evaluation process. Many of these are non-cost factors related to logistics conditions. Furthermore, such concerns as payment by letter of credit can affect logistics costs, since any additional time for the arrangement of payment can result in delays and storage costs.

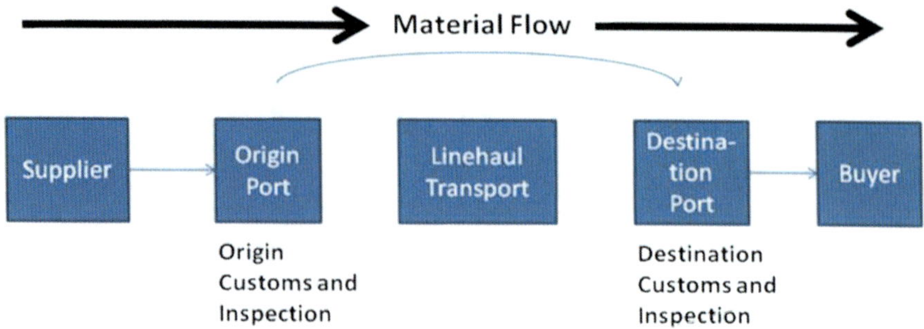

Fig. 12.1 An international purchase and delivery transaction

12.2.6 Customs Regulations and Requirements

Probably the most common impediment to efficient logistics from international suppliers is the complexity and uncertainty surrounding each country's customs and regulatory regime. Negotiations with international suppliers should always include, as a start, agreement on Incoterms[2] for shipments to the customer. Since Incoterms specify both when ownership of the goods is transferred, and who pays for each portion of the international supply chain (see Fig. 12.1), the contract should explicitly lay out exact terms. But other country-specific regulations, from port hours of operation to mandatory product inspections, also affect both direct logistics costs and the need for additional inventory.

As Fig. 12.1 illustrates, there are numerous places in the shipment process where delays are possible because of customs and government regulations. Many supply management organizations seek the assistance of a *custom-house broker*. He/she can provide information on commodity class descriptions that permit the most favorable duties, special tariffs, and the effects, if any, of agricultural regulations and regional differences in the interpretation and/or application of customs rules and procedures. The levying of duties is also affected by international politics and the status of exporting nations as trading partners of the importing country. Understanding and taking advantage of customs and other regulations can be crucial to successful international supply management.

For example, VF Corporation, a seller of apparel, must decide whether to bring goods for sale in Canada directly into Canada, or into the U.S. for some value-add activities and then ship to Canada. This creates the possibility of duty drawback. The *Duty Drawback Statute*, originally passed as the Tariff Act by the United States Congress in 1789, entitles organizations to receive a refund of customs duties paid on imported merchandise that is subsequently exported as part of a finished product. The refund from filing a drawback claim translates into

[2] Incoterms are the terms of sale and shipment payment formulated by the International Chamber of Commerce to govern international purchase transactions.

additional profits, but many organizations fail to take advantage of this unique opportunity. In fact, the law allows a claimant to file a drawback on exports up to 3 years old, thus creating the potential for a substantial recovery amount in the first year of establishing a program.

12.2.7 The Impact of Global Supply Management on Logistics and Other Functions

International supply management sourcing opportunities are changing the mix of activities in manufacturing and service organizations (through make/buy decisions), thereby affecting capital investment requirements and the infrastructure within organizations. For example, transportation is increasingly becoming the responsibility of the supply management function. In a 2005 ISM survey of managers and higher officials in Fortune 1,000 companies, 79 % indicated transportation was part of the supply management department's responsibility. (Philip James, Inc. 2010).

Some unique issues arise when the decision to purchase internationally is made within the organization. Cross-functional input into the procurement process is mandatory, if potential problem areas are to be avoided. A key to effective global sourcing is selecting flexible suppliers of the highest quality. This is often difficult to assess since data concerning suppliers and their respective quality performance are often not readily available. Organizations sourcing internationally should make frequent visits to potential suppliers to assess their capability. Since these visits may require a team assessment, resource allocation constraints become key.

Problems of quality from an international supplier can have an onerous impact on production and customer service perceptions. The pipelines for goods are long, distances are great, languages and cultures are different, and misunderstandings common. All parties, both internal and external, need to clearly understand quality specifications or statements of work before the supplier begins production or service delivery. Engineering, quality assurance, marketing and operations must work together to guarantee the highest level of supplier quality. When poor quality does occur, correcting the customer ill-will, returns, reimbursement, and replacement of the offending items can be quite complex. The bottom line is to avoid defects at all costs.

The longer lead time also complicates the planning and execution of the shipping process. Most international shipments will be made by ocean carrier and the lead-time will be several weeks. This means that the supply management organization must plan capacity and material utilization over a much longer time frame. Schedules must be stabilized or inventories can mount to unacceptable levels. The concept of just-in-time is difficult to attain with an international supplier. When delays occur, expediting that supplier's shipments takes on more urgency due to the extended supply chain. The supply management professional must be on good terms with the personnel of a non-domestic supplier. In fact, the quality of the *management* at such a supplier is probably as important in the selection decision as the quality of the purchased product or service.

12.3 Implications of Global Sourcing for Logistics Costs

Shipments that traverse national and economic boundaries confront costs and delays associated with overcoming political and economic trade barriers. Trade barriers result from government policies or regulations that restrict international commerce. The costs or restraints include tariffs, import permit costs, import duties or licenses, export licenses, local content requirements, subsidies, import quotas, and import and transit taxes. While ordinary trade barriers are the result of a nation's governmental processes, *economic* trade barriers are more often the outcome of less controllable global factors such as a nation's relative position internationally in the world's money and commodity markets. Economic trade barrier costs include those costs associated with monetary exchange rate differences, as well as specialist fees for those who facilitate exchange between different economies (e.g. bank fees, customs-house broker charges, freight forwarder costs, and import broker fees). Governments attempt to manage or remove these trade barriers through a variety of legislative means such as duty free zones, economic development zones, and commercial advice through local attachés.

Thus, cost analysis in global sourcing is more complex than in the domestic arena since additional cost categories and tradeoffs must be considered. For example, the supply management organization now has to decide whether or not to incur customs-house broker fees. Those fees may result in lower duties paid on imports because the broker has a better understanding of the tariff-product classifications than does the importing organization's management. An importer may also be faced with the decision of whether or not to pay higher prices for a freight forwarder with lower damage rates, to allow the organization to reduce packaging costs and/or lessen the risk of an inadequate supply.

The costs and complexity associated with inbound movements including transportation, warehousing, materials handling, packaging, documentation, in-transit inventory carrying, order processing, and communications costs, are usually higher in global sourcing as compared to domestic sourcing. Longer shipment distances, greater order cycles times, multiple transportation modes, and complex documentation requirements associated with the import process can increase costs and the likelihood of delays (see Fig. 12.2). In fact, transport-related costs are such a large factor in international trade that prices are often evaluated in terms of *landed costs*. Landed costs are a subset of the total cost of ownership (TCO), and are defined as the total accumulation of costs for an imported item, including purchase price plus freight, handling, duties, customs clearance and storage to a designated point.

Thus, the benefits of global sourcing must be weighed explicitly against the costs of longer, more variable transportation times. Countries that are contiguous

The importance of logistics-related cost considerations in global sourcing is highlighted by the case of a multi-national manufacturing organization with headquarters in California.

In the past, this organization obtained all the parts required to support production at its cross-border facilities by ordering them from U.S suppliers and shipping them to the organization's California warehouse. From the warehouse, the parts with the required documentation were sent cross-border by air express. Using this two-stage process, it took from three to five days to move a single component from its international supplier through the organization's warehouse to receiving facilities in, for example, Saudi Arabia. In addition, customs clearance at the destination country sometimes took up to a week, and the movement of parts from the airport to the international facility was also costly and time consuming.

To speed the flow of goods through the supply pipeline, the organization turned to DHL International GmbH, and arranged for the air express company to provide door-to-door service from the original supplier to the cross-border facility, bypassing the organization's warehouse. In the new arrangement, the organization continues to be responsible for documentation. DHL plays a double role in the shipment process by moving parts directly from the supplying factory to the carrier's hub at Kennedy International Airport, and at the same time picking up documents from California and attaching them to the freight in New York for express shipment cross-border. In the destination country, DHL handles all customs clearance and payment of duties, in addition to delivering the parts to the receiving facility. By combining domestic and global transportation responsibilities, the manufacturer saves from one to three days of transit time, so that lead times dropped from 10-12 days to 9 days on average.

Fig. 12.2 An example of logistics tradeoffs for global sourcing

can ship goods overland via truck or rail, but most international goods movements must be made by air or sea. Air transport involves relatively high freight charges, yet is the preferred method for international shipments of sensitive items such as electronic equipment and perishables. International ocean carriers feature lower costs for the transportation of goods, but at much slower speeds. Water transportation is typically used for large-volume purchases and the transport of raw materials. When goods are shipped by water, in addition to the transportation charges, inventory carrying costs will increase because of the extra goods in transit required in the supply line due to longer lead times. The additional inventory necessary to support an extended transportation pipeline is one of the frequently overlooked costs of global sourcing. For example, it may take up to 5 weeks for a shipment to move from an Asian supplier via sea to a buyer in the Midwest region of the United States. Continuous use of the product requires an uninterrupted flow from the supplier to the purchasing organization. Thus, there may be five separate weekly shipments at various positions en route to the destination. This five weeks' worth of inventory is costly in terms of its financial investment as well as its transportation. Pipeline inventory costs must be included in comparisons of the total landed cost of distant suppliers versus local suppliers.

12.4 Total Lowest Landed Cost

No matter how the supply management professional obtains price/cost information, he/she cannot adequately identify total cost without factoring in quality, delivery, and many other relevant factors. The importance of these factors varies according to the purchase requirement itself. In buying a sub-element for a missile, quality may well be the overriding concern. Delivery may be extremely critical in another area. For example, when purchasing supplies for ocean carriers and cruise lines, delivery is so important that special delivery controls have been instituted. Two factors—limited dock space at major ports, and the time of day that the ship is scheduled to sail—make delivery schedules very tight. In this case, suppliers may have to meet hourly appointments. Because the delivery schedule is so demanding, the ocean carrier's purchasing manager and the supplier often negotiate a financial penalty for late deliveries.

Similarly, supply managers who purchase complex items requiring significant maintenance must be sure that other indirect costs are included in their calculations of *Total Lowest Landed Cost* (*TLLC*). An aerospace organization listed over 40 factors that could potentially be involved in the TLLC. The most important of these are shown in Table 12.5.

Depending on the situation, each of the factors listed could potentially warrant attention during product development, as well as in the price/cost analysis process. Research could indicate the most relevant costs and the extent to which they could be the focus of a cost reduction effort. For instance, an organization was importing a rare, natural medicinal extract derived from the trees of the Amazon region in South America. The prices were extremely high but the supply management professional believed that it was largely a matter of market supply and demand. The research indicated differently. The supplier had no knowledge of transportation but found it was paying an exorbitant price to a freight forwarder in Brazil. The cost reduction focus turned from the purchase price of the extract to the freight forwarder charges. This is another illustration of the importance of looking for *Total Lowest Landed Cost*. Supply management must work with both internal personnel and external service providers to minimize the sum of all costs, including purchase price, associated with getting the product from the overseas supplier to the buyer's dock.

Table 12.5 Important components of total lowest landed cost

1. Unit price: purchase price per unit of item quoted by the supplier
2. Cash discount: price decrease for early payments during a prescribed period
3. Delivery performance: cost incurred by buyer as a result of early or late delivery
4. Payment period: number of days after shipment or delivery of supplies before payment is due
5. Progress payments: extent to which some payment is required by supplier prior to shipment or delivery
6. Freight costs: costs paid to transportation companies for goods movement
7. Transit inventory: costs of the buying organization associated with goods in transit where buyer has taken title
8. Run interruption costs: costs related to supplier's acceptance of buyer's orders that cause the supplier to replan/alter production runs
9. Tooling costs: cost of obtaining tooling to manufacture the item, expressed as unit cost or lump sum
10. Packaging: cost of customizing packaging based on buyer's request
11. Escalation costs: additional costs above purchase price due to increases in labor, materials or inventory unit prices
12. Cost of non-conforming material: costs incurred by buyer in dealing with and tracking rejected or out-of-specification products
13. Warranty: cost incurred by supplier to provide repair or replacement for a specified period after purchase as requested by buyer

12.5 Evaluation of Logistics Capabilities in Low Cost Countries

The previous sections of this chapter established the reasons for sourcing professionals to consider logistics in their purchasing decisions, and some of the important ways that these decisions can impact logistics cost and service possibilities. Now we turn to findings on how sourcing professionals *actually* evaluate logistics capabilities as part of the decision on where to buy goods to support operations. In particular, we share results of a study by two of the co-authors on sourcing professionals' perceptions of low cost countries/regions. Recent trends clearly favor suppliers from these parts of the world.

12.5.1 Regional Variations in Logistics Capabilities

So-called "low cost countries and geographies" have become a target of opportunity for procurement managers based in developed nations. However, there are clearly major differences between, for example, Mexico and China. It is not immediately clear how to formalize these kinds of comparisons, since sourcing decisions are often multi-dimensional, even if cost is "first among equals". Still, evolving industry practice points to the importance of a "portfolio" of suppliers and locations to minimize supply risk and maximize overall performance.

Table 12.6 Low-cost regions and countries represented in the sourcing survey

- Coastal China (e.g. Beijing, Shanghai, Guangdong)
- Inland China (e.g. Chongquing, Lanzhou, Kunming)
- Less developed Asia (e.g. Vietnam, Cambodia)
- Eastern Europe (e.g. Romania, Bulgaria, Ukraine)
- Russia/Central Asia (e.g. Russia, Kazakhstan, Baluchistan)
- Africa (other than South Africa and Botswana)
- South America (other than Brazil, Chile, and Argentina)
- Mexico
- Urban India (e.g. Bangalore, Mumbai, Delhi)
- Rural India

Understanding the location-specific advantages and disadvantages of various low cost suppliers will facilitate the formation of such portfolios, and evaluation of logistics capabilities is a particularly important step in this process. The following survey and analysis sheds some light on this issue.

12.6 Sourcing Managers' Survey

A survey instrument was formulated by the authors, asking each respondent to rate ten different geographical areas on 12 attributes. A list of the regions and countries and their description on the survey is shown in Table 12.6. Attributes relevant to the evaluation of low cost countries for sourcing purposes appear in Table 12.7.

Sourcing managers were asked to rate the various regions on each attribute using a 1–7 scale, with 7 as the most favorable and 1 the least. The respondents were from a variety of industries, all had experience sourcing from low cost countries, and all were based in either North America or Europe. Each respondent was also asked to rate his/her overall preference for each of the geographies. Note that countries were split in some cases because of the wide variation between regions in those countries. On the other hand, comparison procedures have a practical upper limit in terms of the number of alternatives respondents can evaluate. Therefore regional country groupings were used in the case of Southern Asia, South America, and Eastern Europe. Finally, Mexico was called out separately because of its large volume of trade with the U.S. and the continuing effects of the North American Free Trade Agreement (NAFTA).

Table 12.8 shows how the various geographies were rated on the individual attributes.

Although not the lowest labor cost area, Coastal China is perceived as superior on several criteria, including work ethic, delivery reliability, flexibility, and market attractiveness. The respondents also rated Coastal China the most attractive area for sourcing from the various identified geographies. On the other hand, Africa (other than South Africa and Botswana) was ranked lowest of all the regions and

Table 12.7 Attributes relevant to the low-cost sourcing decision

- Labor cost—unit cost of direct labor, usually per hour or per piece
- Work ethic
- Security of intellectual property
- Attraction of local market
- Meet customer requirements—deliver complete orders, on schedule
- Transportation reliability—consistency of lead times
- Transportation cost—cost from source to buyer's location
- Government support for business
- Political stability
- Flexibility—Ability to react to changes in requirements
- Predictable border clearance times
- Government corruption

countries on 10 of the 12 evaluation criteria. Not surprisingly, Africa was also seen as the least attractive of the geographies by a considerable margin. Further investigation showed that Africa's scores were based on many fewer responses than for any of the other countries or regions, suggesting that lack of knowledge, rather than firsthand experience of poor performance, may have increased the perceived risk of sourcing products and services from Africa.

Figure 12.3 displays the same data on a "perceptual map." This explicitly shows which of the attributes are associated with each other, and how particular regions compare in the minds of experienced sourcing managers (Africa is omitted due to significantly fewer responses).

Perceptual mapping techniques condense large amounts of data on several attributes across multiple alternatives into a two dimensional display, providing insight into how those attributes are jointly considered and what trade-offs are made (Carter et al. 2008). For example, suppose a customer wanted to compare two suppliers based on both cost and service. The perceptual map would combine the ratings of both customers on the two attributes and display the results as a two dimensional vector for each supplier. In this simple two attribute case, each attribute would constitute one dimension on a two dimensional plot. Then if one supplier was perceived to have better service and the other lower cost, the combined cost/service vector would have a different direction for each supplier. Furthermore, if we also mapped the buyer's ideal mix of service and cost, that ideal vector might very well have a third direction on the two dimensional map. Thus, combined with the overall regional ratings, perceptual mapping can provide insight into both the relative attractiveness and the relative competitive positions of the various regions in our survey, based on combining the 12 rated attributes for each region.

There is a variety of methods for transforming multiple evaluation ratings into two-dimensional (or higher) maps, depending on the distance/attribute combination rules used, the availability of overall preferences in addition to individual dimensions, and whether ideal points/vectors are among the goals of the analysis (Hair et al. 1995). Since we were looking at both multiple decision criteria and multiple regions, we used a multidimensional scaling approach. We applied the

Table 12.8 Overview of attribute evaluation by geography (all variables scored from 1 to 7, 7 = most favorable and 1 = least favorable)

Attribute	Mean	Best	Worst
Labor cost	5.19	Less developed Asia (5.96)	South America (4.62)
		Inland China (5.95)	Mexico (4.67)
		Rural India (5.80)	Russia (4.72)
Work ethic	4.95	Coastal China (5.71)	Africa (3.67)
		Inland China (5.52)	Russia (4.42)
		Urban India (5.50)	South America (4.48)
Security of intellectual property	3.57	Mexico (4.59)	Inland China (2.39)
		Urban India (4.35)	Coastal China (2.60)
		South America (4.33)	Less dev. Asia (2.64)
Attraction of local market	4 80	Coastal China (6.13)	Africa (3.44)
		Urban India (5.57)	Russia (4.37)
		Inland China (5.53)	South America (4.49)
Reliably meet customer requirements	4.54	Coastal China (5.18)	Africa (3.53)
		Urban India (5.17)	Russia (4.07
		Inland China (4.69)	Less dev. Asia (4.29)
Transportation reliability	4.30	Coastal China (5.30)	Africa (3.27)
		Mexico (5.08)	Less dev. Asia (3.62)
		Urban India (4.89)	Rural India (3.77)
Transportation cost	3.97	Mexico (5.04)	Africa (3.15)
		Coastal China (4.43)	Rural India (3.43)
		Urban India (4.30)	Less dev. Asia (3.58)
Government support for business	4.46	Coastal China (5.18)	Africa (3.31)
		Urban India (5.06)	Russia (3.73)
		Inland China (4.90)	Less Dev. Asia (4.34)
Political stability	4.37	Urban India (5.35)	Africa (2.56)
		Mexico (5.33)	Russia (3.68)
		Coastal China (5.06)	Less dev. Asia (3.70)
Flexibility	4.32	Coastal China (5.09)	Africa (3.19)
		Urban India (4.98)	Russia (3.83)
		Mexico (4.75)	Less dev. Asia (4.03)
Predictable border clearance times	4.33	Mexico (5.45)	Africa (3.04)
		Urban India (4.94)	Russia (3.67)
		Coastal China (4.92)	Less dev. Asia (3.75)
Government corruption	3.67	Urban India (4.52)	Africa (2.76)
		Mexico (4.27)	Less dev. Asia (3.24)
		Rural India (4.19)	South America (3.54)
Overall attractiveness	4.63	Coastal China (5.88)	Africa (2.82)
		Urban India (5.52)	Russia (3.87)

"CPM System for Composite Product Mapping" from Sawtooth Software to obtain two composite dimensions, and to produce perceptual maps that show the positions of both the regions and the attributes versus the two composite dimensions. These maps are a visual summary of multidimensional evaluations, and a potential guide into how sourcing managers decide to investigate a region.

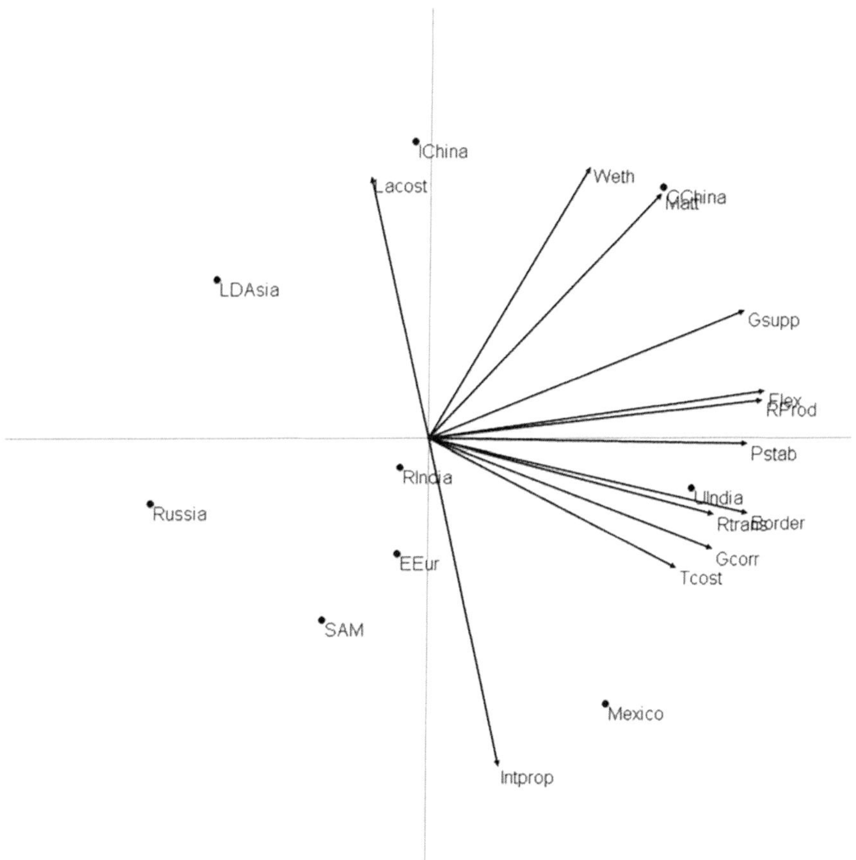

Fig. 12.3 Perceptual map of attributes and geographies

The map highlights a number of points about the role of logistics attributes in the sourcing evaluation decision. Note that the lower right hand quadrant shows that four attributes—transportation cost (Tcost), transportation reliability (Rtran), government corruption (Gcorr), and predictable border clearance times (Border)—appear to be associated with each other in sourcing managers' perceptions. Transportation reliability and predictable border clearance times are straightforward indicators of logistics service quality, and it appears that the level of government corruption is also associated with service quality. Furthermore, the fact that these attributes are in the same general direction as overall reliability (Rprod) and political stability (Pstab) suggests that relatively strong, transparent institutions are necessary for acceptable logistics capabilities in low cost regions. Finally, there seems to be little relationship between labor cost (Lacost) and logistics capabilities. Thus it is not surprising that Inland China (IChina) is associated with labor cost but not with logistics capabilities, since the vector from the origin to Inland China is perpendicular to logistics service attributes. On the other hand, Coastal China (CChina) seems to be moderately associated with both reasonable labor cost and logistics service capacity.

In summary, sourcing managers do see regional differences in logistics capabilities. They also recognize that both institutional and service-provider strengths are involved in evaluating logistics capabilities for potential low-cost suppliers. At the same time, there has been very little published research that can help sourcing managers if they choose to include logistics issues in their supplier selection decisions. The next section of this chapter discusses some of the information resources that are available to sourcing managers who are also considering logistics issues as they evaluate suppliers in low-cost geographies.

12.7 Getting the Information

Although we have established the importance of logistics in sourcing products from other countries, obtaining the necessary information is both difficult and time-consuming, especially for supply managers who do not deal with logistics issues on a routine basis. Supply chain literature has recently asserted that objective data on a country's business environment is important to sourcing decisions, but there are few references for comprehensive logistics data by country. This section of the chapter will point out some of the accessible information and indicate its uses and limitations. We also note that there are other publications on country and regional logistics capabilities (e.g. Bookbinder and Tan 2003; Council of Supply Chain Management Professionals country reports, various dates).

12.7.1 Logistics Performance Index

In 2005 Hausman et al. completed research for the World Bank that attempted to correlate bi-national trade flows with freight-forwarder ratings of country and/or lane logistics capabilities. They formulated an "index" which consisted of objective measures (distances) or forwarder's estimates of the following for specific countries:

- Distance (a surrogate for shipping cost).
- Processing Cost including customs clearance fees, processing fees, port fees, etc.
- Total Time including processing time, inland transport, customs, port, and terminal time.

- Coefficient of variation of total time defined as (maximum time−average time)/(average time) (note the difference between this use of "coefficient of variation" and the standard statistical definition of this term).

Hausman et al. found that their index, appropriately weighted, combined with measures of GDP and perceived corruption, could account for 71 % of the variation in bi-national shipping volumes.

The model of Hausman et al. validates the importance of processing cost, supply chain transit time, and predictability to the level of international trade flows, but has some limitations in its application to sourcing decisions. First, the information was based on the perceptions of *freight forwarders*; it is not clear that their perceptions are completely relevant to the various tradeoffs that procurement managers have to make. Second, the underlying data are built up on a lane by lane basis, so that aggregation to country level may not be straightforward. Third, the model was formulated to support government efforts to improve country competitiveness. Thus, the model indicates that investing in lowering the processing cost may have more potential to increase trade than does lowering overall transit time. Similarly, decreasing variability in lanes that are currently problematic will have a larger impact on trade flows than decreasing variability by a similar amount in relatively predictable lanes. But it is not clear how useful any of these findings are to sourcing managers contemplating low cost suppliers.

Interestingly, the World Bank updated the Logistics Performance Index in 2007 and 2010, (Arvis et al. 2007, 2010). The newer (2010) index includes six components:

- Efficiency of the customs clearance process
- Quality of trade and transport related infrastructure
- Ease of arranging competitively priced shipments
- Competence and quality of logistics services
- Ability to track and trace consignments
- Frequency with which shipments reach the consignee within the scheduled or expected time

For these most recent surveys, data were once again gathered from freight forwarders and the primary express carriers, each providing ratings on the six components for eight selected destination countries. The 1,000 respondents also provided much more detailed information on the international logistics process for the country where they worked. The index was then compiled using Principal Components Analysis to generate weightings for each component. Since it turns out that the six components load on a single factor which accounts for 88 % of the total variance in the data, the final weightings are simply the loadings on this factor. The loadings for the 2010 Logistics Performance Index are shown in Table 12.9, and some sample values of the components and the overall index are shown in Table 12.10.

Table 12.9 Component weightings for 2010 logistics performance index

Component	Weight
Customs clearance	0.42
Transport/trade infrastructure	0.42
Ease of shipment	0.37
Logistics service competence	0.42
Track and trace capability	0.41
On time delivery	0.40

Source Arvis et al. (2010)

Although the reported index does not include specific costs, customs complexities, or transit times by country, the LPI questionnaire did ask for that data, and the country-by-country averages for the most populous city are reported in a separate appendix for the following parameters:

- Distance, lead time, and cost to port or airport (export)
- Distance, lead time, and cost to land crossing (export)
- Distance, lead time, and cost to port or airport (import)
- Distance, lead time, and cost to land crossing (import)
- Number of shipments meeting quality criteria
- Number of agencies involved (import)
- Number of agencies involved (export)
- Number of documents (import)
- Number of documents (export)
- Clearance time with and without physical inspection
- Percent of import shipments physically inspected
- Percent of shipments undergoing multiple inspections

Clearly, most of the above metrics are crucial to the efficiency and cost effectiveness of a freight forwarder. Since forwarders have to satisfy their clients, it is not surprising that many purchasing managers are also interested in these issues. However, those managers have to take a more comprehensive perspective. Thus, the purchasing manager is likely to measure supplier delivery versus. promised delivery date, supplier reliability in terms of order completeness, the likelihood of damage during shipment, and other logistics dimensions related to the needs of the internal group for which the purchasing manager is buying.

12.8 Chapter Summary

The practices of *global sourcing* and *global logistics* are necessarily intertwined. The selection of a supplier in a specific overseas location, for whatever reason, necessarily drives logistics costs and possible service levels. On the other hand, the availability of logistics capabilities (or the lack of these capabilities) is an

Table 12.10 Sample results on logistics performance index (2010) and component scores

Country/score (rank)	Customs	Infrastructure	Ease of shipment	Logistics competence	Track/ trace	On time
Germany 4.11 (1)	4	4.34	3.66	4.14	4.18	4.48
China 3.49 (27)	3.16	3.54	3.31	3.49	3.55	3.91
Costa rica 2.91 (56)	2.61	2.56	2.64	2.80	3.13	3.71
Nigeria 2.59 (100)	2.17	2.43	2.84	2.45	2.45	3.10

important factor in projecting the total costs associated with a supplier and what service level to expect or demand.

This chapter has explored the global sourcing/global logistics relationship by first pointing out that supplier selection cannot be made in a vacuum: understanding the logistics implications of these selections is a logical step in the overall sourcing decision. Recent research has shown that supply managers considering low-cost country sourcing must (and often do) recognize that there are multiple components to logistics competence, and that dealing with international borders can be easy or difficult, depending on the countries involved and their institutional capabilities and transparency. This reality leaves the sourcing manager with the dilemma of finding information on logistics competencies by nation. In that connection, the chapter explored recent efforts to compile and summarize international logistics data through a Logistics Performance Index available through the World Bank. The Appendix to this chapter concerns Purchasing and Logistics in the particular context of the North American Free Trade Agreement (NAFTA). As a case study, it provides opportunities for further analysis and reflection on the interdependency of Purchasing and Logistics.

Global sourcing almost inevitably increases inbound logistics costs, and this chapter has only outlined the issues that need to be addressed by both sourcing and logistics professionals. Lead times, inventory, transportation costs, etc. all affect both functional and total firm results, and they are important "add-ons" to familiar concerns such as purchase price, labor arbitrage, etc. This is particularly true when the possible suppliers are located in emerging markets that may lack infrastructure and capable logistics service providers. If purchasing and logistics are not aligned based on incentives, organization, and outlook, then hidden costs and service failures may discredit global sourcing efforts. In such cases the whole firm suffers, because it is increasingly clear that key growth opportunities are located in exactly those places that may look difficult now, but will almost certainly bloom later.

Appendix A: Logistics and Buying for Maquiladoras-The Chihuahua Automotive Case

Introduction

When the maquiladora program was established, the plants working under this program were located exclusively in Mexican states bordering the United States. As the maquiladora industry developed, some companies ventured into the interior of Mexico, seeking shelter from the high labor turnover rates and more expensive operations costs that had developed in the border cities. The costs for renting a facility in some of the Mexican border cities was up to 50 % more expensive than the rest of Mexico, and even exceeded U.S. rents. Labor turnover rates in excess of 15 % per month have not been unusual in most of the border cities.

Thus, moving to the interior of Mexico was seen as a way to lower production costs and to get a more stable labor force. However, as some maquila plants moved to the interior, they experienced an increase in transportation and inventory beyond their expectations. In addition, certain problems that these plants were trying to solve, such as turnover rates and higher operations costs, started to appear in the new locations.

It turns out that many of these problems could have been either anticipated and/or mitigated if logistics and procurement personnel had shared a larger role in the decision process. Availability of supplies and labor are critical to selecting the proper supplier location, not only based on existing conditions but also based on the conditions that are likely to exist in the medium and longer term. Where prospective suppliers are maquiladoras, it is prudent to determine whether their total costs allow for long term viability. Thus, it is necessary to look at the likelihood that they locate where they can hold on to their work force, as well as economically access a supply base which is still primarily in the United States (see also Rene Villalobos and Ahumada, 2008).

Evaluating Wage Rates for Mexican Locations

One of the primary attractions of Mexican suppliers has been low wage rates, although these are not as low as those available from China or other Asian countries. However, stability of work force is also important, especially in relatively skilled jobs such as electronics assembly or aerospace. Table 12.11 shows average monthly wage rates for major Mexican cities which host maquiladora operations.

Figure 12.4 demonstrates that higher productivity locations are associated, not surprisingly, with higher wages.

Supply managers have often sought out Mexico because of its proximity to markets at a much lower wage rate than standard U.S. wages. At the same time, it is clear that a reliable Mexican supplier should pay the prevailing wage for its

Table 12.11 Prevailing wages and output per employee primary maquiladora locations

City	Monthly output per employee (in U.S. dollars)	Monthly salary per employee (in U.S. dollars)
Mexicali	5,568	658
Apodaca	5,389	784
Nogales	4,832	632
Chihuahua	4,810	749
San Luis Río C.	4,575	443
Cd. Reynosa	4,550	636
Cd. Juárez	4,449	667
Nuevo Laredo	4,246	878
Tijuana	4,015	592
San Nicolas	3,665	579
Matamoros	3,301	622
Guadalupe	3,292	521
Hermosillo	2,967	459
Cd. Acuña	2,720	452
Río Bravo	2,583	587
Santa Catarina	2,324	627
Tecate	2,293	519
Agua Prieta	2,237	622
Ensenada	2,027	439
PiedrasNegras	1,956	470
Delicias	1575	386
Guadalajara	1,493	497
Zacatecas[a]	1,268	281
Torreón	1,134	398
Yucatan[a]	1,131	277
Lerdo	972	370
Goméz Palacio	818	256

[a] State statistics

specific location. As procurement managers continue to evaluate their options among Mexican maquiladoras, one indicator of the suitability of a supplier is its wage level versus. both expected productivity and local conditions.

Inbound Maquiladora Logistics

Beyond labor turnover, maquiladoras should display the ability to handle what are often long supply chains that cross the U.S.-Mexico border. Many of the U.S. component suppliers to the maquiladoras tend to be clustered in areas distant from the US/Mexico border, such as in the US Midwest and Northeast. This clustering of the suppliers in regions far from the assembly plants is not unexpected. Maquiladora plants often assemble products that were transferred from a plant that

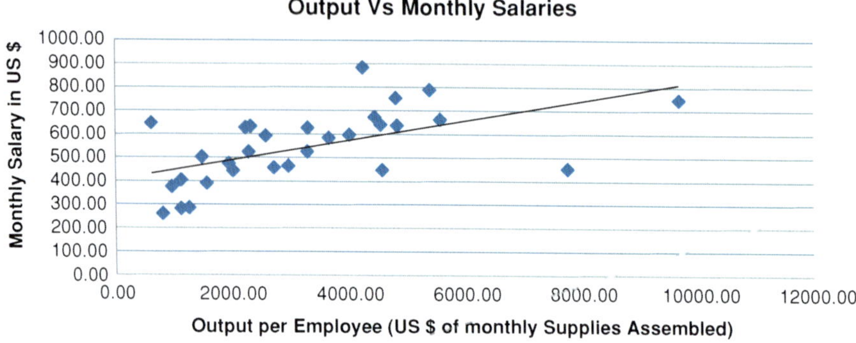

Fig. 12.4 Wages versus. productivity for mexican maquiladora locations

was originally close to those suppliers. When final assembly was moved to Mexico, the suppliers did not follow, although efforts were often made to move the supply base close to the new final assembly location. (The supplier park near the Ford assembly plant in Hermosillo is a notable exception). The longer trans-border supply chain, as well as efforts to set up maquiladoras as just-in-time operations, result in a number of logistics challenges which should be anticipated by anyone planning to source from Mexican locations, especially in the interior. Some strategies for dealing with this complexity are illustrated in the case example below.

Chihuahua Auto Supply

One automotive components supplier recognized the difficulties with locating in a border city such as Ciudad Juarez, and thus chose a site in Chihuahua, some 250 km south of the U.S.-Mexico border. The plant was designed to operate on a just-in-time basis with its suppliers, located largely in the Midwest and Northeast parts of the United States. As a result, frequent deliveries and relatively small shipments were the norm, but the realities of distance and the presence of the border added to the planned cost and complexity of the inbound supply chain. This practice has increased the level of coordination needed between the supplier, the transportation company, and the maquiladora plant. The task was difficult enough that it was turned over to a third party logistics operator.

Since one of the key performance metrics for this plant is minimum inventory, full truckloads are rarely sent from a single supplier, in spite of the distances

[3] The NAFTA provides that U.S. carriers can deliver international shipments into Mexico, and vice-versa. However, the U.S. has never implemented this section of NAFTA, claiming safety concerns. A pilot program was terminated in 2009 based on Congressional opposition. As this is written, a new pilot program has been proposed.

involved. Instead, the third party coordinated multiple pickups of small shipments from the various suppliers and consolidation of these shipments into a single truckload for the long distance from the Midwest to Chihuahua. Three factors increase the complexity of the design of milk runs for a maquiladora plant: the geographical dispersion of the suppliers, the distance from the suppliers to the maquiladora plant, and the requirement for small orders to keep inventory levels down. This resulted in the opening of an El Paso consolidation point that could "feed" the Chihuahua operation. We should also note that under current regulations, the U.S. trucks can take the trailer only to the U.S. side of the border.[3] At that point, a Mexican truck and driver take over to deliver the trailer to the maquiladora plant on the Mexican side of the border. In the case of the final product, this process is reversed: the Mexican truck crosses the trailer to the U.S. side of the border, where an American truck takes over to complete the delivery within the U.S.

Unfortunately, the plant management was not satisfied with the cost and service levels attained by the inbound logistics operation. They suspected a disconnection between the strategies followed to order from the suppliers, and those followed to plan and schedule the transportation resources to take these supplies to the plant. It appeared that this lack of coordination might be resulting in higher overall costs versus those that could be obtained by making joint material management-transportation decisions.

To assess the efficiency and propose areas of improvement for in-bound supply chain operations for the Chihuahua plant, a team was formed between the plant's personnel and Arizona State University (ASU). What follows is a summary of the short and long-term recommendations given by this team, and the plans to implement these recommendations.

- **Short term** Immediate improvement of utilization of transportation resources by:
  - Better designing and monitoring the utilization efficiency of the weekly milk runs used to transport raw material from the Midwest suppliers to the El Paso consolidation warehouse
  - Synchronizing the time and the frequency of orders and shipments of supplies to avoid low truck utilization from the Midwest to El Paso
  - Educating those in Chihuahua who make ordering/traffic decisions as to the cost implications of deviations from transportation policies
- **Long term** Increase efficiency of truck utilization by opening a consolidation site closer to the suppliers.
- **Long term** Develop independent and consolidated metrics of efficiency for transportation and inventory, so that tradeoffs of inventory versus. transportation cost and service are tracked on a regular basis.
- **Long term** Develop enough in-house expertise to evaluate the efforts of the third party logistics company in operating the inbound supply chain.

Conclusions

Traditionally, the relocation of a manufacturing plant from the USA to Mexico under the maquiladora plant program was driven only by labor cost savings. As shown above, the overall relocation strategy needs to consider labor stability and potential competition for the labor pool, as well as the added logistics costs associated with the move. Especially if a long term relationship is desired, supply management professionals should be sure that productivity and labor rates are in synch at the candidate Mexican suppliers.

On the other hand, a careful design of the new supply chain for these proposed suppliers can result in a plant capable of successfully meeting the demands of the original customer base, as well as becoming a strategic supply point for other operations, either in Mexico or farther south. In particular, for the case of a Maquiladora, the logistics strategy should consider the factors that are inherent to the binational transportation environment, such as the time and added cost to cross the border, longer travel distances, higher Mexican transportation costs and less sophisticated logistics infrastructure in Mexico.

Mexican firms are increasingly asking third-party logistics companies to design and manage the different aspects of inbound and outbound supply chains of maquiladoras, especially when the U.S. customer and/or parent has had good success with logistics outsourcing. However, the transborder environment is complex enough that it is unrealistic to expect third-party logistics companies to provide a complete replacement for internal experience and knowledge: they are a *complement*. Adequate internal experience and performance tracking systems should be in place to guarantee the best performance of these companies.

References

Arvis J-F, Mustra M, Panzer J, Ojala L, Naula T (2007) Connecting to compete: trade logistics in the global economy, the logistics performance index and its indicators. The International Bank for Reconstruction and Development/The World Bank

Arvis J-F, Mustra M, Shepherd B, Saslavsky D (2010) Connecting to compete: trade logistics in the global economy, the logistics performance index and its indicators. The International Bank for Reconstruction and Development/The World Bank

Ashenbaum B, Maltz A, Ellram L, Barratt M (2009) Organizational alignment and supply chain governance structure: introduction and construct validation. Int J Logistics Manage 20(2):169–186.

Bhattacharyya K, Datta P, Offodile OF (2010) The contribution of third-party indices in assessing global operational risk. J Supply Chain Manage 46(4):25–43

Bookbinder JH, Tan CS (2003) A Comparison of Asian and European logistics systems. Int J Phys Distrib Logistics Manage 33(1):36–58

Carter JR, Narasimhan R (1990) Purchasing in the international marketplace: principles, practices, and implications for operations. J Purch Mater Manage 26(3):2–11

Carter JR, Narasimhan R, Vickery SK (1988) Global sourcing for manufacturing operations, research monograph no. 3, operations management association. Available through Naman and Schneider Associates Group, Waco Texas

Carter JR, Slaight T, Blascovich J (2007) The future of supply management: technology, collaboration, supply chain design. Supply Chain Manage Rev 11(7):44–50

Carter JR, Maltz A, Yan T, Maltz E (2008) Purchasing managers' perceptions of low cost countries and geographies: a perceptual mapping approach. Int J Phys Distrib Logistics Manage 38(3):224–236

Council of Supply Chain Management Professionals. Global perspectives. To be accessed at http://cscmp.org/perspectives.asp

Hair JF Jr, Anderson RE, Tatham RL, Black WC (1995) Multivariate Data Analysis, 4th edn. Prentice-Hall, New Jersey

Hausman W, Lee HL, Subramanian U (2005) Global logistics indicators, supply chain metrics, and binational trade patterns. World Bank Policy Research Working Paper, Nov 2005

Narasimhan R, Carter JR (1990) Organization, communication and co-ordination of global sourcing. Int Mark Rev 7(2):6–20

Philip James, Inc. (2010) The CPSM Program. Institute for Supply Management

Prahalad CK, Hamel G (1990) The core competence of the corporation. Harvard Bus Rev pp 2–15 (May–June)

Rene Villalobos J, Ahumada O (2008) International plant location decisions under labor scarcity. In: Fowler J, Mason S (eds) Proceedings of the 2008 Industrial Engineering Research Conference

Chapter 13
Innovative Logistics in Extreme Conditions: The Case of Health Care Delivery in Gambia

Hau L. Lee, Sonali V. Rammohan and Lesley Sept

Abstract For millions of people across Africa, health interventions such as vaccines, HIV counseling and treatment, and other public health expertise are out of reach. Barriers to health care can include shortage of health personnel, scarcity of medicines, distance to a health center, terrain, poverty and lack of transportation. The logistical challenges to the delivery of health care in underdeveloped economies are often insurmountable. This case study examines a comprehensive vehicle management model designed by the social enterprise Riders for Health (Riders) to provide African ministries of health with consistently reliable and cost-effective vehicle fleets, thus enabling large-scale health care delivery. The model has been implemented through a public–private partnership between Riders and the Gambian Ministry of Health. When the national vehicle fleet is fully rolled out, Gambia will become the first African country to have sufficient health care delivery vehicles to service its population. The case highlights innovative best practices that can improve the coordination of material, information and financial flows of health logistics in extreme conditions. These innovations require diverse stakeholders such as NGOs, government, and donor organizations to work in close collaboration; incentive alignment is a critical step towards developing these partnerships. What Riders has been able to achieve in Gambia and other parts of Africa can serve as a lesson for business logistics operations in emerging economies.

H. L. Lee (✉) · S. V. Rammohan · L. Sept
Graduate School of Business, Stanford University, 518 Memorial Way, Stanford, CA 94305 USA
e-mail: haulee@stanford.edu

J. H. Bookbinder (ed.), *Handbook of Global Logistics*, International Series in Operations Research & Management Science 181, DOI: 10.1007/978-1-4419-6132-7_13,

13.1 Introduction

Logistics involves the flow of materials, information and money. For the delivery of goods and services in developed economies, organizations can count on having comprehensive transportation systems (such as rail networks, roads, rivers, ocean routes) and transportation conveyances (e.g. rail cars, trucks, container ships, etc.). Coordinating such material flows requires information networks and the appropriate sharing of information. In addition, the flow of money can be taken care of through sophisticated banking systems and complex contract terms and conditions. Improvements in logistics often focus on how those three flows can be made more efficient through new information technologies or coordination schemes with multiple trading partners.

Logistics in underdeveloped economies, however, poses great challenges, since the foundation for managing the three kinds of flows can be weak. This is especially the case when the delivery of goods and services to underserved segments such as rural areas is involved. Transportation networks are often poorly developed or lacking, and as a result, transportation conveyances are often unusable. In addition, many poor nations can ill afford the necessary transportation conveyances to begin with. Data are not available for better planning, or more fundamentally, for performance management. Finally, different kinds of financial flows must be explored to give proper incentives to the multiple organizations involved in logistics. It is often the case that the delivery of goods and services to underserved populations involves some combination of local government, international aid agencies, non-governmental organizations (NGOs), and other local operators.

Managing logistics in extreme conditions where transportation networks and conveyances are minimal, information flows poorly, and economic means are scarce requires innovations that are very different from advances that industry and academics have made in developed economies. The needs, however, are great. Better logistics in extreme conditions can make the difference between life and death.

The literature on logistics management in extreme conditions is just emerging. There has been increased interest on the logistics of disaster relief operations (e.g., Thomas and Fritz 2006; Thomas and Kopczak 2007). Altay and Green (2006) have summarized operations research and management science work in disaster relief operations. Van Wassenhove (2006) has broadened disaster relief logistics to general humanitarian logistics. Given that humanitarian logistics are often linked to nations with extremely inadequate conditions, the work of Van Wassenhove is highly relevant to ours. A number of recent papers have addressed the coordination of responses in disaster relief, particularly in the area of asset and inventory prepositioning (Duran et al. 2013; Balcik et al. 2010; Rawls and Turnquist 2010; Salmerón and Apte 2010). In one of the few books on this subject, Tomasini and Van Wassenhove (2009) presented an integrative approach to managing humanitarian logistics, and gave many examples on how NGOs can mobilize and manage humanitarian logistics relief operations.

In this chapter, we describe an innovative means to manage and operate health care delivery in Gambia. Such a case serves as an illustration that, despite operating in very challenging environments, it is possible to make significant logistics improvements in extreme conditions. The case itself also illuminates some interesting research problems. The case is about the work of Riders for Health, a non-governmental organization based in the United Kingdom that manages vehicles and motorcycles used to deliver health care to rural communities in Africa. We examine the various operating models Riders has used over time, trace the evolution of health transport management in Gambia from the perspective of key stakeholders, note the elements involved in putting the model in place and financing it, and explore the diffusion potential of the vehicle ownership and maintenance model as Riders looks to expand into other African countries. Parts of this chapter are drawn from Tayan (2007) and Rammohan (2010).

13.2 Health Care in Africa

Africa is the poorest continent on the globe, with the standard of living in Sub-Saharan Africa significantly below that of almost every other part of the world. Along with poor economic conditions, Africans have a much lower life expectancy. For example, the average life expectancy for men and women is 53 years versus 78 in the United States (World Health Organization 2010). Among infectious diseases, the most deadly are HIV/AIDS, malaria, measles, pneumonia, tuberculosis, and dehydrating diarrhea (caused by cholera, dysentery, typhoid, and rotavirus). In Sub-Saharan Africa, 22 million adults and children are living with HIV/AIDS, representing 10.5 % of the population. Swaziland, Botswana, Lesotho, Zimbabwe, Namibia, and South Africa are among the hardest hit, with infection rates of 19–33 % (UNAIDS 2007). In 2007, 1.5 million Africans died from AIDS, 0.91 million Africans died from malaria and 0.45 million from tuberculosis.

The increase in financial resources and dedicated efforts of humanitarian organizations to improve health care in Sub-Saharan Africa has made inroads. Many national epidemics have stabilized or begun to decline. However, even though health organizations have expanded the availability of medicines such as antiretroviral drugs, such drugs are reaching less than a third of the patients who need them (LaFraniere 2007).

Experts point to significant obstacles in overcoming infrastructure and other logistical obstacles. First, the number of health care workers is insufficient to support the continent's population. Africa is estimated to have 2.3 health care personnel per 1,000 population, compared to 4.3 in south-east Asia, 18.9 in Europe, and 24.8 in the Americas. To some extent, this shortage is due to the challenge of recruiting and training qualified employees in hard-to-reach locations and for low wages. However, qualified health workers are not easy to retain, and often quit their positions because they find it difficult to fulfill their duties without the necessary supplies, support, and access to patients.

Second, the continent has a severely underdeveloped physical infrastructure system. For example, most African nations lack a modern sewage collection and treatment system. These systems, implemented in developed nations in the second half of the nineteenth century, have been directly responsible for the elimination of water-transmitted diseases such as cholera. By contrast, their absence in Africa contributes to the prevalence of several diseases.

The continent also lacks an integrated road, transportation and logistics network. For example, Zimbabwe has a total area of 390,000 square kilometers but an estimated road system of only 18,300 km (Europa Publications 2000). Although major African cities are connected by paved roads, much of the population lives in remote communities that are accessible only by single-lane sand or dirt paths. According to the United Nations, 62 % of Africans live in rural communities, compared with 19 % in North America and 28 % in Europe (United Nations 2006). In many African countries, only 20–30 % of the rural population lives within 2 km of a road (The World Bank 2006). Furthermore, there is limited existing infrastructure, such as postal services or railroads, reaching into these communities. As a result, health workers cannot easily get to the vast population living in remote locations. People requiring medical attention have to devise their own ways to travel to the closest health clinic. Without motor transportation, they are often forced to walk or rely on a relative to push them in a wheelbarrow. Tragically, those who live five miles or more from a health clinic and are sick, malnourished, or pregnant have significantly lower survival rates than those who live closer to a clinic.

Although Gambia is one of the smallest countries on the African continent, its unique geography offers a number of impediments to health coverage. Located in Western Africa, it covers an area of 11,300 km^2 and is surrounded by Senegal on three sides. The long, narrow geography of the country combined with the Gambia River's prominence make ground transportation quite difficult. Of the 3,742 km of roads extending through the country, 19.3 % are paved. The country has a population of 1.78 million people, and it is estimated that 57 % of the total population lives in urban areas. Figure 13.1 shows the geography of Gambia.

Some of the major health challenges facing Gambia today include malaria, maternal and infant mortality, acute respiratory infections, diarrhea and pneumonia. The United Nations Development Program (Human Development Report 2009) ranks Gambia as 160th among 179 countries in the Human Development Index, which aims to summarize a country's achievement in attaining a long and healthy life, access to knowledge, and a decent standard of living.

Gambia has five hospitals and a mix of public, private and nongovernment organization-operated health facilities. The Gambian health system is relatively centralized, with six regional health teams implementing policies of the Ministry of Health. Each of the six regions in the country has various health care centers, which mainly offer preventive services such as weighing infants, immunizing

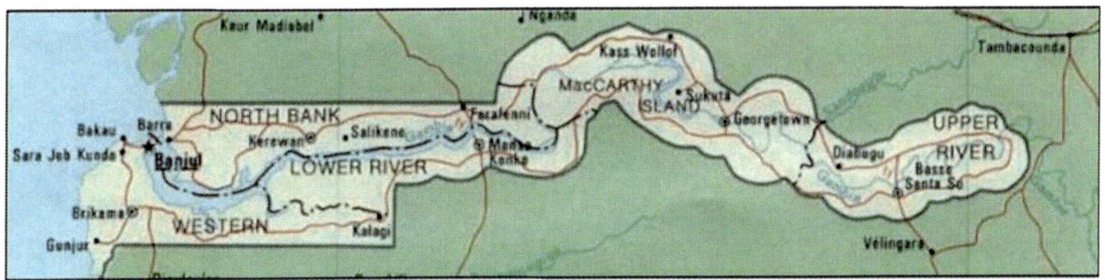

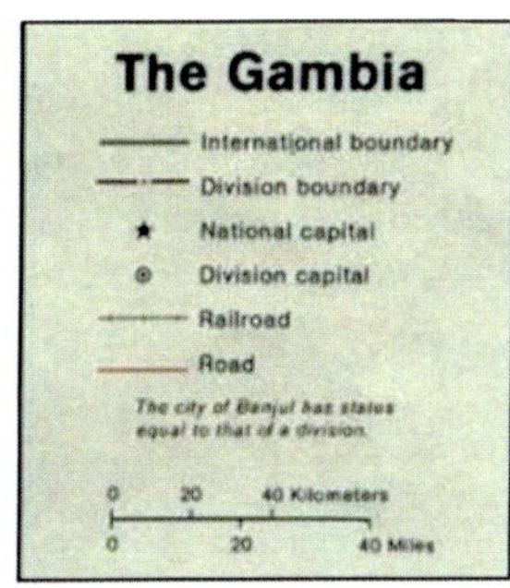

Fig. 13.1 Maps of Gambia. *Source* http://www.lib.utexas.edu/maps/gambia.html produced by the U.S. Central Intelligence Agency 1988

antenatal women and children under the age of five, providing bed nets, and giving health talks.

Before Riders for Health's involvement in Gambia began in 1989, vehicles and motorcycles were often used by officers and health workers for personal purposes, reducing the amount of time vehicle fleets were available for health care delivery. Drivers of health vehicles and health care workers who rode motorcycles received no maintenance training. As a result, the useful life of vehicles, as well as the number of kilometers the vehicles could travel each year, was quite low. Securing funding for up-front vehicle purchase, spare parts, and fuel was also a problem. It was not uncommon for a patient to be asked to pay for the fuel needed to take him or her to a hospital. According to one Gambian medical officer, sometimes medical personnel would pay for fuel out of their own pockets to avoid patients being left without transport (Sonko 2009).

New methods were needed to overcome these obstacles. The most effective solutions would be those that allowed for increased physical presence, or outreach, by health workers into the community itself. Although viable solutions would draw the financial support of international organizations, in the long term, workable solutions would have to become economically self-sustainable.

13.3 Riders for Health

The story of Riders dates back to 1986. Andrea Coleman and United States Grand Prix motorcycle racer Randy Mamola decided to raise money for Save the Children, a United Kingdom-based nonprofit dedicated to helping children in developing nations that suffer from poverty and disease. At the time, Andrea worked in motorcycle team management in the U.K. Andrea's husband, Barry Coleman, worked as a feature writer for the *Guardian* and also covered motorcycle racing for the newspaper on the weekends.

Mamola and Barry Coleman were subsequently invited by Save the Children to observe how the funds they raised were used to immunize children in Somalia. During a visit to a remote community, the health officials accompanying them mentioned that immunization in such locations was rare: insufficient motor transportation made access difficult for health workers. The two noticed several motorcycles left by the side of the road that, according to locals, were no longer operable. Upon inspection, they were shocked to discover that many of the bikes were considered irreparably damaged with odometer readings of only 800 km (500 miles). Health officials explained that the motorcycles broke down prematurely due to dusty and hot conditions. Mamola and Coleman, however, realized that the locals simply had not been trained in basic motorcycle maintenance; many of the bikes were rendered out of commission due to problems that were inexpensive to prevent or repair, such as dust in the carburetor, failure to replace an oil filter, or a broken clutch or brake cable.

Shortly thereafter, Coleman was engaged as a consultant by Save the Children and the World Health Organization to assess its fleet of 86 motorcycles in Gambia. Coleman discovered that only 12 of the bikes were still in operation, with the remainder no longer in use due to similar problems witnessed in Somalia; the 12 in use remained operable because they were regularly maintained by a driver with basic knowledge of mechanics. When Coleman was informed that UNICEF had donated another fleet of 83 motorcycles to the NGOs, he realized that, without parts or training, they would end up being more of a liability than a productive asset, costing much-needed resources while failing to deliver the expected benefits.

Based on his findings, Coleman designed and developed a motorcycle training and maintenance outreach program to ensure that African organizations could utilize vehicles over their estimated useful lives through cost-effective measures. The program, which began as a consulting project for Gambia, was later replicated in Uganda, Lesotho, Nigeria, Zimbabwe and several other countries.

The Riders for Health solution for motorcycle fleet maintenance was called Transport Resource Management (TRM), a program designed to work within the tough conditions and limited resources of many Sub-Saharan African countries. Through routine inspection and the regular replacement of basic parts, significant damage could often be avoided. Because health workers relied on their motorcycles to reach patients in critical need of care, keeping a motorcycle operational directly impacts their ability to save lives. Preventive maintenance provides the best assurance that a motorcycle will not break down while in use.

There are various reasons why motorcycles were effective transportation vehicles in Sub-Saharan Africa. The most important was their ability to access terrain that was inaccessible by four-wheel vehicles. Motorcycles were cheaper to purchase and operate (a health organization could purchase six for the cost of one four-wheel vehicle). Motorcycles also required fewer and less complicated tools to maintain, and they had lower carbon emissions per kilometer than a four-wheel vehicle. Finally, they were less subject to abuse. Because four-wheel vehicles like a Land Cruiser were status symbols, corrupt officials often "borrowed" them for personal purposes, diverting them from their much-needed public mission.

Traditionally, motorcycle fleets owned by African health organizations consisted of a variety of makes and models, many of which were inappropriate for the terrain and conditions of Africa. In order to reduce the cost and complication of TRM, Riders emphasized the importance of standardizing vehicle fleets wherever possible. The bikes most commonly recommended by Riders were agricultural-specification bikes, including the Honda XL125, Honda CTX200, Honda CT110, and the Yamaha AG200. Agricultural-specification bikes were rugged and low tech, making them well suited for the riding conditions in Africa. They had high mud guards above the front and rear wheels, hand guards on the handlebars, and a fully enclosed chain for greater protection against debris and pebbles kicked up by the tires.

Riders had designed a rigorous maintenance program for the motorcycle fleets of its customers, which they were expected to follow closely. Health workers were trained to do routine pre-ride checks every day to ensure their bikes are fit for operation. The checklist included inspection of the tires, oil level, coolant level, the chain, brakes, and lights. They also made certain that nuts and bolts were tight and performed a visual check, looking for signs of damage, excessive dirt or dust, and pebbles lodged in the engine, chain or tires.

Once per month, a Riders-trained technician performed maintenance on the bike and changed parts that were at highest risk from daily wear and tear. Small-dollar parts were replaced before their full useful lives have run out, according to a strict replacement schedule designed for rough riding conditions. Unexpected damage, such as a broken chain or clogged air filter while on the road, could cause significantly more expensive damage to the bike frame or engine, not to mention the risk to the rider and inability to reach patients. Replacement-part maintenance was performed on an outreach basis, meaning that technicians went out into the field to service the motorcycles in the locations in which they were used. Physical inspection of the bikes allowed the technician to plan the parts and service that will be required on the next visit. It also allowed the technician to provide refresher training and riding instructions for health workers.

By having both the health worker and trained technician follow conservative, routine practices, Riders aimed to keep vehicles fully operational between scheduled services.

Operations management is another critical aspect of Riders' TRM program. TRM was run on a hub-and-spoke model within each country. The largest Riders office was usually centered in the country's capital, which served as the bridge to the developed world. The national office was typically staffed 60 % with technicians and 40 % with office administrators. Spare parts were imported into the national office and then redistributed to smaller regional offices. Regional offices tended to have higher levels of technical staff (80 %), leveraging as much as possible the administrative support of the national office. Regional offices, in turn, supported the health workers who are widely distributed among remote communities.

Because spare parts were expensive, Riders applied careful inventory management practices. By maintaining service records on each motorcycle and gathering feedback from technicians in the field, Riders' logisticians had advance knowledge of the parts that would be required and could appropriately time the inventory replenishment. The national office tended to have the highest level of spare parts inventory. Riders provided similar expertise on the management of fuel supplies. They also made sure that all health workers were equipped with the proper protective gear, riding suits, and helmets.

Today, Riders for Health offers three key service-delivery models to clients, and runs one or more of them in each of its seven operational countries. A description of each model follows. We describe a portion of the processes for material flow (vehicle acquisition) and financial flows (payment scheme) under each model.

13.3.1 Interval Servicing

Interval Servicing (IS) utilizes the concept of regular, scheduled vehicle maintenance, and also includes driver and rider training. IS does not incorporate fuel costs, and does not therefore tie its customers as systematically to the preventive service schedule. The IS is offered to ministries of health and other in-country agencies if they are not yet ready to commit to full outsourcing including fuel.

- *Vehicle acquisition process*: Clients purchase their own vehicles or are given vehicles by external funders.
- *Payment scheme*: Clients pay on a per-service basis.

13.3.2 Transport Resource Management

Transport Resource Management (TRM) uses a full logistical support system for fleets that facilitates efficient management. TRM's zero-breakdown preventive maintenance services enable increased mobility, reliability, and safety of health workers. Increased mobility facilitates more frequent access to additional communities to provide prevention, diagnosis, and treatment. TRM depends on training, consistent supervision, and strong supply-chain logistics, with frequent and detailed audits.

- *Vehicle acquisition process*: Clients purchase their own vehicles or are given vehicles by external funders.
- *Payment scheme*: Riders charges a cost-per-kilometer (cpk) fee to the client, which is meant to cover costs for fuel, lubricants, maintenance, driver training, replacement parts, infrastructure and more. A vehicle replenishment fee is also built in (this fee goes into a replacement fund), so that Riders can accumulate capital to enable the client to purchase additional vehicles once existing vehicles come to the end of their useful life.

13.3.3 Transport Asset Management

Transport Asset Management (TAM) is a new system that sets up a means for governments to secure long-term program sustainability and streamlined fleet management. TAM includes all the components of TRM, except that Riders owns the vehicle fleet and can retire a vehicle at its optimal residual value. Riders, as fleet owner, has a greater level of control and enforceability over vehicles. As a result, there is potential for fewer "wasted" kilometers (driven for personal use instead of health purposes) than with TRM. Consider, for example, a situation in which a health worker is found to be using a TRM motorcycle for heavy personal use. While Riders could notify the worker's employer and stop providing TRM, it could not withdraw the vehicle itself since it is not the owner. Under TAM, Riders would have the right to withdraw the motorcycle under the same circumstances

- *Vehicle acquisition process*: To date, TAM has been implemented only in Gambia, where the Skoll Foundation underwrote a loan by GT Bank that enabled Riders to procure its own fleet of vehicles. The Gambian government should no longer need to purchase any vehicles or obtain donated vehicles. In the future, if a donor wants to contribute toward health transport in Gambia, the government would ask the donor for a financial contribution to pay for Riders' TAM cpk fee, instead of asking for an actual vehicle donation. This way, the government could remain uninvolved in the process of vehicle acquisition and management.
- *Payment scheme*: Clients are charged a higher cpk fee than for TRM. The TAM cpk incorporates principal and interest costs for the loan Riders obtains to buy the vehicle fleet. This saves clients the need to set aside large capital budgets for fleet acquisition.

Tables 13.1 and 13.2 provide more detailed comparisons of the features of the three models.

Table 13.1 Comparison of transport models

	No riders	Interval service	Transport resource management	Transport asset management
Worker/driver training	Does not exist	Inconsistent	Strong	Strong
Fuel availability	Inconsistent	Inconsistent	Strong	Strong
Spare parts availability	Inconsistent & questionable quality	Inconsistent	Strong	Strongest (parts are standardized)
Misuse of vehicles	High	High	Low	Lowest
Vehicle resale value	Lowest	Low	Moderate	Highest
Vehicle useful life	Low	Medium	High	High
Km/year	High	High	Medium	Low
Cost control	Weak	Weak	Strong	Strongest
Payment scheme	Self-funded by govt. or govt. pays a private organization per service	Per service and per training payment to riders	Cpk payment to riders	Same cpk components as TRM, plus loan principal & interest added in
Vehicle liability	Client	Client	Client	Riders for health

Table 13.2 Health transport maintenance costs included in riders' charges

	Interval servicing	TRM	TAM
Interventions (Parts and lubricants)	x	x	x
Training		x	x
Fuel		x	x
Direct staff (Technical staff and drivers)	x	x	x
Direct management (Gambia management staff)	x	x	x
Insurance		x	x
Logistics		x	x
Vehicle purchase cost			x
Vehicle loan interest cost			x

In Gambia, Riders has provided varying levels of maintenance services to the Ministry of Health (MoH) since 1989. From 1989 to 2001, Riders performed demand and interval service for various Ministry of Health vehicles and motorcycles. From 2002 to 2005, Riders performed TRM for motorcycles donated to the MoH by the World Bank. TRM service was paid by the MoH on a cost-per-kilometer basis. After 2005, the World Bank program ended, and Riders was again performing demand and interval service for Ministry of Health vehicles. During this period, the government would sometimes run out of funds to pay for its own fuel. Although Riders was supposed to perform basic demand service, which doesn't cover fuel costs, Riders occasionally ended up funding fuel and other items so that vital health services would not be stopped.

The cpk arrangement of the 2002–2005 TRM program had a replacement component, so that reserves could be built up in a special bank account for the government to purchase a new fleet in the future. However, World Bank vehicles were already one year old or more when the TRM program began. Maintenance proved costly over time, and there wasn't enough money to replace the entire fleet by the end of the contract in 2005.

In 2005, Riders initiated discussions with Gambia's MoH regarding an alternative fleet management system where Riders would lease vehicles to the Ministry. This eventually became known as the TAM model. The challenge the MoH faced was to find adequate upfront funds for a large fleet purchase. Riders realized that leasing had several benefits; the fleet and its spare parts could become standardized, Riders would have better control over assets which would result in less personal use of vehicles (as described earlier), and the MoH would be able to make level lease payments to Riders over time, reducing variability in its maintenance budget. To fund a TAM model, the government of Gambia first sought financial support from the Department for International Development and the Global Fund, with no success. Negotiations then began with the Skoll Foundation to work in a three-way partnership with Guaranty Trust (GT) Bank to lend Riders money to purchase the TAM vehicle fleet.

By June of 2009, due to a government funding shortfall, only about two-thirds of the originally-envisioned vehicle fleet was purchased and placed into service.

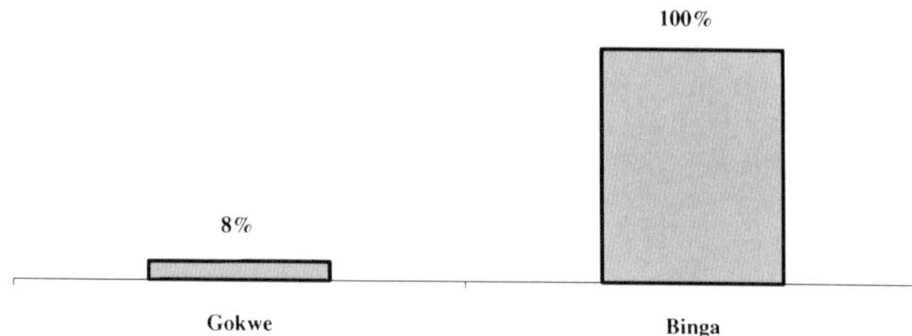

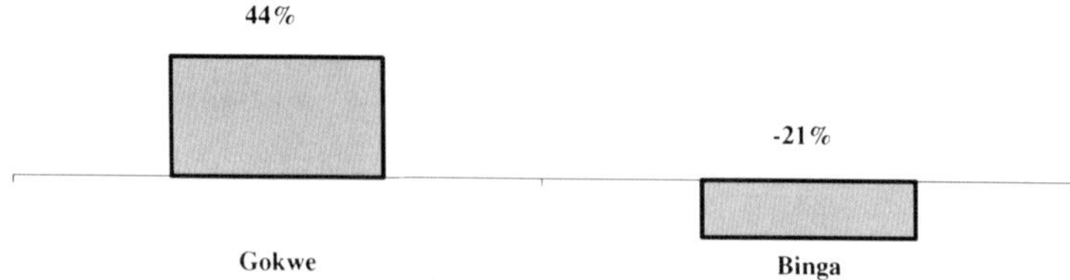

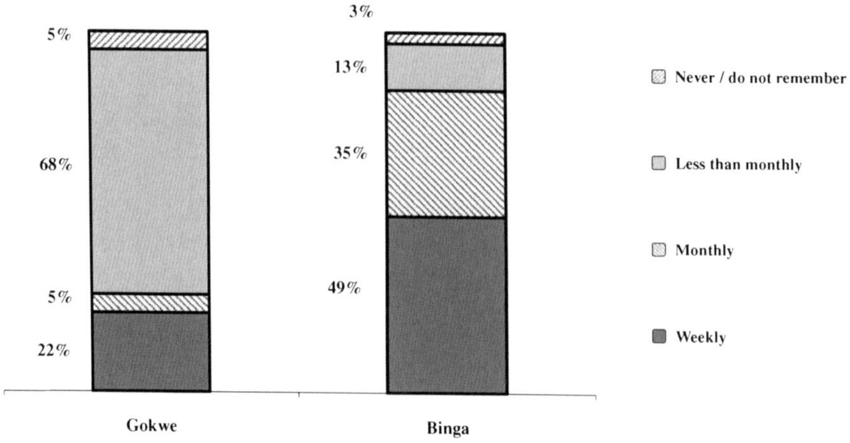

Fig. 13.2 Riders for health: Binga Program, Zimbabwe (2001–2002). *Note* Gokwe region reported no change in motorcycle usage and maintenance. Binga implemented Riders for Health TRM in 2002. *Source* OC&C (2005)

For many of the country's health centers, these vehicles were the first of their kind deployed. In remote areas, ambulance services had been previously unknown. In 2009, TAM motorcycles travelled more than 740,000 km, and ambulances and trekking vehicles travelled in excess of 1 million kilometers. Riders is still working with the MoH on plans to get the remainder of the fleet in service.

13.4 Financing of the TAM Model

The TAM system is described within Riders as a five-legged stool. It requires (1) a funding partner, (2) a financing partner, (3) an underwriting partner, (4) an operational partner, and (5) strong infrastructure. In the case of Gambia, the funding partner is the MoH, which uses internal and donor funds to pay Riders' cpk fee. The operational partner is Riders, which runs fleet management services for the MoH in exchange for the cpk fee. The financing partner is the Gambian branch of the Nigeria-based GT Bank (used by Riders for many years for its standard banking needs), which offered a five-year loan to purchase a standardized fleet. The underwriting partner is the California-based Skoll Foundation, which provided a credit guarantee on the loan. In the case of Gambia, the fifth leg, infrastructure (such as workshops, fuel depots and human resources) was already in place.

The financial arrangement is based on the Skoll Foundation setting up $3.5 million as a credit guarantee for GT Bank, so that, if Riders defaults on its loan, GT could count on the money the Skoll Foundation has deposited with them. Along with the credit guarantee, the Skoll Foundation also provided a companion grant to fund certain infrastructure, such as an additional repair shop in the North Bank (see Fig. 13.1), making the country-wide vehicle maintenance network more functional.

Next, GT paid a below-market rate of interest to Skoll of LIBOR (London Interbank Offered Rate) plus 1 %, capped at 5 %. Riders paid a rate of LIBOR plus 3 % to GT Bank, capped at 8 %. This cap reduced the interest rate risk borne by Riders. The resulting 3 % "spread" went to GT. The rate caps also helped to control the cpk charged to the MoH. In addition, the bank waived its management fee of one percent, and reduced two other fees: one that is usually charged on every debit, and a separate arrangement fee. Because of these concessions, GT saw the loan as having a philanthropic element. Since the Skoll Foundation fully guaranteed the loan, GT Bank dropped concerns it had about credit risk (it had reservations about the ultimate payor of the lease payments, the MoH, defaulting on its obligation).

Skoll also agreed to bear the exchange-rate risk from the arrangement. That risk exists because Riders needed a loan in dollars to purchase vehicles and motorcycles from abroad, yet it was being paid over time by the government in Gambian dalasis, and Riders would be, in turn, paying dalasis back to GT. The dalasi to dollar exchange rate could fluctuate from the time the loan was granted to the intervals at which the loan is paid back. As a result, while Riders could repay GT Bank, it is possible that Skoll ultimately would receive back fewer dollars than originally deposited, because of potential dalasi devaluation over the term of the loan.

From the perspective of Riders, executing the TAM arrangement meant several major shifts for the organization. Dealing with TAM meant Riders would change from a vehicle fleet management organization to an organization that deals with logistics and leasing. Riders owned the vehicles, yet at times it transported goods such as vaccines and bed nets that are owned by other parties. The development of TAM has not only caused an operational shift for Riders, but a shift in funding strategies. While historically, Riders held numerous fundraisers through motorcycle racing events, obtained grants and other more traditional means of funding, the organization has had to raise debt capital with the advent of TAM.

One cannot underestimate the human resources and physical infrastructure costs involved in developing a comprehensive health transport maintenance system. For example, in Gambia, even though most of the infrastructure needed for TAM was already in place, Riders requested a $160,000 grant from the Skoll Foundation for computers, training, a workshop on the North Bank of the country, and more.

Riders for Health expects that, in five years, the second round of the TAM loan will be half the size of that in the first round. This is because a portion of the cpk is a replenishment fee that, over time, will enable the purchase of new vehicles outright. Five years from the start of the TAM program, the fund will have saved up about half of the total purchase cost of the TAM fleet needed. That half-size loan will still, in GT Bank's opinion, require a credit enhancement. However, for the *third* generation fleet (in 8–10 years' time), Gambia should have the funds to purchase the entire replacement fleet outright and avoid obtaining a loan. This is the point at which a self-sustaining fleet will be achieved for the government.

After the TAM program was launched in 2009, the Ministry of Health's existing fleet (33 vehicles donated by UNICEF and others, and 19 Global Fund vehicles) were deployed as backups to be used in emergencies. The TAM program has yet to receive full funding, so plans to purchase an additional 28 vehicles and 60 motorcycles have still not been implemented.

13.5 Cost-Effectiveness and Impact

In 2005 the international business consultancy OC&C carried out a pro-bono due diligence report on Riders for Health's activities in Africa (OC&C 2005). In Zimbabwe, annual motorcycle fleet maintenance costs per thousand people reached by health workers were 62 % lower with Riders versus an unmanaged system. In Gambia, the corresponding reduction was 24 %. These estimates were partly based on assumptions (for example, it was estimated from interviews that managed vehicles lasted 250,000 km versus unmanaged vehicles lasting 100,000 km), and did not use large-scale empirical data. Nevertheless, the figures are in line with the intuitive notion that the cost-effectiveness of a Riders system would be higher than that of an unmanaged system.

Cost savings were derived largely from the fact that health workers were able to reach more patients and therefore achieve better leverage from their resources. For example, Riders' experience in Zimbabwe indicated that a health worker using a motorcycle was able to reach approximately four times as many people as one who travelled on foot. More importantly, health workers in Riders' TRM were better able to make *repeat visits* to patients, ensuring better long- term care.

The impact of TRM is best illustrated by what Riders did in the Binga region of Zimbabwe (Tayan 2007). Located in the northwest region of the country, Binga is one of the poorest districts in Zimbabwe. In 2002, Riders established a TRM program in Binga, training and equipping the 16 health workers responsible for patients in the area. As a result of the TRM program, Riders' equipped health workers were able to make more visits to local communities and increase education on methods to slow the spread of diseases, such as HIV/AIDS, malaria, and cholera. They distributed mosquito nets and provided instruction on use. They also furnished prenatal care as well as education on reproduction and birthing.

As shown in the OC&C report, a comparison between Binga and the Gokwe, a neighboring region to the southeast where no change was made in motorcycle usage and maintenance, highlighted the impact of Riders. Results showed that increased mobility dramatically increased the presence of health workers in local communities. Only 22 % of those surveyed in Gokwe reported weekly visits by health workers, versus 49 % in Binga. Conversely, 68 % of people surveyed in Gokwe said that health workers visited their community less often than monthly, compared to only 13 % in Binga.

Comparisons were also made between malarial deaths in each district in 2001 and 2002. Whereas Gokwe exhibited a 44 % increase in malarial deaths year-over-year, Binga reported a 21 % decrease. Although not a scientifically-controlled study, the results offered strong support for the Riders' TRM solution, and indicated that it was consistent with improved health outcomes (see Fig. 13.2 for results from the Binga-Gokwe study).

Evaluating cost-effectiveness of the Riders' system requires cost performance data before and after the Riders' intervention. However, it is usually very difficult to get a complete cost picture before Riders was involved. Sometimes, vehicles were donated to African countries and therefore the government was not aware of (or especially interested in) their cash value. If or when vehicles broke down, the government felt no special sense of monetary loss. Also, since various transport maintenance costs might reside in different sections of the Ministry of Health budget, and record-keeping could be weak, the total costs of vehicles and vehicle maintenance were not always clear. It was also difficult to assess the benefits of effective transport maintenance. As one former Gambian health minister said, "How much does it cost you to lose a woman and a baby when an ambulance isn't available [during obstructed labor]?"

In fleet management, the standard measure of cost-effectiveness of a vehicle is the cost-per-kilometer. Under TRM in Gambia, Riders charged $0.182 per

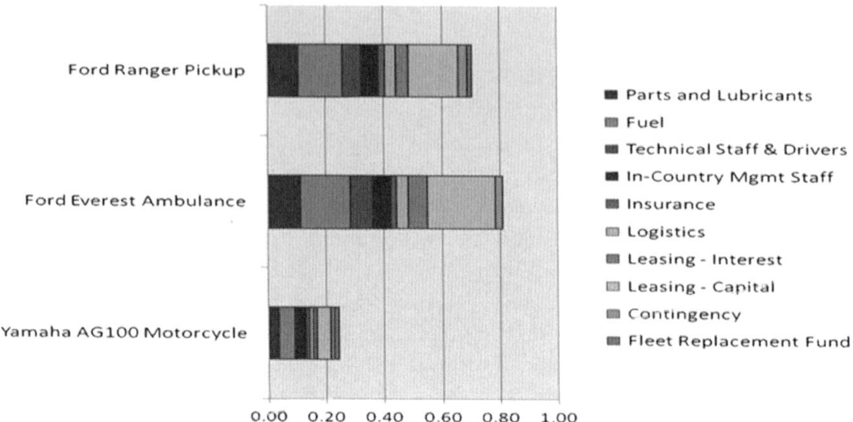

Fig. 13.3 Riders 2009 TAM cpk's in Gambia (in US$) (*Source* Riders for Health 2009)

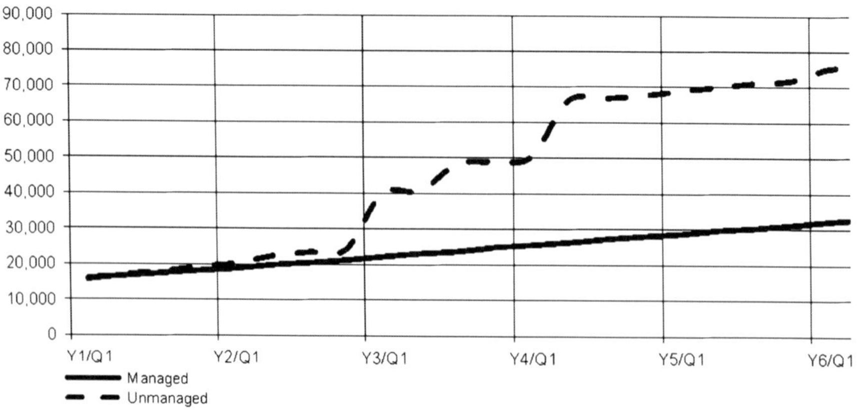

Fig. 13.4 Example–cumulative costs for unmanaged versus managed vehicle for Toyota Land Cruiser (in US$). *Source* Riders for Health (2009)

kilometer for motorcycles, and $0.505 for ambulances. Under TAM, Riders charged $0.241 for motorcycles, $0.807 for ambulances and $0.703 for trekking vehicles (the TAM charges were higher to reflect the principal and interest costs of the loan required to purchase the transport fleet). These cpk charges incorporated infrastructure and setup costs as well. As an indication of the cost-effectiveness of Riders, we can put this into perspective by examining one example in Zambia where an unmanaged motorcycle that cost $3,000 to purchase broke down beyond repair after only 3,000 km. Accounting for fuel and other elements, this motorcycle's cpk was in effect over $1.00 per kilometer, compared to the $0.241 Riders charges for a TAM motorcycle in Gambia. Based on Riders' experience, unmanaged motorcycles last only an average of eight months before having a major breakdown; most unmanaged vehicles last 12–15 months before breaking down.

Some key areas in which Riders could provide value over an unmanaged system include:

- *Reliability*: the goal of Riders is to have zero-breakdown in its motorcycles and vehicles as a result of the rigorous preventive maintenance system.
- *Usage control*: Under TRM and TAM, Riders charges users on a cpk basis and the government typically budgets for a total number of kilometers per month. This enables smooth budgeting. Clients are less likely to use vehicles for non-health related activities (i.e., personal use), because that would reduce the kilometers available in the budget for health activities.
- *Vehicle selection*: Under TAM (and ideally under TRM if Riders is able to influence the government's purchasing decisions), Riders selects appropriate vehicles based on conditions and purpose. For example, Riders may recommend using motorcycles in the place of vehicles if there are fewer health workers that need to use the transport. Also, vehicles and motorcycles suitable for hot, dusty, unpaved roads are selected.
- *Health worker productivity*: As highlighted in the OC&C report, one would expect annual maintenance costs per patient treated to be lower for Riders versus an unmanaged system.
- *Lower costs per kilometer*: Based on feedback from Riders, former Ministry of Health staff and others interviewed in Gambia, unmanaged vehicle fleets have experienced a host of problems. These include premature break-downs and the resulting increase in parts and labor; more accidents due to lack of training; greater transport-replacement costs; and fewer total kilometers driven. These factors, combined with some of the value-drivers mentioned in the bullet points above, suggest that Riders' full cpk would be lower than that of an unmanaged system.

To illustrate the types of costs in health-transport maintenance, the components of Riders' cpk for each of the vehicle types under TAM (ambulance, trekking vehicle and motorcycle) in Gambia are shown in Fig. 13.3.

Figure 13.4 was created by Riders for demonstrative purposes to highlight the cumulative costs of a Toyota Land Cruiser under a managed versus an unmanaged system. Riders conservatively assumed that no breakdowns occur in the unmanaged vehicle for the first two years, and that the vehicle did not altogether break down during the six year period shown in the figure.

13.6 The Diffusion Potential of the Gambian Experience

As Riders works to expand its operations into other African countries, it considers entry strategies best-aligned with government (or other relevant health delivery partners') wishes. For example, if an entity cannot yet commit the will or resources for a full-scale national TRM or TAM program, it may first conduct a pilot project in one region. Or, it may decide to offer a smaller-scale program such as a courier service for medical samples, which involves vehicle management and the employment of drivers/motorcycle riders for specialized blood and sputum sample delivery and collection. In order to obtain a national TAM contract such as the one with Gambia, however, cabinet-level approval of a long-term contract is necessary. Personal connections among Riders staff and government officials played a significant role in obtaining such a contract in Gambia. These types of interconnections are not easily replicable in a larger country. However, there are other elements which could influence governments to consider Riders' services. In this section, we explore the challenges and opportunities involved in expanding TAM.

The first and largest impediment to replicating TAM is likely to be securing the necessary levels of funding for Riders to purchase vehicles and pay for setup and infrastructure costs. Funding a sustainable outsourced leasing model like this requires global health funders to allocate grants to African governments differently. They must agree to pay for Riders' cpk fee instead of donating physical vehicles.

Second, while the Gambia TAM program benefited from Riders' long-standing reputation and track record working with the ministry, in a new territory where Riders has not yet built a working relationship, a larger network of parties must be engaged to encourage a ministry to approve TAM.

Third, a hurdle to both TRM and TAM is that they involve a long-term contract commitment by the government. If a government is highly dependent on a mix of internal revenues and donor funds, creating a long-term agreement for TRM or TAM involves greater perceived risk than requesting one-time vehicle donations and then finding a way to pay for maintenance each year. There is also the attitude toward outsourcing. While governments may outsource some non-core functions such as airport and sea-port management through public-private partnerships, it is not yet common practice to outsource in the health sector in Africa.

Fourth, as is the case with any unmanaged system, those individuals who presently are able to use vehicles for personal purposes in an unregulated manner may not have the incentive to approve a system which puts restrictions on personal use.

Fifth, additional evidence is required on the cost-effectiveness of the Riders system in comparison to unmanaged systems. Riders has made the case to governments that it runs vehicles for the longest possible time at the lowest possible cost. What is clear is that using a cpk mechanism can enable governments to do more transparent budgeting and planning. The Zimbabwean government, for example, approves of the cpk system because of its predictability and the fact that they see vehicles constantly running.

A final challenge to expanding TAM is the organizational shift into fleet management and fleet financing, which will affect the skills needed on staff. Riders is already driving this shift, and bringing in and developing the necessary skills.

Table 13.3 A comparison of best practices in standard versus extreme conditions

	Standard conditions	Extreme conditions
Similar	• Always better to do preventive maintenance before failure • Leverage hub-and-spoke model • Standardize when possible • Utilization of 3PL can be advantageous under the right circumstances	
Different	• Select transportation mode that optimizes flow of materials	• Select transportation vehicle that is well-suited for poor road conditions, and is not expensive to buy or service
	• Implement latest IT advances in order to improve efficiencies	• May not have resources to procure latest IT advances, but introduction of basic system can significantly impact the flow of information
	• Focus on development and implementation of innovative technologies and processes in order to gain a competitive advantage	• Focus on innovative applications of existing (2nd or 3rd generation) technologies and processes; they can have major impact on improvement of material, information, and financial flows
	• Financial flows will be coordinated and negotiated directly between buyers and sellers, or service providers	• Improving financial flows is likely to require the active involvement of diverse stakeholders (donor, NGO, and governmental organizations); this requires careful alignment of incentives

But there are many opportunities. First, once African ministries of health acknowledge that existing vehicle management systems do not consistently deliver strong performance, donor partners could coordinate with each other to advocate to a government the need for TAM. If a contract is secured, then, instead of donating physical vehicles to the government, they would ideally contribute to one pot of funding that could be used to pay the TAM cpk charge to Riders.

Second, governments should examine and understand their existing health transport budgets and actual expenditures more closely. It may be that, as in the case of Gambia, various budgets can be pooled to pay for a TAM system on some scale. When looking at the capital and operating budgets for health transport maintenance, line items might exist for fuel in one place, for spare parts in a second, for vehicles in a third, and for driver salaries in yet another.

Third, the financing mechanism for a new fleet in another country could be modeled on the Gambian example. As the story of GT's involvement becomes more known in the financial community, other African banks may be amenable to participating in such a scheme. As mentioned earlier, an underwriting partner would still be needed to provide a credit guarantee on the loan.

13.7 Logistics Lessons

In standard logistics management, companies must focus on coordinating material, information and financial flows to be successful; the Riders case illustrates that this is also true in extreme conditions. Implementation of an IT system increased Riders' visibility into logistics and tracking, helping them to meet their goal of zero breakdowns. The innovative financing arrangement enabled the financial flows needed to launch their TAM program in Gambia. And, reliance on a self-sustaining business model based on cpk revenues provided a continuous financial flow which has supported the program's long-term sustainability.

To improve these flows, Riders relied on traditional logistics best-practices when they could. When they couldn't, due to extreme conditions (poor transportation network, and lack of financial resources, etc.), Riders developed "new" best practices. Indeed, the Riders case showed that running efficient logistics systems in extreme conditions versus standard environments requires a combination of both common and innovative approaches (see Table 13.3).

First, to ensure a smooth flow of materials, Riders selected a mode of transportation and operating model that was ideally suited for an extreme environment. Due to the poor transportation infrastructure, Riders employed a different mode—motorcycles—to support material flow. In addition, it developed disciplinary measures and operating principles that would minimize the risk of disruptions in material flow. Riders is not the first organization to identify motorcycles as a key means of delivering health care, but it has reaffirmed their usefulness and focused on ways to ensure that vehicles have high reliability. The solution is different, in that it emphasizes the concept of *preventive* maintenance (not just repairs, which take place after a breakdown has occurred) on an outreach basis. Riders' objective is to never let a motorcycle break down, but rather to implement a schedule of maintenance that, if followed, allows the vehicle to always be operable. Part of this involves health workers performing daily vehicle checks to detect and address common problems. Riders relies on the schedule of maintenance work to forecast the demand for replacement parts and to plan the timing of their use. Through preventive maintenance, demand for specific parts is made predictable.

Riders was able to gain leverage through a hub-and-spoke distribution model. That model is based on the idea that certain operational processes can be centralized and therefore done at a larger scale, whereas other processes must remain close to the local needs. In this case, the purchase of motorcycles, the procurement of inventory parts, and the training of health workers and motorcycle mechanics were all centralized. Other processes, such as the actual replacement of parts and oil changes, must be done in the field where the health care workers spend their days. Riders brought the maintenance parts to those personnel in the region, instead of requiring health workers to take their motorcycles to a central office.

Second, by introducing a very simple IT system, Riders was able to successfully manage their information flows. Before Riders began operations in Gambia, data on performance as well as vehicle status and usage were almost non-existent.

Riders started tracking inventory usage and conducting audits of maintenance parts. It created maintenance schedules, and required health workers to complete trip reports. Such data were compiled for two purposes: (1) ensuring that maintenance is done at the correct time, with the right parts being available (the foundation of Riders' value proposition), and (2) enabling accurate calculation of cpk and other payment measures, i.e., these are key performance indicators.

Riders was able to improve their financial flows by implementing an innovative financing arrangement that relied on the careful orchestration of funding from a diverse set of stakeholders. They devised a sophisticated system that enabled the correct payments to go to the right parties at the proper time. To make this work, they had to develop a financial flow process that provided a win–win for all parties.

The unique financing model helped to launch the TAM program, but implementation of a self-sustaining business model has ensured a continuous financial flow. Riders executed a revenue model that recognizes the economic constraints faced by ministries of health. As a social enterprise, Riders is committed to developing a sustainable business model. But many of their best practices apply to corporations operating in a diverse or fragmented market environment. The Riders for Health model thus has general lessons for businesses. Here, we want to share a few.

The model demonstrates the value of standardization. First, standardization facilitates training because complexity is reduced. In the case of Riders, encouraging health ministries to use only a few motorcycle types makes it easier to develop processes for riding instruction and mechanical maintenance. Second, standardization brings economies of scale in the procurement and inventory of replacement parts. Third, standardization allows for better risk management of equipment. This is accomplished in several ways: when a replacement part is required, there is greater stock on hand because all equipment shares the same parts; when maintenance is required on that equipment, there is better availability of trained staff; and if any equipment needs to be swapped out, there is no need for new training by the end user. Southwest Airlines is an example of a company that applies the practice of standardization to its airline fleet.

Riders for Health also demonstrated the benefits of a hub-and-spoke model. These include centralized information, economies of scale, risk pooling at the hub, and decentralized control, responsiveness, and flexibility at the spoke.

Riders acted as a third-party logistics provider, which, if used properly, can add huge value in the supply chain of a service organization. Effectively, Riders can take care of critical logistics that are outside the expertise of the health ministries, permitting the latter to focus on delivering patient care.

Finally, in service supply chains, it is always better to do preventive maintenance before a failure than restoration maintenance after one. The event of a failure is too costly if it entirely shuts down the delivery of service.

The Riders case in Gambia also suggested several interesting research problems linked to performance management, incentive alignment, and integrated operations control. We briefly describe each below.

Performance measurement is important to Riders' long-term sustainability; they must be able to demonstrate their impact and cost-effectiveness, to garner continued support from key partners. The ability to measure the performance of Riders' TAM and TRM models is an important step towards wide adoption of the program. Governments require assurance of Riders' effectiveness, and they certainly need the measurement for budgetary purposes. Donors and aid agencies are increasingly demanding greater transparency of how donated resources are being used, as well as the consequent impact. For Riders and their financial partners, measurements can help to fine-tune the terms and conditions under the TRM or TAM models when they work with health ministries.

It can be a challenge to collect performance data in developing countries. Key data are often missing. For example, before Riders implemented their information system, very limited logistics data existed. Available data were often incomplete or unreliable. Health researchers who focus on emerging economies have noted the lack of quality and comprehensiveness of data from health management information systems (Martinez and Van Wassenhove 2013).

Hence, identifying the key data elements, finding means to collect those data in a cost-efficient manner, and being able to complete the performance measurement with incomplete data, are themselves research issues. The work of Martinez and Van Wassenhove (2011) on vehicle replacement for the International Committee of the Red Cross is a good example of how to develop usable models in the absence of perfect data. Qualitative data collected by the Riders for Health evaluation team suggests that GPS and cell-based technologies and applications can be used to efficiently collect logistics data when information systems are lacking or non-existent. For example, GPS technologies are being used to track information on spatial utilization. These types of technologies can be expensive, but as prices come down they may be viable options on a larger-scale, on-going basis.

Moreover, for a health logistics program like Riders, it is important to develop performance measurement systems that capture both social and business impacts. At least three levels are relevant. First, operational efficiencies of logistics conveyances can be measured. These are the up-time of motorcycles and other managed vehicles, the availabilities of maintenance parts, the duration of downtimes, the useful life of vehicles, fuel efficiencies, costs of repair and maintenance, and inventory of spare parts. Second, we may then examine the operational effectiveness of health care workers as a result of the improved efficiencies of those conveyances. Examples include the number of patients visited, total trips made to remote villages, the number of health interventions (e.g. literature distribution, vaccines or medicines) administered, and the reduced idle time of health workers due to vehicle unavailability. Finally, one can report the impact on health indicators that are closely linked to key health outcomes such as antenatal, tuberculosis DOTS (directly observed treatments), and immunization coverage. This final level can be measured, but its relationship to Riders' program is probably quite indirect: so many other external factors could affect the health outcome of a region. But the design of such a three-level performance measurement system would be an interesting area of research.

The Gambia TAM case clearly shows how the structure of an incentive system influenced behavior. For example, Riders, together with the Skoll Foundation, GT and the MoH had worked intensively to come up with the financial arrangements to implement TAM. The implementation was a success, but was that scheme the ideal one that would be optimal for the whole health system? Was that a scheme that would give the best incentives to *every* party to act in the best interest of the country? In fact, TRM and TAM also give rise to different incentives and behaviors to stakeholders, due to the structure of the payment terms.

Incentive alignment can be a worthwhile avenue of research. As Martinez and Van Wassenhove (2013) demonstrated, incentives may drive some key operational decisions in the management of vehicles in humanitarian logistics; organizations might have to re-align incentive systems to achieve operational improvements. Incentive alignment is beginning to receive interest among operations management researchers, as illustrated in the recent work of Chen (2013), who examined the incentives of Indian farmers in production decisions.

At an operational level, as health workers are armed with a much higher fleet availability, they could have more degrees of freedom to map out their routes and destinations (villages to visit). If the objective is to maximize the number of patients visited, a health worker may select more often those villages nearest to the health center where that worker is based. This could create an inequitable situation in which the most remote villages are not visited, and their needs are not met. Patients in far-flung regions have probably the greatest and gravest needs. Designing an operational schedule that would capture the *equitable* treatment of patients in different areas could be another avenue of research.

Logistics can be the foundation in a business environment, but many other factors are crucial to overall success. In the case of health delivery, logistics is a necessary element, but by no means sufficient. Additional bottlenecks to health delivery in Gambia include an inadequate number of health workers and the occasional lack of supply of drugs. To tackle the complete health care provision problem, all other pieces are necessary.

Integrating the provision of transportation conveyance for the last mile, together with operational controls such as distribution and inventory planning, could be another fruitful area of research. For example, Gallien (2010) addressed the problem of inventory for the resupply and distribution of medicine in Zambia.

Since motorized vehicles in general are not as common in remote areas in Africa, the market for maintenance services in those areas is underdeveloped. Similar to how remotely-located patients are often underserved, remotely-located vehicles are underserved with regard to maintenance. Vehicles play a key role in connecting people within and beyond their communities, and their importance is even greater in remote settings. Is there a potential to replicate the Riders' outreach maintenance model to other services in far-flung areas? Such outreach services may include mobile HIV counseling and testing vans, mobile science labs and mobile libraries. These could make a great impact by bringing services to the point of need. Similarly, can outreach maintenance improve vehicle up-time and utilization in other domains? Determining the diffusion potential of an outreach preventive maintenance model could be another area of research. One can imagine such a model being beneficial for rural school-bus services, local public transportation, and other cases which involve transportation based within remote regions.

On a related note, research could be conducted to determine the potential of mobile applications in general to improve preventive maintenance of remote vehicles. For example, remote motorcycle riders and vehicle drivers might be connected to a central repair hub that would provide focused guidance on preventive maintenance on a regular basis via SMS text messages or other mobile applications.

13.8 Conclusions

Although the extreme environments of many underdeveloped nations are harsh and punishing, logistics innovations like Riders for Health can make a significant difference. The Riders case teaches a few important lessons about achieving logistics excellence in extreme environments.

Utilizing standard best practices can improve logistics efficiencies in extreme conditions. Like many corporations in advanced economies, Riders benefited from standardization and a reliance on a hub-and-spoke model. And, their emphasis on a preventive program showed that it is always better to conduct this maintenance *before* a failure occurs.

Poor transport networks and lack of economic resources mean it is not always possible to apply standard best practices; it will also be important to develop a "new" set of best practices to coordinate material, information, and financial flows. The Riders case points to a few innovative practices that show promise:

- Use advanced technologies and solutions when you can, but do not overlook the power of simple solutions. In extreme conditions, organizations are often starting from square one. Introduction of simple solutions, e.g. a basic IT system or transport mode, can have enormous impact.
- Consider a *longer-term* approach in order to develop sustainable logistics operations. Because material, information, and financial flows are often poorly coordinated and inefficient in extreme conditions, the only way to quickly improve these flows is for an outside organization to provide a basic IT system and financial resources. But, this outsourcing approach can put the long-term sustainability of logistics operations at risk if that partner does not develop the local infrastructure. For example, the outside firm may not provide a continuous financial flow (self-sustaining revenue model). Or, the transportation mode used to improve material flows may be too expensive to maintain, once that outside partner pulls out. Development of local infrastructure can take a few years because it often requires creating partnerships between diverse organizations, building the logistics skills and knowledge of local workers, and potentially

enhancing a market for a product or service. A longer-term approach may mean giving up some speed in the early phases of developing operations, to create a more efficient and lasting logistics system.
- Form substantive partnerships with a diverse set of stakeholders (NGOs, governmental, and donor organizations) to improve financial flows and ensure long-term viability. This requires careful alignment of incentives, providing a "win" for each stakeholder. The more diverse the stakeholders, and hence the goals and objectives, the harder this is to achieve.

To provide a new set of best practices, it is critical to know which approaches are effective; this will require utilization of a robust performance measurement system. That is difficult since data are often unreliable and/or unavailable.

As part of our work with Riders, we are testing different approaches to performance measurement in extreme conditions. We wish to develop a more comprehensive performance measurement system that assesses social and business impacts. As noted previously, Riders' overall impact will be measured by three interrelated levels of performance: logistics efficiencies, health worker productivity, and health intervention coverage. Because logistics data are difficult to obtain, we have to streamline the set of indicators to create a core set of logistics data elements that are relatively easy to capture (and still provide the information we need). This requires balancing the demands of data collection and research priorities; most researchers working in this area will likely have to do so. In addition to identifying key logistics data elements, we have begun experimenting with GPS and cell-based tools for data collection that can be used to automatically capture important logistics and health data such as kilometers driven and health-visits made to remote areas.

What Riders has been able to achieve can thus serve as a lesson for *business* logistics operations in emerging economies.

References

Altay N, Green WG (2006) OR/MS research in disaster operations management. Eur J Oper Res 175(1):475–493

Balcik B, Beamon BM, Krejci CC, Muramatsu KM, Ramirez M (2010) Coordination in humanitarian relief chains: practices, challenges and opportunities. Int J Prod Econ 126:22–34

Chen YJ (2013) Training, production, and channel separation in ITC's e-Choupal network. Production and Operations Management (To appear). doi:10.1111/j.1937-5956.2011.01317.x

Duran S, Eugun O, Keskinocak P, Swann JL (2013) Humanitarian logistics: advanced purchasing and pre-positioning of relief items. In: Bookbinder JH (ed) Global logistics, Springer

Europa Publications (2000) Africa South of the Sahara 2001, London

Gallien J (2010) Improving the public distribution of essential medicines in Sub-Saharan Africa: the case of Zambia. In: 2nd innovations in operations conference, London Business School, London

Human Development Reports (2009) http://hdr.undp.org/en/statistics. Accessed 9 July 2009

LaFraniere S (2007) New AIDS cases in Africa outpace treatment gains. The New York Times, 6 June 2007

Martinez AP, Van Wassenhove L (2013) Vehicle replacement in the international committee of the red cross. Production and Operations Management (To appear)
OC&C (2005) OC&C due diligence report on riders' operations in Africa. Available at http://www.riders.org/downloads/OC&C%20report.pdf
Rammohan S (2010) Riders for health—a fleet leasing model in the Gambia. Stanford Global Supply Chain Management Forum Case Study
Rawls CG, Turnquist MA (2010) Pre-positioning of emergency supplies for disaster response. Trans Res Part B 44:521–534
Salmeron J, Apte A (2010) Stochastic optimization for natural disaster asset prepositioning. Prod Oper Manage 19(5):561–574
Sonko A (2009) Officer in charge at Birkam health center. Gambia, Personal Interview, 12 June 2009
Tayan B (2007) Riders for health: health care distribution solutions in Sub-Saharan Africa. Stanford Graduate School of Business Case, GS-58
Thomas A, Fritz L (2006) Disaster Relief, Inc. Harvard Business Review, Nov 2006
Thomas A, Kopczak LR (2007) Life-saving supply chains—challenges and the path forward, chapter 4. In: Lee HL, Lee CY (eds) Building supply chain excellence in emerging economies. Springer Science, New York
Tomasini R, Van Wassenhove L (2009) Humanitarian logistics. INSEAD Business Press
United Nations (2006) Population division of the Department of Economic and Social Affairs of the United Nations Secretariat. World Population Prospects, The 2006 Revision
The World Bank (2006) Africa development indicators. Washington, DC
UNAIDS (2007) Report on the global AIDS epidemic 2006. http://www.unaids.org/en/HIV_data/2006GlobalReport/default.asp. Accessed 14 June 2007
Van Wassenhove L (2006) Humanitarian aid logistics: supply chain in high gears. J Oper Res Soc 57:475–489
World Health Organization (2010) World health statistics 2010 (part II). http://www.who.int/whosis/whostat/EN_WHS10_Part2.pdf

Part V
Transportation Modes and Their (Land) Interfaces

Chapter 14
Comparative Analysis of Air Freight Networks in Regional Markets Around the Globe

Aisling Reynolds-Feighan

Abstract This chapter examines the Asian, European, North American and Middle East air freight networks of combination passenger and freight and all-freight carriers using air freight capacity datasets for the period 1999–2009. The chapter begins by reviewing some of the key trends that have shaped and characterized air freight markets during the 1990 and 2000s. The impact of air transport market liberalization is identified as a key determinant of changing carrier behavior, particularly in relation to network structure organization. The second major section of the chapter examines the sources of data available for tracking trends in the air freight sector. The lack of comprehensive datasets detailing the activities of the integrated carriers is discussed. Using the Official Airline Guide (OAG) historical databases that list ex-post carrier schedules for each year globally, annual data series indicating freight capacity of all Asian, European and North American and selected Middle Eastern carriers are determined and the general trends are described. The US T-100 Database is used to derive an equivalent distribution for the two largest integrated carriers, FedEx and UPS. The changing nature of industry organization is discussed and the key players in each region are distinguished. For the combination carriers, passenger and freight network structures are compared for the period 1999–2009. The fortunes of the key air freight hubs are reviewed over the same period. The chapter

Funding for this research was provided by the UCD School of Economics and Irish Research Council for the Humanities and Social Sciences (IRCHSS). Thanks to Dr Kieran Feighan for very helpful and insightful comments on earlier versions of this chapter.

A. Reynolds-Feighan (✉)
UCD School of Economics, University College Dublin, Belfield, Dublin 4, Ireland
e-mail: aisling.reynolds@ucd.ie

J. H. Bookbinder (ed.), *Handbook of Global Logistics*, International Series in Operations Research & Management Science 181, DOI: 10.1007/978-1-4419-6132-7_14,

concludes with a discussion about the key driving factors in dictating the future direction of the industry in the coming decade. Consolidation in the airline industry and the role of the integrated carriers receive particular consideration.

14.1 Introduction

This chapter examines the Asian, European and North American air freight networks of combination passenger and freight and all freight carriers using cargo capacity datasets for the period 1999–2009. The air freight industry has received much less attention in the academic literature than the air passenger industry, though it accounted for close to 30 % of global scheduled airline output (by weight) in 2007 (Doganis 2010). The air freight sector is a key component in modern logistical and supply chains at regional, national and global scales, and facilitates the mobility of resources and goods and enhances time-critical access to urban and regional markets. The industry has grown rapidly, particularly in liberalized markets. The air freight sector has evolved in the last decade into a sophisticated set of transport and logistical service offerings at a variety of spatial scales, but increasingly focused on long haul intercontinental time-critical and secure services. These characteristics meet the needs of industries that produce high value-to-volume commodities, and regions with relatively high income levels. Air freight contributes significantly to the 'bottom-line' for most passenger carriers, with the exception of the low-cost carriers.

Research on air freight has focused on analyzing the rapid evolution of this transport sector, particularly in relation to the express or integrated carriers that emerged in the US following air cargo deregulation in 1977 (Reynolds-Feighan 1994, 2001a; Corsi and Boyson 2001; Chiavi 2005). While these carriers developed new markets and products, combination passenger and cargo carriers or more traditional 'heavy freight' carriers make up the majority of operators in the international air transport market. The changing network structures of these carriers is giving rise to shifts in the patterns of trade and economic activity, particularly in the high value and new technology product markets. Gaps in networks, or patterns of redundancy and excess capacity, impact significantly on regional economies by enhancing or reducing accessibility and the mobility of people, resources and goods. Understanding the nature of air carriers' decision making in relation to the structure and organization of their networks helps to explain these patterns of accessibility and mobility. That understanding also helps inform public policy where key regulatory or legislative changes give rise to shifts in the nature and structure of air carrier networks.

In this chapter, the focus is on air carrier freight network structures, and how these may be measured and compared. Significant liberalization of air transport markets has taken place in the last two decades, facilitating new opportunities for airlines to expand, enhance and restructure their networks in international settings. The next section provides an overview of the air freight industry and describes the key players and market characteristics. The important role of carrier networks is highlighted and measures of network structure are presented. Section 14.3 describes the global air freight industry and highlights current trends and characteristics and their recent evolution. The main sources of detailed air freight data are briefly reviewed. In Sect. 14.4, the Asian, European and North American markets are examined in detail. The top 10 carriers operating in these markets are identified, and their network structures are examined closely using a variety of techniques and measures. In the final section, some conclusions and recommendations arising from the chapter are set out.

14.2 Overview of the Air Freight Industry

The transportation system is a key component in the operation and functioning of modern economies. The air transport system has evolved rapidly in the last century to become a critical component in the global flows of people, goods and services. The demand for air freight is derived from a demand for resources, intermediate and final goods and services. Transportation services are consumed as they are produced, and thus are subject to substantial fluctuations as demand varies by location and time. The unit of supply is typically greater than the unit of demand. This has important implications for cost allocation and therefore pricing of transport services.

For most airlines, passenger and freight services are combined and jointly produced. Passenger travel requirements tend to favor direct daytime service with relatively small variations in total space requirements (passengers and their baggage). Passengers tend to travel in roundtrips so that outbound and inbound capacities converge over time. Shipper requirements for freight favor night time services, where routing is less important and travel is in one direction. For combination carriers, the differing requirements have important implications for the allocation of shared costs and optimal pricing of air freight services. Air freight services are high cost, relative to surface transport alternatives. While shippers may have preferences for the speed and lower risk characteristics associated with air transport in the short run, market shares enjoyed by the air transport sector are constantly under pressure from substitution of cheaper surface alternatives. With increasing requirements for safety and security of air freight, particularly when it is carried on passenger aircraft, the extra time imposed erodes the advantages of this mode of transport.

The process of physical distribution of freight has evolved into a highly sophisticated operation, with increasing reliance being placed on the use of new technology to assist in the movement, storage and tracking of consignments. Transport is but one component in this logistics chain. Figure 14.1 illustrates the

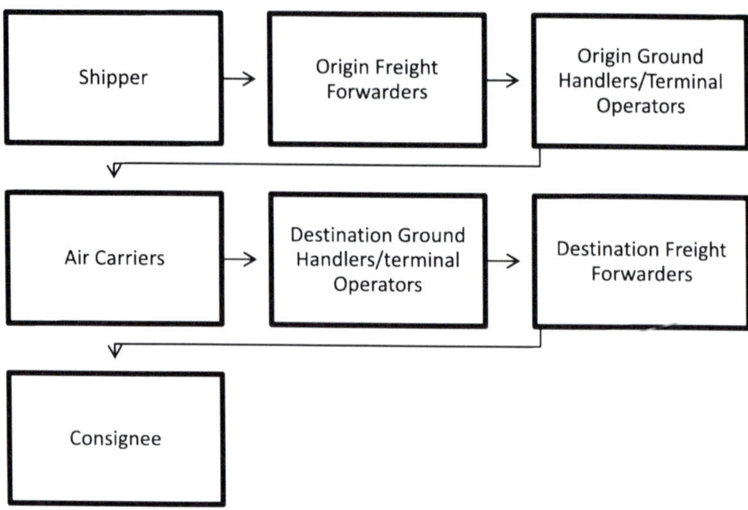

Fig. 14.1 Key players in the movement of air freight consignments

flow of freight from shipper to consignee, and highlights the key players involved in the process.

14.2.1 Air Freight Carriers

The air freight providers are a heterogeneous group of operators, offering different types of services and different levels of logistical expertize. There are three main categories of air freight carriers: these are line haul operators, express (or integrated) carriers, and niche (or specialist) carriers.

1. *Line Haul operators* move cargo from airport to airport and rely on freight forwarders or consolidators to deal directly with customers. Line haul operators can be

    a. *all-cargo operators* (scheduled and non-scheduled/charter), moving only freight in dedicated freighter/cargo aircraft [for example Cargolux (EU) and Polar Air Cargo (USA)]. All-cargo operators offer relatively high reliability and have the capability to move large volumes over long distances. Some all-cargo operators provide ACMI (aircraft, crew, maintenance and insurance) or 'wet lease' services to airlines, whereby scheduled or charter air freight operations may be expanded or developed quickly in response to changing market demand, while not bearing the costs and risks of sourcing new equipment and crews. Atlas Air and Southern Air Cargo are two such ACMI operators.

b. *combination passenger and cargo operators* who use both dedicated freighter aircraft and the belly-holds in passenger aircraft to move freight [for example Lufthansa (EU) and BA (EU)]. For the combination carriers, the cargo operations are mainly long haul, with a significant amount of freight being interlined onto shorter-haul feeder services or 'air trucked'[1] to final destinations. The high utilization of long haul aircraft justifies the purchase of new aircraft for these services.
c. *passenger operators* who use the belly-holds in passenger aircraft. Passenger carriers have tended to view cargo as a by-product of passenger operations. Freight forwarders or Indirect Air Carriers[2] play an important role in consolidating shipments for line haulers. Passenger traffic growth in the domestic North American and internal European markets has been driven by low cost carriers (LCCs) in the last two decades: the LCCs generally do not offer air freight services other than mail.[3]

2. *Integrated/Courier/Express/Parcel operators* move consignments from door-to-door, with time-definite delivery services (examples: UPS, Federal Express, TNT, DHL). Sage (2001) sets out key distinctions and operating characteristics of the different types of services and refers to them collectively as CEP[4] services. In the last decade, many of these operators have expanded the range and scale of their services offerings to cover a broader variety of size, speed and distance coverage. CEP operators operate multimodal networks, combining air services with extensive surface transport to meet customer demands. These CEP operators offer a variety of products to shippers and supplement air services with extensive ground transport to provide time-definite delivery with continuous shipment tracking and, if necessary, logistical expertize to support *Just-In-Time* (JIT) inventory control strategies. In order for CEP operators to be able to offer door-to-door next-day deliveries, they require night-time operations. Accordingly, they need to operate quiet, reliable aircraft with relatively low utilization levels. CEP operators seek to purchase a combination of new aircraft, with high capital costs and better utilization on long haul segments, with less expensive renovated second-hand aircraft for the medium haul operations with lower utilizations.
3. *Niche operators* operate or leverage specialized equipment or indeed expertise in order to fill extraordinary requirements [for example Heavylift Cargo Airlines

[1] "Air trucking" involves the surface transport of freight between airport bonded facilities under airway bill. Air trucking can supplement, complement or replace short haul air freight operations.

[2] "...."Indirect air carrier'' is defined as any person or entity within the United States not in possession of an FAA air carrier operating certificate, that undertakes to engage indirectly in air transportation of property, and uses for all or any part of such transportation the services of a passenger air carrier. This does not include the United States Postal Service (USPS) or its representative while acting on the behalf of the USPS." (US Code 49 CFR Part 1540).

[3] Southwest Airline (US), Ryanair (Europe), Easyjet (Europe) do not offer air freight services.

[4] Courier, express and parcel services.

(Australia) and Air Partner (UK)]. These operators attract business through their capabilities for handling outside freight or special consignments, including line haul to locations with poor infrastructural facilities. These carriers have greater flexibility with respect to choice of airports, hours of operation, load factors, and similar operational characteristics.

14.2.2 Sale of Air Freight Services

Air freight services are sold and marketed in a number of different ways. The line haul operators sell a relatively small proportion of their cargo space directly to their customers. The greater proportion of their space is sold through general sales agents (GSAs) or freight forwarders, who negotiate with the airlines for fixed amounts of space. The agents or forwarders then resell the freight space to customers. As with passenger fares, discounting is widely applied and in the case of cargo, rates will be determined on the basis of a number of characteristics and circumstances, including the following:

- Commodity type
- Volume, density and weight
- Routing
- Season
- Regularity of shipments
- Imports or exports
- Priority or speed of delivery.

Consolidated shipments aggregated by forwarders and carried by the line haul operators typically travel under a single air waybill. Integrated operators offer a variety of products or services depending on (a) the weight of the consignment and (b) the speed of delivery required by the customer. Discounting is applied to these services on the basis of the volume and regularity of business. However, because each consignment is treated as a separate piece of freight, with an individual air waybill and customs declaration, the integrated carriers provide and practice electronic tracking of individual shipments.

Because of the relatively high cost of air freight services, commodities shipped by air tend to be high value, low-volume goods. The safety and security of commodities in shipment is a key concern among operators, with information technology being used to track and trace goods shipped in real time. The disastrous events of September 11th 2001 in the US had a very significant effect on the air transport industry, and have resulted in new procedures and processes to ensure the security and safety of freight transported by air, particularly when carried on passenger aircraft.[5] In 2010, new concerns about the safety of air freight containers[6] resulted in increased screening and documentation of consignments to be carried by air. These security processes introduce delays in the total time between pickup and drop off of cargo, and increase the generalized costs of shippers associated with air transport. In 2010, the US Transportation Security Administration succeeded in moving to screening 100 % of air freight carried on passenger aircraft.

14.2.3 Carriage of Air Freight

Carriage of air cargo has become increasingly standardized with the vast majority of scheduled air freight now being carried on Unit Load Devices (ULDs). ULDs are of two main varieties, namely containers and pallets. IATA (2010) sets out the technical specification for the design, construction, management and handling of ULDs in its *ULD Technical Manual* (IATA 2010).

The dimensions of the container Unit Load Devices depend on the type of aircraft flown and are closed aluminum devices. Their size and shape depend on whether they are loaded on lower or upper aircraft decks and whether they are designed for narrow or wide-bodied jet aircraft. Some container ULDs may be refrigerated. Smaller containers limit the nature of the freight that may be transported.

The pallets are generally sheets of aluminum with hooks that are locked into cargo nets. As with containers, pallet size and shape will vary depending on the aircraft operated by the carrier. Pallets can facilitate the air carriage of larger loads.

The advantages of ULDs are in

1. standardizing equipment for handling and loading of air cargo loads
2. reducing the probability of accidents and damage to personnel, cargo and aircraft, and the associated costs
3. improved safety and security of cargo and aircraft in the carriage of freight. Standardized materials and design specifications maximize utilization of available air freight space on aircraft
4. improved efficiency in the handling and tracking of air freight consignments, due to reduced total aircraft loading times and real time tracking of ULD contents.

---

[5] In 2007, the US Congress passed the implementing recommendations of the 9/11 *Commission Act* (more commonly known as the 9/11 Act), which requires that all cargo transported on a passenger aircraft be screened for explosives as of August 1, 2010.

[6] Goods shipped on an all-cargo flight into the US in October 2010 were packed with explosives: see "Earlier Flight May Have Been Dry Run for Plotters", New York Times, November 1st 2010.

14.2.4 The Importance of Carrier Networks

Network structure is a critical aspect of firm behavior for transportation service providers. The network represents the carrier's production plan and also the carrier's product offerings. Air carrier network activity can be measured by computing aspects of traffic or capacity distribution across the carrier's system of airports. Different measures of network structure emphasize aspects of concentration, dominance, connectivity, circuitry, duplication and centrality. By computing and assessing multiple measures, some important distinctions and conclusions on the nature of accessibility to markets and mobility of goods and resources may be discerned. The share of traffic at a carrier's top 1, 2 and 3 busiest airports can also provide a very useful guide to the number of hubs or focus cities in the network.

The summary traffic measure used in this paper is the Gini Index (Gastwirth 1972). This measure will be used to capture different aspects of a carrier's traffic distribution across its system of airports. The Gini Index may be computed for a continuous variable, x, as

$$G = \frac{2 \quad Cov(x, r_x)}{n\,\overline{x}} \tag{14.1}$$

where n is the number of individual airports in a carrier's network, $\overline{x}$ is the mean of x, $cov(x,r_x)$ is the covariance between the air traffic distribution, x, and the ranks of airports according to their traffic shares (r_x) from the smallest ($r_x = 1$) to the biggest ($r_x = n$).

The Gini Index compares the traffic distribution across the full distribution; it is computed by equally weighting each airport in a carrier's system and compares the actual traffic distribution across the airports with the distribution if each airport had an equal share of the traffic (G = 0). The Gini Index is useful in characterizing multiple hub and spoke networks, where a small number of airports have large numbers of routes (freight tons available, seats or movements), and most other airports have small numbers of links (or just single links to one of the main hubs) or relatively small shares of aircraft movements or seating or freight capacity. Figure 14.2 provides a rough guide to interpreting Gini Index scores computed for airline or airport traffic measures. The Gini Index has been applied widely to measurement of air passenger traffic activity (see Reynolds-Feighan 2001b, 2007; Burghouwt 2007; Huber 2009), and to air freight traffic distributions in the US (Reynolds-Feighan 1994). It will be applied in the next section in order to distinguish different network structures among groups of carriers in the major global air freight markets.

Graph Theory/Social Network Analysis provides measures of the basic structure of a network in terms of (1) number of nodes and links (2) the 'connectedness' of the network (how easy it is to travel between any pair of nodes) (3) the centrality of nodes in the network relative to other nodes (4) the extent of concentration/dispersion in the distribution of links among nodes. Rather than present

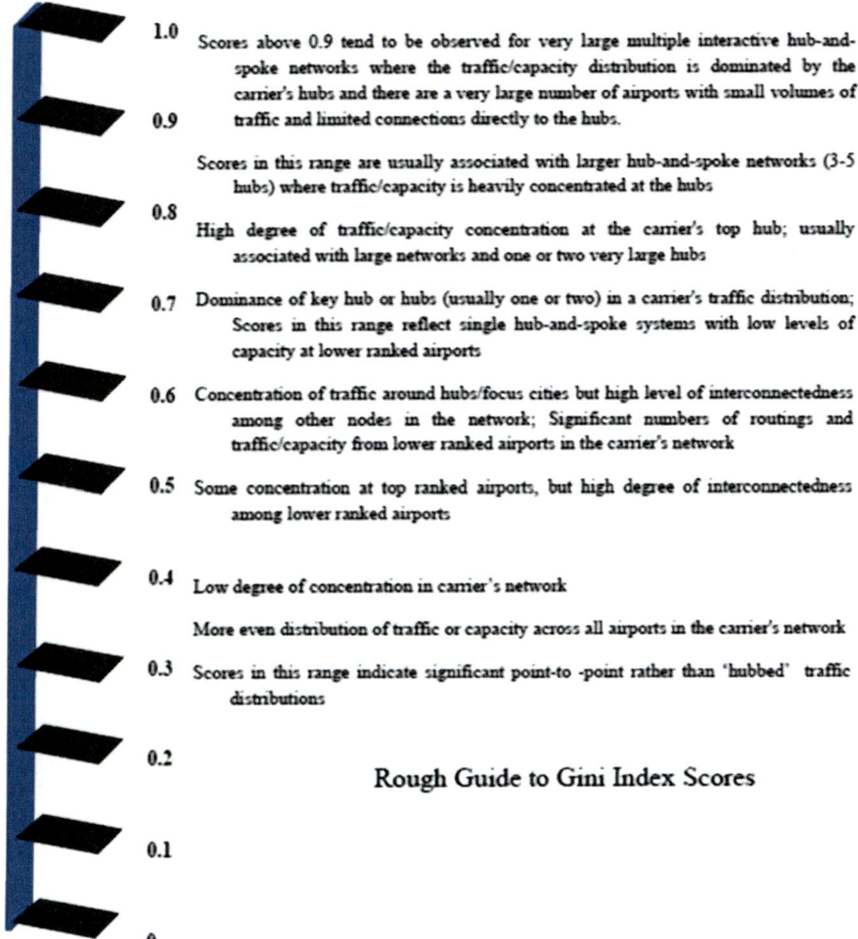

Fig. 14.2 Rough guide to Gini Index scores

these summary measurements in tables, visual displays of linkages within carrier networks will be used in conjunction with the Gini Index described above. The NetDraw[7] software associated with the social network measurement tool UCINET is used to generate stylized graphs of air carrier network linkage structures.

[7] NetDraw is a free program written by Steve Borgatti for visualizing social network data (available at http://www.analytictech.com/netdraw/netdraw.htm).

14.3 Recent Trends in Air Freight

Air freight traffic has grown steadily in the last two decades with average annual growth rates of 5–6 % (IATA 2010). Global freight traffic declined significantly in 2008–2009 due to the impacts of the financial crises in North America and Europe, with some recovery during 2010. Forecasts from ICAO, IATA and Boeing project growth over the next decade: the correlation between world GDP and world air freight traffic forms the basis for forecasts (see Chiavi 2005; MergeGlobal 2009; Boeing 2010 for discussion of this relationship). Accordingly, the growth is expected to be greatest in Asian markets (i.e. intra-Asia, North America–Asia and Europe–Asia and Australasia), with international air cargo traffic continuing to expand faster than domestic air cargo traffic.

Table 14.1 shows the total volume of passenger and air freight activity in 2009, as well as the regional distribution of global scheduled air freight, using IATA defined regions. The North American and European airlines each account for roughly one quarter of total global air freight ton-kilometers, while the Asia–Pacific carriers account for over one-third, at 36 % of the total. The Middle East share has grown to just under 9 % in 2009. Figures 14.3 and 14.4 show the share of air freight and mail carried in the last decade from 1999 to 2009, and the evolution of the regional shares reported in Table 14.1. The share of air mail has fallen from 4.7 to 3.9 % of total global revenue ton-kilometers in the last decade. The US share of total air freight traffic has fallen steadily over the same period. The European share showed a more consistent trend during the 2000s, but fell significantly in 2008–2009. The Asia–Pacific and Middle East carriers showed significant and consistent growth during the decade. The main industry forecasts suggest that these regions will continue to drive expansion in total global air freight activity in the coming decade (Boeing 2010; IATA 2010; ICAO 2010).

In global terms, the dominant air cargo flows are in three main markets, namely (1) the North Atlantic (i.e. North America–Europe), (2) Europe–Asia and (3) North America–Asia (the Pacific Rim). Flows between North and South America, and flows from the Middle East to both Europe and Asia have grown in significance in the later part of the last decade (MergeGlobal 2009). Air freight markets are shifting, as the economic growth patterns of emerging developing countries accelerates past that of industrialized economies.

The main influences or drivers behind these trends are (Reynolds-Feighan 2001a; Boeing 2010):

1. World economic activity (world GDP is the best single measure of global economic activity, with a high correlation between changes in world GDP and changes in world air cargo RTKs).
2. Impact of the range of services in the express and small package market.
3. Inventory management techniques.

Table 14.1 Regional distribution of global scheduled air traffic, 2009

	Aircraft kilometers Millions	Aircraft departures Millions	Passengers carried Millions	Passenger-kilometers performed Millions	Passenger load factor (%)	Ton-kilometers performed		Ton-kilometers available Millions	Weight load factor (%)
						Freight Millions	Total Millions		
Total volumes	33,678	25.85	2,277	4,244,538	76	140,613	531,258	850,883	62
Regional shares of total (international and domestic) services of airlines of ICAO member states (%)									
Europe	26.6	27.8	28	28.1	76	24.4	27	25.5	66
Africa	2.7	2.3	2.1	2.3	66	1.4	2.1	2.5	53
Middle East	4.9	2.9	4.1	6.7	73	8.8	7.4	7.8	59
Asia and Pacific	23.5	21.8	27.5	27.1	74	36.1	29.4	28.7	64
North America	36.8	38.2	32.1	31.4	81	25.9	30	30.8	61
Latin America and Caribbean	5.5	7	6.2	4.5	68	3.5	4	4.6	55

Source ICAO *Annual Report to Council*, 2010
Region ICAO statistical region of airline registration

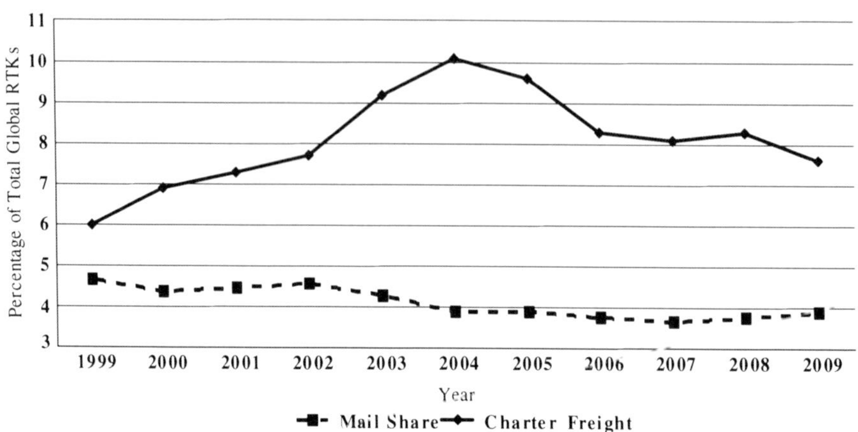

Fig. 14.3 Breakdown of global air freight revenue ton-kilometers by category. *Source* Boeing *World Air cargo Forecast* 2010–2011

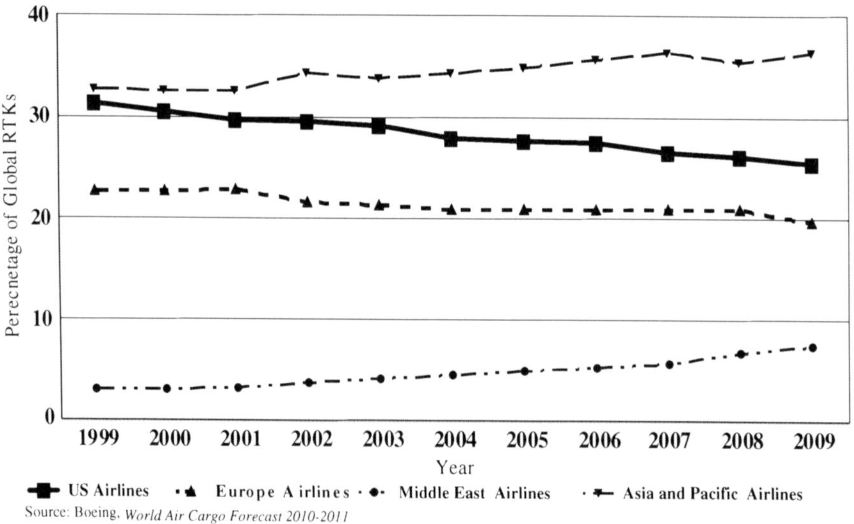

Fig. 14.4 Regional shares of global air freight revenue ton-kilometers, 1999–2009. *Source* Boeing, *World Air Cargo Forecast* 2010–2011

4. Deregulation and liberalization.
5. National development programs.
6. Stream of new air-eligible commodities.

Table 14.2 IATA top 30 cargo carriers in 2009

Rank in 2009	IATA carrier code	Carrier region	Carrier name	Carrier type	Scheduled air freight tons carried ('000)		
					Total	Domestic	International
1	FX	US	Federal express	Express	6912	5021	1891
2	5X	US	UPS	Express	4948	3345	1603
3	KE	AS	Korean air	Pax/cargo	1616	178	1438
4	UA	US	United airlines	Pax/cargo	1494	237	1257
5	EK	ME	Emirates	Pax/cargo	1382	0	1382
6	CX	AS	Cathay pacific airways	Pax/cargo	1339	0	1339
7	SQ	AS	Singapore airlines	Pax/cargo	1274	0	1274
8	LH	EU	Lufthansa	Pax/cargo	1188	31	1157
9	JL	AS	Japan airlines	Pax/cargo	1177	498	679
10	CI	AS	China airways	Pax/cargo	1080	0	1080
11	CA	AS	Air china	Pax/cargo	896	467	429
12	MU	AS	China eastern airlines	Pax/cargo	865	444	421
13	7CV	EU	Cargolux	All-cargo	794	0	794
14	CZ	AS	China southern airlines	Pax/cargo	793	688	105
15	AF	EU	Air france	Pax/cargo	792	6	786
16	NH	AS	All nippon airways	Pax/cargo	764	435	329
17	QY	EU	EAT—European air transport	All-cargo	733	0	733
18	OZ	AS	Asiana airways	Pax/cargo	717	45	672
19	BA	EU	British airways	Pax/cargo	709	0	709
20	BR	AS	EVA air	All-cargo	681	0	681
21	KL	EU	KLM	Pax/cargo	604	0	604
22	TG	AS	Thai airways	Pax/cargo	584	48	536
23	LA	LA	LAN airlines	Pax/cargo	524	21	503
24	MH	AS	Malaysia airlines	Pax/cargo	500	32	468
25	NW	US	Northwest airlines	Pax/cargo	499	154	345

(continued)

Table 14.2 (continued)

Rank in 2009	IATA carrier code	Carrier region	Carrier name	Carrier type	Scheduled air freight tons carried ('000)		
					Total	Domestic	International
26	AA	US	American airlines	Pax/cargo	465	129	336
27	QR	ME	Qatar airways	Pax/cargo	402	0	402
28	QF	SW	Qantas airways	Pax/cargo	386	136	250
29	CK	AS	China cargo airlines	All-cargo	373	66	307
30	SV	ME	Saudi Arabian airlines	Pax/cargo	339	58	281
31	EY	ME	Etihad airways	Pax/cargo	309	0	309
32	DL	US	Delta airlines	Pax/cargo	303	120	183

Source Air Cargo World (2009) "IATA's top 50 cargo carriers", *Air Cargo World*, p 24–30, September 2009

Table 14.3 Top 5 air freight and passenger airports for top 10 European freight carriers, 2009

Carrier code	Carrier name (total number of nodes)	Top 5 freight airports							Top 5 passenger airports			
		Airport code	Airport name	IATA region	Number of routes with freight service	Total number of routes (Pax and freight)	Share of total freight capacity	Cumulative % at top 5 airports	Airport code	Airport name	Share of seating capacity	Cumulative % at top 5 airports
7CV	Cargolux airlines International (70)	LUX	Luxembourg	EU1	57	57	26.7	47.1				
		GYD	Baku Heydar Aliyev International airport	EU2	16	16	9.6					
		HKG	Hong Kong International airport	AS4	12	12	5.5					
		JFK	New York J F Kennedy International airport	NA1	5	5	2.8					
		BKK	Bangkok Suvarnabhumi International airport	AS3	5	5	2.5					
AF	Air France (196)	CDG	Paris Charles de Gaulle airport	EU1	150	216	39.1	51.0	CDG	Paris Charles de Gaulle airport	31.2	51.8
		ORD	Chicago O'Hare International airport	NA1	7	7	4.1		ORY	Paris Orly airport	11.1	
		MEX	Mexico City Juarez International airport	LA2	4	4	3.1		LYS	Lyon St-exupery airport	3.7	
		RUN	St Denis de la Reunion	AF4	4	4	2.8		TLS	Toulouse Blagnac airport	3.2	
		DXB	Dubai	ME1	5	5	1.8		NCE	Nice	2.7	
BA	British Airways (191)	LHR	London Heathrow airport	EU1	136	137	28.4	44.6	LHR	London Heathrow airport	36.3	50.3
		STN	London Stansted airport	EU1	16	16	6.4		LGW	London Gatwick airport	8.0	
		HKG	Hong Kong International airport	AS4	10	10	3.9		JNB	Johannesburg O.r. Tambo International airport	2.7	
		LGW	London Gatwick airport	EU1	59	61	3.7		EDI	Edinburgh	1.7	
		DEL	Delhi	AS1	7	7	2.2		LCY	London City airport	1.6	

(continued)

Table 14.3 (continued)

Carrier code	Carrier name (total number of nodes)	Top 5 freight airports							Top 5 passenger airports			
		Airport code	Airport name	IATA region	Number of routes with freight service	Total number of routes (Pax and freight)	Share of total freight capacity	Cumulative % at top 5 airports	Airport code	Airport name	Share of seating capacity	Cumulative % at top 5 airports
IB	Iberia (130)	MAD	Madrid Barajas airport	EU1	93	127	39.6	52.1	MAD	Madrid Barajas airport	39.5	53.1
		BCN	Barcelona airport	EU1	28	55	5.1		BCN	Barcelona airport	7.6	
		EZE	Buenos Aires Ministro Pistarini	LA4	2	2	2.7		VLC	Valencia (ES)	2.3	
		LPA	Las Palmas	EU1	6	17	2.5		BIO	Bilbao	1.9	
		GRU	Sao Paulo Guarulhos International airport	LA4	2	2	2.2		LHR	London Heathrow airport	1.8	
KL	KLM-Royal Dutch airlines (132)	AMS	Amsterdam	EU1	142	159	46.1	52.7	AMS	Amsterdam	47.7	51.8
		GYE	Guayaquil	LA3	3	3	1.9		LHR	London Heathrow airport	1.2	
		HKG	Hong Kong International airport	AS4	2	2	1.7		GYE	Guayaquil	1.0	
		BON	Bonaire	LA1	4	4	1.6		CDG	Paris Charles de Gaulle airport	1.0	
		DXB	Dubai	ME1	7	7	1.4		CGK	Jakarta Soekarno-Hatta airport	0.9	
LH	Lufthansa German airlines (227)	FRA	Frankfurt International airport	EU1	243	256	29.1	41.4	FRA	Frankfurt International airport	27.1	53.0
		MUC	Munich International airport	EU1	100	119	4.8		MUC	Munich International airport	14.6	
		KJA	Krasnoyarsk	AS4	8	8	3.0		DUS	Duesseldorf International airport	4.4	
		HKG	Hong Kong International airport	AS4	7	7	2.4		HAM	Hamburg airport	3.6	
		VCP	Sao Paulo Viracopos airport	LA4	8	8	2.1		TXL	Berlin Tegel airport	3.1	

(continued)

Table 14.3 (continued)

Carrier code	Carrier name (total number of nodes)	Top 5 freight airports							Top 5 passenger airports			
		Airport code	Airport name	IATA region	Number of routes with freight service	Total number of routes (Pax and freight)	Share of total freight capacity	Cumulative % at top 5 airports	Airport code	Airport name	Share of seating capacity	Cumulative % at top 5 airports
LX	Swiss/Crossair (97)	ZRH	Zurich airport	EU1	96	109	42.2	54.0	ZRH	Zurich airport	43.6	55.1
		GVA	Geneva	EU1	18	21	3.7		GVA	Geneva	5.6	
		JFK	New York J F Kennedy International airport	NA1	2	2	3.5		LCY	London City airport	2.2	
		TLV	Tel Aviv Ben Gurion International airport	ME1	2	2	2.3		DME	Moscow Domodedovo airport	1.9	
		NBO	Nairobi Jomo Kenyatta International airport	AF4	2	2	2.3		LHR	London Heathrow airport	1.8	
MP	Martinair Holland (54)	AMS	Amsterdam	EU1	73	73	26.5	49.3	AMS	Amsterdam	50.0	85.1
		SHJ	Sharjah	ME1	13	13	7.0		AUA	Aruba	15.4	
		NBO	Nairobi Jomo Kenyatta International airport	AF4	8	8	6.3		CUR	Curacao	8.5	
		HKG	Hong Kong International airport	AS4	6	6	4.9		HAV	Havana (CU) 00	5.6	
		UIO	Quito	LA3	11	11	4.6		CUN	Cancun	5.6	
SK	SAS Scandinavian airlines (103)	CPH	Copenhagen Kastrup airport	EU1	53	63	22.5	54.8	CPH	Copenhagen Kastrup airport	18.1	57.4
		ARN	Stockholm Arlanda airport	EU1	45	53	12.1		OSL	Oslo airport	16.8	
		OSL	Oslo airport	EU1	38	47	7.3		ARN	Stockholm Arlanda airport	12.8	
		BGO	Bergen	EU1	9	10	6.6		BGO	Bergen	4.9	
		TRD	Trondheim Vaernes airport	EU1	8	8	6.3		TRD	Trondheim Vaernes airport	4.8	
TK	Turkish airlines (162)	IST	Istanbul Ataturk airport	EU1	221	226	44.2	58.7	IST	Istanbul Ataturk airport	42.2	57.8
		ESB	Ankara Esenboga Airport	EU1	37	43	6.9		ESB	Ankara Esenboga airport	8.2	
		ADB	Izmir Adnan Menderes airport	EU1	7	11	3.4		ADB	Izmir Adnan Menderes airport	3.3	
		AYT	Antalya	EU1	8	8	2.3		AYT	Antalya	2.5	
		ADA	Adana	EU1	7	13	1.8		ADA	Adana	1.7	

Source Author's calculations from OAG Historical Max Plus Database, 2009

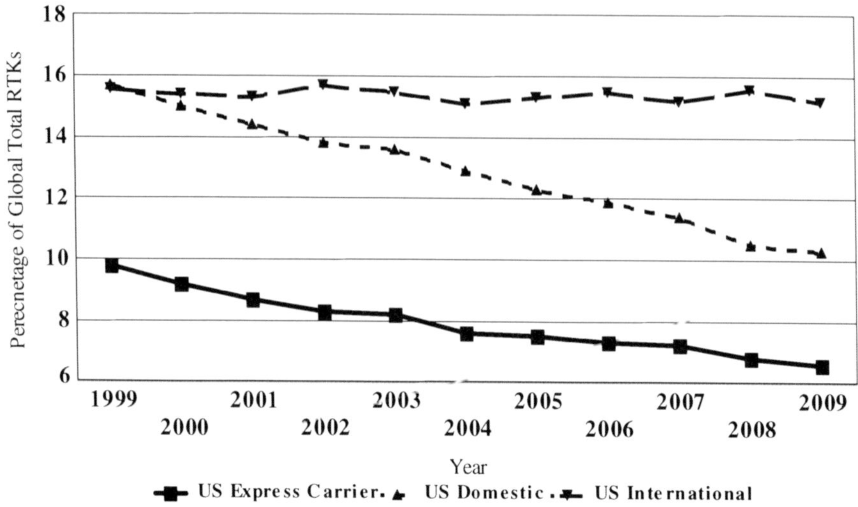

Fig. 14.5 US shares of global air freight revenue ton-kilometers, 1999–2009. *Source* Boeing, *World Air cargo Forecast* 2010–2011

14.3.1 Asian, North American and European Air Freight Markets

Table 14.2 gives the top 30 cargo carriers in 2009 broken down by domestic, international and total traffic performed. Lufthansa, Air France and BA are ranked in the top 20. Cargolux, the Luxembourg-registered all cargo carrier is ranked 13th in 2009. EAT—European Air Transport, which ranked 12th in the IATA listing is a Belgian based carrier wholly owned by Deutsche Post DHL.

Three of the top 5 carriers in Table 14.3 are US registered, with Federal Express and UPS the two largest express carriers/integrators globally. The air freight volumes carried by these two CEP operators are considerably greater than the third and lower ranked carriers. Three US passenger carriers are ranked in the IATA top 30, namely United Airlines, Northwest Airlines[8] and American Airlines. Air Canada was ranked 39th while the US carrier Continental Airlines[9] was ranked 43rd. The dominance of US air freight in global terms has declined steadily since the 1990s and this trend is illustrated in Figs. 14.4 and 14.5 for the period 1999–2009. US express carriers' share of total global revenue ton-kilometers has fallen from 10 % in 1999 to 6.6 % in 2009; US express carriers' traffic still accounted for 26 % of total US carrier revenue ton-kilometers in 2009 (Fig. 14.4). US domestic traffic has declined from 50 % of total US air freight RTKs in 1999 to 40 % in 2009 and this amounted to 10 % of global RTKs. This has occurred

[8] Northwest Airlines completed its merger with Delta Air Lines in December 2009.

[9] Continental Airlines was taken over by United Airlines in October 2010.

because of the dramatic growth in the volume and share of air freight in Asian and more recently Middle East markets.

Among the carriers in Table 14.2, 11 of the top 20 are Asian (14 of the top 30); four are Middle East carriers. Only one Latin American carrier appears in the top 30: LAN Airlines is ranked at 23. In the next section, the availability of cargo data is discussed. Datasets are introduced that in Sect. 14.4 will be used to analyze the leading Asian, North American, European and Middle East carrier freight networks.

14.3.2 Air Freight Data and Statistics

Comprehensive and comparable datasets detailing air transport activity across the major global regions are not readily available. A variety of data sources can be used to present *partial* views of air transport activity in major continental markets or segments. Some of the key data sources are described briefly below and the limitations of these datasets are set out. The two datasets used in the remaining sections of this chapter, namely the Official Airline Guide and US Bureau of Transportation Statistics T100 datasets, are described in more detail.

1. International Civil Aviation Organization (ICAO) Data: ICAO data are compiled on a monthly basis from member country reports detailing domestic and international scheduled and non-scheduled airline passenger, freight and mail activity. Traffic is reported by flight stage (traffic on-board aircraft on international flight stages) and by aggregated origin–destination pairs for all international scheduled city pairs. The flight stage traffic details individual carriers and aircraft operated. Monthly and annual traffic by airport is also reported for major international airports. The main limitations of these ICAO datasets are the incomplete coverage of carriers, the lack of detailed information on domestic services for larger countries, the delay in publication of up-to-date data and the high cost of data access.
2. International Air Transport Association (IATA) Data: These data are compiled from carrier-reported monthly traffic and capacity statistics relating to passenger and freight services for international scheduled operations. The data cover 115 airlines and the dominant share of international scheduled air operations. As with the ICAO data, the IATA data cover a subset of airlines operating in regional markets and access to the datasets is expensive.
3. Official Airline Guide Data: In examining passenger air transport activity, the *Official Airline Guide Historical MaxPlus* datasets give comprehensive coverage of ex-post airline schedules for each year from 1996 to 2009 and cover scheduled and non-scheduled operations. These datasets also include freight capacity available on each flight along with freighter-only services operated by combination carriers and many all-cargo carriers. The services of the US CEP carriers, however, are not included in the schedules. Schedules are published

1 year ahead and the MaxPlus dataset presents the revised ex-post schedules. The OAG coverage of airlines is far more extensive than in either ICAO or IATA, and includes almost all passenger operators globally. The main problems with these datasets are that the activity measured is either seating or freight capacity available, rather than actual traffic performed, and the high access costs. However, the comprehensive and consistent coverage of domestic and international air transport activity globally allows for comparative analysis of major continental air transport markets.

4. US Bureau of Transportation Statistics T100 Data: These present monthly data reported by US certificated carriers and international carriers operating within and between US airports. Scheduled and non-scheduled passenger, freight and mail traffic and capacity are reported along with aircraft type, service class and a variety of operational characteristics such as ramp-to-ramp and airborne aircraft hours. All classes of carriers are covered including detailed information on the CEP carrier network activities. The T100 databases are generated from the preceding traffic reports and are published with 3 month delays at very fine levels of detail by carrier and equipment type for all routes and market pairs. The data are available online from the BTS. The main limitation is that they focus on the US market.

The focus of this chapter is on the comparative analysis of network structures among Asian, North American and European markets. Accordingly, the OAG and T100 datasets were identified as providing the most comprehensive and consistent data to facilitate a comparative analysis of these major continental air transport markets. The ICAO and IATA data will be used to provide the context and give an overview of the relative importance of each of the major air freight markets.

14.4 Analysis of Global Regional Air Freight Networks

The OAG datasets were used to generate annual air freight capacity and seating capacity variables for each of the top 10 Asian, European[10] and North American[11] carriers for the years 2000–2009.[12] The OAG top 10 were compared with the

[10] Europe is broadly defined and includes Austria, Belgium, Denmark, Faroe Islands, Finland, France, Germany, Gibraltar, Greece, Iceland, Ireland, Italy, Luxembourg, Malta, Monaco, Netherlands, Norway, Portugal, Spain, Sweden, Switzerland, United Kingdom, Cyprus, Turkey, Albania, Armenia, Azerbaijan, Bosnia and Herzegovina, Bulgaria, Belarus, Croatia, Czech Republic, Estonia, Georgia, Hungary, Latvia, Lithuania, Macedonia (Former Yugoslav Republic), Moldova Republic of, Montenegro, Poland, Romania, Russian Federation, Serbia, Slovenia, Slovakia, Ukraine. This categorization of Europe is based on IATA definitions of the region.

[11] North America consists of Canada, USA, Greenland and Saint Pierre and Miquelon under the IATA regional classification. It is noted that this definition differs from the NAFTA region: Mexico is included in the IATA Latin America Region.

[12] OAG data were not available for FedEx, UPS, EAT, China Eastern Airlines and China Southern Airlines.

Table 14.4 Top 5 Air Freight and Passenger Airports for Top 10 North American Scheduled Freight Carriers, and Two CEP Carriers, 2009

Carrier code	Carrier name (total number of nodes)	Top 5 freight airports							Top 5 passenger airports			
		Airport code	Airport name	IATA region	Number of routes with freight service	Total number of routes (pax and freight)	Share of total freight capacity	Cumulative % at top 5 airports	Airport code	Airport name	Share of seating capacity	Cumulative % at top 5 airports
78 W	BAX global (41)	TOL	Toledo express airport	NA1	39	39	32.4	43.4				
		PDX	Portland (US) OR	NA1	3	3	3.2					
		BDL	Hartford Bradley International airport	NA1	5	5	2.8					
		IAH	Houston George Bush International airport	NA1	6	6	2.6					
		DFW	Dallas/Fort Worth International airport	NA1	4	4	2.5					
AA	American Airlines (241)	DFW	Dallas/Fort Worth International airport	NA1	107	184	19.7	47.3	DFW	Dallas/Fort Worth International airport	19.3	45.2
		MIA	Miami International airport	NA1	86	133	9.5		ORD	Chicago O'Hare International airport	9.5	
		ORD	Chicago O'Hare International airport	NA1	72	121	8.4		MIA	Miami International airport	9.4	
		JFK	New York J F Kennedy International airport	NA1	55	66	5.0		LAX	Los Angeles International airport	3.9	
		LAX	Los Angeles International airport	NA1	44	57	4.6		JFK	New York J F Kennedy International airport	3.1	
AC	Air Canada (124)	YYZ	Toronto Lester B Pearson International airport	NA1	109	126	29.3	61.5	YYZ	Toronto Lester B Pearson International airport	27.7	59.4
		YVR	Vancouver International airport	NA1	40	47	13.2		YVR	Vancouver International airport	10.5	
		YUL	Montreal Pierre Elliott Trudeau International airport	NA1	53	62	7.7		YUL	Montreal Pierre Elliott Trudeau International airport	9.2	
		LHR	London Heathrow airport	EU1	7	7	6.3		YYC	Calgary	7.5	
		YYC	Calgary	NA1	40	45	5.0		YOW	Ottawa Mcdonald Cartier International airport	4.6	

(continued)

Table 14.4 (continued)

Carrier code	Carrier name (total number of nodes)	Top 5 freight airports							Top 5 passenger airports			
		Airport code	Airport name	IATA region	Number of routes with freight service	Total number of routes (pax and freight)	Share of total freight capacity	Cumulative % at top 5 airports	Airport code	Airport name	Share of seating capacity	Cumulative % at top 5 airports
AS	Alaska Airlines (84)	SEA	Seattle/Tacoma International airport	NA1	69	75	25.3	54.7	SEA	Seattle/Tacoma International airport	28.3	55.6
		ANC	Anchorage International airport	NA1	51	51	13.6		ANC	Anchorage International airport	9.8	
		JNU	Juneau	NA1	18	18	6.4		PDX	Portland (US) OR	8.4	
		LAX	Los Angeles International airport	NA1	22	25	4.9		LAX	Los Angeles International airport	6.0	
		KTN	Ketchikan International airport	NA1	15	15	4.5		JNU	Juneau	3.1	
CO	Continental Airlines (287)	IAH	Houston George Bush International airport	NA1	151	215	22.4	52.2	IAH	Houston George Bush International airport	26.3	52.5
		EWR	Newark Liberty International airport	NA1	166	214	20.8		EWR	Newark Liberty International airport	17.8	
		GUM	Guam Antonio B Won Pat International airport	SW1	48	48	3.3		CLE	Cleveland Hopkins International airport	5.2	
		LHR	London Heathrow airport	EU1	7	7	3.0		LAX	Los Angeles International airport	1.7	
		NRT	Tokyo Narita airport	AS4	10	10	2.8		MCO	Orlando International airport	1.5	
DL	Delta Air Lines (311)	ATL	Atlanta Hartsfield-jackson International airport	NA1	185	304	31.2	49.6	ATL	Atlanta Hartsfield-jackson International airport	27.9	44.6
		JFK	New York J F Kennedy International airport	NA1	91	148	7.0		SLC	Salt Lake City	6.0	
		LAX	Los Angeles International airport	NA1	41	56	4.9		JFK	New York J F Kennedy International airport	4.7	
		SLC	Salt Lake City	NA1	53	129	3.9		CVG	Cincinnati Northern Kentucky International airport	4.0	
		MCO	Orlando International airport	NA1	38	54	2.6		LGA	New York La Guardia airport	1.9	

(continued)

Table 14.4 (continued)

Carrier code	Carrier name (total number of nodes)	Top 5 freight airports							Top 5 passenger airports			
		Airport code	Airport name	IATA region	Number of routes with freight service	Total number of routes (pax and freight)	Share of total freight capacity	Cumulative % at top 5 airports	Airport code	Airport name	Share of seating capacity	Cumulative % at top 5 airports
GB	ABX Air, Inc. (96)	ILN	Wilmington (US) OH	NA1	80	80	28.3	47.0				
		LAX	Los Angeles International airport	NA1	11	11	5.6					
		SFO	San Francisco International airport	NA1	9	9	5.0					
		BFI	Seattle Boeing Field	NA1	7	7	4.7					
		CVG	Cincinnati Northern Kentucky International airport	NA1	20	20	3.3					
NW	Northwest Airlines (232)	MSP	Minneapolis International airport	NA1	104	170	13.2	46.7	MSP	Minneapolis International airport	16.6	42.9
		DTW	Detroit Wayne County	NA1	102	175	11.6		DTW	Detroit Wayne County	16.3	
		NRT	Tokyo Narita airport	AS4	26	34	9.3		MEM	Memphis International airport	5.5	
		ANC	Anchorage International airport	NA1	13	13	7.6		NRT	Tokyo Narita airport	2.7	
		ORD	Chicago O'Hare International airport	NA1	49	64	5.0		LGA	New York La Guardia airport	1.8	
PO	Polar Air Cargo (21)	ICN	Seoul Incheon International airport	AS4	9	9	15.2	60.8				
		HKG	Hong Kong International airport	AS4	10	10	15.1					
		ANC	Anchorage International airport	NA1	11	11	10.7					
		PVG	Shanghai Pudong International airport	AS4	6	6	10.4					
		ORD	Chicago O'Hare International airport	NA1	8	8	9.4					

(continued)

Table 14.4 (continued)

Carrier code	Carrier name (total number of nodes)	Top 5 freight airports: Airport code	Airport name	IATA region	Number of routes with freight service	Total number of routes (pax and freight)	Share of total freight capacity	Cumulative % at top 5 airports	Top 5 passenger airports: Airport code	Airport name	Share of seating capacity	Cumulative % at top 5 airports
UA	United Airlines (199)	IAD	Washington Dulles International airport	NA1	35	111	12.6	46.8	ORD	Chicago O'Hare International airport	17.2	50.5
		ORD	Chicago O'Hare International airport	NA1	72	180	11.0		DEN	Denver International airport	11.8	
		SFO	San Francisco International airport	NA1	39	100	10.1		IAD	Washington Dulles International airport	8.6	
		LHR	London Heathrow Apt	EU1	11	11	6.9		SFO	San Francisco International airport	7.6	
		DEN	Denver International airport	NA1	60	147	6.2		LAX	Los Angeles International airport	5.4	
Note Data for UPS (5X) and FedEx (FX) relate to freight actually carried not capacity. These data were derived from the T100 Database												
5X	UPS (143)	SDF	Louisville, KY	NA1	114	114	30.4	50.0				
		ANC	Anchorage, AK	NA1	18	18	7.2					
		PHL	Philadelphia, PA	NA1	48	48	4.8					
		ONT	Ontario/San Bernardino, CA	NA1	33	33	4.8					
		RFD	Rockford, IL	NA1	33	33	2.7					
FX	FedEx (366)	MEM	Memphis, TN	NA1	151	151	34.2	53.8				
		IND	Indianapolis, IN	NA1	72	72	8.3					
		ANC	Anchorage, AK	NA1	31	31	4.1					
		OAK	Oakland, CA	NA1	44	44	3.7					
		EWR	Newark, NJ	NA1	47	47	3.4					

Source Author's calculations from OAG Historical Max Plus Database and US-BTS T100 Database, 2009

Table 14.5 Top 5 air freight and passenger airports for top 10 Asian scheduled freight carriers, 2009

Carrier code	Carrier Name (Total Number of nodes)	Top 5 freight airports							Top 5 passenger airports			
		Airport Code	Airport name	IATA region	Number of routes with freight service	Total number of routes (pax and freight)	Share of total freight capacity	Cumulative % at top 5 airports	Airport code	Airport name	Share of seating capacity	Cumulative % at top 5 airports
SQ	Singapore airlines (81)	SIN	Singapore Changi airport, Singapore	AS3	104	104	36.8	50.3	SIN	Singapore Changi airport	45.5	55.6
		SHJ	Sharjah, United Arab Emirates	ME1	12	12	3.6		CGK	Jakarta Soekarno-Hatta airport	3.2	
		HKG	Hong Kong International airport, Hong Kong (sar) China	AS4	7	7	3.6		HKG	Hong Kong International airport	2.7	
		LAX	Los Angeles International airport, USA	NA1	16	16	3.1		BKK	Bangkok Suvarnabhumi International airport	2.1	
		BRU	Brussels airport, Belgium	EU1	11	11	3.1		DXB	Dubai	2.1	
TG	Thai Airways International (76)	BKK	Bangkok Suvarnabhumi International airport, Thailand	AS3	84	87	44.3	60.6	BKK	Bangkok Suvarnabhumi International airport	45.4	59.3
		HKT	Phuket, Thailand	AS3	6	6	5.1		HKT	Phuket	5.0	
		CNX	Chiang Mai, Thailand	AS3	4	4	4.2		CNX	Chiang Mai	3.7	
		DXB	Dubai, United Arab Emirates	ME1	5	5	3.6		HKG	Hong Kong International airport	2.8	
		CDG	Paris Charles de Gaulle airport, France	EU1	3	3	3.5		ICN	Seoul Incheon International airport	2.5	
BR	EVA Airways (55)	TPE	Taipei Taiwan Taoyuan International airport, Chinese Taipei	AS4	88	89	41.0	67.0	TPE	Taipei Taiwan Taoyuan International airport	45.3	67.3
		ANC	Anchorage International airport, USA	NA1	7	7	11.4		HKG	Hong Kong International Apt	8.0	
		HKG	Hong Kong International airport, Hong Kong (sar) China	AS4	5	5	6.9		BKK	Bangkok Suvarnabhumi International airport	5.4	
		LAX	Los Angeles International airport, USA	NA1	4	4	4.0		MFM	Macau	4.7	
		BKK	Bangkok Suvarnabhumi International airport, Thailand	AS3	8	8	3.7		LAX	Los Angeles International airport	3.8	

(continued)

Table 14.5 (continued)

Carrier code	Carrier Name (Total Number of nodes)	Top 5 freight airports							Top 5 passenger airports			
		Airport Code	Airport name	IATA region	Number of routes with freight service	Total number of routes (pax and freight)	Share of total freight capacity	Cumulative % at top 5 airports	Airport code	Airport name	Share of seating capacity	Cumulative % at top 5 airports
CA	Air China (139)	PEK	Beijing Capital airport, China	AS4	105	205	32.4	63.3	PEK	Beijing Capital airport	31.8	51.7
		PVG	Shanghai Pudong International airport, China	AS4	29	41	16.8		CTU	Chengdu	8.9	
		JFK	New York J F Kennedy International airport, USA	NA1	5	5	5.5		CAN	Guangzhou	4.0	
		FRA	Frankfurt International airport, Germany	EU1	6	6	5.0		PVG	Shanghai Pudong International airport	3.6	
		CTU	Chengdu, China	AS4	46	88	3.6		HGH	Hangzhou	3.3	
CI	China Airlines (65)	TPE	Taipei Taiwan Taoyuan International airport, Chinese Taipei	AS4	96	117	36.0	59.2	TPE	Taipei Taiwan Taoyuan International airport	42.8	68.7
		ANC	Anchorage International airport, USA	NA1	9	9	11.3		HKG	Hong Kong International airport	12.8	
		JFK	New York J F Kennedy International airport, USA	NA1	7	7	4.3		BKK	Bangkok Suvarnabhumi International airport	6.4	
		HKG	Hong Kong International airport, Hong Kong (sar) China	AS4	9	12	4.0		NRT	Tokyo Narita airport	3.5	
		AUH	Abu Dhabi International airport, United Arab Emirates	ME1	9	9	3.6		KHH	Kaohsiung	3.1	
CK	China Cargo Airlines (20)	PVG	Shanghai Pudong International airport, China	AS4	19	19	34.5	64.5				
		PEK	Beijing Capital airport, China	AS4	4	4	12.1					
		DFW	Dallas/Fort Worth International airport, USA	NA1	4	4	6.2					
		LUX	Luxembourg, Luxembourg	EU1	2	2	6.1					
		CDG	Paris Charles de Gaulle airport, France	EU1	2	2	5.8					

(continued)

Table 14.5 (continued)

Carrier code	Carrier Name (Total Number of nodes)	Top 5 freight airports							Top 5 passenger airports			
		Airport Code	Airport name	IATA region	Number of routes with freight service	Total number of routes (pax and freight)	Share of total freight capacity	Cumulative % at top 5 airports	Airport code	Airport name	Share of seating capacity	Cumulative % at top 5 airports
CX	Cathay Pacific Airways (64)	HKG	Hong Kong International airport, Hong Kong (sar) China	AS4	122	122	34.5	56.2	HKG	Hong Kong International airport	43.9	61.5
		ANC	Anchorage International airport, USA	NA1	21	21	8.4		TPE	Taipei Taiwan Taoyuan International airport	7.8	
		DXB	Dubai, United Arab Emirates	ME1	22	22	6.4		BKK	Bangkok Suvarnabhumi International airport	3.5	
		MAN	Manchester International airport, United Kingdom	EU1	15	15	3.5		SIN	Singapore Changi airport	3.4	
		JFK	New York J F Kennedy International airport, USA	NA1	10	10	3.4		NRT	Tokyo Narita airport	2.9	
JL	Japan Airlines International (86)	HND	Tokyo Haneda airport, Japan	AS4	56	57	25.6	56.7	HND	Tokyo Haneda airport	29.9	55.8
		NRT	Tokyo Narita airport, Japan	AS4	60	67	15.9		NRT	Tokyo Narita airport	7.6	
		CTS	Sapporo Chitose airport, Japan	AS4	21	24	5.6		CTS	Sapporo Chitose airport	6.8	
		FUK	Fukuoka, Japan	AS4	15	17	5.0		FUK	Fukuoka	6.4	
		ITM	Osaka Itami airport, Japan	AS4	18	22	4.7		ITM	Osaka Itami airport	5.1	
KE	Korean Air (121)	ICN	Seoul Incheon International airport, Korea Republic of	AS4	170	177	34.6	56.7	ICN	Seoul Incheon International airport	26.9	63.3
		GMP	Seoul Gimpo International airport, Korea Republic of	AS4	23	23	6.7		GMP	Seoul Gimpo International airport	14.3	
		ANC	Anchorage International airport, USA	NA1	11	11	6.1		CJU	Jeju International	11.4	
		CJU	Jeju International, Korea Republic of	AS4	30	30	5.7		PUS	Busan	8.2	
		PUS	Busan, Korea Republic of	AS4	23	23	3.5		NRT	Tokyo Narita airport	2.4	

(continued)

Table 14.5 (continued)

Carrier code	Carrier Name (Total Number of nodes)	Top 5 freight airports							Top 5 passenger airports			
		Airport Code	Airport name	IATA region	Number of routes with freight service	Total number of routes (pax and freight)	Share of total freight capacity	Cumulative % at top 5 airports	Airport code	Airport name	Share of seating capacity	Cumulative % at top 5 airports
NH	All Nippon Airways (78)	HND	Tokyo Haneda airport, Japan	AS4	57	73	25.9	58.2	HND	Tokyo Haneda airport	30.5	58.8
		NRT	Tokyo Narita airport, Japan	AS4	37	52	11.0		CTS	Sapporo Chitose airport	7.7	
		CTS	Sapporo Chitose airport, Japan	AS4	21	26	7.4		ITM	Osaka Itami airport	7.2	
		ITM	Osaka Itami airport, Japan	AS4	19	29	7.2		OKA	Okinawa Naha airport	6.7	
		OKA	Okinawa Naha airport, Japan	AS4	32	33	6.7		FUK	Fukuoka	6.6	
OZ	Asiana Airlines (105)	ICN	Seoul Incheon International airport, Korea Republic of	AS4	148	153	33.9	58.1	ICN	Seoul Incheon International airport	29.1	60.3
		ANC	Anchorage International airport, USA	NA1	8	8	7.2		GMP	Seoul Gimpo International airport	14.5	
		DME	Moscow Domodedovo airport, Russian Federation	EU2	12	12	6.2		CJU	Jeju International	11.4	
		LAX	Los Angeles International airport, USA	NA1	7	12	5.7		KWJ	Gwangju	2.8	
		JFK	New York J F Kennedy International airport, USA	NA1	5	5	5.1		PUS	Busan	2.4	

Source Author's calculations from OAG Historical Max Plus Database, 2009

Table 14.6 Top 5 air freight and passenger airports for selected Middle East and Latin American scheduled freight carriers, 2009

Carrier code	Carrier Name (total number of nodes)	Top 5 freight airports							Top 5 passenger airports			
		Airport code	Airport name	IATA region	Number of routes with Freight service	Total number of routes (Pax and freight)	Share of total freight capacity	Cumulative % at top 5 airports	Airport code		Share of total Seating capacity	Cumulative % at top 5 airports
EK	Emirates (104)	DXB	Dubai, United Arab Emirates	ME1	126	133	45.3	52.8	DXB	Dubai, United Arab Emirates	45.9	53.6
		HKG	Hong Kong International Apt, Hong Kong (sar) China	AS4	3	3	3.0		BKK	Bangkok Suvarnabhumi International airport, Thailand	2.1	
		BKK	Bangkok Suvarnabhumi International airport, Thailand	AS3	5	6	1.7		LHR	London Heathrow airport, United Kingdom	1.9	
		SIN	Singapore Changi airport, Singapore	AS3	5	5	1.5		AKL	Auckland International airport, New Zealand	1.9	
		FRA	Frankfurt International airport, Germany	EU1	3	3	1.3		SYD	Sydney Kingsford Smith airport, Australia	1.9	
EY	Etihad Airways (78)	AUH	Abu Dhabi International airport, United Arab Emirates	ME1	102	104	42.5	55.3	AUH	Abu Dhabi International airport, United Arab Emirates	49.1	59.6
		PVG	Shanghai Pudong International airport, China	AS4	4	4	4.1		LHR	London Heathrow airport, United Kingdom	3.2	
		NBO	Nairobi Jomo Kenyatta International airport, Kenya	AF4	3	3	3.6		BKK	Bangkok Suvarnabhumi International airport, Thailand	3.0	
		LHR	London Heathrow airport, United Kingdom	EU1	1	1	3.0		BAH	Bahrain, Bahrain	2.1	
		MAA	Chennai, India	AS1	4	4	2.1		DOH	Doha, Qatar	2.2	

(continued)

Table 14.6 (continued)

Carrier code	Carrier Name (total number of nodes)	Top 5 freight airports							Top 5 passenger airports			
		Airport code	Airport name	IATA region	Number of routes with Freight service	Total number of routes (Pax and freight)	Share of total freight capacity	Cumulative % at top 5 airports	Airport code		Share of total Seating capacity	Cumulative % at top 5 airports
QR	Qatar Airways (89)	DOH	Doha, Qatar	ME1	135	136	47.2	57.1	DOH	Doha, Qatar	47.6	58.2
		DXB	Dubai, United Arab Emirates	ME1	3	3	3.8		DXB	Dubai, United Arab Emirates	3.8	
		LHR	London Heathrow airport, United Kingdom	EU1	1	1	2.9		LHR	London Heathrow Apt, United Kingdom	2.3	
		FRA	Frankfurt International airport, Germany	EU1	2	2	1.6		BAH	Bahrain, Bahrain	2.3	
		MAA	Chennai, India	AS1	3	3	1.5		AUH	Abu Dhabi International airport, United Arab Emirates	2.1	
SV	Saudi Arabian Airlines (92)	JED	Jeddah, Saudi Arabia	ME1	98	112	22.6	64.8	JED	Jeddah, Saudi Arabia	27.2	67.0
		RUH	Riyadh, Saudi Arabia	ME1	75	85	20.4		RUH	Riyadh, Saudi Arabia	24.5	
		BRU	Brussels airport, Belgium	EU1	5	5	11.3		DMM	Dammam, Saudi Arabia	6.8	
		DMM	Dammam, Saudi Arabia	ME1	33	39	6.8		MED	Madinah, Saudi Arabia	5.2	
		BKK	Bangkok Suvarnabhumi International airport, Thailand	AS3	3	3	3.7		CAI	Cairo, Egypt	3.2	
LA	Lan Airlines (63)	SCL	Santiago Arturo Merino Benitez, Chile	LA4	46	65	27.1	59.7	SCL	Santiago Arturo Merino Benitez, Chile	28.1	51.8
		LIM	Lima, Peru	LA3	9	23	14.5		LIM	Lima, Peru	8.1	
		EZE	Buenos Aires Ministro Pistarini, Argentina	LA4	6	14	7.3		AEP	Buenos Aires Aeroparque J. Newbery, Argentina	7.3	
		MIA	Miami International Apt, USA	NA1	8	8	5.9		EZE	Buenos Aires Ministro Pistarini, Argentina	5.3	
		FRA	Frankfurt International airport, Germany	EU1	3	3	4.9		PMC	Puerto Montt Chile	3.0	

Source Author's calculations from OAG Historical Max Plus Database, 2009

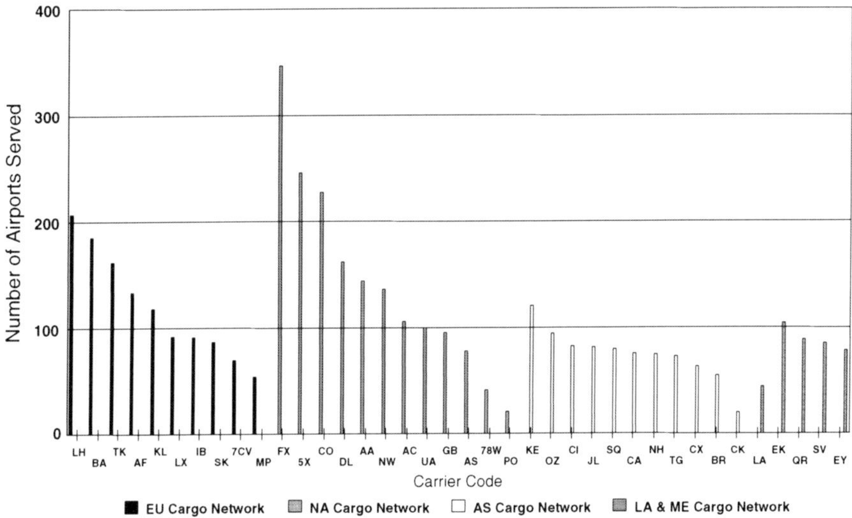

Fig. 14.6 Number of airports served in air freight networks for top 10 European, North American Carriers and Asian carriers and selected Latin American and Middle Eastern Carriers, 2009. *Source* Author's calculations from OAG historical max plus database and T100 database (*UPS* and *FedEx*), 2009

IATA and ICAO rankings of carriers in 2009. Since the data on express/integrated carriers is not listed in OAG, the selected carriers are either combination passenger/cargo carriers or all-cargo carriers. The IATA and ICAO datasets record the actual freight tons carried, while the OAG dataset gives the freight ton capacity available on each route by aircraft type for each carrier. Airports were classified by country and IATA region; summary details for each carrier are reported for 2009 in Tables 14.3, 14.4, and 14.5 for Europe, North America and Asia respectively. Details for the four Middle East carriers and LAN Airlines are included in Table 14.6 for comparative purposes. For each carrier, the top five airports in the freight and passenger networks are recorded, along with the number of routes operated from each airport and the share of the carrier's total freight and seating capacity. The total number of airports in each of the carriers' freight and passenger networks is summarized in Fig. 14.6. Summary measures of each carrier's network structure were computed using the Gini Index described earlier.[13] Figure 14.7 shows the Gini Index scores for cargo (freight tons available) and passenger (seats available) networks for the top 30 Asian, European, North American and Middle East carriers in 2009.

[13] See Reynolds-Feighan (2007) for a detailed discussion on the application of this measure to capture network activity and the spatial distribution of a carrier's traffic.

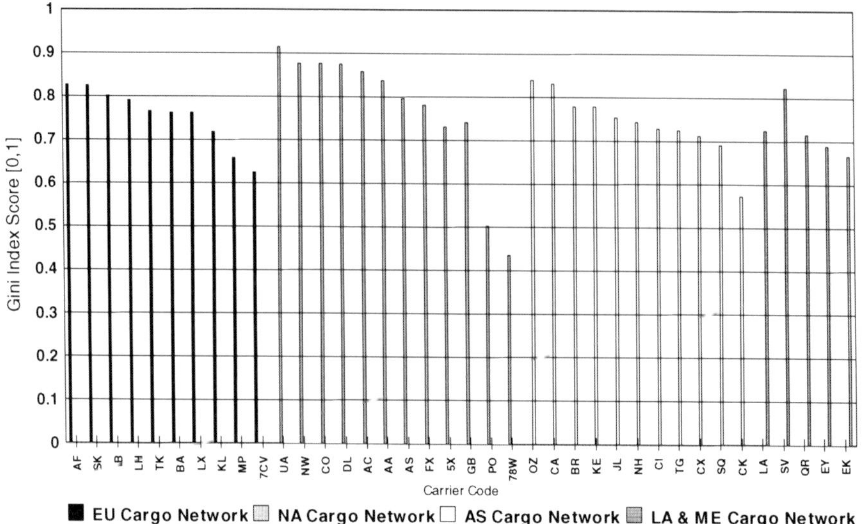

Fig. 14.7 Gini Index scores for air freight (freight tons available) networks for top 10 European, North American carriers and Asian carriers and selected Latin American and Middle Eastern carriers, 2009. *Source* Author's calculations from OAG historical max plus database and T100 (*UPS* and *FedEx*), 2009

14.4.1 European Air Freight Networks

Among the top 10 European carriers described in Table 14.3, Cargolux is the only all-cargo carrier, although Martinair Holland is a predominantly cargo-focused carrier.[14] Cargolux and Martinair Holland are the European carriers with the smallest network of airports in 2009. They are also the carriers with the two lowest Gini Index scores. These measures suggest a greater degree of dispersion in the freight capacity distribution across the network of airports served. The Martinair passenger Gini Index, by contrast, is very high at 0.92. This reflects a very high degree of concentration in the passenger seating capacity, where 50 % of capacity departs from the largest airport in the carrier's network, Amsterdam.

For Lufthansa, and Turkish Airlines, the freight and passenger networks are similar in size and both carriers have expanded their networks since 2000. BA had a slightly larger freight network in 2009, serving 186 airports compared with 171 airports in its passenger network; these networks were smaller than the networks served in 2000. Air France, KLM, Iberia and SAS had smaller freight networks than passenger networks in 2009, and all had experienced contraction in the overall size of their networks between 2000 and 2009.

[14] Martinair Holland ceased its small passenger operation in December 2010 to focus exclusively on cargo. The carrier was acquired by the larger Dutch airline KLM in December 2008.

For the top 7 European carriers, there is relatively small variation in the Gini Index scores: These range from 0.76 to 0.82 for the freight networks, and 0.72 to 0.78 for the passenger networks. That demonstrates a high degree of spatial concentration in both freight and passenger capacity across the networks. KLM has lower Gini Index scores in both networks, at 0.71 and 0.64 in the freight and passenger networks, respectively. The KLM network is a single hub operation focused heavily on the Amsterdam hub. Capacity is relatively evenly distributed across all of the other airports in the carrier's network, and this explains the lower Gini Index score.

The share of freight capacity and passenger capacity at its top airports is recorded for each carrier in Table 14.3. There is close correspondence between the freight and passenger capacity shares for all of the carriers with the exception of BA, Air France and Martinair. BA and Air France operate essentially a single hub network, centred on two airports in the member state capitals where both carriers are registered. While a significant proportion of passenger traffic is distributed between the two airports in Paris, the freight is concentrated at Paris Charles de Gaulle (CDG) airport in the case of Air France. BA has a lower proportion of freight capacity (28.4 %) operated from London Heathrow Airport than passenger capacity (36.3 %). However, London Stansted (6.4 %) and London Gatwick (3.7 %) shared 10 % of BA's total freight capacity between them in 2009.

In Table 14.3, it can be noted that most of the European combination carriers have passenger networks very much focused around airports in their home states. The freight networks, however, include North American, Asian or African airports among the top 5 in each carrier's network, with the exception of Turkish Airlines and SAS. The Turkish Airlines freight capacity very closely matches the passenger capacity and all of its top 5 airports are located in Turkey. SAS is jointly owned by the governments of Denmark, Norway and Sweden, and both passenger and freight networks reflect a relatively even distribution of services from each state's largest cities.

For each carrier, the average number of stops across all routes was computed for the networks in each year. Cargolux and Martinair Holland generally provided multi-stop air freight services. For the combination passenger and cargo carriers, freight services from the home state were generally direct or non-stop services, while services originating in Asia, North America or Africa were often one-stop services.

The class of freight was analyzed. Freight classes listed in the OAG data are distinguished between Unit Load Device (ULD[15])-containers, ULD-Pallets, Other pallets and loose loads. Most of the European carriers' freight capacity is classed as pallets or ULD-Pallets. Iberia and Air France had a significant proportion of

---

[15] Unit Load Devices are defined by OAG as "a load carrying device which interfaces directly with an aircraft loading and restraint systems and meets all the restraint requirements without the use of supplementary equipment. As such, it becomes a component part of the aircraft. The device can be either a combination of components or one complete structural unit. A combination unit is an aircraft pallet plus net plus non-structural igloo, or pallet plus net. A structural unit is a lower deck or main deck cargo container, or a structural igloo assembly."

ULD-container freight, while Turkish Airlines freight capacity was exclusively ULD-container [See Koch and Kraus (2005) for further discussion of the network structures of the major integrators, and the resulting choices of airports, in the European air freight market].

14.4.2 North American Air Freight Networks

Table 14.4 sets out details from the OAG database for the top 10 North American air freight carriers in 2009, excluding the two express carriers FedEx and UPS. Among the top 10, BAX Global, ABX Air Inc. and Polar Air Cargo are all-cargo operators. For the seven passenger and cargo carriers, details of the passenger and freight networks are summarized in Table 14.4. BAX Global operated a 41 node network in 2009 centerd at Toledo Express Airport in Swanton, Ohio. A significant proportion of the carrier's routes were one-stop routings. The same pattern was observed for the other two all-cargo carriers. Polar Air Cargo operated the smallest network with 21 nodes in 2009. ABX Air Inc operated a 96 node network focused on Wilmington, Ohio. Polar Air cargo and BAX Global have reduced the size of their networks since 2000. The three all-cargo carriers had the lowest Gini Index scores, though Polar (0.50) and BAX Global (0.44) were significantly lower than ABX Air Inc (0.74). The all-cargo carriers are focused on airports that are not passenger hubs: this is also the case for the two CEP operators, Fedex and UPS, which have their major hubs in Memphis and Louisville, respectively.

For the combination passenger and freight carriers, the passenger networks are substantially larger than the freight networks. The exceptions are Air Canada and Alaskan Airlines, where the number of airports is closer in the two networks. The largest passenger airport is also the largest freight airport except for United Airlines, where Washington Dulles is the largest freight airport and Chicago O'Hare is the largest passenger airport. In all cases, the Gini Index scores are higher for the freight networks than for the passenger networks and significantly higher than the Gini Index scores for the European carriers. This indicates a very highly concentrated distribution of freight capacity across the networks of the North American combination carriers, a distribution that is particularly focused on a subset of each carrier's hub airports. There is also greater variability in the Gini Index scores for the freight networks (0.79–0.91) compared with the passenger networks (0.74–0.81).

The share of freight capacity at the top airport in each carrier's network is significantly below the passenger capacity shares for many of the European combination carriers. The North American carriers generally operate multiple interactive hub-and-spoke networks that are continental-wide in coverage. Typically there are between three and five hubs in the carrier's network around which service offerings are focused. The European networks, by contrast, are focused on the main cities in the home states of each of the carriers, with relatively small volumes of 'between hub' traffic, and in several instances no between hub air traffic (for example BA and Air France).

Most of the North American carriers reduced the size of their networks between 2000 and 2009, reflecting the economic downturn associated with the financial crisis of 2008. Alaskan Airlines expanded its network over this period. The vast majority of air freight service routings were non-stop for services originating at the combination carriers' main hubs. For Air Canada, there is a very small proportion of routing with stops among the top five airports in its network. For Alaskan Airlines and United Airlines, there are higher proportions of one-stop freight services. In cases where the combination carriers have non-North American airports among their top 5 freight airports, services from these airports have a significant proportion of multi-stop routings.

Finally, the freight class was examined for the North American carriers. In all but one case, the freight capacity was classed as ULD-Containers/pallets. The one exception was with Polar Air Cargo, where significant capacity across its network was classed as 'Other pallets'.

14.4.3 Asian Air Freight Networks

Table 14.5 gives details of air freight and passenger networks for the top 10 Asian carriers and also for China Cargo (CK) Airlines, as this was the highest ranked Asian all-cargo carrier for which OAG data were available.[16] Singapore Airlines, Cathay Pacific Airways, Thai Airways, EVA Airways and China Airways operate similar-sized air freight networks. Each is focused heavily on a single hub, though China Airways have a substantial proportion of its total capacity available from its Anchorage, Alaska base in the US (11 %). As with the European carriers, the Asian carriers have different passenger airports in their top 5 compared with their freight operations. Again, North American, Middle East and European airports are included among the top 5.

The China Cargo Airlines network is the smallest with just 21 airports, and this carrier's services consist of many multi-stop services. The two Japanese carriers, JAL and All Nippon Airways, both operate from the two Tokyo airports [Narita (NRT) and Haneda (HND)] and have smaller shares of their total traffic from their top ranked airport as a result. This pattern is similar to the BA air freight and passenger networks and to the Air France passenger traffic network. Korean Air and Asiana, the two Korean carriers, split their passenger traffic among the two Seoul airports [Incheon (ICN) and Gimpo(GMP)], but like Air France, concentrate their air freight capacity at their top ranked Seoul hub, Incheon. Air China operates a two hub freight network centered on Shanghai Pudong (PVG) and Beijing (PEK) airports. Earlier in the present volume, Chen and Lee (2013) discuss "Logistics in

[16] Data for China Eastern Airlines and China Southern Airlines were incomplete for the domestic air freight market, and are therefore excluded.

China". Their chapter briefly considers air cargo services, and the possible coordination of air freight with sea and rail logistics in China.

The Gini Index scores for the Asian carriers are similar in range to those of the European carriers, varying from 0.69 to 0.83 for the combination carriers. China Cargo Airlines, similar to results for the European and North American all-cargo carriers, has the lowest Gini Index score at 0.52, showing a less concentrated freight capacity distribution across the carrier's network. Air China and Asiana have the two highest Gini Index scores, reflecting a high degree of concentration in air freight capacity across the carrier's networks, and particularly at the top 2 airports.

Air services are generally non-stop from the Asian carrier's main hubs, with a greater tendency for one-stop service from International airports. The Japanese carriers have a very small number of multi-stop routings, while the Chinese carriers have a much higher proportion from all of their top 5 airports. This reflects the greater flexibility afforded to carriers through liberalization of air transport services. Air cargo services have typically been liberalized ahead of air passenger services in domestic and international markets. The air freight capacity for the Asian carriers is generally ULD-container and pallets.

14.4.4 Middle East and Latin American Air Freight Networks

Table 14.6 presents summary details for the four Middle East carriers and LAN Airlines ranked in the top 30 in Table 14.2. Emirates, Ethiad and Qatar Airways operate single hub air freight networks centered on the main hub airport in each carrier's network. The Gini Index scores for these three carriers are very similar and range from 0.66 to 0.71. The top 5 passenger and freight airports in each carrier's network differ significantly for Emirates and Ethiad Airways. For Qatar Airways, the passenger and freight networks coincide more closely. Saudi Arabian Airlines operates a two hub air freight network focused on Jeddah (JED) and Riyadh (RUH). This carrier's passenger network has its top four airports based in Saudi Arabia. As with the European and Asian carriers, the air freight network has greater capacity available at international airports, in Europe and Asia in the case of Saudi Airlines.

LAN Airlines operates from three bases in Chile, Peru and Argentina. LAN Chile was privatized in 1989 and has established new carriers in Peru, Argentina and Ecuador. These carriers have been operated under the single LAN Airlines alliance since 2004. LAN Airlines operates an extensive network throughout Latin America. In line with the rough guide of Fig. 14.2, the Gini Index score of 0.72 indicates the distribution of LAN's air freight capacity across the top 5 airports in its 63 node air freight network. LAN also operates cargo-only services.

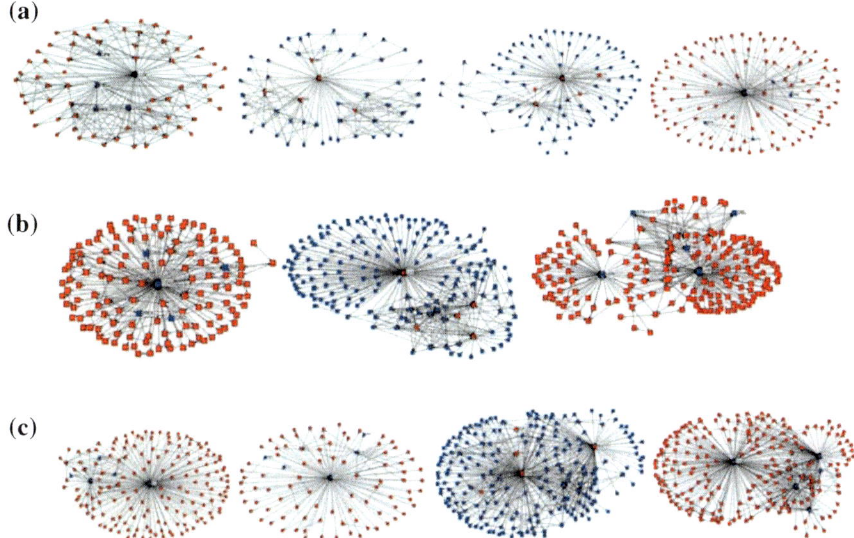

Fig. 14.8 Selected European carrier network structures in 2009. (from *left*) **a** Cargolux freight network, Martinair Holland freight network—Iberia airlines freight network, KLM freight network. **b** Airfrance freight network and passenger network (*middle*), BA freight network. **c** Turkish airlines freight, Swiss/Crossair freight networks, Lufthansa freight and passenger network (*right*)

14.4.5 Visual Representation of Carrier Networks

In order to illustrate the extent of linkages and routings in carrier networks, a stylized diagram showing the nodes and links was generated for each freight and passenger network in 2009 using the Net Draw software. Figure 14.8 presents a set of stylized illustrations of selected European air carrier passenger and freight networks in 2009. Figure 14.9 presents illustrations of North American air carrier networks in 2009. Figures 14.10 and 14.11 illustrate the networks of the Asian and Middle East and Latin American carriers.

The diagrams show the set of linkages in air freight and some air passenger networks: there is no geographic metric or reference in these illustrations. The top five largest airports in each carrier's network are highlighted, and related to those airports detailed in the corresponding Tables 14.3, 14.4, 14.5, 14.6.

In Fig. 14.8a, the extent of multi-stop routings in the Cargolux and Martinair networks is demonstrated and this pattern is also clear in the Lufthansa freight network. This is evident in the chainage of links in the network diagrams. There is a smaller number of multi-stop linkages in the Lufthansa passenger network in Fig. 14.8c. The dominance of the largest hub in all of the European carrier networks is clearly illustrated in every network of Fig. 14.8. This pattern is less pronounced in the case of BA in Fig. 14.8b, but three of the largest airports are in

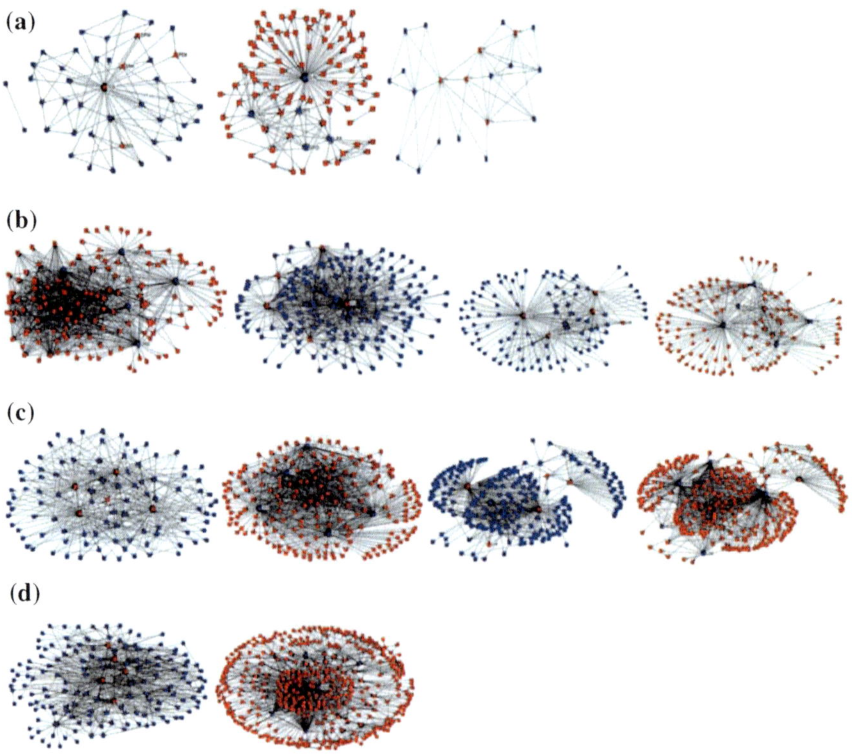

Fig. 14.9 Selected North American carrier network structures in 2009. (from *left*) **a** BAX global freight network, ABX Air Inc. freight network, Polar air cargo network. **b** American airlines freight network—Delta airlines freight network; Air Canada freight and passenger network (*right*). **c** United airlines freight network and passenger networks (*second*); Continental airlines freight and passenger networks. **d** UPS network (*left*) and FedEx network (*right*), 2009

London, and there is no air service operated between London Heathrow (LHR), Gatwick (LGW) and Stansted (STN). The Air France passenger network is analogous [8(b)], where the two largest airports are both in Paris and there is no air service connecting them. Generally speaking, there is a strong similarity among the European carrier networks in terms of their linkage structures and the largely single hub network pattern.

These networks are different to most of the North American networks illustrated in Fig. 14.9. The Air Canada freight and passenger networks are most similar to the European combination-carrier networks, but with greater distances between the largest airports [9(b)]. The US combination carriers operate interactive hub-and-spoke passenger and freight networks with clearly larger passenger networks. The linkages are not weighted by freight volume and merely show the extent of linkages or routes in the network. Using the T100 dataset, the air freight traffic distributions across the networks of FedEx and UPS were determined for 2009.

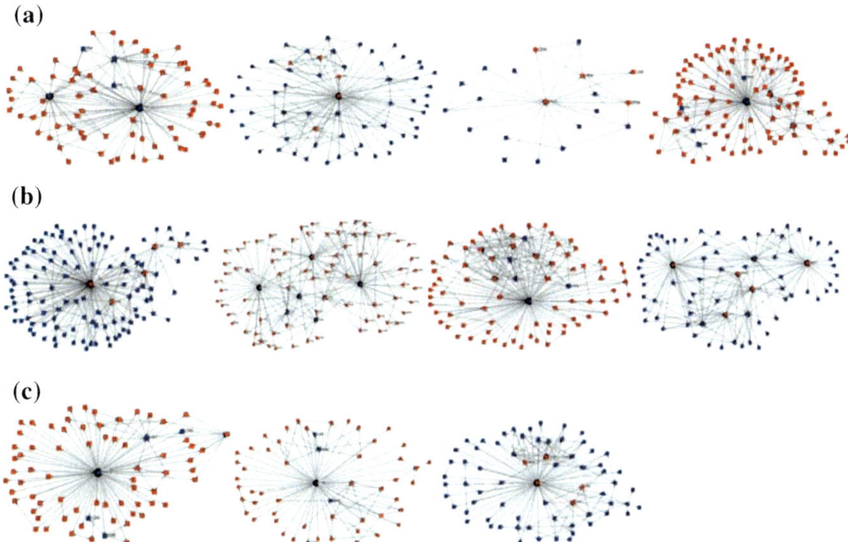

Fig. 14.10 Selected Asian carrier network structures in 2009. (from *left*) **a** Air China (*CA*) network, China airlines (*CI*) Network, China cargo airlines, Asiana airlines (*OZ*). **b** Korean air (*KE*), Japan airlines international (*JL*), Singapore airlines (*SQ*), All Nippon airways (*NH*). **c** Thai airways international, EVA airways, Cathay Pacific (*CX*) network

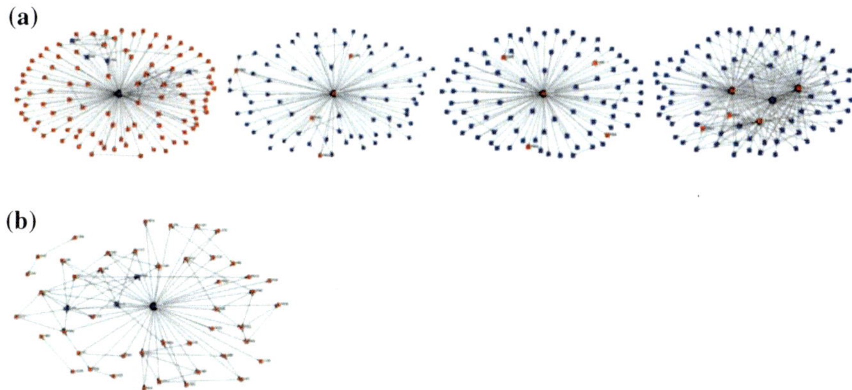

Fig. 14.11 Selected Middle East and Latin American carrier network structures in 2009. (from *left*) **a** Emirates (*ER*), Ethiad airways, Qatar airways (*QR*), Saudi Arabian airlines. **b** LAN Airlines (*LA*)

These networks are illustrated also in Fig. 14.9d. The UPS and FedEx networks are very large and have a high degree of inter-linkages. These networks are more similar to the large US combination carriers, with high degrees of concentration of links focused on multiple hubs.

The three all-cargo carriers have considerably smaller networks. In the case of Polar Air Cargo and BAX Global [9(a)], the largest airport is much less prominent compared with ABX Air Inc. and the combination carrier networks. The relatively high proportion of multi-stop routings may also be discerned from these illustrations in the chaining of linkages; the BAX Global and ABX Air network structures are similar to the CargolLux and Martinair graphs in this regard.

In Fig. 14.10, the Asian networks show the clear prominence of the top hub in the cases of Air China, China Airlines, Asiana Airlines, Korean Air, Singapore, Thai, EVA Airways and Cathay Pacific. The extent of one-stop or (more unusually) multi-stop routings among the second, third and fourth ranked airports is evident in these illustrations in the chaining of linkages. The two Japanese carriers have higher degrees of interconnection among their top 5 airports and within the air freight networks generally, than the other Asian carriers. These networks are somewhat similar to the BA, Air France and Lufthansa networks. The China cargo Airline network is very small, with some multi-stop routings.

The Middle East networks in Fig. 14.11 are dominated by a single node in the case of Emirates, Ethiad and Qatar Airways. LAN Airlines network is also dominated by the top ranked airport, but with significant multi-stop routings visible from the other lower ranked nodes. Saudi Arabian Airlines has a multi-hub structure more similar to the North American carriers with a relatively high degree of interconnections among the nodes.

From these illustrations, the North American carriers stand out as being significantly larger and operating multiple hub nodes, with high numbers of 'spoke' connections and inter-linkages to the other hub nodes. The European, Asian and Middle East carriers are either single hub or 2–3 hub networks, linking their home state capital city or most populous city with a great number of international locations directly. For some of the carriers based in larger states, they operate from multiple airports in the capital/most important city and/or from at least one other major regional capital. The all-cargo carriers operate smaller single hub networks focused on airports that are not significant passenger hubs. China Cargo Airlines would be an exception, based at Shanghai Pudong Airport.

14.5 Summary and Conclusions

Air freight markets consist of three main groups of carriers, namely carrier, express and parcel (CEP) carriers, all-cargo carriers and combination passenger-cargo carriers. The two largest global carriers are two US CEP carriers, FedEx and UPS. These carriers move significantly greater total air freight volumes and perform substantially more revenue freight ton-kilometers than any other carriers worldwide. There are a small number of all-cargo carriers operating large international air freight networks: within the top 30 IATA ranking, there were just four all-cargo carriers. Combination passenger-cargo carriers are the largest group of operators providing domestic and international air freight services.

Air freight networks are structured differently for all-cargo carriers compared to combination carrier networks. The all-cargo networks have a less concentrated distribution of capacity than the combination carriers, and are focused around airports that are not significant passenger hubs. The combination carriers have generally larger passenger networks than freight networks (as illustrated in Figs. 14.8b, 14.8c and 14.9c for example), with the freight capacity focused more on longer-haul routes. Air freight networks have contracted in the last few years, reflecting the downturn in economic activity. North American combination carriers have more highly concentrated air freight and passenger networks than European, Asian and Middle East carriers, with the North American networks focused around key interacting hubs that have large numbers of linkages.

The vast majority of air freight capacity consists of direct routings, although greater liberalization of air service agreements has facilitated multi-country, multi-stop routings. The vast majority of air freight on combination carriers is carried on ULD-containers and pallets, as this speeds up the loading and unloading at airports using standardized handling equipment. This standardization in the use of ULDs has been promoted through IATA.

Air freight networks of European, Asian and Middle East carriers are generally single hub, or 2–3 hub networks in the case of carriers operating in larger states. Despite significant liberalization in the internal European air market and in Asian markets, carrier networks are still focused on hubs within their home states as was illustrated in Figs. 14.8a and 14.8c. Consolidation in the European airline industry is expected to continue apace in the next 5 years, as regulatory and legal constraints that have discouraged cross-border mergers are being removed.

The development and future orientation of the large air freight operators will change to reflect the changing global patterns of economic growth. It is expected that Asia and inter-Asian markets will see the highest growth rates. This pattern is already reflected in the structure of European, North American and Middle East carrier's air freight networks, where Asian airports rank in the top 5 airports for a significant number of carriers.

References

Air Cargo World (2009) IATA's top 50 cargo carriers. Air Cargo World, p 24–30 September 2009

Boeing (2010) World Air Cargo Forecast, Boeing Airplane Company. Available online at http://www.boeing.com/commercial/cargo/wacf.pdf. Accessed 20 Dec 2010

Burghouwt G (2007) Airline network development in Europe and its implications for airport planning. Ashgate, Aldershot

Chen F, Lee C-Y (2013) Logistics in China. In: Bookbinder JH (ed) Global Logistics, Springer, New York

Chiavi R (2005) Airfreight development supporting the strategy of global logistics companies, In: Delfman W, Baum H, Auerbach S, Albers S (Eds) Chapter 21 in Strategic Management in the Aviation Industry, Ashgate, Aldershot

Corsi TM, Boyson S (2001) North America: Insights and challenges, Chapter 4 in Handbooks in Transport 2: In: Brewer AM, Button KJ, Hensher DA (Eds) Handbook of Logistics and Supply-Chain Management, Pergamon, Amsterdam

Doganis R (2010) Flying Off Course: Airline Economics and Marketing (4th edn), Routledge, London

Gastwirth JL (1972) The Estimation of the Lorenz Curve and Gini Index. Rev Econ Stat 54(3):306–316 (The MIT Press)

Huber H (2009) Spatial structure and network behaviour of strategic airline groups: a comparison between Europe and the United States, Transport Policy 16(4):151–162 (August 2009)

ICAO (2010) Annual Report of the Council 2009, International Civil Aviation Organization (Doc 9921), Montreal, October (available online at http://www.icao.int/annualreports/. Accessed Dec 2010)

IATA (2010) ULD Technical Manual. International Air Transport Association, Montreal

Koch B, Kraus A (2005) Integrator network strategies and parameters of airport choice in the European air cargo market, In: Delfman W, Baum H, Auerbach S, Albers S (eds) Chapter 22 in Strategic Management in the Aviation Industry. Ashgate, Aldershot

MergeGlobal (2009) Global Air Freight: Demand Outlook and its Implications, MergeGlobal, Arlington, VA August 2009. Available at www.mergeglobal.com Accessed December 2010

Reynolds-Feighan AJ (1994) EC and US Air Freight Markets: Network Organisation in a Deregulated Environment. Transport Rev 14(3):193–217

Reynolds-Feighan AJ (2001a) Air Freight Logistics. In: Brewer A, Button KJ, Hensher D (Eds) Chapter 28, Handbooks in Transport vol 2: Handbook of Logistics and Supply-Chain Management, Elsevier Science

Reynolds-Feighan AJ (2001b) Traffic distribution in low-cost and full-service carrier networks in the US air transportation market. J Air Transport Manage 7(5):265–275 September 2001

Reynolds-Feighan AJ (2007) Competing networks, spatial and industrial concentration in the US airline industry. Spat Econ Anal 2(3):239–259

Sage D (2001) Express Delivery. In: Brewer AM, Button KJ, Hensher DA (Eds) Chapter 30 in Handbooks in Transport 2: Handbook of Logistics and Supply-Chain Management, Pergamon, Amsterdam

Chapter 15
Business Models and Network Design in Hinterland Transport

Peter W. de Langen, Jan C. Fransoo and Ben van Rooy

Abstract International container transport is the backbone of global supply chains. Hinterland transport, the transport from the port to the final destination and vice versa, is an important component of international container transport. However, academic attention to hinterland transport has emerged only recently. This chapter discusses business models and network design in hinterland transport. Understanding business models is relevant, as many different types of companies (e.g., shipping lines, terminal operating companies and forwarders) play a role in hinterland transport. Their business models influence how they position themselves in the market, their stance concerning cooperation and coordination in hinterland transport, and their scope in network design. Network design is a core issue in hinterland transport. New services need to be designed—and in such a way that they are expected to be profitable. Furthermore, current service patterns only change through deliberate redesign. So competition through the (re)design of transport services is a very important—perhaps the most important—form of competition in intermodal freight transport. One potentially promising innovation in this respect is the *extended gate* concept, where an inland hub becomes the 'virtual gate' of the deep sea terminal.

P. W. de Langen · J. C. Fransoo (✉) · B. van Rooy
School of Industrial Engineering, Eindhoven University of Technology, Eindhoven, The Netherlands
e-mail: j.c.fransoo@tue.nl

P. W. de Langen
Department Corporate Strategy, Port of Rotterdam Authority, Rotterdam, The Netherlands

B. van Rooy
Brabant Intermodal, Brabant, The Netherlands

J. H. Bookbinder (ed.), *Handbook of Global Logistics*, International Series in Operations Research & Management Science 181, DOI: 10.1007/978-1-4419-6132-7_15,

15.1 Introduction: The Hinterland Transport Chain

International container[1] transport is the backbone of global supply chains. Hinterland transport, the transport from the port to the final destination and vice versa, is an important component of international container transport. However, academic attention for hinterland transport from a supply chain perspective has only emerged recently (see e.g., Notteboom and Rodrigue 2005, Notteboom 2008, and Van der Horst and de Langen 2008). The hinterland leg is often more costly than the maritime leg and port costs combined. Furthermore, whereas the efficiency of the maritime leg has improved substantially over the last decades, due to the emergence of global carriers with comprehensive maritime networks, increases in ship size, and the formation of alliances of shipping lines, efficiency of the hinterland leg can still be improved substantially (Van der Horst and de Langen 2008).

This chapter discusses business models and network design in hinterland transport. This issue is relevant for (companies in) ports, and for shippers that benefit from decreased transportation costs. From a societal perspective, improved hinterland access lowers generalized transport costs and thus enables more and cheaper trade (Limao and Venables 2001).

First, we provide a general introduction to hinterland transport chains. Next, we discuss business model innovations in hinterland transport. Third, we discuss changes in network design of intermodal transport networks, more specifically for barge networks.

15.1.1 A Nine-Level Framework of Transport and Logistics

In Fig. 15.1, we present a contrast distinction between nine levels of activities in international door-to-door transport.[2] This figure makes a distinction between activities, not between companies. Companies may offer various bundles of activities.[3] Figure 15.1 provides a basis for analyzing the position of different companies in the door-to-door chain and their business models.

The levels in Fig. 15.1 are in a hierarchy, i.e., the upper levels restrict possible choices at lower levels and deeply influence operations there. Broadly speaking, the levels range from the design of global supply chains (level 1) to the

[1] Even though total transported volumes of bulk goods (iron ore, crude oil, grain etc.) are larger than total container volumes, these container volumes impact more shippers and contain high value intermediates and (semi)finished products.

[2] These nine levels together encompass all direct activities in transport chains. Not included are the many indirect, supportive activities, such as ship finance, transport insurance, customs, and container cleaning and repair.

[3] Figure 15.1 differs from 'conventional' overviews of door-to-door chains (see for instance Van der Horst and de Langen 2008) as these show the core activities of different types of companies (e.g., shipping lines, terminal operators, and forwarders).

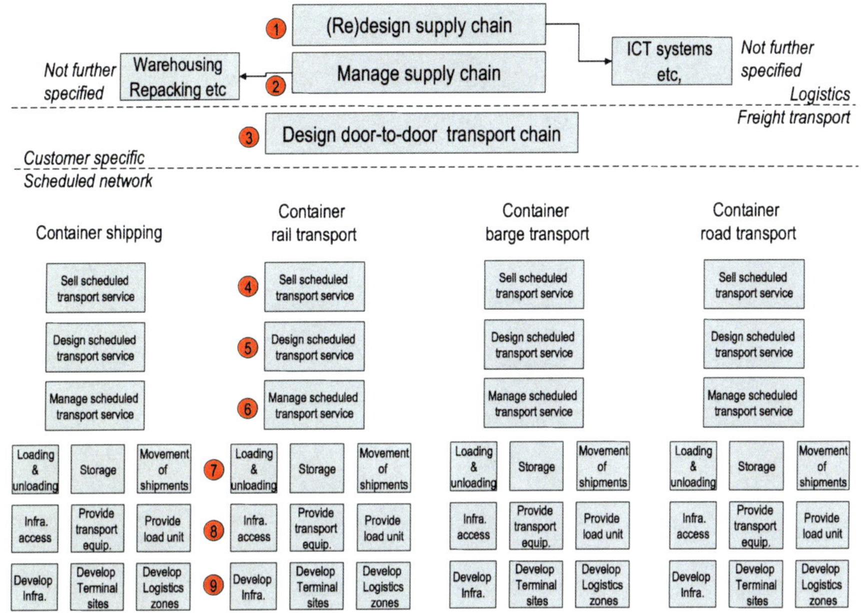

Fig. 15.1 Activities in international container transport (ICT)

development of infrastructure and industrial sites to enable freight transport movements (level 9).

The 'highest level' (Level 1) consists of the design of supply chains. That includes decisions on make-to-order versus make-to-stock (including postponement strategies), number and location of warehouses and distribution centers, and time to market. These are strategic decisions (generally with a time horizon of various years) that have consequences for all operational activities in the supply chain. Level 2 consists of the management of these supply chains, including inventory management and order processing.

Level 3 is about the design of international door-to-door chains for shippers. Shippers have specific door-to-door transport requirements. As an example, a truck service to an inland port in China is followed by a barge service to a Chinese seaport, then ocean shipping to a port in Europe, a rail service to an inland rail port (inland terminal), and a truck service to the final destination.

All parts of a door-to-door chain, except road transport (in this example the barge, ocean shipping and rail services) are offered as *scheduled* transport services. The design of a door-to-door service mainly consists of combining particular scheduled services to create a customer-specific, door-to-door chain.

For each of these scheduled services, a distinction can be made between selling (Level 4), designing (Level 5), and managing (Level 6) scheduled transport services. These are distinct activities that may be carried out by the same firm or different firms. Scheduled transport services furnish capacity in the form of container slots. For instance, an ocean shipping service between Asia and Europe may provide 8,000 container slots. These slots are sold, generally to firms that design door-to-door services. These slots are sold by various firms, such as forwarders or NVOCCs (non-vessel-operating common carriers, see Clott 2000) that purchase large bundles of slots and sell them to shippers. Scheduled services also need to be designed (Level 5). The routes, sailing speed, capacity of equipment, and frequency have to be decided. This design determines the slot capacity provided on particular routes. Design choices are strategic and do not change regularly, partly because of the substantial costs involved in altering the patterns of scheduled services. Scheduled transport is also managed (Level 6). This involves the activities of planning of transport means (such as dealing with delays), chartering transport equipment (e.g., ships) when needed, and coordination with other firms in the transport chain (including the provision of information on arrival and departure times to terminals, forwarders, and shippers).

The *management* of scheduled transport (Level 6) differs from those scheduled operations themselves, e.g., the actual sailing of a ship or the unloading of a train. That is Level 7, which consists of the *operation* of transport services, divided into three parts: loading and unloading, transport and storage.

Level 8 contains three activities that are necessary for the operation of intermodal transport services: the provision of infrastructure and the furnishing of transport equipment and load units (mainly containers). Finally, Level 9 contains the development of infrastructure, terminal sites and logistics zones.

15.1.2 Activities of Companies in the Hinterland Transport Chain

Figure 15.1 allows us to show how a certain type of company (e.g., a shipping line) or a specific firm (e.g. APL) is positioned in the intermodal transport chain. One company may carry out multiple activities in different levels. As an example, many shipping lines have moved beyond managing, designing and selling ocean shipping services, and also engage in terminal operations and selling, designing and managing rail services (see Midoro et al, 2005, and Franc and Van der Horst 2010). Different types of companies engage in the same activities. For instance, shipping lines, deep-sea terminal operators, forwarders, rail operators, port authorities, and inland rail terminal operators all engage in *design* of rail services.

The following companies play a central role in the nine levels of activities described above.

- **Shipper:** The shipper is key in the container shipping supply chain. The shipper generally outsources most (often all) transport activities. In some cases, shippers design door-to-door chains (Level 3) themselves; in other cases, they outsource this activity to others. Some shippers go a step further and outsource the entire management of supply chains (Level 2). Finally, some shippers also outsource the design of logistics (Level 1) as well (See Win 2008).
- **Freight Forwarder:** The freight forwarder typically designs door-to-door chains, and increasingly provides integrated logistics packages to its customers.

Generally, the freight forwarder does not own any vessels, terminals, trains or trucks, but purchases transport services (see Lai and Cheng 2004).

- **Container Shipping Line**: The container shipping line is traditionally responsible for moving containers from one port to the other. Shipping lines increasingly furnish door-to-door services (Level 3), and some shipping lines offer integrated logistics services (Level 2).
- **Terminal Operating Company (TOC):** The TOC provides terminal handling activities and manages the container flows at the terminal. The TOC more often develops a network of inland terminals.
- **Trucking Companies:** furnish road transport services. These companies work for shippers, forwarders or shipping lines. Some trucking firms also offer storage and value-added services.
- **Barge Operator:** The barge operators provide inland transport services by barge; they usually do not own barges, but contract with captain-owners that do own and operate the barges (Douma 2008).
- **Rail Operator:** The rail operator runs scheduled train services connecting the container terminals and inland container terminals.
- **Port Authority:** The port authority is responsible for leasing sites to port-related businesses, and for the efficient and safe movement of ships in the port. Next to that, the port authority develops port infrastructure.

15.2 Business Model Innovations in Hinterland Transport

The overview in Sect. 15.1 shows that various firms have overlapping scopes of activities. They expand into new activities, thereby changing the nature of competition. The interests of different companies in the transport chain are not aligned.[4] Given these overlapping activities, the analysis of the business model innovations is relevant. Such innovations alter the way a company positions itself in a value network.

The term *business model* has become widely used during the last decade (see Margretta 2002; Osterwalder et al. 2005; and Shafer et al. 2005[5]). Companies

---

[4] Three reasons explain why such alignment is problematic (see van der Horst and de Langen 2008). First of all, the lack of contracts between firms in the transport chain constrains the use of incentives to align interests. Secondly, the transaction costs of coordination required to align interests are often very high. Thirdly, strategic behavior may constrain alignment in transport chains. Firms do aim to align interests, and in some cases have been successful, but by and large, alignment is far from perfect

[5] Shafer et al. (2005) define a business model as 'a firm's underlying core logic for creating and capturing value within a value network'. The core logic refers to the coherence of core strategic choices. For example, the business model of a non-asset-based logistics service provider is to minimize investments in assets, whether they are ships, locomotives, warehouses or containers. Capturing value refers to the revenue streams and pricing structure. For example, does a terminal

often stick to the same business model for years, sometimes even decades, but also modify their business model. Such changes impact the organization profoundly. A business model innovation changes the core logic for creating and capturing value within a value network. Below, we describe some important ongoing business model innovations in intermodal hinterland transport, with a focus on examples in the Netherlands.

15.2.1 Inland Barge Terminals: Building a 'Network Proposition'

Four individual inland barge terminal operators in the Netherlands are faced with fierce competition from trucking companies and increasing involvement of large deep-sea TOCs and shipping lines in hinterland transport. These four firms have started to cooperate, under the name Brabant Intermodal, to move from four individual 'terminal propositions' to one shared '*network proposition*'. The idea is to develop an improved proposition towards deep sea TOCs, through a hub-and spoke system that reduces calls to the deep sea terminal, an improved proposition towards shipping lines with regard to empty container management, and an improved proposition to shippers concerning to reliable, fast and frequent services. Central in the innovation is the development of a hub-and-spoke structure. This affects the pricing, as the hub facility would have to operate on a cost-neutral basis.

15.2.2 Terminal Operating Companies: Extended Gates and Terminal Haulage

TOCs develop extended gates to reduce cost and increase customer service. The concept of the *extended gate* is that containers are not cleared, inspected or stored at the port, but that this is done at the extended gate.[6] The most important aspect of the extended gate principle is the bundling of containers at the deep-sea terminal, making it possible to increase the scale of barge transport and reduce the costs per TEU. The possibility to use the inland terminals for this purpose is facilitated by the range of functions these inland terminals can provide to sea terminals. Many inland locations with multimodal access have become broader logistic zones, taking a variety of functional roles by attracting services such as distribution centers, shipping agents, trucking companies and forwarders (Notteboom and

(Footnote 5 continued)
company charge for cargo handling only, or also for storage? The "value network" refers to the position of one firm in the supply chain, and its network relationships with other firms.

[6] One of the logistic concepts of the extended gate is *delayed differentiation* (Lee and Tang 1997). Delayed differentiation increases flexibility and requires less inventory to obtain the same customer service level, since the inventories of end products can be reduced.

Rodrigue 2008). Further, inland terminal operators usually have stronger ties with shippers, hence may have more detailed information on the container's final destination.

Consistent with the extended gate concept, TOCs can offer transport between the deep-sea terminal and the extended gate. That is called *terminal haulage* (see de Langen and Chouly 2009); it enables alignment of quay planning and barge planning.[7]

15.2.3 Shipping Lines: Low Cost Operators

All established shipping lines provide hinterland transport services. The logic of 'bundling' these activities has been analyzed (Acciaro and Haralambides 2007), but not with very clear conclusions. One of the main drivers of these activities is the involvement of shipping lines in empty container flows. Empties need to be collected from shippers at inland destinations.[8] The containers are leased or owned by the shipping lines themselves. To ensure that this repositioning is done efficiently, the shipping lines are forced to engage in hinterland transport.

In a market with over-capacity and low charter prices for container vessels, the preceding business model has been challenged by TCC (The Containership Company). Their business model is focused on simplicity, transparency and responsiveness. This means a port service only. In fact, the current service of TCC is a shuttle operation that calls at just one Chinese (Taicang) and one US (Los Angeles) port. With this low cost-approach, they compete with the established carriers.

15.2.4 Barge Operators: Planning Apart Together

In the port a coordination problem arises, as barge operators and TOCs have to align their operations to tranship containers from a barge to a terminal and vice versa (Douma et al. 2009). Barge and terminal operators attempt this alignment

---

[7] This business model innovation combines two types of business model innovations, distinguished by IBM Consulting (2008): an *enterprise model innovation*, as the 'scope' of the company is changed, as well as a *revenue model innovation*: a new revenue stream is developed. The third IBM type is the *industry model innovation*, where a new industry is developed or an industry is redefined. This has not happened (yet) in international container freight transport. But the introduction of the freight container itself was a true industry model innovation.

[8] Some containers are used for the entire door-to-door chain. But especially in the US, a substantial amount of freight is transloaded from a container to a trailer. The important advantages are that fewer containers need to be repositioned, and that more goods can be transported by a single truck.

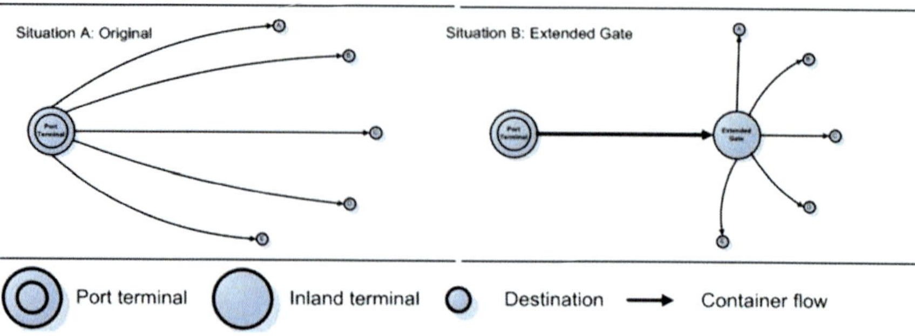

Fig. 15.2 Container flows with extended gate versus with direct calls

through service-level agreements. However, the barge companies want agreements that allow them to function according to schedule, while the TOCs aim for flexibility, to use the quay as efficiently as possible, given unreliable arrival patterns of the seagoing vessels. The result is that barge operators face randomness in waiting and handling times at terminals, and the terminals deal with uncertain arrival times of barges.

The problem cannot be solved by one specific firm. Integrated coordination is hard to achieve because it requires a central trusted party and a form of gain and loss sharing. A 'planning apart together' system may be an effective approach. Douma (2008) developed a real-time multi-agent system that focuses on optimization of the operations of the players involved, with only limited information sharing. Simulation results show that performance of the overall system can be improved significantly. However, next steps are still unclear.

This overview demonstrates the way in which business model innovations in hinterland transport impact door-to-door transport. Central in many business model innovations is the aim to *design* hinterland services, in some cases in partnership, since this has important implications for operational efficiency and the value firms create for their customers.

15.3 Network Design in Hinterland Transport

As discussed in the previous section, TOCs aim to create a competitive edge by offering efficient and effective hinterland connections. Inland terminal operators also aim to formulate a 'network proposition'. These issues will now be explored in greater detail.

TOCs that develop extended gates get more control over connections between the deep sea and the inland terminal. Furthermore, an extended gate can function as an inland hub, from where secondary inland nodes are served (see Fig. 15.2).

In this section, the results of a quantitative analysis of the viability of such a hub-and-spoke (H&S) structure are presented. These results are based on Van

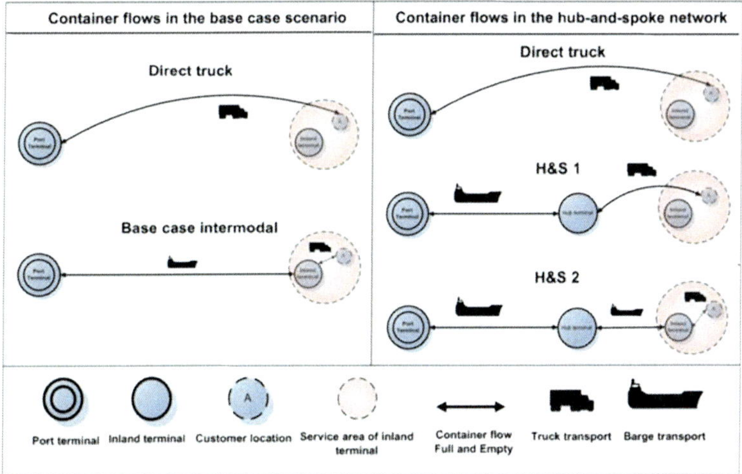

Fig. 15.3 Routing options for containers

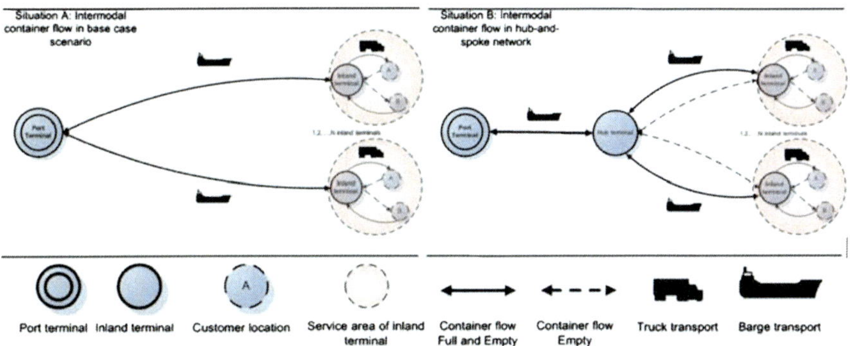

Fig. 15.4 Intermodal container flows in the base case scenario and in the H&S network

Rooy (2010). The left part of Fig. 15.2 is referred to as the base case scenario, whereas the right part will be referred to as the H&S network.

In the model, the costs of the base case and the H&S network are compared; direct truck transport is also considered, as this is another option for hinterland transport. Figure 15.3 shows the simplified container flows that were studied.

Konings (2009) conducted a preliminary analysis concerning the costs of a hub structure. He found that, beyond a distance between port and hub of about 200–300 km, the transportation costs per TEU for the hub-alternative were lower than those of the direct barge connection. On shorter distances, the cost savings in barge transportation are outweighed by the additional handling costs at the hub terminal. However, other issues need to be considered as well, most importantly re-use of empty containers (Choong et al. 2002; Jula et al. 2006).

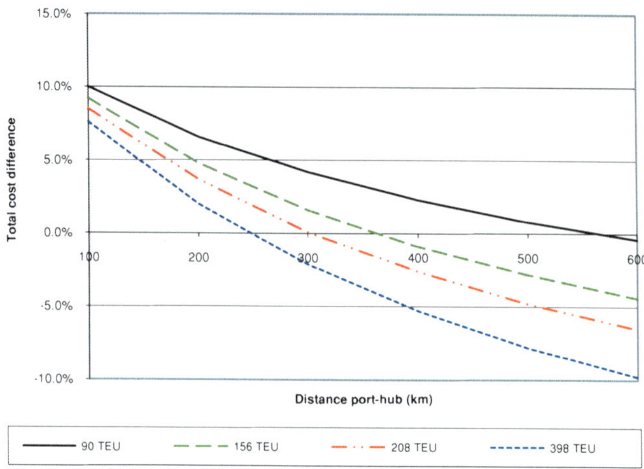

Fig. 15.5 Total-cost differences between the base case and H&S network for varying distances and barge capacities (between the port and the hub). The barge connection between port and inland terminals is kept fixed at 81 TEU)

15.3.1 Empty Container Flows

When terminals cooperate with one another in an H&S concept, container flows of the inland terminals can be combined to increase the re-use of empty containers. Demand for empty containers in one terminal's service area could also be fulfilled using empty equipment originating from the service areas of other terminals (see Fig. 15.4).

Based on this analysis, we have developed a model to quantify and compare the base case and H&S networks. The assumptions and formal model are given in Appendix 1. In the remainder of this section, we discuss the most important findings.

15.3.2 Scale Economies and Distance Between the Seaport and the Inland Hub are Required for a Hub-and-Spoke Network

Figure 15.5 shows the total-cost difference between the base case and the H&S network. The figure indicates the influence of the distance between port and hub, and the impact of the scale of connection between the port and hub.

Figure 15.5 shows that cost savings by the H&S network increase when the barge capacity of the connection between port and hub increases. Costs savings are larger if only smaller vessels can be used on the connection between the inland hub and terminals in the H&S network.[9] Finally, due to economies of scale, a greater distance between the port and hub terminal increases the H&S savings.

15.3.3 *Fuel Costs are Saved in an H&S Network; Higher Fuel Prices Make that Network More Attractive*

The cost effectiveness of the H&S network is positively correlated with the fuel price. That is because of scale economies due to larger ship sizes. This impact of fuel costs on the feasibility of the H&S network is therefore quite significant. Because of the substantial reduction in fuel consumption, the H&S concept can contribute to obtaining a more sustainable supply chain.[10]

15.3.4 *Growth of Transport Volumes has a Limited Impact on Feasibility of a Hub-and-Spoke Network*

The bundling of freight in the H&S network leads to higher vessel utilization, thus to decreased transportation costs. That effect is especially relevant in networks with small volumes. That is in line with results obtained by Konings (2009), who found the cost advantage of a trunk-feeder connection to be greatest when transportation volumes are small. In those cases, the barge connection between the port and hub was more highly utilized.

15.3.5 *The Re-use Fraction of Containers Affects the Feasibility of the H&S Network*

The fraction of empty containers that is re-used is positively related to the total cost savings that could be achieved in the H&S network. These cost savings are due to two factors. Fewer empty containers need be transported between port and hub, and a reduction in empty depot costs at the deep-sea terminal; that function is taken over by the inland hub.

---

[9] Thus, the H&S model generates (more) significant cost savings in situations where the capacity of the waterways to the inland terminal is limited, but the waterway between the port and the hub is not. This is often the case with inland waterways.

[10] The additional handlings at the hub terminal were not accounted for. These will lead to additional fuel consumption by equipment there, but that is likely to be outweighed by fuel reductions of truck and barge transportation. This issue needs to be taken into account when determining the carbon footprint of the supply chain.

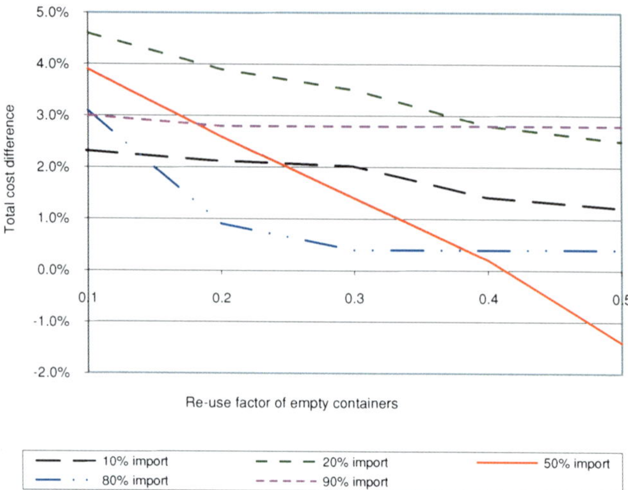

Fig. 15.6 Total cost difference between the base case scenario and the H&S network, for varying fractions of empty container re-use and different levels of import flows

Figure 15.6 shows the relations between cost savings, the percentage of containers that is re-used within the inland network, and the balance between import and export flows. An increase in the re-use fraction in the H&S network always leads to greater cost savings. However, those savings depend significantly on the balance between import and export flows. Take for example the 10 and 20 % import scenarios. Because only a small number of containers transported to the inland terminals are full, few containers are available for re-use.

The impact of the re-use fraction on total cost differences in such situations is limited, as the absolute amount of containers re-used barely increases.[11] The re-use fraction has the most impact on the attractiveness of the H&S network when the import and export flows are completely balanced.

15.3.6 Issues Related to Re-use of Empty Containers

The re-use of empty containers can generate substantial cost savings, but faces two obstacles. First, firms must be capable of matching empties with cargo flows. Carriers have the relevant information and commercial freedom to do this only for the *carrier-haulage* container flows, i.e., those that are managed by the carrier.

[11] In the 80 and 90 % import scenarios (contrary to the 10 and 20 % scenarios), the amount of full containers and therefore the re-use potential is large, but only a few of them are needed to meet empty container demand. This explains why the graphs for the 80 and 90 % scenarios are constant after a certain re-use fraction is reached.

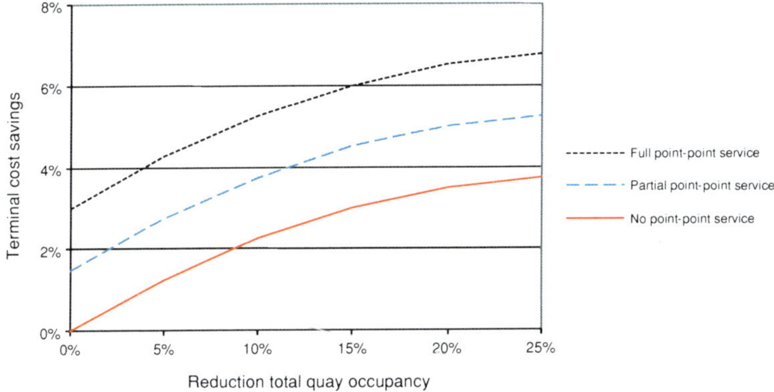

Fig. 15.7 Deep-sea-terminal savings in the H&S network

For the largest part of the flows, the forwarder or shipper manages the inland transport flows (*merchant haulage*). The shipping line (ocean carrier) with no control over merchant-haulage container flows, thus demands that empty containers be returned to the port as soon as possible. Empty container re-use in the case of merchant haulage therefore only occurs when merchants receive permission from the shipping line to pro-actively make matches between imports and exports.

Next to this issue, costing mechanisms significantly influence how and when empty containers are transported. These costing mechanisms are strategic tools used by shipping lines to have control over their container fleet, the merchant container flow, and the container stock at empty depots. Shipping lines charge the so-called demurrage and detention fees to freight forwarders and shippers. *Demurrage* fees are imposed for having a container on storage in the port area. *Detention* fees are paid if the container is not returned to the port within a certain period. These fees aim to reduce the dwell times of containers in the port, and to enable an increase in the number of yearly container shipments. Detention charges are detrimental to the re-use of empty containers, as it often takes a while before a match between import ànd export can be made.

Furthermore, when freight forwarders want to re-use empty equipment at an inland terminal, they often have to pay drop-off and pick-up fees to the shipping line. These fees are not charged when they return an empty container to the sea port. This also hampers empty container re-use at inland terminals.

15.3.7 H&S Networks have a Positive Impact on Quay Occupancy and thus Terminal Efficiency

Douma (2008) argues that the H&S configuration can lead to a reduction of the average number of deep-sea terminal calls in a barge rotation, and an increase of the average call sizes at terminals. Figure 15.7 indeed shows the effect of an H&S network on terminal costs, based on a preliminary assessment. These results are relevant, given the fact that deep-sea-terminal costs account for approximately 10 % of total costs.

15.4 Conclusions

The changing roles of many players in the container supply chain currently leads to a re-definition of the competitive landscape. Large players like freight forwarders, terminal operators, and shipping lines are all attempting to gain more control over hinterland transport. This control serves to increase the efficiency of hinterland transport. Control also permits the respective player to be closer to the final customer, and to be able to offer improved service levels at lower costs. If these players assume different roles in hinterland transport, the network structures are likely to change. While direct connections in the hinterland are still the predominant network design, hub-and-spoke systems have come more into play. In H&S, the efficiency of transportation services is increased, whereas additional costs are incurred due to extra handling. A study of barge hinterland networks in the Netherlands demonstrates that H&S networks are feasible. Utmost care must be taken in their design, however, as these networks are extremely cost sensitive to small changes in the various cost components.

Appendix 1: Assumptions, the Formal Model and Relevant Parameters

Assumptions:

1. Once a container is loaded on a truck in the port area, this truck directly drives to the shipper site, without intermediate handling at the hub or inland terminal, as truck transport is typically used when the container needs to be transported quickly.
2. All empty equipment that can be re-used in the H&S network, but which cannot be used for a terminal's own service area, is transported back to the hub before it is re-distributed, i.e., no mutual empty equipment exchange between inland terminals is assumed.
3. All empty containers not being re-used are transported back to either a port terminal or an empty depot in the port area, but all full containers destined for export are transported back to a port terminal only.
4. Transportation is executed using only standard 20ft and standard 40ft containers. The impact of this assumption on eventual results is negligible. (The share of standard containers in total container volume is very substantial.

Furthermore, other-sized containers only marginally influence costs or are not used for the operations under consideration.)
5. Empty and full containers are shipped between two nodes in the same barge.

Not Included in the Model

6. The handling costs and holding costs of the goods in the container. This follows from the assumption that the overall door-to-door time differs only marginally in both alternatives.
7. Container storage costs are not taken into account explicitly in the model; costs of additional storage capacity are in fact negligible compared to those of handling and transportation.

The Model

See Table 15.1 for a description of parameters and their ranges in value.

A: Direct Call (Base Case)

Volume calculation

The following formula was derived for determining the total volume of containers, $\mathbf{V}_i$, that needs to be transported between the port and the service area of a terminal:

$$\mathbf{V}_i = \mathbf{D}_i - \min(\mathbf{D}_i^f * \alpha^b, \mathbf{D}_i - \mathbf{D}_i^f) \tag{15.1}$$

The *minimum* expression in this function needs to be included, as one cannot re-use more containers than the total demand for empty containers in the service area.

$$\text{Total truck volume,} \quad \mathbf{V}_i^T = \mathbf{V}_i * ut_{P,i} \tag{15.2}$$

$$\text{Total barge volume} \quad \mathbf{V}_i^B = \mathbf{V}_i * \left(1 - ut_{P,i}\right) \tag{15.3}$$

Barge connection calculation

Based on an empirical analysis of a number of inland terminals, it is assumed demand is normally distributed. Thus, the required capacity, $\mathbf{c}_i^{\min}$, of the barge connection can be calculated as follows:

$$\mathbf{c}_i^{\min} = \mu_{v,i} + z(SL_i^{req}) * \sigma_{v,i}, \tag{15.4}$$

Table 15.1 Specification of parameters for the inland barge terminal network in the Netherlands

Parameter	Description	Range	Value if fixed
D_i	Total yearly demand of containers for the service area of terminal i (TEU)	Hub = 30,000–140,000 Terminal = 0.5 * D_H	Hub = 70,000 Terminal = 35,000
a^h	Fraction of empty containers that can be re-used in the H&S network	0.1–0.4	0.1
$ut^h_{P,i}$	Percentage of unimodal transport by truck between the Port and terminal i in the H&S network	0–20 %	20 %
$ut_{H,i}$	Percentage of unimodal transport by truck between the Hub and terminal i	Dependent on $ut^h_{P,i}$	0 %
$d_{P,i}$	Average distance between the Port and shippers in the service area of terminal i (km)	Hub = 100–600 IT = $d_{P,i}$+$d_{H,i}$	200
$d_{H,i}$	Average distance between the Hub and shippers in the service area of terminal i (km)	25–150	75
C_i	Capacity of the barges on the connection between the Port/Hub and terminal i (TEU)	Port-Hub = 90–398 Port - Terminal = 24–156	Port–Hub = 208 Port–IT = 81
$tt_{P,i}$	Transit time in hours of the barge between the Port and terminal i	Dependent on $d_{P,i}$	Port–Hub = 17 Port–IT = 23
$tt_{H,i}$	Transit time in hours of the barge between the Hub and terminal i	Dependent on $d_{H,i}$	8
ρ	Fraction of semi-fixed costs that is considered as variable costs	0.0–1.0	0.5

where $\sigma_{v,i}$ is calculated as

$$\sigma_{v,i} = \mu_{v,i} * cv_v \tag{15.5}$$

Using the value obtained for the required capacity, one can calculate the frequency, f_i, of the barge connection. However, that frequency must be high enough to offer a certain service. Therefore, the formula becomes

$$f_i = \max\left(f_{\min}, \frac{\mathbf{c}_i^{\min}}{C_i}\right) \tag{15.6}$$

The average total round-trip time between port and inland terminal, $TT_{P,i}$, was calculated as

$$TT_{P,i} = 2tt_{P,i} + tw_P^B + tw_i^B + \frac{4(U_i * C_i)/TEUF_i}{r_i^B + r_P^B} \tag{15.7}$$

The final part of the formula shows the average handling time during one round trip.

The slack time, tw_P^B, required to achieve a certain service level, was found via the following formula

$$tw_P^B = \left(\frac{(-Ln(SL_i))^{-\xi} - 1}{\xi}\right) * \sigma + \mu \tag{15.8}$$

The total barging costs per year, $TC_{P,i}^B$ for maintaining the barge connection between the port and terminal i was then calculated as

$$TC_{P,i}^B = \left(FC_{c,i}^B + VC_{c,i}^B\right) * nb_{P,i}, \tag{15.9}$$

where

$$VC_{c,i}^B = P^G * \left(tt_{P,i} * Gt_c + \left(tw_P^B + tw_i^B\right) * Gw_c\right), \tag{15.10}$$

$$FC_{c,i}^B = dc_c^B + pc_c^B + ic_c^B + mc_c^B, \tag{15.11}$$

and

$$nb_{P,i} = \frac{TO}{TT_{P,i}}. \tag{15.12}$$

In the above, $dc_c^B, pc_c^B, ic_c^B, mc_c^B$ stand for yearly depreciation, personnel, insurance and maintenance cost of a barge with capacity c; $nb_{P,i}$ represents the number of barges required per year; and TO denotes the total yearly operating time of terminals and barges.

The total annual costs of barge transport for the base case were then obtained

$$TC^B = \sum_{i=1}^{N} TC_{P,i}^B = \sum_{i=1}^{N} \left(\left(FC_{c,i}^B + VC_{c,i}^B\right) * nb_{P,i}\right) \tag{15.13}$$

Truck connection calculation

The yearly costs $TC_{P,i}^T$ of direct, unimodal transport between the port and the shippers in the service area of terminal i are

$$TC_{P,i}^T = tc_{P,i} * \left(\frac{\mathbf{V}_i^T}{TEU^T}\right) \tag{15.14}$$

With the following formula, the trip cost $tc_{P,i}$ between the port and inland terminal was calculated[12]:

$$tc_{P,i} = vc_d * Td_{P,i} + vc_h\left(\frac{Td_{P,i}}{v_{gem}^T} + tw_{P,i}^T\right) \tag{15.15}$$

[12] Handling time, waiting time at the port terminal, and congestion time on the highway are all included in $tw_{P,i}^T$.

Here $Td_{P,i}$ represents the average total distance travelled for a round trip from the port to the service area of terminal i, and was determined as:

$$Td_{P,i} = 2d_{P,i} + d_O \tag{15.16}$$

The yearly costs of truck transport from the inland terminal to its service area, $TC^T_{t,i}$, were found similarly.

Adding these costs to the costs of direct trucking between the port and the hinterland, the total costs TC^T of truck transport were thus

$$TC^T = \sum_{i=1}^{N} \left(TC^T_{P,i} + TC^T_{t,i} \right) \tag{15.17}$$

Handling costs calculation

The yearly amount of truck handlings, h^T_i, and the yearly amount of barge handlings at inland terminal i, h^B_i, were obtained using the following two formulas;

$$h^T_i = \left(\frac{\mathbf{D}_i * (1 - ut_{P,i})}{TEUF_i} \right) * 2 \tag{15.18}$$

$$h^B_i = \left(\frac{\mathbf{V}^B_i}{TEUF_i} \right) * 2 \tag{15.19}$$

For terminal handlings, the assumption was made that barge handlings are more expensive than truck handlings, due to the use of more expensive equipment and additional resources when handling barges. It was therefore assumed the variable costs for barge handlings were a factor ε larger than the variable costs of truck handling. The total handling costs for terminal i, TC^H_i, could then be calculated as

$$TC^H_i = FC^H_i + SFC^H_i + VC^H_i * \left(h^T_i + \varepsilon h^B_i \right) \tag{15.20}$$

Let h^T_P and h^B_P respectively denote the truck handlings and barge handlings at the port. Equations. (15.21) and (15.22) were employed for the volumes of handling there.

$$h^T_P = \sum_{i=1}^{N} \frac{D_i * ut_{P,i}}{TEUF_i} + \beta * \sum_{i=1}^{N} \frac{ut_{P,i} * (2V_i - D_i)}{TEUF_i} \tag{15.21}$$

$$h^B_P = \sum_{i=1}^{N} \frac{D_i * (1 - ut_{P,i})}{TEUF_i} + \beta * \sum_{i=1}^{N} \frac{(1 - ut_{P,i}) * (2V_i - D_i)}{TEUF_i} \tag{15.22}$$

Now consider the empty-depot handlings, where h^T_E and h^B_E represent truck handlings and barge handlings at the empty depot respectively:

$$h^T_E = (1 - \beta) * \sum_{i=1}^{N} \frac{ut_{P,i} * (2V_i - D_i)}{TEUF_i} \tag{15.23}$$

and

$$h_E^B = (1-\beta) * \sum_{i=1}^{N} \frac{(1 - ut_{P,i}) * (2V_i - D_i)}{TEUF_i} \tag{15.24}$$

In those equations, β is the fraction of empty containers brought back to the port terminal.

The total annual handling costs for the port terminal and the empty depot can then be found from Eqs. (15.25) and (15.26):

$$TC_P^H = VC_P^H * \left(h_P^T + \varepsilon h_P^B\right) \tag{15.25}$$

$$TC_E^H = VC_E^H * \left(h_E^T + \varepsilon h_E^B\right) \tag{15.26}$$

Total costs calculation

The total yearly costs, $TC^{tot}$of the base case can be obtained using the following formula:

$$TC^{tot} = TC_P^H + TC_E^H + \sum_{i=1}^{N} \left(TC_i^H + TC_{P,i}^T + TC_{t,i}^T + TC_{P,i}^B\right) \tag{15.27}$$

B: The hub-and-spoke model

Volume calculation

Because the volumes transported between the port and inland terminals are consolidated at the hub terminal, determination of those volumes differ considerably from that of the base case. The annual volume transported directly between the port and terminal i is given by

$$\mathbf{V}_{P,i}^T = \mathbf{V}_i * ut_{P,i}^H \tag{15.28}$$

The remaining volume that needs to be transported towards the service area of terminal i, $\mathbf{V}_i^{T,B}$, was calculated as:

$$\mathbf{V}_i^{T,B} = \left(\mathbf{D}_i - \min\left(\mathbf{D}_i^f * \alpha^h, \mathbf{D}_i - \mathbf{D}_i^f\right)\right) * \left(1 - ut_{P,i}^h\right) \tag{15.29}$$

The yearly volume transported by truck between the hub and the service area of a terminal is then

$$\mathbf{V}_{H,i}^T = \mathbf{V}_i^{T,B} * ut_{H,i} \tag{15.30}$$

For yearly volume transported by barge between the hub and terminal i, the following equation is used:

$$\mathbf{V}_{H,i}^B = \mathbf{V}_i^{T,B}\left(1 - ut_{H,i}\right) \tag{15.31}$$

For the yearly volume transported by barge between the port and the hub terminal, $\mathbf{V}^{B}_{P,H}$, the calculations are somewhat more difficult, and are based on Eq. (15.32):

$$V^{B}_{P,H} = \sum_{i=1}^{N} \left(D^{f}_{i} * \left(1 - ut^{h}_{P,i}\right)\right) + \max\left(0, \sum_{i=1}^{N} \left(\left(1 - ut^{h}_{P,i}\right) * \left(D_{i} - \left(1 + \alpha^{h}\right)D^{f}_{i}\right)\right)\right) \qquad (15.32)$$

Barge connection calculation

The frequency of the barge connection between the port and hub, and the number of port calls per visit, differ from the base case. This is because the connection needs to be point-to-point in the H&S network, to reduce the uncertainty and risk. That frequency was therefore calculated as follows:

$$f^{h}_{i} = \max\left(2f_{\min}, \frac{\mathbf{c}^{\min}_{i}}{C_{i}}\right) \qquad (15.33)$$

(Note the difference from the number of port calls per visit as given by Eq. (15.6)). Because of the accumulation of demand for inland terminals at the hub, there is decreased variation for the connection between the port and the hub. The expression becomes

$$C^{\min}_{H} = \sum_{i=1}^{N} \mu^{V}_{i} + z(SL^{req}_{i}) * \sqrt{\sum_{i=1}^{N} \left(\sigma^{V}_{i}\right)^{2}} \qquad (15.34)$$

Truck connection calculation

Obtaining the costs of truck transport here is completely similar to the base case, with the exception that the costs of transporting containers between the hub and terminal i must be added. To determine these costs, $TC^{T}_{H,i}$, the following equation was used:

$$TC^{T}_{H,i} = tc_{H,i} * \left(\frac{V^{T}_{H,i}}{TEU^{T}}\right) \qquad (15.35)$$

One can find the trip costs between the hub and inland terminal, $tc_{P,i}$, with the formula

$$tc_{H,i} = vc_{d} * Td_{H,i} + vc_{h}\left(\frac{Td_{H,i}}{v^{T}_{gem}} + tw^{T}_{H,i}\right) \qquad (15.36)$$

Here $Td_{P,i}$, represents the average total distance travelled for a round trip from the hub to the service area of terminal i and is calculated

$$Td_{H,i} = 2d_{H,i} + d_O \tag{15.37}$$

Following this extra container flow by truck between hub and the service areas of inland terminals, the annual costs of truck transport for the H&S network is expressed as follows:

$$TC^T = \sum_{i=1}^{N} \left(TC_{P,i}^T + TC_{t,i}^T + TC_{H,i}^T \right) \tag{15.38}$$

Handling costs calculation

The yearly amount of truck and barge handlings at the hub terminal, h_H^T and h_H^B, are given by Eqs. (15.39) and (15.40):

$$h_H^T = \left(\frac{\mathbf{D}_H * \left(1 - ut_{P,H}^H\right) + \sum_{i=2}^{N} \mathbf{V}_{H,i}^T}{TEUF_i} \right) \tag{15.39}$$

$$h_H^B = \frac{2 * \left(\mathbf{V}_{P,H}^B + \sum_{i=2}^{N} \mathbf{V}_{H,i}^B \right)}{TEUF_i} \tag{15.40}$$

The total amounts of truck and barge handlings at the port terminal and the empty depot, respectively, $h_P^{H,T}, h_P^{H,B}, h_E^{H,T}$ and $h_E^{H,B}$ were found via Eqs. (15.41)–(15.44):

$$h_P^{H,T} = \left(\frac{\sum_{i=1}^{N} ut_{P,i}^H * (2\mathbf{V}_i - \mathbf{D}_i)}{TEUF_i} \right) * \min\left(1, \frac{E_{tot}^C * \beta}{E_{tot}^H}\right) \tag{15.41}$$

$$h_P^{H,B} = \left(\frac{2\mathbf{V}_{P,H}^B - \sum_{i=1}^{N} \left(\mathbf{D}_i * \left(1 - ut_{P,i}^H\right) \right)}{TEUF_i} \right) * \min\left(1, \frac{E_{tot}^C * \beta}{E_{tot}^H}\right) \tag{15.42}$$

$$h_E^{H,T} = \left(\frac{\sum_{i=1}^{N} ut_{P,i}^H * (2\mathbf{V}_i - \mathbf{D}_i)}{TEUF_i} \right) - h_E^{H,B} \tag{15.43}$$

$$h_E^{H,B} = \left(\frac{2\mathbf{V}_{P,H}^B - \sum_{i=1}^{N} \left(\mathbf{D}_i * \left(1 - ut_{P,i}^H\right) \right)}{TEUF_i} \right) - h_P^{H,B} \tag{15.44}$$

In those equations, E_{tot}^{C} and E_{tot}^{H} represent total numbers of available empty containers in the base case and in the hub-and-spoke case.

References

Acciaro M, Haralambides HE (2007) Product bundling in global ocean transportation. In: Proceedings of the International Association of Maritime Economists (IAME) Annual Conference, Athens, Greece

Choong ST, Cole MH, Kutanoglu E (2002) Empty container management for intermodal transportation networks. Transp Res E 38(4):423–438

Clott CB (2000) Non-vessel operating common carriers (NVOCCs) and maritime reform. Transp J 40(2):17–26

Douma A (2008) Aligning the operations of barges and terminals through distributed planning. PhD thesis, University of Twente

Douma AM, Schutten JMJ, Schuur PC (2009) Waiting profiles: an efficient protocol for enabling distributed planning of barge rotations along terminals in the Port of Rotterdam. Transp Res C 17(2):133–148

Franc P, Van der Horst MR (2010) Understanding hinterland service integration by shipping lines and terminal operators: a theoretical and empirical analysis. J Transp Geogr 18(4):557–566

IBM Consulting (2008) Global CEO study: the enterprise of the future, Available at http://www.ibm.com/ibm/ideasfromibm/us/ceo/20080505/resources/IFI_05052008.pdf

Jula H, Chassiakos A, Ioannou P (2006) Port dynamic empty container reuse. Transp Res E 42(1):43–60

Konings JW (2009) Intermodal barge transport: network design, nodes and competitiveness. PhD thesis, Technische Universiteit Delft

Lai KH, Cheng TCE (2004) A study of the freight forwarding industry in Hong Kong. Int J Logistics: Res Appl 7(2): 71–84

Langen PW de, Chouly A (2009) Strategies of terminal operators in changing environments. Int J Logistics: Res Appl 12(6):423–434

Lee HL, Tang CS (1997) Modelling the costs and benefits of delayed product differentiation, Manage Sci 43(1):40–53

Limao N, Venables AJ (2001) Infrastructure, geographical disadvantage and transport costs. World Bank Econ Rev. 15:451–479

Margretta J (2002) Why business models matter. Harvard Bus Rev 80(5):86–92

Midoro R, Musso E, Parola F (2005) Maritime liner shipping and the stevedoring industry: market structure and competition strategies. Marit Policy Manage 32(2):89–106

Notteboom T (2008) The relationship between seaports and the intermodal hinterland in light of global supply chains: European challenges, Discussion Paper No. 2008-10, OECD—International Transport Forum, Paris

Notteboom TE, Rodrigue JP (2005) Port regionalization: towards a new phase in port development. Marit Policy Manage 32(3):297–313

Notteboom T, Rodrigue J-P (2008) Containerization, box logistics and global supply chains: the integration of ports and liner shipping networks. Marit Econ Logistics 10(1–2):152–174

Ostenwalder A, Pigneu Y, Tucci CL (2005) Clarifying business models: origins, present, and future of the concept. Communications of AIS, 15

Shafer SM, Smith HJ, Linder JC (2005) The power of business models. Bus Horiz 48:199–207

Van der Horst MR, de Langen P.W (2008) Coordination in hinterland transport chains: a major challenge for the seaport community. Marit Econ Logistics 10(2):108–129

Van Rooy B (2010) Applying hub-and-spoke networks to inland barge transportation: a quantitative and qualitative analysis for a port terminal operator. Master's thesis, Eindhoven University of Technology

Win A (2008) The value a 4PL provider can contribute to an organisation. Int J Phys Distrib Logistics Manage 38(9):674–684

Chapter 16
Cross-Border Issues and Research

James K. Higginson

Abstract Activities at an international border are meant to ensure the security of the residents of a country. The inevitable results are "cross-border issues" —challenges, decisions, and responsibilities not encountered when movements of freight or people are entirely within one nation. This chapter discusses the most common cross-border events that carriers, shippers, importers, and exporters encounter when products move across an international frontier, with an emphasis on academic research on border issues and operations.

16.1 Introduction

The border between two countries denotes a line of demarcation: a change in policies, procedures, rules, and often cultures and ideologies. As such, a border is inherently a place of disagreement or even conflict, and any person or organization moving people or goods across an international frontier will face challenges and decisions that are not experienced when movements are entirely within one country.

This chapter examines the cross-border movement of freight. To do so, we apply a fairly narrow definition of "border", focussing on what occurs there. Our discussion does not deal with wider questions in international trade logistics.

Activities at a border crossing are intended to maintain the *security* (physical, political, economic, or cultural), and eliminate threats to that security, of the residents of a country. This chapter treats that goal implicitly: we do not examine explicitly the security of a supply chain or a nation. Research on supply chain

J. K. Higginson (✉)
Odette School of Business, University of Windsor, Windsor, ON N9B 3P4, Canada
e-mail: jhiggin@uwindsor.ca

J. H. Bookbinder (ed.), *Handbook of Global Logistics*, International Series in Operations Research & Management Science 181, DOI: 10.1007/978-1-4419-6132-7_16,

security includes Sheffi (2001), Randall and Ammah-Tagoe (2003), Chopra and Sodhi (2004), Closs and McGarrell (2004), Hale and Moberg (2005), and Wright et al. (2006).

The objectives of this chapter are: (1) To describe the most common issues concerning cross-border logistics and transportation that impact shippers, carriers, importers, and exporters; (2) to review and discuss the academic publications on those cross-border questions; (3) to identify areas where further study can be conducted, especially in the application of operations research techniques; and (4) to provide guidance related to the modelling of cross-border processes and activities. While the chapter focuses on the border between Canada and the U.S.A., the discussions herein and the publications surveyed can be applied to analysis of transportation and related factors at many other borders.

This chapter begins with an overview of the major Canada–U.S. issues involving the cross-border movement of goods. That summary is followed by more in-depth discussions of those matters and the corresponding academic literature. We close with comments about future research in cross-border logistics.

16.2 What are the Major Border Issues?

The goal of maintaining the security of residents of a nation through border activities means reducing the illegal movement of persons and goods across that border. This has two major ramifications for individuals and organizations (shippers, carriers, importers/exporters, and third-party logistics service providers) conducting legal business across a frontier: time and cost. Thus, it is convenient to classify the consequences of border activities into those two areas.

Numerous studies and reports (e.g., Taylor et al. 2004; The Canadian Chamber of Commerce et al. 2009) have shown that the cost to a carrier or shipper of crossing the Canada–U.S. border is not insignificant, and the time spent waiting for clearance at these border points can be long. We therefore identify three general categories of cross-border issues:

1. High dollar costs of crossing a border, consisting of:
   - direct border crossing costs, such as administrative fees
   - indirect border crossing costs, such as warehouse costs due to higher inventories caused by unpredictable crossing times
2. Long and unpredictable waiting and inspection times, resulting from (The Canadian Chamber of Commerce et al. 2009):
   - inadequate border infrastructure
   - complex and/or redundant processes and procedures
   - inadequate staffing and training of border personnel
   - insufficient information being provided to cross-border shippers and travellers
   - technology and system malfunctions

3. Miscellaneous issues (which impact either or both of cost or time), such as multiple jurisdictions and overlapping regulations.

We examine each of these general categories of cross-border issues in greater detail, beginning in the next section with discussion of the costs to carriers and shippers of crossing a border.

16.3 Border Crossing Costs

Many studies have attempted to estimate the cost of a border crossing, whether at the macro level (i.e., costs and benefits to a nation, province, or state of establishing border crossings), the micro level (i.e., costs to a community of supporting a specific crossing), or the firm level (i.e., costs to users of a crossing). A list of these costs is lengthy, and includes infrastructure costs (e.g., costs of roads and inspection areas), social costs (e.g., costs of congestion, safety concerns, and air and noise pollution), government costs (e.g., salaries and training costs of border inspectors), and carrier and shipper costs. This section examines the category of firm-level costs. Discussions of costs at the other two levels can be found in, for example, Ontario Chamber of Commerce Border and Trade Committee (2004, 2005) HDR/HLB Decision Economics (2006) and The Canadian Chamber of Commerce et al. (2009).

Taylor et al. (2003, 2004) suggest that a carrier's or shipper's costs of crossing a border can be classified as: (1) transit time and uncertainty costs, and (2) general border costs. These are summarized in Table 16.1. Those papers estimate that, in 2003, the overall annual cost to carriers and shipper of crossing between Canada and the U.S.A. was about $6.3 billion, with the costs of transit time and uncertainty being about $4.0 billion of that total (Taylor et al. 2003, 2004).

In dollar-terms, Taylor et al. (2003, 2004) report that the four largest of these costs are: lost sourcing benefits (shipper/manufacturer cost), extra inventory carrying costs (shipper/manufacturer cost), secondary delays (carrier cost), and primary delays (carrier costs).

Secondary delays refer to delays and costs incurred at the border when a vehicle, container, or shipment, rather than being cleared during primary inspection, must undergo further processing. This most frequently results when documentation accompanying the shipment is not complete; it may also occur when a customs inspector feels that the vehicle and/or its contents and/or its driver warrant more in-depth scrutiny. Total delay due to secondary inspection could be as long as several hours if the vehicle is transporting goods for multiple shippers (as with many courier and less-than-truckload movements). Taylor et al. (2004) comment that many studies of border crossing times consider only delays due to primary inspection and ignore secondary inspection, although the estimated cost of the latter exceeds that of the former.

Taylor et al. (2004) also note that "cross-border trucking freight rates are considerably higher than would be the case for similar domestic U.S. moves… key

Table 16.1 Carrier and shipper costs of border crossing

Carrier costs	
Transit time and uncertainty costs	• Time to complete primary inspection at the border • Time to complete secondary yard processing (if required) at the border (discussed below) • Time added to a drivers' schedule to allow for border delays and uncertainties • Reduced vehicle and driver cycles (= reduced utilization per driver and vehicle) • Time to complete documentation • Missed cargo exchanges with other vehicles and modes • Cancellation of future privileges (e.g., reservations with container ship lines) due to frequent late arrivals
General border costs	• Costs of employees to handle border administration (e.g., documentation processing, staff sited at border, conflict resolution) • Costs due to cabotage prohibition (e.g., causing vehicles to return empty) and other regulations
Shipper (manufacturer) costs	
Transit time and uncertainty costs	• Lost benefits from sourcing internationally (i.e., problematic border crossings may discourage purchasing from vendors outside the country, perhaps forfeiting higher quality or lower priced goods) • Extra warehousing and inventory carrying costs due to larger buffer inventories
General border costs	• Higher carrier rates • Costs of brokerage, customs duties, border fees and penalties, and customs administration

Source Adapted from Taylor et al. (2003, 2004)

reasons relate to border crossing transit time, uncertainty about border crossing times and costs, and the costs of related administration and information systems support." Differences in these rates range from 10 to 35 %. As well, some carriers apply a surcharge for each cross-border shipment transported.

Carrier-related and shipper-related costs are also outlined by The Canadian Chamber of Commerce et al. (2009), including examples of direct costs for crossing the border. These involve user charges such as the U.S. Animal and Plant Health Inspection Fee levied on certain shipments entering the U.S.A., and certification costs of participating in "trusted shipper" programs such as C-TPAT and FAST (discussed in Sect. 16.5 of this chapter). Indirect costs and consequences from border-crossing delays, as identified by Goodchild et al. (2007), include customer dissatisfaction; delaying of a second vehicle that was scheduled to meet and transfer loads to/from the cross-border vehicle; driver problems with hours-of service regulations; unanticipated rail demurrage charges due to delays in transferring cross-border truck freight to rail cars; and loss of future appointment times at water ports. Anderson's (2009) model includes three categories of costs: (1) those due to border crossing delays (e.g., driver wages, fuel, idled capital),

(2) additional inventory holding costs to protect against stockouts, and (3) compliance costs (e.g., membership in C-TPAT and FAST).

Many carrier and shipper costs of crossing a border are a result of lengthy and uncertain processing times (and carrier/shipper actions to reduce this uncertainty). That is the focus of the next section.

16.4 Border Crossing Times and Delays

"Border crossings create delays in transportation and add uncertainty to transit times as customs clearance, traffic congestion, and other operating procedures are often highly variable with respect to time" (Stank and Crum 1997). The interval that a vehicle spends at a border impacts a wide range of carrier and shipper tactical and operational plans, including driver staffing, warehouse usage, vehicle routing and scheduling, and total cost.

A key first step in planning responses to border delays is estimating how long a driver and vehicle will require to cross (or often, *wait*) at a border crossing. Although many border authorities (including Canada Border Services Agency and the U.S. Customs and Border Protection agency) publish estimated wait times, these statistics are for the current instant, and unless one is willing to compile a large number of these observations to create a frequency distribution, they have limited usefulness for modelling purposes. The good news for researchers and modellers is that *summary* border crossing time data are not as difficult to obtain as one might expect. There are, however, several important limitations to those data, as this chapter will identify.

We also should stress that border crossing time data quickly become out-of-date. Recent decline in the number of commercial vehicles crossing the border has led to reduced wait times (to illustrate, in 2009, truck-transported cross-border trade between Canada and the U.S.A. was 31 % less than that in 2008, as reported by The Canadian Chamber of Commerce et al. 2009). The Ambassador Bridge, for example, reported a mean wait time of almost 45 min in February and May 2003, but less than 5 min throughout 2005 and much of 2006 (Bradbury 2010). Although the long waits at the Canada-U.S. border seen in the early 2000s and in 2007 (The Canadian Chamber of Commerce et al. 2009) are not currently being repeated, concerns exist that, as economies improve, border crossing times will also increase.

Once a vehicle has arrived at the border, the major determinants of the interval it will require to cross are:

- its direction of movement (e.g., trucks entering U.S.A from Canada or Mexico experience longer crossing times than trucks leaving U.S.A. (Leore et al. 2003; HDR/HLB Decision Economics 2006)
- the number of inspection lanes open (and hence, the number of inspectors working)

- the time of day, day of week, and season of the year
- whether the crossing provides priority service to qualified carrier or shipments (discussed later in this chapter)
- whether or not the vehicle will be required to undergo secondary inspection at the border crossing (discussed in the previous section).

We now examine the characteristics of border crossing times and how researchers have obtained crossing-time data.

16.4.1 What Do Border-Crossing-Time Data Look Like?

In order to get a feel for the characteristics of border-crossing times and where researchers have obtained such data, we will discuss six empirical studies of border-crossing times. In chronological sequence, the studies are:

1. Paselk and Mannering (1994): Use of duration models for predicting vehicular delay at a US/Canadian border crossing. *Border crossing(s) discussed:* Peace Arch crossing between Surrey, British Columbia and Blaine, Washington. This study examined passenger vehicles only; commercial traffic is not permitted to use the Peace Arch border crossing.
2. Office of Freight Management and Operations, Texas Traffic Institute, and Battelle Memorial Institute (2001): *International Border Crossing Truck Travel Time for 2001. Border crossing(s) discussed:* Ambassador Bridge between Windsor, Ontario and Detroit, Michigan; Peace Arch crossing between Surrey, B.C. and Blaine, Washington; Blue Water Bridge between Sarnia, Ontario and Port Huron, Michigan; Otay Mesa crossing between San Diego, California and Tijuana, Mexico; Peace Bridge between Fort Erie, Ontario and Buffalo, New York; World Trade Bridge, between Laredo, Texas and Nuevo Laredo, Mexico; Zaragoza Bridge, between El Paso, Texas and Ciudad Juárez, Mexico. The results of this study have been used by a number of reports and papers; for example, Lepofsky et al. (2003), HDR/HLB Decision Economics (2006).
3. Leore et al. (2003): Using truck tractor logs to estimate travel times at Canada-U.S. border crossings in Southern Ontario. *Border crossing(s) discussed:* Ambassador Bridge (Windsor, Ontario–Detroit, Michigan); Blue Water Bridge (Sarnia, Ontario–Port Huron, Michigan); Peace Bridge (Fort Erie, Ontario–Buffalo, New York); Queenston–Lewiston Bridge (Queenston, Ontario–Lewiston, New York). This study monitored only Canada-bound traffic on the Peace Bridge and only U.S.A.-bound traffic on the Queenston–Lewiston Bridge.
4. Goodchild et al. (2007): *Service Time Variability at the Blaine, Washington, International Border Crossing and the Impact on Regional Supply Chains. Border crossing(s) discussed:* Blaine, Washington crossing (Surrey, B.C.–Blaine, WA)

5. Anderson and Coates (2010): Delays and uncertainties in freight movements at U.S.–Canada border crossings. *Border crossing(s) discussed:* Ambassador Bridge (Windsor, ON–Detroit, MI); Blue Water Bridge (Sarnia, ON–Port Huron, MI); Peace Bridge (Fort Erie, ON–Buffalo, NY); Queenston–Lewiston Bridge (Queenston, ON–Lewiston, NY).
6. Conroy (2010): Looking for efficiency gains at the Pacific Highway commercial border crossing. *Border crossing(s) discussed:* Pacific Highway truck crossing (Surrey, B.C.–Blaine, WA).

The statistical characteristics of border crossing times are summarized in Table 16.2 (two observations from the U.S.-Mexico border from 2001 are included for comparison). Although most studies contain graphs of crossing times by hour (revealing that the data are positively skewed), only Goodchild et al. (2007) report attempts to fit a theoretical probability distribution to the data; that study found that waiting time followed an approximately lognormal distribution with $\mu = 4.53$ and $\sigma = 0.87$.

As can be seen, most studies report surprisingly low mean and median values. Standard deviations, however, are relatively high. As well, most data sets have very large maximum times, typically resulting when individual trucks are required to move to a separate area of the Customs compound for a more detailed inspection ("secondary inspection").

One would expect that crossing delays would be greatest during passenger rush periods and during the summer (tourist) months. Some studies disagree. Leore et al. (2003) and Anderson and Coates (2010) reported that the bridges in their studies did not experience peaks during the traditional morning and evening rush hours. Anderson and Coates (2010) also found that delays at the Ambassador Bridge did not reflect the month of the year, while the other three bridges peaked during the summer (tourist) months (Blue Water Bridge in June; Peace Bridge and Queenston–Lewiston crossing in August).

It appears, then, that greater concentrations of passenger traffic (by time of day or season of year) do not necessarily result in increased delay in crossing. This probably is due to enhanced staffing by border authorities during peak passenger times. Correlation analysis could verify or disprove this statement; however, such an analysis has not been reported.

What are the major causes of those delays? The Canadian Chamber of Commerce et al. (2009) list five general causes of unpredictable border crossing times: inadequate border infrastructure, systems and technology malfunctions, redundant processes and procedures, inadequate staffing and training of border personnel, and insufficient information being provided to cross-border shippers and travellers. Taylor et al. (2004) comment that, "our analysis over 15 years of observations … is that most of the current delays and uncertainty are the result of institutional failures and not a lack of roadbed crossing capacity…, the biggest cause of problems has been that not all available booths have been staffed when volumes peak". Causes of border delays are discussed in several other works, including, for example, Goodchild et al. (2010).

Table 16.2 Summary of border crossing studies (Canada–U.S. crossings)

	Location	Mean time	Standard deviation	Other statistics
Paselk and Mannering (1994)	Peace Arch	20.2	11.8	Maximum: 59; 90th percentile: 38
Office of Freight Management and Operations (2001)	Ambassador bridge	20.4/8.8	Not reported	95th percentile: 33.9/13.7
	Blaine, WA crossing	17.3/21.5	Not reported	95th percentile: 35.6/35.3
	Blue Water bridge	34.2/6.2	Not reported	95th percentile: 80.3/9.1
	Peace bridge	23.3/21.7	Not reported	95th percentile: 83.4/38.0
	Laredo, Texas	31.2/17.2	Not reported	95th percentile: 54.9/45.0
	Otay Mesa, California	35.0/19.1	Not reported	95th percentile: 64.3/36.9
Leore et al. (2003)	Ambassador bridge	14/10	6.5/5	
	Blue Water bridge	17/10	10/5	
	Peace bridge	18	9.8	
	Queenston–Lewiston bridge	13	11.4	Mode: 6; Median: 9
Goodchild et al. (2007)	Blaine, WA	22.6	22.2	90th percentile: 47.1
Anderson and Coates (2010)	Ambassador bridge	11.3	9.8	Mode: 4.9; median: 7.6; range: 0.8–238.4
	Blue Water bridge	13.8	18.3	Mode: 3.3; median: 7.5; range: 1.0–288.6
	Peace bridge	13.2	24.6	Mode: 5.6; median: 7.9; range: 1.1–732.1
	Queenston–Lewiston bridge	10.8	14.2	Mode: 2.3; median: 5.2; range: 1.0–217.5
Conroy (2010)	Pacific highway	2.0	Not reported	

All numbers are minutes

Notes:

If two numbers, separated by a "/", are given, the first number pertains to trips entering U.S.A., while the second number pertains to trips leaving U.S.A. *nth* percentile indicates the time within which *n* percent of all vehicles travelled through the study area

16.4.2 Responding to Crossing-Time Delays: The Buffer Index

A widely-used measure of travel time reliability/delay is the "buffer index". That index is calculated as the ratio of buffer time to average border crossing time, where "buffer time" is the extra time a driver must add to the average crossing time in order to be x percent certain that he/she will be able to cross the border within the overall interval allowed. For example, Anderson and Coates (2010) reported an average crossing time for the Blue Water Bridge of 13.8 min and a buffer index (with 99 % confidence) of 609.3 %. Thus, a carrier should allow 84 min for delays (i.e., 6.093 times the average crossing time of 13.8 min) and a total crossing time of about 98 min. Taylor et al. (2003, 2004) noted that many carriers at the Blue Water Bridge in 2004 allowed two hours to make the crossing.

Determining the optimal buffer time for passenger traffic has been examined by several researchers (e.g., Norland and Polak 2002). Anderson and Coates (2010) analyze this calculation for freight transportation, noting that the length of the buffer time is directly related to the crossing time variance and the ratio of the late delivery penalty to the early delivery penalty. The paper also discusses those two types of penalties.

16.4.3 Sources of Border-Crossing-Time Data

How, or from where, do researchers obtain data on border-crossing times? Canada Border Services Agency has collected wait-time data at each of the major Canadian border crossings since November 2001 (but see Beeby 2008!); the United States Customs Border Protection agency does the same. Current border-crossing times are posted on the websites of both agencies; these data are only for the current hour and do not represent a probability distribution. As well, as noted previously, crossing-time data become out-of-date quickly, and many studies have preferred to collect new data for their use.

Table 16.3 below lists some of the sources of border-crossing-time data used by researchers.

16.4.4 Comments

Studies on border-crossing times have advanced significantly in the last decade. The use of communication technology to monitor border activities has reduced the effort and cost required to gather sufficient data, while improving analysis by, for example, allowing the division of crossing times into their component activities. Anderson and Coates (2010) collected data from the GPS systems of cross-border

Table 16.3 Sources of border-crossing data

Study/paper	When time data were collected	Source of time data
Paselk and Mannering (1994)	The Wednesday and Thursday after Labour Day 1991	Captured by pneumatic traffic counters and "people collecting data with laptop computers in plain sight of the border agents in the booths"
Leore et al. (2003)	December 2000–April 2002	Obtained from two Ontario trucking companies: one carrier provided GPS-based tractor logs, the other provided engine tachographs
U.S. Office of Freight Management and Operations, Texas Traffic Institute, and Battelle Memorial Institute (2001)	2001	Collected by human observers located (a) where arriving trucks might first become delayed, and (b) immediately after primary inspection booths
Lepofsky et al. (2003)	2001	Obtained from U.S. Office of Freight Management and Operations et al. (2001), *International Border Crossing Truck Travel Time for* 2001
Taylor et al. (2004)	2002	Obtained from Canada Border Services Agency (2002), *Border Delay Archive Database for Commercial and Personal Travel North and Southbound, November* 2001–*August* 2002
HDR/HLB Decision Economics (2006)	2001	Obtained from U.S. Office of Freight Management and Operations et al. (2001), *International Border Crossing Truck Travel Time for* 2001; supplemented by interviews with cross-border trucking companies and customs brokers
Goodchild et al. (2007)	August 2005–July 2006	Collected by observers located near inspection booths, supplemented by reports from drivers employed by a local cross-border fuel delivery company
Bradbury (2010)	November 2001 through December 2006	Obtained from Canada Border Services Agency, supplemented by interviews of border personnel, truck drivers, and businesses
Anderson and Coates (2010)	July 2008 through June 2009	Extracted from digital trip logs of the GPS systems of participating trucking companies as part of the Border Wait Time Measurement Project, a joint project of Transport Canada and Turnpike Global Technologies (a provider of GPS services to trucking companies)
Conroy (2010)	2010	Collected by observers located near commercial vehicle inspection booths

trucking companies; Bluetooth technology and electronic driver log books also have promise for this purpose.

Although the studies listed above have provided useful information for analysis, modelling, and planning, there are several cautions regarding reported data about which users must be aware. First, various reports measure and quote border crossing times in different ways. Some studies give average crossing time (the time from entry to exit of the border crossing), others use average delay time (the difference between the average crossing time and the time that would result at low volumes or with no delay), and some reports are not clear. For example, Anderson and Coates (2010) present average crossing time, Lepofsky et al. (2003) give average delay times, and HR/HLB Decision Economics Inc. (2006) give both.

Second, the geographic extent of the border crossing is defined differently by particular studies. For example, crossing times in Anderson and Coates (2010) measure the time to drive into, through, and out of the Customs plaza (including driving across the bridge, and both primary and secondary inspection), but do not include the length of time trucks waited before entering the Customs plaza. Leore et al. (2003) define the border zone based on the distribution of checkpoint data, resulting in a study area that was 5 km long at the Queenston–Lewiston crossing and 7.5 km at the Peace Bridge. The HDR/HLB Decision Economics (2006) report describes the study area as from "entry to exit" without further details.

Third, as Taylor et al. (2004) state, "the most significant delays occur at secondary yards (inspection), and are partly the result of the large percentage of trucks (20–40 % in 2002) that must enter secondary (inspection) for a variety of reasons". As mentioned previously, some studies (e.g., Lepofsky et al. 2003; Leore et al. 2003) do not consider delays resulting from secondary inspections. Summary statistical data, especially mean crossing times, might be more useful if presented *separately* for trucks that underwent secondary inspection and those that did not.

Fourth, van Lint et al. (2008) note that the skewness of the data, as well as the variance, is an important measure of travel time unreliability. They also add that "most of currently used unreliability measures (which are predominantly based on travel time variance), should be used and interpreted with some reservations, since they only account for a part of the costs of unreliability."

Lastly, Paselk and Mannering (1994) comment that while "queueing analysis can account for standard relationships among vehicle arrival rates, border agents' service times and the number of border agent lanes open", more complex relationships among system elements can render the technique computationally cumbersome. They also claim that border crossing queues are subject to "a duration dependence"—"the probability of ending a wait in a queue soon is a non-monotonic function of the duration of the wait"—that cannot be easily captured in queueing analysis.

The next section discusses two major government programs designed to reduce the time that vehicles wait for Customs clearance at the Canada–U.S. border.

16.5 Border Programs

The list of Canadian and U.S. border programs aimed at tightening border security while reducing crossing times is lengthy; as one carrier commented, "There now are so many different programs and initiatives from government departments and agencies that we need several employees to keep track of them all" (Mark 2008). This section discusses the two border programs that have received the most attention from shippers and carriers: C-TPAT (*Customs-Trade Partnership Against Terrorism*)/PIP (*Partners in Protection*) and FAST (*Free and Secure Trade*).

16.5.1 C-TPAT and PIP Programs

The U.S. *Customs-Trade Partnership Against Terrorism* (C-TPAT) initiative is a voluntary certification program open to manufacturers, shippers, importers, carriers, port authorities, freight consolidators, and other logistics service providers in the U.S.A., Canada, and Mexico (and to selected other foreign manufacturers), regardless of transportation mode. The program requires members to demonstrate compliance with standards by analysing the security and security policies of its facilities, employees, information systems, suppliers, and in-transit activities (Trudeau 2005). C-TPAT-certified shippers supposedly benefit from faster Customs clearance, are less likely to have their shipments selected for physical inspection, are given priority if inspected, and have access to dedicated truck lanes at border crossings. Some C-TPAT members shipping by water have been allowed to take possession of the containers not marked for inspection before the remainder of their shipment has been cleared (Silverman and Seely 2007). As well, "membership in C-TPAT or PIP will yield private benefits to member companies in terms of cargo security and reduced insurance premiums. Members can use program logos, which convey a positive image from a marketing perspective" (Anderson 2010). Although designed as a voluntary program, many importers feel that they are expected to participate and pay the associated costs, but they get few benefits in return (David and Stewart 2008; Anderson 2010).

A number of research studies have attempted to evaluate C-TPAT's effectiveness. Ojah (2005) claimed that while C-TPAT was created to "reconcile supply chain security and trade facilitation goals of the U.S. government, the processes and resources required for these programs are, in themselves, not secure, as well as under-funded and slow." Others have concluded that most members do not receive returns consistent with costs incurred (David and Stewart 2008; Anderson 2010). However, a survey reported in Silverman and Seely (2007) and Diop et al. (2007) indicated major benefits to C-TPAT members of "increased workforce security, fewer cargo inspections and lower inspection release times, and predictability in cargo clearances", and noted that about 96 % of the survey's respondents planned to maintain their membership in the program.

The Canadian version of C-TPAT is *Partners in Protection* (PIP). Although very similar to C-TPAT, the two programs are not yet harmonized, so membership in both is necessary (requiring two separate applications).

16.5.2 FAST Program

Free and Secure Trade (FAST), a joint initiative between Canada, U.S.A., and Mexico, aims at reducing clearance times for commercial shipments at road-based border crossings through improved coordination of Customs processes. FAST is a voluntary program under which drivers, carriers, and shippers apply to be pre-registered as "low risk". At the border crossing, a FAST-registered driver would provide bar-coded documents verifying their FAST registration; in return, the driver benefits from access to dedicated FAST lanes, quicker Customs clearance, and reduced documentation.

Carriers entering U.S.A. from Canada via a FAST lane must be C-TPAT-approved and must be carrying qualified goods from a C-TPAT-approved importer; trucks going from U.S.A. to Canada must be PIP-compliant. In both cases, the driver must also hold a FAST driver registration card. Obtaining a FAST driver registration card can be lengthy, consisting of two risk assessments (one done by Canadian officials and the other by U.S. officials) and an in-person interview. FAST drivers are fingerprinted and photographed before being issued their driver card. (Details change frequently; refer to the U.S. Customs and Border Protection website, www.cbp.gov, or the Canada Border Services Agency website, www.cbsa-asfc.gc.ca, for up-to-date information.)

Anderson (2010) includes a description of how FAST-qualified trucks may (or may not) flow through a border crossing, noting that although FAST-qualified trucks are processed more quickly than those which are not FAST-qualified, there may or may not be a lane for the exclusive use of FAST-qualified trucks. As a result, "since not all shipments are FAST-qualified, a mix of qualified and non-qualified trucks may share a common queue at a border crossing", and if the queue of non-FAST-qualified trucks is long, all vehicles entering the border crossing may be delayed. He concludes that "the existence of a common queue for both FAST-qualified and non-FAST-qualified vehicles reduces the benefits of becoming FAST-qualified", and gives suggestions regarding the physical layout of border-crossing inspection facilities.

The Goodchild et al. (2007) study of border wait times at the Blaine crossing reported that the average time to cross the border (southbound) was "distinctly longer" for non-FAST vehicles than for FAST vehicles (1 h and 23 min versus 23 min, respectively), although the standard deviations were similar (26 versus 22 min). Bradbury (2010) combined statistical analysis of border delays for pre-FAST-implementation versus post-FAST implementation with interviews of border personnel, truck drivers, and businesses to conclude that the FAST program made a positive contribution to reducing border crossing times at four of the five busiest Canada–U.S.A. crossings. The paper also agrees with findings of other reports that larger shippers and carriers have received the most benefit from the FAST program, while small and medium-sized carriers and exporters are "burdened by costs and often unable to capitalize on the program's benefits".

Springer (2010) notes that the FAST lane at the Pacific Highway crossing (Blaine, Washington) often is empty while non-FAST lanes are congested. He examines possible other uses of the FAST lane, including the application of congestion pricing to determine conditions under which opening the FAST lane to toll-paying non-FAST trucks would be justified. The Canadian Chamber of Commerce et al. (2009) include suggestions for improvements to the C-TPAT and FAST programs. Anderson (2009) presents a mathematical model relating a shipper's costs of membership in these programs to shipper costs of border delays and holding additional safety stock.

There is thus clear potential for the application of Operations Research in the preceding design and improvement issues. Moreover, underlying the C-TPAT/PIP and FAST (as well as other border programs) is *risk management*: identifying low-risk organizations, so resources and security efforts can be concentrated on travellers of high or unknown risk. OR clearly can play a major role here as well.

Zhang et al. (2011) study a general two-stage inspection, but where only a fraction of customers at the first stage (inspection) must undergo the further inspection in the second stage. Their queueing model and analysis yield the conditions under which the goals of security and customer service are consistent or in conflict. The approach seems oriented mostly to passengers and passenger cars.

The next section discusses a second approach to reducing border crossing times: improved staff planning at border crossings.

16.6 Staff Planning at Border Crossings

The U.S. Office of Freight Management and Operations (2001) concluded that "the number of inspection and processing booths open at each point-of-entry at any given time had a significant influence on the variability of travel time and delay." The study also reported that there was "a direct correlation between delays and the number of customs/immigration booths open—the greater the number of booths open, the shorter the delay" (quoted from Goodchild et al. 2007). Taylor et al. (2004) stated that "the most common cause of current delays and uncertainty related to the number of available customer primary inspection booths and the staffing of those booths, and the staffing of customs secondary inspection yards." They ranked staffing at border crossings as a "most severe" cause of border delays. It is not surprising, therefore, that a common response to long border crossing times is to call for more inspectors at the crossing (e.g., Canadian Chamber of Commerce et al. 2009).

Although many models for staff planning have been proposed (e.g., Price et al. 1980; Edwards 1983; Ernst et al. 2004), few of these models have been applied to border staffing and, more specifically, to the question of how many booths or lanes to have open at a crossing or how many truck inspectors to have on duty. One such model is that of Haughton and Sapna Isotupa KP (2012), who conducted a simulation study. Employing data on the (time-varying) arrival rates of US-bound trucks at the Ambassador Bridge, they quantified the benefits to the border-crossing system of smoothing the flow of arriving vehicles. The simulation study by Ortiz and Metzler (1998) also addressed border staffing, but now in the deployment of U.S. Border Patrol agents at the U.S–Mexico border in apprehending illegal aliens entering the U.S.A.

An interesting version of the basic Customs staffing questions occurs at small sea ports, where ship arrivals are not continuous and port operators may have to pay Customs for their services. The truck ferry service between Windsor, Ontario, and Detroit, Michigan, for example, operates only ten hours per day, largely because Canada Customs will provide personnel only during those hours. As well, unlike the road crossings between the two cities, the ferry operator must pay Canada Customs to provide border clearance services (estimated in 2005 to be $50,000 per year per Customs agent) (Wright 2005).

16.7 Other Cross-Border Issues

Shippers and carriers experience many cross-border effects other than those related to cost and time. Two age-old concerns are cabotage regulations and the excessive documentation. *Cabotage* refers to rules that permit carriage between domestic points only by carriers of that nation (or more commonly defined as prohibiting transportation of goods or people between two domestic points by a foreign carrier). This would, for example, prohibit a carrier of nation A who is delivering products to customers X and Y in nation B from moving a load from customer X to customer Y. For carriers, this results in empty movements, under-utilized drivers, and additional costs. Cabotage is a worldwide issue, and with the exception of European Union countries, there appears to be little desire among governments to allow the practice.

The number of documents required to move goods across a border often is regarded as being overwhelming, resulting in higher costs, longer times, and greater complexity. Kunimoto and Sawchuk (2004) give the example of some North American firms who purchase NAFTA products (which move duty-free between the three NAFTA countries) preferring to pay the non-NAFTA duty rate rather than complete the additional paperwork required of NAFTA imports.

US President Obama and Canadian Prime Minister Harper jointly made a key announcement in December 2011. The agreement on a new border-security pact has several objectives. By harmonizing some product regulations and synchronizing the inspection procedures in the two countries, freight should flow much more smoothly across the border in either direction. The two nations would also more closely share data on the movements of individuals departing either country.

Excessive documentation is a global complaint and not restricted to land-based transportation. With regard to ocean-carried international trade, *Canadian Transportation and Logistics* (2006) reported that the U.S.A. required five import documents, while Canada needed four, Mexico 8, Denmark 3, and Hong Kong and China 2. These documentary requirements were reflected in the average time for importation, with imports to the U.S.A. taking an average of 9 days, Canada 10, Mexico 26, and Denmark, Hong Kong, and China 5 days. Schinas and Psaraftis (1997) attribute the failure of some European short-sea-shipping endeavours to, among other factors, documentary and procedural requirements; Orton (2001) and Praxiao and Marlow (2002) have also raised this issue in European water transportation.

There are two basic ways of speeding Customs clearance with regard to documentation: reduce the amount of documentation required or speed the processing of those documents. Governments have tended to take the latter approach, and implementing procedures and tools to speed document processing at borders has been a major initiative for many years. Appels and de Swielande (1998) outline a three-stage evolution of a nation's customs programs: Stage I is a labour- and document- intensive focus on physically inspecting all imported goods, Stage II concentrates on verifying import information, while Stage III is to a carrier-driven pre-clearance process featuring collaborative relationships between importers/exporters, carriers, brokers, and Customs agencies.

An early Stage III initiative was Canada Border Services Agency's PARS (Pre-Arrival Review System) and INPARS (Inland Pre-Arrival Review System). Under PARS, an importer or customs broker can submit shipment clearance documents (including estimated time and date of arrival at the border) to Customs prior to arrival of the vehicle at the Canadian border, allowing Customs to decide whether the shipment should be cleared or detained before the vehicle arrives at the border. Another early application—EDI in customs clearance—is discussed by Hellberg and Sannes (1991). Eighteen years later, Hsu et al. (2009) examine the same problem but with RFID. Kuzaljevich (2009, 2010) discusses the current and future states, including problems of regulatory initiatives such as "eManifest", the electronic submission of cargo and conveyance data in place at some border crossings (see also Turnbull 2010).

Khoshons et al. (2006) discuss a computer simulation model for evaluating automated Customs clearance technologies (an example of intelligent transportation systems capabilities). Although the border crossing simulated was hypothetical, truck arrival data from the Pacific Highway crossing was used in the model's development. Simulation models for evaluating automated clearance systems were also developed by Nozick et al. (1999) for the Peace Bridge and Booz Allen Hamilton (2000) for the Ambassador Bridge.

The growth of "e-Customs" has led to research with varying focuses. For example, Raus et al.(2009) identify facilitators and barriers, based on European experience, that influence the adoption of e-customs solutions, whereas Hoepman et al. (2006) and Liercsh (2009) examine the security issues of specific travel documents. On a broader scale, Crainic et al. (2009) discuss the contribution of operations research to intelligent freight-transportation systems. The area of "e-Customs" certainly offers much potential for further study.

Another on-going border issue is the large number of government departments with jurisdiction over transportation matters. This concern applies not only to cross-border traffic, but also to traffic moving across provincial or state boundaries (as in the case with differing maximum truck weights and lengths). For example, in 2010, the U.S. Environmental Protection Agency imposed enhanced vessel emission control rules on those parts of the Great Lakes and St. Lawrence River under U.S. jurisdiction. The potential impact would be to increase water transportation costs to shippers by 25–30 % (Ryan 2010). Canadian Great Lakes water carriers are affected because it is impossible for a ship to remain in one province, state, or country—and hence under one government jurisdiction—during a voyage through the waterway.

Until mid-2010, Canadian cross-border motor carriers disagreed with a now-repealed U.S. requirement that Canadian trucking companies be insured by an American insurer, either directly or through a reinsurance agreement between an American and a Canadian insurance company (Today's Trucking 2010). Further, shippers and carriers have voiced concerns that the proposed enforcement of rules requiring all wood packaging materials to be treated for insect infestation before crossing the Canada–U.S. border will slow international traffic (Canadian Transportation & Logistics 2011).

Lastly, it is well-recognized that the decision to build a new border crossing is controversial and far-reaching, encompassing studies regarding civil engineering, traffic planning, and financial, environmental, social, and political concerns. The problems of the siting of border crossings have received limited attention in the operations research literature. Two examples are Li et al. (2005) and Higginson et al. (2007). In the case of a proposed bridge between Windsor and Detroit, those papers applied conflict analysis techniques to weigh opinions of various stakeholders and suggest how a given party should respond to actions taken by another stakeholder.

16.8 Cross-Border Issues Between Other Countries

Clearly, cross-border questions and problems are worldwide, and are not restricted to the Canada–U.S. border. This section briefly discusses two additional cases: the U.S.–Mexico border and the China–Hong Kong border, and their potential for the application of operations research. As well, examples of problems at several other border crossings elsewhere are given.

16.8.1 U.S.A.–Mexico

The overriding emphasis on controlling the flow of illegal migrants and illegal goods from Mexico to the United States has resulted in many of the same difficulties at the U.S.–Mexico border as at the Canada–U.S. border—specifically, excessive wait times and inflated costs (Gooley 2005; HDR/HLB Decision Economics 2006).

A second, highly-controversial issue is the unwillingness of the U.S. government to allow Mexican truckers to cross into the United States (due to safety, economic, and security concerns), even though cross-border trucking was to have been allowed under the NAFTA agreement since December 18, 1995. The result is that cross-border cargo cannot proceed until drayage carriers (short-haul trucks) move it across the border to long-haul truckers that await, a time-consuming and expensive process. As well, since many of the Mexican drayage carriers are owner-operators with limited financial and technological resources, shippers have voiced concerns over the traceability of their goods, loss-and-damage responsibility, and information filing by carriers during the short-haul movement (Gooley 2005).

Much has been written about this topic from the political side (see, for example, DeJarnette 1998; Haralambides and Londono-Kent 2004; Phaneuf 2007; Cassidy 2010). A more operations-oriented focus, involving discussion of questions related to the actual border-crossing process, is given by Villa (2006). There appear, however, to be few papers discussing operations research techniques applied to problems at the U.S.–Mexico border, including those pertaining to cross-border drayage.

16.8.2 China–Hong Kong

Elsewhere in the present volume, Chen and Lee (2013) give a detailed account of Logistics in China. Cross-border drayage between Hong Kong and the rest of China was examined using operations research by Cheung et al. (2008). (Note that the purpose of the drayage service in the latter paper differs from that at the U.S.–Mexico border. Since most containerized cargo moving between Hong Kong and China travels less than 160 km. (Cheung et al. 2008), drayage carriers are used there for the final delivery of containers, rather than for an intermediate movement between linehaul segments as at the U.S.-Mexico border.)

Hong Kong's closest neighbour in mainland China is Shenzhen, separated by land and water. However, "Hong Kong and Shenzhen are further apart socially and politically because of their vastly different systems"(Chung 2007), and people and freight moving between the two areas must pass through one of three border checkpoints. Chung (2007) noted that "commercial trucks routinely wait lined up for hours" at the border crossing closest to Shenzhen's major commercial district, while newer crossings located further away were virtually empty. Cheung et al. (2008) consider problems created by the Chinese "4-up-4-down" rule (when a driver–tractor–chassis–container combination moves from Hong Kong into China, the exact same combination must return to Hong Kong) and the "one-driver-one-tractor" rule (a Hong Kong driver is licensed to operate one specific tractor only). A similar situation is addressed in Lai et al. (2003). Leung et al. (2002, 2006) consider the case of a manufacturer with facilities in both Hong Kong and China who may use trucks registered in China (which can operate only in China) and trucks registered in Hong Kong (which can operate on both sides of the China–Hong Kong border).

16.8.3 Other Borders, Other Countries

Border crossings between China and neighbouring countries suffer from security concerns, infrastructure deficiencies, and customs inefficiencies. For example, although proposed bridges between China, Laos, and Thailand will eliminate bottlenecks created by the slow and inefficient ferries that currently carry cross-border traffic, some shippers prefer water routes over land-based border crossings to avoid "Lao's notoriously complicated and corrupt customs procedures" and the multiple tariffs charged on goods moving on roads connecting China and Southeast Asia through Laos (McCartan 2010).

As early as November 1999, the governments of Thailand, Laos, and Vietnam agreed to harmonize legislation and procedures relating to cross-border transportation by combining "separate border controls so that inspection can be carried out jointly and speedily" (Thurlow 2000). In May 2010, the governments of Laos, Cambodia, China, Vietnam, Burma (Myanmar), and Thailand met to strike committees to propose improvements to the cross-border movement of goods and people, including transportation, customs, health inspection, and immigration (Vientiane Times 2010). The preceding nations are (essentially) those in the Greater Mekong Sub-region of Southeast Asia, discussed in detail by Banomyong (2013) earlier in this book.

Finally, Fadahunsi and Rosa (2002) list some common border-crossing experiences in Nigeria. They involve high levels of harassment by police and border officials, frequent evasion of customs duty, and recurring demands to pay unofficial "crossing fees".

16.9 Border Issues and Supply Chain Management

To this point, the present chapter has focussed on border-crossing locations. We now move beyond the physical border to consider the impact of border-crossing issues on the wider supply chain.

There are several actions available to shippers and carriers in response to the uncertainties of border crossings. Anderson and Coates (2010) suggest that a buyer dealing with cross-border suppliers may:

- switch suppliers to those who do not have to transport goods across the border; or
- continue with cross-border suppliers but:
  - include penalties for late deliveries in purchase contracts, and/or
  - warehouse product on the buyer's side of the border; and/or
  - include a time buffer when planning purchases and receipts to allow for delays at the border.

Sawhney and Sumukadas (2005), in their study of customs-clearance in developing countries, suggest several strategies that buyers can adopt to reduce the impact of slow customs clearance (these strategies are based on Sheffi's (2001) list of ways to reduce the impact of international terrorism on a logistics system):

- use both local and international suppliers
- hold larger inventories in the buyer's country
- improve shipment data visibility to respond more quickly to product shortages and Customs processes
- apply risk pooling (by, for example, standardizing inputs or reducing the product versions), thus decreasing the variety of items that must be imported.

They note that holding larger inventories in the buyer's country is probably the only border-uncertainty-reduction strategy available to a buyer in lesser-developed nations.

Goodchild et al. (2007) list six possible courses of action by carriers in response to uncertainties in border crossing times:

- allow for longer delays at the border (i.e., increase the buffer time)
- incorporate border delays into planning at intermediate handling facilities (e.g., for transloading of vehicles)
- change vehicle routes to use border crossings that require less time or have smaller time uncertainty
- alter the vehicle schedules as current border conditions dictate
- reduce the amount of cross-border activity (e.g., buyers purchase more products domestically; carriers discontinue cross-border services)
- switch the transportation mode to one that experiences shorter delays and/or less delay uncertainty.

We now discuss the two most common shipper/carrier responses to border crossing uncertainties.

16.9.1 Holding Larger Inventories in the Buyer's Country

Stank and Crum (1997) examined the impact of cross-border transportation on attempts to reduce inventory levels by Just-In-Time (JIT) manufacturers in U.S.–Mexico trade. Through questionnaires completed by 51 maquiladora firms operating in Juarez, Mexico, the study found that the JIT firms had not been very successful in reducing inventory levels, instead adopting a hybrid form of JIT that "may be better suited to cross-border environments. The JIT firms may be sacrificing inventory reductions for improved transit time and reliability. Firms are receiving larger quantities less frequently than one might expect for a JIT environment." Regardless of the extent of JIT adoption, crossing the border was felt to be a challenge, with the major complaint being congestion on Mexican roads. Goodchild et al. (2007) also note that the strategy of changing dispatch and vehicle schedules as current border conditions dictate may increase inventory levels, as more shipments are delivered early in an attempt to avoid arriving at a border crossing during a time period when long delays are common.

A growing body of literature has examined inventory management with supply disruptions. Whereas an unexpected one- or two-hour delay at a road border crossing may not be sufficiently long to fall within the definition of a "supply disruption", a one-*week* delay in delivering a container due to an unexpected Customs inspection might. Examples of works on inventory management with supply disruptions include Lewis et al. (2005), Wilson (2007) and Jeon (2008).

16.9.2 Increasing the Border-Crossing Buffer Time

Based on interviews with commercial carriers, Goodchild et al. (2007) concluded that increasing buffer times was the most common strategy employed by carriers to respond to border crossing uncertainty. Their study noted, for example, "Although the average crossing time southbound [at the Blaine, Washington crossing]... is about 1 h and 23 min, most carriers leave 2 h to cross the border... [thus] building in 37 min of buffer times to accommodate longer than average crossing times." Disadvantages of this strategy include increased transportation and inventory costs, reduced capacity of transportation equipment, and a possible need for more drivers and/or equipment. Further, if a driver is being paid by the trip rather than by the hour, he/she is also suffering an economic loss from increased crossing times.

16.10 Summary and Suggestions for Further Research

This chapter has given an overview of the most common logistics and transportation issues at the Canada–U.S. border, also providing some insight into applications, or potential applications, of Operations Research techniques. This section closes the chapter with a few general comments about OR and cross-border issues.

First, there is not a large body of literature related to operations research applications at border crossings. What exists does report a variety of techniques, going beyond the usual reaction that border crossings are queues, and hence the obvious form of analysis is queueing theory. Other techniques applied in the literature include simulation, risk management, inventory models, resource scheduling, and goal programming.

Second, there is no lack of border-crossing-time data available for analysis or simulation modelling. However, those data become out-of-date quickly as border programs, staffing, and demand for cross-border goods change. For example, the truck queues that clogged Windsor streets leading to the Ambassador Bridge in the early 2000s have since virtually disappeared.

Third, while the major problems at the Canada–U.S. border—cost and time—exist at all border crossings, most other borders put *relatively* more emphasis, and hence more resources, on monitoring and controlling the flow of people rather than freight. As well, the infrastructure supporting many border crossings often is not as fully developed. These factors will impact the problems that could be studied, the data that can be collected, and the analysis that can be done.

Fourth, the majority of cross-border research at the Canada-U.S. border and elsewhere has focussed on truck transportation (followed in popularity by the water mode). However, goods move across borders by a variety of transportation modes. There has been little research published on border-related issues of air shipments or, with the exception of Anderson (2008) (for freight) and The Canadian Chamber of Commerce et al. (2009) (for passengers), rail transportation.

Lastly, much of the research has focussed on the border level (e.g. studies of waiting times) or the national level (such as reviews of economic consequences). Less work has examined regional impacts, especially those affecting supply chains. Not all products or supply chains will be impacted by border issues in the same way (e.g., Klein and Goodchild 2011). Thus, it is important to consider the transportation and supply-chain characteristics of the goods being moved (Goodchild et al. 2009; Kristjansson et al. 2010). Research tying border issues to supply chains can result in valuable contributions to logistics operations and strategy.

Acknowledgments I am indebted to Dr. William Anderson, Director of the Centre for Cross-Border Transportation Studies at the University of Windsor, for his comments and suggestions.

References

Anderson WP (2008) Addressing the potential for increased intermodal freight movements through Canada–US border crossings. In: Proceedings of the 43th annual conference of the Canadian transportation research forum, Fredericton, New Brunswick, pp 597–611

Anderson WP (2009) Cross-border supply chains in the post 9/11 security environment. In: Proceedings of the 44th annual conference of the Canadian transportation research forum, Victoria, British Columbia

Anderson WP (2010) Strategies for increasing the use of the FAST program at Canada–U.S. border crossings. In: Proceedings of the seminar on Canada–US border management policy issues, border policy research institute, Western Washington University, pp 7–11

Anderson WP, Coates A (2010) Delays and uncertainties in freight movements at U.S.–Canada border crossings. In: Proceedings of the 45th annual conference of the Canadian transportation research forum, Toronto, Ontario, pp 129–143

Appels T, de Swieland H (1998) Rolling back the frontiers: the customs clearance revolution. Int J Logistics Manage 9(1):111–118

Banomyong R (2013) The greater Mekong sub-region of Southeast Asia: improving logistics connectivity. In: Bookbinder JH (ed) Global logistics. Springer, New York

Beeby D (2008) Online border-wait times unreliable. The Globe & Mail (September 15). www.theglobeandmail.com/news/technology/online-border-wait-times-unreliable/article709680/

Booz Allen Hamilton (2000) Final evaluation report: Ambassador bridge border crossing system (ABBCS) field operational test. ABBCS Field Operational Test Partners

Bradbury SL (2010) An assessment of the free and secure trade (FAST) program along the Canada–US border. Transp Policy 17(6): 367–380

Canada Border Services Agency (2002) Border delay archive database for commercial and personal travel north and southbound. (November 2001–August 2002)

Canadian Chamber of Commerce and U.S. Chamber of Commerce (2009) Finding the balance: shared border of the future. www.chamber.ca/images/uploads/Reports/sharedborder_0709.pdf

Canadian Transportation & Logistics (2006) Restoring NAFTA: what needs doing? Can Transp Logistics 109(12):19

Canadian Transportation & Logistics (2011) CTA warns new pallet requirements could slow Canada/U.S. trade. Can Transp Logistics. www.ctl.ca/news/cta-warns-new-pallet-requirements-could-slow-canada-us-trade/1000402409

Cassidy WB (2010) Mexico expands retaliatory tariffs in trucks dispute. J Commerce. www.joc.com/trade/mexico-expands-retaliatory-tariffs-truck-dispute

Chen F, Lee C-Y (2013) Logistics in China. In: Bookbinder JH (ed) Global logistics. Springer, New York

Cheung RK, Shi N, Powell WB, Simao HP (2008) An attribute—decision model for cross-border drayage problem. Transp Res Part E 44(2):217–234

Chopra S, Sodhi, MS (2004) Managing risk to avoid supply chain breakdown. MIT Sloan Manage Rev 46(1):53–61

Chung O (2007) Hong Kong pushes for a looser border. Asia Times (August 3). www.Qtimes.com/atimes/China_Business/IH03Cb03.html

Closs DJ, McGarrell EF (2004) Enhancing security throughout the supply chain. IBM center for the business of government

Conroy H (2010) Looking for efficiency gains at the Pacific highway commercial border crossing. In: Proceedings of the seminar on Canada–US border management policy issues, border policy research institute, Western Washington University, pp 1–6

Crainic TG, Gendreau M, Potvin J-Y (2009) Intelligent freight-transportation systems: assessment and the contribution of operations research. Transp Res Part C 17:541–557

David P, Stewart R (2008) International logistics: the management of international trade operations, 2nd edn. Atomic Dog/Thomson, Mason, Ohio

DeJarnette KR (1998) Trucking problems at the US–Mexico border. Congressional research service report, national law center for Inter-American free trade

Diop, A., Hartman, D., and Rexrode, D. (2007). Customs-trade partnership against terrorism cost/benefit survey, Center for Survey Research, University of Virginia, and Eldon Cooper Center for Public Service, University of Virginia

Edwards JS (1983) A survey of manpower planning models and their application. J Oper Res Soc 34(11):1031–1040

Ernst AT, Jiang H, Krishnamoorthy M, Sier D (2004) Staff scheduling and rostering: a review of applications, methods and models. Eur J Oper Res 153(1):3–27

Fadahunsi A, Rosa P (2002) Entrepreneurship and illegality: insights from Nigerian cross-border trade. J Business Ventur 17:397–429

Goodchild A, Albrecht S, Leung L (2009) A description of commercial cross border trips in the cascade gateway and trade corridor. Transp Lett 1(3):213–225

Goodchild A, Globerman S, Albrecht S (2007) Service time variability at the blaine, Washington, International Border Crossing and the Impact on Regional Supply Chains, Border Policy Research Institute, Western Washington University

Goodchild A, Leung L, Albrecht S (2010) An investigation of commercial crossing times at the Pacific highway port-of entry. J Transp Eng 136(10):932–935

Gooley T (2005) Keep it moving. Logistics Manage (June 1)

Hale T, Moberg CR (2005) Improving supply chain disaster preparedness: a decision process for secure site location. Int J Phys Distrib Logistics Manage 35(3):195–207

Haralambides HE, Londono-Kent MP (2004) Supply chain bottlenecks: border crossing inefficiencies between Mexico and the United States. Int J Transp Econ 31(2):171–183

Haughton M, Sapna Isotupa KP (2012) Scheduling commercial vehicle queues at a Canada–US border crossing. Transp Res Part E 48(1):190–201

HDR/HLB Decision Economics (2006) Economic impacts of border wait times at the San Diego–Baja California border region. Final report for San Diego Association of Governments/California Department of Transport

Hellberg R, Sannes R (1991) Customs clearance and electronic data interchange—a study of Norwegian freight forwarders using EDI. Int J Prod Econ 24(1–2):91–101

Higginson JK, Li KW, Friesen D (2007) Analysis of the Windsor–Detroit border crossing problem: an update. In: Canadian operational research society 2007 annual conference, London, Ontario

Hoepman J-H, Hubbers E, Jacobs B, Oostdijk M, Schreur RW (2006) Crossing borders: security and privacy issues of the European e-passport. In: Proceedings of the first international workshop on security, Kyoto, Japan, pp 152–167

Hsu C-I, Shih H-H, Wang W-C (2009) Applying RFID to reduce delay in import cargo customs clearance process. Comput Ind Eng 57(2):506–519

Jeon H-M (2008) Location-inventory models with supply disruptions. Ph.D. dissertation, Lehigh University

Khoshons MK, Lim CC, Sayed T (2006) Simulation and evaluation of international border crossing clearance systems: a Canadian case study. Transp Res Record 2006:1–9

Klein M, Goodchild A (2011) Pacific highway commercial vehicle operations: border policy and logistical efficiency in a regional context. Transp Res Record 2238:15–23

Kristjansson K, Bomba M, Goodchild A (2010) Intra-industry trade analysis of U.S. state–Canadian province pairs: implications for the cost of border delay. Transp Res Record 2162:73–80

Kunimoto R, Sawchuk G (2004) Moving towards a customs union. Horizons 7(1):23–31

Kuzeljevich J (2009) Seeing red. Can Transp Logistics 112(6):19–21

Kuzeljevich J (2010) Cleared to land. Can Transp Logistics 113(6):16–29

Lai KK, Xue J, Xu B (2003) A cross-border transportation system under supply and demand constraints. Comput Oper Res 30(6):861–875

Leore R, Trent M, Shallow T (2003) Using truck tractor logs to estimate travel times at Canada–U.S. border crossings in Southern Ontario. In: Proceedings of the 38th annual conference of the Canadian transportation research forum, Ottawa, Ontario, pp 532–546

Lepofsky M, Ellis DR, Davis REL (2003) Establishing benchmarks for international border crossing truck travel time. In: Proceedings of the 38th annual conference of the Canadian transportation research forum, Ottawa, Ontario, pp 547–561
Liercsh I (2009) Electronic passports—from secure specifications to secure implementations. Inf Secur Tech Report 14(2):96–100
Leung SCH, Wu Y, Lai KK (2002) A robust optimization model for a cross-border logistics problem with fleet composition in an uncertain environment. Math Comput Model 36(11–13):1221–1235
Leung SCH, Wu Y, Lai KK (2006) Cross-border logistics with fleet management: a goal programming approach. Comput Ind Eng 50:263–272
Lewis BM, Erera AL, White CC (2005) An inventory control model with possible border disruptions. Working paper: Georgia Institute of Technology
Li KW, Higginson JK, Friesen D, Levy JK (2005) Windsor–Detroit border crossing problem: conflict analysis of the Schwartz report. In: Proceedings of 2005 IEEE international conference on systems, man, and cybernetics, Waikoloa, Hawaii, pp 1132–1137
Mark L (2008) Crossborder costs soaring out of control? Can Transp Logistics 111(6)
McCartan B (2010) China bridges last Mekong gaps. Asia Times. www.atimes.com/atimes/China/LF18Ad02.html
Norland RB, Polak JW (2002) Travel time variability: a review of theoretical and empirical issues. Transp Rev 22:39–54
Nozick LK, Turnquist MA, Wayno FJ, List GF, Wu TL, Menyuk B (1999) Evaluation of advanced information technology at the Peace bridge. Cornell University and Rensselaer Polytechnic Institute
Office of Freight Management and Operations, Texas Traffic Institute, and Battelle Memorial Institute (2001) International border crossing truck travel time for 2001. Federal Highway Administration, U.S. Department of Transportation. ops.fhwa.dot.gov/freight/border_crossing.htm as 2001 Assessment of Truck Travel Time and Delay at 7 International Ports-of-Entry
Ojah M (2005) Securing and facilitating trade through U.S. land borders: critical analysis of C-TPAT and FAST programs. Transp Res Record 138:30–37
Ontario Chamber of Commerce Border and Trade Committee (2004) Cost of Border Delays to Ontario, Ontario Chamber of Commerce. occ.on.ca/wp-content/uploads/Cost-of-Border-Delays-to-Ontario_May-2004.pdf
Ontario Chamber of Commerce Border and Trade Committee (2005) Cost of Border Delays to the United States Economy, Ontario Chamber of Commerce. occ.on.ca/wp-content/uploads/Cost-of-Border-Delays.pdf
Ortiz R, Metzler T (1998) Planning U.S. border patrol staffing with a modeling and simulation tool. In: Modelling and simulation: proceedings of the IASTED international conference on modelling and simulation, pp 312–316
Orton CW (2001) Going the short sea route. World Trade 14(10):54–55
Paixão AC, Marlow PB (2002) Strengths and weaknesses of short sea shipping. Maritime Policy 26:167–178
Paselk TAQ, Mannering FL (1994) Use of duration models for predicting vehicular delay at a US/Canadian border crossing. Transportation 21:249–270
Phaneuf I (2007) Mexico si? Can Transp Logistics 110(6):28–29
Price WL, Martel A, Lewis KA (1980) A review of mathematical models in human resource planning. Omega 8(6):639–645
Randall L, Ammah-Tagoe F (2003) Emerging security shifts and trends in U.S. trade and border crossings. In: Proceedings of the 38th annual conference of the Canadian transportation research forum, Ottawa, Ontario, pp 333–347
Raus M, Flügge B, Boutellier R (2009) Electronic customs innovation: an improvement of governmental infrastructures. Gov Inf Quart 26:246–256
Ryan L (2010) Canadian great lakes carriers assail unilateral US shipping rules. Can Transp Logistics 113(5):6

Sawhney R, Sumukadis N (2005) Customs clearance uncertainties in global sourcing. Int J Phys Distrib Logistics Manage 35(4):278–295

Schinas OD, Psaraftis HN (1997) New frontiers through short sea shipping. SNAME National Conference, Ottawa

Sheffi Y (2001) Supply chain management under the threat of international terrorism. Int J Logistics Manage 12(2):1–11

Silverman, R.B., and Seely, R.F. (2007). The C-TPAT and CSI supply-chain security initiatives today. *The Metropolitan Corporate Counsel*, www.metrocorporatecounsel.com.

Springer, M. (2010), An update on congestion pricing options for southbound freight at the Pacific Highway crossing. *Research Report #11*, Border Policy Research Institute, Western Washington University.

Stank TP, Crum MR (1997) Just-in-time management and transportation service performance in a cross-border setting. Transp J 36(3):31–42

Taylor JC, Robideaux DR, Jackson GC (2003) Border-related costs attributable to U.S.–Canadian border crossings. In: Proceedings of the 38th annual conference of the Canadian transportation research forum, Ottawa, Ontario, pp 228–242

Taylor JC, Robideaux DR, Jackson GC (2004) U.S.–Canada transportation and logistics: border impacts and costs, causes, and possible solutions. Transp J 43(4):521

Thurlow F (2000) All roads led to Vietnam's Danang. Asia Times (November 30). www.atimes.com/reports/BK30Ai01.html

Today's Trucking (2010) U.S. loosens insurance rules for Canadian truckers. Today's Trucking (July 8). www.todaystrucking.ca

Trudeau M (2005) C-TPAT: our companies have no choice despite enormous costs. Logistics 8(2):32–33

Turnbull L (2010) Prepare for eMainfest. Can Transp Logistics 113(5):30

van Lint JWC, van Zuylen HJ, Tu H (2008) Travel time unreliability on freeways: why measures based on variance tell only half the story. Transp Res Part A 42(1):258–277

Vientiane Times (2010) Mekong countries to boost links through transport agreement. Vientiane Times/Asia News Network (June 18). www.asianewsnet.net/news.php?id=12588&sec=1

Villa JC (2006) Status of the U.S.–Mexico commercial border crossing process: analysis of recent studies and research. Transp Res Record 1966:10–15

Wilson MC (2007) The impact of transportation disruptions on supply chain performance. Transp Res Part E 43:295–320

Wright C (2005) Short sea shipping and the supply chain: a review of cross lake ferry economics and benefits. In: 40th annual conference of the Canadian transportation research forum, Hamilton, Ontario

Wright PD, Liberatore MJ, Nydick RJ (2006) A survey of operations research models and applications in homeland security. Interfaces 36(6):514–529

Zhang ZG, Luh HP, Wang C-H (2011) Modeling security-check queues. Manage Sci 57(11):1979–1995

Chapter 17
On the Relationships Among Facility Location,Transportation Mode Selection and Material Flow Costs in Global Supply Chains

Dong Hee Son, Krishna Patwari, Wilbert E. Wilhelm and Peter Yu

Abstract This chapter, which explores the interplay between three significant factors in global supply chains, holds two research objectives. The first is a model to maximize after tax profit by prescribing facility locations, transportation modes, and material flows in a global supply chain. The second is to demonstrate relationships among these three components through a case study.

17.1 Introduction

Production facilities are typically located near sources of raw materials; assembly facilities, in regions that offer low-cost labor; and distribution centers (DCs), near customers to provide responsive service. Locations determine transport distances, feasible transportation modes, transit times, and material flow cost related to production, inventories and backorders. In general, a transportation mode that offers a shorter transit time (e.g., air) is typically more expensive than one that requires a longer transit time (e.g., rail). However, shorter transit times allow the supply chain to operate with less inventory and fewer backorders, incurring lower material flow costs. Inventory replenishment order quantity is a function of transit time and it is likely that a longer transit time may result in more backorders. In addition, the pipeline inventory that is entailed by transportation transit time adds yet another cost that is less obvious than the others.

D. H. Son · K. Patwari · W. E. Wilhelm (✉) · P. Yu
Department of Industrial and Systems Engineering, Texas A&M University,
College Station, TX 77843-3131, USA
e-mail: Wilhelm@tamu.edu

J. H. Bookbinder (ed.), *Handbook of Global Logistics*, International Series in Operations Research & Management Science 181, DOI: 10.1007/978-1-4419-6132-7_17,

Globalization has increased the complexity of supply chains. There has been a steady trend towards global supply chains becoming longer, so that the competitive advantages of various regions can be more fully exploited. Thus, it is especially important for multi-national corporations to understand the relationships between facility location, transportation mode selection, and material flow costs. Relationships are compounded in the global arena by international financial issues such as tariffs, border crossing costs, transfer prices and income taxes, which can vary greatly from country to country.

However, in spite of their importance in maximizing after-tax profit, the relationships among these three components have not been fully explored. In fact, according to Melo et al. (2009), only a few papers have featured transportation mode selection; and studies on supply chain and facility location have typically focused on the single-period planning horizon, which cannot effectively deal with transit time.

This chapter holds two primary objectives. The first is the formulation of a mixed integer programming model to prescribe facility locations, transportation modes, and material flows in a global supply chain with the goal of maximizing after tax profit. The second is to use this model to demonstrate relationships among these three components in an optimal supply-chain design through a case study.

Strategic level decisions design the structure of a supply chain, prescribing facility locations, the production technologies to be employed at each facility, and the capacity of each. They can also select transportation modes and plan the flow of materials (i.e., production, inventory and backorder levels) through the supply chain (Schmidt and Wilhelm 2000).

The efficiency of trading between countries is defined as the ability to allocate natural, labor, and capital resources, to result in productivity increases and economic gains that improve income and living standards (Wilhelm et al. 2005). According to a recent *Wall Street Journal* editorial (Editorial 2004) "The point of free trade isn't to create jobs per se but to allow resources to find their most efficient use and re-deploy workers to better paying jobs. Manufacturing networks incorporating the comparative advantages of all three NAFTA members have made North America an attractive investment for global capital." Trade agreements have been established around the world (e.g., the North American Free Trade Agreement (NAFTA) and regional trading blocs such as Association of Southeast Asian Nations and European Union) that allow multi-national corporations to allocate resources more efficiently and enhance the living standards in member countries. Thus, it is advantageous for multi-national corporations to design supply chains that can be made more efficient by such trade agreements.

Multi-national corporations can set transfer prices to allocate a disproportionate share of profits to facilities in countries with lower tax rates to increase their total after-tax profit (Vidal and Goetschalckx 2001). However, most countries have laws that prevent such manipulation of transfer prices. For example, the "arm's-length" standard holds that a transfer price should be the same no matter whether the two plants involved are part of the same parent corporation or they are independent companies. Thus, that standard requires each transfer price to be comparable to the price that would be charged on the open market. The U.S. Internal Revenue Code recognizes several methods to determine transfer prices, including comparable uncontrolled price (CUP), resale price, cost plus, comparable profits and profit split (Wilhelm et al. 2000). A transfer price can be determined by any of these approaches, so long as the arm's-length standard is met. Our model reflects the CUP method, by limiting transfer prices to a range according to the market price that would be charged to an unaffiliated facility.

Multi-national corporations locate facilities in different countries to exploit the competitive advantages and markets of various regions (Lee and Wilhelm 2010). Such advantages may include lower labor cost, less expensive raw materials, diminished fixed costs, availability of government subsidies, favorable tax rates, and transfer price regulations. Nevertheless, challenges such as different local cultures and business practices, transportation and telecommunication-infrastructure deficiencies in developing countries, inadequate worker skills, and supplier quality may limit the competitive advantage of a country (Meixell and Gargeya 2005).

Transportation modes compete on the basis of the unique combination of transportation cost and transit time they offer. The relationship between transportation cost and transit time directly affects material flow costs involving inventory levels, backorder costs and pipeline-inventory. Thus, even though a low transportation cost might seem competitive at first glance, it would likely result from a longer transit time, perhaps leading to excessive material flow costs. Further, backorders affect customer satisfaction levels negatively. The result is a loss of trust of and loyalty to the company, an important aspect of the business relationship between that firm and its customers, but which is difficult to estimate as a simple financial penalty. Backorders can be avoided by carrying more inventories, evidencing yet another aspect of the relationships that must be identified.

The body of this chapter is organized into five sections. Section 17.2 reviews relevant literature and clarifies the main differences between traditional models and ours. To address Research Objective 1, Sect. 17.3 presents our mixed-integer programming model and discusses it in detail. Addressing Research Objective 2, Sect. 17.4 describes a case study that demonstrates the linkages between facility location, transportation mode selection, and material flow costs. That section highlights the relationships that an optimal supply chain design must exploit. Section 17.5 summarizes conclusions and recommendations for future research.

17.2 Literature Review

The competitive global economy has led multi-national companies to seek more effective global supply chains to enhance profits, highlighting the importance of the inventory-transport-location tradeoffs that are the subject of this chapter. Previous reviews (Vidal and Goetschalckx 1997; Meixell and Gargeya 2005;

Bookbinder and Matuk 2009) have described the state-of-the-art in designing international supply chains. A substantial literature has addressed strategic decisions (Goetschalckx et al. 2002); papers that prescribe tactical decisions have addressed a subset of relevant factors, including material flows (Erenguc et al. 1999; Sarmiento and Nagi 1999; Schmidt and Wilhelm 2000). Our review focuses on three aspects of the strategic-design literature: facility location, transportation mode selection, and international financial factors (transfer pricing, exchange rates, and tax rates).

17.2.1 Facility Location

Location models prescribe the optimal sites, numbers of facilities and the timing of their openings. The typical supply chain comprises a series of echelons, each with facilities that perform a particular function. For example, the designated roles include those of suppliers, production plants, DCs, and customer zones. Location models typically address a broad set of factors, including facility capacity, inventory holding cost, and the cost of transporting between facilities; and a range of financial issues, including tariffs, tax rates, transfer prices, and exchange rates. Daskin et al. (2002) incorporated cycle inventory, safety stock and economies of scale in a non-linear programming model to locate a DC. They proposed a Lagrangian relaxation solution approach, which performed well in their tests.

Bhutta et al. (2003) formulated a mixed integer linear program to determine the major drivers in optimal facility location. Their model incorporated a variety of parameters such as exchange rates, government policy (tariffs and customer duties), investment, and costs of manufacturing, changing capacity, retaining capacity, and holding inventory. They examined three scenarios to study the influence of global factors such as exchange rates, tariffs rates, and manufacturing costs on the operations of a multi-national corporation. Their findings showed that, although fixed and variable production costs are significant for facility location, tariffs and distribution costs may have even more impact, dominating them. Focusing on DCs, Nozick and Turnquist (2001) studied the effects of distribution center location, inventory, transportation, and service quality over a single time period in the automotive industry.

Robinson and Bookbinder (2007) formulated a mixed-integer programming model to analyze the optimal location for finishing plants and DCs in the international business environment created by NAFTA. Their objective was to minimize total operating costs over a multi-period planning horizon. They discussed the roles of facility capacity on the choice to either centralize or decentralize the locations and management of finishing plants and DCs. Their numerical case study demonstrated that, if satisfying demand is not urgent, the selection of transportation mode depends on the pipeline inventory cost, transportation cost and transit time. Their results continue to serve as a decision support aid for a Canadian manufacturing firm.

Wilhelm et al. (2005) prescribed the strategic design of a supply chain operating under the terms of NAFTA. The strategic design problem aims to recommend a set of production, assembly, and distribution facilities, including their locations, technologies, and capacities, as well as material flows from suppliers through the supply chain to customer zones. With the objective of maximizing after tax profit, the authors formulated a mixed integer program to model a broad set of design complexities, such as bill of materials (BOM) restrictions, international financial factors (exchange rates, transportation cost allocations, transfer prices, and tax rates), and material flow in the supply chain. Their model is unique in that it explores typical international issues (e.g., local-content rules, and border-crossing costs) as well as aspects that are specific to the Canada-Mexico-U.S. business environment (e.g., NAFTA terms, tax rates, and proximity).

17.2.2 Transportation Modes

The selections of facility locations and transportation modes determine the efficiency of a transportation plan, which impacts production, transportation and material flow costs as well as transit time. The choice between transportation modes in a global supply chain is challenging because intermodal transportation is typically involved, and international financial issues (e.g., tariffs, transfer prices, taxes, and border crossing costs) must be considered. Intermodal transportation occurs when more than one transport mode (e.g., vessel, rail, truck) is available to make a shipment, and distinct modes are used on successive links.

Bookbinder and Fox (1998) studied the intermodal transport of containers from Canada to Mexico under NAFTA. They determined optimal routings by examining five origins in Canada and three destinations in Mexico. After obtaining values of transportation costs and transit times from industrial sources, they applied a shortest path algorithm to determine the optimal transportation route between each origin–destination pair. In addition, the authors suggested that, especially under free trade agreements like NAFTA, transportation distance and time may affect inventory needs.

17.2.3 International Financial Issues

In a global supply chain, a multi-national corporation can optimize after-tax profits by setting transfer prices to deal appropriately with tax rates imposed by the countries in which facilities are located. Most countries require transfer prices to be set according to the arm's-length standard. Vidal and Goetschalckx (2001) noted that transfer prices can be optimized within upper and lower bounds to satisfy this legal standard. A number of models have incorporated transfer pricing (e.g., Wilhelm et al. 2005; Miller and de Matta 2008; Perron et al. 2008).

Kouvelis and Gutierrez (1997) studied the two-market "style goods" supply chain, considering a constant transfer price and variable exchange rates. Their objective was to recommend production levels in both primary and secondary markets, as well as the amount of product shipped from the primary market to the secondary one. They concluded that production planning decisions must be made while explicitly addressing uncertainties that affect exchange rates and transfer prices.

Vidal and Goetschalckx (2001) formulated a model to design a global supply chain with the objective of maximizing after-tax profit, allowing transfer price to be a decision variable. They invoked upper and lower bounds on each transfer price to represent the arm's-length principle. In addition to transfer prices, their model prescribed the allocation of transportation costs to shipper and receiver. Deciding both transfer prices and transportation-cost allocation enhanced the flexibility of their model in assisting the multi-national corporation to boost after-tax profit.

Each prior paper has studied an individual aspect of facility location, transportation mode selection, or material flow in the international arena; no study has explored the combination of these factors to understand how they interact. In contrast, we seek to address that overall combination to demonstrate the inter-relationships.

17.3 Model

Our model deals with a complex set of issues to integrate relevant decisions and lead to practical results. This section lists our assumptions, defines the notation we use, presents the model, and then describes it.

17.3.1 Assumptions

We invoke the following assumptions to structure our model:

- The supply chain comprises three echelons: (1) customer zones (CZs), (2) DCs, and (3) production plants
- CZ facilities generally represent (aggregations of) retailers or the collective demands of individuals, acting at a centroid location in a zone
- Locations of all the customer zones are fixed
- The end demand arising in each such zone is known
- A given customer zone must be served by a single DC over all time periods

- All parameters are known deterministically, including the capacities of every production and inventory-holding facility and each transportation mode, the selling and transfer prices, and all fixed and variable (i.e., per unit) costs;
- Transit time, the number of time periods required by each mode to deliver a shipment to its destination, is known deterministically
- Backorders may be incurred at a known penalty
- Each backorder must be satisfied as soon as possible
- Initial and final quantities of inventories are zero
- There are no backorders at time 0 and none can be carried over at the end of the horizon
- The relevant planning horizon comprises $|T|$ time periods
- All costs are represented in U.S. dollars.

17.3.2 Notation

Indices

c	Countries
e	Echelons
f_e	Facility f_e in echelon e
$\bar{f}_c$	Facility $\bar{f}_c$ in country c
i	Products
k	Transportation modes
s	Tax brackets in country c
t	Time periods

Parameters

D_{if_et}	Demand for product i at facility f_e during period t
G_i^B	Penalty cost for each backorder held at the end of a period for product i
$G_{f_e}^F$	Fixed cost for opening facility f_e
$G_{if_e}^I$	Cost to hold one unit of product i in inventory at facility f_e at the end of a time period
$G_{if_e}^P$	Variable cost to produce one unit of product i at production facility f_e
$G_{f_ef_{e-1}k}^T$	Variable cost for transporting one container from facility f_e to f_{e-1} via mode k
$G_{f_ef_{e-1}k}^{TF}$	Fixed cost for transporting containers from facility f_e to f_{e-1} via mode k
$G_{if_ef_{e-1}k}^{TP}$	Pipeline inventory cost/period for transporting a unit of product i from f_e to f_{e-1} via mode k
$G_{if_ef_{e-1}}^{TRF}$	Tariff paid for one unit of product i transported from facility f_e to f_{e-1}, each in a different country
M^{CT}	The maximum number of containers that can be shipped from any facility in any period

$P_{if_ef_{e-1}}$ Transfer (i.e., selling) price of product i when shipped from facility f_e to facility f_{e-1}

R_{cst} Tax rate for bracket s in country c during period t

$R^G_{f_ef_{e-1}}$ Proportion of total shipping cost charged to facility f_e for shipments from f_e to f_{e-1}(i.e., proportion of cost charged to f_{e-1} is $1 - R^G_{f_ef_{e-1}}$)

R^{PW}_t Present worth factor for period t

U_{cst} Upper bound of tax bracket s in country c in period t

V_i Volume (cubic feet) occupied by one unit of product i

V^{CT} Total volume (cubic feet) of a container

$W^I_{f_e}$ Capacity of facility f_e in terms of volume (cubic feet) for holding inventory per time period

$W^P_{if_e}$ Capacity (i.e., number of units each period) of facility f_e to produce product i

$\tau_{f_ef_{e-1}k}$ Transit time (number of periods) to transport from facility f_e to f_{e-1} via mode k

Index Sets

$ARCS1$ Arc (f_e, f_{e-1}), which connects a plant to a DC

$ARCS2$ Arc (f_e, f_{e-1}), which connects a DC to a CZ

$ARSCS$ $= ARCS1 \cup ARCS2$

Note: $ARCS1$and $ARCS2$ distinguish between plant-to-DC and DC-to-CZ transfers, respectively

C Countries $c \in C$

E Echelons $e \in E$

$\bar{F}_c$ Facilities in country c $\bar{f}_c \in \bar{F}_c$

F_1 CZs (facilities)

F_2 DCs (facilities)

F_3 Production plants (facilities)

F Facilities $F = F_1 \cup F_2 \cup F_3 = \bigcup_{c \in C} F_c \quad f_e \in F$

I Products $i \in I$

K Transportation modes $k \in K$

S_c Income tax brackets in country c $s \in S_c$

T Time periods in the planning horizon $t \in T$

Decision Variables

b_{if_et} Number of backorders for product i at facility f_e at the end of period t

q_{if_et} Number of units of product i held in inventory at facility f_e at the end of period t

$r_{f_ef_{e-1}kt}$ 1 if mode k is used to transport from f_e to f_{e-1} in period t, 0 otherwise

$u_{f_ef_{e-1}}$ 1 if f_e serves f_{e-1}, 0 otherwise

$x_{if_ef_{e-1}kt}$ Number of units of product i shipped from f_e to f_{e-1} via mode k in period t

$x^P_{if_et}$ Number of units of product i produced at facility f_e during period t

$y_{f_ef_{e-1}kt}$ Number of containers shipped from f_e to f_{e-1} via mode k in period t

$z_{f_e t}$	1 if facility f_e is opened in period t, 0 otherwise
$\alpha^{+}_{f_e t}$	Total revenue earned by facility f_e during period t
$\alpha^{-}_{f_e t}$	Total cost incurred by facility f_e during period t
β_{ct}	Taxable income of all facilities in country c during period t
β^{s}_{cst}	Taxable income in tax bracket s for all facilities in country c during period t

17.3.3 Formulation

The objective of our mixed integer programming (MIP) model is to maximize after tax profit:

$$\text{Maximize}\, Z = \sum_{c \in C, t \in T} R^{PW}_{t} \left(\beta_{ct} - \sum_{s \in S_c} R_{cs} \beta^{s}_{cst} \right)$$

subject to:

$$\alpha^{+}_{f_e t} = \sum_{i \in I, f_{e-1} \in F_1 \cup F_2, k \in K} P_{if_e} x_{if_e f_{e-1} kt} \quad t \in T, f_e \in F_3 \cup F_2 \tag{17.1}$$

$$\alpha^{+}_{f_e t} = \sum_{i \in I} P_{if_e} (D_{if_e t} - b_{if_e t} + b_{if_e (t-1)}) \quad t \in T \backslash \{1\}, f_e \in F_1 \tag{17.2}$$

$$\alpha^{+}_{f_e t} = \sum_{i \in I} P_{if_e} (D_{if_e t} - b_{if_e t}) \quad t \in \{1\}, f_e \in F_1 \tag{17.3}$$

$$\begin{aligned}
\alpha^{-}_{f_e t} = & \sum_{f_{e-1} \in F_2, k \in K} R^{G}_{f_e f_{e-1}} \Bigg(G^{T}_{f_e f_{e-1} k} y_{f_e f_{e-1} kt} + G^{TF}_{f_e f_{e-1} k} r_{f_e f_{e-1} kt} \\
& + \sum_{i \in I} (G^{TP}_{if_e f_{e-1} k} \tau_{f_e f_{e-1} k} + G^{TRF}_{if_e f_{e-1}}) x_{if_e f_{e-1} kt} \Bigg) \\
& + G^{F}_{f_e} \sum_{v=1}^{t} z_{f_e v} + \sum_{i \in I} G^{P}_{if_e} x^{P}_{if_e t} + \sum_{i \in I} G^{I}_{if_e} q_{if_e t} \quad t \in T, f_e \in F_3
\end{aligned} \tag{17.4}$$

$$\begin{aligned}
\alpha^{-}_{f_{e-1} t} = & \sum_{f_e \in F_3, k \in K} \left(1 - R^{G}_{f_e f_{e-1}}\right) \left(G^{T}_{f_e f_{e-1} k} y_{f_e f_{e-1} kt} + G^{TF}_{f_e f_{e-1} k} r_{f_e f_{e-1} kt} + \sum_{i \in I} (G^{TP}_{if_e f_{e-1} k} \tau_{f_e f_{e-1} k} + G^{TRF}_{if_e f_{e-1}}) x_{if_e f_{e-1} kt} \right) \\
& + \sum_{f_{e-2} \in F_1, k \in K} R^{G}_{f_{e-1} f_{e-2}} \left(G^{T}_{f_{e-1} f_{e-2} k} y_{f_{e-1} f_{e-2} kt} + G^{TF}_{f_{e-1} f_{e-2} k} r_{f_{e-1} f_{e-2} kt} + \sum_{i \in I} (G^{TP}_{if_{e-1} f_{e-2} k} \tau_{f_{e-1} f_{e-2} k} + G^{TRF}_{if_{e-1} f_{e-2}}) x_{if_{e-1} f_{e-2} kt} \right) \\
& + G^{F}_{f_{e-1}} \sum_{v=1}^{t} z_{f_{e-1} v} + \sum_{i \in I, f_e \in F_3, k \in K} P_{if_e} x_{if_e f_{e-1} kt} + \sum_{i \in I} G^{I}_{if_{e-1} t} q_{if_{e-1} t} \quad t \in T, f_{e-1} \in F_2
\end{aligned} \tag{17.5}$$

$$\alpha^-_{f_{e-1}t} = \sum_{f_e \in F_2, k \in K} \left(1 - R^G_{f_e f_{e-1}}\right)\left(G^T_{f_e f_{e-1} k} y_{f_e f_{e-1} kt} + G^{TF}_{f_e f_{e-1} k} r_{f_e f_{e-1} kt} + \sum_{i \in I} (G^{TP}_{if_e f_{e-1} k} \tau_{f_e f_{e-1} k} + G^{TRF}_{if_e f_{e-1}}) x_{if_e f_{e-1} kt}\right) + G^F_{f_{e-1}} + \sum_{i \in I, f_e \in F_2, k \in K} P_{if_e} x_{if_e f_{e-1} kt} + \sum_{i \in I} G^B_i b_{if_{e-1}t} + \sum_{i \in I} G^I_{if} q_{if_{e-1}t} \quad t \in T, f_{e-1} \in F_1 \tag{17.6}$$

$$\beta_{ct} = \sum_{\bar{f}_e \in \bar{F}_c} (\alpha^+_{\bar{f}_e t} - \alpha^-_{\bar{f}_e t}) \quad c \in C, t \in T \tag{17.7}$$

$$\beta_{ct} \le \sum_{s \in S_c} \beta^s_{cst} \quad c \in C, t \in T \tag{7.8}$$

$$\beta^s_{cst} \le U_{cst} - U_{c(s-1)t} \quad c \in C, s \in S_c \backslash \{1\}, t \in T \tag{17.9}$$

$$\beta^s_{cst} \le U_{cst} \quad c \in C, s \in \{1\}, t \in T \tag{17.10}$$

$$x^P_{if_e t} + q_{if_e(t-1)} = \sum_{f_{e-1} \in F_2, k \in K} x_{if_e f_{e-1} kt} + q_{if_e t} \quad i \in I, f_e \in F_3, t \in T \backslash \{1\} \tag{17.11}$$

$$x^P_{if_e t} = \sum_{f_{e-1} \in F_2, k \in K} x_{if_e f_{e-1} kt} + q_{if_e t} \quad i \in I, f_e \in F_3, t \in \{1\} \tag{17.12}$$

$$\sum_{f_e \in F_3, k \in K} x_{if_e f_{e-1} k(t - \tau_{f_e f_{e-1} k})} + q_{if_{e-1}(t-1)} = \sum_{f_{e-2} \in F_1, k \in K} x_{if_{e-1} f_{e-2} kt} + q_{if_{e-1}t} \quad i \in I, f_{e-1} \in F_2, t \in T \backslash \{1\} \tag{17.13}$$

$$\sum_{f_e \in F_3, k \in K} x_{if_e f_{e-1} k(t - \tau_{f_e f_{e-1} k})} = \sum_{f_{e-2} \in F_1, k \in K} x_{if_{e-1} f_{e-2} kt} + q_{if_{e-1}t} \quad i \in I, f_{e-1} \in F_2, t \in \{1\} \tag{17.14}$$

$$\sum_{f_e \in F_2, k \in K} x_{if_e f_{e-1} k(t - \tau_{f_e f_{e-1} k})} - b_{if_{e-1}(t-1)} + q_{if_{e-1}(t-1)} = D_{if_{e-1}t} - b_{if_{e-1}t} + q_{if_{e-1}t} \quad i \in I, f_{e-1} \in F_1, t \in T \backslash \{1\} \tag{17.15}$$

$$\sum_{f_e \in F_2, k \in K} x_{if_e f_{e-1} k(t - \tau_{f_e f_{e-1} k})} = D_{if_{e-1}t} - b_{if_{e-1}t} + q_{if_{e-1}t} \quad i \in I, f_{e-1} \in F_1, t \in \{1\} \tag{17.16}$$

$$\sum_{\forall i \in I} V_i x_{if_e f_{e-1} kt} \le V^{CT} y_{f_e f_{e-1} kt} \quad t \in T, (f_e, f_{e-1}) \in ARCS, k \in K \tag{17.17}$$

$$y_{f_e f_{e-1} kt} \le M^{CT} r_{f_e f_{e-1} kt} \quad t \in T, (f_e, f_{e-1}) \in ARCS, k \in K \tag{17.18}$$

$$x^P_{if_e t} \le W^P_{if_e} \sum_{v=1}^{t} z_{f_e v} \quad i \in I, t \in T, f_e \in F_3 \tag{17.19}$$

$$\sum_{i\in I} V_i q_{if_et} \le W^I_{f_e} \quad t \in T, f_e \in F \tag{17.20}$$

$$\sum_{t\in T} z_{f_et} \le 1 \quad f_e \in F_2 \cup F_3 \tag{17.21}$$

$$r_{f_ef_{e-1}kt} \le \sum_{v=1}^{t} z_{f_{e-1}v} \quad f_{e-1} \in F_2, f_e \in F_3, t \in T, k \in K \tag{17.22}$$

$$r_{f_ef_{e-1}kt} \le u_{f_ef_{e-1}} \quad t = T, k \in K, f_e \in F_2, f_{e-1} \in F_1 \tag{17.23}$$

$$\sum_{f_e\in F_2} u_{f_ef_{e-1}} = 1 \quad f_{e-1} \in F_1 \tag{17.24}$$

$$b_{if_et} = 0 \quad t = |T|, i \in I, f_e \in F_1 \tag{17.25}$$

$$r_{f_ef_{e-1}kt} \in \{0,1\} \quad t = T, k \in K, f_e \in F_2 \cup F_3, f_{e-1} \in F_1 \cup F_2 \tag{17.26}$$

$$u_{f_ef_{e-1}t} \in \{0,1\} \quad t = T, f_e \in F_2, f_{e-1} \in F_1 \tag{17.27}$$

$$z_{f_et} \in \{0,1\} \quad t = T, f_e \in F_2 \cup F_3 \tag{17.28}$$

$$b_{if_et} \ge 0, \text{ Integer } t = T, f_e \in F_1, i \in I \tag{17.29}$$

$$q_{if_et} \ge 0, \text{ Integer } t = T, f_e \in F_e, i \in I \tag{17.30}$$

$$x^P_{if_et} \ge 0, \text{Integer} \quad t = T, f_e \in F_3, i \in I \tag{17.31}$$

$$x_{if_ef_{e-1}kt} \ge 0, \text{Integer} \quad t = T, k \in K, f_e \in F_2 \cup F_3, f_{e-1} \in F_1 \cup F_2, i \in I \tag{17.32}$$

$$y_{f_ef_{e-1}kt} \ge 0, \text{Integer} \quad t = T, k \in K, f_e \in F_2 \cup F_3, f_{e-1} \in F_1 \cup F_2 \tag{17.33}$$

$$\alpha^+_{f_et} \ge 0 \quad t = T, f_e \in F \tag{17.34}$$

$$\alpha^-_{f_et} \ge 0 \quad t = T, f_e \in F \tag{17.35}$$

$$\beta^s_{cst} \ge 0 \quad c \in C, t \in T, s \in S_c \tag{17.36}$$

$$\beta_{ct} \text{ Unrestricted } c \in C, t \in T \tag{17.37}$$

17.3.4 Model Description

The objective function maximizes after tax profit over the planning horizon. β_{ct} denotes the total income of all facilities in country c during the planning horizon and β^s_{cst} represents taxable income in tax bracket s for all facilities in that country during time period t. Since R_{cs} is the tax rate of bracket s in country c, $R_t^{PW}\left(\beta_{ct} - \sum_{s \in S_c} R_{cs}\beta_{cst}^s\right)$ gives the total tax amount in country c in period t. R_t^{PW} is a present worth factor for time period t; multiplying after-tax income by R_t^{PW} yields the present worth of after-tax profit.

Constraints in our model form six categories of features: (17.1)–(17.6) revenues and expenses, (17.7)–(17.10) incomes, (17.11)–(17.16) material flow balance at each facility, (17.17)–(17.22) supply chain capacity, (17.23)–(17.24) single sourcing, and (17.25)–(17.37) integer, sign, and other restrictions. The first category of constraints, (17.1)–(17.6), defines revenues and expenses. The "G parameters" denote discounted costs in U.S. dollars with superscripts representing the type of costs. Ten types of costs are identified by those superscripts: B backorder cost, F fixed cost for using facility, I inventory cost, P cost of production, T variable transportation cost, TF fixed transportation cost, TP pipeline inventory cost, and TRF tariffs.

Equality (17.1) defines revenue at plants and DCs. $x_{if_ef_{e-1}kt}$ prescribes the number of products i shipped from f_e to f_{e-1} via mode k in period t. Here, we adopt the convention that f_e is a facility in echelon e that ships to facility f_{e-1} in echelon $e-1$. The pair (f_e, f_{e-1}) corresponds to a (plant-to-DC) shipment if $e = 3$ and a (DC-CZ) shipment if $e = 2$. Revenue is the product of the selling price per unit and the quantity involved. In other words, revenue at a plant (DC) is the transfer price multiplied by the number of products shipped from that plant to DC (DC to CZ).

Inequalities (17.2)–(17.3) calculate revenue at CZs. (17.1) must be augmented to define revenue at each CZ because any zone may incur backorders. In (17.2), $D_{if_et} - b_{if_et} + b_{if_e(t-1)}$ represents the quantity of product i sold at facility $f_e \in F_1$ during time period t. By multiplying the quantity sold by the selling (or transfer) price of each product, we obtain the revenue in that customer zone. (17.3) is a special case of (17.2) for time period $t = 1$, for which $b_{if_e(t-1)}$ does not exist; $t = 1$ is the first period in which backorders can be incurred. Together, (17.2)–(17.3) define revenue at each CZ.

Equality (17.4) defines total cost at production plant $f_e \in F_3$. Certain expenses, which we call "common costs," are related to facility type (e.g., plant, DC and CZ), including fixed and variable transportation costs; pipeline inventory costs; and tariffs that can be charged to the upstream facility, the downstream facility, or to both. In order to allocate those costs, we introduce parameter $R^G_{f_e,f_{e-1}}$, which specifies the proportion of such costs charged to the upstream facility f_e. For instance, if $R^G_{f_e,f_{e-1}}$ equals 1, the upstream facility f_e pays all of the common costs. The first term in equality (17.4) consists of common costs that are related to the upstream and downstream facilities, f_e and f_{e-1}, respectively. Multiplying these costs by parameter $R^G_{f_ef_{e-1}}$ gives the common costs charged to the upstream facility $f_e \in F_3$. The third term is the fixed cost for using plant f_e, the fourth is the production cost, and the last is the inventory holding cost at facility f_e. Hence, equality (17.4) defines *all* costs charged to plant f_e during time period t.

Equality (17.5) defines the total cost at DC facility $f_{e-1} \in F_2$ during time period t. The first term in (17.5) consists of common costs related to two facilities (a plant and a DC). Multiplying these costs by parameter $(1 - R^G_{f_ef_{e-1}})$ gives the portion of total common cost that is charged to DC f_{e-1}. The second term in (17.5) deals with costs that are common to that DC and its downstream customer zone. The remaining three summation terms define the fixed cost incurred in opening the distribution center, the purchasing cost of all products that arrive from plants, and the cost of holding inventory at the DC, respectively. The summation terms in (17.5), in turn, define total expenses at each DC f_{e-1} during the time period t.

Equality (17.6) defines the total cost at CZ facility $f_{e-1} \in F_1$ during time period t. As in (17.5), the first term in (17.6) deals with costs that are common to DC f_e and CZ f_{e-1}. The remaining four terms define the fixed cost for using CZ f_{e-1} in time period t (CZs are generally retailers, hence always "open"); purchasing costs of all products that arrive from the DC that serves this CZ; and backorder and inventory holding costs, respectively.

The second category (17.7)–(17.10) is the collection of the constraints related to incomes. It is typical that tax rate depends on the amount of income. Since each country has a unique tax rate, the model must identify incomes earned in each country for every time period.

Equality (17.7) defines β_{ct}, the taxable income in country c during period t, as the total revenue minus total cost at facility f_e. The total taxable income in country c is obtained by summing taxable incomes obtained by all facilities located in that country.

Inequality (17.8) defines the amount of income in each tax bracket. Income can be either positive or negative; if it is negative, no tax is paid. To impose this characteristic, an inequality constraint is required. In other words, if income is negative, then all incomes in tax bracket β^s_{cst} are zero. Otherwise, the summation of β^s_{cst} over all tax brackets s applicable in country c during time period t equals β_{ct}, the taxable income of all facilities in country c in period t. The amount of income in tax bracket s in country c during period t is defined by constraint (17.9). (17.10) specializes (17.9) for the first (lowest) tax bracket.

The third category (17.11)–(17.16) assures material flow balance at each facility. $x^P_{if_et}$ denotes the quantity of product i produced at facility f_e during time period t. q_{if_et} is the inventory of product i held at that facility during this time period. $x_{if_ef_{e-1}kt}$ denotes the amount of product i shipped from f_e to f_{e-1} via mode k departing in time period t. Hence, $\sum_{f_e \in F_2(F_3), k \in K} x_{if_ef_{e-1}kt}$ is the total flow of product i from each $f_e \in F_2(F_3)$ to a given downstream facility $f_{e-1} \in F_1(F_2)$ in period t.

Constraints (17.11)–(17.12) define material flow balance at each production plant. (17.12) is a special case of (17.11) for time period $t = 1$, since initial inventory on hand, $q_{if_e(t-1)}$, is assumed to be zero.

This model includes a possibly unique transit time for each transportation mode. Parameter $\tau_{f_ef_{e-1}k}$ denotes the transit time to transport products from f_e to f_{e-1} via mode k. $\sum_{f_e \in F_2(F_3), k \in K} x_{if_ef_{e-1}k(t-\tau_{f_ef_{e-1}k})}$ denotes the flow of product i delivered to facility f_{e-1} in time period t from all facilities $f_e \in F_2(F_3)$ immediately upstream and via all transportation modes $k \in K$.

Equalities (17.13)–(17.14) ensure material flow balance at each DC. Following reasoning similar to that underlining (17.12), (17.14) specializes (17.13) for time period $t = 1$.

Equalities (17.15)–(17.16) guarantee material flow balance at each CZ. In equality (17.15), $b_{if_{e-1}(t-1)}$ $\left(b_{if_{e-1}t}\right)$ denotes the number of backorders incurred for product i at facility $f_{e-1} \in F_1$at the end of period $t-1$. (17.16) specializes (17.15) for time period $t = 1$, for which we assume the initial number of backorders, $b_{if_{e-1}(t-1)}$, is zero.

The fourth category, (17.17)–(17.22), imposes capacities of facilities and transportation modes. Our model is based on the assumption that goods are transported in standard containers. Thus, the number of products that are moved depends on the volume (cubic feet) occupied by one unit of product i, V_i, and the total volume (cubic feet) of a container V^{CT}.

Inequality (17.17) guarantees that the total volume of products shipped via mode k is less than or equal to the capacity of the containers used, where an integer variable $y_{f_ef_{e-1}kt}$ denotes the number of containers shipped via mode k. Inequality (17.18) opens the transportation link from f_e to f_{e-1} for mode k if it is being used to transport containers in period t. $r_{f_ef_{e-1}kt}$ is a binary variable that equals 1 when the transportation link from f_e to f_{e-1} via mode k can be used (i.e., both f_e and f_{e-1} are open) in period t, 0 otherwise.

Inequality (17.19) imposes the production capacity $W^P_{if_e}$ of facility $f_e \in F_3$ in each time period for every product i, and allows a plant to manufacture if and only if it has been opened by period t. Inequality (17.20) limits the capacity of each production plant, DC and CZ to store inventory. $W^I_{f_e}$ is the inventory holding capacity (cubic feet) of facility f_e and V_i is the volume (cubic feet) of each unit of product i.

Inequality (17.21) allows each potential plant and DC to be opened at most once over the planning horizon. Once opened, a facility will remain open for the remainder of the planning horizon. Inequality (17.22) assures that a DC can be opened only if products are shipped to it from an upstream production plant.

Constraints (17.23)–(17.24) assure single sourcing. Inequality (17.23) states that DC facility $f_e \in F_2$ can serve CZ facility $f_{e-1} \in F_1$ only if the route is open during any period t for some transportation mode k (i.e., $r_{f_ef_{e-1}kt} = 1$). Equality (17.24) ensures that each CZ is served by a single DC during all time periods.

The last category, (17.25)–(17.37), gives integer, sign and other restrictions. Equation (17.25) ensures that the initial number of backorders is zero, (17.26)–(17.28) impose binary restrictions, (17.29)–(17.33) give integer requirements, and (17.34)–(17.36) invoke non-negativity. Constraint (17.37) allows β_{cst} to be unrestricted in sign, since taxable income can be either positive or negative.

We note that Robinson and Bookbinder (2007) studied transportation time and its relationship to inventory levels. We hold broader objectives, however, and our model includes a number of issues that theirs did not, as shown in Table 17.1.

Table 17.1 Comparison of Robinson/Bookbinder model to ours

The Robinson/Bookbinder model	Our model
Single product	Multiple products
4-level (maquiladora-plant-DC-customer)	3-level (plant-DC-CZ)
No inventory allowed at CZs	Inventory can be held at each facility
No backorders allowed	Backorders allowed
t represents arriving time of a shipment	t represents departing time of a shipment
No transportation mode has a minimum shipment quantity or a maximum capacity	Each transportation mode has a minimum shipment quantity and a maximum capacity
Minimizes operating costs	Maximizes after tax profit
Single transportation mode chosen on a given link (but mode can change on the link later in the time horizon)	Mixed transportation modes can be used

17.4 Case Study

This section reports a case study that demonstrates relationships among facility location, transportation mode selection, and material flow costs. It contains three subsections. The first describes the structure of the supply chain, the second discusses the data we use, and the third relates case study results.

17.4.1 Supply Chain Structure

The case setting involves an enterprise that manufactures two types of electronic products: 40 inch LCD TVs and 20 inch monitors, respectively product 1 and product 2. These items are delivered through a supply chain that comprises three echelons: production plants; DCs; and CZs, which fulfill customer demands.

The case study involves four alternative production plants, two of which are located in Korea and two in Mexico. Each country has a competitive advantage of either low tax rate or low tariff in comparison with the other (i.e., the U.S. assesses no tariffs on Mexican products under NAFTA). Each country offers a potential site for one *regular* and one *super* production facility. A regular facility does not have sufficient production capacity to meet all demand by itself, forcing it to coordinate with at least one other facility to meet all of the demand. Each *super* facility provides economies of scale and enough production capacity to satisfy all demand by itself. Four alternative DCs are available in the U.S. to serve eight CZs, which, for convenience, we take to be the eight most populous cities in the U.S.

17.4.2 Data and Sources

While our case study is based on an actual industrial decision related to modal selection, we are not at liberty to give specifics. Instead, we use publically available sources of data to reflect the size and scope of the actual industrial setting. This section describes the data we use in our "Base Case" (Case 1), to which we compare results from seven other cases in the sensitivity analyses.

Our test cases define a period to be a week and we employ a planning horizon of $T = 15$ weeks. We begin each case with an empty system (i.e., no inventory in-process at production facilities, at distribution centers or in transit, and no backorders outstanding), representing start-up conditions. Thus, we expect to incur some backorders in the early weeks, until facilities can produce products which in turn can be transported to be in position to respond to demands. This start-up phase appears to last for about three weeks (see Fig. 17.5), and affects results similarly for all cases. Alternatively, we could have measured results for weeks 4–15 to avoid this start-up, or prepositioned inventory in-process at production facilities and at distribution centers to emulate a steady state. However, we elected to use a start-up phase that is consistent for all cases, making comparisons more meaningful by highlighting the relationships we seek to study.

We assume homogeneity so that data can be presented succinctly and results can more readily be interpreted intuitively. For example, the variable production cost parameters are the same for all production plants, as shown in Table 17.2.

Table 17.2 itemizes each of the potential facility locations we use and identifies the type of each facility (i.e., regular (PR) or super (PS) production plant). That table also gives $G^F_{f_e}$ the fixed cost for opening facility f_e; $G^P_{if_e}$, the variable cost of producing one unit of product i; G^B_i, the penalty cost for each backorder held at the end of a week for product i; and $G^I_{if_e}$, the cost of holding one unit of product i in inventory at the end of a week at all types of facilities. We set the cost of carrying pipeline inventory, $G^{TP}_{if_ef_{e-1}k}$, equal to the cost of carrying inventory at the shipment's destination facility for each mode $k : G^{TP}_{if_ef_{e-1}k} = G^I_{if_{e-1}}$. We assume that initial and final quantities of inventories, as well as outstanding backorders, are zero. Thus, backorders are incurred during early weeks until products can be produced and shipped through DCs to CZs.

The demand D_{if_et}, for each product i at any customer zone f_e in every week, was based on annual sales of that product divided by an estimate of the size of the market (Hachman 2008). This resulted in weekly demands for product 1 (flat screen television) of 0.03 % of the CZ population, and 0.01 % of the CZ population for product 2 (monitor).

Given the average selling price of products 1 and 2, $644.97 and $150.45, respectively, we reverse engineer the transfer price at each echelon. Echelons 2 and 1 purchase a product at one price and sell it for a higher price to the downstream echelon and end customer, respectively. Facilities in the CZ echelon pay a transfer price that is 85 % of the price they charge their end customers:

Table 17.2 Alternative facility locations and base-case operation- and production-cost parameters

Facility	Location	Facility type	Fixed facility cost: $G^F_{f_e}$ ($)	Variable production cost of products 1 and 2: $G'^F_{if_e}$ ($/unit)	Backorder cost of products 1 and 2: G^B_i ($/unit)	Inventory cost of products 1 and 2: $G^I_{if_e}$ ($/unit/week)
1	Korea	PR[a]	64,117	266 and 66	N/A	1.7 and 0.4
2	Monterrey	PR	64,136	266 and 66	N/A	1.7 and 0.4
3	Korea	PS[b]	128,233	266 and 66	N/A	1.7 and 0.4
4	Monterrey	PS	128,271	266 and 66	N/A	1.7 and 0.4
5	New York	DC	21,030	N/A	N/A	2.8 and 0.7
6	Los Angeles	DC	21,030	N/A	N/A	2.9 and 0.7
7	San Antonio	DC	21,030	N/A	N/A	2.9 and 0.7
8	Nashville	DC	21,030	N/A	N/A	2.9 and 0.7
9	New York	CZ	21,729	N/A	40 and 10	3.2 and 0.8
10	Los Angeles	CZ	11,110	N/A	40 and 10	3.4 and 0.8
11	Chicago	CZ	12,820	N/A	40 and 10	3.3 and 0.8
12	Houston	CZ	11,908	N/A	40 and 10	3.3 and 0.8
13	Phoenix	CZ	6,631	N/A	40 and 10	3.3 and 0.8
14	Atlanta	CZ	6,655	N/A	40 and 10	3.2 and 0.8
15	Oakland	CZ	7,585	N/A	40 and 10	3.4 and 0.8
16	Wichita	CZ	5,681	N/A	40 and 10	3.3 and 0.8

[a] *PR* Regular Plant
[b] *PS* Super Plant

$P_{if_2f_1} = (0.85)\,(Average\,selling\,price\,of\,product\,i\;to\,end\,customers)$. In turn, the transfer price that DCs pay is 75 % of the price they charge CZs: $P_{if_3f_2} = (0.75)P_{if_2f_1}$. CZs add local sales tax to the selling price they charge (Federation of Tax Administration 2010). We determined the fixed and variable costs of production, seeking a 20 % margin for plants in Korea and a 15 % margin for those in Mexico.

Figure 17.1 depicts the potential transportation links between DCs and CZs in the U.S. We deal with three transportation modes: $k = 1$, ship; $k = 2$, rail; and $k = 3$, truck. We assume that the cost of shipping a 40-foot container from Korea depends upon the destination port, as detailed in Table 17.3. To determine how many 40-foot containers are needed to satisfy demand, we use a container capacity of $V^{CT} = 2720$ cubic feet (see Shipping, logistics management container) and estimate that each unit of product $i = 1$ requires $V_1 = 5.87$ cubic feet and that each unit of product $i = 2$ requires $V_2 = 0.99$ cubic feet, based on dimensions of actual products. We assume that the cost of shipping is borne by the facility f_e that originates a shipment, so that $R^G_{f_ef_{e-1}} = 1$. The maximum number of containers, M^{CT}, that can be shipped from any facility in any week is 50 in our Base Case.

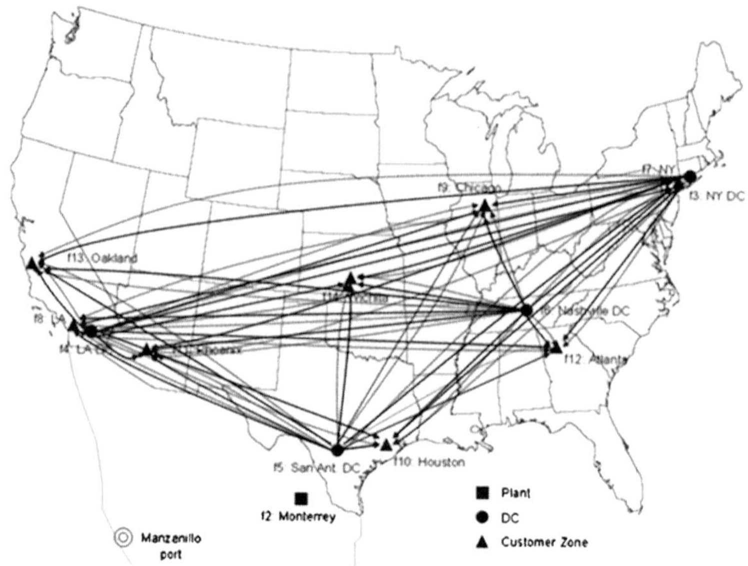

Fig. 17.1 Transportation links between DCs and CZs

Table 17.3 Cost to ship a 40′ container

	Fixed cost($) to ship a 40′ container $G^{TF}_{f_e f_{e-1} k}$
Korea to LA	1,300
Korea to NY	2,100
Korea to Manzanillo	1,500
Korea to Savannah port	2,000

Table 17.4 gives the fixed costs $G^{T}_{f_e f_{e-1} k}$ and variable costs $G^{TF}_{f_e f_{e-1} k}$ we assumed for transportation by each mode, along with the cost of holding pipeline inventory (see also Kehoe 2003).

To calculate transit times for trucks, we used Federal rules (Federal Motor Carrier Safety Administration) on hour-limits for drivers, dividing the distance in miles between facilities by the product of an average speed of 55 miles/h, 9 driving hours a day and 7 days per week (i.e., 55 × 9 × 7 = 3,465 miles/week. We assume that lengthy trips would involve a relief driver, so that regulations regarding driver time behind the wheel would be observed.) The transit time for rail is assumed to be 1.45 times that for truck. We round each resulting value to the nearest integer so that each transit time is an integral number of weeks.

While our model can deal with several tax brackets, each country included in our case study uses only one. Table 17.5 gives annual tax rates for each of the three countries as well as the tariff paid by Korean plants (we assume that Mexican plants operate under NAFTA terms, which assess no tariffs).

Table 17.4 Transportation cost parameter values

Transportation modes	Variable transportation cost: $G^{T}_{f_e f_{e-1} k}$($/container/mile)[a]	Fixed transportation cost: $G^{TF}_{f_e f_{e-1} k}$ ($/shipment)	Pipeline inventory cost: $G^{TP}_{i f_e f_{e-1} k}$ ($/unit/week)
Truck	7.5	150	3
Train	2.5	3,500	3
Ship	0.13	4,000	3

[a] Vidal and Goetschalckx (2001)

Table 17.5 Annual tax rates of all three countries and tariff paid by Korean plants

Countries	Tax rates[a] $R_{cst}(\%)$	Tariff: $G^{TRF}_{i f_e f_{e-1}}$ ($/unit)
US	35	0
Korea	24	1.8
Mexico	30	0

[a] World Tax Rates (2010–2011)

We assume that super facilities 1 and 2 are uncapacitated, and set $W^{P}_{if_e}$, the capacities of facilities 3 and 4 to produce product i in week t, to be 80 % of the average demand per week for all customer zones:

$$W^{P}_{if_e} = (0.80) \times \frac{1}{|T|} \sum_{t \varepsilon T} \sum_{f_e \in F_1} D_{if_e t}.$$

$W^{I}_{f_e}$ gives the capacity of a facility to hold inventory in terms of volume. For plants,

$$W^{I}_{f_e \in F_3} = (0.25) \times \sum_{i \in I} \sum_{f_e \in F_3} D_{if_e t} V_i W^{P}_{if_e};$$

for DCs,

$$W^{I}_{f_e \in F_2} = (0.40) \times \sum_{i \in I} V_i \left(\frac{1}{|T|} \sum_{t \in T} \sum_{f_e \in F_1} D_{if_e t} \right),$$

allowing each to cover 40 % of the average demand per week over all CZs; and for CZs,

$$W^{I}_{f_e \in F_1} = (0.08) \times \frac{1}{|T|} \sum_{i \in I} \sum_{t \in T} D_{if_e t}.$$

It is assumed that DCs are owned by third parties able to provide large capacities.

To discount each future sum to its present worth, we use a nominal interest rate of 0.10, compounded weekly. The present worth factor to discount an amount in week t is thus $R_t^{PW} = (1 + 0.10/52)^{-t}$.

A set of cases is investigated to obtain relationships among facility locations, transportation modes, and material flow costs in supply chain design. In Case 1, the Basic Case, our model prescribes a centralized design, achieving economies of scale by selecting only the super facility in Mexico. Case 2 demonstrates an optimal *decentralized* design: It employs both regular plants, one in Mexico and one in Korea, for comparison. Case 3 explores the effect of variable production cost on production facility locations, while Case 4 studies the impact of fixed costs on those locations. Case 5 evaluates the sensitivity of after-tax profit to the transfer price that production plants charge DCs; Case 6 assesses the impact of demand profile on facility locations. In Case 7, alternative shipping routes from Korea to U.S. DCs are contrasted. Case 8 concludes by examining the relationships between pipeline inventory cost and transportation mode selection.

17.4.3 Study Results

We ran all tests on a PC with *Intel Core 2 Quad®* CPU @ 3.0 GHz with 8.00 GB RAM, using CPLEX 12.1 as a solver. Table 17.6 gives results for the first six cases so that they can be compared easily. Each column records results for one case, including which production facilities are prescribed in Mexico and Korea, which DCs are opened in the U.S., the inventory cost and the number of backorders for each product, and total after tax profit. Finally, run time (RT) (in seconds) and the number of branch and bound nodes that CPLEX requires to solve each case are given.

In the centralized design of Case 1, our model opens two DCs (New York and San Antonio) in the U.S., along with the super production facility in Mexico, as depicted by Fig. 17.2. While the super facility in Korea offers the incentive of a lower tax rate, the one in Mexico is prescribed because its proximity to DCs and CZs resulted in a shorter transit time, reducing the cost of backorders.

In Case 2, we *disallow* use of the super facilities in Mexico and Korea, forcing the model to prescribe an optimal decentralized system to compare with the centralized design of Case 1. Our model, which selected the same set of suppliers and DCs it did in Case 1, shows that the resulting decentralized system is less profitable than the centralized one.

Case 3 studies the influence of material flow cost by reducing the variable production cost at both regular and super production plants in Korea by 10 %. This change could reflect, for example, lower costs there for labor, energy, and/or raw materials. In Case 3, our model prescribes only the super facility in Korea, highlighting the impact that the preceding component of material flow cost can have on facility location. However, the after-tax profit is just 5.6 % higher than in

Table 17.6 Results for six cases

Measure	Case 1	Case 2	Case 3	Case 4	Case 5	Case 6
Plants						
Mexico: regular		X				
Mexico: super	X			X	X	
Korea: regular		X				
Korea: super			X	X		X
DCs						
Los Angeles		X	X	X	X	X
Nashville						
New York	X	X	X	X	X	
San Antonio	X	X	X	X	X	X
Inventory[a] Cost ($)						
Product 1	15,410	6,861	46,440	10,230	6,907	241,273
Product 2	486	128	1,133	8	334	5368
Backorder[b] Cost ($)						
Product 1	1,300,160	2,253,000	1,029,960	3,357,320	1,483,920	979,720
Product 2	80,820	168,210	68,900	264,620	105,190	17,580
After-tax profit ($)	57,268,587	52,151,321	59,844,482	59,222,686	56,856,520	56,298,362
CPLEX measures						
RT Runtime (sec.)	1,020	1,260	1,620	1,560	650	720
B&B nodes	4,415,918	488,623	139,394	414,606	100,449	99,261

[a] Holding cost (dollars)
[b] Number of units short

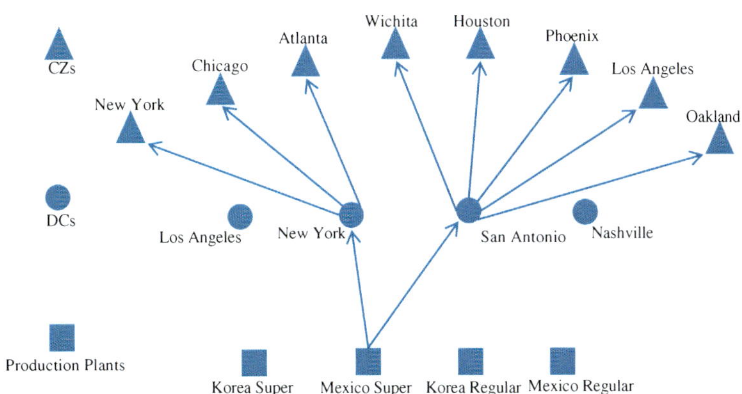

Fig. 17.2 Schematic of the centralized design prescribed in Base Case (Case 1)

Case 1 (the Base Case), even though the tax rate in Korea is only 80 % of that in Mexico. The small percentage gain in profit for Case 3 is due to the longer transportation (transit) time from Korea to the U.S., which results in more back orders during early weeks because the system starts with no inventory. The Korean super plant incurs higher backorder cost, offsetting any savings from the lower variable production cost and the reduced tax rate.

Case 4 investigates the effect of $G_{f_e}^F$, the fixed cost of opening a production plant, on facility location by setting those parameter values at both regular and super facilities in Korea to be 10 % less than their respective values for such facilities in Mexico. Instead of opening solely the super facility in Korea, our model prescribes *both* super facilities, i.e., also the one in Mexico. This illustrates that the profit gain from a 10 % fixed-cost advantage in Korea does not offset the savings that the Mexican facility can achieve by decreasing backorder cost (through a shorter transit time). To explore this relationship further, we continued to lower the fixed cost at both types of Korean facilities to determine the point at which only the Korean super facility would be selected. After several successive reductions of the fixed costs of Korean facilities, our model did not select just the Korean super facility. Even when we reduced fixed costs in Korea *to zero*, our model selected the super facilities in both Korea and Mexico. Economies of scale favor super facilities over regular facilities. We conclude that the fixed costs we used in the Base Case are not high enough to play a major role in determining facility locations. Rather, transit time is a dominant factor because it has a significant influence on the total costs of backorders. To assess this view, we found that our model selected just the Korean super plant only when we *doubled* Base-Case fixed costs for plants in Mexico, and set the fixed costs of plants in Korea to about 50 % of those in Mexico.

Case 5 explores the sensitivity of after-tax profit to transfer price. Transfer pricing is applicable when products are transported between production plants in Korea (Mexico) and the U.S. Because the highest tax bracket in the U.S. is 35 %, which exceeds the Mexican (30 %) and Korean (24 %) rates, an international company sets transfer prices to shift as much revenue as possible to Mexico or Korea to pay less total income tax. To do so, the international firm increases the transfer price that its production plants in Korea and Mexico charge for shipments purchased by its plants in the U.S., so that they account for a larger portion of contributed value and pay tax on it at the lower rate. We actually observed the consequence of changing transfer price from the opposite viewpoint, by decreasing transfer prices at production plants in Mexico or Korea by 10 %. The result is a reduction in after-tax profit, because more revenue is relocated to the U.S., where it incurs a higher tax.

Case 6 assesses the impact of the profile of demand on facility location, comparing the uniform profile of the Base Case with a bell-shaped one that rises to a peak, then reduces to its starting levels (Fig. 17.3). Both Cases 1 and 6 must serve the same total demand over the planning horizon. The bell-shaped profile thus incurs less demand during the beginning and ending weeks, but an extremely high demand during the middle of the horizon. That demand, requiring that inventory be built to accommodate it, is shown in Fig. 17.4. Our model prescribes the super facility in Mexico in Case 1, but the super facility in Korea in Case 6. The latter's lower demand in the early weeks diminishes the impact of the cost of backorders on

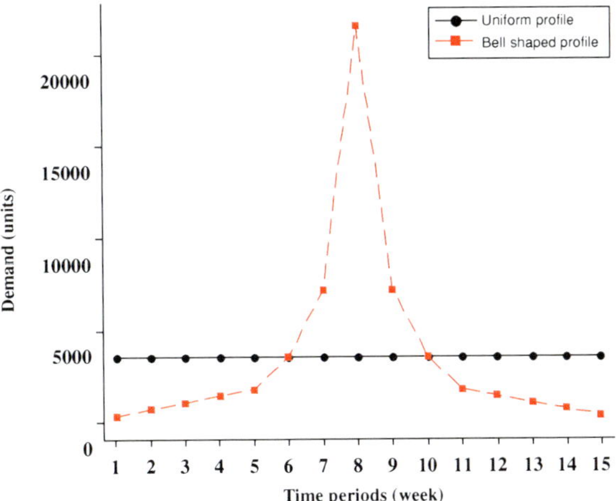

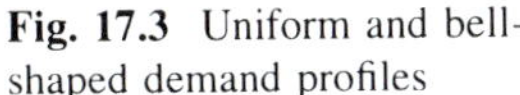
Fig. 17.3 Uniform and bell-shaped demand profiles

facility location (see Fig. 17.5). In Case 6, the competiveness of low tax rates and low (fixed and variable) production costs at Korean plants overcome the transit-time advantage that Mexican plants enjoy. Inventory is built in early weeks (Fig. 17.4), but backorders are still caused by the peak demand (Fig. 17.5) because capacity limits the amount of inventory that can be held. Backorders accumulate in the start-up phase and again at the middle of the planning horizon, because the capacity-limited inventory levels are inadequate to meet peak demands.

Case 7 compares three alternative shipping routes from Korean production plants to U.S. DCs. These routes employ ports in Los Angles, Manzanillo (Mexico), and New York, respectively, then either rail or truck to complete transport to the open DCs. Table 17.7 gives results using each of the three ports as an exclusive entry into the U.S., including DCs selected, total transportation cost, and pipeline inventory cost. The three ports yield comparable results. But the port at New York achieves lower pipeline inventory and transportation costs, due to the use of the Panama Canal, which gives a transit-time advantage to that port. This time advantage is significant because the New York CZ, which has the largest demand, accounting for 26 % of all demand, is near the New York port. While the Manzanillo port gives results that are similar to those of the LA port, our model does not yet reflect infrastructure and security, which must also be considered in making final decisions.

Case 8 examines the relationship between pipeline inventory cost and transportation mode selection. Base Case 1 assumes a variable transportation cost for rail that is approximately one third of that for truck. Base-Case fixed transportation costs are based on transport distance, so that, in comparison to truck, the cost for rail is large enough to favor truck for short transport distances and small enough to favor rail for longer distances. By increasing pipeline inventory cost, rail becomes less competitive, due to its longer transit time. However, the ultimate decision for modal choice also depends on transport distance. A short distance favors truck. On the other hand, modal choice for long-distance transit should not be as sensitive to an increase in pipeline inventory cost, because the advantage of rail (lower

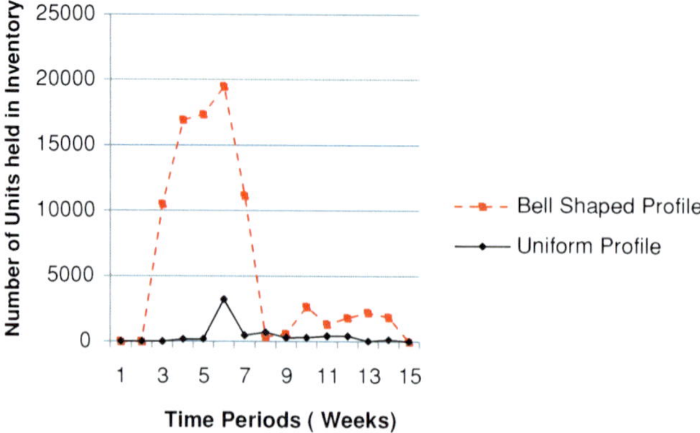

Fig. 17.4 Weekly inventory held for the uniform and bell-shaped demand profiles

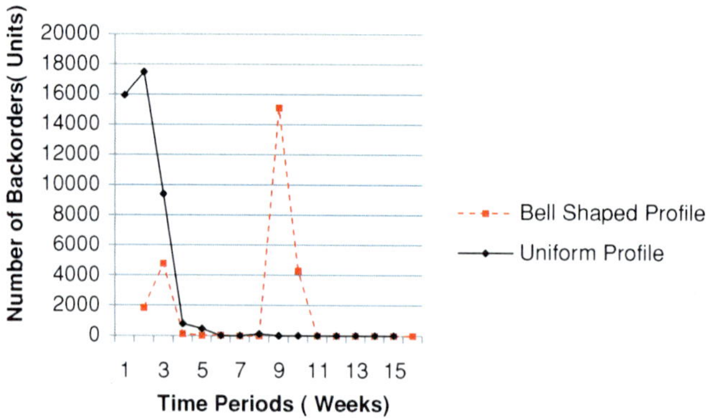

Fig. 17.5 Number of backorders in each week for uniform and bell-shaped demand profiles

Table 17.7 DCs selected and costs of transportation and pipeline inventory using each of three ports

Ports	Los Angles, USA	Manzanillo, Mexico	New York, USA
DCs selected	Los Angles, San Antonio	Los Angles, San Antonio	New York, Los Angles, San Antonio
Total transportation cost ($)	4,889,420	4,832,270	4,564,340
Total pipeline inventory cost ($)	879,368	877,619	847,320
Total ($)	5,768,788	5,709,889	5,411,660

Table 17.8 The number of containers shipped from DCs to CZs at different pipeline inventory costs

(a) Case 1 pipeline inventory cost (See Table 17.1)			CZs							
			New York	Los Angeles	Chicago	Houston	Phoenix	Atlanta	Oakland	Wichita
DCs	Los Angeles	Rail		0			1		0	
		Trucks		140			29		34	
	San Antonio	Rail	76		47	0		24		24
		Trucks	14		10	53		6		5
(b) 2 × (Case 1 pipeline inventory cost)			CZs							
			New York	Los Angeles	Chicago	Houston	Phoenix	Atlanta	Oakland	Wichita
DCs	Los Angeles	Rail		0			0		0	
		Trucks		140			30		34	
	San Antonio	Rail	76		47	0		24		8
		Trucks	14		10	53		6		21
(c) 4 × (Case 1 pipeline inventory cost)			CZs							
			New York	Los Angeles	Chicago	Houston	Phoenix	Atlanta	Oakland	Wichita
DCs	Los Angeles	Rail		0			0		0	
		Trucks		140			30		34	
	San Antonio	Rail	76		45	0		6		0
		Trucks	14		12	53		24		29

transportation cost per mile) increases linearly with distance. Thus, we focus on transportation mode selection for mid-distance transit. Table 17.8 (a, b, c) reports the number of containers shipped by all transportation modes from DCs to CZs as pipeline inventory cost increases, first to double and then to quadruple that of Base Case 1. Our results show that increasing pipeline inventory cost leads to a change in transportation mode from rail to truck for mid-distance transit [e.g., San Antonio (DC) to Wichita (CZ), San Antonio (DC) to Atlanta (CZ)]. Hence, we conclude that pipeline inventory cost affects modal choice for mid-distance transportation. Robinson and Bookbinder (2007) obtained similar results.

17.5 Conclusions and Recommendations for Future Research

We note that our test cases are based on data that reflect current industrial practice but that the reader should be careful about applying our conclusions to any particular supply chain. Rather, this chapter demonstrates the fact that facility location, transportation mode, and material flow costs are related and advocates the use of optimization models to study these relationships in individual applications using actual data that represents that particular setting.

Our model prescribes the locations for (production plant and DC) facilities, and selects transportation modes to design an international supply chain that achieves the maximum after-tax profit. Base Case 1 allows our model to choose between centralized and decentralized supply chain designs, preferring the former because it can achieve economies of scale. The benefit of economies of scale is observed in Case 2 from a different angle: profit reduces dramatically under an optimal decentralized design. Case 4 shows that, even though economies of scale favor super facilities, it is important to achieve an optimal tradeoff between the fixed costs of opening plants and operating (e.g., backorder) cost. Cases 3 and 5 demonstrate the sensitivity of facility location to variable production cost and fixed set-up cost, respectively. In general, our model favors production plants in Mexico over those in Korea because the former offer the advantage of proximity. The result is shorter transit times to the U.S. and significantly fewer backorders (starting with zero initial inventories), offsetting the more competitive tax rates and fixed set-up costs in Korea. However, Case 6 shows that the transit time advantage is diminished if demand is lower in early weeks, so that fewer backorders would be incurred in the startup phase. New ports, such as those under construction in Mexico, provide alternate routes for transportation; pipeline and inventory costs and transit times must be evaluated closely before making decisions, as shown by Case 7. Case 8 shows that pipeline inventory cost can play a major role in determining the optimal transportation mode, especially for mid-distance transports. Case 5 explores the sensitivity of after tax profit to transfer price. Because Korea and Mexico offer lower tax rates than the U.S., increasing transfer prices at foreign production plants shifts more revenue to those countries, reducing the amount of income tax paid, in turn, boosting after tax profit.

Our case study deals with a relatively small supply chain, yet model run times are rather long. We conclude that specialized algorithms are needed to analyze larger supply chains and/or longer planning horizons.

This chapter opens several avenues for future research. We study the deterministic case to identify underlying relationships but other cases may involve uncertainty related to demand, exchange rates and additional factors. Future research could address such uncertainties explicitly. Future research can also model price as a function of quantity produced, or transportation cost as a function of the quantity shipped. Last but not least, future research could devise a specialized solution approach to solve large-scale instances. In particular, the ability to deal with a larger number of time periods would enhance the resolution at which transit times and the preceding relationships can be analyzed. Our continuing research is investigating these avenues.

Acknowledgments This chapter is based upon work supported by the National Science Foundation, Grant number DMI-0529026.

References

Bhutta KS, Huq F, Frazier G, Mohamed Z (2003) An integrated location, production, distribution and investment model for a multinational corporation. Int J Prod Econ 86(3), 201–216

Bookbinder JH, Fox NS (1998) Intermodal routing of Canada-Mexico shipments under NAFTA. Transp Res Part E 34(4), 289–303

Bookbinder JH, Matuk TA (2009) Logistics and transportation in global supply chains: review, critique and prospects. Chapter 9. In: Oskooruchi M (ed) Tutorials in operations research, pp 182–211

Daskin MS, Coullard CR, Shen ZM (2002) An inventory-location model: formulation, solution algorithm and computational results. Ann Oper Res 110, 83–106

Editorial (2004) Review and outlook: triumph of NAFTA. Wall Street Journal, January 12, A14

Erenguc SS, Simpson NC, Vakharia AJ (1999) Integrated production/distribution planning in supply chains: an invited review. Eur J Oper Res 115: 219–236

Federal Motor Carrier Safety Administration, Interstate Truck Driver's Guide to Hours of Service, http://www.fmcsa.dot.gov/rules-regulations/truck/driver/hos/fmcsa-guide-to-hos.PDF

Goetschalckx M, Vidal CJ, Dogan K (2002) Modeling and design of global logistics systems: a review of integrated strategic and tactical models and design algorithms. Eur J Oper Res 143, 1–18

Hachman M (2008) LCD TV sales could fall in 2009 for first time. 18 Dec http://www.pcmag.com/article2/0,2817,2337246,00.asp

Kehoe O (2003) Economics of truck and rail freight transportation. 12 Aug 2003, http://www.kehoe.org/owen/portfolio/truck_vs_rail.pdf.

Kouvelis P, Gutierrez GJ (1997) The newsvendor problem in a global market: optimal centralized and decentralized control policies for a two-market stochastic inventory system. Manage Sci 43(5), 571–585

Lee C, Wilhelm WE (2010) On the role of comparative advantage, competitive advantage, and competitiveness in the strategic planning of international enterprises. Int J Prod Econ 124(1), 225–240

Meixell JM, Gargeya VB (2005) Global supply chain design: a literature review and critique. Transp Res Part E 41(6), 531–550

Melo MT, Nickle S, Saldanha-da-Gama F (2009) Facility location and supply chain management—a review. Eur J Oper Res 196, 401–421

Miller T, de Matta R (2008) A global supply chain profit maximization and transfer pricing model. J Bus Logistics 29(1),175–199

Nozick LK, Turnquist MA (2001) Inventory, transportation, service quality and the location of distribution centers. Eur J Oper Res 129, 362–371

Perron S, Hansen P, Le Digabel S, Mladenovać N (2008) Transfer pricing in a global supply chain, Working paper G-2008-17, Les Cahiers du GERAD

Robinson AG, Bookbinder JH (2007) NAFTA supply chains: facilities location and logistics. Int Trans Oper Res 14(2), 179–199

Sarmiento AM, Nagi R (1999) A review of integrated analysis of production-distribution systems. IIE Trans 31, 1061–1074

Schmidt G, Wilhelm WE (2000) Strategic, tactical and operational decisions in multi-national logistics networks: a review and discussion of modeling issues. Int J Prod Res 38(7), 1501–1523

Shipping, logistics management—container dimensions, container capacity, rating, tare mass and payload of containers. http://www.export911.com/e911/ship/dimen.htm

State Tax Comparisons *FTA* (2010) Federation of tax administrators, 1 Jan 2010. http://www.taxadmin.org/fta/rate/.

Vidal CJ, Goetschalckx M (1997) Strategic production-distribution models: a critical review with emphasis on global supply chain models. Eur J Oper Res 98, 1–18

Vidal CJ, Goetschalckx M (2001) A global supply chain model with transfer pricing and transportation cost allocation. Eur J Oper Res 129(1), 134–158

Wilhelm W, Liang D, Rao B, Warrier D, Zhu X, Bulusu S (2005) Design of international assembly systems and their supply chains under NAFTA. Transp Res Part E 41(6), 467–493

World Tax Rates 2010–2011 http://www.taxrates.cc/

Part VI
Innovative Features and Recent Global Developments

Chapter 18
Humanitarian Logistics: Advanced Purchasing and Pre-Positioning of Relief Items

Serhan Duran, Özlem Ergun, Pınar Keskinocak and Julie L. Swann

Abstract Unfortunately, the world has experienced frequent disasters as well as mega-disasters in the last decade. The challenges faced during the relief efforts to those disasters called for improvements in the area of humanitarian logistics. In this chapter, first we present introductory knowledge on disaster management and humanitarian logistics. The complexities and inefficiencies in the current relief response practice are indicated. To improve the disaster response, we investigate the options of advance purchasing and pre-positioning of the relief items through applied projects performed for different humanitarian organizations.

18.1 Introduction

Unfortunately, the world has experienced mega-disasters in the last decade (2000–2009) such as the Indian Ocean Tsunami (2004), which hit 12 countries affecting 2.5 million people and leaving 226,408 dead and Cyclone Nargis, which killed

S. Duran (✉)
Department of Industrial Engineering, Middle East Technical University, Ankara, Turkey
e-mail: sduran@ie.metu.edu.tr

Ö. Ergun · P. Keskinocak · J. L. Swann
H. Milton Stewart School of Industrial and Systems Engineering, Georgia Institute of Technology, Atlanta, GA 30332-0205, USA
e-mail: oergun@isye.gatech.edu

P. Keskinocak
e-mail: pinar@isye.gatech.edu

J. L. Swann
e-mail: jswann@isye.gatech.edu

J. H. Bookbinder (ed.), *Handbook of Global Logistics*, International Series in Operations Research & Management Science 181, DOI: 10.1007/978-1-4419-6132-7_18,

138,366 people in Myanmar (2008). According to the Center for Research on Epidemiology of the Disasters (CRED, http://www.emdat.be), 3,852 disasters killed more than 780,000 people over the first decade of the third millennium, affected more than two billion others and cost a minimum of $960 billion. The loss of human life in 2010 even exceeds that of the recent decade. The top two most lethal disasters of 2010, the Haiti Earthquake, which killed over 225,500 people, and the Russian Heat Wave, which caused about 56,000 fatalities, by themselves were enough to make 2010 the deadliest year of the two previous decades.

An annual average of 385 catastrophic events, and 200 million people annually seeking relief due to the disasters during 2000–2009, create a need to examine and improve the disaster response of both governmental and non-governmental organizations. One way to enhance the emergency response capacity and preparedness to natural disasters and ensure that there is higher availability of relief supplies is by *pre-positioning* (or stockpiling) inventory through effective advanced purchasing. That is the focus of this chapter. Advanced purchasing can also be used for other health/humanitarian contexts (e.g. sustained food supply chains, Wade et al. 2010) to reduce lead time and procure at better prices.

First we introduce the terminology used, operations executed and parties involved in disaster management. Humanitarian logistics, which constitutes a significant portion of the efforts during a response to a disaster, is the topic of interest in this chapter. We give an overview on humanitarian logistics by discussing its processes, components (such as relief items and supply sources), and unique characteristics and challenges that distinguish it from commercial and military counterparts. Next, we show how advanced purchasing and pre-positioning of the relief items can remedy the issues faced in humanitarian supply chain operations. We give details on how demand and supply can be handled and the methodology that can be followed in pre-positioning studies. Finally, an applied pre-positioning project is discussed in detail and future research directions are indicated.

18.2 Overview of Disaster Management

18.2.1 Definitions

In this section, we introduce the main terms and definitions in the area of disaster management. Naturally, the first definition we need to address is the disaster itself. The United States Federal Emergency Management Agency (FEMA) defines a disaster as an event that causes 100 deaths or 100 human injuries or damage worth US$ 1 million. Disasters can be classified through three aspects: source, location and speed of onset as illustrated in Fig. 18.1 (see Apte 2009; Ergun et al. 2011).

Natural disasters originate from hazardous forces of nature: earthquakes, hurricanes, drought, etc., whereas man-made disasters such as terrorist attacks,

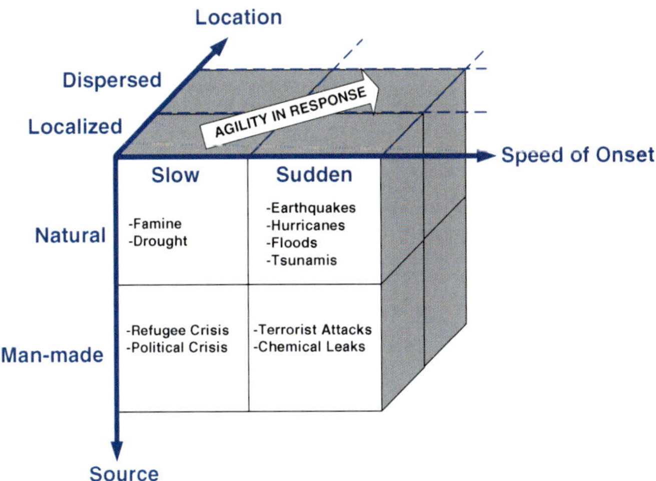

Fig. 18.1 Classification of disasters

refugee crises occur due to the disruptions that humankind cause the environment, resulting in suffering of people. From the humanitarian response perspective, the source characteristic of the disaster—natural or man-made—does not differentiate the funds nor the effort that is dedicated to the relief response. It is the onset speed and location aspects of the disasters that necessitate different levels of agility to achieve the desired success in the response. Slow-onset disasters occur gradually throughout a period of time, providing valuable time to assess the amount and type of relief items needed by the affected. Therefore, in humanitarian responses to slow-onset disasters, the mismatch problem between the relief items delivered and the needs of the affected is less often observed. On the other hand, sudden-onset disasters strike abruptly without a transitional phase, putting a great pressure on initializing the response at once in order to deliver relief items to the affected. Hence, time is a scarce resource and is critical to measure the performance of humanitarian response to a sudden-onset disaster.

The location aspect of the disaster may bring extra distress if the affected people are not *localized* but *dispersed* over different physical or political regions. Such a disaster response requires additional preparation time to mobilize the appropriate means of transportation with the right types of relief items for each disaster zone. No matter the type of the disaster, managing the before and after of a disaster is both a complicated and a critical issue. More specifically, the life cycle of a disaster can be divided into four phases; mitigation, preparedness, response and recovery (Altay and Green 2006). Managing those four stages of a disaster requires a wide variety of operations to be performed. Therefore, we define "disaster management" as the whole of operations aiming to prevent/reduce injuries, fatalities, and damage worth, and to facilitate recovery from the onset of a disaster.

Pre-Disaster		Disaster	Post-Disaster
Mitigation	**Preparedness**	**Response**	**Recovery**
-Barrier Building -Lead Location Choices: -Tax incentives -Tax disincentives -Improving: -Building codes -Risk Analysis -Building resistance -Educating -Community	-Planning -Locations of -Operations centers -Pre-positioned items -Emergency vehicles -Distribution means -Advance Purchasing: -Relief Items -Vehicles -Equipment -Educating -personnel	-Assess relief need -Emergency Rescue -Activating -Operation centers -Rescue teams -Mobilizing Relief Items -First Phase -food, water -Second Phase -Housing -Planning for -the last mile	-Debris removal -Infrastructure rebuild -Designing sustained -medical care -food supply -Assess performance -Feedback to -Planning -Response

Fig. 18.2 Operations in humanitarian logistics over the life cycle of a disaster

18.2.2 Operations

Operations in disaster management aiming to eliminate or alleviate the suffering of the affected spans four sequential stages of the life cycle of a disaster. Each stage has a different target to achieve within disaster operations. A sample of the operations for each of the four phases is illustrated over the life cycle of a disaster in Fig. 18.2. The first phase, mitigation, aims to prevent the onset of disaster or moderate the effects of the disaster. Manipulating the settlement choices of the people away from risky regions through tax incentives is an example of how to avoid large losses in case of a disaster onset. The preparedness stage aims to quicken the response to a disaster. Advance procurement and pre-positioning of relief items improves agility in activating emergency plans significantly. The response stage includes operations related to the implementation of the plans and mobilization of the resources accumulated in the preparedness stage. After assessing the relief requirements, the rescue teams and relief items are marshaled as quickly as possible. The recovery stage involves operations to ensure the sustained retrieval of the affected people, infrastructure and economy. Formation of a sustained food supply chain, rebuilding the infrastructure, and financial assistance to government are the actions that need to be carried out after the response phase, to deliver a complete emergency relief.

18.2.3 Parties Involved

Disaster management operations are executed by parties with different organizational structures, cultures and objectives. The main players in management of a disaster are: governments and governmental organizations, non-governmental (or non-profit) organizations (NGOs), industry (suppliers, distributors and transportation carriers), militaries, and donors (individuals, foundations and private

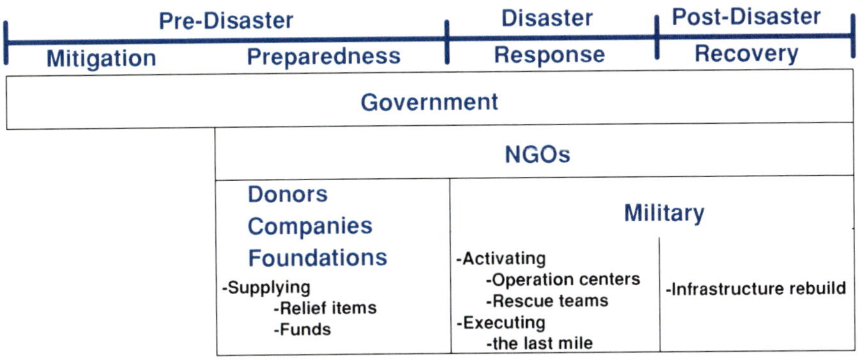

Pre-Disaster | Disaster | Post-Disaster
Mitigation | Preparedness | Response | Recovery

Government

NGOs

Donors
Companies
Foundations
-Supplying
-Relief items
-Funds

Military
-Activating
-Operation centers
-Rescue teams
-Executing
-the last mile
-Infrastructure rebuild

Fig. 18.3 Stakeholders in humanitarian logistics over the life cycle of a disaster

sector companies). Governmental organizations perform all of the operations over the disaster life cycle as seen in Fig. 18.3. Performing the mitigation activities is primarily a duty of the government due to its political and legislative power. A significant amount of emergency supplies provided by donors, foundations and companies are funds or Gifts-in-Kind (non-monetary goods or services). Other than in the mitigation stage, NGOs are also involved with all the humanitarian operations. Those NGOs can be either local or international. The international NGOs (INGOs) such as International Federation of the Red Cross and Red Crescent Societies (IFRC), World Vision, World Food Programme (WFP), OXFAM, and CARE respond to disasters almost all over the world. Often the INGOs collaborate with local NGOs, government and military, or use local logistics companies for the "last mile" operations, the distribution of relief items from the last major supply chain point to the beneficiaries.

18.3 Overview of Humanitarian Logistics

A significant part of the disaster management operations illustrated in Fig. 18.2 can be classified as humanitarian logistics, which acts as a "bridge between disaster preparedness and response, between procurement and distribution and between headquarters and the field" (Thomas 2004, p.3). Humanitarian logistics is formally defined by Thomas and Mizushima (2005) as "the process of planning, implementing and controlling the efficient, cost-effective flow and storage of goods and materials, as well as related information, from the point of origin to the point of consumption for the purpose of meeting the end beneficiary's requirements". In humanitarian terms, the end beneficiaries are the people affected by disasters.

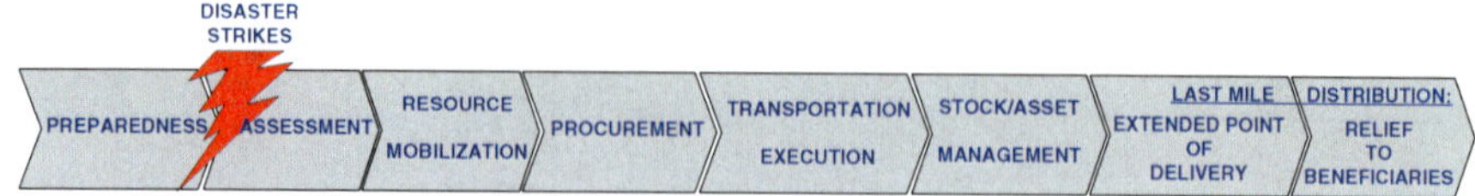

Fig. 18.4 Humanitarian relief supply chain (modified from Thomas 2004)

18.3.1 Humanitarian Relief Supply Chain

Humanitarian logistics ensures that the right relief supplies are delivered to affected people and to disaster zones when they are needed most through the humanitarian relief supply chain. To achieve that, a series of processes throughout humanitarian relief supply chain has to be followed as shown in Fig. 18.4.

In the preparedness stage, national and regional plans are developed for the case of a disaster. These plans should include the tasks to be performed, responsible units for the tasks, and the sources for the relief supplies (Russell 2005). Immediately after the disaster, the first task is to assess the need in the affected region, local resources that can be used, and the current status of the infrastructure. Organizations with local presence or branches are at an advantage in this stage, due to their insider knowledge about the disaster region (Kovacs and Tatham 2009). To set up the regional operation centers, personnel and equipment have to be mobilized as well as the funds to start procurement. The main aim of the procurement stage is to remedy the deficiency between the need of the disaster region and relief supplies already available on hand. The next step is transporting the required relief supplies to the disaster scene. Supplies are carried mostly by sea or air to an entry port of the affected country. Upon arrival, those supplies are gathered at collection sites and stored until the final delivery. The last two stages of the relief supply chain are the *last mile* between an extended delivery point (locations/warehouses near the affected area) and the beneficiaries. The last-mile process is critical to ensure that the relief items are received by the people who really need them. This phase is often challenging, due to damaged infrastructure and road limitations within the affected area.

18.3.2 Relief Supplies

Supplies transferred through the relief supply chain consist of relief items, personnel, transportation vehicles, and construction equipment. Due to their large amounts and wide variety, management of the relief items is a critical issue. As depicted in Fig. 18.5, relief items are categorized as consumable and non-consumable. Consumable relief items need to be fed continuously into affected zones during the relief response. Water, food, hygiene products, and sanitation kits require periodic delivery to the beneficiaries due to storage difficulties experienced by the disaster victims. Non-consumable relief items need to be delivered to the

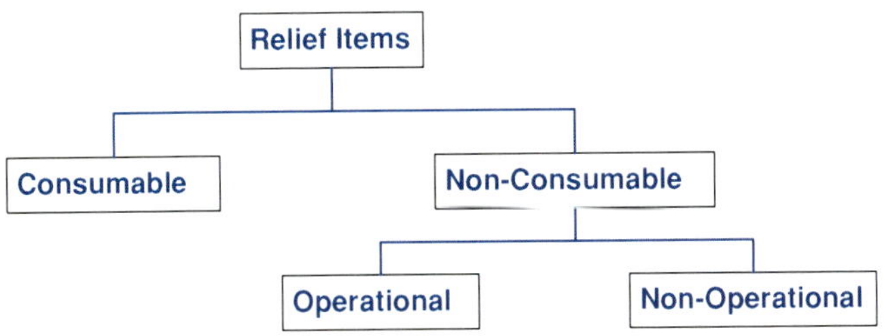

Fig. 18.5 Categorization of relief items

affected areas once, and they are further classified as operational and non-operational. Operational non-consumable relief items are the items such as radios, cellular phones and computers required by relief personnel to set up the operation centers and to communicate efficiently with others. Non-operational non-consumable relief items are supplies such as tents, blankets and utensils that, when received once, can be used by the affected until the effects of the disaster have mitigated.

18.3.3 Supply Sources

Relief items are acquired within the relief supply chain through contributions or procurement. Contributions are composed of donations, grants and Gifts-in-Kind (non-monetary sources). Although they are free of charge, the management of these contributions creates challenges. The majority of contributions are given to humanitarian organizations after onset of the disaster, and frequently a mismatch problem between Gifts-in-Kind donations and the need or requirements is observed. For example, while WFP responded to the South African Food Crisis in 2002, the food donated by the U.S. government was rejected by some of the local governments (Tomasini and Van Wassenhove 2004). Stockpiles of these donations were already in ports or in transit, causing bottlenecks and additional burden in the supply chain. Donations may also cause additional delays in the procurement stage, since the assessment of the quality and quantity of donations has to be determined to decide what needs to be procured from vendors (Fig. 18.6).

Procurement can be done either through global or local vendors. Some relief organizations (such as IFRC, Sowinski 2003) prefer to source relief items from local vendors to stimulate the local economy and to provide faster relief through culturally accepted relief items. But, within a region that was recently hit by a disaster, the quality and amount of relief items provided from local vendors may be low. Prices may be inflated due to scarcity, and purchase of those items may decrease availability or increase prices within the community of non-beneficiaries. Procuring globally has the advantage of lower prices, high quality and capacity, but brings the disadvantages of longer response time and additional transportation costs due to greater distances that have to be traversed. The advantages and disadvantages are shown in Table 18.1.

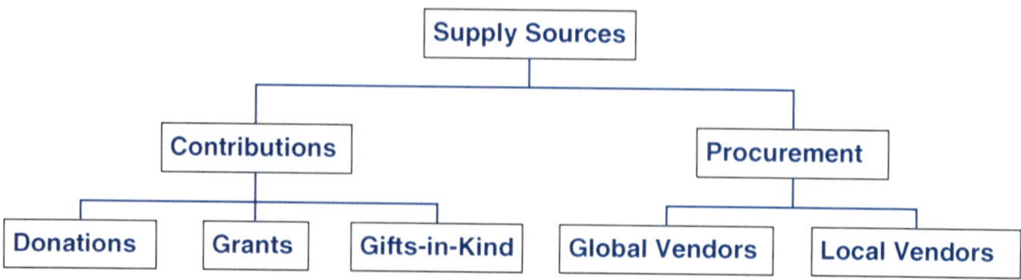

Fig. 18.6 Supply sources of the humanitarian relief chain

Table 18.1 The advantages and disadvantages of procuring locally and globally

PROS	CONS
Local suppliers	
Stimulate economy	Low quality
Low transportation cost	Lower availability
Faster response	Higher prices
Global suppliers	
Higher availability	Slower response
Higher quality	Higher transportation cost
Lower prices	–

18.3.4 Unique Characteristics

Humanitarian logistics has distinctive challenges not seen in military and commercial logistics management. Commercial supply chains are designed to deliver specific products or product groups to certain locations (retailers and warehouses) according to a demand pattern that can be predicted to a certain degree. Although reconfigurations are common, commercial supply chains are utilized for longer periods of time. Therefore, infrastructure investments are more plausible and there is a well-developed supply chain infrastructure ready for utilization. In the humanitarian case, a major proportion of the supply chain structure, such as the last-mile distribution, has to be designed after onset of the disaster. Although response plans are prepared prior to a disaster, infrastructure (roads, bridges and ports) damage that occurred during the disaster onset can require a redesign. As an additional challenge, unlike their commercial counterparts, humanitarian organizations are dependent mostly on donations and grants. Only a small percentage of those contributions can be invested in the infrastructure, due to "donors scrutiny over the usage of funds" (Thomas 2004), and the larger portion is used for direct relief. With such an underdeveloped infrastructure and with funding restrictions, a wide range of relief items has to be delivered to beneficiaries dispersed over the disaster zone. The amount and type of the relief items, and also the locations to distribute them, can only be determined after assessment of the situation. The assessment phase, designing the last mile distribution, and insufficiency of the infrastructure all result in delays in the response in the presence of *pressure of time*. This, in the humanitarian case, "is not just a question of money but a difference between life and death" (Van Wassenhove 2006).

The field of humanitarian logistics also suffers from high personnel turnover and lack of institutional memory that can transfer the experiences from past responses effectively to other personnel. Despite the major differences between commercial sector and humanitarian organizations, according to Thomas and Fritz (2006), "the response to the 2004 tsunami marks a turning point in the involvement of the corporate sector in humanitarian relief." Both parties are looking for opportunities for collaboration.

18.4 Advanced Purchasing and Pre-Positioning

Pre-positioning is broadly defined as the strategic placement of assets such as warehouses, medical facilities, ramp space and temporary shelter space in anticipation of a disaster (Salmeron and Apte 2010). In this chapter, we discuss only pre-positioning of the critical inventory, which will be needed to facilitate an efficient disaster relief response, close to potential disaster regions (Akkihal 2006). This logistical strategy has been adopted from the military, and used along with advanced purchasing, both by humanitarian organizations and private sector companies (see Ergun et al. 2010; Villarreal et al. 2010), due to its potential benefits.

The advance purchasing of relief assests/supplies, and the pre-positioning of them in specific locations to speed up the initial humanitarian response after the disaster strikes, is a strategic decision that requires significant amount of investment both in infrastructure and inventory. The selection of the locations to store the pre-positioned supplies, which supplies to pre-position, in what quantity, and where to pre-position each type of the supply items are critical decisions to be determined. Operations research models in location theory, network flows and inventory management are perfect candidates to be utilized for those strategic decisions, location theory being the dominant one. The well-known problems such as p-median (Akkihal 2006) and covering (Dekle et al. 2005) can be utilized to decide the locations of the pre-positioning warehouses or the emergency centers. These problems consider spatial aspects of operations such as travel cost, population densities and service levels. To include the fact that the hazard of a disaster hitting the same geographic location depends on its magnitude and type, these models are modified to find the optimal locations over disaster-magnitude scenarios created using the historical data (Balcik and Beamon 2008; Duran et al. 2011).

18.4.1 The Need for Pre-Positioning

After the occurrence of a disaster, the initial steps that need to be executed are assessment, resource mobilization and procurement, as seen in Fig. 18.4. The time dedicated to assessing the damage and the corresponding need, and mobilizing the personnel and financial resources, is unavoidable due to high unpredictability of the disaster's magnitude, effect and location. But the procurement phase can be totally or partially eliminated by an established pre-positioning network. Supplies stored in this network can save precious time in alleviating the suffering of the disaster victims, especially in the case of a sudden-onset disaster, where every hour after the disaster strikes is a delay in meeting the needs of the affected people. Advance procurement of the relief items enables the humanitarian organizations to consider local, regional and international suppliers, and to search through all possible suppliers for the best price without the pressure of time in the procurement phase after the disaster onset. By buying in larger volumes, humanitarian organizations can leverage their purchasing power and capitalize on bulk prices (Wade et al. 2010).

Although the benefits of advance procurement and pre-positioning are clear, most of the organizations have to cope with an insufficient supply chain structure and relief supply availability during disaster responses. One of the main reasons for the low level of preparedness is the type of funding received by humanitarian organizations. Sources become available through donations and funds *after* the disaster strikes and receives press coverage. Often these sources are earmarked to be used in a designated disaster response, decreasing the availability of sources for preparedness activities such as advance procurement and pre-positioning. Organizations have to create the resources for those preparedness activities through funding proposals explicitly stating the long term benefits in relief response, and collaborate with other humanitarian organizations to reduce the initial and operational costs of the pre-positioning facilities. As an example of collaboration opportunities, the United Nations Humanitarian Response Depot (UNHRD, http://www.unhrd.org) offers free or at-cost warehouse storage space to the humanitarian organizations through its facilities located around the world (Duran et al. 2011).

18.4.2 Demand

Demand in commercial supply chains can often be measured (or predicted) directly for each item supplied. Similarly, to decide the amount of each specific relief item to supply, the corresponding demand is needed. That should either be measured after the occurrence of the disaster, or predicted from past responses. Unfortunately, direct measurement/surveying of demand for these relief items will take too much time in the wake of the disaster. Forecasting such demand is not straightforward, due to unreliable recording habits of humanitarian organizations, supply deliveries by multiple organizations, and uncertainty on whether the past response corresponds to an over- or under-supplied case.

Therefore, in pre-positioning studies, usually an indirect demand estimation approach is utilized. The numbers of people affected or displaced are the most commonly used demand indicators that can be accessed from databases such as the International Disaster Database (EM-DAT 2010). Akkihal (2006) assumed that humanitarian organizations can arrange non-consumable pre-positioned relief items in unit sets, or item groupings. Demand therefore is proportional to the number of displaced people, and the mean number of displaced people is used as the demand. In the case of constructing a pre-positioning network aiming to respond to multiple disaster types in different climate zones, item groupings cannot capture the climate- and disaster-specific location decisions for the relief items. Duran et al. (2011) estimate the global demand quantities in response to four different types of natural disasters, using the probability of need for distinct relief items and the number of items required by an affected person for each disaster type. For the former data, operational guidelines are from the International Federation of Red Cross and Red Crescent Societies (IFRC 2000), and for the latter CARE International's specifications are used. The expected demand for a specific relief item after the strike of a certain disaster type is calculated by multiplying the probability of need for that relief times the quantity of that item required per affected person, and by the number of affected people.

18.4.3 Supply

In an environment that has just been hit by a disaster, procuring relief items is a complicated process. In the case of no pre-positioned inventory, there is a pressure on the humanitarian organizations to be agile in the procurement process and to proceed to deliver the supply items to the needy at once. This pressure may cause those organizations to end up with low quality and insufficient number of relief items at higher costs, due to incomplete search among suppliers and competition for similar supply items with other organizations who want to respond to the same disaster. In such a case, suppliers hold the upper hand due to uncertainties on the available budget and the desired quantity of the relief items while bargaining for the contracts (Ergun et al. 2011).

Advance purchasing of the relief items and pre-positioning them to be used in the forthcoming disaster responses eliminate the difficulties and disadvantages of procuring after the disaster, with a faster response time. As mentioned before, the challenge is to find the funds needed for the initial pre-positioning warehouse investments, and to acquire supplies not tagged to be used in a *specific* disaster response.

The relief items most appropriate to be pre-positioned in warehouses are those that are costly, durable and difficult to procure quickly (Akkihal 2006). These items are mostly the non-consumable supply items such as shelters, hygiene kits, water purification kits and operational items, such as radios, used by the relief personnel. The global pre-positioning networks that are developed to respond to multiple types of disasters need to have high turnover rates to enable the storage of consumable relief items, such as water and food, without increasing risks of spoilage. In the selection of these consumable relief items, those that are needed for more than one disaster type should be favored.

The source of the pre-positioned relief items is more likely to be international suppliers due to price and quality advantages over local ones. Since time is not a critical issue during advance purchasing, longer delivery lead times from global suppliers are tolerable and organizations have the time to shop around for the best prices around the world. According to Sowinski (2003), IFRC—the world's largest humanitarian network—practices international procurement and maintains agreements with global suppliers for items like blankets, tents, tarps, certain emergency rations, and WHO medical kits that are consistent across disasters.

18.4.4 Optimization Methodology

A humanitarian organization considering to develop a pre-positioning network—warehouses storing relief items to be used in forthcoming disaster responses—has to decide locations of the warehouses it will utilize. The issue of fund availability creates a major difference in the methodology to be followed in selecting the locations of the pre-positioning warehouses within the network. Unlike the commercial counterparts, humanitarian organizations do not have well-defined project budgets for construction of the networks, and instead receive gradual funding from donors. Therefore, they may not have enough funds to set up the desired number of warehouses simultaneously. The more practical approach is to start with an initial warehouse, using the remaining funds to purchase relief supplies to be stocked, and respond to disasters with those resources until the second warehouse's costs are funded.

Hence, the optimal locations for the desired number of pre-positioning warehouses cannot be found by solving the model once, and opening one of them as the first step in construction of the network. If the uncertainties about the amount and time availability of the resources are high, then incremental adding—building each facility at its optimal location incrementally in addition to the ones already in existence, without considering further expansion—will be the best choice (Akkihal 2006). When the desired network size is known with some certainty, the incremental approach should not be used. Rather, different numbers of locations should be considered in the network. Performing a comprehensive sensitivity analysis should be preferred, to measure the sub-optimality created due to the location choices in the initial steps. According to the sensitivity analysis, a gradual expansion plan can be created to perform close to the optimal network configuration of the desired-size if the all required funds were available initially (see Duran et al. 2011).

Table 18.2 Optimal locations for a given number of warehouses (modified from Duran et al. 2011)

	Number of warehouses		
Locations	1	2	3
Hong Kong			√
India	√	√	
Panama		√	√
Dubai			√

18.4.5 An Applied Project

To illustrate the challenges faced during a pre-positioning study and to point out the benefits that can be achieved from completing one, we summarize the applied work of Duran et al. (2011) here in more detail. CARE International is one of the largest humanitarian organizations, providing relief aid to survivors of natural and man-made disasters in more than 65 countries. CARE collaborated with the Center for Health and Humanitarian Logistics of Georgia Institute of Technology to improve its agility in responding to the sudden onset of man-made disasters through the development of a pre-positioning network.

Like most humanitarian organizations, CARE does not have the required financial sources to achieve its desired three-warehouse pre-positioning network while initiating the project. The formulated model focuses on the upfront inventory investment and average response time, and ignores operating costs due to insufficient data on cost of supplies and transportation based on CARE's past responses. Assuming that the costs of warehouse operation can be ignored due to the collaboration with the UNHRD and other humanitarian organizations, the model provides the best warehouse locations and the spread of inventory among them, minimizing the average response time for a given number of warehouses to be opened.

Among the 12 candidate warehouse locations considered, Table 18.2 shows the optimal locations for 1-, 2- and 3-warehouses in the network. The India location that is preferred in the cases of 1- and 2-warehouse networks is replaced with the Dubai location when three warehouses are opened. In such a situation, opening the first warehouse in India as the first step to develop a pre-positioning network would be suboptimal. To provide a roadmap to the managers of CARE, sensitivity analysis was performed to compare the impact of the Dubai versus India warehouse decision, solving the model separately for the cases when the locations of Dubai and India are always forced to be opened.

The authors' final recommendation to CARE was to open the first warehouse in the Middle East, then expand to Central America and then to Southeast Asia and to allocate 35, 15 and 50 % of the available inventory investment among those locations, respectively. Following the recommendations, CARE set up its first pre-positioning facility in Dubai in 2008 and two more in Panama and Cambodia, respectively, in 2009. CARE stocked more than one million sachets of water purification kits in each of these pre-positioning facilities. Those water purification tablets in the Panama warehouse were delivered within a day to the airport in Haiti, and were used during the response to the 2010 Haiti Earthquake to ensure sanitation and safe drinking water (Esterl and Mckay 2010).

18.5 Conclusions and Challenges to Focus on

A comprehensive literature survey on disaster operations management has been prepared by Altay and Green (2006). They state that of all the papers published, 44 % are on mitigation, 21.1 % on preparedness, 23.9 % response and 11 % on recovery phases, indicating a need for research especially on the recovery phase of disaster management. While the recovery phase is the least studied area, it is clear that there is neither lack of need nor opportunity of research on the preparedness phase.

There are few analytical works on procurement processes in the humanitarian relief supply chain. The pioneering work of Ertem et al. (2010) discusses the procurement process of relief items within an auction framework. They compare several scenarios through simulation and measure their effect on the portion of the relief items bought as a result of the procurement auction. The framework developed could be implemented by the humanitarian organizations in order to avoid inefficiencies in resource purchases.

Pre-positioning models mostly utilize the theory developed for locating facilities in commercial supply chains. However, when a disaster strikes, there is a high probability of the destruction of infrastructure facilities (harbors and airports) and transportation paths (roads and bridges) (Larson et al. 2006). Rawls and Turnquist (2010) model the pre-positioning of emergency supplies, considering the uncertainty of survival of the pre-positioned relief items and usability of the transportation network due to potential damage caused by the disaster. They utilize a two-stage mixed integer program to solve this model, and pioneer a much-needed research area: creating location models that provide solutions robust to the infrastructure impairments caused by emergency events.

Another area to focus on is collaboration among multiple responders. Within the disaster zone humanitarian organizations, governmental agencies and local authorities act simultaneously to provide relief to the affected people. Low-level or no coordination among these stakeholders may result in inefficient usage of scare resources such as infrastructure facilities, duplication of the relief efforts and inflated prices for local transportation means. To enable horizontal coordination between relief actors, most of the coordination structures involve a single lead agency (umbrella organization) (Balcik et al. 2010). UN introduced the *cluster approach* in 2005, creating clusters for each key sector of the humanitarian response, and appointed a lead organization to each cluster, which includes a large number of NGOs and agencies with relevant expertise and capacity (Cluster Approach 2011).

Balcik et al. (2010) identified three classes of coordination mechanisms: procurement and warehousing, as currently in use, and transportation as having a future potential. NGOs receive lower prices through joint procurement of relief items due to large-quantity purchases, especially when they are supported by an umbrella organization. Relief organizations can utilize no- or at-cost warehousing space through UNHRD network, benefiting in lower transportation costs due to possessing pre-positioned items closer to disaster-prone areas. During the Afghan crisis, the local transportation costs increased 300 % over a six-month period due to the uncoordinated negotiations by humanitarian agencies. The United Nations Joint Logistics Centre (UNJLC) (later superseded by the Logistics Cluster) engaged in the process and bargained on behalf of all humanitarian agencies. The collective bargaining power resulted in standardizing the prices and saved much needed dollars (Kaatrud et al. 2003). To achieve the high level of transportation (shipper) coordination practiced in commercial supply chains, new contract mechanisms and incentive models need to be developed. These should be tailored specifically to deal with the highly uncertain demand and demand points often observed in humanitarian relief chains.

Acknowledgments This research has been supported in part by the Mary Anne and Harold R. Nash endowment at Georgia Tech.

References

Akkihal A (2006) Inventory pre-positioning for humanitarian operations. Master's thesis, MIT

Altay N, Green W (2006) OR/MS research in disaster operations management. Eur J Oper Res 175(1):475–493

Apte A (2009) Humanitarian logistics: a new field of research and action. Found Trends Technol Inf Oper Manag 3(1):1–100

Balcik B, Beamon B (2008) Facility location in humanitarian relief. Int J Logis: Res Appl 11(2):101–121

Balcik B, Beamon B, Krejci CC, Muramatsu KM, Ramirez M (2010) Coordination in humanitarian relief chains: practice, challenges and opportunities. Int J Prod Econ 126:22–34

Cluster Approach (2011) Humanitarian reform and the global cluster approach. http://www.oneresponse.info/Coordination/ClusterApproach/Pages/ClusterApproach.aspx. Retrieved 14 Febr 2011

Dekle J, Lavieri M, Martin E, Emir-Farinas H, Francis R (2005) A Florida county locates disaster recovery centers. Interfaces 35(2):133–139

Duran S, Gutierrez MA, Keskinocak P (2011) Pre-positioning of emergency items worldwide for CARE international. Interfaces 41(3): 223–237

EM-DAT (2010) Centre for research on the epidemiology of disasters: the international disaster database. http://www.emdat.be

Ergun O, Karakus G, Keskinocak P, Swann J, Villarreal M (2011) Operations research to improve disaster supply chain management. In: Cochran J (ed) Wiley encyclopedia of operations research and management science. Wiley, New York

Ergun O, Stamm J, Keskinocak P, Swann J (2010) Waffle house restaurants hurricane response: a case study. Int J Prod Econ 126:111–120

Ertem MA, Buyurgan N, Rossetti M (2010) Multi-buyer procurement auctions framework for humanitarian supply chain management. Int J Phys Distrib Logis Manag 40(3):202–227
Esterl M, McKay B (2010) Rescuers strain to get safe water to thirsty. Wall Street J (16 Jan 2010)
IFRC (2000) International Federation of the Red Cross and Red Crescent Societies disaster preparedness training manual. http://www.ifrc.org/WHAT/disasters/dp/manual.asp. Retrieved 25 Febr 2008
Kaatrud D, Samii R, Van Wassenhove L (2003) UN joint logistics centre: a coordinated response to common humanitarian logistics concerns. Forced Mig Rev 18:11–14
Kovacs G, Tatham P (2009) Responding to distruptions in the supply network—from dormant to action. J Bus Logis 30(2):215–228
Larson R, Metzger M, Cahn M (2006) Responding to emergencies: lessons learned and the need for analysis. Interfaces 36(6):486–501
Rawls CG, Turnquist MA (2010) Pre-positioning of emergency supplies for disaster response. Transp Res Part B 44:521–534
Russell T (2005) The humanitarian relief supply chain: analysis of the 2004 south east asia earthquake and tsunami. Master's thesis, MIT
Salmeron J, Apte A (2010) Stochastic optimization for natural disaster asset prepositioning. Prod Oper Manag 19(5):561–574
Sowinski L (2003) The lean, mean supply chain and its human counterpart. World Trade 16(6):18
Thomas A (2004) Humanitarian logistics: enabling disaster response. http://www.fritzinstitute.org/PDFs/WhitePaper/EnablingDisasterResponse.pdf. Retrieved 16 Aug 2010
Thomas A, Fritz L (2006) Disaster relief, inc. Harv Bus Rev 84(11):114–122
Thomas A, Mizushima M (2005) Fritz institute: logistics training: necessity or luxury? Forced Mig Rev 22:60–61
Tomasini R, Van Wassenhove L (2004) Genetically modified food donations and the cost of neutrality. Logistics response to the 2002 Southern Africa food crisis. INSEAD Case 03/2004-5169
Van Wassenhove LN (2006) Blackett memorial lecture—humanitarian aid logistics: supply chain management in high gear. J Oper Res Soc 57(5):475–489
Villarreal M, Drake M, Ergun O, Karakus G, Kerl P, Keskinocak P, Swann J (2010) A leading home improvement retailer's commitment to disaster response. Case Study, Georgia Institute of Technology
Wade J, Aviles S, Bah E, Ergun O, Jimenez M, Li L, Morales A, Swann J (2010) Global humanitarian supply chain improvements for the world food programme. Working Paper, H. Milton Stewart School of Industrial and Systems Engineering, Georgia Institute of Technology

Chapter 19
Logistics-Intensive Clusters: Global Competitiveness and Regional Growth

Yossi Sheffi

Abstract Logistics intensive clusters are agglomerations of several types of firms and operations: (1) firms providing logistics services, such as 3PLs, transportation, warehousing and forwarders, (2) the logistics operations of industrial firms, such as the distribution operations of retailers, manufacturers (in many cases after-market parts) and distributors and (3) the operations of companies for whom logistics is a large part of their business. Such logistics clusters also include firms that service logistics companies, such as truck maintenance operations, software providers, specialized law firms, international financial services providers, etc. Logistics clusters exhibit many of the same advantages that general industrial clusters (such as Silicon Valley, Hollywood, or Wall Street) do: increase in productivity due to shared resources and availability of suppliers; improved human networks, including knowledge sharing; tacit communications and understanding; high trust level among companies in the cluster; availability of specialized labor pool as well as educational and training facilities; and knowledge creation centers, such as universities, consulting firms, and think tanks. Logistics clusters, however, exhibit other characteristics which make them unique in terms of cluster formation and their contribution to economic growth. Logistics operations may locate in a logistics cluster due to the cluster's role in supporting economies of scope (mainly for direct operations transport modes) and economies of density (mainly for consolidated transportation modes); their provision of spill-over capacity for warehousing and transportation; and the ability to cooperate between providers when dealing with demand fluctuations. Such clusters provide a range of employment opportunities—from moving boxes to executive, IT and other professional jobs, and they diversify the economic base since they support many

Y. Sheffi (✉)
Elisha Gray II Professor of Engineering Systems, Professor, Civil and Environmental Engineering, MIT, Director, MIT Engineering Systems Division, Director, Center for Transportation and Logistics, MIT, 77 Massachusetts Avenue, Cambridge, MA 02139, USA
e-mail: sheffi@mit.edu

J. H. Bookbinder (ed.), *Handbook of Global Logistics*, International Series in Operations Research & Management Science 181, DOI: 10.1007/978-1-4419-6132-7_19,

other industries, such as manufacturing as well as a range of "mini-clusters." This chapter describes such clusters, based on primary research in several large logistics clusters around the world, interviews with dozens of executives in retail, manufacturing and distribution organizations; with transportation and logistics service providers; with infrastructure operators; with public and private development agencies; and with real estate developers.

19.1 Industrial Clusters

It has long been observed that industries tend to be geographically "clustered." Well known examples of clusters include the concentration of information technology firms in Silicon Valley, California and their counterparts along Route 128 outside Boston, Massachusetts; film studios in Hollywood; wineries in Napa and Sonoma valleys in California; finance and investment banking in Wall Street and around Manhattan, New York City; fashion products in Northern Italy; computer products in Taipei, etc.

In addition, certain corporate functions tend to be clustered. Examples include biotechnology research and development centers in Cambridge, Massachusetts; garments and shoes design in Milan; corporate innovation centers in Silicon Valley; corporate planning and marketing in Zurich and Geneva, etc.

This agglomeration of firms, or corporate functions, that draw economic advantages from their geographic proximity to others in the same industry or stage of value addition is a phenomenon that was originally observed and explained by the British economist Alfred Marshall (1920) in his classic work "Principles of Economics". Marshall hypothesized that the development of industrial complexes implies the existence of positive externalities of co-location. He attributed such externalities to three main forces: (1) knowledge sharing and spillover among the co-located firms; (2) development of specialized and efficient supplier base, and (3) development of local labor pools with specialized skills (see also Peneder 1997).

Michael Porter (1998) expanded on this hypothesis in a landmark paper, providing a detailed framework for cluster analysis, as well as many more examples of clusters in various industries. His paper focuses on the competitive advantages and the increased innovation offered by clusters. He suggests that clusters affect competition by (1) increasing the productivity of the co-located companies, (2) increasing the pace of innovation, and (3) stimulating the formation of new businesses.

Most of the economic literature deals with regional and supra-regional industrial clusters, some of which even span several countries, such as the life science companies in Medicon Valley (extending from Eastern Denmark to Western

Sweden[1]) and the US automotive industry spanning several Midwestern states. A similar phenomenon, however, exists also among retailers on a micro-scale of certain streets or city blocks. Thus, when hairdressers in Boston talk about working on "The Street," they do not mean Wall Street, but rather Newberry Street in the Back Bay of Boston, which is home to dozens of women's beauty salons. There are 25 Italian restaurants on Mulberry Street in Lower Manhattan, in the two block stretch between Broome and Hester Streets.[2] Most British newspapers are located on Fleet Street in London; and six out of the seven concrete plants in Singapore are located in the Port of Jurong, even though the Port of Singapore is significantly larger.

Obviously, many of the economic reasons for clustering used in the literature to explain the advantage and role of clusters do not apply to such "sub clusters," agglomerated along a single street or around a few blocks area. Neither the work force, nor the suppliers' base, nor the customers are located in the vicinity of such clusters. So why aren't they spread all over the urban area in locations where inexpensive real estate and parking would be more available? In reality, some are—there are hundreds of Italian restaurants in Manhattan and many are the only ones on their block; and there are many beauty salons in Boston located in suburbs and shopping malls with few competitors within walking distance. Yet the phenomenon of sub-clusters is evident.

The two major types of inter-firm relationships which contribute to the success of clusters can be defined as "vertical" and "horizontal."

Vertical relationships are links between trading partners. The ultimate examples of vertical clusters are those created by a single "channel master," such as "Toyota City" or the cluster of aviation suppliers servicing Boeing in Everett, Washington. As an example of the wider economic effect of such a channel master, consider Shain's (2009) description of the impact of the BMW plant in Greer, South Carolina. It employs 5,000 workers, yet it supports over 23,000 jobs in the state, as many suppliers decided to co-locate around Greer.

Horizontal relationships are between firms at the same stage of production, such as automobile manufacturing plants in Detroit, Michigan, or film studios in Hollywood, California. Such firms both compete with each other and cooperate along dimensions that benefit them. Horizontal relationships also exit between functions in firms of the same or different industries. Thus, HR, legal, procurement, finance, and supply chain management functions may collaborate across companies and industries.

Clusters grow due to "positive feedback" or "reciprocal reinforcement" forces. As more companies of a certain type (or certain corporate functions) move in, more suppliers and customers move in, making the cluster even more attractive.

---

[1] See the chapter on "Logistics in the Oresund Region of Scandinavia" by Gammelgaard and Kinra in this volume.

[2] Naturally, consumer behavior drives, in part, such retail clusters as they minimize search costs while allowing a variety of options.

Furthermore, as the cluster grows, its influence with government grows, affecting more infrastructure investments as well as advantageous regulations, attracting—again—even more companies.

Naturally, most clusters include both vertical and horizontal types of relationships. Thus, Detroit and its vicinity is composed of not only many automotive plants but also a legion of suppliers and sub-suppliers' plants, as well as educational institutions and a large employee pool. Similarly, Hollywood includes major studios but also a myriad of technical and artistic suppliers, as well as the professional human resources necessary to bring films to life.

19.2 Why Clusters?

In many ways, the existence of such clusters today is surprising. While there are many well-documented examples of clusters in ancient times,[3] it is not intuitive to associate clusters with economic success in today's global economy. In many ways, Tom Friedman's (2005) best seller "The World Is Flat" popularized the ideas that today's efficient processes, supported by advanced communications technologies mean, as earlier authors argue, "The End of Geography" (O'Brien 1992) and "The Death of Distance" (Cairncross 1997).Yet—despite such trends—over half the world's population now live in urban areas, as reported by the UN Population Fund (2007) and that portion is increasing. Commensurate with this trend, Sassen (2001) showed that the economic leadership of mega cities, which are obvious clusters of economic activity, has become more pronounced.[4]

Similarly, data show that industries do tend to cluster; raising the question of why this phenomenon takes place given today's advanced abilities. The answer to this question is that industrial clusters embody certain advantages:

- *Trust.* Clusters include, by and large, people with similar backgrounds, language, culture, religion and customs. It is thus easier to develop trust, among organizations and people, leading to lower transactions costs between firms whether they are trading partners or horizontal collaborators/competitors. In most cases this trust is based on relationships forged outside the work environment. Thus, Hollywood, Wall Street and Silicon Valley are famous for their deal making ability, based on deal participants' reputation and familiarity, giving them a competitive advantage over outsiders.

[3] Examples include the Incense Route along the Horn of Africa, carpet-weaving in North–West Persia, glass-blowing in Phoenicia, the obsidian industry of Teotihuacán, Mexico—the pre-Aztec culture that introduced the world to chocolate—all of which were keys to economic growth.

[4] Naturally, urbanization economics which include also the benefits of concentration of diverse economic activities is somewhat different from the cluster economics which is focused on similar and related industries in the same region. Yet the issues are closely connected.

- *Tacit knowledge exchange.* As systems and services become more complex, much of the knowledge associated with their development and operations cannot be codified in an email attachment sent to a supplier. Such tacit knowledge exchange supports discussions over specifications with a supplier; exchanging benchmarking information with a competitor; or supporting a customer—all made easier, faster, less expensive and more effective when conducted within a cluster—using face-to-face and chance meetings. A related phenomenon is knowledge spillover, which as Rodrı'guez-Posea and Crescenzi (2008) argue "the process of knowledge accumulation gives rise to spillovers that could benefit a whole set of potential (intended or unintended) beneficiaries." Much of this knowledge exchange takes place informally, between programmers, traders, technicians, and growers—depending on the type of cluster involved.
- *Collaboration.* The concentration of firms in the same industry, with their similar needs and concerns, gives natural rise to joint activities. These include lobbying for the provision of infrastructure, regulatory relief, incentives, and other government largesse; development of and participation in organizations dedicated to the cluster development, such as chambers of commerce; developing cluster-focused procurement strategies, leading to lower costs and higher quality for all members; engaging in cluster-specific marketing and branding activities; etc.
- *Research and education.* The strength of engineering and computer science in Stanford University and bio-technology and engineering at MIT mean that companies located in Silicon Valley and "Bio-Cambridge" have access to state of the art research and have a steady supply of educated employees, while faculty and students can work in their laboratories on real problems using actual data. Such symbiotic relationships between university and industry clusters are not limited to the information technology or bio-technology industry. Thus, Sonoma Valley supports the Wine Business Institute in Sonoma State University, while the nearby University of California, Davis offers, arguably, the leading program in the US for viticulture and enology.
- *Supply base.* As mentioned by Marshall almost 100 years ago, clusters attract suppliers who see advantages in locating next to their customers. Even in today's environment, the opportunity for unstructured and chance interaction with customers, the opportunities to learn where their business is heading and the opportunities to forge strong, trusting and collaborative relationships with customers is very important when firms make location decisions.

Given all these advantages, one can ask why firms in a cluster don't end up acquiring each other to form larger enterprises if closeness is so advantageous. Of course, to some extent this takes place in an active merger and acquisition environment. Yet, in many ways a cluster may be an optimal balance between the complexity and bureaucracy that hamper innovation in large enterprises, and the lack of scale that holds back smaller firms. In Porter's (1998) words "A cluster allows each member to benefit *as if* it had greater scale or *as if* it had joined with others formally—without requiring it to sacrifice its flexibility".[5]

19.3 Logistics Clusters

The focus of this chapter is on a particular type of cluster—a cluster of firms with logistics-intensive operations. This includes mainly three types of companies: (1) logistics services providers, such as transportation carriers, warehousemen, forwarders, third party logistics companies (3PLs),[6] customs brokers, and specialized consulting and IT providers, (2) companies with logistics-intensive operations, and (3) the logistics operations of industrial firms, such as the distribution operations of retailers, and after-market parts suppliers.

19.3.1 Examples of Logistics Clusters

There are, literally, thousands of logistics clusters around the world. They are known as "Logistics Villages" in Germany, "Distribution Parks" in Japan, "Logistics Platforms" in Spain and various other names around the world. This section describes some of the largest and most visible logistics clusters, including Memphis, Tennessee; Zaragoza, Spain; Rotterdam in Holland; the Singapore Port area; the Panama Canal Zone; and Alliance in Fort Worth, Texas.

Note that one can define and analyze logistics clusters in several scales. For example, one can view the entire area in the triangle Rotterdam (Holland)-Antwerp (Belgium)-Duisberg (Germany) as a single logistics cluster, covering the two large port complexes and the German rail hub.[7] Or, one can look at the "Dutch Logistics Corridor" stretching from Rotterdam to the German border. This corridor includes, naturally, the port of Rotterdam with its terminals and concentration of logistics service providers; Brabant with its focus on sustainable logistics; Breda, along the main highways connecting the hinterlands of Amsterdam, Rotterdam and Antwerp; and Fresh Park Venlo on the German border, which includes over 70 companies providing trading, transport, warehousing and value

[5] In some cases, leader firms in the cluster discourage mergers in order to foster competition among suppliers. For example, the major chemical plants in Rotterdam encourage competition among industrial gas suppliers (de Langen, 2011, "private communication").

[6] In this chapter the term 3rd Party Logistics ("3PL") is used interchangeably with Logistics Service Provider("LSP") and Integrated Logistics Provider ("ILP") to mean a company offering an array of logistics services, such as transportation, warehousing, custom brokerage, forwarding, return management, part distribution, etc.

[7] Unfortunately, however, trade and economic data can usually be obtained only by province, municipality, state, or country.

added services dealing with fresh products (de Langen 2010). Each of these provinces is, at the same time, a local logistics cluster, comprising several *logistics parks*. Such parks can be classified into two types: (1) managed logistics parks—which are developed and managed by real estate developers, local governments or public authorities, providing a range of value added services—in fact, port authorities are logistics parks according to this definition, and (2) unmanaged agglomeration of logistics facilities. In many cases such facilities operate in the vicinity of managed parks due to the availability of logistics infrastructure.

19.3.1.1 Singapore

The modern history of Singapore dates to 1819 when Sir Thomas Raffles established a British port on the island with the express intent of developing free trade (Josey 1980) and loosen existing Dutch trading monopolies at the time. In 1965 Singapore was separated from Malaysia and lost its hinterland. In order to compete, Singapore redoubled its focus on trade and developed a re-export-oriented manufacturing economy, requiring efficient port operations, continuing Singapore's role as *entrepôt* for Southeast Asia (about 85 % of the containers that come to Port of Singapore never enter the country and over half of the remaining material leaves Singapore as re-export). It is a hub for global corporations, or their subsidiaries, importing raw materials and transforming them into world exports (Choy 2009).

To fulfill this need, first and foremost Singapore developed into a world-class transshipment port, later establishing itself as a world-leading container port. This was naturally followed by the move of logistics-intensive industries into Singapore, transforming it to a regional as well as a global warehousing and distribution center. In parallel, Singapore developed oil port facilities to cater to the needs of oil companies in South East Asia. It is important to note that Singapore development in general, and its logistics and trade in particular, rest upon a virtually corruption-free environment, an educated and motivated workforce, and well-established legal and financial business frameworks. Singapore was rated #2 in the World Bank's (2009) International Logistics Performance Index and #1 in the World Economic Forum's The Global Enabling Trade Index (Lawrence Drzeniek and Moavenzadeh 2009).

At the same time, the Singaporean Port Authority (PSA) kept investing in automation, leading to continuous optimization of port services, reducing time and cost to its tenants. Hand in hand with this policy, the PSA and the government made sure that port services were competitively priced and regulations were simplified and streamlined.

As a result of these policies and investments, Singapore was the world's busiest container port in terms of total shipping containers according to the American Association of Port Authorities (2009), until it was overtaken by the port of Shanghai in 2010. Singapore is still the world's busiest transshipment port, handling one fifth of the world's container transshipment throughput (PSA 2010), as well as handling half of the world's annual supply of crude oil. It is serviced by

200 shipping lines, sailing to and from 600 ports worldwide. The port boasts the fastest customs clearing process in the world.

While the Port of Singapore is a logistics park, including many terminal operators in its midst, there is another, smaller port in Singapore -Jurong. Furthermore, the Air Logistics Park of Singapore (ALPS), on the premises of Changi Airport, houses many logistics operators. Thus, the entire nation-island of Singapore can be considered a logistics cluster as many operators and various logistics services providers, including forwarders, customs agents, and information technology providers, are located in the city itself.

19.3.1.2 Rotterdam, the Netherlands

A coalition of Dutch businesses coined the slogan "Holland is Logistics" to increase awareness to the importance of this sector to the Dutch economy. Like Singapore, re-exports constitute a large fraction of total Dutch export—in this case close to 50 %. It is worthwhile to point out, that Holland has been a trading hub for centuries. Notably, the Dutch East India Company (VOC) was the first multi-national in the world, operating hundreds of vessels throughout Asia and between Asia and Europe in the 16th century and beyond. In fact, in 1770, Holland's re-export share was 70 % of all exports. Today, free trade policies (aided by the creation of the European Union), an educated and multilingual work force, and a sophisticated financial transactions capability support the Dutch trading tradition, creating several strong logistics clusters throughout Holland. Holland is ranked 4th in the World Bank's International Logistics Performance Index (2009).

Rotterdam is the busiest container port in Europe.[8] In addition to several large terminal operators, the port encompasses three logistics parks ("distriparks"): Eemhaven, Maasvlkte, and Botlek. While the logistics service providers in Botlek specialize in chemicals, Eemhaven and Maasvlkte[9] are located next to large container terminals (among others, the ECT Home terminal at Eemhaven and the ECT Delta terminal at Maasvlakte). The land of Eemhaven is owned by the Albrandswaard municipality, while the land owner of Maasvlkte is the Port of Rotterdam, which manages all three distriparks. These distriparks are connected to the European hinterland by highways, rail, inland waterways and short sea shipping,[10] allowing for efficient distribution of shipments from Rotterdam to Europe. A dedicated freight rail line is used to move containers directly from the Rotterdam port to Duisburg, which is a rail hub in Germany close to the Dutch border.

---

[8] Followed by Antwerp and Hamburg (based on 2008 figures). For comparison, however, note that in 2008 the Port of Singapore handled more TEUs than these three ports combined.

[9] The Port of Rotterdam is reclaiming more land for the development of the next phase of Maasvlkte, which will more than double its capacity.

[10] Inland waterways include river transport, while short sea shipping refers to sea-borne freight movement in the same continent.

19.3.1.3 Zaragoza, Spain

The city of Zaragoza is the capital of Aragón. It is the fifth largest city in Spain, located strategically almost equidistant from Spain's four largest cities: Madrid, Barcelona, Valencia and Bilbao, as well as the industrial concentration in Toulouse, France. The logistics cluster in Zaragoza presents a very special case since it was newly conceived and constructed from the ground up, despite not being close to a port, a large city or a main airport. It operates, however, as an inland port,[11] connecting the Mediterranean ports of Barcelona, Tarragona and Valencia, to the Atlantic ports of Bilbao, Gijon, and Aviles y Sines (in Portugal). It is connected to the European rail freight network through a direct rail link to Barcelona.

The logistics park in Zaragoza, PLAZA (Platforma Logistica de Zaragoza) was conceived by the Government of Aragón in the early 2000s in response to the need to diversify the region's economic base away from its reliance on the big Opel plant in the area. The park was built on a green field site, literally from scratch, with investments in high speed roads, rail intermodal facilities, an expanded airport, and supporting services, connecting Zaragoza efficiently to the entire Iberian Peninsula and the rest of Europe.

PLAZA is the largest (and newest) logistics park in Europe (Cambra-Fierro and Ruiz-Benitez 2009); it encompasses more than 12 million square meters (130 million square feet) focused on transportation, distribution and logistics-intensive operations. It provides companies in PLAZA and the surrounding areas with state-of-the-art logistics and, particularly, intermodal services. While it is clear that the Government of Aragón took a significant gamble in developing PLAZA at such a size, deliberately eschewing plans for gradual development, the gamble paid off handsomely.[12] Today, leading companies, including the likes of Inditex, Imaginarium, Porcelanosa, Decathlon, TDN, DHL Express, Acciona Infraestructuras, Memory Set, Caladero and many others moved into the park and established distribution operations there (http://www.plazalogistica.com/index.aspx). As PLAZA grew, new services catering to trucking, as well as shopping and hotels were developed in the park.

The Aragón logistics cluster, however, is more extensive than just PLAZA, large as it is. The Aragón Government has developed other, specialized logistics parks in the vicinity of PLAZA. These include PLATEA in Truel, with a railroad access to the Valencia port; PLHUS in Huesca with connections to the Bilbao and Barcelona ports; and PL FRAGA in Fraga. Private developers also built

[11] An inland port is a location away from a seaport, typically connected to the port by a rail line, where many port operations (customs, bonded warehousing, intermodal operations and distribution infrastructure) can occur. Such inland ports are sited on inexpensive real estate and away from urban areas to avoid the negative externalities of noise, congestion and pollution associated with large scale freight transportation activities.

[12] The huge scale of investment in PLAZA was likely used, in part, to deter the development of competing logistics parks elsewhere in Spain.

specialized logistics parks, including Mercazaragoza, with a focus on agribusiness logistics; PTR Zaragoza, focusing on recycling; CTZ, specializing in automotive logistics; and TMZ, the Zaragoza Maritime Terminal (which is an inland port).

19.3.1.4 Memphis, Tennessee

Folklore suggests that when Fred Smith, the legendary founder of FedEx, proposed a reliable overnight delivery service in a computer information age in a paper at Yale's management School, he got a 'C' grade. The professor wrote: "The concept is interesting and well-formed but in order to get better than 'C' the idea must be feasible..." The paper became the idea for FedEx (for years, the sample package displayed in the company's print advertisements featured a return address at Yale University).

Memphis is the largest cargo airport in the world, handling 3.7 million metric tons of cargo in 2009,[13] largely due to the FedEx operations there (Credeur 2010). FedEx handled an average of over 3.5 million packages every day in 2008, while delivering almost as many in its ground operations segment. The air service offered by FedEx attracted a score of companies who compete based on time-sensitive logistics to Memphis. For example, Mallory Alexander International handles the logistics for 1-800-FLOWERS. It receives flowers from growers in the US, Europe and Latin America into its temperature-controlled warehouse in Memphis. It processes customer orders until 8:00 pm and then picks, packs, and ships more than 100,000 orders a year. These orders can be delivered the next morning anywhere in the US. Flextronics, the US contract manufacturing company headquartered in Singapore, repairs 5,000 laptops every night shipping them to customers for next day delivery; Thomson Technicolor ships 1.2 million DVDs per day from its Memphis location (representing half of all the DVDs purchased in the US), and Advanced Toxicology runs 5,000 lab tests a night for next day delivery of results throughout the US.

The airport-related economic growth generated what Kasarda (2009) has termed an "Aerotropolis." The term refers to a concentration of aviation-intensive businesses around a major airport, creating a new urban form including "shopping malls, office buildings, hotels, hospitals, an international business center, conference and exhibition spaces, warehouses and even a residential community" (Mihm 2006, p. 32). Examples of Aerotropolis developments include Schiphol in Holland, Hong Kong's Chek Lap Kok, Beijing Capital Airport City, Dubai World Central, London's Heathrow, and Suvarnabhumi in Bangkok. Memphis airport supports over 220,000 jobs (over a third of the total area employment).

Memphis, however, is much more than an Aerotropolis built around FedEx services, as a staff report in the trade magazine Inbound Logistics (2008) demonstrates. It is an important trucking hub where interstate highways I-40 and

[13] Hong Kong, the #2 cargo airport, handled 3.35 million tons in 2009.

I-55 intersect and, in the future, I-69 (the "NAFTA Highway") will go through. All major US truck lines operate significant terminals in the Memphis area and it is home to 400 trucking companies, making it possible to ship goods from Memphis by truck to 152 US markets overnight and reach most of the US population with second day service. Memphis is also an important Rail hub: The Canadian National Railway connects Memphis with the Gulf Coast, Chicago, and all of Canada. The Burlington Northern Santa Fe and the Union Pacific connect Memphis with most large cities west of the Mississippi, including the major Pacific ports; and CSX and the Norfolk Southern connect Memphis to most of the Midwest and East Coast cities and ports, as the interactive graphics page put up by the Intermodal Freight Transportation Institute of the University of Memphis (IFTI 2010) demonstrates. Finally, Memphis is the 4th largest inland port in the US and the 2nd largest port on the Mississippi River, handling over 19 million tons annually (Schmitt 2009). These other transportation and logistics options were an important factor in attracting heavy industry to Memphis, such as the Nucor steel plant, which opened in 2008.

19.3.1.5 Panama

The concept of a canal through the Central American Isthmus dates back to the early 16th century. The United States completed the construction in 1914, cutting the sailing distance between New York and San Francisco from 14,000 miles, to go around Cape Horn, to 5,900 miles through the Panama Canal.

On December 31st, 1999 the canal was transferred to Panamanian authority and is now managed by the Autoridad del Canal de Panamá (ACP). In the years since the transfer the ACP has managed the canal independently and professionally. Transit times were cut, fees were set based on market segmentation, more services and accompanying fees were offered. This led to the canal traffic volume more than doubling between 2000 and 2008, reaching 300 million tons per year, while revenue reached over $2 Billion a year.

The largest ships that can fit in the canal are called "Panamax." Panamax container ships can carry up to 4,500 TEU.[14] Many ocean carriers today operate bigger "Post Panamax" vessels that can carry well over 5,000 TEU—in fact, the largest ship operating in 2010, the *Emma Maersk*, can carry 15,200 TEU. In 2007 the ACP embarked on an expansion of the canal aimed at doubling its capacity and allowing it to handle Post Panamax vessels. The project is set to finish in 2014, to mark the 100th anniversary of the opening of the original canal.

In conjunction with the expansion of the canal, the Panamanian Government is investing in the development of several logistics parks, transforming Panama to a significant logistics cluster. In addition to investment in port operations on both sides of the canal (Panama City on the Pacific side and the Port of Colon on the

---

[14] Container ships capacity is measured in TEU-s—Twenty foot-Equivalent Unit (containers come in 20 and 40 ft length).

Atlantic side), the government is investing in the development of Panama Pacifico Industrial and Logistics Park on the Pacific side of the canal.

19.3.1.6 Alliance*Texas

Alliance*Texas is a development by Hillwood, which is a Perot company. The company built and opened the first dedicated cargo airport in the US in 1989 as part of a 17,000 acre development. In 2010, the development featured the Alliance Global Logistics Hub offering inland transportation option via BNSF's Alliance Intermodal facility, two Class I rail lines and connecting Interstate highways. Naturally, the logistics park is in the middle of the Dallas-Fort Worth metro area, with its 6.6 million inhabitants, as well as many millions more within a 250 miles radius—including communities from Oklahoma City to Houston and San Antonio.

The development attracted over 220 companies, creating sub-clusters of such industries as Automotive (Hyundai, Audi, GM, Ford, Bridgestone, Firestone, Tucker Rocky, Enkei, and others); Electronics (e.g. LG Electronics, Texas Instruments, AT&T, Motorola), Health care (e.g. such as Amerisource Bergen, Cardinal Health, Galderma, HCA, Patterson Dental Supplies, US Oncology, Teleflex), and a consumer goods sub-cluster (with Behr, Coca Cola, General Mills, Kraft, Lego, Michaels, Nestle). Some of these companies are running their own logistics operations at Alliance but many others are supported by the services of 3PLs operating in the park, including AmeriCold, BNSF Logistics, Ceva, DSC Logistics, Exel Logistics, KFS, PT, Ryder, Trans-Trade, and UPS.

19.3.2 Classification

One can classify the myriad logistics parks around the world in various ways but these classifications rarely produce mutually exclusive types. Some possible classification schemes can be based on the following factors:

- Modal orientation:
  - Air logistics parks, such as Memphis Airport; Alliance Airport in Fort Worth, Texas; Hong Kong International Airport; Schiphol Airport in The Netherlands; Frankfurt Main Airport; and Changi Airport in Singapore.
  - Port logistics parks, such as Rotterdam in The Netherlands; Elizabeth, New Jersey; Los Angeles-Long Beach area; Singapore Port; Dubai Maritime City; etc.
  - Rail logistics parks, such as BNSF Logistics ParkLogistics Park-Chicago; and the Union Pacific in Dallas. These are built around large intermodal facilities.
  - Trucking is the ultimate distribution mode used by parks dominated by other modes of transport. "Pure" trucking logistics hubs usually serve urban areas or supplement industrial clusters dominated by various industries. Free-standing trucking parks typically serve a short radius of about 100 miles.

The modal orientation generally implies a level of service orientation which is attractive to certain companies. Thus, air logistics parks will tend to attract companies dealing with time-sensitive, high value items; port logistics parks attract enterprises dealing with the large volumes moved by maritime transport and rail, while parks anchored in rail transportation will attract companies dealing with bulk and commodities.

Note that many logistics parks serve as mode-transfer nodes in the global supply chain. Thus ports serve to move freight between ships and rail and/or trucks; airports move freight to/from airplanes from/to trucks; rail intermodal facilities exchange containerized freight between trains and trucks, etc.

- Scope-based classification:
  - International—such as most port and airport-based logistics parks. Other parks, however, also handle significant international freight as globalization means that freight moving in any country may be originated or destined overseas. Specifically, inland ports serve as distribution hubs for containerized international shipments.
  - Regional—handling regional distribution needs, such as the role of the Zaragoza Logistics Park Logistics Park, PLAZA in the Iberian Peninsula and Southwest France, or Greater Richmond Logistics cluster in Virginia, serving the East Coast distribution needs of its tenants.
  - Urban distribution parks are typically set up outside large urban areas to manage the pickup and delivery of goods in and out of the urban area. Such logistics clusters exist and are adjacent to almost all majors cities, such as New York, or, on a much smaller scale, Lyon Logistics, a wholesale and agri-food distribution center.
- Functional classification:
  - Customs and taxation-advantaged places, including:

Foreign Trade Zones (also known as Free Trade Zones)—are areas with special customs procedures. Items that are imported and then re-exported through such locations are not subject to duty.

Bonded logistics parks—include a set of warehouses where imported goods can be stored without duties paid until they are released into the country. Many logistics parks may have a bonded warehousing area within the park—typically near ports and airports.

Export Processing Zones—these are specific areas or sometimes even "virtual zones" that provide a set of export subsidies offered by the government to exporting industries.[15]

[15] The World Trade Organization takes a dim view of such export subsidies, and is working with members countries to phase then out.

- Single commodity logistics parks—specialize in particular commodities, such as food, electronics, chemicals, etc. Such logistics parks support the relevant industry cluster.
- Special services logistics parks—such as those specializing in temperature-controlled storage and distribution; bulk commodity distribution (such as grains, chemicals, and liquids); or hazardous material handling.

19.3.3 Logistics Clusters Around the World

Yu et al. (2005) developed a classification of logistics parks in China, which includes some of the largest such clusters in the world, as shown in Table 19.1.[16]

None of these parks could be described as a "pure" modal or functional park. Thus, port and air parks usually have other transportation modal connections, and multimodal parks simply have no dominant mode. Industrial parks are home to manufacturing industries that rely on a logistics infrastructure for the supply of raw materials and parts, and for the distribution of the finished product. To this table one can add Chinese single commodity/single industry logistics parks, such as the following:

- Agriculture logistics parks—such as Lilijang LP; Nanning Jinqiao LP; Shouguang Agricultural Products LP; and others
- Chemical logistics parks—such as Sinopec LP in Shantou; the Yangtze River International *Chemical* Industrial Park; Nanjing Chemical Industrial Park Logistic Center; etc.
- Pharmaceuticals logistics parks—such as Jingyitang Mediine LP; *Rencheng* Pharmaceutical Logistics Park; etc.

Many other single commodity/single industry logistics parks support clusters in China for automotive, bulk commodities, oil, and other industries. (See also the chapter by Chen and Lee on "Logistics in China," in this book.)

Boile et al. (2009) review 55 "freight villages," 18 intermodal industrial parks and five industrial parks in Europe, North America and Asia. The list of the logistics clusters they review is given in Table 19.2.[17]

---

[16] The table includes a few updates added by the present author as several large logistics parks were opened since the original article was published. In addition, several new logistics parks are under construction. For example, the multi-modal Jinxia Logistics Park in the north of Changsha City which will sport integration of highway, rail, water and air traffic. It will be China's largest logistics park. Construction started at the end of 2009.

[17] The table is based on organizations that participated in this EU research project and is focused on managed logistics parks. It misses, however, many of the large European clusters, such as Duisberg and Hamburg.

Table 19.1 Classification of Chinese Logistics Parks (based on Yu et al. 2005)

Type	Conditions	Main function	Cases
Port logistics park (PLP)	Port	International and domestic distribution	Shenzhen Yantian, Guangzhou Huangpu, Nansha, Shanghai Waigaoqiao LP, Dalian Dahushan Island International LP, Qingdao Qianwan, Wuxi Jiangyin Changjiang, Ningbo Beilun, Zhenjiang, Lianyungang, Suzhou, Nantong PLP
Air logistics park (ALP)	Airport	Air express logistics	Beijing Tianzu, Shanghai Pudong, Tianjin ALP, Guangzhou Baiyun, Shenzhen Baoan, Nanjing ALP, Hong Kong ALP
Multimodal logistics park (LP)	Road hub, Railway hub, Intermodal facilities	Multimodal transport, Distribution	Beijing Liangxiang LP, Majuqiao LP, Ningbo Mingzhou LP, Tianjin Nanjiang Bulk LP, Wuhan Road Hub LP, Zhengzhou Baizhuang LP
Industrial logistics park	Economic development district, industrial district	Manufacturing logistics service	Tianjin Economic developing industrial LP, Wuhan Donghu Guanshan LP, Yizheng petrochemical LP, Suzhou Zhongxin industrial LP
Bonded logistics	Bonded zone	Bonded logistics	Tianjin Bonded International Logistics Operation Zone, Qingdao Bonded LP, Guangzhou Airport Bonded Logistics Center, Dalian Bonded LP, Qianhai Bay Bonded Port
City distribution	Existing warehouses near cities	Urban distribution	Shenzhen Sungag-Qingshuihe LP, Wuhan Duoluokou Distribution LP, Dalian Laogangqu city LP

(continued)

Table 19.1 (continued)

Type	Conditions	Main function	Cases
Integrated logistics park (ILP)	Central location vis-a-vis transport network, market etc	Regional or urban logistics service	Shanghai North-west ILP, Beijing Logistics Port, Nanjing Wangjiawan ILP, Xuzhou Huaihai ILP, Wuxi North-west ILP, Shenzhen Pinghu Logistics Base, Changzhou Xinqu ILP, Suzhou Weiting ILP

19.3.4 Lobbying

Logistics clusters enjoy many, if not all, of the characteristics and advantages of other industrial clusters. Like other clusters, they support joint activities by the cluster's residents. Thus, the Memphis Chamber of Commerce is encouraging more companies to locate their logistics-intensive activities in the Memphis area; the business friendly government of Panama, which came to power in 2009, listed logistics development as one of its four development pillars; the PLAZA organization has been lobbying the Government of Aragón and the central government of Spain for more infrastructure investment; the Port of Rotterdam works together with and on behalf of the terminal operators and the companies in its various logistics parks, lobbying the government of Holland to invest in infrastructure—mainly in the hinterland to alleviate port congestion—and to promote Holland as the logistics and distribution capital of Europe; and Hillwood continues to lobby the Dallas, Fort Worth and other area governments, as well as the Texas Government, to invest in infrastructure. In fact, Hillwood worked closely to remove many hurdles for the construction of Highway 170, connecting the park to the East–West Highway 114 and North–South Interstate 35 W. In addition, all these representative bodies continue to lobby their respective national governments to simplify and ease the bureaucracy and paperwork associated with international trade.

To this end, it is instructive to note the burden of such bureaucracy: Hausman et al. (2005) write that while a typical export transaction requires only a single signature in Germany and only two in Australia, Austria, and Canada, a similar transaction requires 42 approval signatures in the Democratic Republic of Congo, 40 in Azerbaijan, 39 in Nigeria, and 33 in Mali. It is no wonder that Germany leads the world in the World Bank's Logistics Performance Index. In addition to the quality of its infrastructure and services, one of the important dimensions along which countries are scored, is the efficiency of the clearance process by border control agencies.

Table 19.2 Boile et al. list of reviewed logistics clusters

Europe	
Denmark	Denmarks Transport Center, Hoeje-Taastrup Transport Center, Nordic Transport Center, Skandinavisk Transport Center, Taulov Transport Center
France	Rungis-Sogaris
Germany	GVZ-Dresden, GVZ-Bremen NW, GVZ Weil am Rhein, GVZ Nuremberg, GVZ Frankfurt/Oder (ettc), GVZ Osnabruck, GVZ Herne-Emscher, GVZ Kiel, GVZ Kassel, GVZ Hamburg, GVZ Bremen SW, GVZ Rostock, GVZ Koblenz
Greece	Promachon S.A
Hungary	Budapest Intermodal Logistics Center
Italy	Interporto di Bologna, Interporto Marche, Interporto di Novara, Interporto Quadrante Europa, Interporto di Padova, Interporto di Parma, Interporto Rivalta Scrivia, Interporto di Rovigo, Interporto di Torino, Interporto di Venezia, Interporto di Verona
Portugal	Terminal Multimodal Do Vale Do Tejo S.A
Spain	Bilkakobo-Aparcabisa, Centro de Transportes Aduana de Burgos, Centro de Transportes de Coslada, Centro de Transportes de Irun, Centro de Transportes de Madrid, Centro de Transporte de Vitoria, ZAL Port de Barcelona, Zona Franca de Barcelona, ZAL Gran Europa, Centro De Transportes de Benavente, Cimalsa, Ciudad del Transporte de Pamplona, Ciudad del Transporte de Zaragoza, Platforma Logistica de Zaragoza
Ukraine	Liski-Ukrainian State Centre of Transport Service
United Kingdom	DIRFT Logistics Park, Key point: Swindon's premier logistics park, Kingmoor Park, Port of Tyne, Wakefield Europort, Birch Coppice business park
Asia	
Singapore	Keppel Distripark, Pasir Panjiang Distripark, Anexandra Distripark
China	ATL Logistic Center Hong Kong, Beijing Airport Logistics Park, Shenzhen Pinghu Logistics, Husihai Integrated Logistics Park Shanghai North-West ILP, Nanjing Wangjiawan ILP, Tradeport Hong Kong
Korea	Gwangyang Port Distripark, Busan New Port Distripark, Gamcheon Distripark
Taiwan	Far Glory FTZ, Taisugar Logistics Park
Malaysia	Northport Distripark-Port Klang
North America	
US	CenterPoint development in Joliet IL, Alliance TX, Pureland Industrial Complex NJ, Raritan Center NJ, Heller Industrial Park NJ, Hunts Point NY, Winter Haven FL, Mesquite Intermodal Facility/Skyline Business Park TX, Guild's Lake Industrial Sanctuary, Oregon, Dallas Intermodal Terminal/Dallas Logistics Hub TX, Rickenbacker Intermodal Facility OH, California Integrated Logistics Center Shafter CA, Salt Lake City Intermodal Facility UT, Cumberland Valley Business Park PA
Canada	Atlantic Gateway-Halifax Logistics Park

19.3.5 Education and Research

One of the important characteristics and success factors for any cluster is the availability of knowledge creating and education facilities. Some of the leading logistics clusters have invested in specialized university facilities in support of their logistics mission, upgrading their capabilities through partnership with international centers of excellence. Examples include the following:

- *Singapore*. Over the last decade, Singapore's government invested heavily in education and research, both developing its own institutions and through partnering with leading universities. Thus, Nanyang Technical University (NTU) and The National University of Singapore (NUS) partnered with leading universities in multiple scientific and engineering fields, as well as in management education. The various logistics-related higher learning partnerships in Singapore include The Logistics Institute Asia–Pacific, involving Nanyang Technical University and Georgia Institute of Technology, and the MIT-Singapore transportation initiative which is part of the Singapore-MIT Alliance for Research and Technology (SMART). In addition, the *Institut des Sciences Economiques* awards logistics degrees on its Singapore campus, as do several local universities including the School of Business Logistics in Chennai and the Singapore Institute of Purchasing and Material Management.
- *Zaragoza, Spain*. Zaragoza has partnered with the MIT Center for Transportation and Logistics to develop the Zaragoza Logistics Center (ZLC). The ZLC offers international masters and PhD degrees as well as a master's degree in Spanish, aimed at upgrading capabilities of the local work force. The ZLC is situated at the middle of PLAZA, ensuring that students and faculty interact effectively with the 300 + companies in the park.
- *Memphis*. The University of Memphis Fogelman College of Business and Economics offers a degree in Logistics and Supply Chain Management. The university works with local businesses to customize courses and programs to business needs.
- *Holland*. Holland has several strong university programs in logistics and supply chain management. However, in line with the country's emphasis on logistics, it established in 2010 The Dutch Institute for Advanced Logistics (Dinalog). Dinalog's mission is to coordinate the Dutch Research and Development Program for Logistics and Supply Chain Management. Dinalog is envisioned as the (physical and virtual) place where the private sector will cooperate with Universities on tackling logistics challenges and developing technology and processes to enhance the country's efficiency. Dinalog is a cornerstone in the Dutch ambition to propel Holland, by 2020, to a leadership position in controlling flows of goods passing through Europe.
- *Alliance, Texas*. Hillwood and the companies in the park interact with and support in many ways several of the institutions offering logistics education in the area. These include Texas Christian University (TCU) offering undergraduate major and MBA concentration in logistics; and University of North Texas

(UNT) offering an MBA with logistics concentration as well as internship with Alliance companies. Alliance itself offers logistics "Associate" and "Technician" training, in addition to on-site training for forklift certification, manufacturing processes, OSHA, quality management, and more.

19.4 Operational Advantages of Logistics Clusters

While many of the advantages of industrial clusters can be found in logistics clusters, such clusters have several unique characteristics which reinforce the cluster's formation and its advantages. These can be classified into two categories: operational advantages related to transportation and advantages related to sharing of assets among companies. Both types of advantages add significantly to the reciprocal reinforcing feedback mechanism which makes the cluster more attractive as it grows, leading to further growth.

19.4.1 Transportation Advantages of Logistics Clusters

The transportation advantages of logistics parks include economics of scope, scale, density and frequency of transportation services in and out of a logistics cluster.

19.4.1.1 Economies of Scope in Transportation

The cost of transportation can be divided along many dimensions. One of the most important is the direct transportation cost vs. the cost of repositioning vehicles. To understand the issue, note that freight flows are not symmetric—for example, there are many more truckloads of freight going from the US industrial Midwest to Florida than loads available to carry from Florida Northbound. Thus, once a truck has delivered its freight in Florida, it will most likely move back (at least part way) empty to a place where it can be loaded again. Naturally, trucking companies collect revenues only for loaded moves and consequently movements into areas where little freight originates will be expensive, since the carrier has to take into account its next empty repositioning move.

Many (though not all) logistics clusters act as transshipment points where the inbound and outbound flows are balanced.[18] Consequently, carriers—be they truck

---

[18] In other cases trade flows dominate and the flows are not balanced. For example, while freight flows in and out of Singapore Port are fairly balanced, Shanghai is dominated by outbound flows. Note, however, that Shanghai-bound containers have to be repositioned and thus the container flow is balanced.

lines, railroads, airlines, or ocean carriers will charge lower rates for carrying freight in and out of a logistics cluster—since they are not likely to move empty out of there once delivering a load, and not likely to move empty into a logistics park in order to carry a load out of there.

As more companies locate in the park, carriers are more likely to find follow-on loads, leading to lower transportation costs, making the cluster even more attractive to logistics operators.

19.4.1.2 Economies of Scale

The cost of moving a transportation conveyance is almost independent of its load. Equipment amortization and operator wages do not change at all, while fuel consumption and equipment wear and tear are affected only marginally. Consequently, it is advantageous to move the conveyance always loaded at capacity or close to it. When moving in and out of a logistics cluster, where many firms manage bidirectional flows, the likelihood of filling in conveyances is higher than otherwise, leading, again, to lower transportation costs.

In addition, as the volume of freight in and out of the cluster grows, transportation carriers can start using larger and larger conveyances. Since the cost of operating a transportation conveyance does not grow linearly with the size of the vehicle, it costs less to operate a larger vehicle, on a per unit capacity basis, than a smaller vehicle. This is evident by ocean carriers' move to larger and larger ships (resulting in the need to expand the Panama Canal); the use of double stacking and very long trains by railroads; the use of 53′ trailers and double and triple combinations by motor carriers; and the use of large cargo planes by freight airlines. As the size of the logistics cluster grows, this phenomenon generates another positive feedback, since when carriers can use larger conveyances they can reduce their rates, making the cluster more attractive to more companies, increasing the size of the cluster and making it even more attractive to carriers and shippers.

A further advantage of locations where there is a large concentration of freight is that more direct conveyance movements can be operated. For example, LTL movements out of a cluster can utilize more direct movements, bypassing terminals with fully loaded trailers and reducing handling costs (as well as improving service and reducing handling errors and damage to shipments). This phenomenon grows with increasing freight volumes, creating, again, a positive feedback loop.

19.4.1.3 Economies of Density

While in many cases, companies will send a full conveyance directly from origin to destination, this is not always so and thus transportation companies may consolidate a group of less-than-conveyance-loads into a single conveyance load. In some cases, such a load may move directly to a destination but, more often, into a consolidating terminal. In such a terminal the full loads will be built and sent to a destination terminal, where the load will be "broken" and the individual shipments delivered to the specific consignees. Such deliveries will follow a delivery/pickup route in which a truck will conduct a multiple-stop tour at specific shipper locations.

When these pickup/delivery tours are conducted within a logistics cluster, they become more efficient as the cluster grows, since the distances between pickup (or delivery) locations are short. This increases the efficiency of the "last mile" which is usually the most expensive one, allowing motor carriers to charge less for serving the logistics cluster, attracting more companies to the park, increasing further the efficiency of the transportation service.

19.4.1.4 Economies of Frequency

One of the most important factors in providing service by transportation companies is the frequency of departures and arrivals. Such frequency will naturally increase with increased volumes going in and out of the cluster. This is especially important when filling ocean containers since many manufacturing companies will park a container next to their facility and fill it up with shipments destined to a specific place; naturally, sending it to a cluster, the container can be filled with shipments to multiple locations within the cluster. Also, outbound from a cluster, resident companies can cooperate in sending full containers, or a third party logistics company or a carrier can park a container in a cluster, getting it filled up quickly and sending it, thereby increasing frequency without incurring the cost of sending partially-filled containers just to keep the frequency up.

For ocean containers, such frequency increase can mean weeks' worth of reduction in transit time, enhancing the attractiveness of the cluster as the number of firms in it grows.

19.4.2 Operational Advantages of Resource Sharing

In addition to the transportation advantages, logistics clusters offer their members other advantages rooted in their ability to share assets, serve customers better and allow for better adjustment to business volume.

19.4.2.1 Shared Assets

When the daily UPS flights out of Singapore to its Asian hub are full, UPS does not ask its customers to wait 24 h until the next departure. Instead, it can utilize the DHL, FedEx or Kuehne & Nagel airlift capacity to move the package. Having all companies located within the Airport Logistics Park of Singapore (ALPS), makes it easy to arrange for such shipments.

Similarly, warehouse capacity can be used for short periods when one company is running temporarily out of space and another has space to lease. As additional logistics providers join a logistics cluster, these opportunities rise, making the cluster even more valuable to other logistics-intensive operations.

In many logistics parks, a single 3PL may serve multiple customers and thus it can share management, administration, forklifts, and processes across its local customer base. In some cases, customers of a single 3PL provider share the same physical facility and even the same sorting lines, as is the case, for example, with UPS Supply Chain Solutions logistics campus in Louisville, Kentucky.

19.4.2.2 Serving Customers When Providers Change

Logistics is an ultimate global business and the multinationals that operate logistics networks operate on a global scale and serve, in many cases, multinational customers. Such customers routinely move their business from one logistics provider to another, impacting the way their shipments are collected, routed, delivered, tracked and paid for, throughout the world.

When a company changes logistics providers, the new provider has to get up to speed very quickly on the shipper's processes, get familiar with their facilities, hours of operation, personnel, and various special requirements. When the logistics services providers are located next to each other, it is easier for them to coordinate the changes and provide the customer with a smooth transition. The uninitiated may be surprised that the "losing" company will support the change. The reason is that it is understood among all concerned that such changes happen all the time, and the "loser" may be the "winner" next time around. Thus, the logistics providers make sure that above all, the customer gets good service. Naturally, it is another reason for shippers to locate within the logistics cluster, where the presence of multiple logistics providers eases transitions from one to another.

19.4.2.3 Expansion Capabilities

As mentioned above, the flows over a logistics network are not predictable in many cases. The reason is that most strategic changes a company makes, such as spinning off a division; acquisition of other companies; entering new markets; launching new products; or offering new services, manifest themselves immediately in the product flows and the need for storage space. When a company locates its warehousing facilities in a logistics cluster, whether it owns its facilities or uses a public warehouse space, there will be other facilities in the area when there is a need for more space, and its own space may be easier to lease to others if its storage needs contract.

Thus, a location within a cluster gives companies flexibility that can be used when the business expands or contracts. Such flexibility obviates the immediate need to move to a new location, which may be costly due to the need to change the network.

19.4.2.4 Shared Workforce

While companies operating distribution centers may not always share resources directly in a horizontal collaboration, they do it through their 3PL or another external body. Thus, for example, Exel operates multiple customer distribution centers in and around the Alliance Logistics Park north of Fort Worth, Texas. As customer needs fluctuate Exel moves its trained warehouse workers from one facility to the next. Similarly, ATC, in the same park, uses local temporary staffing agencies to move workers not only between its own facilities and customers, but, in fact, to share the pool of trained workers with other 3PLs in the area.

19.5 Conditions Unique to Development of Logistics Clusters

Many economists and other observers argue that government has little or no role in cluster formation. This is especially pronounced in analyzing high technology clusters (Wadhwa 2010) and in the large number of analyses of the most examined cluster of all—Silicon Valley (see, for example, Graham 2006). Others, such as Cortright (2006) and Markusen et al. (1991) take a more nuanced view of the Silicon Valley cluster, acknowledging the role of government, through its early defense spending in the region, the role of higher education institutions (Rogers and Larsen 1984), and the role of individual leadership (Krugman 1991), in addition to the culture and entrepreneurial spirit of people in the area.

Most logistics clusters are developed by a development agent. In many cases, this development agent is the (regional or national) government. In many more of the recent clusters, it is a public–private partnership, a quasi government authority (such as a port authority). But within a logistics cluster, there are likely to be one or several logistics parks, which were developed privately. Unlike many other clusters (such as Silicon Valley, Hollywood, Bio-Cambridge, or Wall Street), logistics parks are typically actively managed by the real estate developer. Furthermore, whether government plays a direct role or not, government regulations and policies play a crucial part in any logistics cluster's operation and success.

An important element in the development of logistics clusters is the natural environment, comprising mainly (but not only) their central geographical location. Thus, many logistics clusters have been a trade junction throughout history.

19.5.1 Natural Conditions and History

Dependency on the natural environment is not unique to logistics clusters. Clearly, agriculturally-based clusters, such as the wine clusters in Napa and Sonoma Valley in California, the coffee growing clusters in Colombia or the banana growing clusters in Ecuador and Costa Rica also depend on natural conditions. For logistics clusters, geography is particularly relevant since it implies a central node in a transportation network with easy accessibility to major trading locations. Other natural conditions, however, also sometimes come into play.

19.5.1.1 Singapore

Singapore is strategically located in a central point on the most important inter-Asian trade lanes; between Japan, China and Korea to the East, Australia to the South and India, as well as the Middle East and all of Europe (through the Suez Canal) to the West. Thus, the Port of Singapore is a natural transshipment location and it is no wonder that Sir Raffles established a port there. The Singapore Port Authority turned the port into one of the most modern and efficient facilities in the world, creating world class maritime infrastructure. It is augmented by the top notch Changi Airport, serving 80 international airlines with 4,500 flights a week to 60 countries, processing 1.9 million tons of cargo annually.

19.5.1.2 Holland

The Dutch Golden Age, during the 17th century, was based on trade with the rest of Europe. The Dutch controlled the North Sea and the Baltics and continuously challenged the English for the Southern trading routes. At that time Amsterdam became the main clearinghouse of bills of exchange as well as a thriving trade center. The Dutch East India Company, founded in 1602 to carry out colonial activities in Asia, was the first multinational corporation and the first to issue stock. This trading culture carries through today with the importance of logistics in Holland, anchored at the Port of Rotterdam.

Rotterdam lies on the Northeast side of the English Channel, which is a major shipping lane. Its main geographical advantage, however, is its location on the estuary of the rivers Rhine and Maas, leading to efficient and inland vessel connections deep into Germany and the heart of Europe. In addition, Holland is a flat country, where transportation operations over land are not faced with natural obstacles and thus distribution networks can be laid out optimally. Building on these advantages, the Port of Rotterdam is now connected to the rest of Europe via five transportation modes: road, rail, pipeline, coastal shipping and inland shipping, The Betuwe Route is the new, 160 km long, freight-dedicated rail line that links Rotterdam directly with Germany. Since trucking is still the major distribution mode, the corridor between Rotterdam and Venlo became, in effect, a logistics-intensive cluster.

19.5.1.3 Zaragoza

Zaragoza was named after Caesar Augustus, who established it in 14 BC as a military outpost and a logistics center. Its importance continued to grow, becoming a central node in the expansion of trade and with it Roman culture. The Muslims conquered Zaragoza in 714, using it also as a logistical base for their excursions into Northwestern Spain and Southern France.

Today Zaragoza is the fifth largest city in Spain with some 700,000 people in the metropolitan area. It lies almost equi-distant to the four largest cities in Spain: Madrid, Barcelona, Valencia and Bilbao. Although far from the sea, at the crossroads between multiple cities, Zaragoza is a natural distribution hub for the Iberian Peninsula and Southwest France, including the industrial region of Toulouse.

The Government of Aragón has capitalized on this location, in addition to leveraging the existence of an old US Air Force base built to support bomb-laden B-52 bombers during the cold war. As such the runway could easily handle the heaviest cargo plane, such as the Boeing 747 freighter and the Antonov An-225. As the park was being built, the Spanish Government completed the high speed rail line connecting Zaragoza to Madrid and Barcelona, thereby increasing the capacity of the existing railway to carry freight. A state-of-the-art intermodal facility, combined with modern freeway connections, completes the physical connectivity. In addition, PLAZA provided a fiber-optic backbone, redundant energy supply and other attractive factors for companies locating in the park. Interestingly, Zaragoza's central in-land location changed one perceived disadvantage of PLAZA—the lack of a seaport—into an advantage, by developing a dry port between the Mediterranean Spanish ports of Barcelona, Tarragona, and Valencia, and the Atlantic ports in Santander, Bilbao and Pasajes. The Government of Aragón astutely noted that while at most major seaports, land was scarce, Zaragoza had no shortage of square meters, thereby building in a cost advantage without which it would have been difficult to compete. As an aside, note that such 'inland ports' logistics clusters have been developed around the world, including Virginia Inland Port, which was the first one in the US.

19.5.1.4 Memphis

From its beginning Memphis' location and the river-based transportation system made it an important trading location, based, for the most part, on cotton trading. In fact, the cotton trade tied Memphis to Northern industry, so much so that many in Memphis did not want to secede from the Union at the beginning of the Civil War.[19]

---

[19] Unfortunately, Memphis also has a sordid past as a hub of the slave trade.

But Memphis became an important node in the modern global supply chains when FedEx moved in. Some of the most important reasons FedEx decided to start operations in the Memphis Airport were the city's central location, central time zone,[20] and the good aviation weather Memphis enjoys throughout the year, allowing FedEx to keep its on-time delivery promise. Memphis is far enough South to be out of the Snow Belt compared to Chicago, Pittsburgh, and other Northern airports, and it is further east from "tornado alley," the region of frequent summer thunderstorms and tornados of Texas, Oklahoma, Kansas, and Nebraska.

Once FedEx moved in and grew, Memphis became a natural location for industries which relied on FedEx for deliveries throughout the US and the world. The excellent railroad, highway and river connections added to Memphis' attractiveness for rail, truck and barge shippers, making a natural distribution hub.

19.5.1.5 Panama

As a Spanish colony from 1501 on, Panama was a major hub of trading and commerce between the North and South, as well as serving as a major trading route between the Atlantic and Pacific islands. In 1513, Spanish traveler Vasco Nunez de Balboa explored the jungle of Panama and discovered a route across Panama to the Pacific Ocean. This route allowed the movement of gold and other treasures from the South American colonies to Spain. In fact, as early as 1532, the Spanish began thinking about digging an all-water route across the Americas, but concluded that it was too difficult and focused on a land route, which was dubbed Camino Real. Gold from Peru was brought to Panama City by ship, transported across the isthmus by slaves and mules along the Camino Real to Portobelo, a port city in the Atlantic, and then by ship to Spain. This trade route became also an important target of pirates such as Francis Drake (between 1572 and 1595) and a century later, Henry Morgan (between 1668 and 1674). The California Gold Rush, which began in 1848, renewed the interest in crossing the Panama Isthmus, as this was the most efficient road from California to the US East Coast. The demand allowed for the construction of the Panama Railroad, which opened in 1855 and followed pretty much the line of the present canal. It cut the crossing time for passengers from several days to one hour; freight, however, still had to be unloaded at one end and loaded at the other, giving the impetus to the construction of the Panama Canal.

The main trading routes using the Panama Canal today are between the Eastern coast of the US and Asia as well as the West Coast of South and Central America;

[20] While Western population centers are further away from Memphis than Eastern ones, the two hour difference, while going westbound, allows FedEx two extra hours to complete its service commitment in the morning. Thus, for example, a flight departing Memphis to New York at 1:00 AM will land around 4:30 local time after about two and half hours of flight. The same flight departing to Portland, Oregon will land at about 4:30 local time after about five and half hours in the air.

between Europe and the West Coasts of the US, Central America, South America, and Asia; and US inter-coastal.

Today, the Panama Canal is in the midst of a significant expansion, slated for completion in 2014,[21] which would allow most Post Panama vessels to use the canal. To complement the expansion, the Panamanian Government is in the process of investing in expanded port facilities and logistics parks.

19.5.2 Government and Regulations

In general, many industrial clusters include and/or are in close contact with government-related entities associated with the type of cluster under consideration. For a logistics cluster this is achieved through local trade associations, export support offices, chambers of commerce offices, etc.

Much of the infrastructure investment exemplified above is financed and advanced by local and central governments, especially in the initial stages of development, unlike other industrial clusters, where government investment increases as the cluster grows and its ability to influence government investment grows.

One of the most important contributions that government can make is not to meddle in the management of the logistics cluster. This is especially the case when the cluster has developed around one facility. In both Singapore and Panama, the government controls the authority that runs the facility—the Port of Singapore (PSA) and the Panama Canal Authority (ACP)—yet both are managed very much like private corporations. In fact, in each case, it is the respective governments' "hands off" policies, that have contributed to the economic success of the two regions. Both the MPA and the ACP are profitable. Similarly, PLAZA in Aragón was established as an independent authority, empowered to act in the best interest of the logistics park—and has been very successful, as is the case with the Memphis Airport Authority. While the Dutch logistics parks are privately managed, in 2004 the Port of Rotterdam was re-organized as a private corporation with public accountability in order to create a "business-driven structure" (see the Port of Rotterdam Annual report 2005). Naturally, there is little concern when the developer and manager of a logistics park is a private corporation to begin with, such as CenterPoint's management of the Joliet Logistics Park outside Chicago, or Hillwood's management of the Alliance Logistics Park outside Fort Worth.

There are five free trade zones in Singapore—four cater to seaborne freight and are adjacent to the port, and one caters to airborne cargo and is located at Changi Airport. All five are focused on facilitating *entrepôt* trade and certain repacking, sorting and reconditioning of goods. As with other free trade zones, transshipped and re-exported goods are exempt from the goods and services tax (GST),

[21] At the 100th anniversary of the completion of the original canal.

and customs and duties are deferred on importation of goods to the FTZ. Other incentives for facilitating entrepôt trade within the FTZs also apply. In addition, the Government of Singapore also signed many bilateral free trade agreements, notably with the US, EU, Japan, India, Korea and Australia.

The Government of The Netherlands has long recognized the importance of the logistics sector to the Dutch economy. To this end, Holland offers customs bonded warehousing, deferring the value added tax until the goods are distributed throughout the European Union, and avoiding it altogether for goods that are destined outside the EU. Holland also offers other VAT deferment mechanisms, as well as a relatively low corporate income tax. In addition, Dutch Customs is highly automated, allowing Dutch distribution centers to operate 24/7. The Holland International Distribution Council represents and promotes the logistics sector in Holland.

Memphis is home to two free trade zones and multiple sub-zones with bonded warehouses available throughout Memphis. The logistics and distribution functions are promoted through the International Division at the Greater Memphis Chamber of Commerce.

The Government of Panama has some of the most business-friendly regulations. Its 1948 Off Shore Company Law allows corporations to establish themselves in Panama and keep ownership and bank dealings secret. This made Panama the leading country for ship registry as well as an important international banking center.[22] The Colon Free Trade Zone was established in 1948 and allows companies to move materials and goods in and out of the Colon FTZ without paying any taxes,[23] known as Panama's Custom Suspense Regime. Panama also set a structure of Export Processing Zones, which can be located anywhere and enjoy no tax for any exports.[24] Panama also encourages corporations to set up headquarters in Panama, with a special law giving tax advantages to the companies and its executives (Law 41 for headquarters), as well as to companies located in the City of Knowledge and in the Panama Pacifico Logistics Park, built on the abandoned American Howard Military Base.

The Alliance-Texas development offers all foreign trade zone advantages, including the elimination of export duty, reduced customs paperwork, no duty on value added in the FTZ, high security status, and the ability to pay on either components or finished products produced in the FTZ, whichever is lower. Alliance also offers complete inventory tax exemption for 175 days, and an on-site

---

[22] The secrecy was weakened when Panama became a signatory to the 2004 Basel II Accord issued by the Basel committee on Banking Supervision.

[23] The Colon FTZ is not compatible with WTO rules since it allows no tax for any export nor on dealings between companies in Panama, amounting to export subsidies. Panama joined the WTO in 1995 and has been tweaking its laws to get into compliance since. The Colon FTZ has been arguing that it provides services, not manufacturing, and thus needs to wait until the WTO will come up with service rules.

[24] The Export Processing Zones scheme is also incompatible with WTO rules, and Panama is in the process of changing some of its rules to comply with the WTO.

US customs and central examination station to streamline administrative processes even further.

19.5.3 Horizontal Collaboration

The supply chain management literature is awash in articles and reports about "collaboration." The majority of these are concerned with collaboration or "partnerships" between trading partners, also referred to as vertical collaboration. Logistics clusters, however, offer companies located in the cluster the opportunity for operational horizontal collaboration– in this case between, say, the distribution operations of shippers (such as retailers, manufacturers and distributors) who locate their distribution centers in the cluster.

Academics, consultants and think tanks have exalted the virtues of such collaboration since in principle it can lead to clear improvements in costs, customer service, and sustainability. For example, Doherty and Hoyle (2009) argue in a World Economic Forum report that optimized transport networks are one of the keys to reduce carbon-based emissions. To support its recommendation, it points out that 24 % of the truck vehicle miles in the EU are empty, and the average utilization of the "full" vehicles is only 57 %. Naturally, much of this can be due to structural imbalance of freight flows, but the authors argue that a third of this inefficiency can be reduced with optimized transportation movements. Since companies can only ship what their customers demand, horizontal collaboration is almost the only approach that can lead to increased utilization without sacrificing service.

Cruijssen et al. (2007) report that in 1993, eight competing medium-sized Dutch producers of sweets and candy agreed to cooperate on transportation deliveries. A logistics service provider was contracted to consolidate and deliver the shipments from these eight companies to 250 retail distribution centers, resulting in reduced costs and improved customer service levels. This cooperation, called Zoetwaren Distributie Nederland (ZDN: Dutch Sweets Distribution) still exists today.

Kees Verwij (2009) reports on several horizontal collaboration activities across the Benelux countries. One of his examples is a joint manufacturing consolidation center between Kimberly-Clark and Unilever for combined deliveries to retail centers, leading to increased service levels and reduced costs.

(Haex, 2010, private communication), of Buck Consultants in The Nederland's, reports on dozens of vertical and horizontal collaborations, including a joint warehousing and distribution operation for Pirelli and Continental Tires, operated by Ewals (a 3PL). van der Meer (2003) reports on the collaboration between four LTL carriers specializing in building materials (Brothers Transport, Vink Internatioal transport, Kluitmans Transport and Twello Verheul), resulting in over 10 % reduction in vehicle-km traveled and 30 % improvement in load factors.

In the late 1990s and early 2000, several cities in Germany launched projects to reduce urban truck traffic. For example, the ISOLDE project in Nuremberg aimed at consolidating urban deliveries of parcel and LTL in "freight villages" ("Gueterverkehrszentrum GVZ") located outside the core urban area. Similar projects were launched around the same time in Heidelberg and Freiburg, as well as Berlin, Duisburg and Frankfurt. Several of these projects included disposal of recyclable material using the trucks going back to the depots.

Unfortunately, these success stories, in Holland, Germany and elsewhere, are few and far between, and many of them have been abandoned.[25] The high tech boom of the 1990s saw many attempts to use the Internet to achieve horizontal collaboration, focusing on collaborative procurement consortia, such as Covisint in the automotive industry and the World Wide Retail Exchange (WWRE). Thousands of procurement sites and digital exchanges tried to connect buyers with sellers in every industry—most, however, failed or changed the business model. The transportation market was no different. Many entrepreneurs developed digital exchanges in every segment and mode of the transportation market, hoping to more efficiently match shippers and carriers. The idea was that carriers would benefit from reduced empty miles and higher utilization, while shippers would benefit from competition between carriers leading to reduced transportation prices. Most of these attempts failed—usually due to carriers' refusal to participate in these online auctions. Using a somewhat different business model, current examples of such exchanges include Manhattan Associates Inc.' Express Bid® application and Open Bid Inc.'s thrice-a-day trucking auction service.

The emphasis during the first decade of the 21st century on global warming and the reduction of carbon footprint has added an extra impetus to the business imperatives of costs and service, yet most businesses do not collaborate with others on logistics-related operations.

Note that in all the collaborations mentioned above, and many others, there is a third party involved. So while digital exchanges can be seen as collaborative efforts (one shipper's head haul is another's back haul), the exchange operator manages the transactions, sets the rules of engagement, executes the financial settlements, and generates reports and analysis. All the above mentioned Dutch examples include a logistics provider to manage the collaborative operation. The German city logistics examples were mandated by local government and thus had to take place as a condition for doing business. Thus, it seems that collaboration can be either mandated or involve a third party.

The companies in Alliance-Texas Logistics Park can be used as an example of the myriad types of collaboration that take place in many logistics clusters. They include space, equipment and worker sharing, but these collaborations are typically neither initiated nor managed by the shippers themselves, but rather operate through the logistics service providers. The approaches to cooperation are

---

[25] In a 2010 presentation at the MSOM conference in Haifa, Israel, Ton de Kok claimed that all horizontal collaborations in The Netherland since 1990 failed.

basically ways in which the logistics suppliers utilize their own resources to provide effective service to their customers. Thus, some of them, such as Ryder and UPS Logistics, provide multi-customer distribution centers, where the space allocation is dynamic and the equipment and workforce are basically shared; others, such as Exel, who operates a dedicated facility for each of its customers, moving their work force from facility to facility when the businesses demand it.

Furthermore, the logistics service providers collaborate with each other, even though they are fierce competitors. Again, they do it through their suppliers—the specialized human resource firms that serve them. All the logistics service providers have unpredictable needs for workers. For example, winning a contract may require several hundred trained workers in short order. Staffing companies like Staff mark, Adecco, Spherion, and others serve this logistics market and in many cases collaborate on locating, recruiting and moving workers to satisfy the needs of the 3PLs.

19.6 Impact of Logistics Clusters

In many cases, when governments (either local or national) look to cluster strategies for economic development, they fix their sights on the "sexy" ones—investing resources in developing the "Silicon Pyramid" in Egypt, Japan's "Science City" in Tsukuba, the Iberian Nanotechnology Laboratory in Portugal, or a film industry in Alaska. Yet logistics clusters provide just as many advantages, and in many cases even more benefits. The agglomeration of companies with logistics-intensive operations in a given location, not only provides these companies with certain competitive advantages, but they also contribute significantly to the economic growth in the regions where they are located, despite logistics rarely being associated with "high technology." The regional economic returns from logistics clusters are rooted in the following factors:

19.6.1 Job Creation

Logistics clusters typically create a large number of jobs. The traditional criticism, that logistics jobs involve "moving boxes" at minimum wage, is an outdated view of the industry. In addition to low-level manual jobs (sorting or hand-picking), the industry includes the following:

Part time jobs—while some warehouse and distribution center jobs involve sorting, loading and unloading, these jobs are usually filled by part time workers for whom such jobs are a stepping stone to another career. Thus, at UPS, the third largest employer in the US with about 465,000 employees in 2010, many of the part time jobs are filled by students and, consequently, UPS' benefit package includes not only medical and retirement benefits but also tuition assistance.[26]

[26] About half of UPS employees are working in these part-time jobs.

- Professional jobs—many other jobs in the industry involve the operations of machinery, ranging from trucks to forklifts, as well as airplanes, trains, and ships, and even sophisticated robotics equipment, such as that used in the Zara distribution center in Zaragoza, Spain.
- Information technology jobs—it may be difficult for those not familiar with the industry to realize how sophisticated are the information technology applications used in supply chain management. Naturally, the need to control millions of parts and finished products, moving throughout the globe, in real time, from sub-suppliers, to suppliers, to manufacturers, distributors and retailers; using all modes of transportation plus an array of brokers, custom agents, and port operators; and as well as the associated contracts' provisions and financial settlements requirements; and endless array of multiple government regulations, security requirements, reporting standards and tax regimes; require an immense information technology infrastructure. In addition, however, supply chain operations have to be optimized in order to balance customer service and costs, in a very uncertain and volatile demand environment. Consequently, companies are spending significant amounts of money on specialized supply chain software applications. In fact, at one point, UPS was spending four times as much on information technology annually as it was spending on buying trucks, raising the question whether it is really a trucking company or an information technology company.
- Executive jobs—as in every other industry, there are many managerial and executive jobs associated with logistics operations.

19.6.2 Advanced Operations and More Jobs

Logistics clusters encourage the development of new and advanced logistics offerings. These include the provision of consulting, planning, network design and information technology services. Naturally, those result in not only more jobs tied to logistics operations but also high paying jobs. For example, YCH Global Logistics started as a transportation company in 1955 in Singapore by Yap Chwee Hock. In 1977 it changed from passenger to cargo transportation under the leadership of Robert Yap, Yap Chwee Hock's son, and became a leading cargo transportation carrier for the Port of Singapore. In the early 1980s it added warehouse leasing, warehouse management and freight forwarding services, and later integrated and added services to become a full service 3PL. In 1992 it opened YCH "DistriPark," as part of the logistics cluster on the intersection of the Kayang Paya Lebar expressway and the Pan Island Expressway in Singapore. In the 1990s the company built a network of distribution centers in logistics clusters around Asia and, at the same time, developed a suite of supply chain management software applications focusing on manufacturing logistics, return management and consumer goods distribution. Today the company offers both logistics execution services and supply chain management consulting/solutions services, with offices in 12 Asian countries. The sophistication of the software drove YCH in the 2000s to set its IT function as a standalone subsidiary, Y3 Technologies, developing and supplying IT application to the logistics industry.

And UPS does not only develop software to optimize its own vast global network. A subsidiary—UPS Supply Chain Solutions—offers shippers consulting, planning, supply chain management and IT services including visibility, tracking and tracing, trade compliance, network design, and more. This subsidiary of UPS has over $6 Billion in sales, employing thousands of high level professionals.

Other directions which logistics service providers have been branching into include light manufacturing and late customization/postponement efforts (see, for example, Sheffi 2005).

Hewlett-Packard reported one of the most-cited success stories of postponement (Lee et al. 1993). It used to distribute six printer models and 23 different country configurations, resulting in 138 versions of the finished printers. To cut down inventory carrying costs and improve service, HP redesigned both the printers and its supply chain. Using a pan-European forecast, it started shipping generic printers to its European distribution center in Holland. As the printers arrive in Holland, an easily accessible side panel in the shipping carton lets HP configure printers for each country once the local demand is known. Logistics clusters are ideal locations for such added-value operations, bringing even more jobs into the local economy.

On a more fundamental level, logistics clusters can be viewed as advanced infrastructure. They serve as the means by which manufacturing industries can move material and finished goods in and out of their plants. For example, both Nucor and Cargill operate large manufacturing plants in Memphis, in large part due to the extensive rail and barge connections available there. Thus, logistics clusters can foster the creation of manufacturing jobs as well.

19.6.3 Diversification

A logistics cluster creates an efficient "infrastructure" for other "sub clusters" of various industries that require strong logistics services. This leads to the seeding of industry clusters and their development, due to the positive feedback mechanisms mentioned above: attracting suppliers, other service providers, being able to lobby as a group, the exchange of tacit knowledge, the ability to consummate "deals" more easily, etc.

For example, Medtronic—a leading US medical devices company, operates a distribution center in Memphis, TN. It chose Memphis because of the ability to ship overnight throughout the US, while tendering shipments very late. Furthermore, Memphis is also a hub for Delta Airlines, which also figures in Medtronic's strategy.

To understand Medtronic's distribution business, consider for example their sale of spinal kits, used by hospitals for spinal procedures. The kit can cost more than $100,000 and hospitals cannot afford to stock them until needed. Furthermore, in any operation, only a small part of the kit is actually used. So when an operation is scheduled for Thursday afternoon say in Boston, Medtronic can put a kit on the FedEx flight on Wednesday night, arriving in Boston Thursday morning and available to the surgeons immediately. After the operation, the unused part of the kit is sent back to Memphis to be cleaned, refurbished, and ready for the next spinal procedure anywhere in the US. Furthermore, when even higher shipping speed is needed, as in the case of an emergency operation following an accident, Medtronic uses a "Next Flight Out" (NFO), involving a Medtronic employee placing the package with the crew of the next flight from Memphis to Boston (there are several flights a day), and a Boston hospital employee will pick up the package at the Delta counter in Boston, rushing it to the operating theatre.

Medtronic is working actively with the Memphis Chamber of Commerce to attract other medical device companies to Memphis. They understand that the presence of a cluster of competitors will attract suppliers and other specialty service providers, creating a positive feedback loop that will benefit all the members of such a medical devices cluster.

Another example is the fashion design cluster in Amsterdam. Having creative talent alone in Amsterdam would not have enabled it to become a fashion design center. Since manufacturing is centered in South East Asia, and mainly China, designers have to be in constant communication with the factories to evaluate apparel color, textures and "feel." To this end, Schiphol airport is the hub of KLM airlines (as well as a few smaller airlines), with nonstop flights to over 260 airports in 91 countries. Furthermore, the logistics cluster around Schiphol includes over 200 logistics services providers. Thus, test fabric swatches can be flown from Hangzhou to Amsterdam, arriving on the same day, ready for a transcontinental design session. This allows factories in Hangzhou to use design shops in Amsterdam, each enjoying cluster advantages of its own industry, while relying on the Schiphol connectivity.

In addition to the fashion cluster, the Schiphol Area Development Company (SADC) is working to seed and develop several other clusters in perishables (based on Holland's logistics prowess in flower distribution); life sciences (again, based on the airport's large number of direct connections), high technology (which also requires fast connectivity), and aerospace, which is a natural cluster for this large airport.

19.6.4 Measuring the Impact

Very few logistics parks or clusters measure their own economic impact. An exception is the Alliance-Texas Logistics Park in Fort Worth, Texas. Alliance has documented with great care the total of all investments—public and private—that

Table 19.3 Investments by regional authorities (figures provided to the author by Alliance-Texas)

Authority	Investment ($)
City of Fort Worth	39,151,482
City of Haslet	597,823
City of Raonoke	3,706,000
Tarrant County	23,172,538
Denton County	2,025,000
Keller ISD	87,366,854
Northwest IAS	14,076,745

went into the park, and the results of these investments (some of the data mentioned in this section can be found on line[27]). For example, the investment by the various regional public authorities was as in Table 19.3.

Figure 19.1 depicts the taxes paid by Alliance companies to the same cities, counties and independent school districts.

By 2008 the average rate of return for the public sector was 11 %. Assuming that the park will continue to grow at the rate it was growing in the last decade, the average rate of return will reach 19 %.

In addition to the direct taxes paid back to these public authorities, Alliance estimated the total economic impact from 1990 to 2008 at $36.4 Billion. This should be compared to a total of $7.1 Billion capital which was in place by 2008, $6.7 of it from private sources and a total of $387 million from public sources (including the State of Texas and the Federal Government, besides the local authorities). A total of 28,000 jobs were created in the park (in addition to the 1,710 construction jobs). The development also led to the creation of 63,388 indirect jobs. In total, 31.2 million sq ft of distribution space was developed by 2008, as well as 7,154 homes, 288 apartments and 200 hotel rooms. The development also planted 36,166 trees.

The impact of the Zaragoza logistics park, PLAZA, was not measured directly but since it was the main investment of Aragón's Government between 2002 and 2008, some performance indicators of Aragón's economy can be used as a (very rough) proxy for the impact of PLAZA. For example, between 2002 and 2008, unemployment in Aragón was only a little over half of the average unemployment in Spain; the index of industrial production rose from 2003 to 2008 by 86.7 % in Aragón, while increasing only by 82.8 % in Spain as a whole; the total ton-miles transported to and from Aragón increased by 58 % from 2002 to 2007; and the number of commercial trucks registered in Argon during this period increased from 7,529 to 19,557.

[27] See, for example, http://www.alliancetexas.com/Research/AllianceTexasFacts/EconomicImpact/tabid/202/Default.aspx. Others are available in various Alliance-Texas publications.

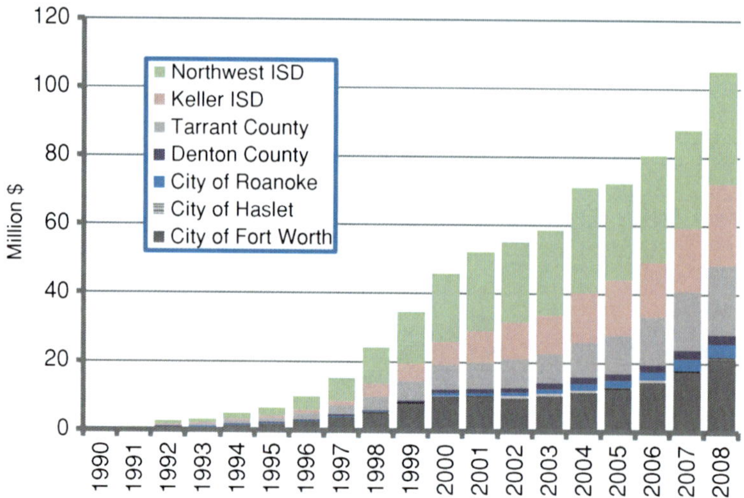

Fig. 19.1 Taxes Paid 1990–2008 (figures provided to the author by Alliance-Texas)

19.7 Conclusions

While the literature dealing with industrial clusters focuses disproportionally on high technology, knowledge-based clusters, this chapter argues and demonstrates that logistics-intensive clusters should occupy an important place in the mind of regional and national governments interested in economic development. These clusters exhibit many of the advantages of all industrial clusters in terms of creating trusting relationships among companies, leading to tacit knowledge exchange among individuals and strong collaborative culture and joint activities to benefit all cluster companies, in addition to attracting suppliers, including knowledge suppliers in terms of research and educational institutions. Such elements help create the positive feedback where more companies in any industrial cluster enhance the benefits and the impact of these elements, attracting even more companies.

Logistics clusters exhibit the same type of advantages (not always to the same extent, though), but they also exhibit other advantages. The main two are (1) the process of positive feedback in the development of a logistics cluster may be stronger than in many other clusters due to the economies of scope, scale, density and frequency involved in the provision of transportation services, and (2) the opportunity to share resources in the face of fluctuating demand for workers, equipment and warehouse space.

As described in this chapter, logistics clusters are typically developed in a geographical hub of transportation; they typically require significant investment in terms of infrastructure; and they require favorable government regulations, such as free trade zones, bonded warehouses and other tax relief.

Most importantly, however, logistics clusters generate a large number of jobs. While many of these jobs are relatively low-paying ones, these jobs serve a large fraction of the population. Logistics services, however, involve global movements of information and cash, in support of the movement of physical goods. Consequently, logistics clusters generate a significant number of higher-paying information technology and banking-related jobs, in addition to managerial and executive jobs (See also Sheffi 2012).

References

American Association of Port Authorities (2009) World port rankings 2008. Retrieved from http://aapa.files.cms-plus.com/Statistics/WORLD%20PORT%20RANKINGS%202008l.pdf

Boile M, Theofanis S, Strauss-Wieder A (2009) Feasibility of freight villages in the NYMTC region: Task 3-Description of how typical freight villages work (2009) Rutgers Center for Advanced Infrastructure and Transportation. (http://www.nymtc.org/project/freight_planning/frtvillage/FrtVillage_files/Task_3_Report_April_2009F2.pdf)

Cairncross R (1997) The death of distance. Harvard Business School Press, Cambridge

Cambra-Fierro J, Ruiz-Benitez R (2009) Advantages of intermodal logistics platforms: insights from a Spanish platform. Supply Chain Manage Int J 14(6):418–421

Choy KM (2009) Trade cycles in the re-export economy: the case of Singapore. WP 2009/05 Economic Growth Center, Division of Economics, Nanyang Technological University, Singapore.

Cortright J (2006) Making sense of clusters: regional competitiveness and economic development. A discussion paper prepared for The Brooking Institution Metropolitan Policy Program

Credeur MJ (2010) FedEx's home airport widens cargo gap over Hong Kong (Update1). *Bloomberg*. Retrieved from http://www.bloomberg.com/apps/news?pid=20601080&sid=aE20.tadEAV4

Cruijssen F, Dullaert W, Fleuren H (2007) Horizontal cooperation in transport and logistics: a literature review. Transp J 22–39

de Langen P (2010) Transport, logistics and the region. Inaugural lecture, Eindhoven University of Technology

de Langen P (2011) Private communication

Doherty S, Hoyle S (2009) Supply chain decarbonization: the role of logistics and transportation in reducing supply chain carbon emission. World Economic Forum

Friedman T (2005) The world is flat: a brief history of the twenty-first century. Farrar, Straus, and Giroux, New York

Graham P (2006) How to be silicon valley. Retrieved from http://www.paulgraham.com/siliconvalley.html

Haex P (2010) Private communication

Hausmann W, Lee H, Subramanian U (2005) Global logistics indicators, supply chain metrics, and bilateral trade patters. World Bank Policy Research Working Paper No. 3773

Inbound Logistics (2008) Memphis: North America's logistics center. Retrieved from http://www.inboundlogistics.com/articles/features/1008_feature04.shtml

IFTY (2010) http://umdrive.memphis.edu/haklim/public/final_the3rd.swf

Josey A (1980) Singapore. Its Past, Present, and Future. Andre Deutsch Ltd

Kasarda J (2009) Airport Cities. Urban Land

Krugman P (1991) Geography and trade. MIT Press, Cambridge

Lawrence R, Drzeniek Hanouz M, Moavenzadeh J (eds) (2009). The global enabling trade report 2009. World Economic Forum, Geneva, Switzerland

Lee H, Corey B, Brent C (1993) Hewlett-Packard gains control of inventory and service through design for localization. Interfaces, July–August 1993, pp 1–11

Markusen A, Hall P, Campbell S, Deitrick S (1991) The Rise of the Gunbelt: The Military Remapping of Industrial America. Oxford University Press, New York

Marshall A (1920) Principles of Economics. Macmillan, London

Mihm S (2006) The 6th annual year in ideas: the Aerotropolis. New York Times Magazine. pp 31–71

O'Brien R (1992) Global financial integration: the end of grography. Royal Institute of International Affairs, London

Peneder M (1997) Creating a coherent design for cluster analysis and related policies, Paper presented at the *OECD Workshop on Cluster Analysis and Cluster Based Policies*, Amsterdam

Port of Rotterdam Annual Report (2005) Retrieved from http://www.portofrotterdam.com/en/Port-authority/finance/Documents/Annual%20report%202005.pdf

Porter M (1998) Clusters and the new economics of competition. Harvard Business Review

PSA (2010) Retrieved from http://www.singaporepsa.com

Rodríguez-Posea A, Crescenzi R (2008) Mountains in a flat world: why proximity still matters for the Location of economic activity. Camb J Reg Econ Soc 1(3):371–388

Rogers EM, Larsen JK (1984) Silicon valley fever: growth of high technology culture. Basic Books, New York

Sassen S (2001) The Global City, 2nd. Princeton University Press, Princeton

Schmitt T (2009) America's Aerotropolis. Special Presentation to the Brookings Institution

Shain A (2009) Boeing jobs: suppliers likely to relocate. The Post and Courier.

Sheffi Y (2005) Maxing the gain: the key is delaying the point of "Differentiation." Chief Executive Magazine

Sheffi Y (2012) Logistics clusters: Delivering value and driving growth, MIT Press

United Nations Population Fund (2007) State of the World's Population. Retrieved from http://www.unfpa.org/swp/2007/english/introduction.html

van der Meer T (2003) Concurrenten gaan Deelladingen Bundelen in project Distribouw (Competitors participate together in cargo project distribouw). LogistiekKrant 16(3):3

Verweij K (2009) TNO. Presentation at the 7th 3PL Summit. Brussels, Belgium

Wadhwa V (2010) Top-down tech clusters often lack key ingredients. Bloomber Business Week. Retrieved from http://www.businessweek.com/technology/content/may2010/tc2010053_047892.htm

World Bank (2009) International logistics performance index. Retrieved from http://info.worldbank.org/etools/tradesurvey/mode1b.asp

Yu W, DingW, LiuK (2005) The planning, building and developing of logistics parks in China: review of theory and practice. Chin USA Bus Rev 4(3):73–78

Chapter 20
Proactive Order Consolidation in Global Sourcing

T. G. Crainic, S. Marcotte, W. Rei and P. M. Takouda

Abstract This chapter discusses *Proactive Order Consolidation* (*POC*), a recently-proposed strategy for wholesalers acquiring goods according to global supply policies. The strategy aims to group orders before they are communicated to suppliers in such a way that the total cost of transportation and inventory of the firm is minimized. We briefly review processes and practices relative to procurement and order management, as well as consolidation activities in logistics. We then detail the POC concept and issues focusing on the associated information and decision systems and processes. Experimental results on data from an actual case study illustrate the interest of the POC strategy.

T. G. Crainic (✉) · S. Marcotte · W. Rei
School of Management, University of Quebec at Montreal,
Interuniversity Research Centre on Enterprise Networks,
Logistics and Transportation (CIRRELT), Montreal, Canada
e-mail: TeodorGabriel.Crainic@cirrelt.ca

S. Marcotte
e-mail: marcotte.suzanne@uqam.ca

W. Rei
e-mail: Walter.Rei@cirrelt.ca

P. M. Takouda
School of Commerce and Administration, Faculty of Management,
Laurentian University, Sudbury, ON, Canada
e-mail: mtakouda@laurentian.ca

J. H. Bookbinder (ed.), *Handbook of Global Logistics*, International Series in Operations Research & Management Science 181, DOI: 10.1007/978-1-4419-6132-7_20,

20.1 Introduction

The retail industry the world over is engaged in selling consumer goods and related services through stores to the general public, goods being typically obtained from another industry sector, the wholesale industry. The two sectors account for a significant part of the economy. To illustrate, the Canadian retail industry accounted for 415 billion CND (Canadian dollars) of sales in 2008, while the figure was 532.5 billion CND for the wholesale industry (Statistics Canada 2009). Corresponding figures for the United States in 2008 were 4,417 and 6,116 billion USD, respectively (US Census Bureau 2010a; US Census Bureau 2010b).

The differentiation between the two sectors is not always clear, however. Wholesalers, whose main activities consist in acquiring large quantities of consumer goods, may also operate their own networks of physical or virtual retail stores. Simultaneously, large retail firms tend to trade directly with suppliers and acquire important quantities of goods "wholesale" (or even to engage in manufacturing operations for the production of private-label goods) to be distributed to stores through their own network of warehousing facilities. In this chapter, we focus on the wholesale procurement activities of both types of firms, which, for the sake of simplicity of exposition, we identify as *wholesalers*.

The procurement function of a wholesaler is charged with acquiring and delivering to its warehousing facilities the goods to be distributed and sold through retail stores or any other channel. These activities come under much pressure from different sources. Clearly, the price and quality of the goods must be adequate for the targeted consumer groups, generally, low and high, respectively. Transportation costs must also be controlled, particularly for firms bringing in goods from distant sources and operating over broad geographic areas. Inventory levels must be sufficiently high to satisfy demand, but low enough to control inventory costs.

Good procurement policies supported by efficient supply chains are required to address these challenges and achieve the profitability goals of the firm. The policies and practices implemented by each organization may differ, however, according to the type of consumer goods distributed and the market targeted. *Global sourcing* has emerged, however, as a strong common trend for the wholesale industry.

Global procurement or sourcing consists in acquiring part or all of the goods sold by the firm from suppliers all over the world. Global sourcing progressed continuously and strongly in the last decades with the setup of broad free-trade economic zones, the liberalization of the economies of several countries (sometimes, but not always, accompanied by changes in the political regime toward a more democratic rule), the introduction of information, communications, and decision technologies, and more liberalized trade rules. The various rounds of multilateral negotiations of the General Agreement on Tariffs and Trade (GATT), the creation of the World Trade Organization following the Uruguay round of the GATT, and the free-trade agreements resulting from bilateral negotiations aimed to define rules and somewhat control the international trade and the exchanges of goods, services, labor, and capital.

Cost control has been the main motivation for global sourcing. Acquiring goods from countries with low manufacturing costs became the usual practice for most of the wholesale industry. Countries like Mexico, the Philippines, Brazil, India, Vietnam, and of course China, have thus become major players in international trade. The result has been a dramatic increase in the number, variety, and volume of products traded, as well as in the distances over which they are moved. Longer supply lines translated into higher total delivery times, while costs fluctuated with the price of oil in an upward trend. Longer supply lines also translated into a significant role for container-based intermodal transportation, both on the seas and on land, which has become the backbone of international trade.

One of the main challenges of logistics and supply chain management in the 21st century is therefore to create innovative processes, practices, and tools to assist firms to efficiently manage their supply chains and, in particular, their global sourcing and procurement. Our objective is to provide such processes and tools. We focus primarily in this chapter on wholesalers carrying durable or non-perishable consumer goods, for which the ratio of goods acquired overseas relative to "local" procurement is increasing steadily. Those wholesalers often deal with suppliers located far away, e.g., in Asia or South America, and thus display extended supply chains and complex procurement decisions.

The main goal of procurement for such firms is to replenish inventories. Advanced inventory-management methods and tools have been developed to help decide when and how much to order, and those methods generally account for the lead time. When long transportation distances are involved, however, one faces a more complex decision problem involving the choice of the appropriate mix of containers (selected from a restricted set of standardized types and dimensions), the quantities to order, and the total cost of long-haul transportation and inventory in storage facilities until products are sold to customers. These decisions are particularly central to the overall profitability of the firm when large volumes of relatively small orders are considered.

"Small" in this context is defined as larger than the size normally moved by small-package delivery services, but much smaller than the volume of a container. Indeed, decisions are relatively simple when they concern few orders with volumes appropriate for small-package delivery services, or when order volumes are relatively close to the capacity of one of the standard-sized containers and *Full-Container-Load* (*FCL*) transportation is appropriate. For all other numerous cases, one must trade off the cost of using a *Less-than-Container-Load* (*LCL*) policy or using only a small part of a full container, both choices resulting in high unit transportation costs not agreeable to most managers. This induces a tendency to order more than indicated by the inventory-management system, to take advantage of the full capacity of low-unit-cost large containers, to the detriment of an increase in inventory costs.

The *Proactive Order Consolidation* (*POC*) strategy aims to avoid these pitfalls. Its goal is to support an integrated and demand-driven supply chain by providing the means to achieve a profitable trade-off between procurement, transportation, and inventory management. POC is inspired by the consolidation idea that has long been successfully applied to transportation and physical distribution. Different from these areas, where consolidation concerns physical flows once movements are already decided, POC aims to group orders **before** they are communicated to suppliers, in such a way that the total cost of transportation and inventory of the firm is minimized. It is in this sense that we describe POC as a *proactive* order-consolidation strategy. According to our best knowledge, this idea has been little, if at all, explored in the literature. We hope this chapter will contribute to increase interest and foster research efforts.

Our work presents the methodological, technological, and managerial aspects of proactive order consolidation, with an illustrative case study in the wholesale-hardware industry (Béliveau 2008; Crainic et al. 2009, 2011).

The chapter is organized as follows. Section 20.2 reviews a number of processes and practices relative to procurement and order management, while Sect. 20.3 discusses consolidation in logistics. Section 20.4 then introduces the proactive order consolidation concept and summarizes a number of related issues focusing, in particular, on the associated information and decision-support system and the processes that have to be set up or modified. The case study is detailed in Sect. 20.5 and we conclude in Sect. 20.6.

20.2 The Procurement Process and Players

Procurement is charged with acquiring the materials required for a firm's operations, and delivering those materials to the appropriate facilities. The procurement function is often mistakenly identified as "purchasing." In traditional logistics, the objective of a purchasing manager was to simply find the lowest-cost supplier. In today's modern integrated-logistics era, successful organizations follow a different approach and develop partnerships with their suppliers of goods and services. They rely on suppliers to improve quality, reduce costs and assist with product design and development. They learn to trust their suppliers. Therefore, other activities, as important as purchasing, are part of procurement. Thus, in general, procurement management groups five main activities: purchasing, consumption management", supplier selection, contract negotiation, and contract management. These activities are inter-related, and coordinated through what is called the "order-management" process. Figure 20.1 illustrates the main information flows associated with these processes, and identifies the corresponding functions and players involved.

Order management in the retail and wholesale industries typically starts, at the tactical level of planning, with consumption management. This consists in understanding how much of each category of products is being bought both centrally and within particular units (e.g., regional distribution centers). These quantities are strongly related to the expected level of sales, and are regularly compared to actual consumption and sales, and updated. The firm then sets up proper inventory-management policies for each product or category of products, and the corresponding order strategies. Supplier selection is also generally associated with the tactical level of planning, the people performing this function being identified as *Merchandisers* in Fig. 20.1. Given the inventory and order policies for each category of product (or for individual products), the merchandiser aims to select the appropriate supplier(s) for the next planning period (e.g., the next year). Decisions are made based on factors such as price, product quality, supplier service level, just-in-time delivery, and value-added services. Those decisions also concern strategic considerations, such as single or multiple sourcing and the geographic balance between local and global sourcing. More than one supplier may be selected to hedge the risks associated with lead time constraints and other uncertainty sources proper to the industrial sector considered. The output of this process is a preferred-supplier list specifying, for each product or category of products, the subset of suppliers to be used during the next planning period, as well as any conditions associated with the particular contract (e.g., minimum and maximum values for the total product volume to be purchased over that planning period, prices ranges, and discounts).

Purchasing occurs at the operational level within the framework set by the order and inventory policies and the preferred-supplier list, and is triggered by a low inventory of a given product (the Inventory form in Fig. 20.1). The *buyer* then determines the quantity of product to be acquired and when it should be received (due date) for the firm to maintain its service level. The buyer also determines whether multiple suppliers should be used, if it appears improbable that a single supplier will meet the specifics of the required purchase (i.e., the specified quantity delivered for the defined due date). One or several contract "negotiation" activities then start with the chosen suppliers.

The scope of these negotiations depends on the type of understanding, agreed to by the firm and the supplier, at the tactical (merchandiser) level (Monczka et al. 2009). In many cases, particularly when orders are repetitively issued to the same supplier, this understanding takes the form of a "blanket purchase order." That is an open order, valid for the length of the planning period, which specifies the terms of the purchase contract. The buyer then simply communicates with the supplier and engages in a routine order release. In many other cases, however, negotiations must be undertaken for each purchase to specify the particular order details, items, prices, deadlines, service levels and so on. Performance targets may be set at this point, as well as bonuses or penalties for meeting those targets, or not. The buyer contacts the first company in the preferred-supplier list and undertakes such a negotiation within the framework of the general understanding. If successful, a *purchase order* (*PO*) is issued. Otherwise, the next supplier on the list is contacted, until the desired items are secured. This second case is particularly present is global sourcing, when suppliers are located in emerging-economy countries, and the buying firm has only a low level of confidence in their reliability. To simplify the presentation, we use PO to indicate the output of this process for both "negotiation" cases.

Management approves the PO and the finance department arranges for payments, which are usually made using letters of credit. The supplier then produces the order (make-to-order strategy), assembles the order from pre-produced modules (assemble-to-order), or picks it from its inventories (make-to-stock strategy).

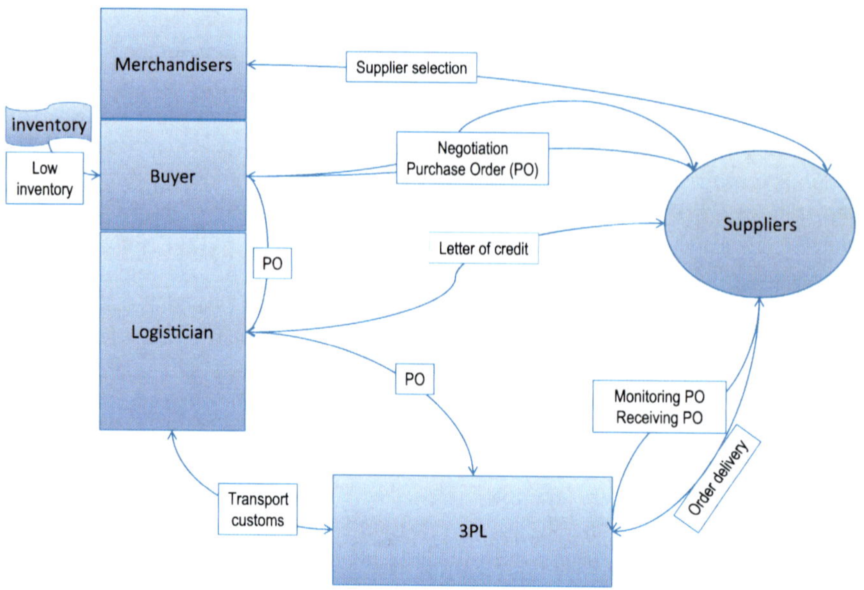

Fig. 20.1 Wholesale procurement process—main players and information flows

Depending on how responsibilities are assigned, transportation arrangements for the goods to be delivered to the wholesaler's facilities are undertaken by the supplier, the firm or both. The *Logistician* box in Fig. 20.1 represents the people within the firm in charge of organizing and supervising these transportation activities.

Those same people also monitor the progress of the order from the time the PO is issued until the goods are in the firm's warehouses. Monitoring provides the firm with the ability to react to delays or other unexpected events, as well as to track the performance of its suppliers and hold them accountable relative to the agreed-upon service level. Part of these activities may be outsourced and be performed by a Third Party Logistics company—the 3PL box in Fig. 20.1—either independently or in close collaboration with the logistician.

The previous description emphasizes the flows of money (financial flow), goods (physical flow), and information between the buyer and its suppliers. These flows are largely determined by the set of decisions made by the players involved, reflecting each firm's practices and strategies. These include continuous supply, inventory-investment minimization, quality improvement, supplier development, lowest total cost of ownership, and gradual volume consolidation (i.e., reduction of the number of suppliers to a rigorously-screened supply base). Other important strategies are supplier operational integration (regarding processes and activities for substantial performance improvement), and value management (advanced planning and operational integration, adding value at each step of the process and resulting in a comprehensive and sustainable relationship) (Bowersox and Closs 2005). Modern information and decision technologies, including Enterprise

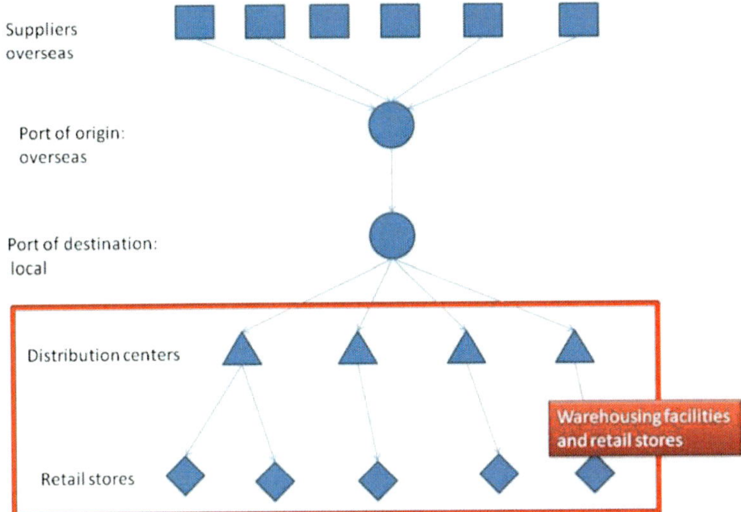

Fig. 20.2 Logistics network for global sourcing

Resource Planning (ERP), Electronic Data Interchange (EDI), and Xnet technologies, usually support the preceding procurement strategies and practices.

Not all those policies may be contemplated when global sourcing is involved, however, particularly when suppliers are located far from where the wholesaler conducts its business. In this context, suppliers are generally sited in less-developed, low-cost manufacturing countries. There, the level of penetration of information technology is lower than in developed countries. Legal and cultural differences induce a number of additional risks that increase uncertainty and compound the logistical challenges (Simchi-Levi et al. 2002; Bowersox and Closs 2005). Of particular interest in this section are issues related to transportation management, and the relationships among various elements that make up the total procurement cost of a given product.

Consider the logistics network corresponding to the global sourcing activities of a wholesaler, very schematically illustrated in Fig. 20.2. Products shipped by suppliers sited in a far-away region, identified as "overseas" in the figure, are transported by means of consolidation-based carriers (Crainic and Kim 2007). Goods are first gathered at a "port of origin" (which may be an actual maritime port, or an inland rail or trucking terminal) to be loaded into containers (if not already packed by the supplier), Those, in turn, are loaded onto a long-haul transportation vehicle, a deep-sea container ship, a train or a truck, to be delivered to a "port of destination" in the area serviced by the wholesale firm. At the destination port, containers are unloaded and sent to the appropriate warehousing facilities for distribution to stores and customers.

Notice that the long-haul transportation link may actually represent an intermodal chain, e.g., a sea-rail combination, which we do not detail for the sake of simplicity of presentation. As for the containers employed to move the freight, they belong to different types defined by their dimensions (standard maritime containers are 20 or 40 ft long, while on land they may reach 53 ft), the particular environment they offer (e.g., regular, thermal, or refrigerated box), their form and type of loading. For our purposes, each variety of container offers a particular volume for shipping goods, and a fixed cost is charged for its utilization on a given trip, regardless of how full it is.

In this setting, when the replenishment quantity issued by the inventory-management system would fill one or several containers, the FCL transportation mode is appropriate. Otherwise, when the replenishment volume is really small and may be handled by regular or express package mail services, the utilization of such services is the way to go. In both cases, the order volume equals the suggested replenishment quantity, and the procurement cycle continues as described previously.

Frequently in wholesale and retail procurement of non-perishable goods, the replenishment quantity falls in between these two extremes. Ordering the preceding quantity means that either one pays the rate for LCL transportation, or for an entire container that one cannot use fully. Both choices result in a high transportation cost per unit of product volume, going against the cost-reducing objective that motivated global sourcing in the first place. One then observes that buyers tend to boost the order volume, to actually fill the container.

Yet, from a global system point of view, this *boosted-FCL* strategy displays several shortcomings. First, larger quantities mean greater warehousing space taken up for longer periods. Second, even ignoring that some products may go out of fashion during this time, inventory costs increase, both in money frozen in the goods bought and in warehousing expenses. The "gain" made on transportation may thus impair the profitability of the firm, or at least that of the respective product.

To illustrate, consider a decorative item with annual sales of 2,642 units. The inventory-management software takes into account the buying pattern and suggests an order quantity of 432 units, which represents a volume of 2.1 cubic-meters (cbm) and an average demand of about 8.5 weeks. According to the boosted-FCL strategy, this quantity is increased to fill a container. The smallest container available, a twenty-foot box, has a capacity of approximately 33 cbm and, thus, a boosted order would result in some 6,788 units. The resulting per-unit shipping cost would be low, but the ordered quantity is more than 10 times larger than the one suggested by the inventory-management software. Actually, this boosted-FCL quantity represents the equivalent of more than 2 years of sales, with huge consequences on the annual inventory costs, which represent a significant part of the value of the goods. Moreover, it is very probable that more than half the items will become obsolete (out of fashion) by the second year.

From the point of view of supply chain management, the boosted-FCL strategy evaluates alternatives from a transportation perspective only, ignoring inventory activities and the finance function of the company. That strategy thus goes against best inventory-management principles. It also contradicts the paradigm of coordination of logistics activities and functional areas of the firm to achieve an efficient and sustainable overall supply chain. Moreover, such a strategy may also result in setting up the supplier as the driver of the supply chain: the supplier would be able to push its products via low-pricing strategies, leaving the retail chain to deal with inventories.

The Proactive Order Consolidation strategy aims to address these shortcomings by consolidating orders before they are communicated to suppliers, in such a way that full containers are used and the total cost of transportation and inventory of the firm is minimized. This strategy is described in Sect. 20.4. But first, the next section presents an overview of the more traditional way of using consolidation in logistics activities.

20.3 Classical Consolidation in Logistics and Transportation

Consolidation in logistics is often defined as the accumulation of several loads to be grouped either in a vehicle (container, truck, plane, ship, rail car) or at a location (warehouse) (Bowersox and Closs 2005). It denotes an active effort to use the available transportation and storage resources more efficiently.

Thus, a program (or policy) of freight consolidation associated with the planning of shipments is defined in Bookbinder and Higginson (2002) as a systematic attempt to decrease the total transportation cost between a given origin and destination. In this context, Çetinkaya (2004) distinguishes *pure* policies, specifically providing dispatching and consolidation rules whenever orders are processed, from *integrated* policies, which combine both inventory and shipping decisions when applying the consolidation strategies.

To implement such policies, an accumulation process is needed to group loads for consolidation. Three strategies have traditionally been used to define such a process: *temporal*, where loads are accumulated during a given fixed-length period; *spatial*, where attaining volume or weight limits stops the process; or *mixed*. The latter is a combination of the first two, accumulation being stopped as soon as one or the other limit is reached (Ford 2001; Bookbinder and Higginson 2002; Tyan et al. 2003). These processes are also referred to in the literature as *time-based*, *quantity-based*, and *hybrid* dispatch/consolidation policies, respectively (Çetinkaya 2004).

Selecting an accumulation strategy very much depends on the criteria used to evaluate it (Mütlü et al. 2010). Thus, a temporal policy is preferable when trying to perform timely shipments to customers within quoted lead times, as opposed to a spatial policy, which minimizes costs. A mixed strategy is useful when trying to strike a balance between the two criteria. It is thus generally acknowledged that the performance of a given accumulation-consolidation strategy depends on the desired customer service level and the order arrival rates (Higginson and Bookbinder 1994). Yet, the particular characteristics of the transportation mode and service used may also influence performance. Thus, for example, a consolidated shipment may be released at any time when road transportation is used, provided that a vehicle is available. When either maritime or rail services are involved, however, the release of a consolidated shipment must match the scheduled departure times of the ship or train being used. Capacity restrictions also differ according to the type of transportation service considered. In the case of road transportation, capacity is usually less restricted, given that vehicles are more readily available. The same cannot be said for maritime and rail transportation, where the number of available container spaces on ships and trains is limited. These transportation considerations are particularly important within global sourcing.

Consolidation may be performed by producers of the goods, shipping those products to their respective warehousing or distribution facilities or directly to customers. Consolidation may be carried out as well as by wholesalers and retailers; purchased products are shipped from their distribution centers to stores. Transportation may be performed by a firm's private fleet, by vehicles hired from a full-load carrier (trucks or ships), or through the services of less-than-vehicle-load consolidation-based carriers such as railroads, LCL, or less-than-truckload motor carriers (See Crainic and Kim (2007) for consolidation in freight transportation.) It is noteworthy that integrated consolidation policies require the coordination of several functions within the supply chain. Thus, selection of suppliers (Aissaoui et al. 2007), order and lot sizing (Aissaoui et al. 2007; Rizk et al. 2008), inventory policies (Bertazzi and Speranza 2005; Bertazzi et al. 2007), and inventory-routing decisions Bertazzi et al. (2008) all impact consolidation strategies.

Consolidation may also be "outsourced", that is, an external firm may take charge of the loads to be shipped or brought. This intermediary, usually a long-haul consolidation-based carrier or a third-party logistics firm, brings the loads into its own terminals, where they are sorted and consolidated with other loads, possibly from different origins and with different destinations, for long-haul transportation (of course, the initial pickup and final delivery are generally performed by dedicated vehicles). Note that most 3PL providers use the services of consolidation-based carriers for this part of the journey, which may take the form of an intermodal path. This business and operations model has proved to be very successful for 3PL firms (Min and Cooper 1990; Chen et al. 2001; Çetinkaya and Bookbinder 2003; Krajewska and Kopfer 2009; Wong et al. 2009).

The broad utilization of consolidation is explained by its benefits (Ford 2001). Freight consolidation provides the means to take advantage of long-haul transportation pricing schemes, where freight rates decrease as the shipment size increases, and may further decrease transportation costs by reducing the total number of shipments. Consolidation also improves speed and reliability by reducing the handling of the products at intermediate terminals.

Without any surprise, load consolidation also comes with some disadvantages. Thus, for example, temporal consolidation imposes additional delays to some loads, which must wait for the entire shipment to be ready, possibly translating into higher inventories and associated costs. Consolidation also requires more sophisticated procedures, processes, and methods for planning, monitoring, and control of operations and deliveries.

Advantages generally outweigh inconveniences, provided the appropriate consolidation strategy is selected (Bookbinder and Higginson 2002). It is noteworthy that all these strategies are concerned with the consolidation of physical flows, once goods are produced and sold, and distribution channels are selected. Such load-consolidation strategies do not address the issues identified in Sect. 20.2, relative to procurement of large numbers of low-volume products through global sourcing. Addressing these issues is the object of the proactive order consolidation strategies presented in Sect. 20.4.

20.4 Proactive Order Consolidation

As previously mentioned, we consider the case of companies that, while using global sourcing, face the problem of managing the procurement of large volumes of relatively small orders placed with a variety of international suppliers. In such a case, companies must manage regular shipments emanating from a series of origin points located in different geographical zones. Each shipment is composed of a container or a set of containers carrying the goods ordered, and traveling long distances through intermodal transportation. How to efficiently manage such shipments, while minimizing overall costs, is at the heart of the POC strategy that is proposed.

The concept of *proactivity* refers here to the role played by a given firm in its own procurement process. Given the functions traditionally carried out by a 3PL in the organization of shipments in the context of global sourcing, a firm usually assumes a somewhat passive role in this respect. A POC strategy furnishes the tools necessary for the firm to play a more active role in the planning and management of those shipments. In turn, POC facilitates and improves the negotiations and interactions with the 3PL that provides the necessary transportation and storage services. By evaluating the capacity required to perform the necessary shipments earlier in the procurement process, a firm can benefit from better rates for the logistics services offered by the 3PL, and can better manage its own operations.

We now present this general strategy and discuss some important factors to consider when applying it in practice. We define the POC strategy in Sect. 20.4.1, discuss some of the expected benefits that justify it, and enumerate important issues to be addressed when applying it. Section 20.4.2 discusses the information and decision support system (IDSS) required by a POC strategy. Issues related to the possible reorganization of the the general procurement process are addressed in Sect. 20.4.3.

20.4.1 Defining the POC Strategy

Within a properly integrated enterprise information system, relevant data concerning quantities of products to buy and the corresponding orders can be accessed at an earlier stage to gain proactivity in the supply chain. In turn, optimization models can be used to extract meaningful and decisive information from this data that will improve the overall procurement process. In the context of global sourcing, "Proactive Order Consolidation" can be defined as a strategy used to group LCL orders that are made through the procurement process, and that share the same origin point for the long haul intermodal transportation. These groups are created to efficiently fill appropriate transportation containers with the objective of minimizing the overall total costs.

Described as such, when using the POC approach, orders are assembled within containers to produce desirable shipments. Given the fact that distinct orders imply possibly different due dates, consolidation is applied here on subsets of orders that can be grouped and dispatched together in the same load. To identify those subsets, a consolidation window is associated with each order. Such a window defines the time period in which an order is available for consolidation. These windows are specified according to the maximum time interval that shipment of the associated order can be delayed, without causing a stockout or other disturbance in the activities of the supply chain.

Note that, as defined here, the POC strategy thus differs from the "classical" load consolidation in logistics literature (Sect. 20.3). First, the wholesaler becomes responsible for implementing and controlling the consolidation strategy used to manage its own shipments. This is an important difference compared to when either the supplier or the 3PL controls the load-consolidation policy. However, this does not necessarily mean that the wholesaler is able to efficiently run such a policy on its own. For example, poor infrastructure (terminals in the supply regions or adequate information systems and decision support tools) or insufficient organization may prevent the company from properly applying the consolidation policy. In such a case, the infrastructure and technical expertise provided by a 3PL may be necessary. Secondly, consolidation is applied to the *information* flows of the supply chain, not only the physical flows. Finally, consolidation influences the company's outbound activities (such as purchasing and contract negotiation), in addition to those inbound (i.e., freight transportation).

Here are the benefits expected from such a strategy. First, note the economies of scale that can still be obtained, even when placing LCL orders. By applying consolidation early in the procurement process, a company can organize shipments that batch orders to be made to a particular supplier. This type of batching thus maintains a high volume of goods ordered from that supplier, enabling those economies of scale. The POC strategy also allows for more efficient transportation operations. In the case of global sourcing, we mentioned that freight travels long distances packed in appropriate containers. By using the proposed strategy, a company obtains an early plan. That specifies the numbers and types of containers required to perform the shipments, as well as a list of specific orders and their assignment to the chosen containers. In turn, this information can be used by the wholesaler to improve the deployment of transportation capacity that is internally available.

Alternatively, the information can be used in negotiations with 3PL firms. A detailed plan, transmitted to the 3PL in advance of the shipping date, enables greater efficiency in transportation. This may then reduce the costs paid by the wholesaler for logistics services provided by the 3PL. Finally, the POC strategy helps in maintaining normal levels of stock. Indeed, because orders are made based on the replenishment needs of the company (as opposed to the FCL strategy), the procurement process follows customer demands more closely, which avoids excessive inventories.

When applying this type of strategy, a series of important issues have to be addressed. A first such question is: How should the subsets of orders used in the POC strategy be defined? Those subsets can be constructed by collecting orders one-by-one, as issued by the procurement process, or in groups. The latter case may be implemented by batching the orders, i.e., when a wholesaler wishes to accumulate orders for a particular supplier before applying POC.

The question of **when** orders should be considered for consolidation, is also very important. As soon as a reordering signal is issued by the firm's inventory-management system, an order can be prepared and becomes available to consolidation. This defines the beginning of the consolidation window for that order, at which point negotiations with suppliers have not yet taken place and the firm is still free to impose lead-time requirements (i.e., the order may be delayed according to the operational policies in use). This point in time may even be forestalled if a company wishes to consider, within the POC approach, orders that are *forthcoming*, in an effort to anticipate shipments. In this case, forecasting is applied to predict both the volumes of those orders and the respective due dates.

Also, orders that are considered for POC will be so for a given period of time. As such, to what extent should a consolidation plan be revisited whenever new orders appear? This also relates to the definition of the subsets used within POC. They either include exclusively new orders, or they take into account orders that have already been consolidated but for which the associated shipment has not yet been made. In all cases, when adjusting consolidation plans, due dates cannot be changed once the POs are issued.

The issue of **how** to decide on what to consolidate, and the way to do so, is also important. As will be explained within the next subsection, Bin Packing models (Martello and Toth 1990a; Wäscher et al. 2007) provide the methodology of choice when addressing the considered problem. However, selection of the particular model to employ will depend on the specific use of the POC strategy.

Finally, issues related to the overall stochastic nature of the procurement process must also be addressed. Uncertainties involving the suppliers (e.g., change in due dates, transportation arrangements) or the transportation activities (containers not available, logistics operation times at the points of origin, etc.) justify both monitoring and control throughout the process. How should this monitoring be applied? What types of controls should be used, to ensure that both the consolidated orders and the chosen containers are available on the day of shipment? These are important points to cover when implementing the POC.

Randomness also entails the need for adjusting the established consolidation plans as new information becomes available. For example, to what extent can the wholesaler company change the consolidation plans to account for delays in delivery to the origin port of a number of orders? That is important to address, since it may impact the efficiency of the procurement process. The availability of the preceding information, however, may impair the analysis. Thus, there is a time limit defining the moment when a planned and filled container (i.e., one to which specific orders have been assigned) can no longer be changed, given the shipping date. Until that time is reached, admissible adjustments should reflect the operational policies of the particular company implementing the POC.

20.4.2 Information and Decision Support System

We turn now to the information and decision support system (IDSS) needed to sustain a POC strategy. We first assume that the general operational processes of the wholesaler are aided by proper information technology tools. Ideally, an integrated ERP system is available, or at the very least, there is an appropriate logistics information system. In addition to the existing tools, the IDSS required for the POC should be able to perform the following general functions:

- Preprocessing: process orders according to their characteristics;
- Consolidation: assign subsets of orders to appropriate containers;
- Monitoring: do the necessary follow up to ensure efficient procurement operations;
- Business analytics: carry out the necessary forecasts, reliability analysis, and evaluation of the procurement process.

The preprocessing function is used to efficiently filter, sort and group orders that are made through the procurement process. Orders must first be characterized according to their volume. This will distinguish those orders that will be shipped by the FCL transportation mode, the regular or express package mail services, or using the POC strategy. Only those orders that would fall in the LCL category are considered for POC. Preprocessing is also employed to sort orders according to the origin and destination points, the supplier, and the consolidation window. Overall, this function serves to produce the subsets of orders utilized in the POC strategy.

Consolidation constitutes the main POC-related function of the IDSS. It aims to establish for each shipment the number and types of containers needed, as well as to assign available orders to those containers. This is done with the overall objective of minimizing costs, based upon the number of containers to be used, or the total fixed (transportation) cost that is paid to use them. This type of problem is well known in the operations research community, and is referred to as the *Bin Packing* (*BP*) problem (Martello and Toth 1990a; Wäscher et al. 2007).

Different BP problems are defined in the literature according to a number of criteria. These include the dimensionality of bins (i.e., containers) and items (orders), how items may be placed within a bin, the assortment of bins and items available, the shape of items, and the optimization objectives. The dimensionality criterion refers here to the characteristics of items and bins that define a feasible item-to-bin assignment (corresponding to constraints in the mathematical BP formulation). These characteristics may simply represent physical attributes, such as volume, length, or height. They may also include placement (e.g., the load weight should be uniformly distributed within the container), or item-to-bin compatibility requirements. The choice of packing model, and associated solution approach, to be included in the IDSS, should therefore reflect the problem specifics faced by the firm implementing the POC strategy.

In addition to the physical packing characteristics considered, the model should also represent the planning context in which the IDSS is implemented. As such, should the model be *deterministic*, possibly employing forecasts to account for upcoming orders, if such orders are considered? Or, should it be *stochastic*, in which case uncertainty is explicitly accounted for in the model formulation? Also, should a static model be utilized (consolidation is applied to distinct subsets of orders at different moments in time), or should it be *dynamic* (orders are consolidated one by one as they are made through the procurement process, and the consolidation plans are adjusted accordingly)?

The monitoring function within the IDSS performs all follow-up activities and controls that are defined by the firm to ensure that consolidation plans are respected. Therefore, such a function is used to track the groups of consolidated orders, flagging delayed orders and adjusting the plan, if necessary. Monitoring also includes verifying with the 3PLs that containers will be available as planned.

Finally, the business analytics function relates to the capacity of the IDSS, both to access historical data and to perform certain specific tasks. The latter include forecasting the upcoming replenishment needs, measuring reliability of suppliers and 3PLs, and evaluating the procurement process.

20.4.3 Reorganizing the Procurement Process

Implementing a POC strategy and incorporating the corresponding IDSS into the procurement process requires revisiting its organization. This calls, in particular, for specifying the people in the firm who will be in charge of deciding on the consolidation, and when to apply POC during the procurement process.

We have identified five possible positions within the procurement process for POC. These five, not necessarily exclusive, positions lead to different versions of the procurement process. Thus, the IDSS can be used, for a given time window and origin-destination pair, every time a new order is being planned, released, paid, or received at the port of origin (POO), according to the option selected among those proposed in this subsection. Each could involve a complete revision or a small adjustment of the consolidation plans already decided upon. Therefore, a deadline can be set on when the consolidation decision is to be reached for the filtered orders that thus far have been assigned to a given group. Afterward, a monitoring mechanism (discussed in the next subsection) reacts to the occurrence of various events and eventually adjusts the consolidation plan.

The five positions of the IDSS within the procurement process are indicated by triangles in Fig. 20.3. The position called Option 0 is for comparison with the

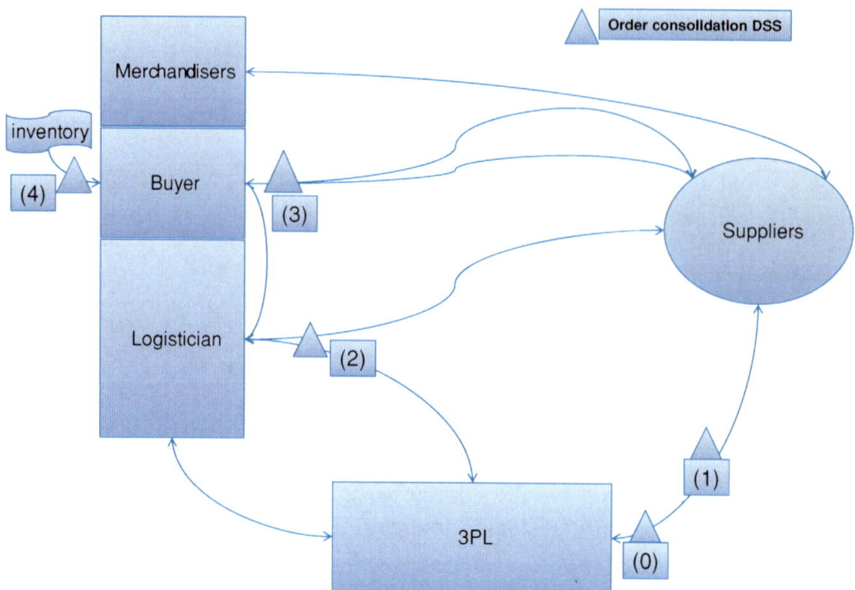

Fig. 20.3 Locating the IDSS within the proactive order consolidation process

other options proposed; there is no POC associated with it. The four other locations refer to different steps of the procurement process. It must be noted that when consolidation is performed after the PO has been released, it is rather a *load* consolidation, not an order consolidation. The intended proactivity within the supply chain is then lost. In all cases, the BP optimization methodology provides the packing of orders within the chosen containers that will be used to carry the shipment, with the goal of minimizing the total cost.

Option 0: **IDSS just before load consolidation of orders**. In this setting, the consolidation is to be performed with the orders that are in hand at the POO at the time containers must be loaded. This consolidation approach is very similar to standard load consolidation, particularly when it is outsourced to the 3PL. As indicated, with this option, the intended proactivity within the supply chain is lost.

Option 1: **IDSS after confirmation of orders**. Similar to Option 0, here the IDSS is called upon just before the packing due dates at the POO. The advantage of Option 1 is that one can consider not only the orders of the given group, but also those for which an on-time delivery "confirmation" was received from the suppliers (even if the goods are not yet at the POO). Of course, there is uncertainty about those latter orders, and they should be monitored carefully. It might even be appropriate to consider only the orders provided by trusted suppliers. If some orders are not received by the due date, an Option 0 consolidation might be required. Similar to Option 0, Option 1 does not support proactivity within the supply chain.

Option 2: **IDSS just after payments**. This setting and the following options enable proactive consolidation. It is the *logistician* who is in charge of POC in this case, and the consolidation strategy is to be applied once (most of) the payments of the POs are confirmed for a given group. Because the IDSS is placed earlier in the procurement process, decisions may be made by considering exclusively those orders already confirmed, or including also the possible incoming orders based on forecasts. These forecasts pertain to regular products, but may also take into account special events such as sales promotions or seasonal items. This option yields two *information* strategies for Option 2, with and without forecasts. The choice, as with the other possible strategies and utilization modes described in this section, must be application-specific, and determined according to the policies of the firm and the level of risk that management is ready to accept. Simulation provides the appropriate tools to assist in making these decisions.

When using the IDSS at this stage, in Option 2, one ends up with "virtual" containers made up of orders already placed but not yet shipped by suppliers. Several sets of such virtual containers may exist simultaneously for various combinations of order consolidation window, origin, and destination. Then, when a new order is placed within the system, a decision must be made to either consolidate that order immediately, within the appropriate group given the characteristics of the order, or wait for other orders with similar characteristics to be available before applying consolidation. This choice yields at least five possible *packing* strategies that, considered with the two information strategies above, yield ten possible utilization modes.

When orders are processed as they appear within the system, the POC packing strategy may be to:

1. Find the best assignment of the order to one of the virtual containers already defined (if no feasible assignment is possible, a new container is to be used);
2. Undo all the previous virtual containers and pack all available orders, including the new one, into a new set of containers.

On the other hand, when orders are collected in groups before being considered for consolidation, the following three packing strategies may be defined:

1. Consider only those orders within the group, and find the best assignment to new containers;
2. Find the best assignment of orders to either new or previous virtual containers (without undoing preceding decisions);
3. Consider all orders (both old and within the new group), and find the best packing into new containers.

An important point must be made if previous decisions are allowed to be changed. In that case, a limit has to be set on which virtual containers can be undone. This limit should reflect the fact that a particular container is less likely to be undone as time passes.

Option 3: **IDSS just after reorder flag**. Consolidation is thus decided at the same time that orders are prepared and placed, both tasks being assigned to the buyer. This option is very similar to the previous one. The main difference arises when forecasts are allowed to be considered for Options 2 and 3. In that case, Option 3 appears potentially more efficient than Option 2.

Indeed, it is the buyer who receives the reordering signals from the firm's inventory-management system, and then proceeds to prepare the corresponding orders. It is the buyer, therefore, who is in the best position to query the system regarding products that are expected to be in need of re-ordering within a short period of time, products from a potential supplier, and so on. It is therefore much easier at this level, compared to Option 2, to decide on advancing some buying decisions or on considering potential buying decisions that could happen in the very near future. Leaving these tasks to the logistician (Option 2) would require either a redefinition of the tasks each function must perform, or an increase in the workload of the buyers, or both.

Option 4: Integrating the IDSS into the inventory management system. This is the "fully automatic" version of Option 3, which may facilitate integrating forecasts into POC. Of course, this does not mean the buyer function is eliminated, far from it. The buyer must still decide whether to call on several suppliers for a given product, and must also interact with the inventory-management system to decide on the consolidated groups. As well, the buyer is still in charge of negotiating and preparing the final orders and associated forms (POs).

To conclude this part, we emphasize that the earlier the proactive consolidation activity is placed within the procurement process, the greater the overview one can have on the entire process. That may lead to a more systemic and global optimization of this component of the supply chain. It could also offer the opportunity to negotiate better terms with the various partners and service providers, in particular with carriers and 3PLs.

On the other hand, early decisions on consolidation imply that uncertainty might play a more important role. Suppose it is forecast that, in the (near) future, one will need to issue orders for other products. That generates some of the preceding uncertainty, which may be important for seasonal or in-promotion products, but much less so for regular ones. Uncertainty also comes from the behavior of suppliers and carriers. Orders can arrive late, incomplete (backorders arriving at some later point in time), and with some items damaged in transport. In most cases, one would need to update and adjust the consolidation plan. Monitoring and observing the progress of orders, to enable the system to react to various events, is required in all cases.

Monitoring is not a new function, of course. All industrial processes must be observed as operations unfold to ensure plans are adjusted (when needed) and followed, such that the stated objectives of the firm are attained. Procurement and the proactive consolidation processes described in this chapter are no different.

One checks whether the forecast orders materialize as planned with respect to time and quantity. One also reports how suppliers take care of the orders received, in particular, if deliveries are expected to be on time. The activities of the other partners, 3PLs in particular, are also supervized to ensure containers are available, and shipments proceed as planned. The particular monitoring processes and actions the firm may implement to react to events and redress the situation are application-specific; an in-depth discussion is beyond the scope of this chapter. We make only three points.

With respect to POC, the main factors that may require updating the consolidation plans are modifications in the quantities ordered and late deliveries of ordered items to the POO. The "do nothing" response to such events does not perform this updating and ships the containers as they are, the extra loads (if any) being shipped by full container or LCL according to the available item volumes. At best, this do-nothing approach applies Option 0 to the loads available at the POO. More proactive strategies would modify the existing consolidated groups, according to one of the previously-defined options, provided sufficient time is available. Obviously, too-frequent updates may rapidly become cumbersome from a management and operations point of view.

Monitoring can also be very useful to assess the quality of service of suppliers, carriers, and 3PLs, as well as to reassess the required lead time associated with a given supplier. If consolidation plans must be done over and over again because a particular supplier is always late in delivering items ordered, then either the lead time should be adjusted in the inventory management system, or that supplier should be dropped from the preferred list. Similar performance measures may be built for the other partners in the supply chain.

Finally, each firm should monitor its own performance with respect to purchasing, ordering and transportation cost, as well as customer service (inventory level versus demand). Other interesting performance measures are the amount of back orders, the value of items that became obsolete because ordered quantities were boosted to fill containers, the number of containers booked but not required, the final cost compared to expected cost, and estimates of the "cost" of uncertainty. Such activities would provide the means to continuously improve the planning capability and operations of the firm.

The design of a proactive order consolidation approach needs to be evaluated before it is implemented. Focus groups help to evaluate qualitative elements such as applicability of the process. Quantitative elements, such as costs, can be evaluated with computer simulations. Discrete-event, Monte-Carlo, object-oriented simulations, and multi-agent based simulation can be used to assess POC. Section 20.5 covers a first simulation evaluation of our proposed approach.

20.5 Case Study

We now illustrate the proactive order consolidation methodology through a number of analyses performed on a case study strongly inspired by the setting of an important North American hardware and home-improvement wholesale-retail chain (Béliveau 2008). We start with a brief description of the case with respect to the procurement processes presented in previous sections. The methodology used to group orders is presented next, followed by the description of the data sets and the Monte Carlo simulation built to perform the experiments. The results of the numerical experiments performed and the corresponding analyses follow.

20.5.1 The Setting

The firm operates as a wholesaler for its nation-wide retail network made up of large and medium-size stores, as well as independent small-size neighborhood shops. It stocks a very large variety of products to serve a numerous and diversified set of customers. Global sourcing is part of the set of strategies the firm deploys to perform within the highly competitive North American market.

The case study concerns the procurement process for a group of products imported from South-East Asia. The procurement process involving the firm, its suppliers, and a 3PL service provider is illustrated in Fig. 20.1, for a logistics network that follows the scheme of Fig. 20.2.

In selecting suppliers, the merchandiser also sets up several agreements. These include the buying conditions (incoterms), port-of-loading/origin (POO), price and the time intervals between orders. Buyers are primarily in charge of maintaining the planned levels of product inventory. Following a signal from the inventory-management software, a buyer negotiates the purchase with a pre-determined supplier. Decisions are made on the order quantity, delivery date, price, incoterms, and POO, the last three being generally only a confirmation of the original contract established by the merchandiser. A PO is then issued, verified, approved by the appropriate services, and transferred to all concerned parties.

The logistician is responsible for the payment aspects, and for monitoring the progress of the order to ensure that the purchased items are delivered on time to the firm's warehouses. This activity is performed in partnership with a 3PL service provider. The 3PL is also in charge of receiving the products from suppliers, and shipping overseas to the company's distribution centers, according to the firm's instructions. Products are typically moved in containers. As noted earlier, two transportation options are generally available, LCL and FCL. Pricing is defined per unit of volume in the former case, while in the latter, the usage of a full container is bought at a fixed price, depending on its type, and filled at will. The logistician decides the transportation option to be used for each order.

When a boosted-FCL strategy is selected, the supplier fills a container with the order, seals it, performs the export functions with the local authorities, and delivers it to the departure yard of the POO so that the 3PL can ship it (a Free-On-Board, FOB, incoterm agreement [Bowersox and Closs (2005)] is generally employed). The POC strategy considered in this study followed Option 3 (buyer based) with an information strategy that did not include forecasts. Orders were considered in groups (by week) according to the first packing strategy (only those orders in the group are to be packed into new containers). It was also assumed that the consolidation strategy was not used to modify due dates. Those were computed given historical data, and assuming loads corresponding to consolidated orders were shipped on a vessel leaving the port of origin each week on the same day. For all strategies considered in the simulation, orders were supposed to be delivered on time.

20.5.2 Grouping Orders: Bin Packing Models

The main decision to be made by the IDSS is the efficient grouping of orders of relatively small volumes into lots with total volumes close to the available container capacity. As indicated earlier, this corresponds to the well-known *Bin Packing* (*BP*) problem class (Martello and Toth 1990a, b; Wäscher et al. 2007). In the case considered in this chapter, containers (bins) and orders (items) are characterized by a single attribute, the volume (usable for the former, and actual for the latter). An assignment of a group of orders to a container is then feasible if the sum of their volumes is less than the usable container capacity (volume).

We analyze two scenarios in this study, and therefore apply two BP models, assuming the availability of a single container type or of two types, respectively. We first address the latter scenario because it is more general than the first. The BP formulation when two (or more) container types are available corresponds to the *Variable Cost and Size Bin Packing* problem of Crainic et al. (2011). Consider a set $\mathcal{I}$ of $|\mathcal{I}|$ orders. Each order $i \in \mathcal{I}$ has a volume v_i smaller than the maximum container capacity (anything larger is to be split into a number of full containers, and a residue to be considered by the order-consolidation process). Let $\mathcal{J}$ be the set of containers, with capacity and cost V_j and $c_j, j = 1, \ldots, |\mathcal{J}|$, respectively. The number of available containers is usually not a constraint, but can be. Moreover, considering an upper bound $|\mathcal{J}|$ tightens the formulation. Define the decision variables:

- y_j, container-selection variable equal to 1 if container $j = 1, \ldots, |\mathcal{J}|$ is selected, and 0 otherwise;
- x_{ij}, loading-decision variable defined for each pair (order i, container j), equal to 1 if order $i = 1, \ldots, |\mathcal{I}|$ is loaded into container $j = 1, \ldots, |\mathcal{J}|$, and 0 otherwise.

The Order Consolidation Bin Packing model (OCM) may then be written as:

$$\text{Minimize}\, Z = \sum_{j \in \mathcal{J}} c_j y_j \tag{20.1}$$

$$\text{s.t.} \sum_{j \in \mathcal{J}} x_{ij} = 1, \forall i \in \mathcal{I}, \tag{20.2}$$

$$\sum_{i \in \mathcal{I}} v_i x_{ij} \leq V_j y_j, \forall j \in \mathcal{J}, \tag{20.3}$$

$$y_j \in \{0, 1\}, \forall j \in \mathcal{J}, \tag{20.4}$$

$$x_{ij} \in \{0, 1\}, \forall i \in \mathcal{I}, \forall j \in \mathcal{J}. \tag{20.5}$$

The objective aims to minimize the total cost of the containers used, while Eq. (20.2) make sure each order is transported (assigned to a container) and constraints (20.3) enforce container-capacity limits. Relations (20.4) and (20.5) guarantee the integrality of decision variables. Notice that when only one type of container is available, all containers are identical, i.e., $V_j = V, j \in \mathcal{J}$, and the container costs may be dropped. The resulting model then corresponds to the classical BP formulation of Martello and Toth (1990a). We use the bounding heuristics proposed by Crainic et al. (2011), which yield very high-quality solutions, for both formulations.

20.5.3 Data and the Monte Carlo Simulations

The goal of the experimentation phase is to evaluate the particular proactive order consolidation process defined above, by comparing it to two options:

1. Boosted-FCL policy, where order volumes are increased to fill up a container for full-container load shipment;
2. LCL policy, where orders, corresponding to quantities computed by the inventory-management policy, are shipped using LCL services.

Experimentation is based on a Monte Carlo simulation, which generates random orders that are processed according to each of the three policies. Comparison is then performed by computing the average total annual procurement and inventory-holding costs.

Based on information provided by the firm, the data used for the simulation correspond to products (SKUs) that originate from the same region in South-East Asia. Items are shipped through the same port, and display regular selling patterns (i.e., promotional and other similar activities were not taken into account). Based on the expertise of the 3PL, we made sure the selected products may be packed together.

The selection process yielded a sample of 109 products. The data available for these products include monthly historical sales for a 13-month span, the packaging information, and selling prices. The annual and the average monthly demand for each product were calculated from this historical data. As for the product packaging information, it was used to compute the order quantity corresponding to a full forty-foot container, which was the type most used by the company.

Forty-foot and twenty-foot containers were available to ship orders to North-America. Each type is characterized by its cost (when fully loaded, forty-foot containers represent the most economical alternative) and maximum loading volume, when used for a single product or for consolidation (approximately 10 % less). The cost per cubic-meter of an order shipped using LCL services was also given. The *transportation-mode break-even point*, defined as the volume for which paying for a full container or shipping LCL yields the same transportation cost, was then found for each container type as its cost divided by the LCL cost per cubic meter.

We assumed the demand for the 109 regular products to be uniform over the year. Three classes of products were defined, corresponding to the total volume ordered, as reflected in the actual data received from the firm. The first class included the 64 SKUs with the greatest annual volume. The high rate of sales implied that each product in this class had to be ordered every month, the order quantity being equal to the corresponding average monthly demand. The second class grouped the 30 SKUs with a medium annual volume of sales, a requirement to buy every two months, and an order quantity twice the mean monthly demand. Half of those 30 SKUs were ordered every odd month (first, third, etc.) and the other 15 every even month. Finally, the 15 SKUs with the lowest annual sales volume made up the third class, with a quantity covering the average demand for 3 months ordered every three months. Five of these products were ordered every first, fourth, seventh, month, etc.; five others every second, fifth month, etc.; and the last five items every third, sixth month, etc. This yielded 84 SKUs to be ordered each month.

The distribution of aggregate orders was assumed to be random within each month. Thus, the total number of orders placed every week was assumed to follow a triangular distribution with parameters 10, 25, and 30, representing the lowest, most-likely (mode), and highest number of orders, respectively. The resulting orders had volumes inferior to the capacity of at least one type of container. By policy, orders could not be split.

Deterministic order lead times were assumed for this series of simulations, meaning the monitoring process is performing well enough to avoid significant delays. Then, each run of the simulation model consisted in developing a procurement plan to satisfy demand for a year, selecting the transportation mode for each order or consolidated group of orders. The simulation (one simulation run) worked as follows:

1. Determine, for each month in the simulated time horizon, a list of products to be ordered according to the 1, 2, and 3-month classes defined above.
2. For every week of the month,
   (a) Determine k, the number of orders to be released that week, based on the Triangular(10, 25, 30) distribution;
   (b) Pick k orders randomly from the updated monthly list (except for the last week, when all remaining ones are shipped); Update the list of remaining orders;
   (c) Solve the OCM model to determine the minimum number of containers (of each type, when appropriate) needed to ship all orders of that week, as well as which orders are to be packed into each container;

(d) Review each container to compare its load (the total volume of the orders it contains) to the breakeven point of the respective container type. Then: send the consolidated container if filled beyond the breakeven point, or else send the orders in the container using LCL services.

20.5.4 Numerical Results and Analyses

Results are provided for three policies: Boosted-FCL, identified as "FCL" in the following tables and figures; all orders shipped by LCL services; and the POC, with LCL for groups of loads whose overall volume is below the breakeven point. The total annual cost of the respective procurement plan is used to compare and assess performance. This cost was computed as the sum of the costs of purchasing, ordering, transportation/brokerage, and inventory holding. We computed these costs according to the actual practice of the firm:

Purchasing = Average total quantity ordered for each product, multiplied by its unit cost, and summed over products. Unit costs are negotiated by the merchandiser for the year and are thus fixed. The annual purchasing cost is therefore computed once, and is the same for the three strategies;

Ordering = Average annual number of orders placed, multiplied by the cost to place an order;

Transportation/brokerage = Sum of the prices paid to ship that average annual number of orders; This includes the cost for transportation and the brokerage fees paid to the 3PL for its services;

Inventory-holding is computed for a given product by multiplying its annual unit inventory carrying cost (viewed as a percentage of the purchase price) and its average inventory level over the year; The total inventory cost is then summed over all products considered.

We performed three sets of experiments, which we identify as

Analysis 1: One type of container, 40 feet, only available for consolidation and no extra costs charged by the 3PL for the potential additional handling caused by consolidation. This corresponds to the actual case studied.

Analysis 2: Two types of containers, 40 and 20 feet, and no extra handling charge.

Analysis 3: One type of container, 40 feet, with additional charges for consolidation. Three cases were considered with an additional 5%, 10%, and 15%, respectively, on the price of the 40-feet container.

The simulation was run over 50 scenarios for each analysis and strategy, a scenario corresponding to one year, 52 weeks, of operations. The Bin Packing method proposed by Crainic et al. (2011) was run on a Lenovo Thinkpad laptop running a 2.4 GHz core i5 processor. Numerical results are reported as averages over all replications. Costs are reported in thousands of dollars. The entire simulation, 52 runs for each analysis corresponding to 12,000 Bin Packing problems, required approximatively 917 CPU seconds, for an average of 0.07 CPU seconds per problem.

Table 20.1 Average annual costs for the three strategies ($K)—Analysis 1

Costs	FCL	LCL	POC
Purchasing	9,517.2	9,517.2	9,517.2
Ordering	6.4	36.3	36.3
Transportation	616.5	1,282.2	794.0
Inventory	941.5	140.4	140.4
Total	11,081.6	10,976.1	10,487.9

Table 20.2 Annual cost comparisons (% of reduction)—Analysis 1

	LCL vs. FCL	POC vs. FCL	POC vs. LCL
Purchasing	0.0	0.0	0.0
Ordering	−470.6	−470.6	0.0
Transportation	−108.0	−28.8	38.1
Inventory	85.1	85.1	0.0
Total	1.0	5.4	4.4

Results of Analysis 1 are displayed in Table 20.1. Ordering costs are lower for the FCL strategy because larger volumes (up to the container volume) are ordered less often. On the other hand, the corresponding inventory cost is significantly higher than for the other two strategies that ship smaller orders more often. Since the number of orders and their volumes are the same for the LCL and POC strategies, the corresponding ordering and inventory costs are also the same. Transportation costs are lower for the POC strategy, which makes it the most cost efficient of the three.

Table 20.2 gives a two-by-two comparison of the performances of the three strategies. Each column, identified as X vs. Y, indicates the reduction, in %, in the cost associated with strategy X relative to that of strategy Y. Thus, reducing the order volumes to the quantities needed does increase the ordering cost significantly, but also reduces the inventory-related costs in a significant manner.

Figure 20.4 illustrates the reduction in inventory-holding cost for the products considered. Those items are displayed by their designated SKU number on the horizontal axis, in increasing order of their average monthly demands (in volume). The holding-cost reduction is at least 40 %, the greatest reductions being obtained for products with low average demands. That confirms the interest of the POC strategy in this respect.

Not surprisingly, the highest transportation cost corresponds to the LCL strategy, where single-shipment costs are paid for each order. Due to the slightly lower loading capacity, the POC strategy yields a somewhat higher unit cost (per cubic-meter) than FCL, as shown in Fig. 20.5. This is however mostly compensated by the large decrease in inventory-holding costs, indicated by the entries in Tables 20.1 and 20.2: a transportation-cost increase of $178K compared to the huge reduction of $801K in inventory costs. The proactive order consolidation strategy is winning in that regard.

Results of Analysis 2, given in Table 20.3, further emphasize the superiority of POC over the other two strategies, yielding substantial economies of 5.4 and 4.5 % compared to FCL and LCL, respectively. This analysis also supports the claim that

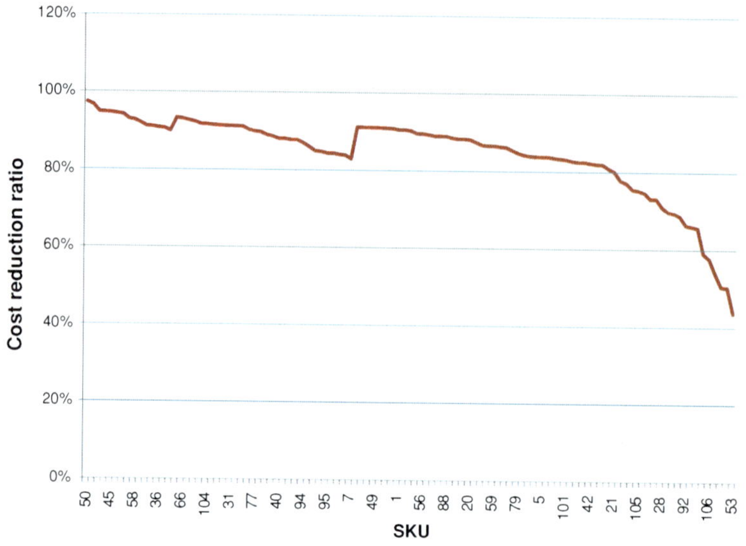

Fig. 20.4 Inventory cost reduction (%) from FCL to POC—Analysis 1

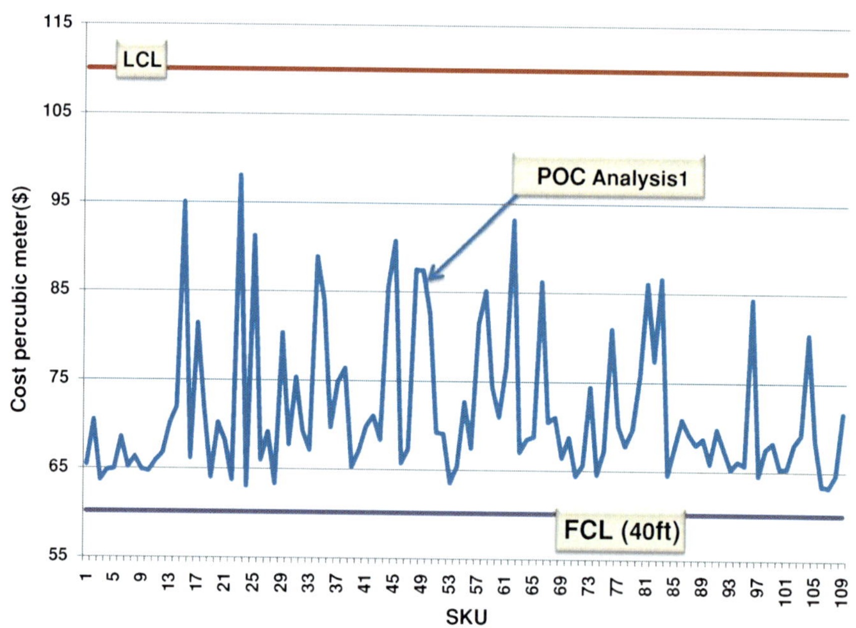

Fig. 20.5 Unit transportation cost per cubic meter for each strategy—Analysis 1

a choice of container types is beneficial. Moving from one to two container types decreases the average transportation cost by $600,000 yearly.

Table 20.3 Average annual costs for the three strategies ($K)—Analysis 2

Costs	FCL	LCL	POC
Purchasing	9,517.2	9,517.2	9,517.2
Ordering	6.4	36.3	36.3
Transportation	616.5	1,282.2	793.4
Inventory	941.5	140.4	140.4
Total	11,081.6	10,976.1	10,487.3

Table 20.4 Average annual total costs ($K)—Analysis 3

	FCL	LCL	POC	POC + 5 %	POC + 10 %	POC + 15 %
Purchasing	9,517.2	9,517.2	9,517.2	9,517.2	9,517.2	9,517.2
Ordering	6.4	36.3	36.3	36.3	36.3	36.3
Transportation	616.5	1,282.2	794.0	831.0	868.0	904.2
Inventory	941.5	140.4	140.4	140.4	140.4	140.4
Total	11,081.6	10,976.1	10,487.9	10,524.9	10,561.9	10,598.1

Table 20.5 Annual cost comparisons (% of reduction)—Analysis 3

	LCL FCL	POC FCL	POC + 5 % FCL	POC + 10 % FCL	POC + 15 % FCL
Purchasing	0.00	0.00	0.00	0.00	0.00
Ordering	−470.6	−470.6	−470.6	−470.6	−470.6
Transportation	−108.0	−28.8	−34.8	−40.8	−46.7
Inventory	85.1	85.1	85.1	85.1	85.1
Total	1.0	5.4	5.0	4.7	4.4

Proactive order consolidation allows wholesalers to give better information, earlier, to their 3PL partners regarding the numbers and types of containers required in future periods. One may thus expect 3PL rates to stay the same or to decrease slightly. Yet, to better characterize the interest of a POC strategy, Analysis 3 takes the opposite view and addresses the case of an *increase* in brokerage fees. A single type of container, 40 ft, is considered. Annual costs are displayed in Table 20.4, while the two-by-two comparison yields Table 20.5. The corresponding product unit transportation cost (per cubic meter) is illustrated in Fig. 20.6. The results of this set of experiments show that, even with raises in transportation/brokerage fees, proactive order consolidation still exhibits significant advantages over the other strategies.

To sum up, the experimental results show that both LCL and POC strategies are better than FCL. Even though they induce an increase in ordering costs, this increase is largely compensated by major savings in inventory cost. FCL appears particularly inappropriate for slow moving products. Proactive order consolidation is clearly the strategy of choice, yielding lower total costs compared to all other strategies considered.

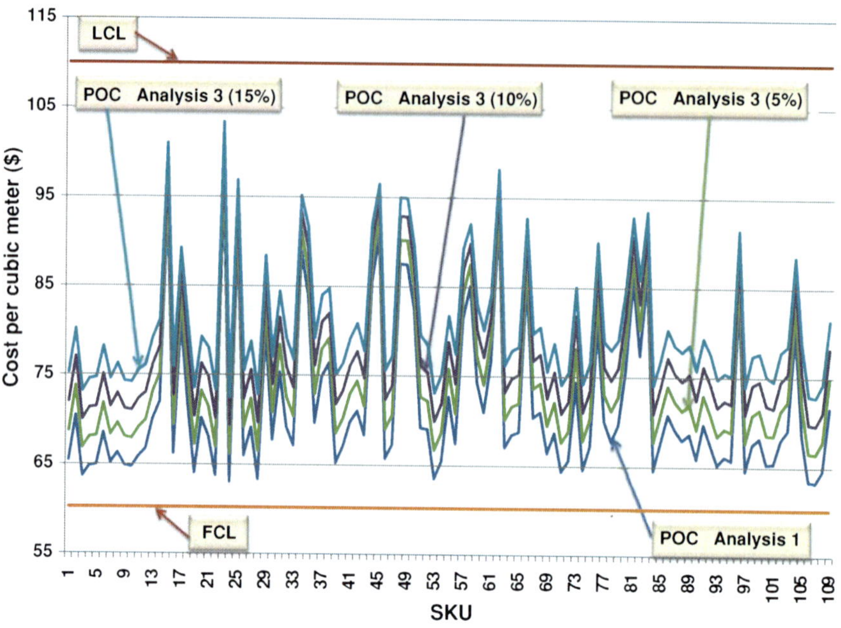

Fig. 20.6 Unit transportation cost per cubic meter, for each strategy—Analysis 3

20.6 Conclusions and Perspectives

We have presented the *Proactive Order Consolidation* strategy for wholesalers acquiring goods according to global supply policies. This strategy aims to group orders before they are communicated to suppliers, in such a way that the total cost of transportation and inventory of the firm is minimized. Experimental results showed the value of this strategy for products with regular demands, but whose volumes are low compared to container capacities. POC provides the means to achieve profitable trade-offs between procurement, transportation, and inventory costs.

Much work and many interesting developments are still ahead. The various alternatives for the POC strategy have to be thoroughly evaluated under a variety of industrial, economic, and partnership settings. Simulation and focus groups with concerned managers appear as the appropriate means to undertake this study. Such comprehensive evaluations are essential in addressing the technology-transfer challenge and building a favorable environment for industry to consider adoption on any large scale.

More advanced POC strategies appear promising and require study and evaluation. A prominent candidate is to consider an integrated decision process that determines order release times and volumes simultaneously with consolidation, to globally minimize the total logistics cost. Methodological developments are still largely to come for most strategies, particularly those explicitly considering time dependencies and uncertainties. The relationships between procurement and the new freight packaging and transportation systems currently being proposed are also worthy of interest. Here is a small illustration.

A container is currently a rigid box. But what if it were transformed to an assembly of smaller boxes of various sizes, adapted to the items transported, which may be combined (without lost space) to make larger transportation units. That would radically change container-based transportation and open very interesting opportunities for proactive order consolidation. We are advancing along some of these research-and-development paths, and plan to report results in the near future.

20.7 Acknowledgments

The authors take this opportunity to thank the Editor and referee for their extensive and very enlightening comments. They helped us write a better chapter.

While working on this project, the first author was the NSERC Industrial Research Chair in Logistics Management, ESG UQAM, and Adjunct Professor with the Department of Computer Science and Operations Research, Université de Montréal, and the Department of Economics and Business Administration, Molde University College, Norway. The fourth author was postdoctoral fellow with the Chair.

Funding for this project has been provided by the Natural Sciences and Engineering Council of Canada (NSERC), through its Industrial Research Chair and Discovery Grants programs, and by the partners of the Chair: CN, Rona, Alimentation Couche-Tard and the Ministry of Transportation of Québec.

References

Aissaoui N, Haouari M, Hassini E (2007) Supplier selection and order lot sizing modelling: a review. Comput Oper Res 34:3516–3540

Béliveau M (2008) Consolidation de commandes dans la grande distribution. MBA Thesis, École des sciences de la gestion, UQAM, Montréal, Canada

Bertazzi L, Chan MA, Speranza MG (2007) Analysis of practical policies for a single link distribution system. Naval Res Logist 54:497–509

Bertazzi L, Savelsbergh MWP, Speranza MG (2008) Inventory routing. In: Golden B, Raghavan S, Wasil E (eds) The vehicle routing problem: latest advances and new challenges. Springer, New York, pp 49–72

Bertazzi L, Speranza MG (2005) Worst-case analysis of the full load policy in the single link distribution system. Int J Prod Econ 93–94:217–224

Bookbinder JH, Higginson JK (2002) Probabilistic modeling of freight consolidation by private carriage. Transp Res Part E 38:305–318

Bowersox DJ, Closs DJ (2005) Cooper supply chain logistics management. Irwin Professional Pub, M.B.

Çetinkaya S (2004) Coordination of inventory and shipment consolidation decisions: a review of premises, models, and justification. In: Guenes J, Alcah E, Pardalos PM, Romeijn HE, Shen ZJM (eds) Applications of supply chain management and E-Commerce research in industry. Springer, NY, p 51

Çetinkaya S, Bookbinder JH (2003) Stochastic models for the dispatch of consolidated shipments. Transp Res Part B 38(8):747–768

Chen F, Federgruen A, Zheng YS (2001) Coordination mechanisms for a distribution system with one supplier and multiple retailers. Manage Sci 47(5):693–708

Crainic TG, Kim KH (2007) Intermodal transportation. In: Barnhart C, Laporte G (eds) Transportation, Handbooks in Operations Research and Management Science, vol 14, chapter 8, North-Holland, Amsterdam, pp 467–537

Crainic TG, Marcotte S, Rei W, Takouda PL (2009) Order consolidation for global sourcing. Publication CIRRELT-2009-37, Centre interuniversitaire de recherche sur les réseaux d'entreprise, la logistique et le transport, Université de Montréal, Montréal, QC, Canada.

Crainic TG, Marcotte S, Rei W, Takouda PL (2011) A case study of proactive order consolidation for global sourcing in the hardware retail industry. Publication CIRRELT-2011, Centre interuniversitaire de recherche sur les réseaux d'entreprise, la logistique et le transport, Université de Montréal, Montréal, QC.

Crainic TG, Perboli G, Rei W, Tadei R (2011) Efficient lower bounds and heuristics for the variable cost and size bin packing problem. Comput Oper Res 38(11):1474–1482

Ford DJ (2001) Inbound freight consolidation: a simulation model to evaluate consolidation rules. Master's thesis, Massachusetts Institute of Technology, Master of Engineering in Logistics

Higginson JK, Bookbinder JH (1994) Policy recommendations for a shipment-consolidation program. J Bus Logist 15(1):87–112

Krajewska M, Kopfer H (2009) Transportation planning in freight forwarding companies: tabu search algorithm for the integrated operational transportation planning problem. Eur J Oper Res 197:86–97

Martello S, Toth P (1990a) Knapsack problems. Wiley, New York

Martello S, Toth P (1990b) Lower bounds and reduction procedures for the bin packing problem. Discret Appl Math 28:59–70

Min H, Cooper M (1990) A comparative review of analytical studies on freight consolidation and backhauling. Logist Transp Rev 26(2):149–169

Monczka RM, Handfield RB, Giunipero LC, Patterson JL (2009) Purchasing and supply chain management. South-Western, part of Cengage, Learning.

Mütlü F, Çetinkaya S, Bookbinder JH (2010) An analytical model for computing the optimal time-and-quantity-based policy for consolidated shipments. IIE Trans 42(5):367–377

Rizk N, Martel A, D'Amours S (2008) Synchronized production-distribution planning in a single-plant multi-destination network. J Oper Res Soc 59:90–104

Simchi-Levi D, Kaminsky P, Simchi-Levi E (2002) Designing and managing the suppy chain. McGraw-Hill, Education.

Statistics Canada: Canada Year Book (2009) Statistics Canada Catalogue no 11–402-X.

Tyan JC, Wang FK, Du TC (2003) An evaluation of freight consolidation policies in global third party logistics. Omega 31:55–62

US Census Bureau (2010a) Annual Retail Trade Survey-2008. Publication, US Census Bureau

US Census Bureau (2010b) Annual Wholesale Trade Survey-2008. Publication, US Census Bureau

Wäscher G, Haußner H, Schumann H (2007) An improved typology of cutting and packing problems. Eur J Oper Res 183:377–389

Wong W, Leung L, Hui Y (2009) Airfreight forwarder shipment planning: a mixed 0–1 model and managerial issues in the integration and consolidation of shipments. Eur J Oper Res 193:86–97

Chapter 21
The Future

James H. Bookbinder and Barry E. Prentice

Abstract We speculate on the prospects for Global Logistics over the next 10–15 years. Three international transformations are emphasized :(1) Global trade will be enhanced, but often shifted to new regions (Asia, Africa). (2) Climate change will negatively affect ports and landside infrastructure, while possibly allowing faster transportation between Europe and Asia (through an Arctic Ocean that may become ice free). (3) Continued digital processing power, wireless communication and the internet will allow tracking of all logistical and transportation movements. *Non-visible* inventory will be the exception. Intelligent transportation technology, including next-generation air traffic control, will increase the efficient utilization of transport infrastructure. We offer considered opinions, backed by examples and references where we can, on the three main changes and others. Particular assumptions that we have made are highlighted throughout.

21.1 Prelude

A number of feasible directions could emerge with respect to transport and logistics. A useful starting point is to imagine a future that is, say, 10–15 years from now. In the world of 2025, what will be the prices of petroleum and

---

J. H. Bookbinder (✉)
Department of Management Sciences, University of Waterloo,
Waterloo, Ontario N2L 3G1, Canada
e-mail: jbookbin@uwaterloo.ca

B. E. Prentice
The Transport Institute, I.H. Asper School of Business, University of Manitoba,
Winnipeg, Manitoba R3T 5V4, Canada
e-mail: Barry.Prentice@ad.umanitoba.ca

J. H. Bookbinder (ed.), *Handbook of Global Logistics*, International Series in Operations Research & Management Science 181, DOI: 10.1007/978-1-4419-6132-7_21,

agricultural commodities? Consider carbon and communications, infrastructure and environment—melting ice caps and rising ocean levels—airships and container networks—export and import flows. All may be important.

About 20 years ago, one of us (JHB) began a Delphi study on "The Future of Logistics in Canada." In that work (Lynch et al. 1994), we attempted to forecast the state of the Industry in 2000 or 2010. It was humbling to re-read the published article. This is the nature of forecasting. Many trends can be extrapolated and some emerging technologies can be recognized, but tipping points generally defy prediction. Even if the prognostications are insightful, the timing of events is unlikely to be correct. Moreover, as defined by Christensen (1997), some technologies are "disruptive". The application of one technological breakthrough leads to a cascade of events. The Internet is an example of a disruptive technology that separates time between a wired-world and a paper-based information society. Few of the changes resulting from the Internet were identified prior to its wide-spread use, and, as evidenced by the "dot-com" bust, most of the projections proved to be incorrect.

The earlier research (Lynch et al. 1994) did employ a recognized methodology, drawing on a Delphi panel of established experts to make "scientific guesses". The present chapter is more intuitive. We call upon our collective experience to speculate on the future of Global Logistics. No official panel of experts exists, but we have gathered input from several knowledgeable colleagues. We did not request that others then attempt to rebut our ideas. Those thoughts are presented as they are, simply conjectures that we hold at the time of writing.

The sections in this final chapter of the book should thus be viewed as food for thought. We offer considered opinions, backed by examples and references where we can. We hope that most readers will agree that the world of transport and logistics has seldom seemed so full of promise or uncertainty as it does in the second decade of the 21st century.

As we get further into the chapter, a section or sub-section will often start with an *assumption.* This is then amplified by several bulleted points which follow. The subsequent text builds on those points.

However, we warn the reader of the following premise: We assume that any war, famine, or disease that may occur between now and 2025 will not be so serious as to negate the remainder of our presentation.

Our remarks are organized around the following themes: New methodologies; Modes and modal integration; and International changes impacting Global Logistics. But we begin with a discussion of those geographical regions that are presently ascending.

21.2 Regions on the Rise

21.2.1 Asia

It is no accident that the first section of this volume concerns Asia. China and India represent a bit more than one third of the world's population. These nations contain billions of potential consumers of the goods made in Europe and North America. Although the rate of population growth has slowed in Asia, the momentum of that growth will dominate the world economy, especially as relative incomes rise. More importantly, the work force in those Asian countries produces many components and sub-assemblies for Western products. The demands for metals, food, fibre and energy in Asia can only be satisfied by continuous imports from the Western hemisphere, Australia and Africa.

So how can business strategists take advantage of the coming predominance of India, China and nearby countries? The key could be "niche markets." Just as the economy and industrial strengths are quite diverse in the United States or the European Union, we should expect the same diversity in Asia. (One source of ongoing and timely commercial announcements regarding new and emerging firms is Supply Chain Asia.[1])

The marine and air-borne trade with Asia is well developed and will undoubtedly increase. Commercial pressure will force economies of size and route improvements. The Airbus 380 and the 18,000 TEU Triple-E class vessels employed by Maersk represent the leading edge of freight transport. It is possible that still larger vehicles will be built, but the size trend could be reaching its upper limits because of infrastructure constraints. Even the newly expanded Panama Canal will not be able to accommodate the Triple-E container ships. Instead, we are likely to see the average size of all fleets increase as more large vehicles replace older equipment.

The demand for timely delivery is encouraging more "near shoring" as some input suppliers are returning to the western hemisphere from Asia. Ships have low freight rates, but are relatively slow, while airplanes are fast, but very expensive. Some goods, like apparel, are time-sensitive, bulky and low in value. Here are three approaches to improved transport from Asia: shorter marine routes, improved land routes, and the next generation of transport airships.

The possibility of new marine routes is a function of climate change. The Arctic Ice Cap has been shrinking for the last 20 years, and the pace appears to be accelerating. Two new routes that can open transport between Asia and Europe are the northeast passage above Russia, and the northwest passage through the Canadian Arctic archipelago. Ships from China have already reached Europe via the northeast passage. The Canadian route is now usable in some years. In the next

[1] www.supplychainasia.org

20 years, if current trends persist, the Arctic Ocean could be ice-free in the summer. These northern routes could cut shipping time by about half.

The Eurasian Land Bridge has been promoted by China since 1997, as a new "Iron Silk Road" (Prentice and Fan 2005). The idea is to connect the rail lines between China and Europe into a 7,000 km double-stack container route. There are a number of stumbling blocks, not the least of which is incompatible rail gauges in the former Soviet Union. Nonetheless, trial experiments have been undertaken by train. It seems only a matter of time before China and Europe have a workable rail link. The other possible land route is a rail link across the Bering Strait between Siberia and Alaska. Although this concept has been floated for many years, a bridge/tunnel would be subject to significant cost and engineering challenges, and is unlikely to be completed within our 10–15 year timeframe. A feasibility study to connect Alaska by rail to the continuous U.S. states has been finished and this link may be a first step toward the land link to Asia (Alaska Canada Rail Link).

The third possibility is large transport airships with payloads greater than 200 tonnes. Several aerospace companies are developing new airships in the 50–200 tonne-lift category, and are planning much larger vehicles. Airships are slower than cargo airplanes, but consume less than a quarter of the fuel. Transport airships will cruise at 80–100 knots, while a Boeing 747 cruises at 591 knots. With an airship, freight shipments over the Pacific would take 5 days and over the Atlantic about 2 days. At half the cost, many shippers will find transport airships an attractive option, especially as heavy fuel consumers start to pay "carbon taxes" in addition to the cost of fuel.

The following are some trends that we feel are likely to be important in supply chains elsewhere in the world.

21.2.2 Latin America

The Panama Canal is being expanded to accommodate larger ships. The eastern ports in the United States are dredging deeper, to allow the possibility that "Post-Panamax" ships can call there. The canal expansion will also impact the market shares of intermodal transport within the US (Hurme 2011). Here is why.

Once the Panama Canal expansion is completed in 2014, the 12,000 TEU containerships will be able to fit. They could therefore go directly to those US east-coast ports that have dredged sufficiently (to a depth of about 50 feet) to now accommodate such huge vessels.

Today, and until canal expansion is done, those Post-Panamax ships with goods destined for the eastern US land at the American west coast. The majority of containers are line-hauled across the country by rail, with individual containers subsequently trucked to destination. Expansion of the Panama Canal thus affects intermodal's market share, by removing the necessity of a cross-country linehaul (e.g. Amadeo 2012).

But according to World City (2011), other eastern ports also will gain increased traffic, via medium-sized ships that can be accommodated there, and do not require the deepest of harbors. (That is, such vessels, formerly going to ports that are now deeper, will be "displaced" to ports whose depth is appropriate to the intermediate dimensions of those ships.)

The new industrial powerhouse of Latin America is Brazil. Long an exporter of agricultural products (e.g. coffee) and raw materials (e.g. iron ore), Brazil is becoming known for Embraer regional jets and other manufactured goods. The growth of Brazil and the "cone" of South America is creating an emerging market that is self-sustaining. One of the greatest impacts of the Panama Canal expansion could thus be enhanced trade between Asia and South America.

21.2.3 Africa

Another region on the rise is Africa. This continent may be the last source of cheap labour as the Asian countries become more expensive. It is also worth noting that Africa has the youngest population, and the most-rapid rate of population growth. Indeed, the Chinese are investing heavily in Africa, particularly in the development of transportation infrastructure. This effect is related to "near-shoring," but where the labour cost can now overcome the extra transportation charges for products that are less technological in nature. Certain manufacturing operations will be outsourced to Africa in the future.

21.3 Targeted Methodologies

Bookbinder and Matuk (2009) summarized a number of approaches that have been employed in the design of global supply chains. Methods such as robust optimization and stochastic programming have been employed by Gutierrez and Kouvelis (1995) and Santoso et al. (2005), respectively. These methodologies were not totally new. Rather, here and in other examples, the approaches had been customized to the International arena.

Research on transfer pricing is quite an important issue in accounting. For global logistics, transfer prices are significant in that off-shoring and outsourcing accent a tendency that is already present: items sold in one continent were assembled in another, and contain raw materials and components fabricated or produced in a third or fourth continent. The proper determination of transfer prices (e.g. Schmidt and Wilhelm 2000; Vidal and Goetschalckx 2001; Kouvelis and Su, 2007, Sect. 4.4) influences the overall profitability of these movements of goods, hence the bottom line of the total supply chain.

Many of the models for global supply chains are *deterministic*. Omission of stochastic features is not surprising in the sense that the formulations are already quite complicated. However, researchers and practitioners have recently emphasized the importance of the modeling of risks and of risk management. The lessening of the likelihood of a "disruption" of the supply chain has become a popular topic, concerning both domestic and international supply chains. But in the latter case, it seems that the issues of risk can lead to the *parallel* use of two modes (the "new intermodal"; see Sect. 21.4.2). Stecke and Kumar (2009) present a comprehensive discussion of the importance of risk mitigation in global supply chains, including the pertinent strategies.

Few applications in global logistics are adequately modeled through a single objective. MCDM (multiple-criteria decision making) is an important area in its own right. But the following examples show the potential significance of MCDM in this application area.

Ding (2009) applies MCDM and ancillary methods to evaluate the strengths of ocean carriers. The purpose of the model is to appraise the relative skill-sets of those transport service providers. The combination of methodologies results in highlighting seven key capabilities and three core competencies. Liou and Chuang (2010) employ MCDM in selecting a logistics provider to which to outsource. Their approach, which takes into account the possible dependencies between two and more criteria, utilizes data from a Taiwanese airline.

Sometimes MCDM can include the subjective beliefs or judgments of decision makers. Tavana et al. (2010) combined intuitive methods with more standard MCDM-based preferences in studying the possible addition of new members to the EU. Chou (2010) applied a similarly-enlarged MCDM approach to the question of which maritime transshipment hub to use in Southeast Asia.

Time/cost tradeoffs are the essence of decisions on transportation and the choice of mode. These tradeoffs could have been listed under MCDM, but are important enough to include on their own. Customer service in Logistics, as perceived by the *customer*, depends on the relative importance placed on the two attributes, time and cost. The majority of published models give priority to cost. It would be good if these two attributes could be calculated together, be treated on the same footing, and allow the key decision maker the opportunity to decide the time/cost tradeoff right from the start, rather than at the end of the analysis.[2]

As the future unfolds, cost may start to trump time in many supply chains because saving time invariably demands faster (more energy-intensive) transport. Several major retailers, like Wal-Mart and IKEA, are emphasizing "green supply chains". Of course, the low rates of interest currently available have made it easier to hold inventory, including inventory in transit, such that the sacrifice of time or cost is an easier tradeoff. Low interest rates cannot persist for the next 10–15 years.

---

[2] Bookbinder and Fox (1998) obtain non-dominated tradeoffs between time and cost in the context of NAFTA logistics. By varying a parameter analogous to the carrying cost of the goods transported, they determine whether a specific decrease in lead time merits the required increment in cost. This is an example of "at the end".

21.4 International Changes Affecting Modes and Modal Integration

21.4.1 Climate Change

Climate change: Assumption—The current trends will continue and the climate change models are approximately right.

- Rising ocean levels will lead to storm-damaged ports and will impair the landside infrastructure, both rail and road.
- Summer navigation across the Arctic Ocean; *year-round* access on the Northeast passage.
- Ice roads only viable in the most northerly Territories.
- Sea barge service available all summer in the Arctic Archipelago.
- Heavier storms, greater snow-fall in the mountains affecting passes and corridors.

Climate change can be viewed as a "wild card" for logistics. Consider the possibility that the Arctic Ocean could become ice free. This may be good in that transportation between Asia and Europe would be faster, as would access to the Arctic region that is known to contain large reserves of oil, gas and mineral deposits.

While melting sea ice does not change ocean levels, the melting of glaciers, particularly in Antarctica and Greenland, will do so. As other oceans rise, ordinary activities may not be much affected, but the advent of more violent storms is also expected. A hurricane or tropical storm during a high tide could create storm surges that might inundate many ports. And near those ports is where large populations reside. The impact of coastal flooding on major metropolitan cities like Tokyo, Los Angeles and Antwerp-Rotterdam could disrupt trade flows and affect millions of people.

Further effects of climate change are the greater temperature swings and increased snowfalls in the north. With the weight of more snow upon the ice, creating greater slush (as the ice sinks) and warmer temperatures, it would thus become increasingly difficult to build ice roads. Remote communities and resource developments that depend on those ice roads will need to utilize more expensive air transport or incur the cost of building all-weather roads.

There is also likely to be more snow in the mountain passes of the United States. Important truck routes traverse those mountains, but the vehicles would now require chains throughout the winter. The difficulty of the journey would thus be compounded. An economic effect of climate change is the trend toward carbon pricing. Concerns about the carbon footprint now play a large role in decisions on sourcing and modal choice. A decreased use of airplanes might then imply an increased reliance on *airships* (Hurme 2011).

Indeed, one of us (BEP) has written and spoken extensively about the potential importance of that new mode (Baluch 2005, p. 221; Janssen 2010; Prentice and Thomson 2010). Melting in the northern latitudes, and heightened ocean levels, are already creating demand for alternative transport. By 2025, will airships be carrying 100 ton loads across oceans and to remote inland locations?

21.4.2 The New Intermodal

Earlier in this chapter, we mentioned the use of two modes together. That is, a fraction α of an order might be dispatched by truck, while *simultaneously* the remaining portion (1—α) of the replenishment is sent by barge. The two shipments represent, respectively, the segment of demand that is less predictable and the remainder that is more stable. The slower mode is appropriate for the latter portion, given the greater reliability attached to the forecast of that demand. Naturally, when materials are procured from a more distant supplier, the transport modes might be air and water, rather than truck and barge. (See, for example, Groothede et al. 2005).

Communications: Assumption—Progress in telecommunications in the next two decades is unlikely to equal that of the past 20 years, but economic applications of this technology will continue to evolve.

- Internet shopping will further expand and diversify—home delivery of goods purchased over the Internet will include shipments of food to a greater extent.
- Working from a home office will persist and grow, especially for professional services.
- All logistical movements will be tracked using RFID tags and wireless internet, such that non-visible inventory will be the exception.
- People will have "embedded" chips—possibly as ear rings, that allow numerous capabilities of identification and communication.
- Electronic markets will be widely used for buying and selling logistical services.

It goes without saying that many of the changes that affect modal integration can occur only because of ICT (Information and Communication Technology; e.g. Shi and Chan 2010; Perego et al. 2011.) There is no shortage of knowledge on the precise location of a load, or even of a particular pallet within it. The challenge is to make efficient use of those data that we receive from satellite or GPS and other sources. The following cases demonstrate some innovations.

Kumar et al. (2007) survey the uses of RFID in logistics and manufacturing. Wal-Mart's early efforts in the monitoring of pallets are described. Hu et al. (2010) propose a system to track the real-time status of individual containers. The supply chain to which each container belongs is supervised through information obtained from modern technologies. Those hardware devices, and the communication and interaction between them, enable management and control of the container supply chain in time and space. Bock (2010) describes an additional approach, also based on real-time control, to enhance the opportunities for consolidated shipments. Freight forwarder networks involving several modes and perhaps multiple transshipments are considered. Possible cooperation between the forwarders, and dynamic response to disturbances involving vehicles or road conditions, are included.

21.4.3 Infrastructure and Containerization

Let us also mention the tyranny of infrastructure. By this we mean the extent to which we are captive to our transportation vehicles, and to the specifications of the track and the highways on which they move. For example, in North America, we are able to employ double-stacking of rail cars. That is not possible in Europe, due mostly to the prevalence of tunnels. Also, the gauge of a railway track determines the maximum size of rail cars that can be used. Russian track has a wider gauge, wider than the "standard gauge." This permits operation of trains that are wider and heavier. Infrastructure thus determines the weight of vehicle that can be employed.

As a further illustration, we are limited by the international standard of container size, viz. 20 or 40 feet. This impedes the use of the 53-foot trailer, which may be viewed as a "domestic container" in North America.

Several additional points, worth noting because they amplify our assumptions on global changes affecting modes and modal integration, concern containerization:

- Container technology will, by 2025, have attained its optimal economy of vehicle size and networks.
- Container networks will become more hub-and-spoke oriented.
- The city of Havana has a very deep port. Cuba could thus become a major North-American hub for container distribution, once the United States eases its 50 year embargo.
- The new Panama Canal will divert container freight from the Los Angeles-Long Beach land bridge to sea routes to the U.S. east coast, and increase container traffic from Brazil.
- Most goods will be shipped in containers, including the majority of commodities that are not too dirty (e.g. coal) or hazardous (e.g. liquid fuels)
- Is it possible that by 2025, the majority of wheat (for human consumption) would move in containers, rather than in bulk?

21.5 International Changes Impacting "Global Logistics" in General

21.5.1 Technology

Vehicle Technology: Assumption—"Greener" transportation will become mandatory, and enforced by carbon taxes/cap and trade and credits that increase the cost of carbon-based fuels. By 2025:

- Plug-in electric and fuel-cell vehicles will become the dominant means of surface transportation.
- Transport airships will serve all current remote communities, and will even provide *intercontinental* freight service.

Baluch (2005, Chap. 16) muses about transport machines of the future. One idea is the Automated Highway System, which would permit a *set* of freight vehicles to operate as a closely coordinated group. This would be the truck-equivalent of the coupling of rail cars. The result should be an increase in the capacity of a motorway to move goods.

Now by analogy to passenger trains, Baluch suggests magnetic levitation for freight transport. Goods would move at 250–300 miles per hour, propelled along a physical guideway by negative magnetic forces. Baluch (2005, Chap. 21) identifies some additional future trends (with no dates), for which the world must prepare. In a less-futuristic light, we wonder whether all delivery vehicles might be electric in 2025.

Intelligent Transportation Technology: Assumption—The marriage of computer algorithms, sensors and wireless technology will permit safer and more efficient use of transportation infrastructure.

- Robotic control and intelligent systems will reduce road accidents and gridlock.
- Next-generation air traffic control will allow UAV (Unmanned Aerial Vehicles), at least for cargo aircraft, and reduce delays and congestion at all airports.

Much technology is of the "incremental" type. As an example, there is the sequence of Boeing aircraft: 747, 757, ..., 787. But technology can also be a "game-changer." The railway opened up the North-American continent. Introduction of the container had a great impact on the speed and safety of goods movement, and also affected the types of employment available at a port.

Indeed, a port itself has become more like a post office: items just pass through. Commercial logistics services may no longer need to be located at the sea port. This observation has led to the implementation of "inland ports" such as SmartPort in Kansas City, MO, USA and the now-operational Centre port in Winnipeg, Manitoba, Canada.

---

[3] Brazil, Russia, India, China.

21.5.2 Macroeconomic Forces

Economic growth and trade: Assumption—The collective economies of the BRIC countries[3] will double in the forecast period (average 5 % annual growth rate), European and North American economies will have half that growth rate (mean of 2.5 % per year), while growth in the rest of the world will average 4 % annually.

- Container-based trade from Southeast Asia to Europe and to North America will double.
- Africa will become a manufacturing sector based on low-wage, labour-intensive industry.
- China will be the largest single economy in the world, and will rely more on internal sales than export demand for growth.
- Resource sectors—food, fibre and metals—will continue to enjoy strong economic performance.
- Cabotage regimes will be extended within most trading blocs; NAFTA countries will have free trade in transportation services.

Although the effects we mention are interconnected through global trade and other economic factors, here we wish to emphasize interest rates, currency valuations, and the prices of commodities.

Worldwide interest rates obviously impact the commercial cycle of a global business. Most industrial firms require credit to smooth the fluctuations between their revenue-generating operations and the cash outflows needed to stimulate sales and produce and deliver the products. This is short-term credit. But naturally, long-term debt is an important component of a firm's capital structure. Because bonds can be bought and sold worldwide, it is indeed the *worldwide* interest rates that are important. And we need not belabour the importance of interest rates on the bottom line of most transportation companies, whatever the mode they operate.

Is there an "intrinsic" value of the US dollar or the Euro? Or is that value simply the daily rate at which the given currency trades with respect to the other international standards? (Let us put aside the big questions in 2011 or 2012 about the future of the Euro-zone, unresolved at this time of writing.) Currency valuations affect logistics in several ways. A supply chain incurs liabilities to suppliers and creditors. Where (in which countries) should those liabilities be recorded? The supply chain creates assets through the manufacture of goods. Where should those assets be produced and stored? Transfer prices and currency valuations are thus major issues for an international supply chain. Its success depends on production and logistics management, but perhaps as much on financial transactions and tax rates.[4]

---

[4] See Henkow and Norrman (2011) for a thorough discussion of the ways in which a tax system can affect the design and operation of a global supply chain.

[5] Carbon dioxide capture and storage.

Energy: Assumption—Fossil fuels will continue to dominate energy production, but with the added expense of sequestration.[5] All other non-carbon energy sources (nuclear, solar, wind) will increase in use, but collectively not account for more than one-third of supply. Horizontal drilling ("fracking") technology will unlock new sources of natural gas and shale oil deposits.

- Carbon sequestration will require retrofitting of coal-fired power plants and encourage construction of nuclear power.
- The "real" cost of fossil-fuel energy will continue to rise faster than the non-inflationary increase in disposable incomes for most of the world.
- Natural gas will occupy a larger share of total energy consumption.

The shift away from gasoline and diesel fuel for transportation is slow but will be propelled by environmental concerns and rising relative prices. The production of natural gas (methane) has been increased significantly by "fracking" technology. Already transport trucks in North America are being converted from diesel fuel to methane because of its lower price. This will be accelerated by carbon taxes. Hydrogen can be blended with methane and utilize similar distribution systems. By 2025, the ubiquity of hydrogen/methane fueling locations will enable road vehicles to operate on all major trade corridors. LNG (liquefied natural gas) transport will expand globally with more ships and port terminals capable of handling overseas supplies.

With the possibility of using *biomass* for fuel, the Boreal Forest becomes a large energy reserve. Baluch (2005, Fig. 18.4) suggests other new fuels for the future.

Consider the costs of petroleum products. In addition to their effect on one's expense for food, energy prices determine the tariffs of the transport modes available today. Transportation charges are a major factor in the trend away from off-shoring, and back to near-shoring.

Various ideas in the latter category have come up throughout this book. Here we will note just a few, beginning with new FTZs (Free Trade Zones). An FTZ can be geographically extensive, as in the EU. But newer zones, when they are just being established, are more likely to include only a few nations. That was generally the case in Latin America. CAFTA (e.g. Jansen et al. 2007) is a free trade agreement between the US and six Central American countries. Other regional FTZs involve, respectively, the four nations (currently) in the Andean Community (Salazar-Xirinachs 2002) and the now-four in MERCOSUR (e.g. Baer et al. 2002). More recently, the latter two FTZs have grown and matured to the point that they have agreed in principle to work towards a merger as "SAFTA." Such an FTZ, spanning South America, would call into question the originally-conceived FTAA (Free Trade Agreement of the Americas; see Brown et al. 2005).

In a different sector of the world, consider the expansion of the European Union. The inclusion of a number of Eastern European countries in a now-27-member EU has led to a new north–south rail route (e.g. Nair et al. 2008). This new route, called the REORIENT Corridor, spanning from Scandinavia to Greece, allows two possibilities. Truck traffic can be diverted from crowded highways, without attempting to increase the freight in the already-crowded, "usual" north–south rail corridor. (The latter is discussed in Vassallo and Fagan (2007), for example).

Elsewhere in this volume, railroad improvements and new railways in China (Chen and Lee 2013) and in the Greater Mekong Sub-region of southeast Asia (Banomyong 2013) have been presented. Naturally, transport network enhancements will have a magnified influence in those cases where the current network is less than world-class in scope. And such upgrades affect trade routes, location choices of manufacturing firms, and the procurement decisions of their customers.

21.5.3 Other Publications on Trends and Futures

Everything else: Assumption–The horrors of the apocalypse—wars, famines and disease—will be limited to regional events.

- The chance of avoiding severe economic disruptions if climate change gets out of hand is likely the strongest assumption. Put another way, peaceful progress appears to be less likely in the next two decades than in the last two.
- No crazy dictators will begin wars that engulf the major powers.
- The emerging powers of India and China will peacefully co-exist.
- Agricultural science will not only cope with climate change—droughts and floods—but we will be able to produce enough food to accommodate another 2 billion people
- Medical science will contain any infectious diseases that begin to spread
- The Toronto Maple Leafs will still not have won another Stanley Cup.[6]

Neither academics nor practitioners are uniformly accurate in forecasting the path of economic growth. Here we do not mean the usual demand forecast, where errors are legion. Rather, we are talking about still more complicated matters. It is thus naturally difficult to foresee the future of the SCM discipline; because of globalization, that is tricky even within a given country. But this does not prevent authors from trying. The following is a small sample.

Hilmola (2011) examines containerized transportation by Finnish and Swedish companies to Russia, China and India. Empirical research enables study of transport volumes, traffic imbalance, and questions of environmental sustainability.

Diaz et al. (2011) contrast the Spanish practices in Logistics/SCM with the best practices documented in the literature. Issues of globalization and competition are among those treated.

Anderson and Leinbach (2007) analyze the prevalence of the Internet and e-commerce, and their impacts on international goods movements. The major roles

[6] *Canadian* hockey fans will especially understand.

of global 3PL providers are noted. The increasing technological sophistication of those firms, and the interactions with the various stakeholders in e-commerce, are highlighted.

Ballou (2007) comments on the future of the disciplines of Logistics and SCM. He emphasizes the evolution of their content as fields of business education and training. That will naturally be reflected in the management activities that a firm performs in practice. But international issues are not discussed.

Bhatnagar and Teo (2009) review the key contributions of *logistics* to ensuring and improving the competiveness of global supply chains. In the present, edited volume, each chapter in its own way furnishes one or more examples of those same points. Memedovic et al. (2008) offer similar remarks regarding global *value* chains. The latter authors propose a new index to track the logistics capabilities of countries. Additional trends are discussed by Straube et al. (2010).

21.5.4 Final Thoughts

Population: Assumption—population will continue to grow towards the 9 billion mark, but the rate of growth will slow and become stable or negative in the current OECD countries.

- The fastest-growing nations are in Africa, with medium-growth countries in Asia and South America, and flat or declining population otherwise.

Population growth is one of the challenges of our time. Will the world's peoples steadily increase to 9 billion? Or will a smaller maximum population be attained, following which there will be a decrease? The answers to these questions do affect logistics and supply chains, but go far beyond.

Now consider the following three occurrences of 2011:

- The earthquake and tsunami in Japan.
- The floods in Thailand.
- The debt crises of Portugal, Iceland, Italy, Greece and Spain (PIIGS countries).

The first two bulleted events affected international supply chains for important products that contain previously-unheard-of components and subassemblies. The third occurrence and its ramifications may impact the Euro-zone and the world's financial system in ways unimagined at time of this writing. The speed at which the three events perturbed global logistics (and the world) should make us realize that the topics in this book will evolve in a manner not yet conceived.

References

Alaska Canada Rail Link (undated). Project feasibility study. http://alaskacanadarail.com/index.html

Amadeo K (2012) Panama canal expansion impact on U.S. economy. Available at http://useconomy.about.com/od/tradepolicy/p/. Accessed 5 Jan 2012

Anderson WP, Leinbach TR (2007) E-commerce, logistics and the future of globalized freight. In: Leinbach TR, Capineri C (eds) Globalized freight transport: intermodality, e-commerce, logistics and sustainability, Chapter 6. Elgar Publishing, Northampton

Baer W, Cavalcanti T, Silva P (2002) Economic integration without policy coordination: the case of Mercosur. Emerg Markets Rev 3:269–291

Ballou RH (2007) The evolution and future of logistics and supply chain management. Eur Bus Rev 19(4): 332–348

Baluch, I. (2005) Transport logistics: past, present and predictions. Winning Books, UAE Dubai

Banomyong R (2013) The Greater Mekong Sub-region of Southeast Asia: improving logistics connectivity. In: Bookbinder JH (ed) Global logistics, Springer, New York

Bhatnagar R , Teo C-C (2009) Role of logistics in enhancing competitive advantage: a value chain framework for global supply chains. Int J Phys Distrib Logistics Manage 39(3): 202–226

Bock S (2010) Real-time control of freight forwarder transportation networks by integrating multimodal transport chains. Eur J Operational Res 200(3): 733–746

Bookbinder JH, Fox NS (1998) Intermodal routing of Canada-Mexico shipments under NAFTA. Transp Res E 34(4): 289–303

Bookbinder JH, Matuk TA (2009) Logistics and transportation in global supply chains: review, critique and prospects. In: M. Oskoorouchi (Ed.), Tutorials in Operations Res, Chapter 9 (82–211). DOI: 10.1287/educ. 1090.0059

Brown DK, Kiyota K, Stern RM (2005) Computational analysis of the free trade area of the Americas (FTAA). North Am J Econ Finance 16(2): 153–185

Chen F, Lee C-Y (2013) Logistics in China. In: Bookbinder JH (ed) Global logistics. Springer, New York

Chou, C-C (2010) Application of FMCDM model to selecting the hub location in the marine transportation: a case study in southeastern Asia. Math Compu Modell 51(5–6): 791–801

Christensen CM (1997) The innovator's dilemma: when new technologies cause great firms to fail. Harvard Business School Press, Boston ISBN 978-0-87584-585-2

Diaz A, Solis L, Claes B (2011) Improving logistics and supply chain management in Spain: an analysis of current practices and future requirements. Int J Logistics Syst Manage 9(2): 150–169

Ding J-F (2009) Identifying key capabilities to determine core competence for ocean carrier-based logistics service providers. Int J Innovative Comput Inf Control 5(9): 2627–2644

Groothede B, Ruijgrok C, Tavasszy L (2005) Towards collaborative, intermodal hub networks: a case study in the fast moving consumer goods market. Transp Res E 41(6): 567–583

Gutierrez GJ, Kouvelis P (1995) A robustness approach to international sourcing. Ann Oper Res 59 165–193

Henkow O, Norrman A (2011) Tax aligned global supply chains: environmental impact illustrations, legal restrictions and cross functional flow charts. Int J Phys Distrib Logistics Manage 41(9): 878–895

Hilmola OP (2011) North European companies and major Eurasian countries—future outlook on logistics flows and their sustainability. Int J Shipping Transport Logistics 3(3): 100–121

Hu ZH, Yang B, Huang YF, Meng YP (2010) Visualization framework for container supply chain by information acquisition and presentation technologies. J Softw 5(11): 1236–1242

Hurme P (2011) Panama Canal vs. West Coast Intermodal? Not Exactly. Cargo Business News, 18–21 June 2011

Jansen HGP, Morley S, Kessler G, Piñeiro V, Sánchez M, Torero M (2007) The Impact of the Central America free trade agreement on the Central American textile maquila industry. International food policy research institute (IFPRI) vol 720

Janssen A (2010) The 6th mode. Logistics magazine, Sep–Oct 19–23
Kouvelis P, Su P (2007) The structure of global supply chains. Now publications, Inc. Hanover
Kumar S, Pauly S, Budin E (2007) Impact of radio frequency identification technology on manufacturing and logistics: challenges and issues. Int J Manuf Technol Manage 10(1): 57–70
Liou JJH, Chuang YT (2010) Developing a hybrid multi-criteria model for selection of outsourcing providers. Expert Syst Appl 37(5): 3755–3761
Lynch ME, Imada SJ, Bookbinder JH (1994) The future of logistics in Canada: a delphi-based forecast. Logistics Transp Rev 30(1): 95–112
Memedovic O, Ojala L, Rodrigue JP, Naula T (2008) Fuelling the global value chains: What role for logistics capabilities? Int J Technol Learn Innov Dev 1(3): 353–374
Nair R, Miller-Hooks ED, Mahmassani HS, Arcot VC, Kuo A, Zhang K, Kozuki A, Ludvigsen J (2008) Market Potential for international rail-based intermodal services in Europe: from sea to shining sea. Transp Res Record 2066(1): 21–30
Perego A, Perotti S, Mangiaracina R (2011) ICT for logistics and freight transportation: a literature review and research agenda. Int J Phys Distrib Logistics Manage 41(5): 457–483
Prentice BE, Fan L (2005) The Eurasian land bridge—an economic perspective of a new transportation corridor between Europe and China Canadian transportation research forum. Proceedings issue: 40th Annual Meeting (2005): 597–610. ISBN 0-9737440-0-6
Prentice BE, Thomson J (2010) Economics of airships for northern resupply. Available at http://isopolar.ca/publications.html Accessed 13 Jan 2012
Salazar-Xirinachs JM (2002) Proliferation of sub-regional trade agreements in the Americas: an assessment of key analytical and policy issues. J Asian Econ 13(2): 181–212
Santoso T, Ahmed S, Goetschalckx M, Shapiro A (2005) A stochastic programming approach for supply chain network design under uncertainty. Eur J Operational Res 167(1): 96–115
Schmidt G, Wilhelm WE (2000) Strategic, tactical and operational decisions in multinational logistics networks: a review and discussion of modelling issues. Int J Prod Res 38(7): 1501–1523
Shi X, Chan S (2010) information systems and information technologies for supply chain management. Chap. 13 , 208–226 in Waters
Stecke KE, Kumar S (2009) Sources of supply chain disruptions, factors that breed vulnerability, and mitigating strategies. J Marketing Channels 16(3): 193–226
Straube F, Nagel A, Rief D (2010) Trends and strategies in global logistics. Chap. 3 in Waters (2010), 31–48
Tavana M, Sodenkamp MA, Suhl L (2010) A soft multi-criteria decision analysis model with application to the European Union enlargement. Ann Oper Res 181 393–421
Vassallo JM, Fagan M (2007) Nature or nurture: why do railroads carry greater freight share in the United States than in Europe? Transportation 34(2): 177–193
Vidal CJ, Goetschalckx M (2001) A global supply chain model with transfer pricing and transportation cost allocation. Eur J Operational Res 129(1): 134–158
Waters D (ed) (2010) Global logistics: new directions in supply chain management. Philadelphia 6th edn Kogan Page Ltd
World City (2011) Panama Canal expansion potentially a 'game changer' for Miami, South Florida. 15 Mar 2011. Available at www.worldcityweb.com/trade-connections-listing/781 Accessed 30 Jan 2012

Index

J. H. Bookbinder (ed.), *Handbook of Global Logistics*, International Series in Operations Research & Management Science 181, DOI: 10.1007/978-1-4419-6132-7,

Printed by Publishers' Graphics LLC
ICISO130703.15.13.1